A Daoist Theory of Chinese

WITHDRAWN FROM
MACALESTER COLLEGE
LIBRARY

A Daoist Theory
of Chinese Thought

A Philosophical Interpretation

CHAD HANSEN

OXFORD
UNIVERSITY PRESS

OXFORD
UNIVERSITY PRESS

Oxford   New York
Athens   Auckland   Bangkok   Bogotá   Buenos Aires   Calcutta
Cape Town   Chennai   Dar es Salaam   Delhi   Florence   Hong Kong   Istanbul
Karachi   Kuala Lampur   Madrid   Melbourne   Mexico City   Mumbai
Nairobi   Paris   São Paulo   Singapore   Taipei   Tokyo   Toronto   Warsaw

and associated companies in
Berlin   Ibadan

Copyright © 1992 by Chad Hansen

First published in 1992 by Oxford University Press, Inc.
198 Madison Avenue, New York, New York 10016

First issued as Oxford University Press paperback 2000

Oxford is a registered trademark of Oxford University Press

All rights reserved. No part of this publication may be reproduced,
stored in a retrieval system, or transmitted, in any form or by any means,
electronic, mechanical, photocopying, recording or otherwise,
without the prior permission of Oxford University Press.

Library of Congress Cataloging-in-Publication Data
Hansen, Chad, 1942–   .
A Daoist theory of Chinese thought :
a philosophical interpretation / Chad Hansen.
p.   cm.   Includes bibliographical references and index.
ISBN 0-19-506729-0; ISBN 0-19-513419-2 (pbk.)
1. Philosophy, Chinese.   2. Philosophy, Taoist
3. Chinese language—Philosophy.   I. Title.
B126.H277 1992   181'.114—dc20   91-3645

1 3 5 7 9 8 6 4 2
Printed in the United States of America
on acid-free paper

To Joyce Wong

ACKNOWLEDGMENTS

I have drawn on a rich fund of accumulated wisdom about Chinese thought as I studied and reflected on it over three decades. I worry that the explicit acknowledgments in the text and footnotes will barely begin to express my debt to earlier scholars. I welcome this format to mention a few of the most prominent influences and sources of insight and ideas. Some, I am sure, I will still miss. For those listed, I must add this caveat: they are entitled to claim credit for the fertilizing my thought, but bear no responsibility for any deviant uses I may have made of their contributions.

At the top of the list I place Donald Munro. He gave me my first comprehensive picture of the classical period. I realized then how much clarity he contributed to the subject because I had already despaired of making sense of the standard accounts in Chinese and English. But my appreciation of the clarity and depth of his insights has grown as I have worked out more and more of my theory. I continually discover the seeds of it in his first work. In particular, I cite his insight that Chinese thinkers focus more on the behavioral implications of a theory than on its *correspondence truth*. In a sense, this entire account merely defends and develops this central insight of his *The Concept of Man in Ancient China*. My book footnotes what I learned from my teacher and friend.

My professional attention has been focused on different, less orthodox areas and aspects of the classical period—the philosophy of language. And for my understanding of these areas I owe an immeasurable debt to Professor A. C. Graham. This debt is not mine alone. The entire field of Chinese thought could not have advanced to the point of being philosophically interesting without his magnificent lifelong contribution. Without any hesitation, I rank his publication of *Later Mohist Logic, Ethics and Science* as a far more important event in understanding Chinese thought than the unearthing of the Mawang-dui tombs. His unraveling of the analytic Mohist theory defines the state of the art in textual reconstruction and grammatical analysis. He reconstructed the details of a long-lost theory of language and showed its direct and immediate impact on the thought of Zhuangzi and Xunzi. This study is motivated primarily by the goal of working Graham's discovery into a unified theory of the philosophy of the entire classical period.

David Nivison has been an invaluable source of support and promotion during lean and threatening years. His positive evaluation of my various fragmentary insights and early results were especially important. My respect for him is such that I treated his opinion as essential confirmation that gave me the confidence to continue. If this study shows an inadequate fondness for the doctrines of Mencius, it cannot be his fault. Professor Nivison gave me a splendid opportunity to understand the idealist position. He gave me the main clue to Mencius' theory of language and the line that would link the mainline Confucians with the analytic Mohists. His careful and thoughtful analysis of the Mencius-Gaozi debate has served as a model to me as it has to all of his students.

These three giants of Anglo-American sinology are links in the chain of creative transmission. Each link depends on the former ones. And the presence of the passion and commitment to preserving *dao* is a debt we all owe to Confucianism—and its first great innovative transmitter, Confucius. Without that transmission, there would be no possibility of this odyssey of the mind. It gives the resources for traversing the greatest conceptual, linguistic, and space-time distance possible in the actual world.

Two figures stand out as important in bridging the cultural gulf (at least from our side). They are Fung Yu-lan and Hu Shih. My first exposure to Chinese thought came from the first Chinese book I ever read all the way through. It was a middle-school adaptation of Fung Yu-lan's theory of Chinese thought. His magnificent two-volume *History of Chinese Thought* (with thanks to his translator, Derk Bodde) is the basis from which many of us begin. Fung dared advance a holistic theory of the period while most scholars prefer the safety of specialization in one thinker. His life required courage in many ways.

Hu Shih championed the notion that Chinese thought could be understood rationally. I read his *Development of Logical Method in Ancient China* for my first term paper on Chinese philosophy and read his *Outline of the History of Chinese Philosophy* as the first step in my dissertation research. Much of this theory derives from that early attempt at the philosophical project of making respectable philosophical sense of classical Chinese thought.

Many nonphilosophers have contributed to the cultural transmission. These include the incomparable James Legge, the father of all sinologists. The great triumvirate of Wing-tsit Chan, Burton Watson, and Theodore De Bary produced translations and publications which were the texts for my generation. I still use them for my students. Joseph Needham's lifelong dedication and his works are well known. The second volume of his *Science and Civilisation in China* represents an English model of someone willing to produce a holistic theory of the period. Bernard Karlgren launched the serious theoretical study of the classical Chinese language.

My first philosophy teachers in China were Fang Dong-mei and Chen Guying at the National Taiwan University. At the Stanford Center on that same campus, I studied and argued about philosophy with many of my teachers. All provided light-bulb-like insights that eventually fit into the larger theory. I especially thank Gregory Chang, with whom I first read Hu Shih. He was not only patient with my Cantonese accent, but willing to bend the then-strict rules to allow free philosophical discussion. I was honored later to attend classes taught by the Mo Zongsan and Tang Junyi at New Asia College in Hong Kong. The richness of my opportunities to learn far outstripped the meager conscious capacity of my brain to comprehend and store what was available. I find many of what I thought were my original insights in Tang's wide-ranging *Yuan-Dao*.

My best ideas often come after animated conversations with professional friends. Frequently those long leisurely talks plant the seed of an idea (or embarrassingly often, they fully communicate it to one's subconscious where it is later "rediscovered"). But the greater value of those friends lies in the stimulation of thought, defence, elaboration. They also offer the immense luxury of enjoying what one does for a living. Some of my most enjoyable moments came while I was at Stanford University and regularly attending seminars at Berkeley. These were organized by Tu Wei-ming, who has always impressed me as the most articulate spokesman for Neo-Confucian ideas in American academe. My companions for the delightful discussions, besides David Nivison, included my colleague Lee Yearley, and students P. J. Ivanhoe and Sally Gressens. My conversations with each have continued with equal pleasure, but regrettably less frequency, over the years.

I owe a similar debt to a more scattered group: Michael Martin at the University of Hong Kong, Roger Ames at the University of Hawaii, Henry Rosemont at St. Mary's College, Robert Eno at Indiana University, who gave helpful and stimulating comments on the text, Kwong-loi Shun at the University of California at Berkeley, and Bao Zhiming at Fudan University and MIT. They have all listened patiently to various aspects of my theory and reacted alternately with enthusiasm or reasoned criticism. Both reactions have helped enormously as I struggled to clarify and support the overall theory.

I have been exposed to the ideas of several scholars after my own ideas had mostly taken shape. Still I benefited from reflecting on their general outlook and have drawn heavily on their works for detailed insights in fleshing out my own view. These include Benjamin Schwartz, Frederick Mote, Raymond Smullyan, and Herbert Fingarette. Schwartz's early paper on "The Absence of Reductionism in Chinese Thought" excited me a great deal and I have constantly enjoyed his gentle but stimulating insights and questions at conferences and gatherings. His imposing *World of Chinese Thought* was published between the first and second drafts of this attempt at a related but rival project. This stimulus to clearer and better elaboration of my view was invaluable. It will be obvious how much I have drawn from and reacted to that rich work. Mote's admirably clear picture of Chinese thought made me wish I had discovered it far earlier. I still incorporated many elements of his theory easily into my overall picture. Smullyan delighted me in showing that another analytically inclined philosopher who happened not to be a sinologist should anticipate what I take to be the real nature of Daoist mysticism. Similarly for Fingarette's picture of Confucius, to which my review was too unkind. I have always appreciated his groundbreaking vision of the depth of Confucius' reliance on convention.

I owe debts of many kinds to my colleagues at the University of Vermont, especially Bill Mann, the chairman. The university and department have been generous with sabbatical and release time. My colleagues there include most notably Hilary Kornblith, George Sher, the departed Philip and Patricia Kitcher, David Christensen, and Derk Perebloom. They all demonstrate the openness that belies the prejudice held among sinologists that philosophers—especially analytic philosophers—are narrow minded about Chinese thought. They stimulate me to clear thought and hold me to high standards. Each has contributed important philosophical insights that sharpen the presentation. Peter Seybolt, who heads the Asian Studies Group at the University of Vermont engages me regularly in those debates that foment whole new section headings. Vermont is the ideal environment for an American Daoist.

I have benefitted from sabbatical release funds from a Fulbright sabbatical grant and summer research support from the University of Vermont. The University of Hong Kong offered some housing support, a forum for my verbal exposition, a position at the Center for Asian Studies, and regular opportunities for enrichment attending their seminars and conferences. They have also graciously invited me to deliver bits and pieces of my theory in their Traditional China Seminar. The philosophy department provided other opportunities for discussing my ideas about Chinese thought and lots of encouragement. Special thanks to Professor Tim Moore, Lawrence Goldstein, and Chris New.

I cannot begin to trace and credit the sources of the Western philosophical ideas I use here in explaining Chinese philosophy. Obviously, not much is original. In addition to the ancient masters, my ability to distance myself from the traditional Western psychology and philosophy of language owes much to Wittgenstein, Quine, and Sellars. I have drawn especially from the more recent writings of Stephen Stitch, David Lewis, Daniel Dennett, Richard Montague, Michael Sandel, Saul Kripke, Richard Rorty, Hilary Putnam, John Rawls, Richard Grandy, Tyler Burge, Thomas Nagel, and Derek Parfit.

I must thank my students through the years at the universities of Pittsburgh, Michigan, Stanford, Vermont, Hong Kong, Hawaii, and U.C.L.A. Their questions, their interest, and their enthusiasm all helped. But mostly it helps to reflect on how they have restated what they learned from my attempt to make Chinese philosophy accessible. I collect those restatements and use them to improve the presentation and this account.

My thanks to my wife, Joyce, who unlike most wives noted in acknowledgments, didn't type a word of the manuscript. But she tolerated my temper as I ran the gauntlet of computer word processing. She encouraged and made space for my bizarre work habits and curious interest in wildly different ways of thinking. Then she guided me with what, as soon as I heard them, I instantly recognized as incredibly sensible techniques for working on the text.

Lest I forget what we must all learn from Confucians, let me also thank my parents. They provide the basis on which we all build. In my case they gave me both a habit of early rising and hard work and a love of learning. They also gave me a dose of the life of a dairy farmer that helped me acquire a passion to be an academic instead. And my entire family gave me the confidence that comes from life-long acceptance that good Freudians and good Confucians both agree is essential for our development. The inner freedom to be an eccentric is frequently a consequence of such orthodox systems of support and a wonderful gift from my family.

If this is to become thanks to the causal antecedents, a Daoist acknowledgment must now follow. If personal history and transmission of culture is a cause, then so is evolution. My thanks to the primates, large mammals, the plant kingdom, and the unfathomable natural forces on which they rest. The electromagnetic field coursing through my computer no doubt flows from the Big Bang. (Mysticism is an easy matter these days of black holes and singularity.)

No serious skeptic can cite natural causes and ignore supernatural ones. A special footnote of thanks to Dan Hoffman for originating the theory that I am a reincarnation of Zhuangzi. Apparently Zhuangzi decided that the distortion and misunderstanding of his doctrine had gone on long enough and needed a missionary. What better than to use the barbarian system? He chose rebirth in the Rocky plateaus of the High Uintah mountains of Utah where one can grow to outward maturity acquiring a minimal cultural endowment. (My ninth-grade English teacher read *Horton the Elephant* to us aloud for cultural enrichment!) It also provided an institution that would send the scion to Hong Kong in this relatively unformed state. So from a place where our nearest neighbors were three miles away I found myself whisked to a place where I saw more people in fifteen minutes than I had seen my whole life. There I quickly learned there was more gospel to learn than to teach.

Of course in order for Zhuangzi's plan to work, one had to have such a religious institution. Zhuangzi had a plan. A Vermont farmer possessed of his New England Yankee independence could create a religion. But he needed the impetus. History used the Chinese ginseng root. A mysterious stranger proposed to Joseph Smith, Sr., that he plant his farm to ginseng and sell it to China. I don't know if it was ever delivered, but no money came back and Smith lost his Vermont farm. He fell back on his mystical Vermont tradition of water dowsing but added the special claim that he could douse for gold. His son learned the trade as they wandered to Upstate New York. There Joseph Smith, Jr., continued his fascination with finding buried gold and an interest in ancient, exotic cultures and people. He found gold plates with a theory of the American Indians. Based on this book, he founded his iconoclastic, freethinking, quintessentially American religion. The chain of events leading to founding of the Mormon empire in Utah and my own eventual return to Vermont is all fairly ordinary history. Those who sense a continuity with Mormonism in my thought patterns, despite my professed atheism, don't have it all wrong.

I do not intend to put much weight on this story. I shall rest my case on the explanatory power of the interpretive theory. I offer it here for those more impressed with pedigree and credentials than argument.

Shelburne, Vermont
May 1992   C. H.

CONTENTS

1. An Introduction with Work to Do, 1

The New Perspective and Philosophical Progress, 2
The Ruling Interpretive Theory, 5
The Translation Paradigm, 7
The Fragmented–Schools View, 11
The Meaning-Change Hypothesis, 13
Indo-European Theory of Language and Mind, 14
The Philosophical Worth of Chinese Thought, 26
The Rehabilitation of Daoism, 26
Summary, 28

2. The Context of Chinese Philosophy: Language and Theory of Language, 30

Geographical Setting, 30
Prehistoric Influences, 31
Language, 33
The Social Context: Some Conclusions, 53

Part I   The Positive Dao Period

3. Confucius: The Baseline, 57

The Confucian *Analects:* Some Preliminary Hypotheses, 57
The Well-Ordered Society, 60
Theory of Human Nature, 71
The Confucian Conceptual Scheme: Dao, 83
Ren and Confucian Theory of Language, 87
Miscellaneous Other Topics, 94

4. Mozi: Setting the Philosophical Agenda, 95

Rehabilitation, 95
Life of Mozi, 98
Crafts and Guiding, Objective Standards, 99
The Process of Enculturation, 100
The Attack on Traditionalism, 106
The Utilitarian Standard, 108
The Conceptual Structure of Mozi's Utilitarianism, 115
The Role of the Natural Urge, 121
Morality: Motivation and Justification, 124
Universal Love in Interpersonal Relations, 128

The Doctrine of Agreement with the Superior,130
Miscellaneous Consequences of Utilitarianism,135
Reason and Right in *The Mozi*,138
Pragmatics versus Semantics,139
Mozi's Theory of Language,143
The Three Standards of Language,143

Part II   The Antilanguage Period

5.   Mencius: The Establishment Strikes Back,153

Background: The Double Challenge to Confucianism,153
Mencius' Philosophical Calling,157
Mencius' Theory of Moral Psychology,162
Reflections on Mencius' Moral Psychology,167
Mencius' Attitude toward Language and the Heart-Mind,183
Mencius' Lasting Influence,193

6.   Laozi: Language and Society,196

Theoretical Interpretation,196
The Text of the *Daode Jing*,200
Historical Background of Daoism,204
Laozi: Nonlife and Tradition,210
The First Chapter: The Interpretation,214
Reversal of Opposites in the *Daode Jing*,222
Primitive Daoism: Mysticism and Mencius,227

Part III   The Analytic Period

7.   The School of Names: Linguistic Analysis in China,233

The Neo-Mohist Text: Importance and Problems,235
The Realist Move,239
Strings and Reference: Extending the System,244
Ethics and Realist Language,247
Neo-Mohist Epistemology,252
Neo-Mohist Logic,254
Gongsun Long: The Defense of Confucian Language,257
Hui Shi's Paradoxes—The World Is One,261
Summary: The School of Names,263

8.   Zhuangzi: Discriminating about Discriminating,265

An Interpretive Manifesto,265
Zhuangzi's Place in the Pre-Han Dialogue,269
Zhuangzi: Textual and Historical Issues,272
Language and Its Adequacy,273
The Refutation of Mencius,277
The Refutation of the Neo-Mohists,280
The Refutation of Absolute Monism (Primitive Daoism),285

Dreaming and Skepticism in Zhuangzi,292
Science and the Division of Fact and Value,296
Practical Advice,299

Part IV   The Authoritarian Response

9. Xunzi: Pragmatic Confucianism,307

The Interpretive Dilemma,307
Xunzi's Intellectual Influences,309
Outline of Xunzi's Thought,310
New Rectifying Names,319
Is Human Nature Evil?,334
Philosophy of Heart-Mind,338

10. Han Feizi: The Ruler's Interpretation,344

Han Feizi's Life and the Ruling Image,344
Confucian Rule of Man and Western Rule of Law,351
Historical Survey of Statecraft in China,357
Language and the Danger of Interpretive Anarchy,361
Authoritarian Daoism,370
The Aftermath,374

*Notes,*377

*Glossary of Chinese Characters,*423

*Bibliography,*431

*Index,*437

1

An Introduction with Work to Do

A missing text is always an exciting discovery. The later Mohist dialectic chapters are a unique case. They form a missing text that was not physically lost. Chinese archivists had copied and transmitted it down through two millennia after a textual accident had turned it into an incoherent jigsaw puzzle. The interpretive tradition lost the ability to understand the text. A Qing scholar first discovered the key to the puzzle near the end of the nineteenth century. Angus Graham completed the systematic reconstruction of the text in his *Later Mohist Logic, Ethics, and Science* in 1978.

The Mohist text gives us access to a detailed classical Chinese theory of language. It thus poses a rare challenge and an opportunity. The Mohists exemplify the opposite of the ruling stereotype of Chinese thought. That stereotype treats *analytic thought* and *Chinese thought* as virtual opposites. Now Graham has shown that many Chinese philosophers of the period knew the basic principles of Chinese linguistic analysis. They both understood and applied its technical terminology. Any coherent account of the period must now shoulder a new task. We must explain how that intense interest in language analysis arose out of the philosophical context. This missing text challenges us to revise our entire view of the classical period of Chinese philosophy.

Coincidentally, general studies of the entire classical period are beginning to come back in style. Benjamin Schwartz published his monumental *The World of Thought in Ancient China* in 1985 and Angus Graham followed in 1989 with his *Disputers of Tao: Philosophical Argument in Ancient China*. Both studies, however, mainly develop the ruling stereotype. Schwartz surveys several new approaches to the classical thinkers but he consistently finds the reasons for departing from traditional interpretations deficient. Graham is intentionally more revisionist. (His theories are among those that Schwartz rejects.) Still, he structures his account around the familiar reason-intuition dichotomy that devotees of Eastern wisdom have used to explain Chinese thought since Northrup first proposed it.[1] I regard both as differing versions of a deeper standard interpretation. Bifurcating the tradition into separate analytic and intuitive components is the trademark of the traditional standard view. Schwartz treats Chinese linguistic analysis as a minor and irrelevant aberration and largely ignores it. Graham, of course, gives it more extensive treatment. Still, he treats analytic reason and intuitive mysticism (spontaneity) as two distinct and incompatible philosophical styles. Analytic reason, he argues, lost out in ancient China.

Both scorn the challenge to revise and unify the interpretive theory that was dominant before we understood the analytic Chinese philosophers. Neither challenges our familiar romantic assumptions that antirational mysticism is distinctive of Chinese thought. Both, in different ways, relegate the language theorists to an out-of-tune limbo in Chinese thought. A *unified interpretation* should try *to explain* how these different philosophical directions in Chinese thought emerged from a shared philosophical perspective and problems.

Unifying our interpretive theory of the period requires that we thoroughly rethink the background beliefs we attribute to the preanalytic philosophers. A unified theory must show both how earlier philosophical issues led to the interest in linguistic analysis *and* to the particular line of analysis they followed. The view that Chinese linguistic analysis is an inexplicable aberration in Chinese thought should raise our skeptical eyebrows.

The New Perspective and Philosophical Progress

My motivation in writing differs from that of the two giants of sinology who preceded me. Confucius posed the classic polarity, "To study without thinking is worthless, to think without study is dangerous." The trick, of course, is to find where the balance lies. My instincts are philosophical, not historical. I depend heavily on what other scholars have learned about Chinese thought. But for me, the challenge has always been to make some sense of it. My response to the challenge is also philosophical. Philosophers construct *thought experiments* when exploring theoretical frameworks. We test philosophical positions by detailing how they would *spin out*. We test our intuitions or considered judgments by imagining alternative theories.

In one sense, the philosopher's urge is to start from scratch—the view from nowhere.[2] We can't, of course. But classical Chinese philosophy gave me a chance to do the next best thing. What would it be like to do philosophy with a *radically different* set of assumptions? The assumptions I trace are constrained, but not by the limits on my imagination or current theoretical purposes. Chinese philosophy allowed me to perform a thought experiment removed from the immediate task of solving some outstanding philosophical problem. At the same time, it allowed me to *start over* in a sense—but not from nowhere. The new starting point is a real place that is just very different. I imagine myself retracing the rise of philosophy in *the one place in the actual world* most removed from our own in spatial, temporal, linguistic, cultural, and conceptual terms.

The texts and the language set real and rich limits on this exercise of philosophical imagination. The philosophical and conceptual theories I attribute to Chinese thinkers should meet two explanatory goals. Those theories should both *explain* and *be explainable*. That is, it must explain the text as expressing a theory, and it must explain why thinkers using that language and addressing those philosophical issues would adopt the theory.

My quarrel with the current state of interpretative theory thus goes far beyond its failure to explain Chinese analytic theory of language. It fails adequately to explain a host of things. It has notoriously (and admittedly) failed to make sense of Daoism, it denigrates Mohism as shallow, boring or *excessively Western*, and makes

Legalism an implausible ideology of official cruelty. So it not only marginalizes the analytic school; it marginalizes *all* the classical thinkers except Confucians. The Confucian theory even fails to make much sense of Confucianism itself. It tends to be filled with defensive claims that objecting to its obvious inadequacies reveals a modern or Western or (horrors!) analytic bias.

I don't quite see the point of denying my guilt. There are many modern, Western, analytic views of many different things. I believe some and disbelieve others. One of the things I believe is that no one I know personally has successfully adopted the view from nowhere. I doubt that my pretending to have done so would increase my credibility except among the gullible, who, I suppose, will already have stopped reading. So I will neither adopt a ''Just the facts, Ma'am'' tone nor represent what follows as the shared conclusions of all serious and competent scholars. I am aware, and the reader will be soon, that I disagree with the wise men of the realm.

Given our inherent limitations, objectivity must take the form of explaining why our perspective would vary. I came to the study of Chinese philosophy just as Graham was working out his account of the Analytic school, with its rich theory of language. I thought about that *first*. Having made some sense of that, I looked at Daoism. It looked philosophically interesting! Then early Mohism, out of which this study grew, looked much richer and more pivotal. Even Legalism seemed more sensible. The conventional theory of Confucianism seemed to fit into a coherent picture that unified the whole period.

The key to my view of Chinese thought is this. I attribute a theory of language and mind to Chinese thinkers that differs fundamentally from the popular Western view. This theory of language makes sense of the philosophical disputes between the ancient philosophers. It is a very different theory. We can explain those differences either as prima facie plausible or as a tenable theory of language for this philosophical tradition—given the Chinese language and their other philosophical presuppositions. It both explains and can be explained.

Attributing a radically different theory of language and mind to the classical tradition reveals good, albeit also radically different, philosophy. But more important, it reveals a unified philosophical point of view that develops and matures in an interesting way until banned, buried, and burned by political authority. The only cost of this new perspective is that Confucianism does not come out on top philosophically. In fact it ends up near the bottom. The same political authority that stifled further philosophical development also awarded Confucianism its high position in history. One of my Daoist biases is against argument from authority—especially political authority.

I will attribute the following perspective on language to all Chinese philosophers of the period: Language is a social practice. Its basic function is guiding action. The smallest units of guiding discourse are *ming*^names.* We string *ming*^names together in progressively larger units. The salient compositional linguistic structure is a *dao*^guiding

---

*I will use this superscript notation to refer to Chinese characters in my interpretive metalanguage. When I use such a notation, I am using (or mentioning) the Chinese concept. The translation in superscript is to help readers who know Chinese identify the concept and to help others follow the theory. Use of this notation does not mean that the supplied translation is identical to the intended concept. This whole book, not the superscripts, is my interpretive theory. A change in superscripts does not mean a change in character. I include a glossary of characters with the different superscripts at the end of the book.

^{discourse}.* The Chinese counterpart of interpretation is not an account of the truth conditions. Rather, to *interpret* a *dao* is to *perform* it. The interpretation of a *dao*^{guiding discourse} starts from the interpretation of the *ming*^{names} that compose it. In learning a conventional name, you learn a socially shared way of making discriminations in guiding your action according to a *dao*^{way}.

The issues that provoke skepticism and drive philosophical reflection in this perspective differ from their counterparts in the Western tradition in intelligibly related ways. These issues include: (1) what standards should guide the social conventions for discriminating and applying a term† (2) whether there are extralinguistic sources or standards of guidance and (3) whether we can find any constant (objective) way of fixing which language to use in guiding behavior or the ways of interpreting it. These questions, I will argue, both motivated the early philosophers and led to the newly discovered Neo-Mohists' theory of language. The Later Mohists proposed a referential semantics for names and embedded it in the larger pragmatic project. All the ancient thinkers viewed languages as a way to coordinate and regulate behavior. No one in this tradition developed a theory that the central function of language was representing or picturing facts or reality.

My theory identifies four progressive stages in Classical doctrines about language and mind. The first stage is the positive *dao*^{way} period, what the Daoists call the *Ru-Mo*^{Confucian – Mohist} period. The philosophical dispute in this stage concerned what language we should use in guiding a society. Should tradition set the standards of discourse or should we reform those standards? If we are to reform them, we need a standard or criterion such as utility. How could we justify using such a standard? Tradition would reject it and utilitarian justification presupposes it.

The perceived futility of the *Ru-Mo* debate led to the second stage—the antilanguage *dao* period. Both Confucian and Daoist thinkers from this period rejected the earlier ideal of guiding behavior by social conventional discourse. They appealed to a natural, intuitive, or innate guide to behavior. This development led to the doctrines of Mencius and the Laozi form of Daoism.

The third period—the analytic period—exposed the incoherence of the antilanguage position. It led to the realist analysis of the Later Mohist school. But the school of names also included a strain of relativist-skepticism about language. This motivated the skepticism of Zhuangzi.

---

*The obvious contrast here with Western thought lies in the absence of compositional units corresponding to sentences. Chinese thinkers did not distinguish sentential units as an intermediate structure. Thus they did not focus on truth conditions. Similarly, their philosophy of mind did not include the theory of beliefs (sentences in mentalese). And their moral theory did not focus on rules (universal prescriptive sentences). The Later Mohists did begin to analyze compositionality but mainly analyzed how names are compounded and included in noun and verb phrases.

†The issue of realism versus conventionalism (of word use) still drives ancient Chinese versions of skepticism. Classical Chinese skepticism questioned the constancy of naming, not the descriptive accuracy of beliefs or perception. That skeptical premise lead to the conclusion that no scheme of linguistic guidance was constant or reliable in guiding action. The postanalytic philosophers faced this specter of skepticism with two results. Daoists, like Zhuang zi, playfully romped in skeptical freedom from convention. Confucians and their offspring, the Legalists, viewed linguistic skepticism as criminally dangerous and disorderly. Since language played a role in coordinating and regulating cooperative behavior, skepticism threatened society with a deep kind of anarchy. They advocated using authoritarian methods to impose and stabilize social control of how people use names.

The perception that analysis bred conceptual anarchy motivated the final, authoritarian period. Xunzi's conventional authoritarianism filtered through his ruling class student, Han Feizi, yielding the ideology of controlling language and expression exclusively in the interest of the political ruler.

This unified theory thus identifies a central and dominant philosophical problem that informs classical discussion of a whole range of issues. I shall argue that the problem of practical interpretation of terms—How do we project the distinctions associated with a term in concrete settings to guide our behavior?*—dominated the classical Chinese period.

In using words, we must make distinctions correctly in new settings.† The guiding ideal of this classical period of Chinese thought is to get a constant *dao*—a form of discourse that *reliably* guides behavior. The crux of the issue in the Daoist analysis is that a constant *dao* requires constant naming. There are many possible standards. Any actual *dao* arbitrarily picks out one of the possible standards as the constant guide to naming.

Normally an introduction should end here. But as my title suggests, this introduction has much more work to do. I propose to do more than merely state a novel view. I shall argue that the theory I attribute to Chinese thinkers better explains their writings as a unified and coherent philosophical tradition. This argument requires identifying a rival theory and explaining in what sense the theory I will set out is better. The arguments are based on a theory of the connection between philosophy of language and philosophy of mind. The casual reader may find the going a bit heavy in what follows. I suggest three possible routes through the rest of this argumentative preface and introduction. The first is to skip it entirely and go directly to the narrative, starting with Confucius. The second is to read only the main text and skip the footnotes. I have tried to place the more recondite lines of argument and analysis in those notes. I warmly invite potential critics and rival interpretive theorists to follow the third route.

The Ruling Interpretive Theory

I present my new interpretive theory in contrast to what I will variously call the *standard,* or *orthodox,* or *traditional,* or *ruling* theory of Chinese thought. Of course, other interpreters have proposed *many* theories with significant differences. Together they make up the received view of the classics of Chinese philosophy. No one specifically is a model of the standard theory. From the perspective of this Daoist theory, all the different interpretive theories with which I am familiar have some strong

---

*My assumption is that any productive, energetic philosophical period has a central dominant focus. The search for an account of meaning and truth in metaphysical terms dominated the classical Greek philosophical period. The problem of sense skepticism and conceptualist philosophy of mind and meaning dominated the early modern European period. Similarly, describing the metaphysical attitude that characterizes the awareness of the sage dominated the Neo-Confucian period.

†This is a Chinese version of Kripke's Wittgenstein puzzle. See Kripke (1963). What counts as following a rule for the use of a term? How do we project the term correctly into situations that are different from the learning situation?

similarities. They share a set of related features and assumptions. The shared assumptions of these theories constitute *the ruling theory*.

I will state the features of the ruling theory that most concern me besides the introductory one—that they bifurcate the tradition. They are all (perhaps unwittingly) pro-Confucian. To varying degrees, they identify Chinese philosophy with Confucian philosophy. Either they talk only or mainly of Confucianism, or their explanations exaggerate the centrality of Confucianism. They discuss other schools mainly from the perspective of Confucian thinkers. A standard account typically includes defensive apologies for Confucianism. For example, it dismisses obvious philosophical objections to Confucianism as Western or modern anachronisms and hints that critics who raise these objections have an unfair analytic bias.

Standard theories commonly take a philosophical stand in favor of doctrines congenial to Confucianism, for example, intuitionism, traditionalism, elitism, right-brain aesthetic sensitivity, antiutilitarianism, virtue and special-relations ethics, and so forth. Taking a position, again, is not objectionable on its face. I am simply less sympathetic to the alleged Confucian positions. But I am sympathetic to other positions that I take to be common to the entire tradition: naturalistic theories of mind and pragmatic theories of language.

My objection, accordingly, is not merely to the defects that I see in these philosophical positions. Nor is it directly to the pro-Confucian bias. My objection is that the ruling strategy for making Confucianism look good exacts too high a theoretical cost *on the rest of our interpretive theory* of the period.* Standard theories buttress

---

*Schwartz warns us of the dangers in proposing to revise the received interpretation as I do. To propose a basic revision of the received view, he warns, commits us to what the calls "the doctrine of the privileged or transcendental vantage point" (Schwartz, 1985, p. 50). His skepticism of our ability to take a radically detached perspective grounds his own comfortable acceptance of the inherited ruling interpretive theory. But this is to *retain* the ideal of the privileged vantage point. It *privileges* the tradition and *burdens* any proposed alternative.

Treating interpretation as theory allows us to understand interpretive progress *without* assuming a privileged or transcendantal viewpoint. Schwartz is correct that we can never start from a blank slate and assume an unmediated direct access to Chinese thought. Theoretical advance in interpretation is like theoretical advance in any scientific theory. We float, as Neurath's famous metaphor has it, in the ship of previous theory even as we repair it. We rely on the received theory to justify the very hypotheses we use in revising it. As scholarship progresses, we find ways to make the interpretive theory explain the texts better. We work for more adequate interpretive explanations. My interpretive hypotheses, however radical, do not amount to a totally new theory. The revisions I propose start at a higher level of abstraction, but my Daoist version still follows the logical form of a progressive revision of received theory to eliminate problems in that theory.

The riddle each interpreter must face is what to revise and how to revise it. The scientific parallel gives us the account of *confirming* any proposed theory. That same model also reminds us that we still have no plausible account of the logic of discovery. Perhaps Schwartz's worry is about how we could imagine the alternative theory to subject to the test of explanatory adequacy. When we find a consistency problem in the standard theory, which of the two incoherent elements do we reject? What do we put in its place? Since we do not have any direct privileged access to the original facts, how are we to tackle these problems?

I do have a strategy. I do not start from a privileged transcendental point of view. I practice Daoist reversal of opposites. The standard theory seeks primarily to make sense of Confucianism and accepts the consequence that the rivals are vulnerable to criticism. I start by making sense of Daoism. The discovery comes by systematically removing pro-Confucian (anti-Daoist, anti-Mohist, anti-Legalist) bias from the standard theory. That is the discovery strategy. The *proof* strategy comes from the scientific parallel—comparative evaluation of the explanatory power of the new theory.

this tilt toward Confucianism with a theory of other schools that makes them, at best, hard to motivate. Mohism becomes a shallow, unattractive, low-class, hyperreligious moralism and Daoism becomes a notoriously incomprehensible and contradictory mysticism. The analytic school of names becomes pointless logic chopping, and Legalism becomes an implausibly horrific and baseless celebration of cruel despotism. Even Confucianism does not fare all that well—hence the need for apologetics. The problem is that the standard theory is deficient in explanatory power.

The advantage of abandoning Confucian bias is that we can still make the *same* sense of Confucianism that the standard accounts do. We simply avoid lavish approbation and defensive claims that its predilections are quintessentially Chinese. The Confucian positions may be defended, but there are some obvious attacks. Did no one in the tradition think to make them? If we look for the natural philosophical criticisms of Confucianism, we will find that contemporary philosophical rivals of Confucianism did make them. Thus, we can make these rivals straightforwardly intelligible. Clearly developing these criticisms of the philosophical positions of standard theories will give us the handle we need to make clear sense of the entire tradition. The standard strategy makes only partial sense of Confucianism.

Another feature of the standard theories is that they attribute the conceptual structure of a Western theory of mind and language to Confucian writers. This results from the translation paradigm that tempts us to regard English as fixing the possible meaning structure of Chinese.* Linking Chinese and English words further tempts us to view their philosophical theories as straightforward counterparts of our own. I shall discuss this feature of standard theories further in the next section.

The ruling interpretive theory of Chinese thought is an evolutionary product of the theory Westerners first learned in the initial encounters of our two cultures. We became conscious of China during the late medieval dominance of what Western historians call the Neo-Confucian school.† The Neo-Confucian period came after a long period of Buddhist domination of Chinese thought. Our description, *Neo-Confucian,* introduces the skeptical possibility that those medieval Confucians *did not correctly* interpret classical philosophy.[3]

The Translation Paradigm

A standard methodology accompanies the standard interpretive theory. The implicit methodology is part of our training in Chinese. It instills a translation focus. The translation tradition camouflaged the theoretical nature of translation. We assumed

---

*I call this the English-is-the-only-real-language fallacy in honor of my son, who first formulated it in those words. "Why," I asked him, "do you say that English is the only real language?" "Because every other language means something in English."

†Chinese accounts speak instead of at least three late medieval Confucian schools: of principle, of mind, and of Han learning. There were significant internal disagreements among these schools. Clustering the three in one classification endures among Western scholars for good theoretical reasons. It draws on the historical theory current in the Neo-Confucian traditional schools. That historical theory suggests that a philosophical dark age brought on by political oppression followed the classical age. An eight-hundred-year period of Buddhist intellectual domination followed. So this is a Confucianism separated from its own classical tradition by two radical intellectual gaps in transmission.

we were learning *the* meaning of a term when we consulted a dictionary. From a realist perspective, a dictionary is a widely accepted interpretive theory—albeit in an inelegant and unargued form.* We learned that translation precedes interpretation. When you propose an interpretation, you should cite a translation as *evidence*. That makes translations analogous to observations. But the translation itself presupposes an interpretive theory. The alleged *evidence* is circular unless we can independently support the interpretive theory embodied in the translation. Being in a dictionary is not the support we need. The dictionary is an inherited, piecemeal, fragmented interpretive theory.†

*Students of Chinese learn a set of dictionary equivalents among which we choose in different contexts. We also learn grammar in the form of a vague set of conventionally accepted heuristics for generating sentences of English from sentences of classical Chinese. A scientifically adequate grammar should consist of a set of recursive rules for generating a potentially infinite set of meaningful strings. A translation manual for pre-Han philosophical Chinese embodies a model for generating functionally equivalent sentences of English. The rules for translation thus follow from an interpretive model or theory of *both* languages. We assume that we natively know the interpretion of English.

English in this case, is the language in which we construct our interpretive theory—the metalanguage in contrast to the target language that we are interpreting. It does not presuppose that English is privileged. We construct a theory of a language that we strive to explain using the resources of one we know. Our idiomatic ways of talking about meaning together with the translation paradigm tempt us to what I have called the English-is-the-only-real-language fallacy. We talk as if the meaning *is* an English language structure.

Sinological training is dominated by the translation paradigm. Sinologists focus attention and analysis on what term to use more than on what theory to adopt. Searching for the closest possible familiar term, they unwittingly translate the conventional conceptual assumptions into their accounts. They accept each seemingly small incoherence that results from translation. They dismiss these with the conventional line, "Translation can, after all, never be exact." They never pursue the hypothesis that the accumulation of small errors might be an indication of a quite different conceptual scheme. If we imaginatively and coherently elaborated an alternative, it may turn out to fit the texts better.

The deeper problem is the translation paradigm itself. Whether one accepts conventional dictionary equivalents or suggests new ones, the translation paradigm confuses theory and observation. Translators assume that determining the right English translation equivalent is a relatively straightforward, empirical matter that *precedes* interpretation. We simply check that the expression *makes sense of* each context where the Chinese term is used. What the translation paradigm ignores is that many alternative translation equivalents could make sense of each isolated sentence containing the term. To decide among these requires some principle for evaluating the implied theory of what beliefs the writers held. Meaning cannot be determined independently from belief.

†The translation model motivates the conventional cliché, but the problem with this cliché becomes acute when the translator proceeds with the interpretation. She assumes that what she did before—the translation—is objectively verifiable and what she is about to do is subjective and speculative. The translator's speculations are then guided by inferences that she draws from the scheme of beliefs and theories in which *the English word* functions. This naturally tempts us to the interpretive hypothesis that Chinese philosophical theories are like our own. The result is a circular argument that their philosophy must have the same conceptual structure that ours does.

There are two manifestations of the translation-priority malady. One arises because the translator has chosen an ambiguous English word as the translation. The translation always works because there is always *a meaning* of the English term that makes sense. But then the interpreter draws inferences from the other meanings. An example is *know*. I will argue that Chinse *zhi*[know] works only like English *know-how*, *know-to*, or *know-about*—but not *know-that*. The translations therefore always make sense, but interpreters end up attributing Western epistemological assumptions to Chinese thinkers despite the fact that there is no equivalent *belief* verb or a concept of *truth*. They are talking about knowledge, they reason, so Chinese writers must be talking about the same thing Western philosophers talk about (true belief) when *they* talk about knowledge.

Another example is *argument*. It has two distinct senses in English. In one sense it is roughly syn-

I remember fondly how often the phrase "that's not the way it is traditionally understood" came up in all my classical Chinese classes. Our training thus inculcated a Confucian cognitive strategy—conformity to traditional or conventional interpretive standards. The accepted standard of *good* scholarly translation is that one must consult and cite commentary supporting one's translation.* This suggests to students that the correct form of argument is appeal to traditional authority.

The personal nature of this work is a consequence of my focus on theory. I cannot claim to report a scholarly consensus or the conclusions of the last fifty years of sinology. This sometimes feels more like a confession of frustrated inadequacy. Those who claimed to know Chinese assured me that if I knew Chinese, I would see that *this* is the meaning. After years of study, it never happened to me. I *always* had to *theorize* about the meaning and then test my theories. To attribute a particular meaning to a section seemed to require that I attribute a certain doctrine to the author.

onymous with *quarrel*. In another it is synonymous with *proof*. Graham translates *bian*^dispute as *argument* and deduces himself into finding the study of logic and a theory of reason in Chinese philosophy. If they were talking about argument, then this must be the theory of argumentation—proofs and reasons.

The opposite error occurs when we find ourselves using several English terms for different uses of a Chinese concept. When translators choose which term to use, they assume that the Chinse writer is using it in the sense of the chosen English word—as if he had English in his mind. They fail to try proposing a unified theory of the conceptual role of the term. This leads them to the sinological shibboleth that Chinese words have lots of separate meanings, and, in turn, to the fragmentation to which I have been objecting. The translation paradigm buries the conceptual connections between different theorists and the different aspects of their theories. The examples here are a multitude but some important examples include *ming*^to name:command:fate, *shi*^this:right:assent:is, *dao*^doctrine:way:speak:guide, *fa*^standard:laws, *yan*^words:language:doctrine, *wei*^do:deem:make:for the sake of, etc. We must remember that the speaker uses the same term in these different contexts, he need not suppose that there are *two* concepts merely because we use two different English equivalents. Nor must he even suppose that what we identify as nominal and verbal uses are different. Of course, we may conclude that he is wrong about this. But it is not plausible to attribute *even our allegedly true belief* about the character to the Chinese writer. It is motivated for us mainly by the requirement that we use the appopriate part of speech when we translate it to English. No Chinese writer will have had his attention focused in that way.

In deciding on an interpretation, further, it is not enough to make sense of individual sentences. We must make sense of the attributed scheme of inferentially related beliefs and philosophical theories. The translation is a good one *only* if we can argue that the pattern of inferences among attributed beliefs is intelligible. We can say that a philosopher has a certain concept *only if* we can give a reason for him to adopt the theory associated with the concept. The pattern of inference among attributed concepts must explain the Chinese philosophical texts better than available alternatives. If the pattern of inferences among terms is not intelligible, then the translation is mistaken.

The dictionary model of translation merely bungles this issue a bit worse than the translation model by itself. It takes the dictionary writer's theory of meaning as given. Then, when faced with the lack of the confirming pattern of inference among concepts, it concludes that Chinese thinkers have special, exotic inference strategies. Thus, reliance on the dictionary paradigm leads quickly to the conclusion that Chinese thinkers use a special logic. Dictionary translation virtually guarantees that one's interpretative theory will be unoriginal, wooden, inconsistent, and obscure. Philosophers regard a dictionary, therefore, as nothing more than a choppy, unstructured, unreflective, and theoretically irresponsible semantic theory.

*The state of art in accounts of Chinese syntax consists mainly of heuristics for translation in connection with a dictionary. Otherwise, specialists in Chinese language concentrate either on phonology or etymology. They construct rival theories of *the* original pronunciation of various characters or trace how graphic shapes developed from hypothetical ideographs or actual graphs on oracle bones and bronzes. In the absence of any credible recursive semantic or interpretive theory, scholars tend to treat theoretical approaches to interpretation as inherently undisciplined unless buttressed by claims from phonology or etymology.

To do that, I needed to see a plausible reason why the author would hold such a theory. I could see little plausibility in what the commentaries said was the obvious reason.

Unable to see either the obvious meaning or make any sense of the attributed obvious doctrine that those who knew Chinese saw, I felt like the youngster viewing the emperor's new clothes. Was I meaning-blind? Was I narrow-minded? Should I just accept that fundamentally different kinds of things could be reasons for Chinese thinkers? How could I discover that liberating truth unless I had that elusive direct access to the gossamer threads of meaning that others seemed to see? But try after try, I could only see characters. No aura, no shimmering flashes of meaning met my eyes. The challenge was to say what else it could reasonably mean. That is what I will now attempt to do.

My instinctive assumptions are realistic. An expression has a meaning. Commentaries propose *a theory* of what that meaning is. The dictionary is a theory. A translation of a passage *presupposes* the translator's theory; it is not evidence for it. When we adopt different meaning theories we attribute to the writer different beliefs. If I say that the character *niu*[ox] means *dog* and you say that it means *horse,* I attribute to the writer the belief that there is a dog over there and you attribute to him the belief that there is a horse over there. An interpretive theory of a language is more plausible when it better explains the beliefs it attributes to those who wrote it.

The standard theory attributes an incoherent, mystical, irrational set of beliefs to Daoists. I will propose a theory that makes them not only reasonable but incisive in critique of Confucianism. That, and not appeal to authority or circular citation of translations, is the evidence for my revised interpretive theory.

Suppose a defender of the standard theory says, "But it's not a failure of our interpretive theory that the Daoists seem irrational. They in fact are!" This simply begs the question. If they add, "Look, here is what they say," and produce a translation, they rely on the very interpretive theory that is in dispute. Suppose they add, "Chinese may reason differently from the way we reason." We simply ask how they could know such a thing. "Well, look at the Daoists!" That begs the question again. The only way to confirm the "it doesn't matter if Daoism seems irrational" hypothesis is to show that *on no plausible interpretive theory* can we make sense of it.

I propose to show that it is possible to make sense of Daoism. This meta-argument shows that, if possible, such a theory is in that regard better than the standard theory. It shows why appeals to authority or tradition in meaning theory are invalid. A better theory of meaning and background beliefs is a better theory—period. Nothing, of course, can force one to give up bad theories. But if it is a better theory, we ought to adopt it.*

---

*A simple question clarifies this realistic instinct. What makes an interpretive theory the correct one? The answer is not as simple. We need some principle to select among alternate interpretive theories: for example, the Confucian principle is conformity to tradition. What feature of one interpretive theory makes it scientifically better than some alternative?

Philosophers have proposed and discussed two such principles: the principle of charity and the principle of humanity. The principle of charity is a natural extension of the motivation of the formal logic-based origin of the philosophical theory. It endorses the interpretive theory that makes more of the corpus of expressions of the target language *true*.

Advocates of the principle of humanity worry that application of the principle of charity poses a danger, since in practice, it foists upon users of that language a body of truths which we (with a com-

The Fragmented-Schools View

My list of possible Confucian prejudices is incomplete and, as I argued, inconclusive. On their face, they do not make the ruling theory objectionable. I object to them because they undermine our ability to make sense of the rest of the tradition. I want now to focus on other bias-inducing structural features of the ruling interpretive theory.

Our current versions of the Neo-Confucian theory have two related dubious assumptions. First, they accept in varying degrees a piecemeal- or isolated-schools view of the classical period. They exaggerate similarities within schools and de-emphasize influence among the schools. The Neo-Confucian orthodoxy minimizes the degree to which philosophical projects and assumptions cross school boundaries. It also downplays philosophical progress. Schools analysis treats typical philosophical progress as merely deepening or elaborating the insights of the semi-divine founder. It tends to downplay how engaging in philosophical debate with rival doctrines motivates theory change.

The fragmented-schools view underlies a static presentation of classical Chinese thought. A typical account discusses Chinese philosophy with an encyclopedia organization in which Confucianism and Daoism are simply two different entries.*

pletely different scientific and cultural background) accept. So, they proposed that we maximize *reasonableness* rather than truth. We assume that humans reason in similar enough ways that we can understand them. We should be able to appreciate what would motivate a Chinese philosopher to adopt one theory instead of another. We can recognize what would count as a motivating reason for another rational human to adopt or express a doctrine. The principle of humanity thus allows us to attribute philosophical doctrines that are different from any we now adopt or have historically adopted. Our interpretive theory must simply explain why, given people's other beliefs, they accept the belief in question. That it now seems (or ever seemed) true to us is not crucial.

Because they begin with the notion of an interpretive *theory* of a language, both principles reinforce the assumption of the holistic nature of meaning. We attribute meaning to *a language* in a single systematic theory. The principle of charity selects that translation manual that makes the greatest number of the expressions true. Still, the effect of the principle of charity in the ordinary sinological method puts quicksand under piecemeal studies. An interpreter purports to prove an interpretive hypothesis (e.g., that a certain translation is correct for this character). He cites a sentence containing the character and translates it using the chosen term or phrase. If it seems true to the translator (or if it resembles a familiar Western philosophical doctrine), then he rests his case. The result is that we tend to attribute to Chinese philosophers a cluster of familiar but unsystematic philosophical doctrines.

The principle of humanity also requires that the interpretation makes sense of a fragment of the text. The sense conferred by the proposed interpretation is, however, not the immediate sense it makes to the translator *now*, pondering the sentence *in isolation*. The sense required is counterfactual. Using the principle of humanity, we implicitly ask the question. "Would that passage so construed make sense to a philosopher who accepted the background doctrines and operated with the theory-laden terms current in her time?" The principle of humanity, thus, forces us to recognize that we presuppose an interpretive theory of the whole tradition in each translation. We attribute beliefs and meaning in the same theory. So a fundamental revision of the interpretive theory is unlikely to emerge as a summary of more focused research topics. A researcher is likely to take the outlines of the received theory for granted in narrower studies.

Thus the idea of interpretation as an explanatory theory plus the principle of humanity makes the importance of interpretive holism inescapable. We presuppose an entire theory of the classical period in our interpretation of any part.

*Confucius invented Confucianism. Mencius and Xunzi elaborated and filled out the theory with a slightly different emphasis. Laozi invented Daoism, which again, is a single theory. Laozi and Zhuangzi

The other schools are simply object lessons in the necessary failure of any alternative theoretical path. The ruling theory brooks no hint that Confucianism may have grown from reacting to criticisms of opponents—especially the much-despised Mozi. Thus the ruling theory fragments the classical period into theoretically isolated schools.

I shall not reject school analysis entirely. The traditional assignment of schools represents some shared attitudes. The closest things to schools were text-based communities focused on texts. They studied, maintained, and updated the master's words and debated with other communities. When we collect these communities into the traditional schools we group together different, often incompatible, and progressively more advanced theories. I propose to understand the advances and changes as a result of their debate with other such communities.[4] They do not consist of a few core ideas that simply mature in an internal and unexplained process of theory growth. Philosophy advances through conversation, not private reflection. As Laozi puts it, each *dao* changes. I shall stress the developmental view and trace the growth of philosophical sophistication and understanding through all the schools.*

Even if we cannot occupy Schwartz's neutral vantage point, we should at least experiment with this interpretive theory that reverses the standard bias. Daoist method may recover Daoist content. We should explore the possibility that the rival theories have more depth and value than the standard interpretation recognizes. We look carefully and sympathetically at the criticisms of Confucian opponents and look critically at the adequacy of Confucian defenses. We treat the entire period as an ongoing dialogue in which the motive to philosophical progress comes from criticism and skepticism. The ruling interpretations, by contrast, undercut the force of each opponent's criticism. I shall try to sharpen those criticisms. The ruling interpretation may

accept the same core beliefs. They, too, differ only in emphasis. Now, in addition, there was Mohism (a strange and shallow doctrine), Legalism (a despotic and dirty one), and the Logicians (who were both impenetrable and irrelevant).

Chan's *Source Book* is the paradigm of this organization. But Schwartz's more historically organized *World* still exemplifies the residual tendency. Both Schwartz and Graham start with Confucius and follow historically with Mozi. But then Schwartz isolates Laozi and Zhuangzi in a chapter called "The Ways of Taoism" and Mencius and Xunzi are treated together in "The Defense of the Confucian Faith." Graham has an even more historical and original organization. But again, his middle section chapters are "From Confucius to Mencius . . ." "From Mozi to Later Mohism . . ." and "From Yangism to Chuang-tzu's Taoism . . . ." Each suggests that philosophical progress is some kind of self-contained maturation process of thought. The main beneficiary of these organizational schemes is Mencius. It buries the weakness of his case against Mozi and loses sight of Laozi and Zhuang-zi's attack on innatism.

*My developmental view of the philosophy of the period will spotlight instead the ways Confucius is similar to Mozi, Mencius to Laozi, and Zhuang zi to Xunzi. Confucius and Mozi both agreed that the task of social leadership is to foster some guiding discourse. They disagreed about what linguistic content public guiding discourse should officially promote and encourage. Mencius and Laozi form an antilanguage reaction to the irresolvability of the *Ru-Mo* Confucian–Mohist dispute. They share an appeal to naturalness and an aversion to letting language distort natural dispositions. Laozi, moreover, gives an account of how we might get apparent intuitions in the very process of learning a language. The Later Mohists formulated a decisive refutation of the antilanguage views and argued for basing language on the similarities and differences in the world. Zhuang zi argued that the world favored no unique way of marking similarity and difference. He showed that the arguments for both innatist intuitionism and Mohist realism presupposed disputed standards. Xunzi rehabilitiated traditionalism on relativist pragmatic grounds as an attempted solution to Zhuang zi's challenge. Han Fei zi followed Xunzi's pragmatic and conventionalist argument and scraped historical traditionalism. He simply urged that the ruler promote any discourse that is useful to the ruler and the state and ban all others.

remove the motivation or clarity of an opponent's rival theory. I shall try to restore it. The ruling theory may distort even Confucian theory to make it immune to the attacks of its contemporary critics. I shall note the weaknesses in Confucian arguments with emphasis and undisguised Daoist glee.

The Meaning-Change Hypothesis

A second metatheoretical feature of the ruling interpretation buttresses this *isolated schools analysis*. Standard accounts use *meaning-change* hypotheses promiscuously. Meaning-change hypotheses make the isolation of the schools from common concerns a matter of language. Each meaning-change hypothesis entails that the schools were talking about fundamentally different things. The two most prominent examples of meaning change hypotheses concern the terms *dao*$^{\text{guiding discourse}}$ and *fa*^{standards}. Standard interpretations say that *dao-jia*^{Daoists} and *fa-jia*^{Legalists} changed the meaning of their focal terms. When Daoists spoke of *dao*$^{\text{metaphysical absolute}}$ or Legalists spoke of *fa*^{laws} they changed the subject. Thus, the meaning-change ploy effectively isolated Confucianism from its critics and rivals.

The isolated-schools approach of the ruling theory needs to render Daoist, Mohist, and Legalist arguments irrelevant to Confucianism. We persist in the classifications despite recognizing that neither Daoism nor Legalism was a school in the standard sense. Intellectual historians during the Han dynasty (which established Confucian political orthodoxy) retrospectively invented both these names and used them to identify and distinguish certain trends in classical thought. These historians named each school with a term that they took to be the unifying concern of a set of thinkers, *dao*^{way} for the Daoists and *fa*^{law} for the legalists.

The ruling theory artificially forces these writers together and separates them from the mainstream of philosophical discourse. The standard view not only gives them a single conceptual focus, but also a single core theory about that key concept. Daoists, they allege, changed the meaning of *dao*^{way} from moral doctrine to metaphysical monistic absolute—the Chinese equivalent of Parmenidean being. Legalists also changed the meaning of the term that defines their school from *fa*^{standards} to positive *fa*^{law}.*

---

*These are only the most egregious uses of the meaning-change hypothesis. The shibboleth that Chinese words have many meanings dominates the sinological mythology of Chinese language. The most common diagnosis of this analysis is that the interpreters have confused a writer's *theory* about some topic with the meaning of the word he uses in expressing that theory. So Confucius says that a gentleman is concerned with *yi*^{morality}, a small man is concerned with *li*^{benefit}. The common practice is to suggest that for Confucius *yi*^{morality} *meant* the opposite of benefit. When the Mohists define *yi*^{morality} as *li*^{benefit}, that forces us to say that either the meaning has changed or one of these two is misusing it. For the tradition, Confucius defines correst usage. Mozi is derided as lacking linguistic and sylistic expertise; he is semantically confused. Respect for Confucians entails that Mozi's moral theory must be an oxymoron.

We should say, instead, that Confucius has one theory of morality and Mozi proposes a rival theory of morality. An adequate theory of meaning should treat *yi*^{morality} as having the common meaning that explains how rival theorists could adopt these two contrasting moral theories. That enables us to see substantive disagreement between the schools. The Confucian strategy of asserting meaning change when-

The ideological effect of illicit use of the meaning-change hypothesis is this. We cannot see the theories of the rival schools as critical comments about and attempts to improve on Confucian theories. Sinologists present the meaning-change hypothesis (words change meanings in China as actors change costumes in plays) as empirical, observational fact. It is as if meanings were perceptible auras that surrounded the character. Those who *know* Chinese have learned to see the aura and can directly perceive when it has changed. As I have admitted, I cannot claim to have seen the gossamer threads of meaning. So I cannot empirically prove that they have not changed. But any theory of meaning that makes words change meaning whenever we find a rival theory makes philosophical disagreement hard to explain. It reinforces the tendency to treat schools as self-contained points of view with only an internal dynamic—effectively different languages.

We have reason, therefore, to suspect ideologically motivated biases in both the standard interpretation's details and structure. The meaning-change hypothesis props up the fragmentary account imposed by the isolated-schools view. These feed into the practice of characterizing Confucian rivals in ways that protect Confucianism from local philosophical criticism. Apologetic Confucian accounts then dismiss most philosophical criticism of Confucianism as reflecting Western philosophical bias. If we treat meaning as shared between rival theories, however, we will find that the obvious criticisms were clearly stated within China's own classical tradition.

Indo-European Theory of Language and Mind

A different type of suspicion arises from our awareness of the Buddhist influence on Neo-Confucianism. This source of distortion is considerably more complex and difficult to sort out because Western biases collaborate with Neo-Confucianism in imposing it on Classical thinkers. Buddhism came from a philosophical culture with extensive historical contact with ancient Greek and Middle Eastern civilizations. The conceptual structure of its theory of language and mind closely resembles that of our own Western folk psychology. The Neo-Confucian absorption of this theory of language and of mind would, therefore, be harder for us to isolate and neutralize. We fail to bracket and examine it precisely because it seems like obvious common sense. It too closely resembles our own, two-thousand-year-old tradition of beliefs. We hardly even notice it.

ever there is a disagreement makes all philosophical dispute merely verbal. Then, by hypothesis, they expect us to acknowledge that Confucian usage is correct.

Another source of this widespread view of Chinese comes from confusing our theories of dictionaries. The Western dictionary tradition flows out of our Euclidean and Platonic heritage. We assume the notion of a *meaning* that the definition should express. The Chinese dictionary tradition is more historical. It collects different historical examples of use and lists possible character (or phrase) substitutes in each use. It also gives a causal-historical theory of the character—a purported etymology and routinely a pictographic or ideographic analysis. We tend to treat each such entry as a different meaning.

Now, the notion of meaning is vague enough to allow us to run different uses together with different meanings. But, our interpretive theory will be more coherent if we propose a core meaning that explains the different uses. That way, when different philosophers disagree with each other about philosophical topics, we will not dismiss their dispute as merely verbal. Not all philosophical disagreement is the result of using their key terms with different meanings.

Neo-Confucianism was a scholastic Confucian movement with *only* Buddhism as a serious philosophical foe.* In its attempt to recover the ancient Confucian *dao,* it typically painted Buddhism and Daoism as functional twins—the foil against which it distinguished Confucianism. It used Daoism as the classical place-marker against which to present its theory of the special merit of Confucianism. This colored the entire presentation of the classical period. Buddhist metaphysics and the presupposed similarity between Daoism and Buddhism dominated the Neo-Confucian reconstruction of philosophical issues. These familiar facts suggest that the orthodox interpretation might have *two* sources of inaccuracy: (1) it may favor Confucian theory or (2) it may presuppose a Buddhist conceptual framework.

The schools analysis leads us to postulate an obscure and mystical Chinese logic that is irrational by Western lights. The Buddhist influence leads us to assume the Chinese thinkers shared Western traditional psychological theories. On the face of things, one could make a more plausible case for precisely the opposite analysis that their inference strategies (their actual cognitive psychology) resembles ours more than their psychological theory does. It is possible to have different theories of our shared linguistic, intellectual, and social capacities. Western popular mentalist psychological theory is dubious and seriously controversial even among Western thinkers and cognitive psychologists. It is far less likely to be true than is Western logic.

The Buddhist impact on the standard theory coincides with the loss of the Chinese linguistic analysis in China's philosophical dark age. Dark-age philosophers clearly failed to appreciate the highly technical, deep, and involved theories of the Later Mohist theory of language. The long period of Buddhist intellectual domination of medieval China that followed the dark age thus takes on special significance. The Confucianism that reemerges from the Buddhist overlay may interpret its own ancient theories in terms of a *Buddhist theory of language and mind.* Western transmitters would unconsciously perpetuate and exaggerate this distortion. The Buddhist theory shares so much with that of ancient Greece that the result looks very much like our own inherited philosophical views on language and mind.

The Neo-Confucian movement and Western theorists are unwitting coconspirators in this inadvertent self-deception. But, unlike the Confucian bias I targeted earlier, this slant does *not necessarily* favor Confucianism. The framework set by alien assumptions about language may also distort Confucianism's philosophical base.

We know of substantial prehistorical cultural contact between India and the birthplace of Western philosophy in Western Asia. The recognized boundaries of the Indo-European language family are only one indication of the pattern of early cultural

---

*The received theory's own account of Chinese intellectual history guides our skepticism. Its abiding obsession lay in revitalizing classical Confucianism against a changed intellectual background. The emergence from the philosophical dark age was gradual. The Han dynasty changed the focus of Chinese philosophy to an eclectic, yin-yang cosmology. The *Dark Learning* school of the Wei emerged next. It reinterpreted Daoism by combining it with the yin-yang and tai-ji cosmology of the *Yi Jing* and tried to make the result compatible with Confucianism. Buddhism spread in China by putting its doctrines in a *Dark Learning* framework and dominated the long period up to the Tang dynasty. The Wei, cosmological prototype shaped Buddhism and in turn Neo-Confucianism. It gave them a model for making Mencius' innatism into a cosmology. They viewed Daoism on that same model distinguished only by its amoral cosmic view. Thus, the Neo-Confucians reconstructed their account of classical Confucianism and Daoism on a Buddhist metaphysical and mystical model. Ancient Confucianism was to Daoism as their Confucianism was to Buddhism.

migration. Our history of Greek philosophy traces its origins to contact with cultures in the Middle East in the Ionian parts of Asia Minor.* Historians also assign an Aryan origin to the philosophical Brahmin class in India. Finally, we know from history that Aristotle tutored Alexander the Great, who spread Greek military and political power as far as India.

Not surprisingly, therefore, Indian philosophy shares many vital concepts with Greek linguistic and psychological theory.† At root, Indian thought views the function of language as primarily representative or descriptive. Buddhist logic shows a clear conception of an argument or a proof as a series of sentences with subject-predicate structure. It has a full-blown sense of logic as a theory of the structure of argument. Indian logic, like Aristotle's, focused on a syllogistic form.

Its theory of mind shows striking parallels as well. It revolves around the intentional notions of belief and of reason as the way beliefs are arrived at, modified, and discarded. Beliefs are contrasted with desires. Together belief and desire explain human action. Indian thought, like more modern Western thought, developed a mind-body metaphysics. Mind is a realm of mental objects just as the physical world is a realm of material bodies. The skeptics in both traditions challenged the alleged correspondence between the realms. Were the mental objects illusions? Do mental objects correspond to the objects in the physical world?

The common Indo-European theory of mind centered on the cognitive faculty. The model of knowing was representing accurately through mental contents—true beliefs. The mental items arrange themselves into beliefs—mental compositions or sentences of *mentalese*. These mental constructions (thoughts) picture possible physical configurations of objects. Beliefs are true if the pictures are accurate, false if they are not. This model breeds skepticism of belief through doubt of the senses as causes of (evidence for) our beliefs. Radical skepticism ensues because we can never objectively test whether our mental contents correspond to the world. Our only access to the world is through our senses, which are under skeptical attack.

Like traditional Western thought, the Buddhist view of language meshes with its view of mind. It similarly concentrates on how language relates to reality. The theory treats the mental ideas as interpretations of words. Ideas have pictorial content. That pictorial content relates them to sensed objects. Thus the language has semantic value in virtue of its link to ideas. The theory of ideas explains meaning and it explains how we understand the words or sounds of language and apply them in the world.‡

---

*The philosophical similarities of Indian and Greek philosophies of language and mind can be explained by either cultural transmission or independent discovery *or both*. Since the languages have a family resemblances, we can easily understand their adopting similar theories of their language. Cultural transmission could be from India to Greece or Greece to India or from some other common origin (the Middle East) to both.

†I make this claim with some trepidation, since I am not a Sanskrit scholar. I rely on other's description of Indian philosophy. See for example Zimmer (1951), pp. 4 and 333–63, and Chaudhuri (1979), pp. 22–24 and 64–83, Obviously someone who did the same with Chinese would conclude, with the standard theory, that Chinese thinkers had a theory of consciousness, meanings, beliefs, sentences, mind-body, sense data, etc.

‡The focus on pictorial correspondence led Buddhists, like the Greeks, to give reality (like logic) a subject-predicate form. The subject corresponds to things and the predicate to features, attributes, properties, essences, and characteristics. They assumed, as the Greeks did, that using a word presupposed the

The familiar Western conceptual separation of mind and body that also marks Indian thought carries in its wake other familiar mental concepts. Indian thought, like Western thought, blends semantics and psychology with subjectivist theoretical terms like *experience* and *consciousness*. These structure a subjective picture of individual psychology. As we noted, these inner pictures of a world generate, in Buddhism as in England, a radical phenomenological skepticism about the external world. The lever of philosophical discourse pries against the fulcrum of a contrast between an inner, private subjectivity and an outer, abstract, objective, transcendental reality.*

Thus Indian thought and Greek and Western thought share a focus on metaphysics and epistemology. They view the function of language as communicating informational content. It does this because words refer to particulars (objects) in the world. Words do this by means of some semantic mediator—an idea, essence, or meaning. Since many objects bear the same name, the name must relate directly to some essence or property that each object has. That shared essence puts them into a natural collection of objects. Mental ideas link names to these collections. Buddhist thought, like Western thought, thus accepted what Blackburn has called the *dogleg* theory of meaning.[5] A meaning is something that mediates between a word and particulars in the world.

Translation of Indian mental theory into Western terms has been relatively straightforward. Semantic content (meanings, concepts) are carried in mental objects (ideas).[6] Syllogistic logic and the proof model of reasoning bolster this mental semantic theory. Reasoning operates on beliefs (the cognitive, semantic, subjective contents of mind). The mind constructs mental proofs with its beliefs and desires as premises. This practical reasoning produces deliberate, morally responsible action.

The shared-proof model carries in its wake the concept of truth. Truth is the semantic value of sentences and therefore of beliefs. The concluding sentence in a proof inherits truth from the sentences that make up the premises of the proof. Reasons are premises. In a practical syllogism the conclusion is an action, and desires and beliefs are reasons for action.

---

existence of permanent substances. When an ordinary object changes we use different predicates with the same subject. We uttered "Peter is young" years ago. Now we utter "Peter is old." Peter must refer via our ideas to some underlying, unchanging thing that once had the property of being young and now has its opposite property. Change thus presupposes some underlying permanence that *has* the changing attributes. For similar reasons, the appearance of multiplicity demands explanation in terms of an underlying unity. This is a chair. That is a chair. There must be some deep essence that they share that justifies calling them by the same name. That one behind many essence is the unchanging essence. That abstract essence, this reasoning goes, is what our idea is an idea *of*.

Like the Greeks, therefore, Indian philosophers drew on a contrast between reality and mental appearance. Their full-blown conception of proof and argument gave them a familiar notion of reason which, like the Greeks, they contrasted with experience. The function of reason in revising beliefs was to make them accurate pictures of the real world. That meant passing suspicious judgment on the world of changing appearance. The result was the striking assumption that Greek and Indian rationalism share: reality is permanent. Anything that changes is, to that degree, unreal.

*The contrast of reason with emotion (and the consequent deprecation of the latter) arises from the same structure. The psychology of belief and desire correlates with mind-body dualism. Belief and desire together cause action. But beliefs are paradigm mental entities. They could not directly act on physical objects. So we theorize that desires arise from our physical nature. They are like perceptions which reality introduces into the mind. The are perceptions of the state of our body. Desires conflict with the idealized activity of reason. They tend to disorder, disrupt, and distort its generation of an accurate, philosophical inner picture of the external world.

I have tried in this brief account to emphasize how this cluster of concepts in semantics, logic, psychology, and moral theory work together. These are not random, isolated notions, but part of the central conceptual structure of both Western and Indian philosophy.*

The reader may now appreciate my motive in this section. These ideas are not separate items like packages of cereal that one may take off the shelves of the supermarket of ideas. To attribute one of these ideas to a philosophical culture is to attribute the *network* of ideas to them. The reasonableness of attributing one belief from the set depends on their having a theory in which it functions along with the others. Something counts as the same idea only if it has the same theoretical connections. Obviously, I intend to deny that Chinese thought has *the entire network* of this Indo-European subjectivist psychology and linguistic theory.

Even in the ruling theory, it is a commonplace that Chinese thought does not exhibit a mind-body dichotomy. The ruling theory, however, treats that dichotomy as an isolated doctrine. It does not notice these deep connections to our familiar folk psychology of private mental contents, the distinction of ideas and emotions, consciousness, awareness, and experience. It ignores how central mind-body dualism is to our conventional view of meaning in language—that is, our theory of ideas. The result is that we uncritically interpret the thinkers of the pre-Buddhist period against the background of an Indo-European theory of psychology and language.

So, again, my strategy experiments with reversal of opposites. Where the ruling theory uses our familiar psychological assumptions in explanation, I work for an interpretation free from those assumptions. Still, this second source of skepticism presents a deep problem. I can target any assumption that attributes this Indo-European theory of language and mind to ancient Chinese philosophers. But how do we improve on mentalist theory? Can we conceive of an alternate model? Our difficulty lies in constructing and stating an intelligible alternate. Our Indo-European conceptual perspective is so familiar that any alternate seems blatantly wrong. We can only confirm it if we can construct it.

The Computer Analogy

Why do we experience such difficulty in entertaining the hypothesis of deep differences in another culture's thought? One reason might be that our own beliefs have changed so little over our history. We assume a similar psychological theory because we can hardly imagine believing other than what Indo-European culture has *always* believed. These evidently *eternal truths* must be universal and obvious truths.†

*It even has echoes in Indo-European religious thought. This metaphysical conception of the mind as a realm in which ideas are the objects helps validate the philosophical proofs of immortality in both traditions. It generates the familiar association of death with body, desire, and sin. Life, meaning, and value correlate with consciousness, the mind, thought, and reason. The aspiration to purity in mental transcendence stems from the parallel-world structure of the theory of mind.

†Our folk psychology has changed, but only slightly, from its Greek origins. The main change came in the seventeenth and eighteenth centuries. Cartesianism made the realm of meaning and thought private and subjective. Plato's version was of an objective, intellectual realm of cognitive and semantic *forms*. Modern *common sense* about psychology, language learning, and meaning has remained largely unchanged since Descartes's individualistic, subjectivist revision. Modern cognitive psychology is a different matter. See Stich (1983).

We have reason to be suspicious that the ruling interpretation has imposed an Indo-European theory of language and mind on the text. What other philosophical psychology could we substitute? We are lucky, in this regard, that very recent philosophy and empirical psychology have not only cast doubt on the traditional Western view, but have also begun to develop an alternative conception of mental functioning.* We now have a way to characterize reasoning without assuming the *arguments-on-paper* view of the mind.[7] Substitute the notion of a computational program for the familiar picture of the mental-arguments concept of reasoning. Use the computer model to explain how a physical being can process language and how language guides action in a real world context. We need not explain a computer's operating by attributing to it mental or semantic content, inner consciousness, or experience.

A computer operates with a program. We input the program—load it into the computer. That process changes the computer's *dispositions* in complex ways. It will now behave differently to different inputs. We may use the language of stimulus-response or even of intuition, but the relation of input and output need not be simple minded. It can come from a very complicated program. The computer's dispositional state has a physical realization (an electronic functional state) that may produce very subtle behavioral responses after a complicated calculation.

The explanation of the computer's behavior does not require our habitual contrast of belief and desire. The program itself causes the behavior (of course, using energy supplied as electricity and oil, requiring a dust-free environment, and resting—cooling off). The now-familiar science-fiction images of robots, cyborgs, or droids have made this new model somewhat familiar. (I suspect that it also creates some image problems that I will address below.)

If we accept that the Chinese philosophy of mind did not rest on a mind-body dichotomy, then we surely could use something like the computer analogy to explain intelligent human behavior. The computer analogy illustrates how a physical thing could reason, act, be moral, and function in the world as humans do. A computer can print out the result of a complicated calculation when we input the data. It does a calculation though it does not have beliefs.[8] We do not suppose that the computer reflects on the meaning of the premises and sees the conclusion of its proof in a kind of rational insight.† Informally, it helps us see why we do not *need* to assume that Chinese philosophers took the traditional Western theory of the relation of mind, language, and the world for granted.

This is not to suggest that the ancient Chinese had invented computers. The computer analogy of mind helps mainly because it frees us from reliance on our inherited Greek view of psychology. It allows us to imagine an alternative to this doctrine of a mysterious, internal mental realm. It gives us a model for understanding

---

*I propose to use the resources of these modern philosophical challenges to the semantic-centered theory of language and traditional Western folk psychology. We draw on naturalistic epistemology, cognitive psychology, and the computer analogy of mind. Together, these give us a *syntactic* analysis of the nature of thinking to replace the *arguments on paper* (Kornblith, 1985) view of reasoning.

†That is what I mean by saying that the model of the mind is syntactic rather than semantic. What we call reasoning can be understood as calculating according to a program. We understand computers as having a *physical* potential to do the caclulation. We created that potential when we altered its electromagnetic state by loading our program. That physical state explains how it can reliably take the input and yield a correct output.

both how our minds might work while conceptually identifying mind and body. It does not require a separate inner mental realm to parallel the natural physical realm. Rational and emotional outputs are equally physical responses to inputs.

Trying this out on the classical Chinese philosophers, we get a model that explains the central position of dao^{way} in Chinese philosophy. A dao is analogous to a program. Confucius viewed education as inputting the inherited $dao^{guiding\ discourse}$ of the sages. We study and practice a dao. We learn to speak and act properly by studying the *Book of Poetry* or the *Book of Rites*. This view accounts for Confucius' distinctively non-Western attitude that instilling tradition is a realization and fulfillment of human nature instead of a limiting constraint. The $de^{virtuosity}$, as the traditional formula had it, is the dao^{way} within a person. It is the physical realization of the program that generates the behaviors. When we have good $de^{virtuosity}$, our behavior will follow the dao^{way}. The program runs as intended in us. Good $de^{virtuosity}$, therefore, is like a combination of virtue (when compiling a moral dao^{way}) and like power (because executing instructional programs enables us to do things). Our virtuosity is the translation of an instruction set into a physical, dispositional potential.

Daoist thinkers make this view of things especially clear. The *Laozi* introduces the idea that we create desires by learning guiding discourse—gaining knowledge of what to do (know-to). The programming model explains many issues of classical Chinese thought. Notice first that we are, in a sense, programming each other. Our outputs include language that is input to others. The importance of maintaining cultural traditions, the family, the father model of the ruler and the educational role of political society all have clear motivations once we adopt this model. Let us look briefly at more of the explanatory value of the computer model of mind.

Instantly this model gives us a new conception of the roles of language and mind. Pragmatic (action centered) rather than semantic analyses now make more sense. Language guides and controls behavior. It does this by restructuring our behavior guiding mechanism, the $xin^{heart-mind}$. The common translation of xin as *heart-mind* reflects the blending of belief and desire (thought and feeling, ideas and emotions) into a single complex dispositional potential. We need not attribute separate structures of reasoning and feeling to computers to explain their behavior.

Now what do we say of the source of mental, cognitive content in the Greek psychology—experience or consciousness? This question reveals a deep difference between these explanatory models. Western thought, in effect, treats experience as the programming step: experience generates the inner language of ideas with which we calculate. Chinese thought treats the programming as the social process of reading in guiding discourse. Experience then merely triggers execution of the program. The computer has *program control* tied to the external state of affairs. The senses provide discrimination—branching input to trigger different parts of the socialized program.*

---

*The program works by stimulus-response but not necessarily *simple-minded* stimulus-response (see Dennett, 1981). We can imagine fine-tuning the response and making it as complicated as we think human behavior to be. Certainly, we would expect the model to include an account of thinking. It need not be an account of inner reflection on meanings or thoughts. It would instead amount to calculating and adjusting response to reflect the complex situation. Still we would not need the internalist, consciousness-based view of thinking. Experience, similarly, need not be a picturelike inner world. The programming model requires only that our sense organs discriminate between features of the outer world. Experience is not data but an interface (input-output device). We would respond to the actual situation insofar as our

So this model gives us what we wanted. We can explain the focus on *ming*^names and *bian*^distinctions in the school of names in a way that is continuous with the surrounding philosophical tradition. The crucial philosophical problem lying in the path of this social theory is that of the projectability of names. What counts as having used a name correctly? How do we project the distinction we make here to future cases?*

The computer analogy also gives us a way to interpret classical Chinese disputes about innateness without importing our reason-intuition distinction. We can convert a *dao*^way to our machine language only if we already have a compiler or translator in the machine. Obviously someone must have hard-wired some structure into the unit before we can input any programs. One question about human nature that dominates this period amounts to asking how much behavior guidance is hard-wired (innate)? Do we need *any* social *dao*^guiding discourse? Is it appropriate to use *dao*^guiding discourse or *yan*^language to change the behavioral features that *tian*^heaven has hard-wired in us?

---

senses could provide discriminatory categories for use in program control. So our *xin*^heart–mind and the sense receptors together explain how we can test for a condition in following the program. Does the name "father" apply here? Then execute the instruction that lowers your eyes and say "father" in a respectful tone.

Instead of cognitive content, then, we have cognitive-response sensitivity. Executing a *dao*-program requires that we correctly register the external conditions and sensitively adjust our responses. At the base of that requirement is this: we should know the boundary conditions for applying each name used in the guiding discourse. This explains the role of rectifying names and its importance in the Confucian model. Confucius does not use definitions. His concern would be with correct behavioral response, not with cognitive content or meaning. Having control of the word amounts to triggering the *right procedure* in response to external conditions. Besides, giving a definition would merely duplicate the interface problem. More words or internal programming can help only if the programmer has already properly adjusted our *de*^virtuosity to the external conditions for application of those words. A definition can only help if we correctly apply the words in the definition, so it cannot be the general solution to the problem of adjusting behavior. The basic solution is the equivalent of debugging. Run the program in real time and have the teacher (programmer) correct errors. Rectifying names is essential to achieving the goal of a *dao*^guiding discourse. It is the job of the social elite.

*The computer analogy yields many interesting corollaries that explain other features of Chinese thought. We think of programs in sentencelike units (commands) with sentential syntax. The *machine language* translations, however, consist of a *stack of words*. The order in the stack is important from top to bottom, not just in sentences. Sentential segments of the stack have no uniquely important status. The Indo-European fascination with the sentence reflects two interesting differences in our theory of language. One is inflectional grammar that operates mainly within sentence boundaries. Sentential role-marking (part-of-speech inflections) directs our attention to the sentence as the linguistic unit in which each part of speech plays a role. The syntactical rules requiring both a subject and a predicate also draw our attention to the notion of a complete, freestanding unit. The other difference is the theoretical focus on semantic content—truth. Here the sentence represents the complete thought, the map of a state of affairs, the fact. Truth is a property primarily of sentences. It should not, therefore, surprise us if we do not discover this cluster of linguistic concepts in Chinese thought.

The lack of sentential focus will also have implications for ethics. Our conception of an obligation makes it the prescriptive correlate of a fact. The is-ought distinction postulates two different sentence types. The types suggest two different roles that language plays (describing and prescribing). The computer model, by contrast, suggests that language is primarily prescriptive, behavior guiding. If we attribute a picture of reality to the computer, it will only be as a guide to generating some output. Chinese moral debates will not be analytical theories of rules or duties. Moral debate will be about what *dao*^guiding discourse to use in social programming and how to adjust names and distinctions to guide execution of that *dao*.

The Computer Analogy and Human Dignity

A problem now arises that is almost as difficult as conceiving of a different psychological model than the one we traditionally take for granted. Being able to understand
the model may mean that we find it emotionally cold and evaluatively demeaning.
The problem is not merely in the science-fiction cliché of intelligent androids that
lack feelings and emotions. Conventional wisdom ties our notion of the special status
of being human to our theory of mind, intellect, and reason. The model of an alternate psychological theory that I am offering is likely to evoke cries that it deprives
us of humanity and dignity: that it makes us just like animals—merely responding to
external stimulation (albeit with somewhat more complexity than other animals). This
model, religiously inclined champions of human dignity will insist, denies the unique
human ability to transcend our nature that makes us better than animals. It denies us
the Godlike results of our having partaken of the tree of knowledge and lost our
innocence. We paid a terrible price for the biblical choice between knowledge and
everlasting life. We can hardly imagine giving up the model of ourselves as knowers
or of our minds as cognitive.

Ancient Greek humanism took the now familiar road of elevating humans out
of nature into the intellectual realm. It placed us in a hybrid tension between the
physical world of common sense and experience and an intellectual, rational world
of meaning, knowledge, and value. We are neither of this world nor free from it
(until we die). The identification of human worth with the impulse to transcendence
has a flip side, since we accordingly devalue the physical, the material. These twin
elements of Greek thought became the mainstays of Christianity and our view of our
special relation to God.

Our tradition also contrasted the reasoning faculty (the mind) with the irrational,
base, physical desires and passions (the heart). Our beliefs, our ideas, come from
the mind—from the reasoning faculty. Our bodies supply us with our desires. We
tied our conception of dignity to our possible independence from natural desires.
Rational worth lies in obedience to the law of reason alone. Only then can we understand our actions as free, voluntary actions. To be free is for our reasoning faculty
to control us. We detach ourselves from mere bodily, physical determination.

The ruling interpretive theory of Chinese thought reacts defensively to this impulse to value transcendence in Western thought. That defensive reaction mistakes
having the theory of reason (and worshiping it) with being capable of reasoning.
Clearly, I believe that Chinese thinkers reasoned competently, but I do not think that
they developed *a theory of reason*. To suggest that Chinese thinkers did not have the
reason-emotion dichotomy amounts, in the view of some, to a condemnation—almost
a racist one. Reason is the source of our moral dignity. Certainly the idea of philosophy without the theory of reason would challenge our deepest assumptions.

The Eastern-guru theory of Chinese philosophy deals with this issue in a thoroughly confusing way. First, it defensively insists that classical thinkers *implicitly*
had a theory of reason. However, they say, the Chinese philosophers consciously
rejected the notion of controlling one's life by reason. They did so, the theory goes,
for good reasons. They appreciated a mysteriously higher, more profound view of
the value of the right brain, of intuition.[9] This response reveals a failure to appreciate
both the complex and the deeply normative character of the Western theory of rea-

son. It is not merely a descriptive term for an isolated psychological faculty (the left brain). Its textual problem, however, is sufficient reason to reject it until we see if an alternate theory can explain the texts. We will find no clear formulation of any reason-intuition dichotomy in classical Chinese writings.

I would like further to meet the ruling theory's valuation of transcendence head on. It is now commonplace both to recognize and appreciate the Daoist view of the unity of humanity and nature. Understanding ourselves as continuous with nature, as animals in a natural ecological brotherhood, is currently fashionable enough to defy this medieval distaste for the *natural man*. The antitranscendence view is surely consistent with science—no doubt, still opposing Western religion on this issue. Plenty of room remains for religious awe in the mysteries and complexity of nature, the working of our marvelous minds and language. If we are to worship, it makes sense to worship the wonders that lie before us. Why worship an imagined and unseen creator of them? We no longer need transcendence for awe.*

Mentalese and Conventional Language

Resistance to the computer model may come from still another direction. It may still seem that the mental content view is the only (or the best) way to explain our mastery of language. The current disputes in philosophical psychology and psycholinguistics address just this issue. These disputes offer us the chance to take a new perspective on our traditional assumptions about mind and language. Some philosophers and cognitive psychologists suggest that the ancient Greek picture of the relation of mind, language, and the world is simply false.[10] That old, useless theory is destined for the same historical fate as the theory of phlogiston, Newtonian absolute space-time, witches, and magic. I certainly do not hope to settle that issue here. I shall merely summarize the kinds of puzzles that first drew critical attention to the deep problems in the common-sense, received version of the theory of ideas.

Part of the source of the controversy is that different philosophers disagree on

*The emerging ecological consciousness surely will find Daoism a more congenial home than the Christian transcendent scorn for *this world*. Even before that, it should have been obvious that this Greek and Christian conception of human dignity not only cut us off from animals, but also made our relation to our earlier selves and our children conceptually puzzling. It was used historically to distinguish men from women and freeholders from slaves. We castigate those inferiors as lacking in sufficient cognitive rational ability to deserve our elevated status. The historical track record of this unique conception of human dignity has not been as stellar from our present perspective as its remaining religious defenders pretend. It perhaps took a mind as unorthodox as Nietzsche to show us this Christian attitude as a *sick* moral psychology, a form of self-hate. We learn to hate all natural passions and desires. We long for *the other life* only half conscious that we are implicitly hoping for death. Perhaps only Nietzsche could have shown us this deep kinship of Buddhism and Christianity. The hoped for transcendence, as Socrates first recognized, is possible only with death—the natural man is an enemy of God!

I expect I will not have totally blunted the tendency to think of human dignity and worth as tied to transcendent reason and cognition. This is one of those places where I can merely openly announce my perspective. I, therefore, give fair notice to critics. This theoretical focus may tempt them to accuse me, as Graham did, of "cretinizing" Chinese philosophy (Graham 1985, p. 698) and of promoting an anti-Chinese bias. If it does, let me turn the pointing finger of attribution of bias back on them. It is precisely this Western *evaluative bias* that needs defense, not my interpretation of Chinese philosophers. What bias lies behind the view that this model demeans us? Daoist nature worship certainly appeals more to *me* than Christian otherworldly transcendence does.

what phenomenon the theory of ideas is to explain. For our purposes, let us look at one aspect of the use of language that Chinese thinkers share with us. How can we make the distinctions needed to use a word correctly in following directions? A traditional Western mental account goes as follows. Merely learning a word (a mere sound or visual representation of a sound) cannot explain this ability. We theorize that, from our experience and memory traces of a class of things, we have abstracted a vague image—an idea of the *type*. Only after we have this idea or concept can we hope to learn the English (or German, or Chinese) word for that type. We learn to associate the word with the idea, and the idea helps us to make the distinction among the objects we see. The analysis has two parts: (1) it associates the inert, meaningless sound with an idea in the mind, and (2) something like pictorial resemblance links the idea and the class of intended objects.

Ludwig Wittgenstein, accordingly, raised two serious problems for this view—one for each side of the explanation. First, consider the relation of the words and ideas. The original ability we intended to explain was the ability to distinguish some object, say an eel, from others, say a fish. We must do this to follow a program or a command using the word. This proposed solution assumes that on hearing the word *eel* we can pick the idea of an eel out from all the other ideas stocked in our mind. Now, the analysis set out *to explain* how we pick out the eel from the fish in front of me. The proposed explanation merely puts the same puzzle into my mind. How do I pick out my *mental picture* of the eel from my mental picture of a fish? If we think of the mental items as objects in a mental world, the proposed explanation assumes the very ability it purports to explain: the ability to distinguish eels from fish.

The other side of the explanation raises a similar problem. The ideas themselves, as we saw, work like a language. The ideas, corresponding to words, combine into thoughts or beliefs, which correspond to sentences. Philosophers[11] have dubbed this language of thought *mentalese*. We explain meaning as translation into mentalese. Notice that on the received view, mentalese is similar to a pictographic or ideographic language. We assume that the pictographic nature of this language removes the interpretive problem. But on reflection we will see that it doesn't. The pictures, after all, do not look exactly like the items before us and the question of whether to extrapolate from the eel picture or the fish picture remains. An ideographic or pictographic language needs standards of interpretation as much as does the ordinary language. (Chinese philosophers would surely appreciate this fact!) If a deep puzzle about how language can guide discrimination exists, it applies to pictographic mentalese as well.*

This familiar Western solution to the problem of explaining our ability to use language simply divides it into two related problems. One is how sounds pick out types, and the other is how language can consistently project to new or novel cases from past examples. Instead of solving the problem, it merely duplicates it on two sides of the mysterious, postulated, mental entity. We envision a kind of translation from a phonemic to a pictographic language that requires the very ability we seek to

---

*In the Chinese case, the possibility that one can misapply a pictograph to an object would have been obvious to them. They recognized their graphs as both social and conventional. Mentalese theory postulates *a private language* of semantic signs. This removes the normal criteria for identifying a correct and incorrect application of a sign. No one can *catch us* making a mistake in applying our own mental signs. So we assume that we cannot apply them incorrectly.

explain. Then it merely recreates the problem of explaining how a language (now pictographic) refers to the world.

I should note that the computer analogy and the Chinese theory of language are not intended as a solution to this problem. Their use here lies in showing that the traditional, Western, mentalese solution begs the question. So if our reason for believing it is that it explains how language works, then we have no reason for believing it. Better to accept that language learning simply requires that humans can learn to discriminate using names. It is part of our physiological hard-wiring.*

The Theory of Ideas and Chinese Language

We have seen that the theory of ideas begs the question. It assumes what it seeks to explain. It still seems an alluring theory. Even if it is wrong, it is too naturally tempting an explanation not to have occurred to anyone thinking philosophically. How could it possibly not even occur to Chinese philosophers? We can only answer that question by analyzing the historical lines of argument that have led to the theory. The only way to explain the absence of something is by showing the absence of its normal causes. If these arguments would not have tempted a Chinese philosopher, then their conclusion would not naturally have occurred to him.

In the next chapter, I consider the philosophical relevance of the Chinese language. I will describe some interesting features of Chinese spoken and written expression. There I will contrast the common-sense theory of language in China with our own conventional wisdom about language. This, I hope, will allay the sense of the inevitability of our folk theory of language and psychology. Then I will explain how the distinctive Chinese theory of how language works motivates their more social, naturalistic theory of heart-mind. My hypothesis is that real differences in the languages can explain differences in the popular theories of language. Since theory of language and theory of mind influence each other, a different language can inspire a different theory of the mind.†

*This argument, however, should give us an important liberating insight. The theory of mentalese is not only a theory of mind and language; it spills over into other philosophical theories, in particular epistemology. We assume not only that the ideas are private, but also that they are self-evident and incorrigible. It should be impossible for anyone to doubt them. This feature of our inherited psychology led critics to worry that my earlier theories were a form of linguistic determinism. If Chinese had no account of things that were so obvious, something must *stop them* from thinking of them. Our own acceptance of the theory made it inconceivable that others did not accept it.

Even if we do not settle this question (whether a computer analogy better explains our use of language), it has this advantage: it does show that our inherited Greek psychological theory *is one of many possible explanatory theories* and is not pure observation. It may or may not be a good theory, but it is not obvious and inescapable to anyone who thinks about the human use of language. Even if we go on accepting that theory, our conception of it as a theory should give us the distance we need. We can at least imagine a philosophical culture with a radically different view of the relation of human beings to their language and the world.

†I realistically expect that this strategy will again evoke accusations of *linguistic determinism*. The careful reader of this introduction will, I trust, remember that I argue that classical Chinese thinkers had a different *theory of* psychology, not a different *psychology*. Similarly, I shall not be arguing that our languages are as different as are our *theories* of languages. The Chinese theory can be applied to English just as the Western theory can be applied to Chinese. I shall argue that we can raise serious doubts about aspects of the common-sense Western theory when we consider classical Chinese. But I focus on the conclusion that the Western theory would not be either natural or obvious given certain other prima facie plausible beliefs about Chinese language.

The Philosophical Worth of Chinese Thought

Clearly, Chinese thought has a conceptual content drastically different from that of Western thought. This wide gulf in conceptual structure and interest has fueled skepticism that Chinese has any real philosophy. That skepticism generates a defensive reaction in the standard accounts. The defense consists typically of insisting that "this is an example of some familiar Western philosophical doctrine or theory" or "this is a rebuttal of some familiar Western theory." My approach undermines that defensive strategy.

The strategy was never worth much, in my view. The piecemeal tactic of defending the worth of Chinese philosophy by finding here and there a doctrine that is "just the same as . . ." defeats itself if the goal is to get acknowledgment from the discipline of philosophy. Philosophers are not looking merely for well-known or traditional puzzles. They value coherent unified philosophical points of view. The defensive tactic backfires because it saddles classical thinkers with a list of unconnected, ad hoc, unmotivated, curiously stated, undigested, and undeveloped fragments of the allegedly *same theory.*

A unified theory based on the theory of language offers much more promise to rehabilitate the flagging image of Chinese thought. Language is a central interest of modern and ancient philosophers. If the classical Chinese philosophers held a radically different theory of language, that fact could explain many other differences in a coherent, unified way. It would reveal their doctrines as a fully coherent alternative to the Western philosophical perspective. It could do so without having to resort to uncritical praise or even to the assumption that they got it right. It is enough that they had a credible theory and developed it in philosophically challenging and interesting ways.

The ruling account, relying on their prior sense of philosophical worth, tended to downplay the linguistic import of these doctrines. Often they translate them away. Paradoxically, the mistake is due to the ruling theorists' uncritical acceptance of traditional Indo-European theories of ideas. The interpreters thought literal renderings of Chinese doctrines would turn them into superstitious views of *word magic.* They downplayed the linguistic doctrine and translated them into the more sophisticated sounding language of *ideas, meaning,* and *belief.*

This study, by contrast, starts with the faith that we can have a unified conception of what philosophy is and still appreciate two quite different philosophical traditions. What makes them both philosophy is not their content or shared theories. It is their shared interest in and philosophical analysis of how language, mind, and society interact.

The Rehabilitation of Daoism

I call this a Daoist theory because the linguistic insight yields a new way to understand Daoism. The ruling theory has treated Daoism as the essence of Chinese antirational mysticism. Daoists, it alleges, theorize about *dao* and their theory of *dao* is that language cannot express it. The ruling theory's explanatory strategy in conveying this paradoxical view is *itself* paradoxical. The interpretive theory tries to discuss what *dao is* such that discussing it is impossible. That strategy, predictably, simply befuddles us more. They suppose that their failure to make any sense of Daoism with this strategy confirms their interpretation of Daoism as rationally inaccessible. How unintelligible is Daoism? It is so unintelligible that we cannot intelligibly explain why it is unintelligible.

The proposed focus on the theory of language allows us to turn our attention from *dao* to language. If language cannot express *dao* it must be due both to something about *dao and* something about language. Now we can look at the other, possibly intelligible, side of the Daoist puzzle. What do Daoists take to be the function and limits of language? Why is language so limited? An intelligible Daoist theory of the limits of language can explain in what sense something might resist linguistic expression.

I shall argue that if we change the implicit theory of language we attribute to Daoists their position will become much more lucid. The ruling theory had understood ineffability through the Buddhist theory of language with its metaphysical focus. Language is about the world, so *dao* must be a metaphysical object. It must be an unchanging, abstract one behind the many. The Neo-Confucians triggered this view because they understood the Daoists as similar to Buddhists. Daoism thus inherited Buddhism's mysticism of the one, permanent, ineffable Buddha-nature. They structured that mysticism along the lines of the Greek one-many, permanence-change contrasts. We have learned to read Daoism as if Daoists were Parmenideans, characterizing *dao* as a monistic or unchanging pure being—except that, paradoxically, it is also nonbeing.*

Getting a philosophically lucid Daoism is an unexpected by-product of spelling out a naturalist Chinese theory of mind and language. The Daoist love of nature should have given us the hint. Daoism contrasts starkly with the Platonic and Kantian myths of transcendent realms of meaning. Where Western theorists talk of having a concept or knowing the meaning, Daoism begins with a naturalistic focus on a socially learned skill at discriminating. The Daoist theory *does* tend toward relativism. The Confucians reacted as our own cultural conservatives would: A little relativism is a dangerous thing! Let us ban it! We must act as if our local parochial ideas are

---

*The ruling theory has it that the appearance of multiplicity and change required Daoists to reject sense experience, as Parmenides did. Interpreters have therefore read an aversion to the physical senses into Daoism that blatantly conflicts with its obvious naturalism (and its exuberantly libidinous sexual practices). Inevitably, they filled out the story with all the rest of the traditional Western theory-laden terminology that accompanies our theory of language: subjective-objective, subject-predicate, object-property, noun-adjective, and member-set. They also rely heavily on the Buddhist importation of the Western mind-body, reason-emotion, belief-desire, reality-appearance dichotomies. For none of this do we find any sound textual basis in the Daoist classics themselves.

The ruling theory chose a line of explanation that led to the impenetrable mysticism of a single subject. A *One* exists that embraces the *many* and yet is not a collection. It never changes and yet embraces all changes. Westerners understood Buddhist mysticism, therefore, as similar to Christian mysticism. They, accordingly, treated *dao* as a rough counterpart of God. This forces typical accounts to speak of Daoism using the subjectivist language of a mystical *experience*. They assume that Daoists must have had such a mystical experience of ineffable oneness. This familiar assimilation forces us, next, to attribute skepticism of the senses to Daoists. Medieval Western biases conspired perfectly with the Buddhist distortion to hide Daoism from us.

universally appropriate from a cosmic point of view! We must ban all this philosophical controversy! Love the old doctrines and accept conventional standards or face anarchy!

It is probably just a coincidence that Daoists seem to value iconoclasm and presenting unconventional views. It only serves the Confucian interest to treat them as incomprehensible. The proclivity to iconoclasm makes the present project Daoist in form and content. If the awareness that our conventions might be very different leads to anarchy, then we should give anarchy a try. Philosophers may react more fondly to Daoists than to Confucians. Confucians have an affinity for history. Starting from Confucius himself, they interested themselves more in transmitting than creating. Daoists incline in the opposite direction. That does not *make* Daoists better philosophers. But they are better philosophers!

Summary

This study sets out to revise the standard theory to make the later Mohist theory of language consistent with its larger tradition. I must admit that independent considerations also motivate my revision. The standard theory is notoriously incoherent, philosophically murky, and intellectually insipid. The challenge that Graham's work set us is also an opportunity. We can finally make philosophical sense of classical Chinese thought. The strategy for constructing the alternate theory depends on some preliminary hypotheses. One of these is that the standard theory, derived from Neo-Confucians, may have a Confucian bias. Another is that it may have an undetected Buddhist influence. The Confucian bias may emerge in many details of the interpretation both of Confucian thinkers and of their rivals. I further identified two systemic features of the standard theory that protect Confucianism. The isolated-schools view and the meaning-change hypotheses tend to isolate Confucianism from theoretical challenge.

The second source of skepticism about the ruling theory is both more directly involved in theory of language *and* more difficult to correct. Its difficulty comes from the almost inevitable familiarity of the theory in our own common sense. Our philosophical psychology of consciousness, experience, ideas, beliefs, emotions, reason, mind has been with us since the dawn of Western philosophy. I have argued that the theory has deep problems and suggested that we use the computer analogy in its place.

In the chapters that follow, I will argue for attributing different assumptions about psychology and language to the classical Chinese tradition. Doing so will make the rival theories of the Daoists, the Mohists, the dialecticians and the Legalists more intelligible. This result should tend to confirm the hypothesis since it bears out our initial suspicion. The twin Neo-Confucian biases explain the persistence of the view that Chinese thought is rationally inaccessible. This defensiveness in the standard theory has made it *seem* unintelligible and inaccessible to Western thought. We found three kinds of defensiveness. The first is the Confucian defensiveness. The second is defensively trying to import our most familiar assumptions about ourselves and our language and human dignity into their philosophical motivations. The third is trying to force parallels of traditional Western philosophical doctrines on the texts. The awareness of the bad fit totally overcomes any comfort we get from the familiarity. Precisely the failure of these defensive explanations required the additional assumption that Chinese thought was rationally inaccessible.

In the abstract, we have no reason to expect more similarity between Chinese and Western philosophy than we have to expect similarity between Chinese music and Western music. Many current writers follow Needham in accepting the possibility that Chinese conceptions might be more like modern physics than Newtonian physics. Yet, other historians who criticize trying to do this still tend to a connected mistake. They suppose that something fixes *the course* of rational philosophical or scientific thought. I cannot count the number of times others have lectured me that the only appropriate comparison for classical Chinese is ancient Greek thought! I remain unconvinced and unrepentant. I know of no argument that shows that ancient Chinese music, physics, or philosophy should any more resemble ancient Greek philosophy, music, or physics than it does modern versions of each. I reject the Hegelian myth of the unfolding of reason in history. No law of theories dictates that all early societies must adopt the same theories in the same order.

The unified theory, of course, will not take the form of laws and mathematical deductions. That should further calm those worried about the determination of ideas. I strive for the modest goal of a more coherent narrative explanation of the fertile initial period of Chinese thought. Significantly, it is the period before the invasion of Buddhism with its Indo-European conceptual structure. Confucianism was a powerful school in that context. Yet it did not have the dominance that it held throughout most of the Neo-Confucian medieval and early modern period in China. The other schools in classical China constantly had Confucianism on the defensive. Later, its political orthodoxy secure, Confucianism tended more to eclectic incorporation of those other schools.

The strategy opens, I hope, an exciting possibility. We can come to understand a radically different theory of language. With that basis, we can journey through time and space and have a philosophical conversation with an unusually rich philosophical tradition. These philosophers are linguistically and conceptually as far as possible from us—while we stay in the real historical world. This conversation began in the sixteenth century between various Western travelers and the late-medieval Neo-Confucian scholars of China. This is merely another interpretive step. The standard Western theory is already an accretion of insights transmitted from generation to generation of Western theories. We have gradually refined our theory of classical thought through a process not unlike that seen in scientific theories. Open discussion and criticism is the engine of theoretical insight. It is in the spirit of that progress that I offer these revised interpretive hypotheses.

2

The Context of Chinese Philosophy: Language and Theory of Language

Geographical Setting

I do not suppose that language is the only explanation of features of philosophical thought. I have heard plausible, suggestive accounts of how geography, for example, might contribute to a culture's having a certain broad philosophical direction. I am a philosopher of language, and neither a geographer nor a historian, so I cannot vouch for the accuracy of these suggestive accounts. But they can serve to give us some general sense of the context in which philosophy played its role in Chinese culture.

One obviously significant feature of Chinese geography—a physical barrier—explains the relative lack of philosophical exchange between China and the Indo-European tradition. Philosophical tenets are social products. They spread as technology, sculpture, language and music do. When two cultures come in contact they may talk about things. In this way they learn each other's technology, religion, philosophy, astronomy and so forth. A physical barrier to travel normally inhibits the spread of philosophical theories because it inhibits the wandering of philosophers—who are, after all, not notoriously physically adventurous.

Early Chinese and Greco-Indian philosophical traditions materialized on opposite divides of a great physical barrier—the Himalaya mountains and Xinjiang barrens. Greece and India formed the extreme poles of a Middle Eastern philosophical world. They shared a conceptual perspective. Chinese philosophy had a similar relation to Japan, Korea, and Southeast Asia. Each large region, however, apparently exerted far less influence on the other.[1] Sinologists have noted that early Chinese philosophers show startlingly little interest in the familiar staples of early Western thought. They were not enchanted with the creation myths and cosmology that pervaded ancient Indo-European culture.[2]

Agriculture dominated Chinese economic life. This may explain the pervasive emphasis on natural cycles, interest in the constancy of nature, and the stress on harmony with nature. Greek thought, by contrast, grew up where shipping, trade, and commerce dominated the economy. We suppose that contributed to their early interest in the stars, astronomy, navigation, and eventually geometry that fed into Classical Western philosophy and science.

The natural tendency of agriculture is toward self-sufficient small units. Yet, a large-scale challenge countered this natural tendency in ancient China. Chinese civilization grew up along the Yellow River. It is yellow because its contents are (and were) one-third earth. This meant that river channels silted quickly and the river frequently shifted course and flooded farms. Flood control required wide-scale social cooperation and therefore large political units. Significantly, the Chinese culture hero myths focus on their control of water (despite the apparent absence of a myth of a worldwide flood).

Prehistoric Influences

Any explanatory theory must leave something unexplained. History of philosophy must start somewhere and assume that some religious or other doctrines that explain philosophical developments are in place. Again conventional accounts of Chinese prehistory have suggestive explanations for some features of Chinese philosophy. As a nonhistorian, I cannot vouch here for the accuracy of these historical claims, but offer them to give some historical context for the emergence of philosophy in China.

Written history in China began in the Zhou period (1111–249 B.C.). We know an unusual amount, still, about the immediately preceding (technically prehistorical) Shang dynasty (1700?–1112 B.C.), deriving our knowledge largely accidentally from their divination practice. Shang priests used oracle bones (turtle shells or large mammal scapulae) in divination, heating the bones until they cracked and *reading* the cracks. They carved questions on the bones and sometimes added instructions gained from the divination. Typically a question asked for guidance and the divination helped select one course of action from alternatives. The diviners stored the bones and shells, probably both as sacred objects, as a record, and as an accumulated store of guidance. Frequently the inscription would also include a record of the outcome—what validity the divination had—on the bone. The discovery of these oracle bone collections has provided scholars with an accidental, indirect, prescriptive history.

If we think of this practice as the origin of Chinese written language, then it suggests one reason why the priests would think of language as guiding behavior. The record keeping would be viewed as accumulating valuable guidance rather than a descriptive history. The practical Chinese conception of divination survives in popular form in the *I Ching*. It instructs us to start by formulating a practical ("Should I . . . ?") question. Typical Western divination, by contrast, focuses, like science, on prediction of future events.

We regard the Shang characters carved on the oracle bones as the etymological ancestors of the Chinese writing system.[3] This descent contributes to a traditional Chinese theory of the pictographic origin of language. Many of these Shang graphs were more recognizably pictographs than are the more stylized descendants. The modern graphs became standard around the Han dynasty (221 B.C.–220 A.D.). A higher proportion of early Chinese graphs were pictographic and those more obviously picturelike than the now standard graphs.

The storing of the result of past divination signals another, equally important and enduring Chinese attitude toward language. Chinese culture values the historical accumulation of guiding literature—*dao*. Good guiding words are a precious resource and culture accumulates guiding knowledge as a capital investment and a cultural inheritance.

The divination practice also suggests a pre-historic precedent for the importance and power of an educated priest class in giving guidance and advice to rulers. The divining priests may have been the precursor of the *Ru*^{Confucian} school.[4] The traditional birthplace of Confucius is in a region that many scholars have argued was a seat of the late Shang culture.

Other features of Shang religion also survived the Zhou conquest, which traditionally marked the beginning of historical China. Its influence on Zhou thought radiated enduring Shang attitudes throughout Chinese history. Especially important, the traditional Chinese religion of ancestor worship appears already to have existed in the Shang. It signaled a religious view that society is continuous across even the boundary of life and death. It contributed to the view of the spiritual realm as continuous with the natural world. The doctrine underwrote the Confucian view of society as an extended family. It also gave religious sanction to the family-role morality that marks Confucianism.

The ultimate ancestor was the Shang deity, the Emperor on High. The Zhou substituted their own deity—*tian*^{heaven} as the source of guidance. The character suggests an anthropomorphic origin of the concept.[5] Theoretically, however, Zhou thinkers tended steadily to depersonalize *tian*^{heaven}. Ultimately the Zhou *tian*^{heaven} cult came to resemble nature worship, although *tian*^{nature:heaven} retained its role as the source of the guiding *dao*^{way} except among Daoists.[6]

Tian^{nature:heaven} played a central role in the Zhou theory justifying their conquest of the Shang. The doctrine of the Mandate of Heaven gave the Zhou a moral and religious claim to social authority. Heaven *ming*^{commands} the most virtuous family to rule. The command may pass to another family when the ruling virtue of the old dynastic family declines. This doctrine became the underpinning for the interpretation of the Chinese history as dynastic cycles. The decline in family virtue is apparently inevitable, a Chinese law of moral entropy.

Students of comparative political rationalizations will note interesting contrasts with the Western *divine right of kings*. The mandate is a command, not a right, and it implicitly justifies revolution by the same mechanism that justifies rule.

The history of *tian*^{nature:heaven} signals the tendency in Chinese philosophy to naturalize norms. Heaven comes to stand for the constant course of things. Moral conclusions follow from the natural context of social action. Normative concepts, such as legitimacy, come to depend on implied conformity with nature (or natural will). Ultimately, the tradition will give naturalistic explanations of the mandate itself, which derives from the natural consequences of running a well-ordered state. Causal explanations regularly displace magical connections in Chinese philosophy.

Language

I have a good deal more to say about language than about either geography or history, since language lies in the background of my argument for much of the theory that follows. I will adopt the practice, again, of putting argument that draws on extensive familiarity with Western philosophy or Chinese in footnotes. The reader may, again, choose three routes through this material. She may read the text *and* notes, read the text and skip the notes, or, again, skip directly to the narrative chapters that follow. This discussion is necessary more to the argument for my position than to understanding the later narrative. Again the detailed argument is necessary because I am challenging widely held assumptions within sinology about classical Chinese and its relation to Chinese philosophy. The ruling theory, as I outlined it in the preface, assumes that Chinese thinkers all implicitly adopted the familiar Indo-European view of language and mind. Potential defenders of that standard view, therefore, are not invited to skip this section.

In the Introduction (pages 16–18), I introduced that Western dogleg semantic theory of language, meaning, ideas, and the mind. I said there that in this chapter, we would look at some features of Chinese languages that would motivate a different theory on these matters. Indo-European languages are part of the context that influences Indo-European mental theory. In this presentation, I will highlight some ways in which Chinese common sense about language differs from our own. I assume that some general features of modern Chinese spoken languages (tonality, regional variation, sentence final particles) had analogues in ancient times.* The features of writ-

---

*These assumptions are defeasible, of course, but the evidence, at this point, seems to support their initial plausibility. *The Analects* has passages that suggest that Confucius used an official pronunciation in preference to a colloquial local one. Some thinkers seem to deny these assumptions on a priori grounds. Linguists regularly represent themselves as reconstructing *the* sound of ancient Chinese. Some such systems regard it as important to *explain the emergence of tonality* from other features of language. In the absence of empirical argument for these contrary assumptions, we should assume continuity with current Chinese rather than with Western languages.

The linquistic diversity of China poses a terminological problem. The ordinary criteria for appying both *word* and *language* in English are linked to the written form. We tend to individuate words mainly by their written form. (When we say, "That is one word, not two!" we are normally giving instruction on how to write, not how to speak.) This criterion partly explains why English speakers refer to Chinese characters as words. We also tend to individuate languages by written form. Where speakers share a written form, ordinary usage terms the spoken variations as dialects. Thus we characterize Chinese regional variations as dialects, despite the fact that the actual linguistic diversity in the spoken languages of China is roughly equivalent to that of Europe. I assume that the classical period had analogous linguistic variety.

The theoretically best linguistic chracterization of a *word* and a *language* is a different, difficult, and unsettled matter. The first step is to distinguish a word-token from a word-type. The previous two sentences contained five tokens of the word(-type) *a*. Some tokens of word-types are spoken tokens; some are written tokens. A word-type is an abstract theoretical object. So, therefore, is a language that consists of words. Written and spoken language are different embodiments of the abstract language.

Chinese linguists frequently criticize anyone who describes Chinese as monosyllabic. That characterization is appropriate if we individuate words by spaces in writing—as *zi*^{characters}. I do not find the available arguments for rejecting the view that characters are words particularly compelling. A phrase-structure grammar and a semantic model of ancient Chinese, particularly, could quite consistently place single characters at terminal nodes. That character compounds are more frequent in modern Chinese does not

ten language I will be describing apply mainly to classical written grammar. I do not necessarily assume that classical written grammar can be identified with the spoken grammar of any particular region of that time. Classical written grammar may have differed from the various ancient spoken grammars as much as it does now.*

The ancient Chinese theory of language was systematically different from Western popular theories. Our respective assumptions about language are not the result of private observation and empirical experience. We learn our theory of language from our community and absorb a shared communal set of assumptions about language from our elders as we learn the language. When others correct our speech, they frequently give us a conventional rationalization for the instruction. Thus they teach us a bit of the conventional theory of language. When they train us to read and write, our teachers may impart a widely accepted theory of writing.

These socially imparted theories of language are not necessarily descriptively accurate.† Consider our Western grammar school theory of language—the one that

---

convince me that a character base would not work for modern languages as well. The modern compounds mainly have systematic syntactic and semantic structures: verb-object, resultative verb compound, synonym compound, contrastive compound, etc. The fact that translators normally render these compounds with single English words does not settle the theoretical issue.

*Paradoxically, many writers on Chinese language seem to make the opposite assumption. I have tried to trace the source of this surprising view among its adherents. Their objection relies more on conforming to an alleged linguistic consensus than on its explanatory power in dealing with Chinese. They take the priority of spoken language to be a settled linguistic universal and deal with the Chinese counterexample only by struggling to bring it into line with this linguistic generalization. A scientific inference procedure would have stimulated someone to raise doubt about the generalization in the face of the classical Chinese counterexample. As far as I know, only Rosemont (1970) has done this.

The linguistic school that sinologists take to be orthodox assumes that all written languages must be transcriptions of spoken language. Once we understand the type-token distinction, this view seems to lose all plausibility. The written tokens are indeed tokens of word-types in the language. But it does not follow that they must be transcriptions of spoken tokens to play this role. My sources, in any case, suggest that this bias is far from established doctrine in linguistics. Even if it were, we should wonder how the generalization stands in the face of classical Chinese. (Other problems for the generalization include logic, mathematics, sign languages for the deaf, computer languages, drums, smoke signals, and so forth.)

John DeFrancis has led the sinological crusade to accept this generalization and reinterpret the Chinese case to conform to it. His argument seems to rely mainly on citing the emphatic rhetoric of Bloomfield. His pleonisms seem to have become orthodoxy among Chinese language teachers. Bloomfield suggests, somewhat tongue in cheek, that "written language"is an oxymoron. "Writing is not language, but merely a way of recording language by visible marks." See DeFrancis 1989, p. 48. With the type-token distinction in hand, we can say the same thing about spoken language. Spoken language is not language, but a way of tokening language in an oral-aural medium. But DeFrancis clearly interprets Bloomfield's generalization to mean that written tokens can only be transcriptions of spoken tokens of language. So interpreted, Bloomfield's linguistic generalization is implausible and controversial even for European languages. In the case of Chinese, it simply directly contradicts the normal interpretation of the phenomenon. Searching DeFrancis at length for a justification, just when I would hope to find an argument, I find only appeal to authority: "Most linguists believe this." Therefore, on pain of embarrassing Chinese, we twist and turn to make the appearance conform to the perceived orthodoxy.

Writing grew in China as a ritual practice connected to divination and constrained by its medium— carving on bones. Its telegraphic terseness could reflect ordinary speech only if every Chinese speaker were far more laconic than any Gary Cooper character.

†Note, therefore, that we do not really have to decide whether Bloomfield's claims about the priority of spoken language are true. The relevant question here is whether they are likely to be part of the theory of a culture with Chinese written language and regionally diverse spoken languages. Whether these Western claims are true or not, they are far more likely to become conventional wisdom in a culture with a phonetic alphabet than one with Chinese characters.

acompanies our linguistic training. Our high school grammar is notoriously not a scientifically sound account of English syntax. Its role is different: to explicate and induce a conception of *correct* formal usage. So we would naturally expect school and folk ideologies of language to exaggerate some features of their respective languages and ignore others. When languages differ, therefore, we may expect their teaching theories to differ perhaps even more markedly. Understandably, we further tend to generalize our own teaching theory. We tend to understand the theory not merely as an account of *our* language, but of the *nature of language* itself.

So we have quite nonmysterious reasons to suppose, then, that where our languages differ, our popular theory of language also will differ. In Western language socialization, for example, spelling accuracy plays a more important role in our evaluation of a person's linguistic competence than does calligraphy. We not only tolerate that well educated people might have unattractive handwriting, we even expect it in doctors. In Chinese language socialization, good calligraphy plays a much more important evaluative social role; their training theory emphasizes calligraphy more than our own.

To understand the background assumptions about language in classical China, we should note the features of our respective languages that contribute to these different popular ideologies. Let me describe some features of Chinese that illustrate the different folk theory of language in classical China.

Pictographs and Ideographs

For Westerners the most familiar element of Chinese is that it is a pictographic or ideographic. The nonalphabetic character of Chinese writing immediately captures our attention—as it does traditional Chinese theory. Unfortunately, the sinologists under Bloomfield's spell assume that the development of writing traces an inevitable path from primitive pictographs to modern phonemic structures. To characterize Chinese as ideographic suggests the demeaning conclusion that Chinese writing is primitive. As a result, some self-styled historical linguists have virtually made a cottage industry of challenging the established use of *ideographic* to describe Chinese.* They bend over backward to keep from taking the unique nature of Chinese writing at face value.† So we find Chinese linguists indignantly trumpeting the Western folk theory that *all* writing is merely a recording of speech.‡

---

*John DeFrancis's corpus of writings are the locus classicus of this reaction: "The cumulative effects of a professional lifetime in which I have had to put up with error about Chinese have finally propelled me to take up arms against the misrepresentation of its system of writing" (1989, p. xi). His sense of isolation puzzles me. In fact, his view seems to be the conventional wisdom of Anglo-American sinology—which, of course, leads me to question it.

†DeFrancis, for example, insists that all full written languages are "visible speech." He represents Chinese as continuous with German, French, and English, different only in its degree of phonemic accuracy. Correspondence between sounds and symbols "decreases somewhat for systems such as German, Spanish, and Russian. It drops further for French, still further for English, and even further for Chinese" (ibid., p. 51).

‡DeFrancis, as I noted above, openly embraces Bloomfield's dictim: "Writing is not language, but merely a way of recording language by visible marks" (ibid., p. 48). He acknowledges (1989) that other linguists dissent from this view even as it applies to Western languages. DeFrancis adopts the posture of defending the honor of Chinese against the offensive biases he sees lurking in the accepted characterization

The slender factual basis of this frenzy of debunking is straightforward. We conventionally divide Chinese graphs into pictographs, ideographs, and phonetic compounds. The pictographs include characters for horse, sun, moon, oxen, sheep, person, and mountain—most of the radicals. The ideographs include such obvious ones as numbers, above and below, middle, and also complex graphs formed from pictographic radicals such as *shen*[forest] (three trees) and *ming*[bright] (sun and moon). The phonetic compounds typically have a pictographic radical and a component that contributes phonetic information.*

DeFrancis's opponents in this mortal struggle are not, as he pretends, Western thinkers bent on ridiculing China. They include Chinese folk theory itself. Popular Chinese language learning aids construct elaborate purported etymologies of most of the phonetic graphs. It assigns a meaning-based rationale to the entire character even while characterizing those elements as phonetics.† As we noted, Chinese language ideology links language, poetry, and painting in a way that contradicts the assumptions of Western folk theory. For our purposes, this hostility to using words like *ideograph* is blind to a distinctive character of the traditional Chinese style of thinking about language. DeFrancis's distaste for this characterization of Chinese comes from his uncritical acceptance of the Western folk theory.

Presumably, the Chinese advocates of the significance of written Chinese do not share our Western ideology of language as a system of sounds. Our popular history of the *invention of (Western) written language* tempts us to view pictographic languages as primitive. DeFrancis's passionate assimilation of Chinese writing to ''re-

---

of Chinese as ideographic. Yet, paradoxically, DeFrancis openly *embraces* the offending *evaluative* premise. Ideographic writing systems, he says, are primitive and phonemic ones are mature. This makes his defense of the honor of Chinese less than ringing. He characterizes Chinese as a grossly ''defective'' and ''abysmally bad'' phonemic writing system that is ''incomparably more deficient than English'' (DeFrancis 1984, p. 128–29). This reminds one of the condemnations of sexism that insist that there are no physical differences between females and males. Surely, the reasonable place to correct such prejudice lies in the evaluative premise that insists that male physiology has special value, not the descriptive premise that states the difference. Let us simply deny the bias: phonemic writing systems are no better than those based on ideographic principles. Then we can accept the normal English characterization of Chinese without moral indignation.

*The DeFrancis line is that since it contributes phonetic information, the graphic structure and meaning of the phonetic element is irrelevant. Since it contributes phonetic information it contributes *only* phonetic information. I can find no justification for this persistent non sequitur.

†Studies have argued that these popular etymologies are not always reliable history. Nonetheless, DeFrancis's puritanical conclusion about phonetic compounds is implausible on its face. The phonemic part may also contribute semantic information. Possible phonetic elements for the sound *li*, for example, include *li*[road], *li*[profit], and *li*[sacrificial vessel]. It hardly seems irrelevant that *li*[ritual] uses *li*[ceremonial vessel] with a religion radical and *li*[pattern] uses the *li*[road] with a jade radical and *li*[clever] uses *li*[profit] with a human radical.

Graham has argued that philosophers apparently designed many characters for expressing philosophical distinctions they thought important. He notes that the phonetic in both *zhong*[loyalty] and *shu*[reciprocity] are relevant to the implicit theory of each (the phoentic *ru*[be like] as explaining *shu*[reciprocity] as likening to oneself, and the phonetic *zhong*[center] for a notion both of loyalty to the ruler *and* wholeheartedness on behalf of inferiors) (Graham 1989, p. 21). He offers similar arguments for *qing*[feelings] (p. 98), *xing*[nature] (p. 56), *cheng*[sincerity] (p. 133), *bian*[dispute] (p. 36), and a host of other important terms in classical philosophy. Graham argues that the Mohists used character-construction techniques deliberately to make what they took to be important philosophical dinstinctions. Even if DeFrancis *were* right about the bad consequences of allowing ourselves to call Chinese characters *ideographs,* the view of language enshrined in such a characterization is very plausibly that of the classical philosophers themselves, not merely of Western dilettantes.

cording of speech" shares this bias. He writes, "Error about the Chinese system of writing can subtly lead to bias against the Chinese people themselves." * The proper attack, again, on this bias is the premise that phonemic writing is more highly developed writing. Leaving that premise in place will demean Chinese writing even if we manage to "correct" the quaint view of Chinese as totally pictographic to a more accurate view that it is 25 percent phonetic. It will still seem relatively primitive until we dethrone that baseless value assumption about possible writing systems.

The real culprit here is the assumption that sound and speech are integral to the very concept of language. The proper corrective, as the type-token distinction directs, is to treat language as an abstract symbolic system. Sounds are *one familiar example* of linguistic symbols, not their essence. Pictures, gestures, electromagnetic modulations, graphs, map conventions, eyebrow movements, ideographs, logical notation and so forth are other possible symbol systems that can token words of a language. The assumption that language consists essentially of sounds—even without the Chinese example—has seldom captivated philosophers. We refer to our logical systems, to mathematics, and to computer languages as *languages.*† The argument that we should stop speaking our accustomed way about these things is far from compelling.

Suppose we speak only of natural languages, those that children can learn *at their mother's knee*. This turns out empirically to be mainly spoken, verbal language. But that seems largely an accident of physiology, not a consequence of the very concept of a language. Deaf children, for example, can learn a first language that is not based on sound.‡

The deeper problem is that the sinologists, shying away from acknowledging any significance of Chinese writing, miss the ways it could be philosophically interesting. First, the issue here is not whether "pictographic" or "ideographic" is a *correct* description of written Chinese. Our question is whether the Chinese language ideology would naturally so describe it. DeFrancis's treatment would make it seem that our tendency (and the traditional Chinese tendency) to characterize Chinese as ideographic lacks *any* factual basis. The alleged error is a total fantasy. I would think that something in the difference between written English and written Chinese demands an alternate explanation. It will hardly do to say written Chinese is just like English, only deficiently so.

What tempts us to remark on the uniqueness of Chinese characters is not merely

---

*Ibid., p. xi. As we noted, this is not subtle. It is a consequence of the bias that DeFrancis embraces: the view that the natural line of development of writing is from pictographs to phonemic systems. See, for example, his comment on page 221 that all systems of writing are alike in "tracing their ancestry back to pictographic symbols. . . ."

†DeFrancis dismisses formal languages like mathematics on the grounds that they are *incomplete*. He does not give this claim a clear alternative sense from that used in logic. Given the logical sense, all languages complex enough to include ordinary arithmetic are incomplete. Given the common-sense reading, his argument would be easily derailed by formal results in metalogic. The Lowenheim-Skolem theorem shows that *any* language with denumerably many sentences has an interpretive model in first-order logic plus arithmetic. I presume that a language would count as complete in DeFrancis's sense if it has *infinitely many possibilities* for the expression of thoughts.

‡DeFrancis dismisses sign language used by deaf people with the observation that all actual communities of deaf people have incorporated elements of the language of their larger society. That does nothing to show that a natural gesture language is either conceptually or even humanly impossible.

that they look like pictures of their object (they don't, normally). Nor is it that historically, they seem to be derived from pictures. What really tempts us is the interlanguage aspect of Chinese graphs. DeFrancis's parallels with English and Finnish are misleading because Chinese seems a hybrid between a single language and a language family. *Many different* Chinese languages share a *single* written form. A Chinese written graph no more represents a sound in one of those languages than in any other.

Chinese writing thus plays the interlanguage role of Plato's realm of meanings and its philosophical descendant, private mentalese ideas.* Chinese writing tempts us to describe it as ideographic or pictographic because it plays the interlanguage role that Western theory envisions for its pictographic mental ideas. Chinese graphs give a model that explains how to relate the sounds of different spoken languages. But the model is a social-conventional model, not a mental, abstract, or metaphysical one.

In theory, we need not limit the possibility that characters play such a role to languages in the Chinese family. For a long time in early Japanese history, the main writing system (for males) was classical Chinese. It had as little relation to Japanese spoken language as it would to English. We could also write English in Chinese characters using similar techniques.†

I find the implicit Chinese view eminently reasonable. Our ability at language

---

*This is what makes the word *ideograph* seem appropriate. Ideographs do not *represent* ideas; they play the analogous explanatory role in Chinese theories of language that ideas play in the Western counterparts. Chinese $zi^{characters}$ are in this sense analogous to ideas. The theory of ideas treats them as picture-like, interlanguage items. A causal chain ties both ideas and $zi^{characters}$ to the objects in the world to which the words of language refer. They anchor the dog-leg theory because they *purport to* substitute straightforward pictorial representation for the mysterious power of semantic representation.

The main difference is that Plato's version paints the ideas as the ultimately *real objects* in an objective realm of reason. He treats only the sound as constituting the *conventional* aspect of language. Our seventeenth-century mentalese version of Platonism also makes the pictographic language in the head nonconventional. This individualist version makes the mental ideographs purely subjective and private. (They are still, however, the product of reason—now combined with experience.)

Chinese $zi^{characters}$ are unmistakably conventional, social, and public. Classical Chinese theorists do not give into the temptation to make picturing the explanation of the language-world relation. History (Sage king's coining) and convention (our intentions to conform to their usage) tie language to the world. The Chinese counterpart of this pictographic interlanguage language is different mainly in being an on-the-earth, conventional language rather than a private, mental, intellectual or other-worldly one. Chinese writers easily recognize that even a pictographic orthography is a social convention. A picture language stands in need of intentional interpretation as much as does a system of sounds. They would not be tempted to the naive assumption that postulating a pictographic mental language into which one translated sounds would solve the riddle of language. It could not provide the required *constant* relation of language and the world. Even if they were pictures, their usage still would depend on the surrounding conventions, not on their pure pictographic content.

†DeFrancis lampoons this possibility in a burlesque titled "The Singlish Affair." He describes an fictional plot by the Japanese, together with Koreans and Vietnamese, to force Westerners to write in Chinese characters after the war. DeFrancis apparently hoped that the account would lay this *silly idea* to rest as a bit of quaint chinoiserie. Unfortunately, he reports, many readers took the spoof seriously. He seems to have missed the point of that reaction. What it shows is that the story has just enough *conceptual plausibility to make a good hoax.* DeFrancis thinks the story shows the incoherence of the idea and just how it is supposed to do that is an enormous mystery. Of course, the story does show political, social, and cultural naïveté. It is certainly bizarre to think that this particular conceptual possibility is sensible policy. To note the *conceptual possibility* of such a thing is not to *advocate it as linguistic policy.*

presupposes a distinctive human ability to identify categories of shapes, what artificial intelligence theorists characterize as *pattern recognition*. Our ability to read presupposes this ability to recognize categories of shapes. So does our ability to apply language in guiding our behavior in the world. Both require that we can recognize a set of *similar* shape tokens as a type. We learn to recognize a conventional shape or to assign a word to a conventionally determined range of shapes. Pictographs are early forms of writing because a communally shared shape recognition capacity must exist for any language development.*

The popular Chinese ideology is not unlike our own in this regard. The written form influences both folk theories of language. Even illiterates will learn their respective culture's theories. They would adopt their culture's theory of language as they their culture's theory of the sun, the moon, psychology and spirits, and death. They need not have learned to write themselves to acquire the community's ideology of their language. All they must do is talk about language with others who do accept the theory.

Meaning, Translation, and the Mental

So the feature of Chinese that tempts us (even if mistakenly) to describe it as pictographic or ideographic is philosophically important. It shows why Chinese language theorists would *not be tempted* to anything like the Western dogleg theory of meaning. Western ideology introduces meaning to explain interlanguage translation. Since the theory of meaning has such extensive historical and theoretical links to the notoriously obscure notion of an idea, we lack one important motivation to postulate Chinese counterparts of ideas, beliefs, meanings, thoughts, or the apparatus of mental, cognitive content.

To show this, consider a typical, standard account of how our folk theory generates puzzles about meaning. Notice that implicit in our grammar-school ideology is a requirement that meanings be objects of some sort. Our assuming language has a descriptive function and our focus on objects as the building blocks of reality inclines us to require objects for any meaningful term in our language.†

> How can a word—a noise or a set of marks on paper—*mean* something? There
> are some words, like "bang" or "whisper," which sound a bit like what they

---

*Neutrally, we can say that language consists of intelligible symbols. Gestures, sounds, pictures, smoke puffs, and dance steps can be symbols. The only a priori limit on symbols is that humans be able to learn to recognize them: can we make sense of the principles of combination that allow the generation of new symbols and complex symbols from simple ones? Beyond that, contrary to sinological dogma, we find no a priori objection to treating a language of conventional written symbols as distinct from any particular spoken language.

In English, as I argued above, we individuate words and languages by criteria based on the written form. We regard *fit out* as two words and *outfit* as one. We do not say that *biscuit* and *cookie* are the same word in British and American English. We tend to say, instead, that *the same word* means something different in British English. Chinese speakers refer to the character to disambiguate their utterances. When someone asks what they mean, they may write the character on their hands, in the air or describe it. Some characters have familiar descriptions such as "three-line Wong." They also can use character combinations to identify the character such as "the *zhong* in *zhongguo.*"

†Actually, more sophisticated versions of the representational theory require that there be objects backing up only the *logically proper* names of the language. Other terms are then construed as complex names. This analysis is necessary to deal with the problem of reference to nonexistent objects.

> refer to, but usually there is no resemblance between a name and the thing it is
> the name of. The relation in general must be something entirely different. . . .
> The mystery of meaning is that it doesn't seem to be located anywhere—not in
> the word, not in the mind, not in a separate concept or idea hovering between
> the word, the mind and the things we are talking about.[7]

However familiar and intuitive this notion of a meaning hovering around our use of language may seem to us, we need not attribute it to classical Chinese philosophers. The Western theory came to invoke the private pictographic language. Since, unlike sounds, ideas *do* resemble their objects, they form the explanatory link between sounds and objects in the world. We identify those mental pictographs as the person's meanings for the words of whatever language she learns. These mental objects explain our ability to learn conventional languages. Western folk theory supposes that we translate our mother tongue into this private language of mental pictographs.

Traditional Chinese theorists would have no parallel motivation to postulate private, subjective meanings. Chinese folk theory treats the alleged pictographs as having a historical, causal relation to the world (as do our ideas). But the history is the history of a linguistic community, not that of an individual, and the Chinese use of the graphs conforms to historical conventions. Their theories note explicitly the conventional nature of language and the crucial role of acceptability of use. Chinese theorists emphasize the relation of language and society, perhaps even more than they emphasize the relation of language and the world.

Chinese thinkers don't get caught up in the familiar problems of meaning. They do not start with a conception of philosophy as a search for definitions. That doesn't mean they are not philosophical. They simply adopt an intuitively more social theory of language. Social conventions govern all aspects of language—the graphs themselves, the distinctions, and the sounds we have for the character. Language depends on social agreement, convention, or coincidence. The shared pattern of use has customary normative status. These conventions, Chinese skeptics note, could be different from what they are. Chinese skeptics draw on cultural relativism for their doubts instead of inner, private subjectivity.

Emotionless Tone

The Western student's difficulty with spoken Chinese usually comes before she deals with characters. It starts with tones. This is not because tone is an inherently difficult aspect of pronunciation or even that tone is lacking in English. The problem is that our early linguistic training taught us to disregard tone in identifying words. Our grammar school ideology of language normally overlooks tone. We learn pronunciation and grammar while focusing on our written symbols—alphabet letters. Tone does play a role in speaking English but not in writing it. The intonation on a sentence signals different speech roles—expressing sarcasm or skepticism, accusing, flirting questioning, persuading, demanding, and so forth. This, however, we seldom teach in our grammar books. The role of tone strikes us as too amorphous to train explicitly; we assume that one gets it naturally or not at all. Sincerity cannot be taught. In our popular theory, we effectively treat tone as extralinguistic.

We instead use the word *tone* in the denotation-connotation distinction. In our folk theory of language, the tone of voice does not change the *substance* of what we say. It only changes the affective overlay, what we call *emotional* tone. One may adopt a sneering tone, a questioning tone, a surprised tone, and so on. Westerners thus learn a folk theory of language that links the phenomenon of tone to another aspect of our philosophy of mind. It reinforces the folk theory's split between intellect and emotion, idea and feeling, belief and desire, reason and passion. Words express pure rational ideas. Tone expresses emotion or feeling. You learn words, but the emotional tone is just a natural result of your emotional state.

In modern Chinese languages (presumably also in classical Chinese languages) tone plays a linguistic role more like that of letter-phonemes in Indo-European languages.* This feature of Chinese is a source of the stereotype that Chinese has a singsong quality.† This also may have contributed to the stereotype of Oriental inscrutability. In fact, Chinese speakers may be as uncomfortable with allowing the tone to vary *emotionally* as Western students are with making the tone constant.

Given that tone plays the word-identifying role, we might wonder how one can *express emotions* in Chinese? For example, Cantonese—a modern language closer to ancient Chinese—has a rich vocabulary of words in sentence final position that convey sarcasm, surprise, doubt, persuasive force, and so forth. One simply adds that word to the end of an utterance to change what we would call its *emotive* role.‡

One could say that Chinese language exhibits the social, or emotive, impact of what we say straightforwardly. This feature of language reveals explicitly that we do things with language, especially social things. Western language ideology, by contrast, treats the key role of language as conveying ideas, facts and descriptive content. Chinese language training more naturally portrays language as a way people interact with and influence each other. In Chinese we use a particular explicit word to quote, to command, to persuade, and otherwise to affect people.

My hypothesis is that Chinese language training would not motivate the Western bias toward understanding language as descriptive.§ Chinese theorists could plausibly

---

*That is, tone is crucial to word identification. The phonetic qualities associated with letters—rounded versus unrounded (*o* versus *e*), bilabial versus dental (*b* versus *d*), are important distinctions in English. They determine which English word we token. In Chinese, level versus rising, upper versus lower tone do that as much does change in vowel quality or consonant.

† This is especially true of Cantonese, from which many of our stereotypes descend. Cantonese has more tones, a greater tonal range, and less tone sandhi than Mandarin, so that each word is usually said in its full tone. The conversational enthusiasm of Cantonese speakers reinforces the impression.

‡ I believe that this phenomenon is less an expression of emotion than signaling the speech-act role or illocutionary force of a sentence. The same sentence with the addition of a final word may be used to persuade, to order, to question, to criticize, etc. My describing this as expressing an emotion is a temporary concession to the Western folk-theory of language.

§ I do not assume that this feature of Chinese is the *cause* of their viewing language in its social context. Chinese philosophy arose in a context of prior interest in transmission, conformity, mastery, and practice of ritual as means of socialization. Western philosophy arose in the context of prior interest in astronomy, navigation, geometry, etc. These dominant interests probably account most directly for the different context in which the two traditions viewed language. Western thinkers looked at language in its relation with the world (semantics), Chinese thinkers looked at language and its relation to language users

assume that language socializes us.* I will argue that Chinese thinkers treat skill in applying names as a learned ability. We conform to the community in marking distinctions. This shared linguistic skill enables the community to coordinate behavior. In philosophical terms, the Chinese theory of language starts from pragmatics—the relation of language and user; Western theory focuses first on semantics—the relation of language and the world.

Ordered Grammar

For the struggling Western student, the simplicity of Chinese grammar may partly compensate for the tonal difficulty. Students sometimes put the point inaccurately by saying Chinese lacks grammar. The kernel of truth in this cliché is that Chinese grammar does not use grammatical inflection.† Our conventional expression comes, again, from our grammar-school ideology of language. Our formal language training focused strongly on number, tense, and case inflections. Since we seldom find it necessary to teach word-order to native speakers, we emphasize grammatical agreement in urging students to speak correctly. The conventional examples of bad grammar are such things as absence of subject-verb agreement and mistakes in case and number. So we tend to think of these features as exhausting the range of *grammar*. Our struggle with the grammar of other Indo-European languages also focuses on the tedium of declining verbs for tense and number and mastering the gender and case inflections.‡

　　Chinese, in this respect, resembles logic more than English does.§ In ancient written Chinese especially, word order determines grammatical role.‖ As long we order terms strictly, case inflections are superfluous.

and social convention (pragmatics). This feature merely reveals a particular way that each culture elaborated that direction of analysis.

　　*Classical Chinese thinkers eventually do *derive* a theory of the descriptive role of language *from* this more basic role of guiding behavior. Their theory of term reference grows from accounting for how we should make social usage *constant*. External reference was one theory of how to regularize name use.

　　† This statement of the difference depends on a restrictive conception of an inflection. Chinese uses characters—sometimes after verbs, sometimes as sentence finals—that might be described as tense markers. I would describe them as aspect markers (completion, continuation) rather than tense markers. A completion marker may be used grammatically along with the word *tomorrow,* for example. If we think of inflection as affecting a word *and* think of a character as a word, then these would not count as inflections. Of course the same could be said of the plural pronoun $zi^{character}$, *men* (Mandarin), or *dei* (Cantonese).

　　‡ Our grammar-school folk-theory rationalizes our investment in mastering these perplexing features of Indo-European languages. We believe that this complicated system of inflections is essential to clear communication. Studying Chinese liberates us from this prejudice. The Indo-European way of marking sentence functions will come to seem unnecessary. Studying logic would have had the same effect. Logical notations also dispense with most inflections. (I say "most" because we could regard the difference between variable and predicate letters [usually capitalized and small letters] as a counterpart of syntactical inflection.) Logical notations rely mainly on order and operators. If your sentence contains words like *yesterday,* tense is redundant. If *seven* precedes a noun, we hardly need a *marker* on the verb to tell us it is that seven is *two or more*. Nouns occur in subject and object position (in English) without case marking. Pronouns *could* do the same.

　　§ Linguists call languages which rely on word order rather than inflections *analytic*. English is among the most analytic of Western languages. Classical Chinese may well be the most analytic of actual human languages.

　　‖ As in logic, classical Chinese predicates have several ordered *slots* or *places* for terms. A transitive

Our folk theory of language stresses another accidental feature, especially of English. Our grammatical training includes the imperative to speak and write in complete sentences. A complete *sentence* expresses a complete *thought*. Our ideology emphasizes that a complete sentence has both a subject and a predicate. In English, even in slightly bizarre contexts, we grammatically require the subject term (as in "It is raining"). Although, logically, the typical sentence is equally *about* all the terms used in it, our grammar ideology teaches us that the predicate says something about the subject. Thus a standard thought is *about* some object and describes that object in a certain way.

Classical Chinese written language regularly omits the subject *and* other preverbal nouns. We should not, therefore, assume that our sentence-based ideology will be part of the intuitive Chinese theory of their language. If we do not attribute a belief in a subject-predicate distinction to Chinese philosophers, then we would have no reason to attribute its elaboration in ontology or theory of mind to them. Chinese philosophers need not believe that expressions are *about particular objects*. We need not assume their ontology analyzes reality as consisting of substances (objects, particulars) with attributes (properties, characteristics). We need not assume that they share the psychological theory of *subjectivity* versus *objectivity*. We need not assume they will treat language as conveying a unit of thought (belief or other counterpart of a sentence) or a fact.

These familiar, almost instinctive, aspects of our folk theories surrounding language training need not be part of the folk theory conveyed in teaching a language as different as Chinese. We cannot treat these as default assumptions in our interpretive theory. Each attribution would require constructive argument from the text.

Building Blocks of Language

We learn our grammar by means of a theory that breaks language down into several individual structural parts. Our grammar-school ideology does closely associate spoken and written language. So we individuate first the letters (sounds) that compose words in the written form. Our theory then individuates words mainly by our writing conventions—where we leave spaces. Our theory treats a word as a string of sounds with a syntactical role (part of speech) and a meaning (an association with an idea). Words (parts of speech) fit together to make sentences. The sentence is a key structural fragment in our linguistic ideology. Sentence boundaries govern most grammatical agreement. We think of grammar as the rules for constructing sentences. Our way of teaching our grammar therefore stresses the sentence.* Sentences express

verb has two ordered places, a verb that takes an indirect object has three, an intransitive verb one, and so forth. Prepositions increase the number of places in a predicate where terms can be inserted. The instrumental preposition i^{with} comes between the subject position and the verb. The locative preposition yu^{in} comes after the objects. The preverbal term-slots may be emply. The postverbal ones require variables (pronouns) if the term is missing.

*Wittgenstein treated our concept of *a fact* as a structure of reality that shares its logical form with the structure of a sentence. A typical sentence consists of a set of terms and a relational element. A fact consists of the corresponding configuration of the objects referred to by the terms. A fairly recent trend in Western syntax is dialogue-based grammar. Logicians can be said to study the grammar of a *series of sentences,* an argument.

Western semantic thought gave Western thinkers other reasons for treating sentences as important.

beliefs (complete thoughts composed of ideas). Sentences map onto our mental world. Sentences share a logical form with our inner thoughts and beliefs.

Chinese theories of the structural units that make up language would, of course, differ. If the Chinese also drew on their written form, they would not treat sound as the basic building block. As they learn to write, they learn a different theory about the origin and nature of writing, a theory that would not start with phonemic letters or an analysis of syllables into components. The Chinese merely note that the $zi^{\text{characters}}$ are pronounced in a certain way in their dialect. They would not describe themselves as *writing sounds*. The basic structural unit Chinese language training emphasizes is the brush stroke.*

The next unit in Chinese folk theory is the radical—the graph or that part of a graph that contributes meaning.† There are radicals for *human, water, tree, mouth, heart, language, fish, bone, knife,* and so forth. Complex characters contain radicals in configurations with character elements that contain the phonetic information.‡

Here Chinese popular theory links writing up with spoken language in a different way. Characters do *not* represent sounds. They note, simply, that different Chinese

Our concept of truth applies properly only to sentences. Our traditional theory of language dealt mainly with semantics or theory of meaning. As these developed, we understood the meaning to depend on the notion of the truth of a sentence. Similarly our epistemology focused on propositional attitudes—the difference between belief and knowledge. Belief and knowledge contrast only at the level of the sentence or proposition, the complete thought. We also call them *sentential* or *propositional* attitudes.

Chinese pragmatic linguistic theory, by contrast, deals with assertability more than truth. This contrast is a genus-species contrast, not an exclusive one. We can think of *truth* as a species of *assertability*. Distinguishing truth pragmatically from other species of assertability appeals to the theory of the faculty of reason and the doctrine of belief-content. We do not limit assertability, as we do truth, to sentences. We may assess words, phrases, sentences, arguments, even whole dialogues for assertability.

Chinese thought does deal with $zhi^{\text{knowledge}}$ but not with propositional knowledge. Classical Chinese has no grammatically parallel verb for propositional belief. The grammatical object of zhi^{know} is always a noun or a verb phrase, not a subject-predicate sentence. The kind of knowledge that makes sense of Chinese views is knowing-how to do something, knowing-to-do something, or knowing-of (about) something.

The closest counterparts to a belief context in classical Chinese also focuses on the term, not the sentence. Where we would say, "He believes it is good," classical Chinese would use a structure something like, "He goods it" or "He, yi^{with} (with regard to) that, wei^{deems} [it] good." We capture its theoretical force best by talking about a disposition to use a term of some object. Some translators render this belieflike structure as *deeming* or *regarding* something as being of a kind.

*The brush stroke links calligraphy and painting in Chinese folk theory. It obviously does not emphasize the alleged gap between words and pictures familiar to Western students. Chinese painting, conversely, comfortably includes language in the frame. Even landscapes scrolls typically incorporate a peom, proverb, or couplet. The continuity of calligraphy and painting is a deep and important cultural feature of Chinese aesthetics and theory of character. The Chinese theory of excellence in painting and calligraphy stress the *quality* of the brush strokes. That accounts partly for the emphasis noted above on the importance of calligraphy as revealing a person's character. The stark dichotomy of pictures and words, so familiar in our "worth a thousand" proverb would hardly make sense as a feature of Chinese language teaching.

†Traditional dictionary organization uses radicals and Chinese folk etymology stress the pictographic origin of the radical component of characters.

‡The phonetic information may be more accurate for some characters and in some dialects (languages) than others. As I noted above, Chinese folk theory typically assigns meaning to the phonetic element as well. Historians of Chinese language, remember, regard these folk etymologies as mostly fanciful. Whether or not we agree, the Chinese folk theory is certainly easy enough to motivate. Typically a number of phonetic structures are available to signal the approximate sound of a character. It is hardly obvious that the phonetic element selected from the range available has nothing to do with meaning.

languages have different ways of saying a $zi^{\text{character}}$. Correctly ordered strings of characters constitute the ci^{phrase}. The ancient Chinese concept of ci^{phrase} ranges across any linguistic strings that we intentionally structure.[8] It includes what we would call a compound word, a noun or verb phrase, duplicated verbs, whole sentences, and even pairs or groups of related sentences (couplets).

Classical writers did not use the modern term ju^{sentence} in their theories of language.* The next larger unit of language they spoke of was a $shuo^{\text{explanation}}$, and then a $dao^{\text{guiding discourse}}$.

Chinese writing depends heavily on elegant parallelism to convey structural information. Structural agreement partially replaces inflectional agreement as a way of disambiguating expressions. Structural parallelism may extend over whole essays. Thus, Chinese language ideology draws more closely together what our popular language ideology separates: it blends prose and poetry just as its artistic decoration blends words and pictures.† We illegitimately conflate language ideologies when we conclude that the frequency of poetic structure in Chinese philosophy signals its emotional or irrational character.[9] Poetic structure in Chinese is a means to clarity, not to mysticism, obscurity, or romanticism.

Structure and Interpretation

Classical Chinese characters have great syntactic mobility. We could say they can play many part-of-speech roles. This way of putting it, however, overstates the dif-

---

*Graham has claimed that the Mohists discovered the sentence and changed the meaning of ci^{phrase} to refer exclusively to sentences. His evidence for this is basically that the Mohists discovered that word order is important in strings of words. Beyond that, he relies suspiciously on a reconstructed passage that looks more like a malleable field for Graham's own linguistic intuitions than a theory of the sentence. Graham says that at first sight it looks like an unintelligible list of samenesses, but "on closer inspection" it turns out to be a statement of Graham's own grammatical analysis of classical Chinese sentences—an analysis of nominal and verbal sentences (Graham 1978 , p. 474). Even Graham admits that the key heading "sameness of the same root" is "mysterious" (ibid., p. 475).

The Mohists did indeed discover that word order was important in ci^{phrases}. But that does not mean they discovered the sentence. All linguistic strings have functional compositionality. That is, the unit is made up of functional parts. A noun phrase, for example, may have an article, an adjective, and a noun. Even people's names have syntactic structure.

Our Western grammatical theory emphasizes the complete sentence and a theory of its basic functional parts. Our theory of a sentence postulates a set of *parts of speech*. The functional parts play important roles in our syntax and also in our semantics. The meaning of a part is the role it plays in making a sentence true. The root-declension structure of Indo-European languages draws our attention to these functional roles.

Chinese linguistic theorists did not have this kind of reason to develop the theory of a sentence or its complement, parts of speech. Chinese linguistic theorists did notice that word order was important in discourse. Word order, pauses, beginning and ending points are important for any meaningful string of characters. Chinese theorists did not theorize that word order distinguished sentential strings from either smaller or larger language structures. In their statement of the importance of order, they did not invoke sentential functions. The importance of word order lay in how language guides us, not in how it expresses a truth.

†Traditional accounts of the word wen^{language} claim that it originally referred to decoration. One of the more interesting and revealing compounds in Chinese is $wen^{\text{literature:decoration}}$ + hua^{change} which is conventionally translated as *civilization*. The idea that civilizing is decorating or embellishing human nature by means of an accumulated literature or written langauge is a revealing look into the Chinese point of view. It also reminds us again of the observation made above of the importance of calligraphy in evaluation of one's character, one's educational and cultural development.

ference. In English, as well, any word-*root* can play many part-of-speech roles. The contrast is that for an English root to do this requires an appropriate inflection. A proper noun can become an adjective, for example, *Einsteinian*. We can make a noun into a verb with *-ize*. We can make a general noun into a singular abstract noun with *-ness* or *-hood* and so on. We use a root-inflection structure to make our words play different roles in the sentence. The difference is merely that Chinese does this *without* inflections. *Word order* determines the syntactic role of the characters in a string.

Characters, like word roots, do have dominant sentential roles.* *Bai*^{white} is normally adjectival. *Ma*^{horse} is normally a noun. We interpret a character's use in other positions in the sentence via that root use. So ''I white it'' corresponds roughly to ''I regard it as white.'' (Translations aiming at familiarity would use ''I believe it is white'' or ''I make it white.'')† That characters can function in different part-of-speech roles explains a bit of Western ideology about Chinese. It contributes to the general Western impression that characters have many meanings (see above, pages 13–14).

Mass Terms and Scope Metaphysics

Huge parts of our ideology of language may seem to have little relevance to language. We have already mentioned the Western doctrine of substance and attributes, particular objects and their shared (and changing) properties. A related distinction in early Western thought was that between an enduring object and its changing *constituents*. This distinction between objects and the stuff of which it is made also figures in the Western philosophical problems of one and many, permanence and change. The contrast has become a stock tool in linguistic analysis.

Ordinary school grammar, however, barely recognizes that English has a syntactic feature that traces this distinction between an object and its stuff. Western languages mark this intuitive distinction with different kinds of nouns—count nouns and mass nouns. *River* is a count noun. *Water* is a mass noun. We believe that the

---

*This fact, along with structurally specialized characters like *zhe*^{one who} and *zhi*^{it:it's} (used as an object pronoun or in apposition) make it possible to confirm hypotheses about the structure of a sentence. Otherwise it would be harder to argue that any parsing is better than another on syntactic grounds. Obviously, the assignment of sentential role is relative to a hypothesis about where the string begins and ends and what the main verb is. The notorious grammatical obscurity of Classical Chinese stems from this relativity. Arguments for parsing hypotheses frequently depend heavily, therefore, on interpretive hypotheses.

In practice, given the lack of punctuation, the optional character of the subject, and the syntactic mobility of characters, grammatical parsing and interpretation are interwoven. This helps, again, explain how common poetic structure is in Chinese philosophy. As I suggested above, poetic structure may actually be clearer than prose. This celebrated feature of Chinese philosophical style may be motivated by an urge to clarity more than mystical obscurity. A writer can guide interpretation via poetic parallelism. If two phrases have parallel structures, we usually assume the same parsing hypothesis for both; this helps rule out some of what would be plausible interpretive theories for either sentence in isolation. Note, for example, the argument about lines 3 to 6 of chapter one of the *Daode Jing* below. Stylistic parallelism *between* phrases thus plays a vital role in guiding the reader's analysis. We use interpretive *intelligibility* and *parallelism* together to cull out parsing hypotheses.

†Our language-class grammar of Chinese distinguishes between *causative* and *putative* uses of this structure. We usually elaborate the distinction with the Western theory of belief. But we could as well talk about the social versus physical cause of a distinction.

river is water. Heraclitus asked how he could bathe in the same river twice since he obviously did not bathe in the same *water* twice.[10]

The mass-count distinction in nouns underlies the different concepts of identity and individuality of things that inform the famous Western problem of flux. A count noun has a principle of *individuality* built in. To understand the noun is to know how to count the objects it refers to. The principle of *identity* for a count noun allows that it can gain and lose *matter* and still remain the *very same individual*. Thus we can count rivers and they remain the same even as the water flows in and out of them.

A mass noun, like *water* refers cumulatively. The concept has no *particular* principle for individuating (counting or measuring). Its principle of identity, by contrast, is much more strict. If some parts of it have changed, it is no longer the very same water.

Western languages use both kinds of nouns. *River, car, dog, spoon,* for example are count nouns, since we can count them. They typically have a plural form and can be modified directly by numbers and by phrases like *many* and *few*. The count nouns dominate our commonsense view of reality. These nouns correspond to the commonsense objects of our world. The noun itself contains a principle for identifying the *individual* of a common type. The ordinary world of Western common sense is a collection of particulars or individual objects.

Water, gold, grass, wood, furniture, and *beef* are English mass nouns. We measure them rather than count them. Depending on which measure or principle of individuation we choose, we can *count* the same quantity in indefinitely many ways. We think of these objects as more amorphous, variable *components* of our world— stuffs instead of objects. Grammatically they normally resist pluralization and direct numbering. We modify them using *much* and *little* instead of *many* and *few*. These nouns have principles of identity, but do not have an inherent principle of individualization. We know what counts as *the same X* but not what counts as *an individual X*.

If we want to measure or count stuffs, we combine the mass noun with a count sortal such as *cup of, ounce of, blade of, cord of, piece of,* and *head of*. What counts as an individual is relative to our measuring purpose. We may measure water by using drops of water, cups of water, buckets of water, or bodies of water, or any other measure. Further, unlike objects, stuffs are cumulative. We refer to several spatially isolated bits of stuff by one of these mass nouns. We can refer to the sum of the bits with the same word we use for each part.

So the conceptual puzzle about permanence and change in Western philosophy is reflected in this grammatical distinction. Western common sense assimilates stuffs to qualities in its solution to the problem of change and leaves particular objects as the foundation of reality. It seems that objects are stable and unchanging, yet the stuff out of which they are made constantly changes. Like the water running in and out of the river, living things take in and breathe out stuff as they grow and change. Yet they remain the same thing. What is it that remains stable or unchanged? This answer gives rise to, among others, the doctrine of essences that I discussed above. The constituents of a thing may change while its essence remains the same. Like Indian thought, Greek thought assumed that reality must be unchanging.

Both this stuff-object distinction and the object-property distinction feed into the traditional Western focus on particular objects. The Western particular is, in fact, an abstraction. The world of Western conventional common sense is a collection of stable abstract individuals or particulars which change constituents or properties and yet remain the same underlying, pure individuality. We distinguish this abstract particular from its many different features, attributes, accidents, modes, properties or characteristics as well as from its matter, substance or atoms.*

So much of Western philosophical theory derives from this model that we have trouble imagining any other. Our concept of a thing, an object or entity is essentially that of the countable particular. We thus attribute our cultural analysis of reality to Chinese philosophers without noticing its grammatical base. We baldly assume that is inevitable common sense.

I propose a radical hypothesis. Suppose Chinese philosophers assumed something more like an ontology of stuffs.† When they talk of 10,000 wu^{things} they probably do not mean 10,000 countable objects, but 10,000 nameable stuff kinds. Modern philosophers have called this alternative ontology a mereology.[11] It is an ontology of noncontiguous stuffs with a part-whole structure.

Modern Chinese languages appear to have few grammatical count nouns.[12] Nearly all common nouns of modern Chinese require sortals when used with numbers or demonstratives. Chinese nouns do not take pluralization.‡ Chinese lacks the *many/ much, few/little* distinction.§ In classical Chinese the case was not so clear. Nouns

---

*One thrust of Western thought has been a search for ultimate particulars—atoms, then protons and neutrons, then quarks then . . . The doctrine of the abstract particular still guides our cultural search for the ultimate building blocks of the universe. The reductive physicalist analysis assumed until Einstein and quantum mechanics that reality must consist of particular objects in space-time. The nonreductive realist insisted that the shared properties must also be real—there must also be abstract universals. The common-sense objects of appearance were complexes of the underlying abstract realities. They are metaphysically constituted of these more basic objects. These, we traditionally thought, would be the unchanging elements. Realists use them to explain change as combinations or modifications of abstract particulars and universals.

†My mass-noun hypothesis has been widely misinterpreted, partly, I suppose, because I called it the mass-*noun* hypothesis. It was not a syntactic claim that Chinese nouns have mass-noun grammar. I in fact argued (1983), as I do below, that Classical grammar is *not* a mass-noun *grammar*. The mass-noun hypothesis, as its Quinian ancestry suggests, is an interpretive hypothesis, a theory about the meaning of these terms. I hypothesized that the *semantics* of Chinese nouns may be like those of mass-nouns. The test of the hypothesis is not grammatical, but whether the attribution of meaning makes more rational sense of the beliefs we attribute to the Chinese philosophers. Graham (1989, p. 402) cites Harbsmeier's tentative grammatical classification of Classical nouns into three groups. Harbsmeier labels the alleged grammatical groups in a question-begging way as *count, mass,* and *generic* in an attempt to rebut a mass-noun grammatical hypothesis. Graham seems to think that if Harbsmeier decides to commit himself to this classification in print, it will show that "the mass-noun hypothesis is no longer tenable, at least in its original form." Aside from the questionable criteria of truth (that is, whatever Harbsmeier is eventually willing to commit himself to in print), this declaration muddles the issue. Graham allows that the "insight of Hansen which seemed especially valuable survives the upheaval." But that insight is the *whole* of the mass-noun hypothesis. I had already denied that classical Chinese nouns were grammatical mass-nouns. I made the interpretive claim that we would understand their theory of language and related doctrines better on the hypothesis that their implicit ontology was a mereology. Harbsmeier systematically confuses syntax and semantics.

‡Modern pronouns do and there are reduplicative forms for universal scope: ren^{human} ren^{human} = everyone. To say that nouns do not admit pluralization is different from simply saying they lack a plural. For example, *fish* and *deer* both accept pluralization even though their plural form is identical to their singular. The important thing is that we can number or count them.

§One can, however, ask questions about amount in a way that signals that one expects the answer to

lacked plural forms and a *many/much* distinction but numbers *could* modify some nouns directly. However, they could also use number-sortal ("five head of") structures to modify them. These masslike structures typically came after the noun (*ma*^{horse} *wu*^{five} *bi*^{teams}).

Arguably, Classical Chinese ontological assumptions may have affected Chinese language development. Gradually nouns came to have a more uniform mass-noun syntax. The number-sortal forms became standardized during the Han dynasty (221 B.C. to A.D. 220) shortly after the classical period we are discussing.

Scope and Grammatical Categories

One salient way in which Chinese nouns resemble English mass nouns is that they can fill a term place in a predicate without article modifiers.* This grammatical feature helps blur any distinction between different kinds of nouns.† Chinese theory of language, accordingly, distinguished nouns mainly by their range or scope.

Adjectives also have scope. Classical Chinese adjectives also can fill a term position, either as subject or object.‡ Chinese theorists, accordingly, draw no explicit distinction between nouns and adjectives.§

Adjectives, in turn, are not clearly distinct from intransitive verbs.‖ In English grammar, we require an *is* verb with adjectives but not with intransitive verbs. In logic and in Chinese, adjectives and intransitive verbs function alike grammatically.

This string of assimilations further helps explain why Chinese theorists did not note what seem to us obvious functional distinctions (parts of speech) among their characters.# Chinese writers in the classical period speak of words only as *ming*^{names}. Given these facts about their language, we can appreciate that this is neither a mistranslation nor grammatically naive.**

---

use a sortal: *ji*^{how many} *zhi*^{pieces} *bi*^{pen}?" But the standard contrast *duo*^{much:many} *shao*^{few:little} may be read either way. "*Duo*^{much:many} *shao*^{little:few} *yu*^{fish}?" could be answered with either an individual fish sortal or a weight (or volume) measure. "*Hen*^{very} *duo*^{much:many} *yu*^{fish}" does not commit itself beteen a mass or count reading.

*In English, only a logically singular noun (a proper noun, abstract noun, or mass-noun) can fill a term slot. We must embed count nouns in noun phrases ("*The* Cat," "*A* young person").

†There *is* a grammatical difference, however. Proper nouns cannot be modified. Mass-nouns can form new mass-nouns with a modifier. *Muddy water* is a mass noun with a different scope from *water*. *Cleaver Jane* is an exclamation, not a noun with a different scope from *Jane*.

‡Classical (and modern) grammar does not require any copula with either adjectives or noun complements. They effectively replace mass nouns. The technical semantic difference between adjectives and mass nouns is that masses have identity. (We understand the notion of the very same water that was in this cup and is now in the pot.) But given their focus on the question of how to make the distinction, this common-sense English grammatical distinction was not important for their theory.

§The distinction that Chinese language theorists do note involves whether the scopes overlap or interpenetrate. This is the closest they come to differentiating adjectives and stuff nouns. And even here, they mainly distinguish between kinds of compounds—hard-white compounds and ox-horse compounds. Gongsun Long at one point may suggest a nonreflexive dependence. White, he hints, depends on horse in a way that horse does not depend on white.

‖Again this situation is similar to that of logic, where intransitive verbs, adjectives, common nouns, and mass-nouns would all be represented by predicate letters and interpreted as a set of objects or mereological sets. Our Chinese class grammars called adjectives *stative verbs* to mark this assimilation.

#They eventually note a distinction between *shi*^{reality} names and *xu*^{empty} names. They would include common and proper nouns, adjectives, and verbs (all terms with a referential scope) in the former category and functional or emotive finals in the latter.

**One could argue that *mass noun* would be a better translation for *ming*^{name}, though less colloquial.

Scope and Ontological Relativity

Scope is the salient semantic feature of any character (word) that draws the most attention in ancient Chinese theories. The theorists notice that some names apply to a small range or portion of reality and others apply to a wider range. So, Chinese ontologies do not use the familiar Greek realist one-many structure. They draw on a more relative part-whole view of reality. In Chinese ontology we see no reductive thrust toward atoms or unchanging particulars and no grammatical object-property distinction. Their ontologies conform to the mass-stuff model.

The importance of this model, however does not lie in the scattered nature of the object referred to. It lies in the conception of language mastery that goes along with it. Chinese linguistic theory emphasized the ability to distinguish or mark the boundaries between stuffs. Reality is not a multitude of independent, fixed objects, but a ground out of which a linguistic community *carves* distinctions and marks them with names. Each part-whole assignment is relative to some presupposed standard and purpose. A part, in turn, has parts. Any whole can be a part of some larger whole.

The familiar individual object of Western ontology fits in a part-whole scheme as one of many possible ways of partitioning a whole. Western thought emphasized the ability to recognize or classify an object as of a type. Even when Chinese thinkers did turn to semantic issues such as reference, they retained the pragmatic focus. How do skilled users of the names project these distinctions in new situations?

The mass hypothesis explains one source of the relativism in Chinese theory of language. Stuffs can be numbered and counted from a plurality of perspectives and for different purposes. We can discuss individuals of human-stuff, families of human-stuff, and cities or states of human-stuff. Objecthood is derivative in this conceptual scheme. The primitive particular objects of Western ontology emerge as a result of dividing stuffs into smaller (and incidentally, contiguous) clusters for some purposes (see pages 528–29 below. Xunzi's argument here expressly relies on the theoretical purpose of explaining a kind of sameness that allows numerical sameness through time.). They do not regard those unit clusters as the ultimately *real* building blocks of the wholes out of which they are carved. The part-whole structure marked by language is pragmatically relative.

The standard interpretive theory frequently attributes a Heraclitus-like problem of change to Chinese philosophers (especially Daoists). I object. *No* philosophical problem arises from the mere fact that change takes place in a *part-whole* ontology. Stuff changes. But that observation, by itself, raises no philosophical difficulty. The perennial *Western* problem lies in explaining how the object can remain *the very same object* while its constituent stuff flows in and out. Daoist worries about con-

---

But, for these purposes, I regard mass nouns as logically singular, like names. Of course, they are not proper names. The grammatical distinction, as I noted above, is that proper names cannot be modified and mass-nouns can. While we might plausibly regard all extensional predicates as names, the Chinese theorist is, admittedly, wrong in regarding operators *(all, some, exists, exists-not)* as names. It is wrong, but still not naive. Those operators frequently filled term positions too, like pronouns. In any case, the proper analysis of quantifiers is an advanced subject in the development of logic and these operators behave in many ways more like nouns or relational verbs than do their counterparts in English. The existential operator and its opposite (yu^{have} wu^{lack}) for example, normally function grammatically as two-place verbs.

stancy and inconstancy, however, did not arise out of that familiar Western conceptual framework. They derive rather from the *relativity* of the part-whole distinctions implicit in any community's language. They worry about linguistic constancy, not object constancy. Our standards for projecting a partitioning distinction—carving a stuff out of the world—may change. This is a radically different problem of change. It could provoke philosophical reflection even if there were *no* real or metaphysical change.

Chinese skepticism also has its locus there. The theorists debate about our standards for partitioning reality in one way instead of another. Chinese relativists claim that the reasons are pragmatic and not in the nature of things. Chinese realists argue that nature or innate intuition guides the partitions. The fundamental question is whether there is a correct way to partition the whole into named parts. Skeptics doubt that there is any right solution. When Chinese philosophers worry about change, they do not worry about what object or individual *survives* substantial or property change. They notice how we might change linguistic practices. We might draw the partitioning boundaries in the world in different ways. Constancy is an issue of linguistic pragmatism, not metaphysics.

The Regulative Role of Language

As I suggested above (pages 41–42), all the Classical thinkers shared a deep assumption that buttressed their pragmatic approach to language. Their folk ideology assumes that language guides behavior. We can approximate this perspective if we think of the prescriptive sentence as the basic form. This goes against Western grammar-school ideology. In English, we learn that we *omit the subject* to make the sentence into an imperative or a command. Our *complete-sentence* ideology treats imperatives as mutilated sentences (with an implied subject). We regard the descriptive form as the normal, complete form, the one that illustrates the real role of language.

Classical Chinese does not have explicit descriptive and prescriptive forms.* Students of comparative translation, therefore, will find huge chunks of text that one translator renders in declarative English and another in imperative English. Behind this apparent ambiguity, I suggest, lies this assumption about the function of language. *All* language functions to guide behavior. Given that assumption, a community would not require an explicit prescriptive marker.

That does not mean that all sentences are prescriptive sentences. It means only that, like a computer program, the input as a whole guides our action in the world. We use *all* the distinctions made in language in guiding action. The communication of information is a subtask of language. Information is always information in relation to a program that guides action.

Society uses language to guide our behavior. Elders teach us to conform to conventional ways of making distinctions among thing kinds in choosing and rejecting courses of action. We do not learn language in isolation from other ritual practices. Language guides behavior because learning the community's language induces

---

*We can often translate with some confidence from the context. Other times the context leaves it ambiguous. We have already noted that in classical Chinese, grammatical subjects are optional even in declarative sentences. Subjects may, by contrast, be present where the context clearly requires translation with an imperative. Also, classical Chinese lacks explicit *ought* or *should* verbs.

us to adopt a socially shared way of reacting differentially to the world. Chinese thinkers explain this function of language in terms of the scope structure that dominated their attention.

Western philosophy, as we have noted, began by assuming a descriptive role for language. Western thinkers thus needed to postulate a modification of that normal function to explain how language guides us. They postulated the existence of obligations, rights, values, and so forth. This was another realm of *objects* to be *described* by value language. Western ethical philosophers, accordingly, looked for the relations or properties of things to which words like *ought, good,* or *should* refer. Ethical skepticism in the West gets much of its mileage out of denying that anything real lies behind these prescriptive terms.

Western philosophy includes a long tradition of dispute about the reality of these value properties and relations. We view description as the function even of evaluative language. This view leads to the assumption that objectivity or validity depend on reality. We puzzle at how sentences with prescriptive function can be explained in a scheme of descriptive properties and relations. If my pragmatic hypothesis is correct, we will not find this style of ethical discourse in classical China.

We do, in fact, find no parallel philosophical concern in classical China. There, the objectivity concern will focus on the standards for making guiding distinctions. Are there constant names that can make up a constant *dao* ^{guiding discourse:way}? What standard justifies distinguishing things *here* rather than *there* in social, guiding discourse? The central realist problem in China is the irresolvability of disputes about which standard to use. How could we arrive at noncontroversial standards for this project? Must we presuppose the conventional ones? Are there natural standards and distinctions? Another problem comes from raising the identical question about the standard itself. How do we decide the correct way to apply *the standard* to things? Is there a standard for interpreting the standard? How do we project *it* in making distinctions between correct and incorrect uses of other terms?

Language and Psychology

So we have seen several justifiable differences in Chinese ideology of language. Chinese theorists justifiably blur our rigid separation of language and painting, prose and poetry, or poetry and music. They would not draw a sharp distinction between language and feeling or emotion. They need not postulate an inner mental life with its distinction between thinking and feeling to explain language. They certainly should not think that the basis of language is private, individualized experience or consciousness. They are, overall, not drawn to any of the details of our familiar mind-body view of ourselves.

So we find little trace of the ways Western thinkers spell out the rest of mentalist psychology: experience, consciousness, inner pictures, mental substance, and objects in a mental realm. Dream arguments and sense skepticism play major roles in Western thought, they are at best minor refrains in Chinese thought. Chinese thinkers do note the phenomenon of mental imagery in both memory and imagination. But they had little reason to assign it the role of explaining meaning. Their dominating problem is not explaining how an individual uses language. They ask, instead, how society should sustain or change its guiding discourse.

In particular, Chinese thinkers do not attribute mental sentences to individual minds as beliefs. They postulate a heart-mind that guides behavior. Internalizing a conventional language influences how the heart-mind does that job. Society programs us with a social morality as we learn our language. The process does not draw on the Euclidean model of a series of sentences arranged in a proof. Chinese thinkers do not characterize the process in terms of the sentential notions of premises or reasons. They do not represent desires as propositional (as we must to explain their function in practical reasoning).

Western theories of action focus on *voluntary* action. We use beliefs and desires or reasons-for-acting to explain this special, restricted kind of action. That distinction would not seem to Chinese thinkers to carve the moral world at its joints. The idea of a moral agent, a person, as someone with a faculty of reason, who can process inner sentences (beliefs) and desires on the Euclidean model belongs to Indo-European philosophical traditions. The *reasoning* model of mental functioning does not dominate Chinese theory of mind.

The Social Context: Some Conclusions

Chinese theories clearly recognize the public, social nature of language and thought. They can hardly fail to note that pictures are not self-interpreting. Little would tempt them to try to solve the riddle of language with a system of *private* pictures. For popular Chinese learning theory, language is pictures and yet the problems of reliable projection remain. Whatever problem there is in understanding how words relate to the world is still there when we use pictures in place of words. The Chinese tend to accept the irreducible conventionality of language and its essentially social influence on our lives. We program our heart-minds with terms and distinctions learned from society and inherited from a historical culture. Society, history and convention, not private experience, shape our minds.

Western philosophy began where astronomy and navigation were central concerns. They first confronted issues of explanatory metaphysics. The model of geometrical (Euclidean) proof structure dominated the Western conception of mental functioning. Ethical thought began in the world's first democracy and borrowed the conceptual structure of pre-Socratic metaphysics. Legal debate (developed as theater) then influenced the development of Western philosophical activity.

Chinese thought, by contrast, emerged in schools that started as ritual and then text-based communities. They moved in the direction of political-religious movements. These partisan movements vied for political influence in a feudal and then in an imperial hierarchy. Their dominant concerns, from the beginning, were the issues of proper social organization and motivation. Philosophy emerged from something more like our policy think-tanks than from legal and scientific debates; when Chinese thinkers moved away from that model, as Daoism did, it moved in the direction of literature and poetry, not argumentative theatre.

Despite these differences in context, their disputes still focused on language, its relation to the heart-mind, and realism versus relativism in ethical guidance. They gradually developed carefully elaborated philosophical theories of language and its social role. These shaped their analysis of moral psychology and political and social ethics. Chinese philosophy was not static. It traced an exciting intellectual journey and the engine pushing the dialectic was the unique Chinese theory of language.

I

THE POSITIVE DAO PERIOD

3

Confucius: The Baseline

These texts included statements about the world subject to judgments of truth and falsity, but they differed from statements that characterize Western philosophy because the evidence of their validity could only be obtained through mastery of the practices that lay behind them. No text of theoretical cogency could be relevant because the practitioners of *taos* assumed that the conceptual frameworks we use to determine truth are not generated analytically, but are the product of practical interaction with the world through experience. As a *tao* structures experience, it synthesizes a perspective and the truth of a text's explicit claims cannot be evaluated outside of that perspective.

ROBERT ENO[1]

While none of us comes to such an enterprise without deep-laid assumptions about necessary logical relations and compatibilities, we should at least hold before ourselves the constant injunction to mistrust all our unexamined preconceptions on these matters when dealing with comparative thought. One of the liberating functions of comparative thought lies in its ability to challenge precisely such examined assumptions concerning logical consistency and doctrinal compatibility.

BENJAMIN SCHWARTZ[2]

He was not a philosopher in the technical sense.

WING-TSIT CHAN[3]

The Confucian *Analects:* Some Preliminary Hypotheses

At the dawn of recorded history in China, a social group known as the *Ru* dominated the intellectual scene. The *Ru* were concentrated in the Shang cultural area. They may have originated from the Shang elite. Having withdrawn from political activity, the *Ru* communities may have buried themselves in learning, transmitting, performing, and thus preserving traditional ritual forms. They sought virtuosity in all traditional arts. They chanted. They danced. They cultivated ceremonial and they lost themselves in the *flow of performance*.[4]

We acknowledge Confucius, the most famous *Ru,* as the first scholar and educator in China. Confucius considered *Ru* status a matter of education, not birth. No doubt, the *Ru* had teachers (models, leaders) before Confucius. Confucius' apparent innovation was to transform the focus of his *Ru* group from pure ritual mastery to include the study of texts. His training included mastering a syllabus of traditional texts. Confucius made up his reading list from the classics of the *Ru* heritage: historical writings, poetry, and ritual.[5] This shift to a texual focus in the context of training in chanting, dance, poetry recitation, and so forth, led to a performance conception of language.

Like modern university professors, Confucius thought that teachers should also be scholars. His scholarship lay in intellectual and ritual history. Schwartz speculates that Confucius belonged to "the scribal wing of the service class," the "custodians of all the cultural traditions preserved in the state archival documents."[6] Tradition holds that he collected, studied, and edited ritual texts while traveling with his *school*. Tradition also holds that Confucius' wandering was a frustrated search for political employment. Robert Eno has argued that this image is a projection from later Confucian concerns. Confucius' political ideology, he suggests, actually justified the continued political withdrawal of the *Ru*.[7]

Some of Confucius' students aspired to official careers (employment in the court of some feudal lord) and some succeeded. Politics had produced a demand for education. The lords also needed experts in ritual. Ritual held the feudal state together and governed diplomacy. Confucius' *Ru* training also stressed elegance in speech[8] and knowledge of history. Confucius emphasized political loyalty and obedient self-control. Rulers in those volatile times appreciated such virtues.

Other disciples followed Confucius' example and became teachers of the textual tradition. Confucius must have been an inspiring teacher. The adulation of Confucius continued to the second or third generation of disciples, who introduced the next innovation. They began collecting memorable conversation fragments attributed to Confucius into a text, which became the famous *Analects of Confucius*, literally *Lun-yu* [discussion words]. This compilation is the chief source of our knowledge of Confucius' *dao* [way]. It also marks the emergence of the institutional structure in which philosophy in China developed—the school based on studying, preserving, transmitting and gradually augmenting a text of the teachings of a *zi* [master].

This would commonly be the place to present a portrait of Confucius in the style of a good novel: "Confucius was kindly man who loved his mother. He had a trauma at school when . . ." This story-telling style urges us to adopt a personalized view of philosophy. It says that philosophical method is like the self-described methods of Descartes, the father of modern European philosophy. The stereotype has a wise person surveying the contents of her brain in her armchair. She reasons her way to a philosophical position. Descartes called it *meditations*. She then puts pen to paper and writes the system down to enlighten of the rest of us.[9]

This familiar model is an exaggeration, certainly in the case of Descartes, who borrows heavily both arguments and doctrines from medieval thinkers. But in China, in the case of Confucius, it distorts the social role of a *zi* [master's] text. Starting with *The Analects* of Confucius, the study, preservation, transmission and selected editing of a text was the focus of small intellectual *communities* in China. Many texts have a larger authentic core than others (*The Mencius* and *The Mozi*). The *jia* [schools:families] of Ancient China recited, preserved, and were guided by a text. The textual communities cared for and typically augmented the text as their dialogue with other schools required better theory. So in the place of a personalized portrait of Confucius, I offer only the above portrait of the $Ru^{\text{Confucian}}$ community.[10]

The Analects of Confucius justifies classical *Ru* training, in essence a ritualists's philosophy of education. The educational theory rests on assumptions about language, society, and psychology. Some of these assumptions inform all classical Chinese philosophy. *The Analects'* defense of traditional *Ru* training gave Kungzi$^{\text{master Confucius}}$ founder status in the school. The aphorisms collected formed the basic defense of the school against other text-based schools with other masters. Eventually every *Ru* identified with Confucius. Now we simply translate *Ru* as *Confucian*. After the classical period (550–200 B.C.) political structure selected Ruism as the official orthodoxy and the political system virtually deified Confucius.

That Confucius himself did not write his own philosophical text is important to the ritualist view. Confucius[11] describes his role as transmitting; not creating (7:1). He set out simply to study and transmit the tradition. The *Lun-Yu*^{Analects} reports his conception of his own scholarly activity as more historical than philosophical. He viewed the *dao* he taught his disciples as a historically stored guide for ritualized conduct (4:9; 11:22).

Confucius did not share Plato's interest in debate, and particularly in legal debate. The two culture's philosophical pioneers viewed their scholarly activity differently. Plato's style used the model of a debate. Confucius' model was the concert performance. We find debates in *The Analects* but Confucius did not encourage debating as a method, Confucius did not view himself as participating in or resolving a debate between schools.[12]

Notoriously, however, *a kind* of debate does emerges in the *Lun-yu*. Unsympathetic commentators have suggested that the text is so riddled with contradiction, Confucius must have been debating himself.[13] For example, one notorious puzzle is whether li^{ritual} or ren^{humanity} is more important in guiding people. Some passages make *li* seem the key to all virtues (2:3, 2:5, and 8:2) and others (3:3) suggest that ren^{humanity} is. Still other passages say Confucius seldom spoke of *ren* (9:1)! His attitudes toward punishment also seem ambivalent. Some passages suggest comfortable acceptance[14] and others total opposition.[15]

Still, the crime of contradiction is not easy to prove. Given the snippets-of-conversation structure, *explicit* contradictions are hard to find. Further, as Wang Cong (a Han dynasty critic of the text, b. A.D. 27) suggests, the fault could lie totally with the disciples and their editing process. The main tension in *The Analects*—the question of *li* and *ren*—may reflect an interpretive split among the disciples. The collection of aphorisms were certainly subject to *selective* memory. The *li* versus *ren* question, in any case, generated a continuing split between two different Confucian schools in classical China, traditionalists and innatists.[16]

Textual detectives find evidence of this division among Confucius' immediate disciples. Schwartz[17] gives an admirable account of the differences in outlook among the disciples mentioned in *The Analects*. The first, represented mainly by Zixia and Ziyou, held that following the *dao* required studying, practicing, and internalizing a traditional code, the *li*. The other, represented by Zizhang and perhaps the elusive Yan Hui, stressed the internal guide, *ren*. The goal was not simply to master the li^{ritual}, but to cultivate the more abstract and intuitive ren^{humanity}. What we read in *The Analects* is a *disagreement* about mainly this issue in Confucius' *dao*.

Faced with their divergent interpretations of what they had been taught, the disciples apparently collected statements and fragments of conversation with Confucius. These include passages rebuking various disciples for their mistaken emphasis and others where the disciples themselves complain to Confucius about his vagueness or inconsistency.[18] The title, *Lun-yu,* suggests this collection is a *dialogue.*[19] The aphorisms seem to war with one another, I conclude, because the disciples were quoting Confucius to support their contrasting, partisan interpretations of what Confucianism holds. *The Analects* is not Confucius's *dao,* but at least two warring theories of Confucius's *dao.*[20]

Accordingly, in reconstructing Confucius' teaching, we have access only to an already divided, factional account. We can still use the text for important purposes: (1) to elicit the assumptions the two factions shared and (2) to focus on the conceptual structure in which they cast their dispute. We may attribute these shared assumptions to Confucius, but the book is evidence, not authority for such a conclusion. His view might have been something distinct from either of these partisan lines.[21]

Further, we could theorize about the way such a dispute may have arisen and thus identify a plausible *original Confucian* position that might have led to the dispute.[22] This yields the conceptual baseline from which Chinese philosophy grows We will not worry whether Confucius held a consistent theory of either distinct type. We don't need to resolve the intraschool dispute about which side Confucius was actually on. We must, still, wonder why the quotations from Confucius never hint that he might have sensed the tension and conflicts in his doctrine.[23] We should treat an interpretation that claims Confucius had resolved it as a priori unrealistic. Such an interpretation makes the later split in Confucianism harder to explain except on the assumption that he deliberately allowed his disciples to remain confused.

The Well-Ordered Society

Confucius did not teach an explicit social-political philosophy. His teachings, however, signal a set of attitudes about the well-ordered society. We can, therefore, tentatively generate an implicit theory for him based on his acceptance of Zhou political institutions and theory of legitimacy.[24] Both wings of the Confucian school share these basic attitudes. Moreover, in broad outline, the perspective is shared by all the Classical thinkers. Democrats were rare in ancient China. Reconstructing the point of view suits my expository purpose because, despite its general acceptance in China, it differs radically from familiar Western conceptions of how society should be ordered.[25]

Chinese social philosophy strikes us as singularly naturalistic. It reminds us that the Western *autonomous individual* is as much an idealization as angels and devils are. To Confucius, an isolated individual means that some disaster has occurred; the natural, healthy state of humans is in social structures. If we assume that a political philosophy must justify social-political structures from the point of view of egoistic individuals, Confucius will seem to have no political philosophy.

The Educational Hierarchy

Chinese philosophers take for granted that human beings are social animals. Humans do not straddle some metaphysical divide between the natural and the divine. The natural social structure, furthermore, is a hierarchy. Our social organizations focus on training and transmitting proficiency at some cultural activity. Confucius treats the family as the basic social pattern. Political organizations copy the family in form and function. The rulers is like the father, having responsibility for the education and protection of those in his care. As Hsiao says, "the entire corpus of government and society in themselves was nothing more than a vast organization for the nurturing of men's character."[26]

Confucius' social philosophy and his philosophy of education are one. The child learns to walk, talk, eat, sleep, greet, insult, play, and work in just the way her family does. She acquires this repertoire of performances mainly by copying the behavior of her father, mother, and older siblings. Politics simply expands and extends this natural process to larger contexts and to more complex and specialized conduct.

The conduct we model in the family depends on our conventional social status. A girl learns different verbal and body language from a boy. We model ourselves on those who play the status roles to which we either aspire or are fated. In the larger context, we model ourselves on artists, craftsmen, teachers, bus drivers, television personalities, baseball stars, and politicians. We don't, properly speaking, *choose* the basic roles we come to play; they are so tied up with our identity that they are prior to choice. When those basic roles include further choices, we may conform to our initial role in making other role-defined choices.

Confucius therefore accepted the notion of family virtuosity. Modes of behavior and artistic proficiency tend to run in families, but not as necessarily genetically inherited patterns. Inherited training produces a family's shared character. This assumption lies behind the Chinese political theory of family dynasties. The Duke of Zhou first formulated the *Mandate of Heaven* doctrine. That Chinese justification of political legitimacy differs from its nearest Western analog, the divine right of kings. Legitimacy is not an unaccountable, mystical grant of right; it is tied to family excellence. The ruling family's status follows from its educational role as a model of appropriate behavior. The family with virtuosity in conduct deserves the mandate because it is suited to the hierarchy's natural purpose—serving as an educational model. The ruling family must exemplify *de*[virtuosity].

So, while authority is hereditary, lack of family merit may alienate the mandate. The mandate of Heaven also differs from divine right of kings in that it is implicitly a doctrine of revolution. Revolution occurs when another family has more *de*[virtuosity] than the ruling family. The mandate is not a right to make laws and punish people; it is a command to educate and shape people's character.

Confucius' interest, perhaps, was not in politics per se. He envisioned a continuous, hierarchical *social* structure. Politics simply concerns the higher levels of that

social organization. The political aspect of his education mission—training government functionaries—grew out of this guiding perspective on society. His political
dao ties the mandate of heaven to a conception of a natural social order. Following
the social *dao will* serve the mandate by preserving social order. The model ruler's
way is the natural way societies work.

The dispute that divides the disciples did not stem from any differences in this
social outlook. They shared, in outline, the same social *dao*. For that matter, as I
suggested above, so do Mencius, Mozi, and Xunzi. I shall characterize this orthodox
baseline as the Confucian social-political *dao*. From this base we can measure disagreement in details.

Confucius' policy conclusions do differ from those of other philosophers. His
prescriptive views are refreshingly free from supernaturalism[27] and yet classically
conservative. The realpolitik way to preserve the mandate is to preserve order—not
law and order, but simple *order*. Order, for Confucius, involved more than mere
domestic peace, however. A state was ordered when it had a *correct* structure, a
particular ritualized order. Traditional accounts of the rule of the sage kings laid out
the model of this order for Confucius.

His scholarly activities gave him some expertise on the order the sage kings
followed and intended to transmit. The aim or goal of Confucius' political way was
the specific social pattern embodied in the traditional *wen*[literature]. The *dao* of the sage
kings could be known by studying literature from the past. We must, therefore, study
both the *Book of History* and *The Book of Li* to discover the political *dao*. The core
of his policy recommendations is *follow tradition.* He assumed that current social
problems stemmed from departure from the ancient ritual model and theorized mainly
about how to resurrect and then preserve the traditional social order.

Society consists of a ritual structure, a system of roles. The social way is a
composite of all the component roles. To play a role in society is to follow the *li*[ritual]
of that role. Its conventions—its *li*[ritual]—exhausted the content of those roles. When
we fill a role we conform to its *li*. Confucius, the historical scholar, found *li* in the
transmitted literature of the *Ru*[Confucian] scholarly tradition.

Ordinarily, ritual actors fill multiple roles, some at the same time and some at
different times. I am simultaneously father and son, husband and friend, teacher and
student. The roles set up reciprocal and complementary normative relationships. This
conventionalist position does not rest on personhood or moral agency. Society is the
sum of its roles, not the sum of its individuals. Confucius did not base his humanism
on the abstract conception of the human individual engaged in choosing a morality
to guide his relations with others. He roots his accounts of the way to act in the
transmitted social practices. Our humanity consists in playing whatever role we find
ourselves in. The role is a conventional one and the criterion of virtuosity in performing the role is *ren*[humanity].

The reciprocal structure of Confucius' traditional code of conduct dictates a
natural hierarchy. Social rituals all have analogues of superior and inferior.[28] This
does not mean that some people are born naturally superior; the code assigns no value
comparisons to bare individuals. We may, as I noted, alternately fill complementary
roles in different contexts. To each upper-role position there corresponds a lower
one. *Li* gives the behavior of each party in terms of the complementary position. The
father treats the son one way and the mother another. Further, the appropriate behav-

ior for father and son must be in harmony. When both fulfill their roles, they *realize* the *dao* expressed in the *li*.

A particular kind of optimism about all human nature distinguishes Confucianism and Chinese thought from both ancient Greek and Indian thought. Confucius' position suggests that we not use hereditary status to assign people to ritual roles. He stressed instead that we *appoint* by merit based on *de*^{virtuosity}. Merit does run in families, but it is presumably a result of nurture, not nature. It can decline or rise over generations. In the well-ordered society, as pictured in Confucian writings, people and families rise through the role hierarchy by acquiring and transmitting virtuosity or excellence. Later political institutions determined excellence by either recommendation or open competitive examination.[29]

For the most part, Confucianism seemed committed to the view that people begin from an equal base—an equal innate ability to acquire and become expert in their *li* roles. All are capable of attaining excellence in traditional terms. Therefore, those who reach the higher ranks in that practice both deserve it and benefit others by being there. They model correct behavior for the rest of us. Submission to *li*^{ritual} is the key that justifies promotion to higher roles and status.

The Role of Rulers

At the top of the ritual hierarchy, the king obeys his mandate and plays his role. The king does not have a *right* to rule, but a *ming*^{command} to order the system. The *ming*^{mandate} (same character) of heaven gives him a pivotal ritual role. At the apex of the hierarchy, he starts the chain of behavior modeling. He triggers the entire ritual structure. His concern is conformity with *tian*^{heaven:nature}. Human ritual takes place in a natural context. Ritual *succeeds* only if it is in harmony with nature. The king is the liaison between heaven:nature and human society. He sets society on the ritual path necessary to keep it in harmony with nature. Only that path will result in human flourishing. Human flourishing preserves order. Order preserves nature's approval and the mandate remains.

The king *is* responsible for the efficient and smooth running of the ritual system. He does not (indeed, could not) directly supervise all repertoires of conventional behavior. His main task, therefore, is naming role models. He *names* those who fill roles at the second tier of the ritual hierarchy (2:19–20). Beyond this quasi-linguistic task of appointing role experts, the king is mainly responsible for setting an example of decorum in his own behavior. He thus instills ritual conformity in those directly below him. They, in turn, model social behavior down through the hierarchy. He does not meddle in day to day administration.[30]

> Confucius said, "Ruling undeliberately: This was Shun! What did he do? He made himself reverent and faced south." (15:5)

> Qi Kangzi asked Confucius about *zheng*^{regulating}. Confucius replied, "One who *zheng*^{regulates} *zheng*^{rectifies}. If you model rectification, who will dare not rectify?" (12:17)

> Qi Kangzi in asking Confucius about *regulation* said, "What about killing those with no *dao* in order to bring about having *dao*?" Confucius replied, "In your

regulating, why use killing? If you desire proficiency, the people will be proficient. The character of the rules is the wind and the people are grass. The wind over the grass always bends it'' (12:19).

Confucian Opposition to Law and Punishment

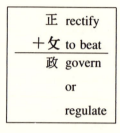

In particular, early Confucianism made it no part of the king's duty to pass laws and enforce them. The closest counterpart to the notion of law was the concept of coercive regulating—*zheng*—used in 12:17 and 12:19. We can partly unpack Confucius' koanlike answer in 12:17 (above) by noting that the two *zhengs* are related in both structure and pronunciation. The character translated here as *regulate* (also *government administration* etc.) consists of the character for *rectify* with a radical with a core meaning of *to beat*. The pun suggests that rulers should dispense with beating and merely educate. Confucius preferred education and opposed using coercion to get social order. If the opportunity to learn and the social models are present, people *will* absorb the dominant social practices for their roles. The use of punishment is not merely cruel, it is positively counterproductive if the goal is ritual order.

> Confucius said, ''*Dao*[lead] the people with *zheng*[coercion] and order them with punishment, and they will avoid wrongdoing but will have no shame. *Dao*[lead] them with *de*[virtuosity] and order them by *li*[ritual] and they will have shame and moreover fit their places.'' (2:3)

Confucius' reasoning is instructive. He accepts the proposition that legal motivations *will work*. People will avoid wrongdoing. He objects that, in working, coercive regulation subverts the innate inclination to absorb social programming. The more we regulate behavior by fear, the less people will develop spontaneous social practices such as *li*. Our potential for conventional social intercourse depends on our having a sense of shame—the inclination to conformity. We can explain Confucius' rationale by two assumptions: (1) humans have inclinations both to social conformity and to self-interested calculation and (2) exercise of an inclination strengthens it. Regulating coercively exercises the people's inclination to prudence or self-interest, since avoiding punishment is in our self-interest. Coercion requires this self-regarding disposition, the disposition to prudence. Punitive regulation strengthens the tendency to egoism and correspondingly weakens, by inattention, our natural social instincts. Law undermines our tendency to ritual conformity and emulation of models. It thus endangers the very root of the *natural* social order.

Further, because laws have a fixed, canonical formulation, they encourage disputation. Every law has interpretive ambiguities. Some person must determine whether any specific action violates the words of the law. Litigation is therefore inevitable. Confucius noted that, although he was as good as anyone at *litigation,* his goal was to eliminate litigation not to encourage it (12:13). Litigation is like a drug: once society gets hooked on it, it becomes impossible to withdraw. The law generates self-regarding motivations. The self-regarding person will cultivate cleverness at litigation to avoid punishment. He will argue (or hire someone to argue for him) that the law does not apply to his case. His case is special, or an exception, or covered under a different law. Sometimes he will succeed. More elaborate formulations will then be needed to refine the regulations. Ever more clever and glib people will emerge, trained by practice in this unnatural social institution. The laws will need to become ever more detailed and complex, resulting in an endless cycle of more laws, more lawyers, and more litigation.

A famous *sophist* of the period, Dengxi, may have heightened this awareness of the gap between codes and concrete guidance. He was a popular specialist in litigation in the state of Cheng who aided people in avoiding punishments. He gave clever, legalistic interpretations which "made right wrong and wrong right, the permissible impermissible and impermissible permissible."

Law thus stimulates the development of glib, clever, aberrant use of language rather than conforming use.[31] The development of law in China, as in Greece, produced a class of sophists ready to argue for both sides of any issue.[32] As Dawson notes, "it was conventionally accepted that the words could be taken out of context and made to bear any meaning required by the speaker."[33] Embarrassingly, given all these drawbacks, legal institutions will not result in a more orderly society. By undermining the social, ritual-conforming nature of people, this *quick-fix* solution to the problem of social order becomes self-defeating. The society with much litigation will, paradoxically, also be the society with many crimes. Its leaders may even hide behind the law and say "What I did may have been immoral, but it was not illegal!" Better in the long run to choose social forms that downplay natural egoism. Better to cultivate the contrasting natural instinct to social conformity.

This Confucian case against law has two components. The first is a motivational argument and the second an interpretive component. Law undermines social motivations and stimulates litigiousness. The second of these problems, however, also plagues rule by *li.* Specific *li* require contextual interpretation as much as do laws. The interpretive problem applied to *li* provides the motivation for the Confucian doctrine of rectifying names.

Rectifying Names

The most striking feature of the Confucian theory of the well-ordered society is its proposal to *rectify names.* Here educational theory, theory of language, and political theory merge.[34] Rectifying names is a practical political answer to the problem of interpreting codes. By carefully modeling language distinctions, social-political authorities try to make us follow the traditional codes correctly. Language is a convention transmitted by copying the performance of experts. Natural authorities (opinion leaders) determine usage by modeling language and behavior together (1:14). Language, thus, is merely a particularly central convention, one on which other conventions, especially the *Book of Li,* rely.

Confucius' students, in their arguments about what correct ritual behavior is, must have discovered what Confucius discovered about law codes. Given a codebook filled with rules, it is not obvious whether a given action conforms with or conflicts with those rules. The disagreement may come from the rules themselves being in conflict. For example we may have a rule to allow old people to get on the bus first and a rule to get on the bus promptly. If the old person happens to be slow or hesitant, the rules are in conflict.

We may have a simple *li* ^{ritual} entry that says "pass to the left of a king and to the right of a commoner." I meet someone coming down the road. For that rule to guide me, I need both to know both which rule governs the case and what the rule dictates. I must be able to distinguish a person's rank from his appearance. Even if I have that skill, applying the rules may be difficult. The person may be a king in disguise making a clandestine survey of his realm, or a deposed king from another country in a democratic realm, or an illegitimate tyrant rather than a true king. Unless I can put the right name on the object, I cannot correctly apply the rules.

Even after I decide which rule to apply, I still have to decide what the rule tells me to do. I must be able to distinguish right from left in the way the rule-writer intended. Again, even if I have learned the left-right distinction, I can have further questions. Does the rule mean *my* right or *the commoner's* right? We have to make distinction about both the object and the action for each item in the code in the appropriate way before the rules can guide us.

The rules by themselves cannot settle these interpretive issues. Further rules for their interpretation only compound the problem. Becoming an expert in the rules cannot provide a non-question-begging answer to this skepticism. I cannot hoist myself by my educational bootstraps and try to generalize from the rules. This line of skeptical argument casts doubt upon my understanding of each specific rule I profess to have learned. Without prior knowledge of how to make the linguistic distinctions, I cannot even apply one of the rules in even one instance. My profession of expertise simply begs the question.

Confucius mentions rectifying names explicitly only once in the collected fragments. The context suggests it is the duty of social leadership, specifically of a scholar like himself who attained the position of prime minister.

> Tzu-lu said, "Suppose the rule of Wei makes you *zheng* ^{administrator}, what will you do first?" Confucius said, "Necessarily, *zheng* ^{rectify} *ming* ^{names}." Tzu-lu said, "Is that so? You exaggerate. Why rectify?" Confucius said, "Yu! How uncouth you are! With regard to what he does not know, the superior man should maintain an attitude of reserve. If names are not rectified, the language will not flow smoothly. If language does not flow smoothly, then social acts cannot be carried out. If social acts cannot be carried out, then ritual and music will not thrive. If ritual and music do not thrive, then punishment will miss the mark. If punishments miss the mark, then the people will not know how to move hand or foot. Therefore the superior man will utter a name only in appropriate language and use language only in appropriate conduct. With regard to his speech, the superior man is not careless. That is all" (13.3).

This doctrine underlies all the features of Confucian political theory that make it unique. The role of administration is education in *li* and music. That education cannot succeed if people are misusing the names in the texts. Provisionally, we shall consider a misuse any use the sage kings (the authors of the *li*) would not make. So, if we use the word *gu* of the wrong ritual object, we will not be carrying out the ceremony in the correct way (6:23).

Implicitly this passage acknowledges that the same problem plagues both *li* and laws. Any fixed formulae that guide behavior can be misinterpreted in action. If society does not use the names correctly, the people will not derive guidance from the transmitted linguistic formulae.

No less interesting is the inclusion of music among the traditional literature forms that can go awry if we misuse names. A simple explanation is that, in effect, if names (symbols) are not rectified, we will play the wrong notes. If we don't know how to translate the marks into fingerings we won't play the song intended by the composer. Later, we will consider how an interpretation may be deficient without involving so gross a mistake as a wrong note.

Though Confucius says why he must rectify names, he does not say how. But, given his analysis of the need, it could not plausibly consist in publishing a list of definitions. If Confucius worried about the ability to interpret language, publishing a dictionary in a language would merely compound the problem. Most likely the ruler rectifies names the way parents do for their children. Model their correct use and then *shi*[right] the child's own correct uses and *fei*[wrong] his mistakes. Modeling the correct use will involve using them correctly as one *skillfully* practices and performs one's *li*-ordained role. We simply set examples by publically identifying objects and by naming our modeling behaviors as we do them.

Confucianism's classical rival, Mohism, reacting to a consequence of the Confucian theory, proposes a slightly modified theory of rectifying names. In order to prevent conflict among the rules of the fixed code like the *li*, the Confucian theory would require that only one term can apply to a thing *at a time*. Thus, since different rules address the treatment of a human and a thief, we must describe any actual being before us as either a thief or a human, but not both. Otherwise, the rules give us ambiguous guidance. The Mohists find the Confucian consequence, "a thief is not human," unacceptable, given their realistic theory of names. They propose instead to rectify only action descriptions. A thief is human, but killing-thieves is not killing-humans (see the discussion below, pages 250–51).

This gives us a way to elaborate on Confucius' other statements about *zheng*[governing]. The way in which governing is rectifying is mainly by rectifying names. Rectifying names is the key to the ruler's educational modeling role. That is what should be substituted for beating and killing.

Another famous passage may give us further insight into the relation of rectifying names and the political theory of hierarchical model emulation. The ruling interpretation treats this passage as a discussion of rectifying names, although Confucius does not mention the phrase in the passage and it is interpretively ambiguous. Confucius is again asked about the homophonic *zheng*[governing] as he is in all the earlier passages.

Duke Qing of Qi asked Confucius about *zheng*[governing]. Confucius replied, *"Ruler* rulers; *minister* ministers; *father* fathers; *son* sons." The duke said, "Excellent! Indeed when the ruler is not a ruler, the minister not a minister, the father not a father, and the son not a son, then even were grain around, how would I get anything to eat?'' (12:11)

This passage takes up the interpretive issue about models where the earlier one addressed interpretation of *li*. The duke's task in *zheng*^{governing} is to *name* people to roles based on their merit—to give the name *ruler* to rules, *minister* to ministers, and so forth.[35] Confucius is charging the duke with what he saw was the role of political leadership, identifying models and naming them. He thus rectifies the names of models so that emulation will be morally accurate. We may suppose that without such an identification, the people could not innately distinguish good from bad models. Rectifying names corrects the performance of *li,* music, laws, and any other transmitted instructions in literature. Society must also correctly identify the *models* of the ritual roles. The educational purposes of government thus depend on rectifying names.

The task of political leaders is to model the correct use of terminology, not to modify the rules, that is, to legislate. The rules are in the inherited transmitted *dao.* Rectifying provides the conditions for the transmitted *dao* to yield appropriate behavior. As a corollary, rulers must *name* or *identify* models of social roles correctly. The *dao* of each role is a settled matter.

Still a third way of rectifying names becomes important in later Confucianism. It concerns how historical scholars use language, not how political leaders do. In writing history, one can put the appropriate terms on the heroes and villains regardless of the status or rank they actually achieved. The tradition credits Confucius, the uncrowned sage king, with writing history on such a model. Tradition claims he rectified names in his *Spring and Autumn Annals.* Even if one cannot be a model to one's contemporary community, one can be a model to later inheritors of the transmission through literature.[36]

We can hardly even state this theory without noticing a problem. We began with the worry that people may not follow the rules correctly. We propose that the political and social leadership have the responsibility to set the example. Now, how are they to know that they have followed the rules correctly? All the grounds for skepticism apply to those at the top of the hierarchy as well as to those on the lower rungs. They apply to our teachers and past models as well as to present actors and performers.

My hypothesis is that this skepticism lies behind the elevation of the mysterious, undefined, intuitive doctrine of *ren*^{humanity} to a central position in Confucianism. Confucius himself perhaps had little to say about *ren*^{humanity} because he had not yet fully appreciated the problem. The disciples, confronted with their obvious disagreement about interpretation, began to focus on every mention of the word *ren* for clues to the intuitive standard that could resolve the problem of how to rectify names and guide interpretation of the *li*^{ritual}. They saw *ren*^{humanity} as the interpretive intuition that would enable them to see *specifically* what the *li*^{ritual} required in any particular situation. The ruler (or their scholarly advisers) should cultivate that intuition. With it, they could behave correctly while citing the language of the *li*^{ritual} and thus model the correct use of names in guiding action. The rectifiers of names must have some intuitive access to the right actions in these situations of doubt about what the rules require. Some kind of intuitive theory like that of *ren*^{humanity} is required if rectifying names is to serve as a solution to the interpretive problem.

That role for *ren* explains why it would be so important—why Confucius would worry aloud about what would become of *li* if people did not have *ren*[humanity]. Confucius describes *ren* as controlling yourself and conforming to *li*. He says that *ren* enables one to class people as good and bad (4:3) and that if you set your mind on *ren,* you will be free from evil (4:4).

I shall return to this issue below. Eventually, I think, both the traditionalist and the innatist rely on the doctrine of *ren*[humanity] as an intuitive guide. They disagree about the source and nature of *ren*[humanity]. Was it innate or learned? And they disagree about the degree to which it displaces formal written traditions. Does *ren*[humanity] require *li*[ritual] or does it displace it?

A Familiar Western Analogue to Rectifying Names. The American legal tradition provides a familiar counterpart of rectifying names. Confucius' view of government is like that of a purely judicial hierarchy, that does not make law, but only interprets it. A series of Supreme Court decisions upholds or reverses lower courts' uses of the legal phrase *freedom of speech.* The Supreme Court's decisions fix (for the judiciary) the acceptable reference of that constitutional term essentially by modeling the appropriate use in the specific case. They may never define *obscenity,* but they name it when they see it. Logically, all legal interpretation involves fixing the scope of names. Deciding to describe a case as *free speech* rather than *obscenity* determines which legal rule or provision applies to the case.

There are several points of positive analogy:

Fixed code. In both cases, we inherit the guiding linguistic form in a canonical, fixed, public form. We do not invite the interpreters to alter the wording in order to conform to some abstract conception. This feature of law and *li* contrasts with Western rational morality and science. The intellectual goal of the latter is to refine, change, and improve the *actual statement* of the *dao* in question. The Supreme Court cannot alter the constitution; it can alter only its theory of interpretation—the scope of its terms. The Constitution may be regarded as the United States' *li* of government. It is a canonical form inherited from sagelike founding fathers.

Modeling by concrete use. The court decides in only concrete, actual cases and controversies—actual contexts of official government action. Its decisions consist essentially in saying the right legal words here and now. For the Supreme Court, saying it makes it legally so.[37] Other courts attempt to model their legal language on the linguistic behavior of the Supreme Court. The legal system is a system of model emulation. Lower courts conform to the precedents of higher courts. All attempt to conform to past precedent.

Authority hierarchy. Those lower in the guiding hierarchy (the judiciary) model their interpretive use of the code on those who are higher. Again, this contrasts with morality and science, where we acknowledge no performative authorities. No one can *make* something moral or true by declaring it so. Our conception of these rationally based social institutions informs and reinforces the Western ideal of individual autonomy and integrity.[38]

Idealized authors and intentions. There are also traditional and idealist lines or schools of interpretation in judicial theory. The traditionalist idealizes the historical authors of the *dao* in question. They understand themselves as conforming to the founding fathers' (or sage-kings') intentions. They conform consciously to the past as the social practice conforms upward.

Special interpretive sense. The idealist line stresses that the social models of use of the fixed code should have an internal standard to guide their interpretation. We call a Supreme Court justice's guiding intuition *a sense of justice.* Innatist Confucianism emphasizes *ren* [humanity] as an intuitive guide to interpretation. The traditionalist also requires it. But traditionalism stresses intuition's instrumentality. It is a means of access and conformity to the founder's intention. For the innatist, it is an assertion of a standard which is right in itself and *explains* the authority of the founders and, happily, coincides with their judgments.

There are important disanalogies, of course, which are rooted in more general contrasts between our traditions. In our tradition, the concept of justice has a more focused content than merely an intuition to correct evaluation. Our Platonic tradition links justice to reason and theoretical coherence. The courts have the un-Confucian responsibility to give reasons or arguments for their interpretive actions. They operate with the notions of *meaning* and *definition.* The court relies on a distinctly juridical conception of morality in guiding its legal interpretations. Our justification of the entire system of rule of law rests on a morality of deontological individualism.

The controversies in the Supreme Court focus on what standard makes an interpretation correct. The conservative position, again, trumpets conformity with the intentions of America's sage kings. Reformers appeal to an intuitive sense of justice, general benevolence, or some rational standard, such as coherence, evidence, or objective morality. Carrying out the total rationalization of rectifying decisions is acknowledged to be a task of an idealized mental Hercules.[39] Practically speaking, limited, human judges rely on a rational intuition. The Confucian reforming ideal has similar directions, but without having generated a guiding concept of reason. Politically, a sense of justice is our rectifying counterpart of Confucian *ren* [humanity].

The proper *contrast* to rectifying names is the Socratic conception of critical morality. Socratic method, based on Euclidean indirect proof, aims at *revision* of the rules. No authoritative text records the principles of morality. We use reason to arrive at them. The idealized rule structure must coherently resolve all conflicts and exceptions. The moral axioms and the rules of inference should produce the concrete answers to particular moral questions. The formulation of the highest guiding rules is the focus of intellectual activity. The Socratic approach buries interpretive ambiguity.[40]

Frequently, however, even Western moral disputes take the form of rectifying names. This happens especially when we have conventionally accepted a canonical moral rule. Consider the abortion debate. We have an apparent conflict between our conventionally accepted rule that we do not kill innocent people and the conventionally accepted rule that people shall have the freedom to make choices affecting their own lives. Few participants in the public debate question either of the rules. Their dispute turns on a rectification of names. What is the scope of *person?* Does it include or exclude fetuses? If a fetus is a person, then the provisions of our morality involving killing apply. If it is not a person, they do not apply and the freedom of choice rule applies to the only person concerned—the woman. If you have an intuition that abortion is permissible, you will not include fetuses in the scope of *persons*. If your moral intuition goes the other way, you do.

Theory of Human Nature

Injecting Human Nature

The traditional focus of dispute between the two wings of Confucianism concerns human nature. Mencius came to hold an extreme idealist view that inclinations of human nature are innately good. He thus made the theory of human nature the basis of his system. Confucius seems not have focused on the issue. (Recall the passages in *The Analects* that complains that the disciples did not hear his views on nature, heaven, or *ren*^{humanity}.) I shall argue that his social-education theory logically presupposed a theory of human nature different from that of Mencius.

Several passages bear on the question and, although Confucian orthodoxy follows Mencius, even the disciples who stressed *ren* seemed to regard human nature as more neutral than Mencius did (6:19, 16:9, 17:2, and 17:3). Many human traits, such as selfishness, are subject to educational influence. Much of human nature is acquired. That doesn't mean there are no innate dispositions, but the ones that matter the Confucian conception of *de*^{virtuosity} are transmitted as part of a cultural *dao*^{way}. Thus the disciples note that Confucius stressed *wen*^{literature} more than nature and the natural *dao* (5:13). The important dispositions to behavior came mainly from practice and cultivation (see pages 80–81 below).

Early Confucians thought of humans as ritual-acquiring animals that naturally tend to teach and learn *li*^{ritual}. Confucius explicitly cites only a few specific *li* which range from etiquette to ceremonial appropriateness. We suppose specialized sacrificial, funereal, and official ceremonies dominated his compendium of *li*. Given its centrality, most interpreters attribute a much broader scope to Confucius' *li*. Herbert Fingarette is typical when he treats *li*^{ritual} as standing for convention, institution, or social practice in general.[41]

Consider Fingarette's example of a commonplace *li* of modern Western culture—the act of shaking hands.[42] It takes two to act; the act requires reciprocity. The initiator, someone in the appropriate social context, extends his hand, and the other, a cooperating respondent, joins. Their joint physical behavior in the appropriate context constitutes hand-shaking *by virtue of* the existence of a hand-shaking *li* in our culture. Conventions, so to speak, create act-types. The act of shaking hands is not a purely physical act. No merely physical state could be an act of hand-shaking unless a historical community had a convention to respond to the physical configuration as a nonaggressive gesture.

We can grasp Confucius' view of the role of *li* in human nature if we think of Wittgenstein's analogy of social practices to games. Humans have a natural inclination to participate in structured social interactions. Notice a child's natural delight at simple games like peek-a-boo, pat-a-cake, and bye-bye. Think of *li* as embracing such responsive rituals as conversational ones:

"How are you?" "Fine. And you?" "Just fine, thank you."

Notice that the *li* of these greeting games with their standard moves are culturally variable. The counterpart game in China (before foreigners introduced "Ni hau ma?") goes as follows:

"Have you eaten yet?" "I've eaten. Have you?" "I've eaten."

We naturally strive to copy and mimic these ritualized interactions. We tend, that is, to acquire conventional social behavior by playing the games with others. We push and practice and value becoming reliable performers. If our teacher (or other accepted *performers*) recognize our performance as an instance of the practice, then we experience the natural satisfaction of having learned it. The ritualized interaction is humanly fulfilling. On the other side of the social hierarchy, we derive pleasure not only from practice and performance, but also from teaching our acquired skills. We enjoy becoming models of the skills we have acquired.

My child, for example, carries a picture book and tugs on my hand. I sit on the floor. He sits on my lap, opens the book, extends his index finger and says "Utsah." Whatever he thought he was doing, I recognize this as the conversational move, "What is that?" and respond with the next move—to name the objects on the page. We are practicing an elementary form of the reading ritual. We successfully play the language game whether or not he knew that he was asking a question with three words.

Or consider how a child learns to count. First he learns to recite the numbers one to ten. What is the next step? Open the book to the page with ten balloons. I extend my index finger, point to the page and recite the numbers in order. He mimics me. He taps the page absently while reciting the numbers. I do not *shi*[this:right] this performance. There was something he did not notice. (At this stage, I surely cannot *explain* the matter!) He has to tap once per number. When he catches on to that, he has to notice that I touch a different balloon with each number, then that I never touch the same one twice. Counting is a complex ritual that builds on many simpler rituals.

Again, Wittgenstein gives us a parallel insight. In the learning of social language games, we do not normally rely on explicit rules. In the interpretation of any rules we may be given, we always rely on some *deeper human abilities simply to catch on and continue*. (Imagine trying to spell out the rules of peek-a-boo to a child.) Thus the transmission of games or *li* requires both modeling *and* some basic human tendencies. The tendency that aids transmission of games is mimicry and this instinct to *catch on to* human forms of ritualized interaction. Notice, also, that this ability is continuous to some degree with the whole animal kingdom. We play simple games quite satisfactorily with cats and dogs. The abilities that ground this conception of humanity have nothing to do with transcendental intelligence or proof-structure rationality!

We need the teacher, but not merely as a model, since the teacher also serves to certify or reject our *moves*. This may, but need not, take some explicit assent and dissent form like *shi*[this:right] or *fei*[not this:wrong] (yes or no). It more typically consists in making the next move in response to the child's move. Thus the teachers' responsive uptake is the criteria of virtuosity. The game goes forward.

The Importance of Modeling. We seldom, therefore, learn ritual behavior solely by rules. Arguably (see pages 65–67 above) we cannot. Learning requires modeling by teachers and intelligent mimicry by students. The Confucian baseline views education in this broader context as socialization. Education is a natural part of *growing up*. Analogues of the formal teacher-pupil relation pervade society. Confucius' own impact on his students stemmed as much from their admiration of him as a model as from his teachings. Confucius' social-political theory, as we saw, stressed the importance of learning by example. *Jiaoyu*^{teaching:nourishing}, that is, character building, requires modeling. Upright officials contribute to moral education just by being seen in proficient action (2:1). Without this modeling of proficiency, teaching of *li* cannot succeed (4:13).

Ultimately, our ritual know-how comes from emulating others, not from book learning. Table manners, no matter how carefully taught, are almost hereditary. Children learn mostly by example. Most of us need to *play it once* before we understand a game. Beyond a point, more time studying the rules is wasted.

We recognize in our own popular culture the force and power of learning by example: "What you are speaks so loudly, I can't hear what you say." It is commonplace among marriage counselors that the way we saw our parents and other adults behave with each other has more influence on our marital behavior than does our theorizing and teaching. Excellence in sports is notoriously incapable of discursive direction; we need to be shown (and shown and shown) how to do it. We use apprenticeships for learning most major crafts.

Modeling is important for another reason. We unconsciously process so many clues from the environment in acting, we could never learn a skill from a finite set of instructions. We must see exemplars model in actual contexts. However much we can learn to do from descriptions and instructions, we can never get the kind of exhaustive detail to guarantee skillful and successful performance of such repertoires. Each instance of a performance has a unique context to which we must respond.

The Role of Intuition. What we call *intuition* is usually the acquired skill to process contextual clues and react to them quickly enough to adjust our action to ever-changing circumstances. We could not practically include all the required detail in a theoretical account of how to do a thing. Precisely because we need to adjust our action to an endless variety in a myriad of factors, practice is required.

Practice builds an intuition—an ability quickly to process and respond to clues, to environmental features that affect the performance. *Michael Jordan drives to the hoop* . . . He doesn't plan that spectacular shot. It emerges from the circumstances. He has highly developed feedback mechanisms, peripheral vision, a sense of what the defenders will do, an ability to extrapolate present motion, etc. His skill lies in adjusting his performance of a well-practiced ritual in response to that feedback. Intuition yields not propositional knowledge, but timely responses. We become a reliable mechanism for detailed registration of clues and response in performance by modeling and practicing skills.

Notice that, for our purposes, we are concerned with intuitive ability, not intuitive beliefs. We require that kind of intuition to perform with virtuosity. I may redescribe my intuition to turn right while herding cows as an intuitive belief *that the cow will turn right*. That redescription plays a role in the Western theory of action. However, it plays no explanatory role in the Confucian context. My accomplished practical intuition *explains* my turning right by itself. I do not process a cognitive thought (even an intuitive one) and *then* turn right![43] Confucius envisions that the ritual behaviors will become spontaneous. That kind of cultural acquisition *fulfills* our nature as social animals. However, he also observes that at early stages of learning, performance requires more obvious concentration than when we are virtuosos (2:4). To understand the skeptical reaction to Mencius, we need merely remind ourselves that *even early Confucians* noticed that we normally *learn our guiding intuitions* through practice.

The guiding intuition consists in a dispositional faculty realized in our actual physical structures. It does not belong to some purely intellectual or mental realm. Its typical output is the appropriate performance (physical movement) in the circumstances. Confucians traditionally regarded *de*[virtuosity] as being visible in physical form.[44] Acquiring a transmitted competence *changes* us. Or, as Confucius says, training and education in *li shapes and polishes* us (1:15).

Early Confucians thus supposed that people learn most effectively by emulating skilled practitioners, what Munro calls model emulation. The roots of the intuitive wing's antilanguage position also lurk in this outlook. Without modeling, no amount of rule giving can convey the detail necessary for a good interpretive performance. We saw traces of this antilanguage attitude in Confucius' opposition to law and punishment. The interpretive looseness of codified rules generates glibness and cleverness in *rectifying names* to escape punishment.

Language: A Paradigm. Most readers of this English prose will have been raised with a Western attitude toward convention. We can appreciate the Confucian position better if we look at language as an example of a convention. Language ability is a conventionally defined skill. We learn language by modeling. We consider achieving skill at language as fulfilling a natural human function. A newborn (some experiments suggest even a fetus) responds more to language than to other sounds in his environment. Young children mimic brilliantly and relish language play. We learn grammar rules, if ever, long after we have already largely mastered our language. Formal training, to English teachers' eternal frustration, has a minimal effect on our actual language use. In natural language acquisition, children learn simple skills and build these into more complex skills. Most important for Confucius' attitude, we seldom worry that in shaping language behavior we constrain the child's free nature.

Among rituals, language has a special status. It is a particularly pivotal conventional social practice. Language plays a role in almost all highly complex social rituals. Language learning comes early in our programmed agenda for culture shaping—though not alone. We do not learn language as an abstract prerequisite of rituals. We learn language in a framework set by other rituals: greeting and farewell rituals, rituals of kinship classification, eating rituals, permission-asking and rights-claiming rituals.

Note this difference in Chinese and Western views of the function of language. The written form—*wen*[literature]—not spoken language, fascinates Confucius.(1:6) *Wen*[literature] also refers to artistic decoration and embellishment.[45] Confucius, the scholar-transmitter, fixes on how language functions in transmitting and preserving aesthetic embellishments. We usually regard written language as parasitic on spoken language, as Western languages are. What we think of as words, Confucius would regard as a way of pronouncing words, not as the words themselves. (7:18)

We learn content (lexical items) and form (correct or artistic word order) together. The linguistic community accumulates names and different ritual uses over time. Literature is the *flow chart* of a civilization. Confucius' social project is programming and embellishing people with literature. Chinese called the result *wen*^{literature} *hua*^{changed} which we translate as *civilized*. Confucius said, "If you do not study *The Book of Poetry* you will have nothing with which to speak"(16:13; see also 17:19).

Word mastery thus underlies all acquired cultural refinement. We develop *abilities* to stage the rituals or play the games that constitute our *form of life*.[46] We model others' speech as we model their ritual behavior. Learning and practice thus *realizes* our natural human potential. It creates our human nature; it does not constrict it. Learning to recite a verse, to shake hands, and to whistle a tune are alike. "Let a man be stimulated by poetry, established by *li,* and perfected by music"(8:8).

Confucian Conventionalism and Western Folk Psychology. Western thought takes its attitude toward language and its folk psychology[47] to be self-evident. That makes it hard to see the appeal of the Confucian view. I want to trace why it seems *self-evident* to us so we can appreciate how ancient Chinese thinkers could have missed what we take to be obvious *truths* about psychology and language.

Confucius' having focused on written language, in contrast to spoken language, carried other contrasts in its wake. Since Chinese philosophers thought of their language as pictures, they saw immediately that a picturing language rests on conventions as much as sounds do. Pictographic symbols are not self interpreting. Chinese philosophers would not have thought that postulating mental pictures could explain the meaning of language. Their language was pictures. These pictures were conventional and public, conveyed and learned as civilization's adornment. The language of thought was public, shared and acquired through history. And further they recognized the need for interpretive conventions.

Popular Western accounts of language mythologize the process of language learning. We hide the process in the obscure and inaccessible realm of the private, inner mind. We postulate that a prelinguistic rational process creates invisible, intangible, inaccessible, obscure, and somewhat mysterious mental objects. We call these ideas or concepts. And then, with a logic that would delight Nietzsche, we insist that these mysterious, unseen things are the most immediate, obvious, and basic objects of knowledge. No one can fail to have total, perfect, unmediated knowledge of them!

These mental objects are the characters in our private ideographic language. Let us call this language mentalese.[48] Our individualist theory of language learning then insists that we have to generate this private ideographic language before we can grasp a shared community language. The model of language learning is translation: we see ourselves as understanding a public language by translating it into our private mental graphs. We communicate when we trigger in someone else's mind an occurrence of sufficiently similar pictographs of his version of mentalese.

The ideas form *strings* in our mind as words form sentences on paper. A string of ideas is a complete thought when it corresponds to a grammatically complete sentence. If we have a certain, undefinable attitude (analogous to a desire—a sort of Buddhist *clinging*) toward a mental sentence, we call that complete thought *a belief.*

A consequence of psychological *clinging* is that belief can function in our theory of action. The belief together with a desire (think of a desire as a thought with which we have a different kind of *clinging*) causes our action. When this happens the beliefs and the desires are *reasons* and the process by which they lead to action is *reasoning*. Most of the attention of Western philosophy concentrates on voluntary actions, which we treat as the product of reasoning. Hence our enshrined contrast of *rational* and *ritual-following* animals makes us see Confucius' view of ritual as manipulative.

Elaborating our account of language learning leads us to encourage people to resist socialization. We resort to egoistic assumptions and mechanisms to explain how society socializes someone as if it were a trick or a subterfuge. A linguistic community, using subtle reward and punishment, trains us to translate our ideas and beliefs correctly. This makes language learning look manipulative and unnatural. We prefer the theory according to which an inner language is completely individual and we merely translate our fully individual ideas into the socially shared language for our own advantage.

Notorious puzzles lurk in Western grammar-school ideology. One puzzle is how the linguistic community knows *when* we have learned language correctly. Only I can compare my words to my thoughts. A similar puzzle plagues our image of communication. How can we ever know if it is successful? How can a theory raise doubt about our ability to connect a sound with a shape in the world and solve it by assuming we can connect a sound with a shape in the mind? How can it solve the puzzle of the relation of word and world when it gives us two puzzles back: (1) how do we connect the word to the mental pictograph and (2) how do we connect the mental pictograph (which, as Chinese reminds us, is merely another word) to the world? Finally, it tries to explain these puzzles while ignoring the conventional, social-practice character of language. It treats meanings as strange objects in a mystical, mental medium. These intellectual objects are accessible to individual minds independent of all their social practices.

Finally, the folk theory is at odds with things we widely recognize about language. If in England I say "I want a biscuit," I will get a cookie. If I say it in Kansas, I will get a puffy cooked dough. What my request meant had nothing to do with what I wanted. Its meaning was fixed by the linguistic community. What goes on in my inner psychology cannot change what words mean in a community. Our way of objecting to this kind of misunderstanding contributes to our confusion about meaning. We are likely to say, "I meant this, not that!" This equivocates with the word *meaning*. In one case it concerns a word's relation to the world and in the other it concerns our intentions or desires ("I didn't mean to hurt you"). The correct description of the case is, "I wanted one of these, not those"; "I wish I had said something different and I now correct my request." Our psychological state cannot change the meaning of a word in a community.

These reflections help explain Fingarette's controversial views on the absence of psychology in Confucius. Western common-sense psychology of beliefs and desires will not help our understanding of Chinese theories of human nature. Confucius' theories do not require any dogma about an inner mental, cognitive life in explaining human nature. My son plays the "utsah" game whatever his inner state is. The success lies in the social surroundings. I respond to him. He doesn't need to believe himself to be uttering a three word interrogatory sentence, "What is that?" to have mastered this simple *li*.[49] Inner psychological states are not what give conventional forms their life or language its meaning.

Again, I do not intend a thorough refutation of the *language-of-thought* view. I shall rest with my having described it in a way that shows its connection with superstitions that we cannot take seriously. I want to present it so that we can at least appreciate how someone might regard it as a troublesome, popular myth rather than as something self-evident and obvious. I want mainly to alert readers of this English prose that their ordinary way of talking about such matters is not self-evident nor is it inescapable common sense. Whatever the merits of the belief-desire folk psychology of inner mental states, that psychological theory is not inevitable. It is not a theory which anyone who thinks about human behavior has to adopt.[50] We ourselves have trouble avoiding this view, even given its problems and puzzles, because it is deeply embedded in our language. The point is that we should not assume that people on the other side of the world, two thousand years ago shared this psycholinguistic mythology. Classical Chinese thought certainly does not.

We shouldn't elaborate the Confucian view using the mythology of the inner individual. We have no evidence of the beliefs and desires of a child aside from her behavioral tendencies. Let us speak directly of those tendencies, of natural human inclinations and capacities.[51] Put simply, we have both the inclination and capacity to learn language.[52] Language acquisition is a key part of our natural sociability.

Now we can see the relation of Fingarette's examples to his claims about the absence of psychology in Confucian thought. Notice that the significance of Fingarette's handshake does not rest on any mental or psychological act. The two parties shake hands even if they are sleep-walking, in a coma, or, under the influence of hypnosis, think they are eating potato soup. They shake hands even if they don't like each other and shake hands even if they are insincere about the meaning of the gesture. If they are shaking on a business deal, the deal is made whatever schemes the parties may harbor in their minds. What makes this action handshaking is the existence of a social practice and not the psychological state or cognitive assumptions of either participant. Similarly, what makes language meaningful is a historical linguistic community and not some private subjective experiences.

For most of us, explaining our handshaking behavior (especially if we are the responder) in terms of beliefs, desires, and decisions is slightly bizarre. We seldom have time to form a belief (''Oh, he wants to shake hands'') and check our desires when a hand is thrust out to us. It is equally strange to explain it in terms of a habit—shaking hands is not strongly analogous to stroking my beard. In fact, any focus that is psychological (in the sense of explaining behavior purely by what goes on inside the individual body) explains such behaviors poorly. The explanation has a crucially social and historical character.

Confucius offers neither psychological nor other explanations. To understand Confucius, it is best to think of *ren*[human] as a single scattered object. Humanity directs its parts (states, cities, families, individuals) by a system of conventions; it is as if the conventions were the central nervous system of the humanity organism. Think of the motivating impulse as in the social unit, not in the individual. The parts are functional pieces of the whole. Individuals emerge as interstices in the framework delineated by social *li*. The emphasis, remember, is on ritual roles, not on the individuals who fill them. We learn to become daughter, brother, teacher, ruler, lover, priest, friend, and so forth as we master socially defined patterns of behavior. The important features of our being are the roles we take on from society, not the personality we bring to it.

Applied Psychology of Education. The picture we are drawing of Confucius' theory of humans as ritual animals informs his special view of education. In educating, we do not communicate a cognitive content such as scientific facts and mathematical theorems. Rather, education is applied moral psychology. Its purpose is to give a population competence in conventionalized conduct. Education internalizes behavior patterns. Education most resembles behavioral training—character building.[53] Social education inculcates inclinations to follow *li*. The goal of education is mastery of the *li* roles we are to play.

We could, however, construct a plausible naturalistic psychological theory that would cohere with Confucius' social theory. We would not postulate any nonphysical substance or properties or events. We *could* talk of a heart-mind, but treat it as an organ that effects bodily movement in conformity to *li*[ritual]. The physical state of the well-trained heart-mind would literally *embody* competence at staging social rituals. This state is what Chinese thinkers call *de*[virtuosity]. The conventional explanation of *de* is *dao* within. We can understand this as the translation of *dao* into our actual physical dispositions.

Individuals have skills. We each learn a repertoire of skills at executing various roles. The psychology simply attributes to us the physically realized dispositional state that consists in our being able to generate—at appropriate places and times—some acceptable move.

We can attribute to Confucius the necessary assumptions about individual human psychology needed to explain enculturation. We need not attribute Western mentalistic folk psychology to him. The psychology does not explain the meaning or life of ritual, but it explains how we acquire a capacity to perform them well. The interesting *content* governing our lives is social.

Confucius' claims about *li* and its inherent involvement in human social life are claims about *humanity*, not strictly claims about individual persons. He does not assume, as we do, that claims about society must be explained by talking about the behavior of the *atoms* of society—human individuals and their psychology.[54] Confucius' claims about human nature are most plausibly regarded as being about human-stuff nature, not about human-individual nature. Humans are distinct from other animals not merely in being social, but in having their sociability rest on learned, inherited, conventions rather than instinct.[55]

Confucius' disciples condense his *psychological* theory regarding the practice of *li* into a pithy opening passage of *The Analects*. "To study and constantly practice—Is that not pleasant?" (1:1) The human tendency to learn these rituals and practice them with one another—and to enjoy it—is one part of the content of Confucius' assumption about the goodness of human nature. We are instinctively inclined to get satisfaction from acquiring ritual behaviors.

Human Nature and the Role of Ren

Confucian views of human intellectual functioning center on ritual. Confucius offers an account that requires no assumptions about a supernatural or mental component in human nature.[56] Confucian views are compatible with modern biological accounts. We are social animals. What uniquely distinguishes humans from other social animals is the way we socialize. We accumulate culture and transmit it through language and literature. Nature does not print how people fit together in society in their genes. The way is accumulated; it is cultural; it is historical. We pass the forms down through history in written or oral traditions. Humans, thus, are ritual-following animals who are naturally shaped by historical literature.

Nothing, however, imposes conventions on a recalcitrant, reluctant human spirit. Conventions do not constrain an *autonomous* agent. The conventions *make us* who we are. Our very identity as persons is bound up with our roles. They fulfill and constitute our nature rather than control it. Human nature is good—not because good behavior is innately natural, but because internalizing good—that is, social, conforming—dispositions is natural.

From a late twentieth-century perspective, Confucius' theory counts as being very optimistic about human nature. The social explanation undeniably rests on an assumption that human nature is naturally social. For a culture imbued by assumptions of psychological egoism, this counts as a theory that human nature is good. By our lights, Confucius and Mencius will not seem far apart. But in the intramural Confucian disputes, Confucius seems never to have gone as far as Mencius goes.

In the intramural dispute between innatists and conventionalists, we need more argument to show that Confucius belonged to the "Human nature is *originally* good" school. Mencius' slogan is:

(A) Human nature is *ben*^originally good.

Confucius, I suggest, might plausibly be committed to two closely related claims about human social nature.

(A^1) Humans are social, ritual-abiding animals.

(A^2) Humans are social, behavior-copying animals.

Being *good* in the sense of being inherently social and conformist is a weaker claim than is Mencius' slogan. We can imagine a social animal learning rituals, but (1) learning the wrong ones or (2) learning from bad performances, or mimicking the bad aspects of some performance. This suggests that we would have to add something to Confucius' theory to get closer to that of Mencius.

(A$^{1'}$) The human, ritual-abiding tendency tends to be morally correct.

A$^{1'}$ is ambiguous between the two ways that learning ritual may go wrong. On one interpretation, it raises a question that Confucius pointedly avoids: the question of the ethical status of the *li*. "Might we have learned from the wrong book of rituals?" We will suspend discussion of this issue until Mozi raises it in the next chapter. On the other interpretation, A$^{1'}$ reminds us of a problem Confucius *has* raised: the issue generated in criticizing laws. People may disagree about what the *li* prescribe. Do we have a natural tendency to interpret codes correctly? If we had such a harmonious interpretive inclination for the code of *li*, it would undermine Confucius' criticism of law. It would be hard to explain why a penal code would produce litigation and disputes if we natively tended toward interpretive goodness.

If we allow that there can be both good and bad interpretations of *li*, then we would require some independent standard of the *shi*[this:right] interpretation. We could not rest with a purely literature-based notion of value.

Notice that a parallel problem arises in regard to model emulation. We can move in Mencius' direction by reinterpreting A^2 as:

(A$^{2'}$) Human behavior modeling correctly values good models.

Let us concentrate on the claim that humans *correctly* evaluate when they select actors and performances to imitate.[57] Again, a mere tendency to imitate social superiors is not sufficient to guarantee a *good* outcome. If we emulate bad models, we will be bad. Our concern is not merely, in Mencius' phrase, do humans *shi-fei?* Our concern is, do they do so *correctly?* One version of the question, "did Confucius teach A" is "did Confucius teach $A^{2'}$." Again, there are two components of $A^{2'}$.

(A$^{2.1}$) Humans distinguish good performance from bad.

(A$^{2.2}$) Humans only copy behavior which they class as good.

Without optimism in this matter, one would have to defend Confucianism by accepting an authoritarian social practice of teacher worship. There would be no guarantee the result would be the absolutely correct *dao even if we accepted the sage-king's dao as correct.* We would have to settle for the relativism inherent in conventions of interpretation. If a later tradition went wrong, then wrong would become right and right would be wrong.

So this version of the question about the goodness of human nature translates as: Did Confucius teach that humans have inclinations to recognize and prefer positive as opposed to negative models? The answer is unclear. Confucius' most cited passages on human nature are these:

> Confucius said, "In nature [humans] are close to each other. In practice they distance themselves [from each other]." (17:2)

> Confucius said, "Humans' growth is toward being upright (right). If he lives in violation of that, then if he is lucky, he may escape."(6:19)

The first passage hints that we are capable of bad practice as well as good—or at least of relatively *less good* practice. It expresses an optimistic view of humanity's potential but allows the possibility that requires rectification of names for both use of *li* and models. The second is among the strongest claims of natural morality in the text.[58] But in another passage, Confucius suggests the standards of *upright* are relative to region and conventional standards (see pp. 82–83). His position can also be interpreted in light of a much revered passage in *The Analects* where Confucius discusses the process of scholarly human maturity. That passage suggests that Confucius viewed *intuitive* effortless conformity to ritual rules as something acquired over a lifetime of study and practice.

> Confucius said, "At fifteen you should set your intention on learning; at thirty you should be accomplished; at forty you will have no doubts; at fifty understand fate; at sixty hear anything comfortably; at seventy follow your heart-mind's desires and do nothing wrong."(2:4)

Confucius' quoted statements, then, suggest that excellence in interpretive performance is a natural *achievement,* but that it is an achievement that relies on internalizing a transmitted form. He seems comfortably assured that it will be correct, but gives no way to remove the worry that we might have cultivated the wrong intuitions. The fragments are not explicit enough to show that Confucius held anything as strong as an innatist version of $A^{2'}$. One reason not to include an innatist version of $A^{2'}$ in the system is that it generates a Confucian problem of evil. Ex Confucian hypothesi, there were sage kings and a golden age. Now, if humans can distinguish good and bad models and naturally incline to emulate the good ones, then we should never have fallen to the present state. Further, note that in the political assumptions, Confucius regarded it as necessary to have authority designate the models. This should not be necessary if Confucius accepted innatist $A^{2'}$. Similarly the political theory of rectifying names suggests that people can go wrong in interpreting ritual codes.

Defenders of Confucian orthodoxy claim that Mencius' doctrine (that the entire repertoire of social behaviors is innate) merely embellishes on Confucius. To get this result, they have to confuse *intuitive* and *innate.* I intuitively know which way to turn when herding cattle. I don't stop to calculate probabilities they will run left or right. I don't hesitate or wonder about it. I process clues in their behavior and the environment that I could probably never recite—no doubt some of which I am not even aware. (They may even include the reactions of my horse.) But, however natural and obvious I find this activity, it is surely not innate.

We no doubt have innate abilities—balance, the ability to follow motion, pattern recognition, language, etc. The innate abilities are *also* intuitive and may be involved in acquiring other intuitions. But most of what we call intuitive behavior is most plausibly repeatedly practiced to the point of spontaneity. Consider, again, speaking our mother tongue. We speak spontaneously. It becomes unconscious background processing to most of our conscious processing. But we do not consider it innate. Contrary to conventional wisdom, females probably do not have *more* intuitions than males, but have quite *different* ones. Again some of these may be innate, but most are probably acquired as we internalize our respective cultural roles.

Morality and Human Nature

The stereotype of Chinese philosophy is that its neglect of metaphysics and epistemology is accompanied with a greater focus on ethics. Recently Rosemont has argued that following Fingarette's analysis results in questioning whether Chinese philosophy deals with morality at all. Fingarette characterizes Confucius' *dao* as a "way without a crossroads." [59] As Rosemont notes, Confucius' views on human nature seem to rule out the autonomy necessary for moral reasoning.[60] Confucius, Fingarette argued, did not even have a concept of *choice*.

I will have more to say about the conceptual issue in discussing Mozi. But at this point we can note first that the meaning of *dao* is clearly more general than is the term *morality*. Morality, arguably, is a part of *dao* (16:11). Moral discourse is one of many forms of guiding discourse. But not all *dao* is moral: *dao* includes all practical guidance—ritual, music, speech, and so forth.

Second, Chinese language seems to have a perfectly adequate term for what we think of as morality. Confucius' concept of *yi*[morality] [61] seems to play the relevant theoretical role. He says (1:13) that *xin*[trust] is close to *yi*[morality]. He regards *yi*[morality] as important to *zhi*[know] and to follow. *Yi*[morality] presents a limit to pursuit of the good (14:12 16:10) and guides choice (14:13) and language (15:17).

But, given that Confucius has a concept like *yi* available, it is significant that he focuses his attention on a *dao* of conventional propriety—*li*. Confucius seems to have stressed *li*[etiquette] to his disciples more than *yi*[morality]. Given the nature of Confucius' references to *yi*[morality], we cannot tell if he distinguished between real morality and a community's social mores. Mores are formally like *li*[etiquette]. They are relative to a historical community and its social agreement. We can use empirical research to discover them. They do not tell us what is finally morally correct.

It is seriously to be doubted that historical, sociological research of the kind that characterized Confucius' scholarship can ever answer the real moral question.[62] Some historians believe that history can substitute for philosophy and provide moral guidance. Interpreters tend to assume that Confucius is such a historian.[63] Confucius, however, does not raise the debater's metaquestion of justification and provide a historian's answer. Indeed, he seems to have no cognizance of the metaquestion at all. When it is raised in his presence, he pointedly avoids it. His traditionalism is nowhere more pronounced.

> Duke She said to Confucius, "In my group there is an upright Gong. His father took a sheep and the son bore witness of it." Confucius said "The upright in my group are different from this. The son is screened by the father and the father by the son. Uprightness is in that behavior."(13:18)

Rather than tackle the question of what morality really requires in the conflict of duties, Confucius retreats here to social mores—my group's are just different from yours. This suggests that Confucius thinks of *yi*[morality] as a convention, as mores rather than moral reasoning. This, of course, is consistent with his view of *dao*. The *Analects'* conception of *dao* is such that history *could* provide a *dao*. The discourse in *The Antalects* makes no distinction between moral *dao* and conventional mores.[64]

Apologists for Confucious have argued that Confucius did not have the resources or world experience to make the distinction between accepted convention of China and universal morality. That defense fails. The issue can be formulated in Chinese as effortlessly as in English. The sheep case poses the question adequately, Confucius simply dodges it. Confucius knows that *li* are different in different periods.[65] He announces this along with his choice to follow the specific *li* of Zhou culture.[66]

The Chinese *language* does have simple words available to make the distinction.

Mozi, the first anti-Confucian figure, effortlessly makes the contrast between su^{custom} and yi^{morality} explicit. Later Confucians follow Mozi, and the debate between traditionalists and innatists is cast as a contrast between a $ren^{\text{benevolence}}$-yi^{morality} and a $li^{\text{etiquette}}$-yi^{morality}. As we have seen, the interpretive issue itself provokes questions of realism in ethics. $Li^{\text{etiquette}}$ yi^{morality} is conventional mores.

Confucius, despite secularizing rituals, was intensely and unquestioningly committed to them: "I love the ritual" (3:16).[67] He does not appear to have taught his disciples a discipline of arguing for a position. His conception of careful thought is more like taking good aim than it is like proceeding from premise to conclusion. If he is to be compared to Socrates, it should be observed that his *dao*, his discourse, insofar as his disciples mastered it, exemplified neither Socratic doubt nor Socratic method.[68]

Neither wing of his disciples saw the moral issue clearly. They had not been trained to worry about the criteria of morality. Their concern was correct performance of a given historical, literature-based *dao*. They paid attention specifically to the problem of the correct interpretation of *li*. This led them to their intramural dispute about ren^{humanity}. The early Confucian theory of *ren* played a different role from that of Mencius. It was *not* designed to answer Mozi's question about the criteria of morality. It was designed to answer the question, "What constitutes following *li* correctly?" They never seemed to worry about the question, "Are the *li*, after all, what we ought to follow?"

Confucius is less concerned with the criteria of morality than with its efficacy. The *dao* is given in the literature. Our task is simply to learn it and follow it. Accordingly, he discourses about etiquette more than about yi^{morality}. In this preliminary sense, then, we can see the point of Fingarette's and Rosemont's claims that Confucius has no moral theory.

The Confucian Conceptual Scheme: Dao

The key concept in traditional Chinese philosophy has virtually become an English word—dao^{way}. Conventional wisdom treats *dao* as a most difficult term to understand, and yet translators render it more consistently than almost any other philosophical term: *way*. Our difficulty remains because *way* is a singularly nebulous English term. English uses of *way* run a wide spectrum and our philosophers have never given the concept the analytic attention accorded to metaphysical and ethical concepts such as *reality, knowledge, good,* etc.

Way is a primitive term in the sense that it resists easy analysis. It has many partial synonyms. But I can think of no genus of which *way* is the species. We are normally reduced to explaining it by subtypes: a method, route, skill, custom, or practice. In the traditional sense of *definition, way* does not have a definition in English any more than *dao* does in Chinese. Fortunately, however philosophers have outgrown the Greek fetish for genus-species definitions! We can explain *way* adequately by formulae such as:

(1) X is a way $=_{\text{df}}$ S follows X in going from point y to point z

or

> (2) S uses X in ———ing.

We link a way with actions, walking is the most concrete one. A way can be specified by what it aims at: its goal. *Dao* is strongly analogous to *way* in this regard. Its most concrete meaning is a path or road. This extends to the general notion of an answer to any *how* question, to practical guidance in general.

We can see why translating *dao* as *way* works and start to get a sense of Confucius' use of *dao* by surveying the predicates and modifiers Confucius applied to *dao*. In *The Analects,* Confucius treats a *dao* as the kind of thing that could be heard (4:8), spoken, (6:12) studied, corrected (1:4), modeled, walked (5:7) or wasted, that could be present or absent (3:24). A *dao* can be born and grow (1:2), strengthened (15:29); it can be small or great (19:4). One can master a *dao. Dao*s guide the skills (16:5), including the skill of speaking (17:12). A *dao* performance is a source of pleasure (13:25, 16:5). Different people interpret *dao*s differently in their performance and attitudes (17:3).

Dao, like other Chinese nouns, works roughly the way a mass noun works in English. We can count the chosen thing-kind in many ways.[69] *Dao*s do not have a single inherent principle of individuation.[70] So *dao* differs from *way* in that we cannot treat it as either singular or plural. Instead, we treat *dao* as having parts that are *dao* and being a part in some greater whole that is also a *dao*. If X is *dao* and Y is *dao,* then the sum of X and Y is *dao*. The way I get to work is a sum of the way I walk and the way I drive my car. Chinese writers sometimes discuss the *dao* of particular role actors and other times of the entire course of social life.

Confucius' use shows *dao* to be a general mass term as opposed to a proper name. A proper name may not be modified; *dao* can be. Confucius distinguishes part of *dao* from the whole by adding reference to specific historical individuals (4:15). Thus we may speak of your father's *dao,* Confucius' *dao,* the former Kings' *dao,* or a village's *dao,* and *tian*[heaven:nature]'s *dao*. We can also distinguish different *dao* by periods of history (3:16) or by reference to specific skills (4:5) or normative systems (16:11). There are ways to do all manner of things and there is the straight and narrow *way*.

Each partial *dao* may have its own parts (8:4) and each can be seen as part of a greater *dao*. Naturalizing heaven affects the important concept of *tian*[heaven's] *dao*. It begins as something like a specific deity's prescriptions or commands and comes to embrace the sum of all *dao* that occur in nature, all paths followed in or by nature. In this naturalistic shift, the notion of *tian-dao*[natural way] preserves its normative force (except for Zhuangzi).

Another grammatical way *dao* and *way* differ, besides individuation, is this: *dao* can be used as a verb. You can *dao*[guide] states, clans, families, individuals, and even arms and legs. One *dao*[guides], for example, with regulations or charisma or doctrines. The most common translation of this verbal use is *to speak*. Thinking of the nominal use as discourse helps explain this connection between the verbal and nominal use of *dao*. It conveniently has a mass-noun structure. Your discourse and my discourse make our discourse. The sum of the discourse of each political actor is a society's political discourse.

Still, *speech* seems both too broad and too narrow to capture this verbal use. It is too broad because not just any speech is *dao*ing, but only speech that *guides behavior*. However, speech is also too *narrow* because we can guide behavior by gesture and example (and obviously by written symbol) as well as by speech.

This caution about *speech* as a translation of *dao* signals some general warnings about language and symbolism that we need to keep in mind. We should think of language as broadly as we do when we speak of *body language* and the language of dance or of music. Then we should remember the assumption that the role of language and discourse is to guide behavior (1:4).

Dao comprises all meaningful, behavior-guiding practices. *Dao* models not reality but value. We *translate* a model into a performance when we follow the value model. *Dao* is to be performed. Gestures, looks, dances, songs, poems, legal rules, and rules of etiquette are all subject to interpretative performance. Following a rule is an analytically important model but performing a symphony may more sympathetically capture Confucius' conception of *dao*.[71] For a poem, an interpretation may be a reading. For dances and music an interpretation is a performance. We understand Confucius' *li* better if we think of it as performed rather than obeyed or followed. These *dao*, intended to guide action, do so via an interpretive performance.

Dao and Metaphysics

These reflections about *dao* help highlight how the baseline concerns of Chinese philosophy differ from those of Indo-European philosophy. The deep parallel is that both traditions are interested in language. But the Greek and Hindu theories of language depend on the semantic concepts of meaning and truth. The Indo-European approach tries to explain linguistic meaning in relation to individuals and to a real world. We apprehend the meaning *in* the objective world. Language is *about* the real world. This Indo-European perspective treats the main function of language as descriptive or representative. The role of language assumed in these theories is the communication of information about the world from one speaker to another.

As a result, Indo-European philosophy has a particular kind of interest in metaphysics and epistemology. Its epistemologies address the question of how an individual can comprehend meaning and how we can know the world. This leads both Western traditions (Indian and Greek) to a notion of a mind populated with inherently representative mental items: ideas. As we have seen, ideas constitute a kind of private language. Conventional languages, thus, become superficial in the Indo-European model.

It is hardly controversial that Chinese philosophy does not have the classical mind-body dualism of Western philosophy. We also accept that it has far less concern with epistemology. We certainly find none of the worry about the individual's experience of the world and its accuracy as a representation. The concern with knowledge in Confucius is linked directly to *dao*. Knowledge is knowledge of *dao*, knowledge of what to do. (The modern term for *know* is *zhi-dao*[know way].) *Zhi*[knowing] and ignorance are determined by *dao* (5:21). To study is to study some *dao*. To know is to know some *dao*; to be ignorant is to be ignorant of some *dao*. Thus, in *The Analects*, translators frequently render *zhi*[know] as *clever*. *Zhi*[knowing] is more akin to skill than to information processing.[72] We should understand *zhi*[know] as *know-how* or *know-to* rather than *know-that*. To *zhi*^{know} *dao* is to know (how) to perform it properly.

Finally, therefore, the focus at the early Confucian baseline is not on metaphysics, but on guidance. *Dao* does not communicate scientific truths, but ways to perform. *Dao* is initially and basically a prescriptive, not a descriptive concept. The role of language is not representing a reality that is external to our inner psyche. Its role is communicating and transmitting guidance to society from social leaders through history.

Literature: Li, *Music, and Poetry*

Value-discourse clearly may be written discourse—*wen*^{literature}. Literature shares the wide interpretation we just gave *discourse*. We speak of musical literature, for example. The value-discourse presented in *The Analects,* Confucius' *dao,* consists of a literature curriculum designed to shape character. Two of the central texts in the disciples' education are the *Book of Li* and the *Book of Poetry. Li* is very frequently paired with *yue*^{music} in Confucius' aphorisms. *Yue*^{music} really suggested an elaborate concert including dancers. (We may also read the character for *music* as *enjoyment.*) This suggests an attitude toward *li* that elaborates the Western model of following rules that we used in explaining rectification of names. Confucius may view all of his training on the model of the performing arts—poetry, music, and dance. The *Book of Li* consists of ceremonies that are performed by ceremonial role players in stylized chanting, singing, and dancing.

Generalized to society, then, this attitude toward *li* underlies Confucius' intriguingly optimistic attitude toward the relation of society and people. The model of *li*^{etiquette} presupposes a system of roles or ranks. *The Analects* stresses appropriate performance of these roles. But the appropriateness may be further understood in an aesthetic sense as well as a semantic sense. The important feature that music and *li* share is that we interpret both in a performance. One practices and learns these different *dao* and takes delight in performing them. Some performances, recognizable as performances of the same song, are better than others. We prefer certain performative interpretations without necessarily classing one as wrong.

Rather than limiting our view, then, to the structure of discourse as consisting of sentences or rules, we should heed those recent accounts that stress aesthetic models. In particular, given Confucius' penchant for pairing *li*^{ritual} and *yue*^{music}, we should experiment with a score-performance model of the relation between discourse and behavior.[73] Our explanatory focus will shift to the process of pleasing interpretation. If interpretation of a social practice replaces belief-desire and practical-reasoning models in explaining behavior, this blending of correct and aesthetically pleasing is natural. Interpretation and *dao* together explain action. An actor naturally tends to acquire and perform social forms. His human ability to do this explains his performances. Performances, not actions, are the objects to be explained in the Confucian model.

An interpretation, then, is minimally captured in the notion of following a rule. *Ren*^{humanity} may not only help us follow the rule, but to do so with style. We not only play the right note, but also combine them with the proper duration, intensity, flow, and smoothness that makes a performance not merely right but spectacular. We take as given that we guide our behavior by social, meaningful codes (music scores, ritual instructions, and signposts). When we concentrate on this kind of conduct, the Greek model of voluntary actions seems irrelevant. Belief-desire and reasons-for-action analysis would strike us as beside the point in this aesthetic model.

Ren and Confucian Theory of Language

These reflections, then, have introduced a crucial explanatory role for the important but elusive concept of *ren*^{humanity}. Confucius' pivotal saying with regard to *ren* and *li* is "If *ren*^{people} were not *ren*^{humane}, what would become of *li*^{ritual}?" (3:3) Confucius, paradoxically, regarded *ren* as something easily and almost universally available to people, and yet was reluctant ever to credit anyone with being a person of *ren*" (4:6).

The idealist wing argues that all humans have *ren* and offers that as the basis of its strengthened optimism about human nature. *Ren* enables us correctly to select models and the aspects of their behavior worth modeling. A conventional or traditional *dao* seems to require such an ability. But, I shall argue, that appeal to *ren* is available to conventionalists as well as innatists.

Confucius' theory of *ren* is notoriously mysterious. As we noted above, some disciples even complained that they heard nothing about it. Others must have heard enough for it to be one of the most frequently used theoretical terms in *The Analects*. The standard view is that Confucius did not (or could not) define *ren*. If it is an interpretive ability then it is either primitive or mystical. Minimally, we can say that Confucius' vagueness left the dispute between the historical conventionalist and the innatist unresolved.

The political act of rectifying names seems to depend on the rectifiers having an interpretive insight of *some sort*. If *ren* is this insight, then it explains why *li* would be worthless without *ren*. As we saw, *ren* seems formally necessary to guide the interpretation of *li*. It is not an empty, behaviorally inert right *feeling* we have while conforming, but a crucial element in governing the course, the *dao,* of a performance. It is part not of Confucius' psychology, but of his intuitive hermeneutics of practice.

The debate in *The Analects* could only have arisen if it is possible to be mistaken about the *dao* represented in the *li*. *Some* of the disciples exposed to Confucius' divine teaching must have missed the point. It is clearly possible to listen to the same discourse from the same teacher and disagree about what constitutes a proper performance. The possibility is an embarrassment to any form of traditionalism. An ethical theory based simply on conformity to a code, as we have argued above, seems to have no answer to this route into relativism and skepticism. The concept of *ren* is not, therefore, an inherently innatist concept. No traditionalist account could be adequate without it.

After I know the texts, what constitutes following them? Humans who know the text still disagree. This reflection makes the question of the missing definition of *ren* particularly urgent. Many candidates for an alternative standard of correct interpretation come to mind. We might think that the *correct* interpretation of any fragment of a code was one that was:

1. rationally correct (coherent and consistent)
2. best warranted by the evidence
3. authentic to your nature
4. closer to the meaning of the founder
5. personally advantageous
6. in the best interest of everyone concerned
7. morally correct
8. intuitively correct

None of these conceptions of an interpretive standard requires that we think of the standard as innate. But this does show that Confucius *needs* some notion of *ren* to accompany the *li*. What the disciples did not hear was any detail of Confucius' conception of this interpretive ability. The different answers to this question can give us a convenient philosophical typology.

We can assume that Confucius would have preferred (7) to (5). Egoism had not been raised or refuted in Confucius' time, but neither Mencius' nor Confucius' use of *ren* suggests much affinity for egoism. (Later we shall discuss Yang Zhu, who might be more favorable to such a solution.) Still (7) poses a problem for Confucianism. So far, we have no reason to think that Confucius has the notion of an independent morality. The only Confucian guide to behavior is a traditional code. If that is thought of as the standard of morality, then (7) offers only a circular answer to the problem of interpreting the code. We need to understand the code in order to know what is moral and we need to know what is moral in order to be able to understand the code.

A utilitarian could interpret (7) as (6) and interpret guiding discourse in ways that made everyone better off. Confucius has a stronger tendency toward this answer than the orthodoxy is usually willing to admit (see 1:12). This specific answer was selected by Confucius' most vociferous opponent, Mozi, and the affinity would be embarassing. But as Graham has suggested, Confucius' negative golden rule seems to lead directly to Mozi's universalist utilitarian position. Mozi, in turn, seems to have been followed to an embarrassing degree by Mencius (for whom *benevolence* is an appropriate translation of *ren*).

The traditionalist and innatist may both agree on (8). That distinguishes both from Western rational moralists who would supposedly prefer (1) or (2) as an elaboration of (7).[74] The serendipitous translation of *ren* as *humanity* reminds us of the role of (1) in the Western theory of semantic interpretation. One interprets by assuming we share some characteristically human inference strategies. We search for the fundamental assumptions from which the rest of their *dao* seems to follow. We interpret one rule by asking what way of applying that rule will make it most coherent with the entire body of rules.

Wittgenstein reminded us that the appeal to humanity is not merely bound up with the coherence of beliefs and doctrines. His famous aphorism, "If a lion could speak, we could not understand him," suggests that we share with those we interpret not merely logical abilities but basic motivational and attitudinal outlooks. We could not communicate effectively with a being who views us as either an irrelevant annoyance or a meal.

The Confucian version of humanity reminds us of this Wittgensteinian model.

At least Confucians do not characterize *ren* as a reasoning structure, but as a set of specifically human social inclinations. In their view, a key element in this dispositional structure is family affection. Hence the slogan that *xiao*^filiality is the root of *ren*^humanity (1:2). Still the issue within the tradition is about the status of those intuitive inclinations. Are they innate or inborn, or are they the result of training in a tradition of guidance? The pure traditionalist should give *ren* a conventional analysis. The tradition is the final guide; the moral intuition necessary for its interpretation comes from *within* that tradition. We acquire it, as Confucius indicated, by internalizing a scheme of guidance.

The tempting traditionalist's answer, in the spirit of the "at seventy follow your heart's desire" passage (2:4) and the implicit ideals of rectifying names, is (4): "pick out the action *intended* by the authors of the text." Operationally, this may amount to the counterfactual claim that the sage kings would not have corrected your performance had they been teaching you and watching you critically.

The innatist disagrees. He would interpret (8) as (3), perhaps with emphasis on the familial structure of our moral feelings. Then, on the additional assumption that we all share the same nature, he could accept (4) as derived from (3). The Confucian orthodoxy, following Mencius, accepts this innatist reading of *ren*. Defenders of the orthodoxy would argue that that outcome is implicit in Confucius' doctrine. *Ren*^humanity does seem to be required, as I argued above, even by a traditionalist attitude toward human guidance. However, the above reflections show only that *some* prior standard to a fixed code is required. It does not show that the standard must be innate. It need not even be an intuition. Even when we assume an intuitive standard, the intuition we credit judges or sages with having might be learned through practice. It may be the acquired intuition we discussed before—an ability to register many clues in the situation and use these clues in fine-tuning our action.

If by *ren* we mean this acquired intuition, then an intuitive solution to the puzzle is also available to the traditionalist. It is a solution that is true to Confucius' pronouncements: *Ren* is acquired but only after long practice. You'll get it when you're seventy if you start as a teenager. Anyone, however, could acquire it in that way.

Philosophers of mind note that people can get and teach know-how which they cannot even begin to formulate: riding a bicycle, chicken sexing, speaking correctly, reasoning philosophically. Our ability to speak language is merely the most famous example. The test of whether you have native speaker's know-how is relative to other native speakers. The relevant authorities (e.g., native speakers) recognize or declare (name) you as one who has *got it*. This solution preserves the communitarian spirit of Confucius' guiding *dao*.

Obviously, we can still raise our *philosophical* puzzles. This *learned* intuition begs the question of how to *justify* traditional conventions themselves. Our intuition is essentially a product of training in precisely the traditions in question. If *ren* is treated as an acquired intuition, as Confucius does in his account of his moral growth, the position remains deeply traditionalist. Being raised in a Kantian tradition would give you Kantian moral intuitions. *Ru* training would give you Confucian intuitions. The appeal to those intuitions in rejecting utilitarian or other moral reform proposals would beg the question. This intuition could not defend against a challenge from a rival moral system. Mozi proposes changing the content of the guiding intuitions that society instills in us. He objects to the content of the Confucian Dao even before interpretation. The innatist solution seems stronger as a response to a rival *dao*. If the question is merely about having a way to interpret tradition, then a traditionalist answer seems possible.

We can raise, however, a group of puzzles that favor the innatist position. First, this learned intuition cannot settle which interpretation of the code is correct. We began with the dispute between different interpretive schools of Confucianism. If I am a student of school A, I will develop one type of interpretive intuitions. Appealing to these intuitions in dispute with a student of school B about the *li* will not settle anything. His intuitions will be as strong as mine and yet contrary to mine. As between rival interpretive lines, the traditionalist solution cannot justify one line as correct. It explains *how* we transmit interpretive intuitions, but cannot justify any one of them.

Second, even if we allow that we learn our intuitions, we must have some innate capacity that enables us to take the first step. Most of us have innate abilities to learn to distinguish left from right, up from down, sweet from sour, and so forth. Some innate or presocial human dispositions are presupposed in our ability to learn conventions.

Finally, if we accept the intended-by-the-author theory of what is a correct performance, we have to face Euthyphro's question: Do the sage kings intend this performance because it is right, or is it right because the sage kings intend it? Which should we say? Is the traditional code, the *li,* the standard of behavior or is the intention of the sage kings? Hiding behind a tradition merely postpones the philosophical questions. It does not eliminate them. No Confucian liked pursuing such questions. Mencius and the innatists did, at least, *attempt* an answer.

However, the innatist intuitive solution has its own problems. It cures the disease but kills the patient. It tends to dissolve completely the need for the code of rules in the first place. Supposedly, as we have argued, these intuitive abilities work to rectify names in concrete cases. That suggests that we have an ability to sense in the concrete case before us what is right and what is wrong. Only if we have some code-independent way to know that abortion is permissible or wrong can we rectify the terms *fetus* and *person* in the conventional code.

If the Confucian officials have this sense of *ren* and if it works to tell them what is right or wrong in concrete cases, then one begins to wonder why they need the *li* after all. If those officials are so good at telling what is right in the concrete case, that's all they need to know. Technically they are not *following* the *li*. Their actions *coincide with* the allegedly correct interpretation of *li,* but they *follow ren*. The real standard of right and wrong becomes the intuition of the sage. The study of history has its use, but the way I know my interpretation is correct is *ren*. They had *ren* which inspired them to write it. I have *ren* which allows me to follow it.

One compromise solution to this problem is elitist and contrary, I believe, to the egalitarian spirit of early Confucianism. It requires *li* for ordinary people and *ren* for the sages. The sages rectify names for the masses of people who have no *ren* and can be lead only by the *li* and their respect for authority. This preserves the role of tradition for social guidance and the social authoritarian structure. It undermines Mencius' claim that *all* humans have *ren* innately. We Daoists are not surprised that the authorities would pose this *solution*. We are surprised that they expect us to take them seriously.

In any case, the deeper problems remains for the elite. For them, now, the *li* would be superfluous. The deeper problem has no solution within the innatist system. If it starts out to determine the relative importance of *ren* and *li,* it ends by giving *li* no importance whatsoever except as a summary of historically correct judgments made by the sage kings. A summary of their correct judgments has the same ethical status as a summary of yours or mine.

The innate version also doesn't answer the philosophical puzzle. The innate version purports to offer an independent justification of tradition. Innatists ground conventions in human nature rather than in accidents of history. We can still ask, however, why we should regard our natural reactions as correct ones? Neither the innate nor the acquired intuition is self-warranting. All the innate version does is give us an independent standard from social conventions. It gives no reason for taking that standard to be the correct one. It is quite possible that some of our innate natural reactions, like vengeance and greed, may be blatantly immoral.

Innatism and the Unspoken Dao

This dependence on intuition in general in Confucianism and Chinese thought is a consequence of an implicit skepticism of language. Ultimately the commitment to *li* could not survive Confucius' argument against law (as our analogy to legal interpretation shows). The possibility of rectifying comes from the awareness of ambiguity in a code. That awareness undermines the very idea of code-guided conduct. The simple code *can't* guide conduct. Guidance by a code requires some interpretive guidance that is external to the code.

However, if we focus on conventional learning in general, we are tempted to say that *at some point* we must assume an innate intuitive ability. This is especially true when the conventional system is language, as Wittgenstein taught us. At some point humans just do *catch on and continue* in learning rules. Chomsky argues that we need an innate grammar to be able to learn any particular conventional language. Could this intuition be codified (written, say as a computer program)? Perhaps, but the computer must still have *some* unmodified interpretive structure (the hard wiring). There must be something that is there before any language can be used. The capacity to be programmed by some language must be in the innate hard-wiring.

De ^{virtuosity} is something that we can acquire. Education can change our dispositional structure. But our reflections reveal the consequence that there must be *some* innate *de*. Simply and centrally, we must have the innate disposition to engage in learning and mastering conventions. We must incline to mimicry and enjoy positive feedback. We must enjoy ritualized games as we enjoy babbling conversations with adults. It is this psychological *hard-wiring* that makes social programming possible.

This is a *dao* within us, a *de* ^{virtuosity} that is presupposed in our ability to absorb socialization. We may think of it as a natural *dao,* an unspoken *dao.* It is the program that is not programmed. Without the capacity, instinct, and predilection we have to acquire languages, no language could ever guide our behavior.

Perhaps we similarly need an innate grammar of morality to be able to follow a conventional morality *correctly.* It would be an unacquired *de* ^{virtuosity} that embodied a *dao* that must be prior to language. The way to use language must be prior to language. Thus some minimal *moral* humanity must be innate. I will argue below that Mencius identifies a plausible list of candidates of innate moral humanity.

These reflections yield another sense in which a *dao* must be extralinguistic. If we think of a body of guiding discourse as a guiding *dao,* we can now draw a distinction between that *dao* in language and the *range of* actual behaviors that may result from following it. Supposedly, only some of these courses of behavior follow it correctly. Of these, only some are truly superb aesthetic performative interpretations. No guiding discourse can point to a unique, specific performative interpretation. No amount of elaboration could guarantee that an interpretation would be either beautiful or correct. This physical realization of a *dao* cannot, in that sense, be adequately specified merely by language.

Consequently, no *dao* can ensure that ones *de*^{virtuosity} will produce one or another physical realization. The physical realization of programming with a social *dao* affects how we physically realize the *dao* in the world, the actual path we follow. The machine-language translation of the public guiding discourse cannot be specified in that guiding discourse. The *dao* within is also extralinguistic.

Philosophy and Code Skepticism

The philosophical issue that clearly emerges in *The Analects* arises after we have identified a codified *dao.* The issues in philosophy of education and philosophy of language start from the shared position of the two lines. We have our code; now what constitutes following it? What constitutes understanding *li* and can it be taught?

Thus, the rectifying-names theory as a solution to the problem of how to fill the gap between discourse and action triggers a central theme of classical Chinese philosophy, which Schwartz dubs "the language crisis."[75] This language crisis has radically different characteristics from Plato's. It concerns following an instruction set, not a theory of meaning. It motivates a kind of skepticism about language that cannot be mitigated by definitions (further instructions for use). It raises the worry that we could not tell if we had gone wrong in our use of language. We *intend* to use language as our teachers used it and our teachers' teachers used it and so on back to the sage kings. We *intend* to conform. But there can be no way to be sure that we have done so.

This is not merely a problem between generations. I may be unable to tell whether I have adhered to *my own* resolved and announced intentions to follow some rule. If I have reinterpreted the rule, I will be unable to notice that I have done it.

Traditional defenders of both Confucian systems tend to glorify the flexibility of Confucianism. That flexibility is signaled by the intuitive solution to the problem of linguistic skepticism. It means that they ignore their own rules whenever they intuitively think it proper to do so. It gives them a defense against the Western perception that Confucius' guide to conduct seems rigid by our Socratic, philosophical standards of creative autonomy.

The problem lies in finding a middle position between making Confucianism rigid (because *one* naturally correct way to interpret the code was set by historical anachronisms) and turning it into relativistic quicksand. The flexibility interpretation allows us to read any moral attitude into the *li*. The flexibility becomes authoritarian normlessness. True, rectifying names does introduce flexibility in the fixed code, but without more specification about the intuition, it supplies no limit to the degree of flexibility. Unless we pick some non-Confucian standard such as reason or utility, the code can be compatible with any action whatever. Yet, if we do pick another standard, we have the problem of justifying it. The justification runs the danger of presupposing the standard. Then we face the original problem of interpreting the standard. It is no easier than interpreting the first-level guiding discourse. In addition we still have the problem of explaining why, given the standard, we still need the code that it is to interpret. Why not use the standard directly to evaluate actions?

The doctrine of rectifying names set a trend in Chinese philosophy. That trend was as puissant as Plato's search for definitions was in Western philosophy. Furthermore, it marks the major distinction in analytic reasoning style between the two traditions. The Platonic tradition was searching for some universal intellectual content; the Confucian took the content for granted. The Confucian baseline launched a search for some constant, unchanging way to adhere to a given guiding content. The skeptical vertigo sets in because we can ask about the *way* to interpret every *way* we presuppose. This means we can raise the question about interpreting any higher-level standards that we proposed to interpret the level-one *dao*.

Each tradition, as we shall see, had its skeptics. The nature of the philosophical projects Chinese philosophers criticized affected the shape of Chinese skepticism. Where Western skeptics argued that we can never know any formula to be *true*, Chinese skeptics said that no set of rules or intuitions yields a *constantly reliable guide* to action (a constant *dao*). Chinese skepticism does not focus on the truth of some expression, but on how it guides behavior.

Western philosophy started with the Socratic challenge. That challenge came to be almost part of the conception of philosophy. "I know," Socrates said, "that this is the accepted thing to do, but should I follow what is the accepted thing to do?" Confucius, by this standard, does not seem to be a philosopher at all. He never raises this kind of challenge to the accepted mores. But Chinese philosophy seems to have started instead embroiled in the Wittgensteinian challenge: Even given my acceptance of this traditional way of acting, how shall I know if I have followed it correctly?

This structural contrast in moral theory spawned a pronounced difference in philosophical direction. Western philosophy absorbed Socrates' and Plato's distrust of conventional wisdom, that is, hearsay. That sent Western thought on an endless quest for perfectly universal principles. The worry about what constitutes following a principle became central in the twentieth century. Meanwhile, the search for the correct formulae led to the notions of *sentential reason, proofs, falsification,* and the basic apparatus of scientific theory structure. Chinese philosophy began with a Confucian respect for *transmitted formulae* and emphasized *interpretive variation*. Chinese thought has opted for meaning change over theory change. This search led to a more intensive focus on names and on the conventionality of the scope or application of names. Confucianism carried this emphasis into scholasticism that became the long-term orthodoxy in China. Rival schools, as we shall see, challenged the traditionalist piety but without developing any authoritative concept of reason.[76]

Miscellaneous Other Topics

This discussion of Confucius lacks many of the subtopics you will find in most accounts; there is little detail here about the centrality of filial piety, the five great social relationships, the three family bonds, and so forth. I have barely touched on Confucian pragmatic views of spirits, ghosts, and the afterlife. I have instead concentrated on the systematic contrasts with the Western philosophical tradition and the shared assumptions of classical Chinese thought. This is important if we are to avoid distorting and trivializing Confucius' point of view.

It is also important because it is the part that survives in modern China. It is also the part that explains the dynamics of the growth and development of philosophy in this period and Confucianism over two millennia. It is also the part that figures in the development of the other schools during the Hundred Schools era.

The basis of that development is the concentration on our social nature. Social nature is acquired in learning conventions. Traditional Western intellectual culture relatively downplays the inescapable conventional element in language and the social element in human satisfaction and fulfillment. We stress individual, private, subjective things. We concentrate on a faculty of reason that we understand as precultural. Even our talk about pleasure seems to presuppose that it is totally private, though most of us who have experienced both kinds know that shared pleasures are better. There are rituals underlying most delightful forms of sharing—playing in a band, talking with close friends, Christmas caroling, and scuba diving, for example.

Confucius' ideal is not an utterly alien one.

4

Mozi: Setting The Philosophical Agenda

One thing is certain, and that is, philosophically Mohism is shallow and unimportant.

Wing-Tsit Chan[1]

And yet, as we have seen, he defends it in the same pedestrian and uninspired way in which he defends every other doctrine he preaches—by an appeal to material benefit, to authoritarianism, and to the dubious account of an ancient golden age.

Burton Watson[2]

Rehabilitation

Confucius's presuppositions form the background. Mozi, the first opponent of Confucianism, starts the process of philosophical reflection. So he sets the philosophical agenda and the terms of debate. Most of the central concepts of Daoist philosophy actually stem from Mozi's statement of his argument with Confucianism.

Confucian accounts have routinely maligned Mozi.[3] He is *the most important* philosopher in the early half of the classical period. Analyzing his thought carefully gives us a more accurate view of the direction of philosophical thought in China. China, in the fifth century B.C. had no tradition of philosophical reflection or of theory building. The $Ru^{\text{Confucians}}$ practiced their dances and wondered if there might be a central thread to tradition. They were trained to recite poetry, not to write arguments. Writing argumentative essays and engaging in philosophical reflection both start with Mozi. He distinguishes between traditional mores and morality proper. He formulates a unique version of utilitarianism and argues for that theory and for an explicit political theory. He offers an interesting version of a state of nature justification for social organization. He works out a coherent pragmatic epistemology and both an operational and a historical theory of language. *And* he gives arguments![4]

Mozi's school did not survive the Confucian hegemony that launched China's philosophical dark age. Maligning Mozi has become a litmus test of Confucian profundity. Despite the final decline of his school, Mozi's philosophical impact rivals that of Confucius. Mozi's arguments forced Confucianism into a philosophical debate, forced it to learn a little philosophy. Without Mozi's provocation, Confucianism might never have progressed beyond the *wise saying* style found in *The Analects*. His skeptical challenge changed both the content and the style of Confucian theory. Mencius, despite his bitter, distorted attack on Mozi, defended Confucianism by making it more universal. Mozi's attack on Confucian traditionalism is the catalyst of Chinese philosophical development. Daoists have recognized this implicitly by basing their analysis on the $ru^{\text{Confucian}}$-mo^{Mohist} debate.

Daoism draws heavily on the conflict between Confucians and Mohists for crucial metaphilosophical insights and concepts central to its theory of language. Mozi starts questioning which language to use in cultivating character and raises the issue of an Ur-standard of choice. He develops the concepts of $bian^{\text{distinctions}}$, shi-$fei^{\text{this–not}}$ ^{this}, yi^{morality}, $zhi^{\text{know – how}}$, $xin^{\text{heart – mind}}$, $ke^{\text{admissible}}$, and dao^{way}. These form the conceptual framework for philosophical discussion throughout the period. The Daoist theory especially depends on these Mohist concepts. Mozi continues the use of dao^{guiding} ^{discourse} as a general term, not a proper name, but clearly conceived of alternate *dao*, providing the notion of choice missing in Confucius. He launched the development of the theoretical goal of a natural, constant dao^{way}.

The school Mozi founded eventually spawned the analytic study of language, of ethics, an early form of science, and some moves toward logic. This school triggered the philosophical zenith of the Classical period. I divide Classical philosophy into two periods—a formative period before the Later Mohists, and a mature, analytic period after. Mozi towers philosophically over the formative period and his movement opens the way for the mature period.

The Effect of Confucian Ideology on Translation

The earlier list of philosophical accomplishments contests Chan's judgment. Yet his Neo-Confucian attitude toward Mozi pervades the ruling theory. The persistence of a negative view of Mozi among sinologists is an object lesson in interpretive inertia. Translators, accepting the dominant Confucian scholarship about the meaning of terms, accept Confucian commentaries on the texts as following from the meanings of the terms. The partisan commentary glosses explain terms in ways that insulate Confucius from criticism and undermine his most vociferous critics. Since each of us strives to conform to his teacher, sinological training even in the West is rooted in these Neo-Confucian attitudes. As Confucius taught us, in learning a language, we conform to the practices of our teachers. Translators and scholars begin by confusing Confucian *theories* about terms with the *meaning* of those terms. We confirm our mastery of Chinese by conforming to the dominant, traditional Neo-Confucian interpretation *and the valuation* of Mozi.[5]

The standard way of talking about Mozi assumes that terms like ren^{humanity} and yi^{morality} are *Confucian* terms. Translators theorize about how many Confucian terms Mozi uses and how he changes the meanings of these Confucian terms.[6] The terms are terms of Chinese, not Confucianese. All the schools used them to state their disagreements. Their meaning is what allows them to be so used. The particular positions of the different schools presuppose, but do not fix, the meaning of the terms. The straightforward way to report on these matters is to say, "Confucius thought morality was X and Mozi thought it was Y.'' But sinologists are addicted to saying, ''For Confucius morality meant X, while for Mozi it meant Y.'' The strategy is to leave the implication that Confucians use the language correctly and Mozi is a linguistic deviant. This is a recipe for confusion.

Confucius, as we have noted, never theorized clearly about key terms like *ren* and he used *yi*^{morality} rarely and informally. Numerical frequency suggests that Mozi was the philosopher who made both terms central to moral theory. He uses *ren*^{benevolence} roughly twice as often as Confucius did and *yi*^{morality} three times as much. Mencius' own focus on these two terms probably owes more to Mozi than to Confucius. Mencius, like Mozi, makes both terms more central to his theory than the Confucian *li*^{ritual}. He follows Mozi in treating *ren*^{benevolence} as an altruistic other-regarding attitude rather than merely as an undefined intuition.

Mozi uses *ren*^{benevolence} and *yi*^{morality} as central concepts in his *criticism* of Confucianism. He never hints that he regards these as terms over which the *ru* have some special proprietary license. He uses *yi* in the sense in which we use morality—as a critical, reflective guide to action—in contrast to mere mores. He proposes the distinction *li-hai*$^{benefit-harm}$ as the standard to guide reflective moral evaluation. Yet, Confucian interpretations treat *yi*^{morality} and *li*^{utility} as conceptually incompatible. They declare Mencius' criticism of Mozi to be analytically true in Chinese, thus making Mozi's utilitarian morality an oxymoron. Finally, many translations of Mozi use *profit* to translate *li*^{utility}. This attempts to turn the baseless Confucian distortion of Mozi as an egoist into another meaning-postulate of Chinese.

Confucius, as we saw, did not stress *yi*^{morality}. He stressed *li*^{convention}. This fact raises embarrassing questions about his very credentials as a philosopher. Here again, Western accounts generate an issue obscuring apology offered as a meaning postulate. It distorts our view of both Confucians and Mohists. Convention, the Western accounts argue, includes morality.[7] Since this is false in English, one must assume that Chinese is very different. Then, since *morality* is taken, they translate *yi* with the prudish religious term *righteousness*. When required to face Confucius' traditionalist naïveté about reflective morality, they argue that *the whole culture* fails to make the distinction between morality and tradition. They attribute Confucius' philosophical failure to the supposed homogeneity of Chinese culture.

This apology fails. Precisely that distinction lies at the core of Mozi's thinking. The first *real* philosopher in China makes the distinction as explicitly and simply as Socrates does in Greece. Confucian training did not instill the most basic distinction in ethical philosophy.[8] But that statement is about Confucian educational practice, not about Chinese language!

Style Slander

The orthodoxy's disdain for Mozi has unwittingly contributed to the bad philosophical reputation of Chinese thought. Chan's puzzling put-down, for example, prompts those looking for serious philosophy in China to skip Mozi.[9] Even in Chan's translation, however, the impressive list of Mozi's philosophical accomplishments shines through. Faced with the undeniable evidence of Mozi's philosophical advances on the Confucian tradition, scholarly disdain needed a crutch. As Watson's comment shows, the fallback position focuses on Mozi's allegedly boring style, his repetitiveness, and his passionless, uninspired expression. Schwartz[10] and Graham[11] chime in. It has become almost impossible to write of Mozi without making some irrelevant remark about his style. This practice obviously buttresses the "Mozi doesn't know Chinese" strategy.

We have long had perfectly plausible explanations of the alleged repetitiveness we find in Mozi's writing. Chinese depends on intricate parallelism to mark complex argument structures. Further, some accounts suggest that members of Mozi's school used repetitive recitation to learn his theses. He was not writing for a university press and public circulation. He used a presummary-then-parallel-argument-then-recapitulation style to make his arguments easier both to follow and to memorize. A philosopher can't help thinking the *real objection* of the standard theory is that Mozi *argued* for his positions. If you think Chinese is a language in which all philosophy must be done in obscure aphorisms, veiled allusions to ancient poetry, and impenetrable gnosis, you will find Mozi's style objectionable. Mozi pioneered the philosophical essay style in China. Confucians must choose between the feeling that they are incapable of sustained argument and the feeling that such literary activity is beneath them!

It is, of course, difficult to rebut judgments of taste. I find the tone of these stylistic criticisms petty and irrelevant when one is discussing philosophy. But, more important, I cannot even understand the basis for it. Consider this passage in Watson's own vivid translation. Many adjectives could apply to it, but *boring* and *pedestrian* would be among the last to occur to me.

> Moreover, the Confucians corrupt men with their elaborate and showy rites and music and deceive parents with lengthy mournings and hypocritical grief. They propound fatalism, ignore poverty, and behave with the greatest arrogance. They turn their backs on what is important, abandon their tasks, and find contentment in idleness and pride. They are greedy for food and drink and too lazy to work, but though they find themselves threatened by hunger and cold, they refuse to change their ways. They behave like beggars, stuff away food like hamsters, stare like he-goats, and walk around like castrated pigs. When superior men laugh at them, they reply angrily "What do you fools know about good Confucians?"[12]

One can appreciate why Confucians would not like such writing. However, that it has no style is a controversial judgment of taste. Calling it *passionless* cuts close to the acceptable limit of the use of *that* term.

Life of Mozi

We know little about Mozi's life. The ruling theory speculates wildly to try to construct a persona for the doctrines. The character *mo* means ink. Tattooing uses ink. Slave owners and punishers in China used tattooing on their victims. Hence some have concluded that Mozi was a slave or a criminal. More credible theories, however, draw their inferences from the content of his writings, their style, and the social context.

We surmise from the detailed knowledge contained in his attacks that Mozi had studied Confucianism.[13] Given his dates (around 480 B.C.), we can suppose that one of Confucius' disciples (or disciples of disciples) taught Mozi—probably someone from the traditionalist wing of Confucianism.[14] However, while the aristocracy spawned Confucius and most of his students, Mozi most likely came from the opposite direction, a rising middle class of craftsmen. Apparently he studied the tradition as taught by Confucians and grew to loathe it, as a practical man would.

Mohism grew when the crafts became important in China. It declined when they lost power to the imperial system that bestowed orthodoxy on Confucianism. Histories of the period record the emergence of a craft consciousness, of activist guilds, and even of strikes. Mozi fills his writings with examples of craftsman's tools—compasses, rulers, turning wheels, measuring instruments, etc.[15] Economic groups, as Marx argued, spawn their own intellectuals. The most feasible hypothesis, then, treats Mozi as the intellectual representative of a growing craft class.

Again we go from trying to focus on an individual to focusing on the social group. The school that coalesced around Mozi's text fragmented in a different way. Their interest seemed to lie in moral theory and justification, not in performance. We have three formulations of the core doctrines of Mozi. Graham has noticed that they differ essentially in their degree of political purity,[16] and labels them the purist, the compromisers, and the reactionaries. It seems that, like Eno's Confucians, Mohists were gradually adjusting their doctrines to make them more palatable to rulers. The interesting difference is that the different schools of Mohism altered the text. They did not dispute merely about interpretation, but reworked the formulae themselves. That is an important clue to the difference between the two schools.

This Marxist sociological explanation of the birth of Mohism conveniently explains its final demise as well. The Qin and Han dynasties transformed China into an imperial bureaucratic state. They brought an end to the classical period of dynamic thought and the start of China's dark age. The more totalitarian state repressed the guilds, while it provided a convenient home (the bureaucracy) for the Confucians. The craft hypothesis explains why what little science did develop in China came from the Mohist school. Optics (especially mirror optics), geometry, and economics developed out of the period's crafts. China abandoned its move toward scientific theorizing when it subjected all schools and thinking to political domination and evaluation.

Crafts and Guiding, Objective Standards

Mozi's craft background shows in his philosophical style and his substance. The *Ru* were priests specializing in cultural and ritual performance. Confucians emphasize conventional approval and authentication. The Mohists were carpenters, engineers, military strategists. The standards of success for them are more world-guided and less socially dependent. Mozi sought standards of objective measurement in philosophy. His most frequent examples are of measurement tools.

> It makes no difference whether a craftsman is skilled or not: all alike use these
> five (devices) as standards, only the skilled are accurate. But, although the un-

skilled fail to be as accurate, they nevertheless get much better results if they
follow these standards in the work which they do. Thus it is that craftsmen in
their work have the measurements which these standards give.[17]

Mozi contrasts this objectivity of measurement with reliance on imitation of
teachers and parents. He treats the social acceptance criterion of correct action as
unreliable. Mere imitation, he insists, stands as the basis of *ren*. The quest for more
objectivity and realism are the cornerstone of Mozi's *dao*. He urges more constant,
universal, and natural standards in evaluation. He advocates using *tian*[nature:heaveen] to
substitute for social superiors as a standard of behavior.

Mozi thus buttressed his internal criticism of the tradition by appealing to a
traditionally important external authority—*tian*[nature:heaven]. *Tian*[nature] becomes a paradigm of what is constant, reliable, and measurable. *Tian*'s perspective is neutral
between rival evaluative communities. Mozi thus implicitly accepts the Confucian
psychological need for an authoritarian structure to guide how we instill human character. He seeks to universalize authority and to make the standard equally accessible
to all. Thus the appeal to *tian* is an extension of the search for reliable, consistent,
definitive standards. He constantly alleges that *tian* is objective and definitive—more
like a craftsman's measuring standards than an artist's intuitive reaction. The skilled
and the unskilled can get similar measurement results. You don't need an esoteric
cultivated insight to determine whether the standard has been met.

Confucian tradition came to accept Mozi's contrast of universal versus partial as
their key disagreement. Defending their stress on filial relationships, Confucians began directly to advocate a differential moral treatment based on social distance. It is
not clear that Confucius himself thought so highly of partiality, as signaled by his
various versions of the golden rule. Graham speculates that Mozi's universalism derives from Confucius' teaching of the golden rule.[18] But the fact that Confucianism
came to criticize Mozi on this ground underlines Rosemont's worry that their school
might never have learned any clear conception of morality. Their view of practical
principles led them to blur morality, social mores, politeness, style, etiquette, and
simple obedience. The theory of reflective morality, stemming from Socrates in the
West and Mozi in China, tends to postulate an impartial and consistent or constant
standard of human action.

Morality's purpose is to provide a more reliable and constant guide to behavior
than our normal clan instincts. I will argue that when Mozi brings *tian*[nature:heaven] into
the justification phase of his argument, it is to exploit nature's associations with
constancy, reliability, objectivity, and fairness

The Process of Enculturation

This emphasis on constant measurable standards is the crucial element in Mohism. It
contributes to the impression that he is a Westernlike thinker. But his assumptions
about society, psychology, language, and mind are essentially the same as those of
the *Ru*. Despite his yearning for objective standards, Mozi accepts the Confucian
description of the natural education process. Humans learn and develop their char-

acter in social hierarchies. He does not, however, use li^{ritual} as a general term for all conventions; for that he uses su^{custom}. Mozi offers no defense of the specific conventions of *Ru* devotional dancing societies. He does accept that we are shaped by training and models. We imitate social superiors and conform to their examples of language, of practice, and of interpretation. He retains the father-authority model of moral education but pushes the father analogy beyond the ruler. The ultimate model—the model for the ruler—is $tian^{\text{nature:heaven}}$.

Mozi shifts emphasis from the specifics of li^{ritual} to the crucial core of conventional practices, yan^{language}. *Dao* is public guiding discourse—yan^{language}. Mozi develops a rich language for characterizing how social guidance takes place. He has no doubt that it *does* take place.

Cultivation, Character, and the Heart-mind

The Mozi opens with familiar arguments for the importance of having scholars and worthies in the polity for instilling moral character. We show our character in action; character is the sum of our behavioral motivations. These motivations arise from the $xin^{\text{heart-mind}}$. The *xin* distinguishes between $shi\text{-}fei^{\text{this/not-this}}$ and thus guides conduct.[19] The *shi-fei* reaction of the *xin* consists in this. We characterize a course of action, a state of affairs or an object as *it* or *not it*. We see it as satisfying or not satisfying a descriptive term. I identify a sign as a yellow diamond shape. In accordance with my learned program, my dispositional state becomes more cautious. The *shi-fei* assignment triggers a behavioral impulse, a program.

Like Confucius, Mozi assumes that we get our character as we learn and gain skills. Learning a skill trains the heart-mind's behavioral guidance system, thus Mozi speaks of heart-skills.[20] We gather *shi-fei* reactions that we can use to direct behavior. These reactions are the nearest counterparts of motivations. Our motivations and character come from language and social practice. Behavioral motivations are not innate. What we would call *feelings* are the heart's action-causing *shi-fei* reactions to things. The composite of all our dispositions to react is our character. Mozi's concern is *how* to hone and shape these behavioral impulses. He does not suppose that society can drop character cultivation. Instead, he asked how we *ought to* cultivate character: Should we use a traditional *way* or some new *way*?

We call the successful programming of heart-mind *wisdom*. The term implies a real, objective standard. Language plays a crucial role in gaining skill or wisdom.[21] But if our use of language does not coincide with the structure of things, our *reactions* will not be *skills*. We gain skill by adjusting performance to the real context. That practice in adjustment distinguishes skill from clumsiness. So we must, Mozi argues, be good at picking out thing-kinds before we can claim to transmit real knowledge.[22]

This is a crucial premise in Mozi's criticism of Confucians. Confucians cultivate skill in using words without skill in discriminating realities by those words. Their focus on a teacher's certification of learning diverts attention from the world. Confucius, thus, never fixed the reference of *ren* and *yi*. As a result, though Confucians babbled endlessly using these moral terms, they could never agree on what counted as satisfying them. The result is that the terms became so flexible that Confucians could mouth their slogans while participating as advisers in governments that fostered horrible evils.

Mozi again agrees with Confucius that the rulers are appropriate targets of language socialization. The words they zhi^{grasp} (take as central in their guiding *dao*) determine how they will act. Changing the programming language changes their behavior. We may use language to change even natural, universal human attitudes. The Confucian partiality for one's own family and relationships is an example of an allegedly natural, but still changeable, behavioral attitude.

> Let us take two rulers. Make one of them zhi^{grasp} $jian^{\text{universal}}$ and the other grasp bie^{partial}. Then the *bie* ruler's language will say, "How can I be as concerned about all my subjects' well-being as I am about my own? This radically conflicts with the reality of the world. People have no choice but to live on this earth— like galloping horses through a slit." Thus he retires and sees his people starve and does not feed them, they freeze and he does not clothe them, are ill and he does not nourish them, die and he does not bury them. The *bie* ruler's words are like this and his actions the same. The *jian* ruler's language is different as is his action. He says, "I have heard that, concerning the kingdom, an enlightened ruler puts the well-being of the populace before his own. He only then counts as an enlightened ruler." Accordingly he retires and sees his people starve and feeds them, they freeze and he clothes them, are ill and he nourishes them, die and he buries them. The *jian* ruler's words are like this and his actions the same (26/16/35–41).

Mozi viewed his moral reform as an issue about the content used in the language-based, social engineering project. He saw language as a central aspect of socialization. The models of language and social practice (the social elite) should speak a language that will yield a beneficial result when the populace mimics the models. Language is the main manipulable variable in regulating human behavior since it interacts with every identifiable social practice. Socialization involves learning speech behavior and social behavior together.

Mozi thus accepted the main outlines of Confucian moral psychology. Familial partiality and graded social loyalty *are* natural human traits. It is precisely because we instinctively care so much that the family is so effective in shaping our socialization. This provides the essential tension in Mozi's view. Mozi accepts the *naturalness* of graded love, but questioned its ethical value. Maybe we should amend this natural disposition with directed language socialization. Yet it is the very disposition that provides the mechanism for altering natural dispositions in general.

Mozi further agrees with Confucius that the central type of moral training is model emulation. We follow hierarchical superiors in learning both socializing discourse *and* proper behavior linked to the discourse. Confucius and Mozi share the sense that we learn morality and language in the same way. They are aspects of the same process. We mimic the speech and the associated practice of those *above* us. The people tend to revere their leaders. They store the language standards modeled by the social leaders. The behavior of the leaders fixes the meaning of those standards. He saw the role of political society precisely as Confucius did. Its main justification is that it provides education by modeling and rectifying the social *dao*. Again, both use *dao* in the sense of public, guiding discourse.

Within these structuring assumptions, Mozi's disagreement with Confucius is clear. He wants a more constant, more realistic *dao* ^{way} to guide that training process. If the leaders would cultivate utilitarian standards in behavior, the people would also. Mozi seeks both to exploit that emulating tendency and to change both traditional values and natural dispositions. He argues for instilling universalist language and practical dispositions. This would alter both human nature and historically accepted patterns of behavior.

> Within less than a single generation, people can be changed. They will seek to affiliate themselves with those above them.[23]

Mozi agrees with Confucius. The elite's model of correct language use instills new, moral attitudes in the people. For him, however, this opens the possibility of changing language as well.

> Whenever words tend to promote good behavior, *chang* ^{constant} those words.[24]

Mozi's emphasis on objectivity in measurement and the real context of language combines with a Confucian awareness of the social nature of *yan* $^{language:words}$ and *dao* $^{guiding\ discourse}$. Both *social* and *real or natural* standards should fix the terms in guiding discourse. Some things are what they are because a community recognizes them as such. What constitutes a negotiable check depends on the acceptance by the proper social institutions—banks and courts. A check could be written on a basketball. Other things are what they are independently of social standards. A whale is not a fish even if a whole society classifies it as such. Most terms are a mixture. There are social standards for application of most terms but these social standards depend on the presence of real measurable features. The mastery of these terms requires both social inculcation *and* knowledge of the world.

I will call such terms *thick* guiding terms.[25] Thick concepts include words like *honest* and *lazy*. They direct pro and con attitudes but also have descriptive content beyond their prescriptive roles. Purely prescriptive words are the thin guiding concepts—*shi* ^{right} and *fei* ^{wrong}. They have no further world-guided content beyond their guiding role. *Shi* and *fei* are also the thin descriptive terms in Chinese language—*this* and *not-this*. In either role, as Zhuangzi will note, they can be applied to anything.

We can represent Mozi's position as taking the collection of thick guiding concepts to be a *dao* $^{guiding\ discourse}$. The salient constituent parts of a *dao* are words, not sentences or rules. We learn a complex ability to divide the world into *shi* $^{this:right}$ and *fei* $^{not\ this:wrong}$ in the ways our teachers approve. *All* terms guide behavior. Our linguistic and behavioral mastery, the entire repertoire of skills, is our *de* ^{virtuosity}. Translators are, accordingly, torn between *virtue* and *power* in translating the term. As I noted above, the traditional formula is "*de* ^{virtuosity} is *dao* ^{way} as realized in the individual." (Actually Mozi uses *de* ^{virtuosity} as realized in *any* system. States, periods, families, individuals, and even nature may have *de* ^{virtuosity}.) Reflecting on the relation of *dao* and *de* keyed the argument in the last chapter that any linguistic *dao* requires an unspoken *dao*.

As Mozi understands the system, then, moral choice operates at the name level.

The actor learns to *shi* something as the relevant kind or to *fei* it as not of the kind. The implicit assumption is that applying one of these thin action guiding terms to an object triggers different behavior toward the object. We execute an internalized *dao* differently when we apply the opposite term. The word for discriminating something in the environment that triggers a disposition associated with a *ming*[names] is *bian*[discrimination]. *Bian*[discrimination] is the closest counterpart of our notion of moral choice. In distinguishing between X and not-X, one classifies situations or results and thus guides behavior. How it guides behavior depends on the total program—the *dao*—our system of guiding discourse. To *bian* is to know how to *shi* and *fei* things as satisfying a name in the process of executing our programming.

Western philosophers traditionally have tried to explain the ability to use thick terms by either metaphysical or epistemological theory. Western tradition postulates that there are repeatable items (characteristics, properties, or attributes) that inhere in similar particulars. The presence of these shared properties explains their being *similar*. Plato's metaphysics postulated the existence of a form. Each thing in the range of the name embodies that repeatable form. Our minds recognize the form and thus use the name correctly. The more familiar alternative is epistemological. We get (innately or through experience) a *mental representation* of the things in the scope of a name. That idea becomes the meaning of the term and explains our ability to *shi*[this:right] the right things.

Mozi's account, like Confucius', depends on neither of these approaches. His explanation stops with the notion of learning a discrimination skill *(bian)*. This underscores the social nature of his view of language. We gain our disposition to *bian* from social training. Our social superiors certify us as competent when that pattern of discriminating agrees with theirs. Mozi does not postulate any inner cognitive content. Nor does he offer a metaphysical analysis of similarity. He does take for granted that things really are similar and different. On the basis of objective similarity and difference, we make socially approved distinctions. Once we have achieved virtuosity or competence in discriminating, we assume that our use is correct. Similarly trained members of our society should use the guiding term in a *constant* way.

Thus it is that Mozi cannot dispense with Confucius' teacher-student method of transmission even though he wants a more objective, realistic content. Our basic linguistic skill in making distinctions requires a string of teacher-student embodiments. We can change it, but only through the same process of modeling and training. Mozi does not propose rationalist definitions or an empiricist epistemology to ground his *bian*[discriminations].

The term *zhi*[know] thus plays a different role in Mozi's system than it plays in our familiar discourse about language. Again his use is like that of Confucius. *Zhi* is not an inner representation of content but a type of mastery. The object of knowledge is a *dao*. We can convey a *dao* in conversation or through the study of literature.[26] We know a *dao* when we make it *real* in our *xin*. If we have internalized its pattern of *shi-fei* distinctions and can follow it in action in real contexts, then we know that *dao*. We regard other's cultivation as *skillful* or as *knowledge* when we *endorse* the *dao* that their heart-mind's behavioral discriminations and motivations expresses.[27]

Language is both a tool and a trap in this process. Because we adjust language to reflect the important differences in the world so it can guide us properly, we must analyze reality. We cannot accomplish that merely by cultivating mastery of texts, of poetry, and proper form and style. The cultivation of decorative language that Confucius advocates as a route to character cultivation is dangerous.[28] Mozi wants to increase the contribution of objective measurable reality in the process of guiding behavior with names.

Furthermore, teachers must join their language with some behavior toward the things they *shi*. Their behavior is the model that fixes the guiding *shi-fei* reactions that underlie language. Even after you have made a correct distinction, only if your action is skillful—properly adjusted to the objective world—will the student grasp that distinction.[29] Language is a cultivation tool wedged between reality and skillful action. If your language is not reliable, your actions will not be effective.

Models of Dao

Our traditional Western metaphysics or epistemology of language is going to tempt us here. To help avoid this, I have suggested that we make use of the computer analogy of mind. We can then provide a naturalistic theory of how language guides behavior without attributing our familiar theory of mind to Mozi. Think of the terms of a language as embedded in a program, a string or stream of language. We internalize the language of our community and execute the social program when we act deliberately. Society *types* the program into us as we master society's guiding discourse, its *dao*. The order of terms—the syntax—in the *dao* therefore matters. But Mozi does not focus on the syntax of sentences or rules. He segments language only at the *ming*[names] level. Chinese thinkers, as I have argued, have little motivation to mark the joints in the program as sentential commands or rules. (Classical Chinese has two related characters pronounced *ming*. The ruling theory treats *ming*[command:name:fate] as the verb form of *ming*[names].)[30]

Think of machine language with its *stack* of computer *words* (bytes). The command stack is the computer's machine interpretation of the sentential programming languages. It is a physical embodiment of the program in the machine—the machine's *de*[virtuosity]. We must *translate* or *compile* a programming language into a machine language before *running* it. Similarly, we socialize ourselves by internalizing a language. Our internal translation of it interacts with our natural dispositions (our machine structure) to give us our actual patterns of proper socialized action—the machine language program. Our ability to absorb programming in language presupposes a hard-wiring. The inner realization of the program is an ordered stack of words. The order matters. But given the overall order, segmentation into sentences is irrelevant. Even if we do segment the command stack into sentences, the order among sentences is as important as the order of words within a sentence.

Our hard-wiring must include both dispositions to learn language *and* some patterns of behavior toward *natural* unprogrammed distinctions such as pleasure and pain or benefit and harm. Human hard-wiring must include at least the tendency to mimic and cultivate social, conventional practices. How well any social program can be made to work depends on the prior wiring. We can think of *dao* as the program and *de* as the physical potential of the human who has internalized it. The *dao* within us is an internal, physical realization of public discourse.

With this incomplete but helpful modern picture, we must leave this puzzle aside. The classical thinkers do not give us a computer theory of how *dao* is related to *de*. The computer analogy mainly helps us to refrain from attributing our familiar mental theory of sentential beliefs and desires to them. Let us concentrate instead on the concerns which classical thinkers did directly address. Mastery of *ming*[terms] allows us to *bian*[discriminate] and *qu*[select] in *ke*[appropriate] ways. We treat *dao* as a word-based moral guide. Its core consists of world-guided, behavior-relevant terms. Roughly, the terms guide us in *shi*ing and *fei*ing value-relevant objects, situations, states of affairs. Where we represent directives as guiding us, these early Chinese philosophers took guiding to depend on apprehending value. To follow *dao* is to track value. Morality does not consist in a set of duties or obligations.

A term-based (as opposed to sentence-based) *dao* guides by evaluations rather than duties or obligations. In a word, it is a *dao* of the good rather than the right.[31] The way *dao* guides us is not by obedience to sentential laws, but by something resembling Nozick's notion of tracking value.[32] A scientific picture of a rule-guided, sentential *dao* would be of a space-time ribbon consisting of actions and events. It would be the possible world path through history brought about by following the rules in action. A more apt image for this early phase of classical Chinese rhetoric is of paths through a forest: the trees are values and disvalues. Social, inherited, transmitted language is a way of blazing the trees. The ethical questions are "What marks should we put on which trees?" and "How should we act on seeing a mark?"

When we gain a new skill—a dispositional potential—we do it with effort, deliberation, and difficulty. Once we have mastered a behavior, it does seem easy. It is as if our mind farms the acquired procedure out to a parallel processor: it drops from consciousness and becomes spontaneous. It seems indistinguishable from natural or hard-wired dispositions. From the internal deliberation perspective, the skilled behavior gradually becomes an intuition—second nature. It becomes a basic action to which we can refer in instructions conveying new, more advanced skills. When we have thus internalized a *dao*, the guiding force appears to come from the world rather than from us. Thus *dao*, the public guiding discourse, leads to *de*, our realization or translation of that *dao* into character, personality or skill—dispositional structure.

In summary, we train people by exploiting their natural tendency to emulate the people they look up to. We emulate both socializing discourse *and* proper behavior linked to the discourse. The master Mozi saw the role of political society precisely as Confucius did. It provides moral education through modeling and rectifying discourse. Again both use *dao* in the sense of public, guiding discourse. But Mozi conceived of the inconstancy of *dao*[way]. *Dao* could be bad, crooked, wasteful or, like Confucius' *dao*, simply wrong. Mozi wanted a new and more beneficial *dao*[way] to guide that training process.

The Attack on Traditionalism

Mozi's attitude toward cultivation of the heart is thus implicitly reflective. It is potentially critical of accepted tradition. The transmitted content, the language of the traditional texts, might be poorly adjusted to the real world in which we act. Mozi's stress on the importance of analysis and investigation challenges the traditionalist attitude. Nonetheless, Mozi does regard his *dao* as an alternate tradition to which he appeals to counter the traditional authority that Confucians cite.[33] Like the authority of *tian*[natur-heaven], this probably reflects Mozi's acknowledgement that learning from tradition is inevitable. We cannot eliminate appeal to tradition, but we can choose which tradition to appeal to.

Nonetheless, Mozi launched a Socratic attack on *Confucian* tradition. He represents an explicit departure from the hypertraditional attitude that permeated early Confucianism. He made his critical point by a thought-experiment (masquerading as a bit of anthropology). Consider a shockingly conflicting accepted practice such as rending and eating the first-born son. Our *intuitive,* shared, even *Confucian,* reaction is that the practice is neither *yi*[moral] nor *ren*[benevolent]. That we all accept something as a tradition does not make it *yi*[moral].

> Mozi said: This is what is called "treating their practice as dependable and their *su*[customs] as *yi*[moral]." In ancient times, east of Yue there was the city-state of Kaishu. When their elder son was born, they rent and ate him. They said it would be beneficial to the younger brother. When their fathers died, they carried their mothers on their backs and abandoned them. They said "The wife of a ghost can not live in the same place with us." These practices were taken by the superiors to be correct administratively and those below took them to be custom. Everyone acted this way all the time. They practiced these rituals and did not give them up. And yet how can these be the way of *ren*[humanity] and *yi*[morality]? This is what is called "treating their practice as dependable and their customs as moral" (39/25/75–78).

Once we think to ask Mozi's or Socrates' question ("Are our accepted practices correct?"), we embark on a road where moral reform becomes possible. We have seen that Confucius' standpoint did not involve reflectively checking itself. He did not encourage making transtraditional judgments. Confucius' explicit concern was rather with the interpretive question. Given a transmitted guiding discourse, how do we select one of the different ways to *xing*[perform] it. Rectifying names was the short answer.[34] We must socially model the distinctions we want people to make using the names.

The content question about *which words* to include in the public *dao* and in what order had to await Mozi. Mozi first formulated the reflective detachment from conventional moral literature. To argue in this way, the language he shared with those to whom he addressed the argument (the Confucians) must include a term such as *yi*[morality]. That term must license the contrast of morality and custom. Mozi's argument for moral innovation uses traditional moral language. He made his case in terms that already had roles in Confucian ethical discourse. Even good Confucians must agree that these traditions are neither moral nor benevolent. In our shared language, saying that something is traditional is not equivalent to saying that it is *yi*[moral].[35]

Yi[morality] is a term that can be used, like *morality,* to formulate the perspective of reflective philosophical ethics. *Li*[ritual] may or may not be consistent with *yi*[morality]. Only in Confucian accounts should we identify *yi*[morality] with a religious, devotional attitude toward holy rites. But note that using *yi*[moral] does not suggest that the source or nature of the critical ethical perspective is individual rational autonomy. Mozi, like the Confucians, does not put the crucial moral issue at the point of the individual choice of action. Mozi's individuals are as much products of socialization and training as are Confucius'. Choice is simply triggering program control according to the circumstances. The moral question is raised from the *social* point of view, not from the individual.

Mozi attacks primarily the traditionalist version of Confucianism. None of his arguments target the innatist position. Indeed, I shall argue that the attempt to answer Mozi is what motivated Confucian innatism. Mozi's challenge was more important than the internal tension we noticed in *The Analects*. The Mencian innatist position, as I argued above, also borrowed heavily from the conceptual and theoretical structure of Mozi.

So, Mozi finally makes the crucial Socratic distinction between customary mores and morality proper. He asks the question that almost defines philosophical reflection: "Why should we follow the traditional value system?" Mozi's question is, however, different from that of Socrates in interesting ways. The Socratic question *is* essentially individualistic: "How should *I* live?" Mozi's is "What system should *we* follow?" Socrates' question focused on an individual's life as the locus of moral reflection. Mozi asks his question from a shared, social point of view and his question focuses on social order and the nature of public guiding discourse. But both share an implicitly anticonventionalist essence. For neither is it enough to have someone tell us, "This is what one does!"

Mozi thus inherits the Confucian focus on the social as opposed to the individual point of view. Neither his theory of language nor his conception of moral objectivity starts from internalist, subjectivist, individualist concepts. He suggests that neither the language nor the moral issue is essentially individual; both are social. Individuals, institutions, schools, or other systems may physically embody a *dao* as that system's *de*^{virtuosity}. The reflective question concerns what should be in the *dao* that we are to realize.

We have to consider the possibility that a traditional practice might not be *yi*, Mozi argues. His point is not that we should decide whether to follow social practices but whether we should reform them. Society, Mozi argues, must adopt some test *other* than *customary* or *transmitted* for judging its *dao*. When we have the right standards, then we can use them to *shi* some social *dao*s and *fei* others.[36] Immediately, however, a counterpart of Plato's educational paradox grips us. What can make a standard of *shi-fei* right other than the community's shared usage? How can we recognize a traditional point of view as falling short of morality when our moral attitudes come from that point of view? How can we recognize *our own* moral practices as inadequate?

The Utilitarian Standard

The standard that Mozi proposes for guiding the *shi-fei* pattern that constitutes the social *dao*^{way} is *li*^{utility} and its opposite *hai*^{harm}. As he puts it, these are necessary if we are to be *ming*^{clear} about *shi*$^{\text{this:right}}$ and *fei*$^{\text{not this:wrong}}$. We use this core *bian*^{discrimination} to guide our social reform of language and with it the accepted *dao*^{way}. Mozi tells us to promote and make constant guiding discourse, social practices, language, and customs that benefit the people and the state. Those that do not we must eschew and drop.

We feel a sense of familiarity here. Mozi's antitraditional impulse—like that of many moral reformers in the West—is to substitute a utilitarian standard for conventional moral attitudes. The familiar clash between a settled, intuitive morality and utilitarianism stems from two general features of utilitarianism:

Projectability: First, a utilitarian *dao* provides measurementlike simplicity, clarity, and precision. We can reliably project the new moral concepts to different contexts from those in which we learn them. Such projectability helps us envision the moral reformer's alternative. Otherwise its unorthodox recommendations would seem too vague to guide us reliably in our evaluation and action. Since it faces an ancestral morality that has a robust scheme of *thick* concepts, people must be able to apply it reliably without being raised in it. Easy projectability partly compensates for the absence of a tradition. A moral-reform proposal runs a danger that its guiding concepts will lack constancy—Mozi's main theoretical requirement. People will therefore have no consistency in interpreting the moral concepts in action. The advantage of the utility standard thus lies in its *measurability*. It conforms to standards that, like a craftsman's plumb line, any person can use with reliable accuracy.

Natural Grounding: Second, the benefit-harm distinction strikes us as a natural (as opposed to conventional) guiding distinction. It seems to be a presocial guide as opposed to a socially programmed one. It gives a neutral basis for ordering proposals for what guiding concepts we would want to adopt. It yields a natural basis for revising conventional standards. The desire for benefit and aversion to harm are not relative to a society. The choice of benefit over harm seem to come from a natural, presocial will (*tian-zhi*[natural will]).

A corollary is that Mozi's standard should be accessible to people from different social groupings. We use the standard in the social choice of a *dao* for guiding our behavior. A universal, *natural* will, he thinks, underlies the *li-hai*[benefit-harm] distinction. Our natural preference for this distinction, however, is not egoistic. Like Hume, Mozi regards this natural preference for benefit to apply quite generally to other people. The standard is, as it should be, universally accessible.

As both Confucians and Kantians note, utilitarianism conflicts with conventional intuitions about what is moral. It does not follow that, other than their opposition to utilitarianism, Confucianism and Kantianism embody a similar attitude toward morality.[37] From either traditional point of view (for their different reasons) utilitarianism appears immoral. Its calculations or measurements conflict with our considered moral judgments. That is precisely how we would show that a moral reform is wrong.

Utilitarian critics of either of those traditional moralities, on the other hand, find our reliance on our moral intuitions naively nonreflective. Our reliance strikes utilitarians as moral dogmatism. At best, once we have formulated the Socratic or Mohist question, this appeal to moral intuitions is circular. But any utilitarian criticism of accepted morality seems to assume that utility *is* the moral standard. And, speaking in the language of our shared, thick, conventional moral concepts, that is a wrong assumption.

Can there be a neutral perspective from which to judge these warring ethical standards? Can there be either a criticism of traditional ethics that does not beg the question or a noncircular disproof of utilitarianism?

The Paradox of Moral Reform

Philosophical reflection and doubt thus have a price. Once we raise the culture-transcending question, answering it may come to seem hopeless. How are we to decide what principles to follow? If we use a conventional standard, we get no reform. If we use another standard, it will seem arbitrary and immoral. Any other standard we use will be ethically controversial. If the standard the reformer proposes differs from our tradition, our cultivated moral intuitions will judge the results of applying that standard *immoral*. Since the proposer of the standard rejects the view that our cultivated intuitions are really moral, this does not impress him; following our *traditional* morality is immoral by *his* lights.

The paradox is even more recalcitrant for Mozi because Chinese evaluative terminology emphasizes the social, pragmatic point of view. Where Socrates reflected on what ethical principles were true—as opposed to those that the masses accept—Chinese thinkers relied instead on the term $ke^{\text{admissible}}$, a concept that favors the argument for traditional, accepted standards.

This explains Mozi's introducing the term $chang^{\text{constant}}$ into the debate. It gives his standard of *dao*s a point of contact with reality. As with any realistic term, it also became the focus of skepticism, particularly Daoist skepticism. Mozi launched the ideal of the constant *dao*. Hu Shi, who noticed this link between Mozi and Daoism, suggested that *chang* meant *truth* because it was intended to be more realistic than the concept $ke^{\text{admissible}}$. But it is still a more pragmatic concept than is *truth*. Although the constancy of a *dao* might depend crucially on the *real world*, it is not a concept of the *representational correspondence* of a doctrine and the world. Mozi still understands a *dao* as a guiding discourse. The world is the context in which a *dao* guides. If, in that real world a *dao* reliably and successfully guides a society, we may never need to change it. Hence it is a constant *dao*.

Varieties of Constancy

There are a variety of ways in which a *dao* may fail to be constant. I group them under three main heads: (1) inheritance constancy, (2) projection constancy, and (3) pragmatic constancy.

Inheritance Constancy. Inheritance constancy is the problem that worried Confucians about *dao*s. The rectification of names is a bid to preserve the transmitted *dao*. It makes the discourse guide us in a constant way, the way the sage-kings (founding fathers) intended. The worry is that language changes across generations. Pronunciation change, of course, worries no one. Confucians worry instead that the *behaviors* associated with terms or the artifacts or objects picked out by the guiding terms may change. The traditions and ceremonies may thus go astray. The problem is that no one within the tradition *would be able to tell* that it had changed. Thus, even in the most faithful community of conformists there may be a problem of inheritance constancy. What I now *shi*[this:right] in applying the *li*[ritual] may not be what Confucius would have chosen had he been here.

Projection Constancy. The problem of projection constancy is a generalization of the inheritance problem. I may become skeptical about even my own application of a term in different cases. Suppose my teacher has certified my *de*[virtuosity.] in using a term. I may worry that pattern of *shi* and *fei* associated with the term was only accidentally right.[38] I just happened to project correctly around her long enough to gain her endorsement. Or, perhaps, I really did have the pattern, but since certification, I have lost it. Despite my social credentials—my graduation from school—my application of the term might have wandered. I would not now conform to my teacher's use. This worry has a different version. I may find that I *shi*[this:right] what my teacher *feis*[not this:wrong]. But then I would not be sure if my usage is wrong or if my teacher has changed—perhaps lost her competence because of old age.

We suppose that the Western metaphysical and epistemological accounts of mind and ideas provide answers to the worry about projection constancy. The appearance that they do so, however, is an illusion. If I worry about whether I discriminate objects consistently from one time to another, the mentalese theory is unlikely to comfort me. It merely allows me to worry if I discriminate mental objects consistently as well. All the mentalese theory does is to remove the *practical possibility* that someone would catch me in an error. No teacher can check if I made a mistake with regard to the application of English terms to my inner ideas. Far from solving the problem, this mental theory just gives skepticism another level to chew on: How do I know I have picked the right *idea* to go with the word?

One variety of projective constancy is performance constancy. Terms apply not only to objects (artifacts, kin, social roles) but also to actions, rituals, and performances. I may, thus, wonder if my *performance,* my interpretation, continues to be a correct one. Do I *father* my father correctly? Is this extension of my past performance of this named behavior still within the acceptable range?

It is an interesting feature of Mozi's language utilitarianism that it automatically adjusts for performance and projective constancy at the social level. The projective and performance defects people have in general are given. Mozi proposes that we adopt the guiding discourse that optimizes the benefit of programming those people (with their actual interpretive tendencies). If people regularly *misinterpret* their roles in some way, that factors into the calculation of the best *dao*.

We can, therefore, distinguish between the discourse-level *dao* and a performance-level *dao* to understand this feature of Mozi's theory. He proposes a discourse level *dao* but tests it by applying the utility standard to the performance-level *dao*—the course of actions people actually undertake. The discourse-level *dao* that he advocates is whatever will produce the performance-level *dao* with the greatest utility. The interpretive problem is short-circuited by the condition specifying that the discourse-level *dao* should maximize benefit.

Pragmatic Constancy. The third type of constancy is pragmatic constancy. A social *dao* that encourages people to jump in front of speeding buses will not be constant. The world and our bodies are a given context. Those who adopt a *dao* that regularly grinds its users' bodies up in the world will not be likely to convey that *dao* through too many generations. A *dao* may or may not promote social harmony. If it promotes disharmony, that disharmony will likely result in the social change. Its *dao* will change. Doubtless some *dao*s will be more stable, given human nature and natural conditions, than others.

Defenders of Mencius may argue that, given human nature, a family-based morality is more stable than a universal one. At an abstract level, Mozi should accept the relevance of that consideration. If that *were* empirically true, the constant *dao* should be familial. If that is the Confucian position, Confucianism is basically as consequentialist as Mozi is. Mozi differs mainly in rejecting the empirical assumption.

The Self-Defeating Nature of a Dao of Partiality

A particularly embarrassing kind of instability results when complying correctly with a *dao* commits us to advocating that the public should heed a *different, rival dao*. Following Parfit, we can call any *dao* with this consequence a self-defeating *dao*.[39] Mozi argued that Confucianism was such a self-defeating *dao*. As we saw, the conflict between Confucian moral intuitions and Mozi's utilitarianism centers on the issue of universal versus partial moral concern. Confucianism champions primary concern for the family and only derivative concern for progressively larger domains of moral concern. Mozi argues that morality must involve equal concern for all people. Many of Mozi's arguments, accordingly, are arguments for universal moral concern. In this context, Mozi stumbles on a partial solution to the paradox of moral reform. He offers a nonquestion begging argument for universal concern *as against* the Confucian traditional morality in the following story.[40]

> Suppose here is a broad plain, a vast wilderness and a man is buckling on his armor and donning his helmet to set out for the field of battle, where the fortunes of life and death are unknown; or he is setting out in his lord's name upon a distant mission to Ba or Yue, Qi or Jing, and his return is uncertain. Now let us ask, to whom would he entrust the support of his parents and the care of his wife and children? Would it be to the universal minded man, or to the partial man? It seems to me that on occasions like these, there are no fools in the world. Though one may disapprove of universality himself, he would surely think it best to entrust his family to the universal-minded man. Thus people condemn universality in words but adopt it in practice, and word and deed belie each other. I cannot understand how the men of the world can hear about this doctrine of universality and still criticize it!

The case is not perfectly convincing. The Confucian soldier may protect his family *better* by putting them with a relative. Even though they *come after* the original family, they still *come before* starving strangers. But we may understand Mozi's conclusion with a ceteris paribus clause. Given two brothers, two neighbors, or two strangers with whom the soldier can leave his family, he would choose one more likely to moderate the special affection for his own family. Then he would treat the soldier's family better. We can generate many cases like this one whenever we consider social-coordination problems that extend beyond the range of our partiality. Each of us benefits our family by throwing our trash in our neighbor's yard. The result, when all families do this is bad for each family. Each family would be better off if all had a broader range of concern. Where the partiality is for the individual self, it generates the Hobbesian argument. Where it is familial, the Mozi version follows. Nationalism is similarly self-defeating. Many environmentalists accept a parallel argument about speciesism. Given straightforward empirical assumptions, we can derive a coordination problem that undermines any *partial* evaluative standard.

So Mozi makes a powerful and pertinent point. The issue is what *dao*-type should we instill socially. If we were properly to instill a Confucian *dao* in someone we would expect him to seek correctly to achieve its goal. To behave correctly according to a Confucian *dao* would be to instill a *different dao* in others. In particular, he should instill a more universal *dao* than the *dao* he himself follows.

Now, there would be no *contradiction* here if the reflective moral question were the Socratic one: "What should *I* do?" Then, with perfect consistency, the soldier could accept one morality and, based on that value system, decide to motivate others to have a different one. However, Mozi asks the reflective moral question in a more social way: "What *dao*-type should society teach to all people?" Someone who judges from a Confucian point of view should still see the merit of teaching the universal moral perspective to others. Thus Mozi can justify the universalist utilitarian standard without having to presuppose it. He *can* justify it from within the Confucian *dao*. We take the moral goals of the Confucian *dao* for granted. We can still see circumstances in which it would lead us to Mozi's public *dao*. We would achieve Confucian goals more effectively if the social morality were universal than if it were partial.

The case shows the internal incoherence of a special-relations morality. Moreover, it appeals to something like neutral rationality. ("At times like these, there are no fools.") Still, Mozi does not develop a theory of a faculty or a process of reason. In particular, though often accused of it, he never depends on an egoistic conception of practical rationality.[41] He makes the argument from the perspective of the partial-minded Confucian gentleman motivated by Confucian moral standards—the concern for his family. It is his standard of judgment, not his desires and beliefs, that yields the pragmatic inconstancy.

In sum, this argument against Confucian common-sense morality has special and little noticed significance. It is crucial to any theory of moral reform. Mozi attacks the partial, family centered moral system *through its own presuppositions*. Even someone who accepted the family based morality would still prefer that society cultivate universal attitudes in others.[42] Achieving the goals of the Confucian morality is more likely if the rest of us cultivate our characters in utilitarian ways. The widespread adoption of *natural,* family-centered moral attitudes results in a less acceptable outcome *from a Confucian perspective*. Common morality, Confucian morality, is, in Parfit's phrase, collectively self-defeating.[43] Practiced collectively, its outcome is worse *for its own goals* than the alternative—universal utilitarianism.

Might Mozi's Dao *Be Self-Effacing?* Consider, now, the actual stream of words and the problem we raised above. People will interpret any given discourse into varying patterns of behavior. Mencius (1A:1) will accuse Mozi of still another kind of inconstancy. His *dao* fails its built-in publicity condition. It is *self-effacing*. Applying the *li-hai*[benefit-harm] standard could lead to the paradoxical conclusion that we ought *not* to cite the actual words *li-hai*[benefit-harm] in the public *dao*.[44] People might *mis*interpret talk of *li*[utility] in ways that lead them to behave selfishly. Utility uses a principle of choice that is appropriate for an individual and generalizes it to the community. It may be that including that principle in the community's language stimulates selfish utility calculation. The utilitarian *dao* could be more likely to achieve its goal if it did not allow anyone to make the *li-hai*[benefit-harm] distinction in ordinary discourse.

This is a different kind of criticism.[45] It does not strictly show any incoherence in the *guidance* the Mohist *dao* gives. Mozi would still appropriately use the standard of *li-hai*[benefit-harm] to evaluate the results of socially performing the discourse *dao*. But the discourse *dao* would not ever make the standard explicit—if Mencius' pessimistic empirical assumptions about people's interpretive tendencies are correct. Mencius conclusion depends on our (predictable) *mis*use of the standard. The king can continue to *use li*[benefit] as a standard to guide his use of language. he expects others to emulate his use of other language terms. For precisely this reason, he cannot include the *li-hai* pair among the terms he *models*.

Being self-effacing technically does not prove that utilitarianism is faulty, but it is an embarrassing consequence. The correct discourse may turn out *not* to include its own basic distinction. If Mozi was serious about his *dao,* perhaps he should never have advocated it openly. If the empirical assumptions are correct, it is a constant *dao*[way] that must not be spoken.

The Natural or Heavenly Dao. These reflections give us a regulative ideal for *dao*. A *dao* should not be self-defeating or self-effacing. Any self-defeating *dao* is an inconstant *dao*. A *dao* ought to be one that can govern people with a single standard.[46] Universal, utilitarian attitudes, character, and motivation are more constant than partial, familial moralities. If our goal is a constant *dao,* then we ought to change the existing morality. People have to undergo a psychological change and cultivate different *shi-fei* reactions. They must adopt altruistic, universalist attitudes.

A *dao* can fail to have pragmatic constancy even if it is not self-defeating. Rawls suggests similar requirements for his *dao:* the two principles of justice. A *dao* should settle into a kind of reflective equilibrium. Reflection and practice should lead to homeostasis. Our principles should come into equilibrium with reality, including human reactions and natural facts. Successive adjustments should converge on a constant *dao*. Further, correct principles should lead to a more spontaneous commitment to them. The sense of justice should tend toward natural harmony with human feeling.[47]

The ideal of pragmatic constancy suggests a way of understanding the term *natural* (or *heavenly*) *dao*. One sense of a natural *dao* is that it is one that is pragmatically perfectly constant. We may take it to be chosen, in *that sense,* by nature through a kind of evolutionary process. That nature prefers it is shown by its universal survival as an impulse in our natural constitution. This explains Mozi's suggestion that the constant natural *dao* is universal and transcends particular cultures.

The conventional moral *dao* and the words that make it up are not constant. The associated attitudes and behaviors are self-defeating. Their status as conventionally accepted does not mean that they are right. We can come to see this and seek reform in a tradition. The notion of a *chang*[constant] *dao* gives us a way out of circular use of traditional standards. A tradition can elevate itself by its own bootstraps. We can come to see that traditional standards are unacceptable by their own lights. When that happens, what we classed as acceptable we may come to see as unacceptable.

We now need a new standard and we can show that even by appealing to the old standard.

So Mozi concludes that we need to inculcate a new standard to shape moral attitudes. He chooses *universal* and *constant* as positive features, both of which characterize utilitarianism.[48] We should make the utilitarian *dao* constant. (Notice that this formulation suggests that Mozi did not think of the *naturally* constant *dao* as *inherently or innately* constant.)

It turns out, then, that Mozi can justify his anti-Confucianism without begging the question. His normal appeal to *tian*[nature] does beg the question since *both* schools claim that *tian* endorses their favorite standard. His usual pragmatic argument, on the other hand, begs the question because it uses the utilitarian standard in judging the pragmatic results. The argument that Confucianism is self-defeating has no such defect. He need not start by assuming his own moral point of view. He shows how to get to his universalist conclusion from the Confucian partial point of view. That does not show it is *absolutely* correct, but a Confucian could hardly object to the starting point of the argument. The argument does show one way that Mozi's morality is more *constant* than that of Confucianism.

The Conceptual Structure of Mozi's Utilitarianism

Philosophers typically distinguish between two varieties of utilitarianism. Act utilitarianism (AU) requires that we calculate the benefit of each act we might perform and choose the optimal one. Rule utilitarianism (RU) allows us to calculate the effect of adopting different rules. When we act, we obey *the rule* that passes the utilitarian test. The Chinese version of utilitarianism differs from both of these. It does not focus on rules or acts, but on the *words* in public discourse.[49]

We could coin *system utilitarianism* (SU) as a neutral type that embraces RU and Mozi's word utilitarianism. It evaluates a guiding language game. System utilitarianism does not commit itself to any privileged way of parsing or segmenting guiding discourse. The order among rules in the *dao* may be as important as the order of words within rules. We may also think of it as *language utilitarianism* (LU) or *program utilitarianism* (PU). It consists of using language to direct people's character. But it does not do so through statements of obligation—sentential prescriptions. Guiding discourse is a string of words along with a social model of how to apply them in regulating our behavior. The language or program we should use in this project is the one that has optimific results given a natural and human context. The population cultivated by that *dao* should realize maximal benefit.

Confucian traditionalism may itself turn out to be a version of SU. We treat Confucian *li*[ritual] as a discourse *dao*. Confucius, however, did not theorize about his norms in sentential or rule form nor did he use duty words such as *ought* or *should*. His notion of *dao* was not of a set of prescriptive sentences. It was a notion of behavior-guiding discourse in which the segments of discourse were the words—just as Mozi's are. Whenever Confucius gave us any hint of the makeup of *dao*, the salient parts or units were *ming*[words]. Typical words are role terms such as *father, son, ruler, minister* or the names of artifacts and ceremonial objects. Words do refer to things, but the reference of words is embedded in guiding discourse, not in factual discourse. Proper discrimination of roles or objects involves a *way* of acting toward them.

Mozi's discussion of language, mind, and action similarly centers on *ming*^{words}. The linked notions we discussed above—*bian*^{distinctions}, *shi-fei*$^{\text{this–not this}}$, *ke*^{assertability}, and *chang*^{constant}—all apply to terms used in guiding behavior. The account of how words work is indirectly referential—guidance depends on our making distinctions in the real world. But the overarching *prescriptive* role of discourse shapes the account of *how* words refer. As we noted above, one verbal form of *ming*^{names} is *ming*^{command}. Mozi's focus is on how words guide distinctions which in turn guide a person's reaction. And he emphasizes the role of society in instilling the guiding discourse.

This focus on names may seem purely formal, but it has interesting consequences. Western philosophy divides discourse into prescriptive and descriptive functions. We normally think of both as being made up of sentences. Prescriptive sentences are rules or statements of obligation, right or value. We treat the imperative sentence form as parasitic on the descriptive form. We explain the meaning of a command or rule by first translating it to the descriptive form. We understand the command as guided by its corresponding descriptive form. We are commanded to try to make the descriptive sentence true.

This adds an important element to the cluster of related formal differences we have noticed. Classical Chinese philosophers usually focus on words rather than sentences, prescriptive rather than descriptive language, and assertability rather than regular semantic truth.[50] If we keep these formal differences in mind, we can better appreciate the workings of Chinese ethics.

The proper dichotomy for understanding Chinese guiding discourse is Laozi's pairing of *ming*^{names} and *dao*. A *dao* guides behavior by using names. Names are at the root of the guiding discourse systems. The language can work without prescriptive verbs like *ought* in part because classical Chinese philosophers all viewed the core role of language as governing action. Representing or describing things was a derivative means to that basic end. At the heart of the guidance system are the *ming*-$_{\text{names}}$.

After Mozi, philosophers began to pay more attention to the descriptive function of *ming*^{names}. His school eventually worked out the most realistic system of the classical period. But Mozi's own moral views commit him to a pragmatic antirealism. We seek to instill the pattern of *bian* for any given term in a way that optimizes *li-hai*$^{\text{benefit-harm}}$. We identify object types pragmatically. What counts as an object type—a *wu*$^{\text{thing:kind}}$—depends on human practical purposes. Each competing *dao* would segment the world differently. Thus Chinese thinkers understand their disagreements as rooted in *bian*^{discrimination}. This is another way in which the classical Chinese conceptual scheme is more pragmatic than realistic. Consider, again, Mozi's formula:

> Language which can repeatedly be practiced, make it constant; that which cannot pick out [good conduct] conduct, do not make it constant.[51]

Pursuing the sentential, descriptively based model of ethics focuses our attention on a state of affairs, That, remember, suggests a picture of a *dao* as a possible history that following the rules brings about. Above I preferred to treat the early Chinese conception as the path through the world that guiding discourse helps us recognize. Mozi agrees that we must learn to discriminate in ways that enable us to execute our guiding program in the actual world. That is the interpretive worry. But he also directs our attention to the *content* of the guiding program. He critically questions the traditional content of social guidance, the words. The words that make up the *dao* are the key to real-life application. The question is which words in what order in the *dao* will lead to the best outcome?

Guidance by Name-Pairs

Mozi's ethical standard is utilitarian. He does not, however, use an additional subjective *bian*[discrimination] between *pleasure* and *pain* or *happiness* and *sadness*. His is neither hedonistic nor subjective utilitarianism. He never treats *li*[benefit] as the satisfaction of desire or as pleasure or happiness. Normally, he thinks of benefit as straightforward material well-being. He contemplates our applying it to all the people or the social whole—the state.

The *li-hai*[benefit-harm] distinction is his primitive distinction, the one on which all other distinctions rest. He gives no deeper justification for the use of this standard. He thinks it is natural and everyone implicitly accepts it. The people *are* presumably happier when they have benefits, but he does not define benefit by the causal power to produce pleasure or happiness. He takes it for granted that we obviously know what benefiting the people is. (For the people of ancient China, it was a comparably simple matter: starvation versus survival.) As I will argue on pages 125–28, Mozi assumes that *li*[benefit], like *life,* is a naturally *constant* term.

The Malleability of Human Moral Character. Three kinds of language reform seem germane to how language affects us. One involves the introduction of new lexical items. Zhuangzi delights in this antitraditional activity, but Mozi does not suggest using new words. The second is the activity of rectifying names. That Mozi's is a parallel activity is signaled by his terms, *bian*[discriminate], *shi*[this:right], and *fei*[not this:wrong]. This language reform comes by changing existing language habits involving the same lexical items. Here we change the distinctions marked by the names and thus affect behavior.

The third reform also uses the same lexical items. However, it changes the order of the *ming*[names] in the stream of discourse. This explains how we can use the same words to recommend opposite actions. Think of *yan*[language], of discourse, as consisting of a stream of names. Mozi may not segment discourse into sentences, but the order in which we use words in public discourse does make a difference. A different order affects behavior differently. The order, like a command stack in machine language, determines how inputs will affect outputs. The scheme of words will alter the way that an input triggers branching in the program.

Sentential linguists deny that we have a fixed repertoire of sentences. Mozi, by contrast, seems committed to the view that we use language as our society does—the pronunciation, the distinction marking, and the ordering of compounds.[52] It is up to social leaders to model and enforce the use of language. They supplement their natural authority with approval, promotion, reward and punishment, and other social sanctions. They train us to make the proper distinctions and to guide our acts using those distinctions.

Spirits and Fate. Mozi's discussion of spirits and fate illustrates the pragmatic temper of his language reform proposal. His theory of *bian*[discrimination] embraces both distinction marking and word order. To see how word order can be included in *bian*, consider two possible string orders. In one, the character *you*[exists] precedes *spirits* and *wu*[not exist] precedes *fate*. In the other the converse pattern holds. Mozi understands knowing which strings to accept as knowing the way to *bian*[discriminate] between *you*[have] and *wu*[lack]. Word order is a special case of knowing to apply a word to a thing. Mozi argues that we (the cultural leaders) should *zhi*[grasp] *exist* of spirits and *not exist* of fate.

The standard for testing this word order is also benefit-harm. If we cling to *exist* before *spirits,* people are more likely to act in fitting ways. The test of correct language is not that it semantically states the actual or true principle of morality. (The test is certainly not whether language is an accurate picture of objective facts.) Mozi asks only which of the alternative pairings best promotes beneficial conduct.

Mozi calls this utilitarian insight into ordering as knowing the *dao* of an opposing name pair. For example, the *dao* of *you-wu* guides how they combine with such other words such as *spirits* and *fate*.[53] He proposes using the *li-hai bian* to determine the *dao* of *you-wu*. Society should adopt a public guiding discourse—a *dao*—with agreement on these ordering *bian*. They will affect everyone's behavior. His proposal is to adjust each distinction and the felicitous combinations of distinctions in a way that generates maximum *li*[utility].

Thus Mozi argues that one has to be clear on the *bian* between *li-hai* to get clear on the *bian* between *shi-fei;* that *bian* interprets all other name pairs. For any name, to know the name is to know how to *shi-fei* using it. It includes knowing whether to *shi* it of spirits or fate. How we construct *ming*[names] into strings in discourse relies on the *li-hai*[benefit-harm] distinction.

Notice, in particular, that we have no reason to characterize the strings in the *dao* as being *true.* Mozi's *dao* will include strings that have *you*[have] before *spirits* and *wu*[lack] before *fate.* He does not literally argue *for believing in spirits* any more than Confucius does! He points to the pragmatic benefits of speaking this way. He especially worries about wasting the traditional moralizing literature that describes spirits redressing injustice. How, he asks, can it be appropriate in this linguistic tradition to *wu* spirits? After a string of such literature based arguments, Mozi concludes with an argument that pointedly stresses the pragmatic nature of the issue. He adopts a tone that suggests he himself *actually doubts* that there are spirits. He is arguing that we have to adopt and follow this *dao* of *you-wu.* Because of the popular literature, folk beliefs, word of mouth, and so on, the proper and utilitarian guiding language will use *you* of spirits.

David Nivison has suggested an updated and Westernized version of the Confucian critique of Mozi that focuses on this point by drawing on Plato's paradox of education.[54] This *is* helpful because Chinese thinkers focused on education and the heart's cultivated choices, not on logical presupposition. How, Nivison asks, could we *recognize* when we are being given moral knowledge unless, in some sense, it is already innate in us? Some version of this argument, I have already argued, most probably lies behind innatist Confucianism. How could we be motivated to submit ourselves to socialization unless we had some prior moral affinity to it? When Nivison contemplates Mozi, using our usual concepts of human action, belief, and desire, he finds a deep puzzle: How can Mozi, like Pascal, suppose that *by a simple act of will* humans can change their beliefs?

The paradox of education is a counterpart of what I am calling the paradox of moral reform. If you can recognize that the reform proposal is indeed a moral improvement, you must already have that new moral inclination in you in some way. Plato argued that to learn anything is to gain knowledge. If you can recognize anything as true, you must be comparing it with something. So you can only gain knowledge if it is already implicit in you. You must already believe it to recognize it as true.

Nivison's analysis gives a plausible link between Plato's doctrine of recollection and Mencius' slogan about innate goodness. But his criticism of Mozi's position is faulty. Mozi does not argue that we ought to "believe in ghosts" and "disbelieve in fate." He does argue that the society ought constantly to say "there are ghosts" and "there is no fate." That is the constant language pattern that society should inculcate.

The contrast lies here. Beliefs figure in Western folk psychology's explanations of ordinary human action. But language figures in Mozi's theory of ordinary human action. It is not that Mozi has a theory that we "think in language." He simply assumes that people execute linguistic instructions. Executing the program explains action. If we change the instructions, we change the behavior. The Western folk-psychology elaboration of this point finds no expression in Mozi.

Now we may, again, be tempted to insist, "But he must believe that language influences behavior *through* beliefs." As I have argued, he says nothing of the sort and, however familiar and necessary our folk psychology seems, we have no reason to insist that Chinese thinkers must have adopted it without noticing. We have found good reason to take at face value the way that they actually express their own language-based theory.

Thus Pascal's problem is irrelevant to Mozi. Pascal can be criticized because he has misused the concept of *belief.* Belief is not the sort of thing that is chosen, but the precondition of other action choice. Mozi is not making a proposal to individuals about what they should believe. He is making a proposal to a *society* about what should be included in the public discourse—the *dao.* That raises a problem about how existing public discourse can undertake to evaluate and adopt the proposal. That is the paradox of moral reform. But it does not raise Pascal's problem.

However, Nivison's analysis is correct in suggesting that there is a motivation as well as a justification version of the paradox of moral reform. The paradox has resonances in Hume's two famous slogans: "You can't get an ought from an is" and "Reason can only be the slave of the passions." The logical point could be stated as a counterpart of Zhuangzi's version, "You can't get an ought out of reason without presupposing an ought." But the Chinese version is not obviously about logical consequence. It is about standards for applying words, for making the discriminations that underlie linguistic distinctions. You can't arrive at a standard of *shi-fei* without presupposing one.

Each standard is itself a linguistic distinction and asserting a correct way to *shi*[that's it] and *fei*[that's not] using any distinction also depends on a standard. One way of putting the problem, anticipating Daoist terminology, is to say that Mozi treats *li*[benefit] as the constant (positive) term. It remains fixed while he proposes changing the rest of the distinctions we make in guiding discourse. He supposes the *bian* between *li-hai* will fix how we *shi-fei*. Yet we have to make a *shi-fei* assignment to justify using *li-hai* in this way.

Mozi has two Daoist problems. One is the problem of fixing standards for picking out one distinction as the basic one—the justification problem. The other is an interpretative or projectability problem in using *li-hai* in moral reform. Mozi seems to assume that there will be no controversy about fixing the scope or point of discrimination for the *li-hai* pair itself. He does not worry about how we will *shi-fei*[this–not this] *using* the *li-hai* distinction. Clearly, however, interpretive debate is likely. Mozi, for example, regarded a large population to be a benefit. China now sees it as a harm. We can say similar things about the availability of alcohol, milk, red meat, and religion. People will disagree about what counts as benefit and harm. Thus, in a second way, Mozi presupposed a *shi-fei* in applying the *li-hai* distinction in moral reform. We need a standard to apply *that* distinction before we can, in turn, use *it* to fix other *shi-fei* distinctions. Given Mozi's understanding of *bian*, he should have worried about whether he had deployed the *li-hai* distinction *correctly* in classing the outcomes of saying *you spirits* as *li* and *wu spirits* as *hai*.

The Chinese version of the infinite regress is like Hume's second slogan in having a motivational element. *Shi* and *fei* are not merely assignments, but assignments with behavioral consequences—like pro and con attitudes. Thus *shi* may be translated in different contexts as *this, right,* or *assent; fei* as *not this, wrong,* or *denial. Shi* and *fei* are the baseline primitives of the Chinese conception of language. As such, they ground the theory that language guides behavior. They are both the thin prescriptive *and* descriptive terms.

Mozi's position has an objectivist ring because he emphasizes external permanence as guiding our use of language. He advocates measurementlike standards. Such standards are *one* component of a scientific perspective. Theories of measurement accompanied by operations that yield constant, reliable, results for different evaluators are as crucial to science as is mathematics. In fact, it is only through the measurement hypotheses and the observer invarience of measurement operations that mathematics can be used in science.

The measurement component makes Mozi's position seem universal, realistic, constant, objective, and therefore rational. But Mozi has no conception of proof structure, premises, or conclusions nor does he have the mental apparatus of belief-desire practical rationality. His basic view is that language socialization directs human behavior. He proposes that we reform the process of socialization in accord a standard that he thinks is natural, measurable, and therefore both universal and tied to external constancy.

Mozi does rely on the malleability of human motivation by language. But that does not mean that he thinks humans are born as motivational tabulae rasae. First he clearly thinks they are born with the programming that makes them malleable to social superiors and example. Second, he also thinks his basic standard of *li-hai*[benefit-harm] is a natural impulse. So he is not in the position of denying that there is any innate human nature.

But the impulse to *li-hai* need not be regarded as the innate impulse of each individual. It is an impulse of nature which tends to be manifested in each of its systems. The natural order, as Mozi sees it, is an order designed to maximize benefit. Each animal type seeks its own benefit as does each human level of organization. Mozi's is not a claim about specifically the psychological level. Thus Mozi, like Hume, treats the natural urge to benefit as an urge to favor the concept in general, not an egoistic concern for partial or individual benefit.

The Role of the Natural Urge

We noted above that there is both a justification and an interpretation aspect to the Daoist paradox of moral reform. For both aspects there are separate questions of standards and motivation. Mozi appeals to *tian*[nature] to solve the entire complex of problems. Let us focus first on the justification problems.

Open standard. What is the Ur-standard of morality? How can we show that the universal standard of moral distinctions should be *li-hai*[benefit-harm]? How can we justify uniquely taking *it* as the constant term-pair.

Mozi often seems to confuse that question with a motivational question.

Motivation/Obligation. Why should we care about utility morality? What makes any answer to a question about standards matter? Why should we worry about how to answer it?

As understood in both traditions, morality involves two aspects: (1) an external, evidential aspect and (2) an internal, emotive, motivational aspect. These aspects answer two questions in moral theory: "What is moral?" and "Why be moral?" We must both have standards for distinguishing between moral and immoral and have impulses to conform to those standards in making action-guiding distinctions. In Western moral philosophy, we blend the standard and the motivation to action in the notion of *a reason to*. We harmonize the two questions by means of our theory of how reasons can also be causes. This route, however familiar it seems to us, is not Mozi's.

Tian[nature:heaven] thus plays a complex role in the *Mozi*. On the one hand, it seems to be a justification; on the other, like the term *spirits, tian* plays a motivational role. Mozi refers to *tian* in justifying the Ur-choice of his utilitarian moral standard. Utility is the answer to "What is moral?" *Tian*[nature:heaven] *authorizes* that standard. So *tian*[nature] plays the familiar dual role of authority, settling questions and effecting the solution. The motivation comes partly from threat, but also from the natural desire to conform to superiors. *Tian* also answers "Why be moral?"

These roles flow inextricably together in Mozi's discussion. He certainly does not clearly distinguish them. As a source of obligation, *tian* is akin to (but *higher than*) other social leaders—elders, rulers, parents. *Tian*[nature:heaven] plays an analogous role for all Chinese thinkers (except perhaps the Neo-Mohists and Zhuangzi). It extends the authority hierarchy beyond the actual community.

The confusing this is that Mozi seems both to cling to the authority perspective, but to reject the doctrine of *tian-ming*$^{\text{mandate of heaven}}$. The phrase *tian-ming* has a puzzling array of translations. On the one hand, as we have noted, *ming*^{command} is understood to be a verbal form of *ming*^{name}. It suggests that names play the prescriptive role of commands but without invoking the sentential structure of a command, a law, or a rule. Then, again, translations regularly render *ming*$^{\text{name:command}}$ as *fate*. I suggest that the *fate* translation is misleading. The issue in classical China is not so much causal determinism as it is *name* determinism. *Ming*^{name} plays a theoretical role that embraces that of *rank, fame, accomplishment, status*. The name is the recognition to which one can aspire. To say that names are fixed by nature is the closest theoretical counterpart of Western causal *property* determinism.

Confucius' use is continuous with his political theory. *Tian-ming*$^{\text{mandate of heaven}}$ *names* the king, who then *names* the high ministers who *name* the lower functionaries. All are supposed to do their naming based on *de*^{virtuosity}. But *tian-ming*$^{\text{natural naming}}$ has fatalistic overtones in Confucianism because it suggests that nature provides the crucial condition for the operation of the system in which we get our appropriate moral status. If heaven has not done *its* naming, even a sagelike Confucian may go unrecognized. This is blaming *tian*^{nature} for our lack of *ming*$^{\text{name:status}}$.

Understanding *tian-ming* in this way helps explain why Mozi opposes the doctrine of *tian-ming*$^{\text{natural naming}}$ while he claims to follow *tian-zhi*$^{\text{natural intent}}$. Mozi's theory would be that arranging and achieving names is a social function, not a natural one. All names are determined by social, human processes. They should be determined in accordance to a discrimination standard which follows natural intent—*li-hai*$^{\text{benefit-harm}}$. *Tian-zhi*$^{\text{natural intent}}$ is constant. If there is a failure, it is ours. So he opposes *tian-ming*$^{\text{natural naming}}$ on pragmatic, utilitarian grounds. Espousing such a theory will interfere with our moral ambition and make us unwilling to work to change both the structure of status and our moral *name* within the structure. We are responsible for ordering the *dao* that guides society's naming. We should do it so one's status depends on how beneficial they are to society. They should get the name that best contributes to general well-being.

Confucian passivity is at the social more than the individual level. They are unwilling to take responsibility for reforming the scheme of names. They take those as fixed by nature and past history. Confucius taught the attitude of accepting the traditional training in his various arts, practicing them rigorously and waiting for heaven to set the conditions under which they will be properly recognized in the political structure. Accepting the Confucian theory of natural names makes us socially passive. Individually, Confucians did cultivate themselves, but their ritual purity led them to shun responsibility for reforming society. As we noted, Confucians play their roles and leave it to *tian* to conduct the concert.

So Mozi rejects *tian-ming*^{fate}, yet he accepts *tian-zhi*$^{\text{natural will}}$. He accepts nature's will about the constant *standard* for naming, but not the notion that nature fixes names. Society fixes the names using the standard *approved* by nature. The natural will (the presocial preference pattern) selects the standard of *li*^{utility}. That sets the basis for moral reform. Aside from the name pair *li-hai*$^{\text{benefit-harm}}$, nature does not lock the name system in place nor are named roles divinely assigned to people.

We name the ruler using the natural *li-hai* standard.[55] From there on the system looks Confucian. The ruler then names subordinates. The subordinates name the next tier and so on. They also name actions, events, etc. They *shi-fei* them. Mozi argues for standard constancy for these *shi-fei*, action-guiding acts of naming. Each level relays its authority to the next level. The source of overall authority is nature. Hence nature's constant measurement standard, *li-hai,* should govern all the subordinate naming and valuing. Nature gives us the standard, but it is up to us to apply it in our cultural forms.

Tian^nature thus differs from lower-level authorities. We can exhort each level of authority to performance guided by values using the standards of a higher level. In nature's case, we do not exhort it to adopt the ideal standards. Nature or heaven is where appeals to authority end. It sets the measurable real context for moral reflection.

Thus Mozi's use of *tian*^nature inferentially leads to the notion of *universality.* Mozi takes for granted the Confucian notion of an essentially social structure using a *dao.* But *tian* draws our attention away from the conventional and changeable. It gives us a more universal perspective from which to make and reform conventional *shi-fei* distinctions. If we base a *dao* merely on social consensus, then we lack warrant for treating it as *yi*^moral. *Yi*^morality shares the Mohist ideal of being constant, measurable, and universal. As Mozi puts it, we can leave a family if we do not like meeting the expectations there and we can even leave a whole state. However, we cannot leave the natural world. Nature's motivational force is universal, not limited to any particular social structure (from which one could, in principle, escape).[56]

Thus we do not have to attribute to Mozi an explicit notion of autonomous or independent rational motivation—motivation that comes from the faculty for deductive reasoning. The Confucian tradition certainly has not bequeathed that element of a Kantian deontological point of view. For them, all direction comes from some kind of social structure, from social leaders. Now, if moral knowledge is of this sort, then where do the leaders get *their yi?* The chain of authority reaches through the social leaders and back to nature. Mozi gets his universalism from the analogy of a cosmic community.

Tian^nature:heaven also appears to play the required justifying role. It does not justify a *dao* type directly, but justifies the utility standard for choosing one. The natural urge is for what results in human life, prosperity, and order. The motivation to morality is that it leads to the goals that nature has willed. These goals are the standards of choice among social paths. The evidence of *tian*'s accepting the utility standard is all the evidence there can be for using the standard as a metastandard of choice among *dao*^ways.

Mozi claims to know that *tian* approves the utility standard because (1) it follows the standard in natural action, and (2) it is an objective, measurable, obvious standard. *Tian* causes rain to fall, the crops to grow, and so on. These are clearly beneficial to the people and the state. Nature, further, does not limit its benefit to any particular state or culture. All social groups, Mozi asserts, receive the same blessings from nature. They recognize and sacrifice to some deity in gratitude. This shows that heaven's or nature's concern is universal and not limited to one culture.

We hardly need to dwell on the weakness of this justification. The human tendency to think that nature is arranged for our benefit still plagues even our popular interpretations of the theory of evolution, which we think proves that humans are the fittest creatures: evolution has intended or pointed to the survival of humans rather than that of dinosaurs. This familiar human-centered bias in arguments about nature, fortunately, is not Mozi's only analysis. His reasoning just as frequently reverses the direction of explanation. He attributes his utility standard to nature *because* it is easy to know.[57] *Tian*'s will has this desirable feature. We can measure it precisely, as a craftsman does with his compass or plumb line. Nature's standard is accessible and projectable. It does not depend on a relativist interpretive tradition. Mozi alleges that he can determine the will of nature with the precision of a craftsman at his trade. The utility standard is natural precisely in being simple and objectively measurable.

The argument seems to suggest that simplicity and objectivity are the marks of the natural and universal. Complexity and controversy are marks of the social, conventional and historical. His best argument for using the *li-hai* distinction as the Ur-distinction, then, really relies on the claim that it is precise and clear. We are justified *and* motivated to select the standard because it lends itself to more widely accessible, precise interpretation.

Thinking of *tian*'s role both in motivating and justifying morality reminds us of a parallel point about language. I have proposed a hypothesis explaining how Chinese philosophers thought that language influenced behavior. That hypothesis postulates a natural link between moral standards and moral motivation. Our internal motivation for action is in language. We can think of ourselves as operating a program—the social prescriptive discourse. We have, so far, not relied on the intentional concept of a *desire*. Our motivation comes with our nature. We are operating systems for social programs. Our species naturally conforms to social practices that center on language. The closest thing to an appeal to desire comes in the claim of a natural will consisting of the *li-hai* distinction. The people also naturally *tend* (desire?) to conform to their superiors. These two natural inclinations provide Mozi's engine of social-moral *dao* reform.

The rest of the story focuses on the conventionality of language. The social leaders start to speak differently, to make new distinctions, to evaluate and act differently. That catches on and spreads through the natural social hierarchy. It changes everyone else's programming and behavior. It is heavenly, natural, and inherent that we do operate with language and master and perform social practices. Belief-desire explanations per se play little role here once we have established the base standard.

Finally, then, the appeal to *tian* is a reflection of Mozi's incomplete, struggling urge toward realism in ethics. He wants a standard that is more universal than culture and society, a standard that does not depend for its application on a tradition of interpretation. It must resolve vagueness or culturally relative assumptions about *shi-fei*. Still, his concept of *tian*[nature:heaven] draws heavily on the social-authority model.

Morality: Motivation and Justification

I have argued that Mozi's theory of heart-mind and language is pragmatic and that this theory generates a dual account of the doctrine of nature's will. Treat nature and utility as answering two different questions: (1) "What standard do we use to test a tradition's *dao?*" and (2) "Why should we inculcate a *dao* that passes the test?"

Universal utility answers the first question. "Nature commands it" answers the second, insofar as anyone *can* answer it.

Nature thus does not act as a *standard* of morality *independent of* universal utility. It explains our *motivation* to take utility's guidance seriously. Mozi appeals to nature and uses the natural human attraction to its transsocial authority. The point is not so much that *tian*[nature] intends human well being as that humans pre-socially have that motivation. His arguments about the role of *tian*[nature] parallel those he makes about spirits, ghosts, and fate. He argues that our saying certain things about *tian*[nature] plays a beneficial role in motivating people. That is, Mozi argues for the beneficial effects of saying *exists* of spirits and *non-exist* of fate as he argues for the beneficial effects of retaining talk of *tian*'s knowledge and authority. All these traditional religious ways of speaking play important pragmatic roles. He does not directly argue for the truth of these claims. The benefits of talking of spirits as existing and *tian*[nature] as knowing and willing arise because society traditionally has accepted a divine command theory of (political) obligation. Traditional culture has accepted and relied on stories and moral fables which use the language of *shen*[spirit], *guei*[ghost], and *tian*[nature] to motivate moral conformity. Mozi does not advocate wasting these traditional *dao* in the process of reforming *dao* to make it more beneficial.[58]

Because he does not distinguish clearly between utility as the criterion and nature as the motivation, Mozi has the classic problem that comes from mixing divine command with other normative theories. Is something right because commanded or willed by nature or is it commanded or willed by nature because it is right? Mere extensional equivalence does not remove the objection that one has two distinct theories of morality. This leaves the *theoretical* chance that they might conflict. That opens the door to Mencian and Daoist criticism. Graham argues that the later Mohists pointedly avoid the appeal to *tian*[nature:heaven] because they see the danger of anarchism in appeals to being natural.

Mozi's alternate appeal to measurable projectability which I have preferred may be as good a *justification* as is possible for accepting the universalist utility criteria. If its coherence, and the incoherence of the alternative, is not enough to justify adopting it, nature's command does not help. It can motivate but not justify. Further motivation may be psychologically necessary, but it can not rationally improve the status of the proposal.

We can see why the appeal to heaven or nature to *justify* a standard fails if we consider the open question argument again. The appeal to heaven allows asking (as Zhuangzi does), "Why obey heaven?" Asked seriously (especially from the moral point of view), the question "Why be moral?" may have no answer.

The Meeting of Fact and Value

We could also explain the twin Daoist problems of justification and interpretation using G. E. Moore's open-question argument. Moore argued that for any alleged naturalistic definition (X) of *good,* we can intelligibly ask "Is X good?" Thus no naturalistic definition of good is uncontroversially correct. The Chinese version may be stated as: for any alleged natural standard of *shi–fei*[right-wrong] like *li-hai*[benefit-harm], we can ask "What standard justifies and guides *shi-fei*ing with this distinction?" That formula asks both why we select it as the dominant distinction and why we should apply it in any particular way in guiding the rest of our use of language.

Each *dao* presents a different value path. We understand the appeal to nature or heaven as an urge toward realism or objectivism in value. Western folk tradition addresses this issue under the guise of a *fact-value* distinction in which facts are objective and values are subjective. Further, given our preoccupation with descriptive sententials, we tend to blur the *fact-value* and the *is-ought* distinctions. Is-ought refers to different types of *sentences*—factual statement and statements of obligation. Thus we treat the argument-based slogan "You can't get an *ought* from an *is*" as a proof that we cannot bridge the fact-value gap.[59]

From a pragmatic, action-guiding, and word-based point of view, however, value words and distinctions work much like descriptive ones. Thick ethical terms and descriptive or natural kind terms are both *world guided*. Their application depends on responding to public features of the real world. To absorb any term, say X, that guides action, we learn to discriminate appropriately between what is X and what is not X. Then, depending on our program, we run a subroutine triggered by our sensing the presence of X. Given this description, it does not matter whether X is a natural kind term like *water,* an artifact term like *check,* or an evaluative term like *benevolent.* To learn the term is to learn to make the distinction and to use it in guiding action *in a certain way.*

All the distinctions that we master help prescriptive discourse to guide behavior. We soak up dispositions to behavior from the social practices that surround our use of a term. Along with learning skill at discriminating, we learn *to respond* to the discriminants in culturally given ways. In learning *ming*[names], we learn a distinction and certain ways of using it in action. The dispositions I have acquired to choose water from its environment or to take a check are undeniably very complex dispositions. In some situations we do favor the X in question; in others we do not.

We do not learn the dispositions in discourse form. We learn them as *similar* behavior. We extrapolate from examples. Usually, we cannot describe what we do except in the most general terms. The application of all such terms involves many layers of acquired intuition so that our guidance by terms strikes us as dictated from the outside, a natural response to the things.

Mozi concentrated directly on the ability to discriminate, *bie*[distinguish], *bian*[discriminate], *fen*[divisions], or *bian*[divide].[60] Every *bian*[discrimination] involves a *shi-fei*[this:right-not this:wrong] assignment. Every *bian*[discrimination] is apropos some *ming*[name]. To know how to use a name is to know how to *shi*[this:right] something (apply the name to it) and how to *fei*[not this:wrong] other things. We do this distinguishing and naming in the course of performing or executing an acquired competence at some social practice.

The dual translation of *shi* as *this* and *right* flows from this theoretical perspective. Language and words guide action by marking things. Finding a *this* is finding the *right* thing in the context to trigger one of the learned dispositions. *This* is a thin descriptive term, as *right* is a thin ethical term. We call it thin because the term *this* relies minimally on features of the world. It picks out[61] the contextually appropriate thing in each situation. The heart runs its distinction making program with a particular term and returns a *shi-fei.*

When the circumstances call for a *shi*[this] assignment, we have called the term that triggers our learned disposition *dominant.* When we treat a term as dominant,

Mohists say we *zhi*^{grasp} the term (as the rulers in the quotation on page 102 *grasp universal* and *partial*). Making each term assignment triggers a complex performance.

In any plausible *dao, water* and *check* are not constantly dominant terms. Sometimes we trigger positive behavior toward them, and sometimes negative, rejecting behavior. However, some thick terms are more constant; these include what we normally call value terms. The disposition to prefer kindness to cruelty is largely stable or constant. Any *dao* with a term for kindness will *relatively* constantly interact with social practices to induce us to choose kindness over cruelty. *Kind* is (almost) constantly dominant in most human *dao*s. *Water* and *check* are less constant in their guidance.

We might think the constant-inconstant distinction corresponds to the fact-value distinction. Some descriptive terms, however, are also constantly dominant. We almost always prefer life to death, benefit to harm, and pleasure to pain.

Mozi thought the constancy of preferences guided by these terms showed they were nonconventional or presocial preferences. Presumably, we do not learn these preferences as we do our preferences for negotiable checks and college degrees. No doubt any actual disposition to take water is partly natural and partly instilled by some traditional *dao*. A tradition, furthermore, can temper behavior flowing from even these *natural* preferences. A given *dao* can induce us to prefer death to dishonor or liberty to life. Notoriously, even our taste for food and sex show class-induced differences.

I have been using Bernard Williams's notion of *thick* ethical concepts in making sense of this early theorizing about language and *dao*. Williams claims that we learn these terms along with a rich traditional *way* of acting toward the values the terms symbolize. The values are world-guided and therefore regarded as objective by the relevant linguistic community. We learn to apply the distinction in the real world using accessible properties. We seldom dispute about the application of those words.

Williams contrasts these to *thin* ethical concepts, those that give us the means to state our disagreements about value. Examples are *right, wrong, ought,* and *should*. Even within a given community, we have controversies about the use of these terms. Our community comes to state and debate its disagreements using *thin* terms. We use thick concepts by way of a strongly shared intuition and a sense that the values are *world guided*. We hold the thick terms in common when we debate about the application of the thin ones.

This gives us another perspective on the link between Mozi's reliance on *tian* and the priority he assigns *li-hai*. *Li-hai* is a naturally guiding distinction. It guides all people no matter what the other content of their tradition. So it gives us a fulcrum outside any particular tradition to use in testing that tradition. It is a naturally constant guiding term. As such, Mozi regards it as heaven's will—a natural preference.

Our fact-value distinction, then, translates into two distinctions in Mozi's analysis: constant-inconstant and natural-conventional. Constancy and naturalness characterize different ways in which terms may be dominant action-guiding terms. Had he engaged in playing *our* scientific, descriptive-language game, Mozi would have reasons of *descriptive* or explanatory constancy for a distinction that plays a minimal role in China: that of causally natural kinds. Because Chinese philosophers theorized mainly about language as guiding behavior, we can understand their different focus.

Neither Mozi nor Confucius thought about the difference between natural kind divisions and evaluative ones.[62] Mozi's prototypical abuse of Confucian gentlemen assimilates these two kinds of divisions. Judgments about what is moral and what is not are similar to judgments of what is black and white, bitter and sweet.

> Consider someone who, on seeing a little bit of black, called it black but, on seeing a lot of black, called it white. Then we would regard this person as not knowing the black-white *bian*[distinction]. If on tasting a little bitter, he called it bitter and on tasting a lot called it sweet, then we would, of course, regard him as not knowing the bitter-sweet *bian*[distinction]. Now someone does a little *fei*[not this:wrong] then [the gentlemen] know to *fei* it, but, on doing a lot of *fei* like attacking a state, then they do not know to *fei* it. They go along and praise it and call it *yi*[morality]. Can we call this knowing the moral-immoral distinction? This is how I know the gentlemen of the world are confused about how to *bian*[discriminating] *yi*[morality] and its opposite (28/17/11–29/17/14).

The Chinese philosophical tradition focuses on pragmatics in place of semantics. It dissolves what we would call the fact-value distinction into a matter of degree of constancy and naturalness. It has *no sentential* counterpart of the *is-ought* distinction.

Universal Love in Interpersonal Relations

Let us summarize our conclusions to this point about the structure of Mozi's utilitarianism. His ethical theory starts from noticing the limits of traditionalism. Traditional moral theories are not self-justifying. In some cases, particularly the Confucian partial-love versions, they are self-defeating. The Chinese tradition did have a clear conception of moral reform. Mozi clearly raised the issue. From Mozi on Chinese thinkers accepted the requirement that any perspective *dao* requires some kind of nontraditional gauge of correctness. Mozi accepts that traditional authority is necessary to teaching but he advocates a universal, constant *content*. This leads him to the *bian* between *li* and *hai,* with li seeming to be a naturally constant guiding term. It becomes the base for all *shi-fei* distinctions, determining the scope of names and the way to order name-pairs and longer strings in the community discourse. The leaders should make that language with its utilitarian effects the *constant* language.

Mozi's signature in Chinese *popular consciousness* is his doctrine of universal love. Applying the *li-hai* standard, he says society should stress universal love rather than the Confucian partial love. People will internalize whichever pattern of guidance the leaders adopt and model in their language and behavior. This will change their prior dispositions, which, Mozi admits, are in the direction of partial love.

The justification of this social project takes the standard of utility for granted. That moral criterion is the root from which both the well-known doctrines of universal love and agreement with the superior branch. One is in the interpersonal sphere, the other in the political sphere.

Partisan Confucian accounts sometimes present Mozi's position as *based on* universal love.[63] They suggest that utilitarianism follows from universal love rather than vice versa. This is textually indefensible and theoretically confused. In the passage quoted above and throughout the chapter on universal love, Mozi follows a perfectly clear argumentative line. From the opening sentence—"It is the business of the benevolent man to try to promote what is beneficial to the world and to eliminate what is harmful"—to the ending sentence—"It is the way of the sage kings and a great benefit to the people"—Mozi clearly argues *for* universal love using the natural, constant, measurable criterion of utility.

The Confucian tendency to focus on universal love instead of utilitarianism reflects a characteristic *Confucian confusion*. Confucians systematically confuse moral psychology with normative ethics. Mozi acknowledges that his normative moral reform involves changing natural dispositions. He relies on both a natural *will* for benefit over harm and the natural tendency to master social practices. These *effect* the changes dictated by the *normative theory*. Normative theory is not a Confucian strong point. Confucius, as we saw, did not have a particularly clear notion of normative ethics. His disciples *yearned for* a single thread of moral theory. All they got was an unexamined dedication to ritual and a mysterious, inexplicable *ren*[humanity] gained from unquestioning practice. Mozi has convincingly undermined existing social practice as a standard of the moral *dao* and the early Confucians have no obvious normative response.

The response came from Mencius. He shifted Confucian attention to moral psychology, the theory of human nature. Confucian accounts treat this as a philosophical breakthrough.[64] But, although an interesting issue, it is an irrelevant dodge of Mozi's challenge. By focusing on universal love, Confucian critics of Mozi shift the spotlight from normative ethics to descriptive sociology, where they feel on stronger grounds. They word the dispute in descriptive terms: "Are humans naturally partial or naturally universal?" Confucians can certainly point to evidence of the natural family partiality of our emotions. They assume that in doing so, they are refuting Mozi. In fact, this is simply to miss the point of normative theory.

All this Confucian focus on human nature ignores that Mozi had already met the strategy. He put the Confucian claim in the mouth of the *partial* ruler (above pages 102–3): "This violates the feelings of all under heaven!"[65] Then Mozi calmly traced the effect of someone who talks in that way as opposed to someone who uses the language of universal love. Each cultivates his emotional structure by the distinctions he *grasps* or treats as *constant*.

He both met the criticism that the normative reform he suggests would change natural feelings, and the more pertinent criticism that the theory is unrealistic. This first criticism claims simply that universal utilitarianism requires changing natural reactions. The answer is, "So what? Training in *li*[ritual] also shapes and polishes human nature. The issue is *which* changes should we effect."

The second criticism is that it requires changing them in ways that we could never accomplish. The form of the second criticism resembles our own platitude, "It's all right in theory but not in practice." Mozi's response[66] is sound. How could a *dao* be a good *dao* if it was not practical! *Daos are* schemes of *practical* guidance. If a *dao* were not practical it would not *be* a good *dao*. We don't ask if a *dao* contains the phrase *greatest utility;* we ask, "does it bring about the greatest utility?" The practical effects of a dao do not assume perfect conformity to the discourse. We compare behaviors of those who adopt a language of universal concern to behaviors of those who adopt partial language standards. Do they behave differently? Yes. Is one pattern of behavior preferable? Yes. The test is not "Do people perfectly conform to this *dao?*" but "Does social endorsement of this *dao* tend to better results?"[67]

Mozi's account of how we *can change* society starts from Confucian assumptions about human nature that were implicit in the rectifying-names strategy. He assumes, with Confucius, that our affections are naturally *filial*. However, he argues, humans can best accomplish their filial goals by practicing universal love. He bases this conclusion on the faith that society influences and shapes people through modeling the use of language and competent performance of the *dao* by acknowledged masters.

If this is Confucianism's defense against Mohist optimism, it suggests a surprising and uncharacteristic cynicism about human nature. It implies that no one can transcend natural partiality. Mozi's optimistic response appeals to human *intelligence:* "Do they intend to suggest that the filial sons of the world are all stupid and incapable of doing right?"[68] An intelligent person motivated by filial concern ought to practice and promote universal concern. That will make our filial goals easier to accomplish. Mozi's arguments frequently start with filial concern. He opposed only its vapid, short-sighted implementation. An intelligent, reflective filialist, he argued, would join him in advocating a more universal *dao.*

Mozi's argument also draws on Confucian assumptions about the power of models. It draws on the view that following traditions is natural. Practicing universal concern will change society because people respond to models. If you display altruistic behavior to other people (such as caring for someone else's parents), they will adopt altruistic behavior. A universalist language can become the accepted social convention "within a single generation" by having the rulers adopt, practice, and model that language. Mozi takes for granted the Confucian assumption that humans naturally conform to accepted social practice and model themselves on social superiors. Given these assumptions, there is no clear reason to oppose altering the guiding traditions toward this more reflective ethical standard. The Confucian attempt to shift the focus of debate from normative ethics to moral psychology fails in part because Mozi's moral psychology is not markedly different from Confucius'. Mencius' moral psychology, as we shall see, is a different matter.

The Doctrine of Agreement with the Superior

The theory of how to gain social acceptance for universal love thus leads naturally to the political sphere. Here Mozi uses another ordered name pair as a slogan: *shang-tong*[agreement with the superior]. He assumes that *li-hai*[benefit-harm] is the key normative distinction, that the application of that distinction to *shi* some political *dao* is natural, and that its outcome is obvious.

Mozi's argument is a familiar one. On the surface, it reminds us of the classical social-contract argument of the English political philosopher, Thomas Hobbes.

> Mozi said, From today go back to when humans began to live, when there were no proper elders. We may say that people in the world had different *yi*[moralities].

One person had one *yi;* ten people had ten *yi:* a hundred people a hundred *yi*. The more people, the more things we would call *yi*. Accordingly, people assented to their own *yi* and dissented from the *yi* of others. They ended in mutual disagreement.

Within, fathers and sons, older and younger brother had angry words and an impulse to disperse. They could not engage in mutual aid. It got to the point that mutual labor could not use left over energy. People hid advantageous *dao*s and did not share them. They would not divide and share rotting excess foodstuffs. The disorder in the world got to be like that of wild animals. There were no conventions of ruler-minister, superior-inferior, elder-younger and no rituals governing father-son and elder and younger brothers.

So the world was disordered. Clearly the people lacked a rectifying leader to unify the world's *yi* and thus the world was disordered. As a result they selected the most worthy, good, sagely, knowledgeable, discriminating and wise person in the world. They set him up as the zi^{master} of $tian^{\text{nature:heaven}}$ with the job of unifying the *yi* of the world. (12/15/1–16/7)

Notice that the argument for unifying *yi* is a utilitarian argument. It presupposes that we ought to do what will optimize li^{benefit}. Now we could insert the self-defeating argument discussed earlier between the lines of this doctrine. Mozi could be suggesting that *each* particular *yi* point of view would fail to achieve its goal in this state of conflict of goals. However, given the plenitude of $yi^{\text{moralities}}$ he postulates, a *self-defeating* argument for each would be unmanageable. We could remove the appearance of appeal to his own particular moral standard by assuming that the different $yi^{\text{moralities}}$ will each have a conception of *li-hai*. Each will be able to see the point of the political proposal. Everyone, Mozi thinks, will agree that the conditions he describes are hai^{harms}.

I will focus on two points in analyzing Mozi's political doctrine: (1) the comparison and contrast with the English philosopher Thomas Hobbes (and other Western hypothetical-choice political theorists) and (2) the comparison and contrast with Confucius.

First, note that Mozi, like Hobbes and unlike Confucius, does not rely on the mandate of heaven (the divine right of kings) to justify political structures.[69] The form of Mozi's use of *tian* thus illustrates the point I made earlier. He takes a natural *will* as the base of his system but rejects natural or heavenly $ming^{\text{name:command}}$. He regards the assignment of names to be an essentially social matter guided by the natural impulse to benefit.

Still, though he derives it rather than presupposes it, Mozi accepts the general outline of Confucian presuppositions about what counts as a well-ordered society. He justifies an ordered hierarchy of merit. The hierarchical structure is not directly mandated by nature, but is a consequence of the natural will to utility. The hierarchy influences behavior by modeling words and deeds. Mozi's disagreement with Confucius concerns mainly the *content* of the moral teaching that should come from this social hierarchy. He rejects the three-thousand odd rules of li^{ritual} as the ordering principles and substitutes the single principle of universal utility—li^{benefit}. Agreement with the superior is a *sociological* constant. It explains *how* we can be made to use language and act in accord with utilitarian altruism. Thus, the agreement with the superior deals with the motivation to moral distinction making and performance, not with the criteria or standard. In this respect, it is like the appeal to heaven or nature. That appeal endorses the criterion and effects it. But the criterion is simple benefit. Mozi does not envision that social authorities will challenge a standard endorsed by nature.

Comparison to Hobbes

Mozi's story describes a situation superficially resembling one that Hobbes describes as the *state of nature*. Let us call an argument of this form a hypothetical-choice justification of government. A hypothetical-choice justification presupposes that we will (intelligently) choose a government when faced with a choice between government and a *state of nature*. To see the parallels *and contrasts* with Hobbes theory, let me summarize the Hobbesian argument.

Hobbes begins with a mechanistic materialist view of the world and of human psychology. Human individuals make up society as atomic particles make up ordinary physical objects. Each individual element acts according to its own principles and the whole takes shape as the sum of the individual actions. The principles of action of the human atoms are pleasure and pain. Nature motivates human beings to maximize the one and minimize the other. Hobbes' theory is the classic example of psychological egoism, and specifically the hedonistic version.

The individual pursuit of self-interest is a *law* of nature. Self-defense by punishing aggressors is a natural *right*. However, absent any laws and government, this pursuit of self-interest and self-defense would inevitably lead to a state of war of each person against every other person. In that warlike state, life would be solitary, poor, nasty, brutish, and short. All rational self-interested people would inevitably want to sign a truce. They would make a covenant with each other to abandon the war of the state of nature. The covenant transfers a *natural* right to punish aggressors to a sovereign. He therefore *justifiably* has a monopoly on the right to punish. The sovereign then makes laws and inflicts punishments. Whatever the content of those laws, the order and security gained by this arrangement justifies abiding by the covenant and obeying the sovereign.

The general outline of a hypothetical-choice theory forms the backbone of modern Western political theory. We can find different versions in Locke, Rousseau, Kant, Jefferson, and constitutional writers in general. So familiar is the argument to us, that on meeting Mozi's discussion our familiarity inclines us to treat it as a version of Hobbes. Thus historians have assumed that Mozi is a Chinese Hobbes— an instructive case of familiarity-induced distortion and an example of the principle of charity gone wrong.

One result of identifying Hobbes and Mozi's argument too closely is that it confirms the Confucian distortion by suggesting that Mozi's system rests on psychological egoism.[70] In fact, Mozi's assumptions about human nature parallel those of Confucius. Humans are social animals motivated by social practices and conventions, including language conventions. We have seen no more hint of individualistic, egoistic psychology in Mozi than we saw in Confucius.

Mozi does not say that everyone is an egoist motivated by his own desire. Each person is motivated by a $yi^{morality}$! The problem he is discussing is the disorder which arises from the plethora of different *moral motives*. The culprit is conflicting conceptions of *yi,* not selfishness. Each group uses a different guiding discourse for their moral behavior. Moral disagreement, not egoism, causes the destruction of social order. The presocial condition described is, accordingly, less drastic than the Hobbesian state of total internecine warfare.

What we see in Mozi's state of nature is not that egoism is self-defeating, but that moral *agreement* about what actions are proper is more efficient. Disagreement wastes human labor power, good doctrines, and foodstuffs. *In the extreme,* it can lead to warfare. Again, this is warfare of conflicting moral conceptions, not of selfish interests. Each side feels righteous motivation, as it must to justify dying for its moral conceptions. No pure egoist would choose to die in battle. Furthermore, Mozi introduces no doctrine of rights, specifically no natural right to punish in self-defense. And his solution does not come from either a promise, a contract, or a covenant. He treats the outcome as the natural result of reflecting on the inefficiency of the state of nature. The people act on their sure acceptance of the need for a social arrangement that unifies *yi*[moralities].

Hobbes justifies the rule of law, but Mozi never refers to law or to retributive institutions per se. As Confucius does, he regards the state as an educating institution. He does accept the use of punishment as one of the social sanctions that promotes participation in the social scheme of emulation. Those who will not accept the authority structure supporting the common *yi*[morality] may be punished. But they are not punished for specific violations of particular rules.

Note that the content of Hobbes' laws need not meet any moral standard. Hobbes justifies allegiance to a ruling scheme in which the content is arbitrary. Mozi's argument for the scheme carries over into its content. The utility criterion governs moral judgments, the *shi-fei,* that are modeled up and down the system.

This observation reinforces the impression that Mozi relies on nature only for its motivational force. His theory does not offer a divine-command *criterion* of morality. Similarly, agreement with the superior is not a political criterion for *yi*[morality]; the criterion remains *li*[benefit]. The argument here is for a social-motivational structure that instills that criterion and governs its beneficial interpretation in more particular judgments of *shi-fei.* Mozi does not argue that the base distinction is whatever the superior (or nature) says. The hierarchy merely assures moral agreement. The content of the agreement is given by utility. According with that basic standard requires that we participate in an agreed social pattern of *shi-fei* judgments.

Mozi stresses repeatedly that only those above can correct people. That is a claim in psychology or sociology, not a criterion of a correct *yi*[morality]. It is not that the superiors *make* something *shi* in *shi*ing it. The objectively correct criterion that governs all *shi-fei* activity is utility. (The *tian-zi*[natural master] must conform to nature, and nature's criterion is utilitarian.) The *shang-tong*[agreement upward] is not a relativistic standard of the good (whatever the superior says). It is social answer to the interpretation-and-motivation problem. The political system provides the structure to *effect* that standard. It provides punishment, reward, advocacy, praise, approval—a social counterpart to the motivation of *tian.*

Comparison to Confucius

Mozi's state, as I noted, signals a Confucian view of the role of organized society. He lacks a Western, legal conception of the role of the state as separate from society.

The chief implicit purpose of social organization is moral education—character building. Mozi has analyzed this as the harmonization of guiding language, of our dispositions to *shi*[this:right] and *fei*[not this:wrong]. This analysis parallels the purpose behind rectifying names except that it does not presuppose a traditional code. Confucians share Mozi's conception of human psychology and the goal of a well-ordered state. Confucius also had a *superiors' example* mechanism for rectifying names. The two schools offer us conflicting *contents* to use in that social mechanism. Mozi's agreement similarly concerns applying guiding terms. But he also would change the order of terms in the guiding discourse. The social hierarchy manipulates content *and* interpretation to bring about the most beneficial social patterns of prescriptive discourse.

Thus, as Mozi spells out his theory, we see it diverge even more from Hobbes. It resembles a Confucian well-ordered society. First, rather than justifying a single legislating sovereign, his argument is really for a hierarchy of official educating models. "Considering how extensive the realm was and that for distant states and different peoples, it was not a simple matter to distinguish clearly between *shi-fei* and benefit and harm,"[71] and so the top figure selects wise and virtuous men as high officials. He cannot extend his educational influence broadly enough by himself. Perhaps this is because Mozi still thinks of the training task as resting on modeling the use of these distinctions.

When the system is in place then:

> Hearing of good or evil, one shall report it to his superior. What the superior *shi*s, all shall *shi;* what the superior *fei*s, all shall *fei*.

This upward agreement, remember, does not separate value judgment and application of terms. The system of agreement is more explicit than in Confucius' rectifying names. We attribute it to Confucius by inference. He has a hierarchical, emulation theory of government that makes rectifying names the focal point in administration. We infer that rectification works by guiding conventions of usage. It comes about by example and by gradual acceptance and conformity with the usage of superiors. Both imagine that the process consists in conformity of usage in a hierarchical system.

Further, although Mozi does not express explicit opposition to law, as Confucius did, his system does not rely on retribution. His morality is not based on what one deserves. He does not, that is, have the *tian-zi*[natural master] writing or pronouncing law and enforcing it with punishment for specific violations. The ideal is more of a common-law judicial system in which each lower *court* bases its judgments in conformity with the *court* above. Here the agreement is in evaluations, not duties. Confucius similarly builds rectifying names, as we noted, on a judicial paradigm.

Mozi does allow the use of reward and punishment in getting people to accept and participate in the whole system of agreement. "To identify oneself with one's superior and not to form cliques on the lower levels—those above will reward such conduct as this and those below will praise it. . . . If the subordinates make common cause among themselves and fail to identify themselves with their superiors—if there is such conduct as this, those above will punish it and the people at large will condemn it.[72] This use of punishment, however, is not classically retributive. One is not punished for a specific *fei* act but for refusing to participate in the unifying project.

Society does not attach punishment to specific laws and grade it according to the seriousness of the wrong and the culprit's degree of responsibility.

So Mozi's system is deeply Chinese despite its surface similarity to Hobbes. Like Confucius, he treats government's function as providing a hierarchy of models of correct language and behavior. He justifies authority by the threat of anarchy. Note, however, that the final authority is not the *tian-zi*[natural master] or any special sagelike intuition. That authority is nature or heaven and its natural urge to utility.[73] Beyond that constant, natural measurable value, all other *shi-fei*s are calculated or measured by *li*[utility]. The *tian-zi*[natural master] (the emperor) himself should agree with his superior, heaven. And what does his superior want? Universal utility! Thus Mozi's system amounts to a political demand that everyone maximize utility in language and action. He proposes to ritualize or make constant utilitarian language usage and behavior. The agreement with the superior is a social mechanism to achieve his linguistic goal of making constant the language that promotes utility.

The person at a lower level can, in principle, chide his superior for faults. This suggests that the utilitarian standard is still more basic than the political obligation. Only with access to such a standard can he report good and bad to his superior and remonstrate with him when he is wrong. The superior sets the standard of right and wrong, thus, only when he judges correctly according to the heavenly approved standard of utility.

Miscellaneous Consequences of Utilitarianism

Some of the unfamiliar consequences Mozi draws from his utilitarianism signal deep differences between the Chinese and the Western cultural perspectives about what counts as utility or benefit. We have already noted that Mozi does not even mention the kinds of subjectivist standards of value that dominate Western utilitarian philosophy—happiness or pleasure.[74] These individualist, internal, subjectivist perspectives seldom emerge in Chinese philosophy. No one in classical China seemed even tempted to the view that all activity aims at some kind of subjective satisfaction or that a person directs all her actions toward her own happiness or pleasure.[75]

Mozi exemplified a social, objective view of value. The standard of value does not have to be something private, inner, and individual. He presumes that *li*[utility] has a straightforward, public scope. It does not refer to an inner feeling. The examples of utility are adequate food and shelter, peace, and objective, material conditions of life.

The Opposition to Music

Mozi's opposition to music is a good illustration that such subjectivist standards of value are not Mozi's. We would expect a Western utilitarian to approve music as a *good*. We would expect Mozi to *shi* it if he accepted a pleasure conception of utility. In fact, he *fei*s it.

The first instruction we draw from Mozi's opposition to music is that his utilitarianism is not hedonistic.[76] The second instruction is, again, about familiarity-induced misunderstanding.

When someone translates *yue* as *music,* we may treat a lone cowboy strumming his guitar by the campfire as a typical case. That is hardly the social convention Mozi criticized. His criticism parallels his criticism of *li*[ritual]. (Confucius' advocacy, remember, also links the two.) His basic argument is a social-cost argument. His condemnation of music is an instance of advocating frugality in expenditure. *Yue*[music] in ancient China typically involved a ritual musical extravaganza for the rulers—concerts complete with dancers and acrobats. They were (from an antiaristocratic point of view) lavish and profligate luxuries for the aristocracy. We need not suppose that he condemns peasants singing (or listening to their Walkmans) in the fields. (He might insist that they *are* in the fields working and not dancing around.) Of course, he does not advocate such pleasures either.

Finally, that *yue* is a term which Confucius' language most frequently paired with *li* may help explain Mozi's opposition to music. Confucius regarded *yue* as having a strong effect on our emotions and therefore on our behavioral attitudes. Ritual music cultivates traditional Confucian moral character. In addition, musical forms, like language, are conventional forms. Their performance and preservation delights in the same way any other practice of conventional forms delights. Finally, music and chanting may have been closely linked. Confucianism celebrated the intoxication of chanting the ancient books, engaging in ritual dance, and undergoing the sublime states of mind that accompany total involvement in these activities.

Placing the words of the ancient tradition in a chanting cadence or musical refrain, we enhance their power to capture human attention, mesmerize us, and shape human attitudes. (This is a view familiar enough to us with conservatives and communists alike blaming modern music for the degeneration of morals.) Unlike Plato, Confucius had no ideal of reason, so he favored using any craft to shape and polish human nature. Mozi, in this regard as well, comes closer to our rationalist roots in opposing music. Music is mainly only wasteful. Its link to *li*[ritual] marks it as potentially objectionable in content as well.

The Opposition to Aggressive War

Another straightforward application of Mozi's altruistic utilitarianism is his opposition to aggressive warfare. Here again, cost analysis is the core of the argument.

> Take the case of a country about to go to war. In winter one fears the cold, in summer the heat. This means that neither winter nor summer is the time for such action. But, if in the spring then the people miss their sowing and planting; if in the autumn, they miss reaping and harvesting. If they miss only one season, then the number of people who will die of cold and hunger is incalculable. Now let us calculate the army's equipment, the arrows, standards, tents, armor, shields, and sword hilts; the number of these which will break and perish and not come back is beyond calculation. So also with the spears, lances, swords, daggers, war chariots, and baggage wagons; the number of those which will get smashed and ruined and never come back is beyond calculation. So also with oxen and horses

who go out fat and come back lean, or die there and do not come back at all—a number beyond calculation. So also with people; the incalculable number who die, owing to cutting off the food supply or from lack of logistical support. Also consider the number who, living under bad conditions with irregular means and excesses of hunger and repletion, fall sick by the road and die. The army casualties also are incalculably large. Whole armies may perish.[77]

Criticism of Confucius

The final *fei* is the emphatic attack on the *Ru* school. Mozi's criticism of Confucians is so extreme that it tempts us to say he deserves the Confucian misinterpretation of his doctrines. (See the example above, page 98.) To grasp the significance of Mozi's view of Confucians, we must remind ourselves that Confucianism developed theoretically *after* Mozi. Our current view is of a Confucianism refined by two millennia of that development. Much of that development came in response to Mohist and Daoist challenges. Confucians in Mozi's time, with their chanting and ritual fanaticism, may have seemed fully as inane as Mozi makes them out to be.

Mozi's criticizes mainly the traditional ritual content of Confucian theory and the Confucian language and action. Confucians spoke in eloquent, polished ways about *ren* and *yi*. But their actions showed they did not act with proper discrimination in using moral terms. (See above, pages 127–28.) Mozi shared Confucian political assumptions and most of the optimistic estimate of human nature and the theory of cultivation that he elaborated. These doctrines, which divide China and Indo-European thought, are shared between even such bitter rivals in China. They represent deep and enduring distinctions between Chinese and Western thought.

In broad outline, even Mao Zedong and the revolutionary radicals in modern China share the Confucian and Mohist political and sociological postulates. Some challenge them at scattered times in history, but seldom successfully. Mostly, Chinese thinkers take the doctrine of a meritocracy and the essentially social nature of humanity for granted in nearly all their social-political philosophy. At the root of these postulates lies a characteristic view of intelligent human behavior and especially of linguistic behavior.

The telling aspect of Mozi's criticism, however, lies in its emotional fervor. His theory of measurement standards relies on operations that anyone can perform to determine the application of a term. He does not formulate an account of nor exemplify *cool, dispassionate, reason.* He does not conceive of an interpersonally valid deduction or proof as a method of determining if sentences as true and false. As a result, Zhuangzi draws a skeptical moral from Mozi's criticism and the ongoing dispute between the two schools. It illustrates the insoluble fruitlessness of dispute about distinctions. The Daoists view the exchange between these two bitter enemies as the inevitable outcome of starting from different conceptual perspectives. They start from different ways of making the basic distinctions like *ren* and *yi*. Their *dao*s follow those different ways of drawing distinctions. Each distinction alters the situation of choice for the next distinction. Following each *dao*, therefore is like finding one's way on different roads after having chosen the first branch. Neither has any neutral way to justify their basic standards. Confucians rely on tradition, Mohists on naturalistic, mechanistic measurements.

The division between Mohists and Confucians thus seems to Daoists to reduce to a matter of different ultimate standards. The Mohists have a *natural* taste for utility, the Confucians for ritual and music. Both assume that their taste is natural. Their sages project their *shi-fei* on heaven. Each assumes that its standard can be the basis for erecting, imposing, and making constant their preferred social guiding discourse, what each views as a constant *dao*. They assume that one can posit a constant *dao*.

Reason and Right in *The Mozi*

Commentators frequently notice suggestions of a belief in Western *reason* in Mozi.[78] That, I have suggested, is a misleading illusion. Mozi does not say that reason tells us that his doctrine is true. He does allege that no one can resist his words or alternately that he cannot understand how people can hear his *dao* and still criticize it. Or he remarks that even the stupidest of people will say thus and so when asked a question. He considers certain strategies of behavior *obviously* right or wrong.

However, Western thinkers typically buttress such assertions with a theory of a universal human faculty of reason. This faculty involves the ability to recognize and the disposition to accept good arguments. In Western philosophy, reason forms an integral part of our philosophy of mind. Mozi's account differs. His philosophy of mind involves only the universal preference for benefit and the potential to be programmed with a social *dao*. Utility becomes a universal standard for his way of making other distinctions and of pairing terms. We can make sense of his argument without presupposing the details of Western theory of rationality. We all simply recognize and prefer benefit to harm. The other element of universality comes from the accessibility of measurement standards. All can get similar interpretive results without needing to appeal to skilled performers as interpretive authorities.

We can continue to understand Mozi's theory of human social nature as we did Confucius'. He argues for a different *dao* and a different standard of practical interpretation. But his is not the Western folk theory that practical reason structures our psychology. What people say and do, what they accept and reject, results from their internalizing a *dao,* a system of behavior guiding language. Society adopts a certain language and thus affects behavior or performance. It makes the language constant using models, social practices, leadership, and punishment and reward. No early Chinese thinker cites a psychological faculty of reason as a motivating factor.

Education or socialization builds in dispositions and motivations. Cultivation, not individual reasoning, creates motivations. We need no distinction of rational versus irrational motivations. We do need a distinction between utilitarian and nonutilitarian ones and perhaps between presocial and socially engineered ones. The only part of the concept of rationality that Mozi's system inherently requires is the practical adjustment of means to ends and its simple, projectible, measurementlike standards.

Pragmatics versus Semantics

Mozi's theory of language, then, differs from Western (and Indian) rationalism. *Dao* is the central concept of Chinese philosophy. *Dao* does stand at the center of philosophical controversy. However, it is a mistake to assume that *dao* is therefore a *metaphysical* concept. In fact, the converse is true. That *dao* is the main term for understanding language shows that Chinese do not view the role of language as description of metaphysical reality. The issue in Chinese theory of language is not the relation of names and reality. The view of language is practical. The issue is the relation of names and the way we act—our *dao*. The purpose of language is to guide action—to show us *the way*. Language is not a tool of protoscientists but of practical, social engineers whose goal is to program us properly.

Our tendency to treat *dao* as metaphysical comes from our own tradition, in which the main issue in theory of language is semantics—meaning and truth. Semantic theory (truth) and metaphysics (reality) are intimately connected. Again the best way to deal with these assumptions is first to make them explicit. Indo-European rationalism was born in intimacy with the semantic concepts of truth and meaning, metaphysics, and epistemology. It dealt with a Euclidean model of a proof structure. That structure operated on a set of sentential judgments—opinions and beliefs. Western theory assumed that the role of mind was processing proofs *about the world* and practical proofs that resulted in rational voluntary action. It took the paradigm rational process to be deductive inference and argument.

We construct an argument out of sentences—premises and conclusions. In deductive inference the concluding sentence *inherits* truth from the sentences that form the premises. Reason leads to knowledge. Western philosophy's traditional concept of knowledge stressed deductive form, which was built on sentences. Following Plato, Western tradition has defined knowledge as true belief backed by good reasoning.

Western thinkers focused on truth and on meaning. The truth of a sentence is a function of its meaning, which in turn depends on the meaning of the words that make it up. In Socrates and Plato this focus becomes a preoccupation that stereotypes Western philosophy: the search for definitions. Definitions turn words into sentences that can function in proofs. Platonism treated definitions as the foundations of knowledge. The meaning of a term is the contribution it makes to a sentence's truth. Without knowing the term's meaning (and therefore the definitions) it is impossible to know any sentence to be true or false.

Fixing on truth and meaning is a hallmark of Western folk semantics. Western tradition focused on fact-stating discourse, which informed both Western epistemology and philosophical psychology. The entire Indo-European cultural area shares this semantic approach to the study of descriptive language. The Chinese philosophers approached language pragmatically and concentrated on language as guiding action—its prescriptive role.

The central issue in a semantic tradition is the relation of words to some stable objects in the allegedly unique real world. A pragmatic tradition concerns mainly the relation between words and society. It views language as a social practice with social effects. A semantic tradition deals in truth, a pragmatic one in appropriateness or acceptability of utterances.[79] A semantic tradition focuses on meaning, a pragmatic one on patterns of usage and the effects of usage on the users. I am arguing that the pragmatic rather than semantic focus dominated both Confucius and Mozi.

Euclidean Rationality and Duty Ethics

I want to argue that the Western concept of proof rationality—the Euclidean model of reason—explains some of the radical differences between Western and Chinese ethics. The depth of the difference has given rise to speculations that Chinese philosophers are not talking about moral theory at all. (See pages 81–83.) These speculations grow out of the centrality of the notion of rational agents and voluntary individual choices in Western ethical theory.

Philosophical orthodoxy divides moralities into two types: duty ethics and virtue ethics. My analysis suggests that Chinese ethics is a structure of a third type. I do not know its name. Forced to give it a name, I will call it *dao* ethics. Virtue ethics is *de* ethics. I have argued that in Chinese theories, *dao*^way is basic and *de*^virtuosity derivative. So Chinese ethics is not strictly virtue ethics. At the same time, *dao* is not a system of duties, obligations, or rules. It simply assigns *shi-fei* to objects or acts according to their behavioral significance. It identifies the values we are to track.

Assuming *daode* is a correct translation of *ethics,* then, Chinese ethics differs from either variety of Western ethics as duty ethics differs from *dao* ethics. The difference corresponds to the difference between voluntary rational action and skill. A *dao* guides a skill. For free, rational agents, duties guide voluntary rational actions.

Let me draw the contrast by elaborating the linked views of language and the mind behind the two different conceptions. We individuate actions roughly as we do sentences, but we name skills. We choose actions, but we cultivate and trigger skills. Skills consist of a structure of dispositions, not of actions *per se*. We can repeat actions but we perform skills. A skillful performance is more sensitive to the different triggering states of affairs.

The Euclidean Model. Western ethical philosophy was rocked in the cradle of Euclidean geometry, which still stands as our model of *thinking*. Geometry works with the notion of a proof, a sequence of statements, sentences, or equations (linguistic items with truth value). We divide the sentences into a set of premises and a conclusion. The premises are axioms or definitions. The conclusion is a hypothesis, theorem, or lemma. If we have constructed the proof properly—validly—then the conclusion inherits truth from the premises. It is true if they are true.

We took the content of the Euclidean system to be a powerful representational model of spatial reality. The proof-structure model gave the initial shape to the concept of reason and our view of the objectively real world. It then became the pillar of Western philosophy and eventually of science. *A* reason is a premise in a proof. *To* reason is to recite a proof in one's own mind. *Being* reasonable is thinking, saying, and doing what valid proofs justify our thinking, saying, and doing. Mostly the Euclidean model was a model of what to say about the world—a model for scientific theories. Axiomatic deductive structure remains the heart of a Western conception of reasoning.

The Euclidean model introduced the notion of the definition. Definitions played a central role in reasoning. Their status was like that of the axioms. They were to undergird the entire knowledge structure. From the *dao* perspective, a definition is superfluous since the central problem is how discourse guides behavior. A definition looks like just another bit of discourse to guide *language* behavior. It is a rule—a prescription—for the use of a word. The Chinese thinkers had no use for a technique that turns words into sentences. A definition simply pushes the problem of guidance back one level. Interpretation of *dao* does require a standard, but the standard, like the other elements of *dao* is a distinction. The infinite regress still beckons but its structure is not a string of definitions but a string of interpretive distinctions guiding the application of *shi-fei*[it–not it] to lower-level distinctions.

The Euclidean Model in Practical Reasoning—The Practical Syllogism. The Euclidean model of rationality informs the development of Western logic. The model, as I noted above, was initially a powerfully condensed way to represent all truths about the spatial world in a finite series of axioms and definitions and a rule-guided process of inference. Western ethical philosophy then borrowed the Euclidean model to explain and to justify actions. When we reason about what to do, we call it practical (as opposed to theoretical) reasoning.

Aristotle postulated a special proof form called the practical syllogism. The premises of a practical syllogism include prescriptive sentences. These may be either prescriptive expressions of desires or basic moral principles. This triggered the concept of ethical theories as a search for the highest moral axioms. Other premises state relevant facts—descriptive sentences or beliefs. Formally, the practical syllogism yields a prescription that follows from the moral principle in the factual circumstances.

For Aristotle to Kant, the form was required not only to justify, but also to explain action. The conclusion of a practical syllogism was action. In adapting the syllogism to explain action, we require a mind that has rational logical structure. The mind performs logical operations on premises. The Humean analysis said that premises may include mental translations of psychological states. The factual premises correspond to our beliefs and the prescriptive ones to our desires. Our desires, of course, may be moral. If we are rational, there is a valid argument *model* for our psychological *process* of guiding action.

This Greek psychology has become the common-sense psychology of the West—and of India. We find the Greek syllogism embedded in ancient Buddhist logic. Because it is so widespread, we tend, as I have argued, to assume that everyone implicitly follows this Greek psychological theory. We buttress this conviction with a powerfully persuasive theoretical feature of the theory. If it is true, then it must be immediately obvious that it is true. If we accept it, we can not imagine that any culture or civilization could possibly miss it.

The inevitability of this psychology comes partly from Aristotle and partly from later philosophy. Aristotle made the psychology prior to language. He said that we make mental images of things in the world and that words are the signs or symbols of these images. Modern (seventeenth- and eighteenth-century) European and British philosophy added the claims that we know these images or ideas immediately and indubitably. The ideas combine as words do into mental sentences or beliefs. About these as well, we must inevitably be perfectly aware. No one can fail to believe in beliefs!

Obviously, what goes for beliefs, goes for their counterpart, desires. These, also, must be sentencelike. Although we normally describe them as desires for objects, logically they must be desires "that I have some object." Otherwise, how could they function in practical syllogisms to explain action? In any case, the desire for an object has to consist of the mental representation of the object. How could anyone fail to see that?

This theory-proof conception is a powerful Western cultural invention. I do not mean to repudiate or minimize it. But it *is a cultural invention*—along with related cultural inventions such as beliefs, ideas, and propositional desires. Ancient Chinese psycholinguists did not build an *arguments-on-paper* model of thinking.[80] They constructed a quite different psycholinguistic theory that had different strengths and different weaknesses.

The main weakness of the Western belief-desire model for explaining human action lies in explaining skills. A computer can exemplify Euclidean rationality and solve mathematical and logical problems. So far no one has managed to make a computer that can walk upstairs on two feet or produce reliably grammatical English. The very idea of a practical syllogism for skills seems almost deliberately perverse. I cannot make my putting more consistent by coming to believe and desire what Jack Nicklaus believes and desires.

Where translators use *belief* in translating Chinese, there might be several flexible grammatical structures in the text. They all focus attention on dispositions, skills, or abilities, for example, the ability to use words or make distinctions. They do not suggest the familiar subjectivist view of an inner representation of a sentencelike content—a thought or belief. The classical Chinese grammatical structure typically uses dispositional verbs constructed from ordinary predicates (verbs, adjectives, and common nouns). For example, where we would say that Ronnie believes the table is blue, classical Chinese says Ronnie *blues* the table or $yi^{\text{with regard to}}$ the table, $wei^{\text{deems:makes}}$ it blue. That is, Ronnie is likely to apply the term *blue* to the table. He is both disposed to discriminate between blue and green in such and such a way and to use the term *blue* of things on the right side of the dividing line.

This word skill or disposition figures in explaining action or performance. The way Ronnie draws the line between colors affects how he follows orders, instructions, requests, rules, etc. His tendencies to discriminate determine the way he acts, his names make up his *dao*.

Thus we must be careful in talking of both *knowledge* and *belief* in the Chinese tradition. We may impose a familiar modern Western conceptual scheme in the face of evidence that Chinese thinkers had a different language for discussing the relations of mind, language and the world. The closest Chinese counterpart of zhi^{know} is *know-how*. The closest counterpart of *belief* is this doctrine of a disposition to discriminate between types and use ordinary terms. We speak of this disposition approvingly (as know-how) when we *endorse* the discrimination. *We affirm* the person's competence, acuity, judgment, and skill. Some of us *know to* discriminate between two colors of sunsets. But sometimes one of us looking at the same sunset will *red* it and the other will *gray* it. Some of us *know to* match certain colors in our wardrobe; others never master that *refinement*.

Belief and knowledge, as they function in Western philosophy, apply more naturally to sentences than to words. What we can either believe or know are sentence-like objects (propositions, complete thoughts, beliefs, statements, etc.). The English word *know* has nonpropositional uses that play almost no role in traditional Western epistemology. Belief is not applicable when we consider these other uses of *know*. For example, I can know the capital of New Zealand but cannot appropriately say that I *believe* the capital of New Zealand. I can know how to do a seat-drop on a trampoline, but we do not talk about anything resembling believing how to do it.

In talking of sentences, we usually concern ourselves with knowledge-that. In talking of words, we are more likely to use the concept of know-how or know-of than of propositional knowledge. We know that word; we know how to use or pronounce it.[81] These nonpropositional uses allow the use of *know* in translations of Chinese. Once we have the word *know* in our translations, we play on the ambiguity of the English word *know* and attribute the theory of propositional knowledge and belief to Chinese philosophers. The belief-knowledge contrast, however, does not figure in Chinese theories of knowledge.

In the place of definitions and meanings, Chinese theorists focus on an assimilated capacity to make a *bian*[discrimination]. Since disagreement about how to make distinctions is the core explanation of disagreement among schools, we can translate *bian* as *argument*. Then confusing two senses of argument, translators assume it therefore means proof rather than quarrel.[82] And they conclude the school of names was dealing with logic! Our assuming an *obvious* psychology combined with assuming that English words are univocal makes for an interpretive quicksand that keeps translators from explaining the real structure of Chinese theories.

Mozi's Theory of Language

The interesting differences in Mozi's utilitarianism, then, arise from his embedding it in a different implicit theory of language and theory of mind. We have seen that it shares with utilitarianism in the West the characteristic of being antitraditional in tone. It tends toward universalism as opposed to a morality of special relations. It is a product of a reflective doubt of tradition. It is a clearly philosophical bid at making the moral point of view more coherent and *constant* than the prephilosophical traditionalist morality. It prides itself on giving clear and consistent answers where the conventional morality gives ambiguous guidance or no guidance. It would still be a mistake to think that Mozi's utilitarianism fits into the same conceptual space that utilitarianism occupies in Western rationalistic thought. It does not.

The Three Standards of Language

The ruling interpretation has missed Mozi's importance in Chinese philosophy. His similarity to Western thinkers impressed the interpreters too much. They have missed the basic, radical difference. This makes him look like a brief irrelevant aberration in the essentially Confucian tradition. In fact, as I have been arguing, he shapes the philosophical tradition more than Confucius does. His word focus fixes the framework of Chinese philosophy. It is the key to understanding most of the ethical disputes of the Classical period. We can understand how language and ethics interact by looking at Mozi's ethically motivated proposals for language reform.

In *Understanding Spirits* and *Against Fate,* Mozi uses his famous *three tests of language* to propose *making* certain ways of speaking *constant.* This theory forcefully illustrates the difference between the Western truth-based scheme and the Chinese pragmatic one. Translators have not appreciated Mozi's point. They have persisted in projecting sentential and truth-based considerations on him and have treated his doctrine as a test of the truth of theories. A popular translation that illustrates this danger is the following:

> Therefore a theory must be judged by three tests. What are these three tests of a theory? Its origin, its validity, and its applicability. How do we judge its origin? We judge it by comparing the theory with the deeds of the sage kings of antiquity. How do we judge its validity? We judge it by comparing the theory with the evidence of the eyes and ears of the people. And how do we judge its applicability? We judge it by observing whether, when the theory is put into practice in the administration, it brings benefit to the state and the people. This is what is meant by the three tests of a theory.[83]

The treatment rings familiar because we think about modern American pragmatists and their pragmatic definition of truth. Mozi appears to make a parallel point. However, Western pragmatists were facing a two-thousand-year-old truth-focused tradition. They had a well-entrenched notion of scientific *truth* to kick around, to define, and to explain. Questions of knowledge and belief virtually defined the philosophical training of American pragmatists. Such questions, I have argued, were never even formulated in China. Since none of these theoretical concerns are explicit in Mozi's language, we have no reason to attribute such a concern to him.[84] He gives a pragmatic standard for *something.* Since we are most familiar with pragmatic arguments for truth, translators assume that *truth* must be the something.

Similarly, as soon as we identify his interest as concerning spirits, we want to understand Mozi as saying something familiar about spirits: that we should believe in them. The absence of explicit belief language, again, does not bother translators because they regard the theory of beliefs and other mental objects to be obvious and inescapable. We can therefore assume that this mentalistic psychology of language lies in the background of Mozi's argument. He must be saying that belief in spirits has pragmatically beneficial effects.

Now we all agree that when we interpret him this way, we make his doctrine less plausible. So translators inevitably throw in critical, tongue-clucking remarks about Mozi's naïveté. In fairness, then, we had best take a closer and more careful look at the structure of Mozi's language and his translation to see if it requires attributing such a naive mistake to him. I will present a summary account of my interpretation first by focusing on the actual words used in formulating the doctrine and then I will argue for it on a more general level.

Two words in the above translation twist the issue to make it seem to be truth: *theories* and *tests*. Mozi talks of three *fa*[standards] or three *biao*[gnomen]. Graham identifies the latter as a reference to a system for marking and measuring where the sun rises or sets. *Fa* and *biao* are standards of accuracy, not definitions or tests of truth of sentences. And what they are standards of is *yan*[words:language].[85] Mozi advocates objective reference points or standards for the use of *yan*.

The first standard is a historical criterion of appropriate usage. We normally try to use words as our teachers did. They, in turn, tried to follow the model of their teachers. One social standard of language appropriateness traces conformity back to the coiners of the terms. We conform to past usage in making a discrimination—in projecting the term to new uses. Mozi also wants us to conform to past usage in linking words. That is part of getting the distinction right. We should, for example, follow the sage-king language coiners and existing literature in putting *exists* before *spirits*.

It is very tempting to treat the second standard, the way ordinary people report with their eyes and ears, as an incipient *scientific* test of truth. The reference to eyes and ears strikes a familiar cord and suggests empirical confirmation of scientific theories. Mozi, however, never uses the standard as an empiricist would. He does not discuss inferences from evidence of the senses to the truth of some theoretical sentence. In fact, he does not use the notion of inference or sense data at all. If this is empiricism, it is empiricism without the philosophical, subjectivist notion of *experience*. It coheres better with the context if we treat it as a social standard of appropriate usage. We should use language as ordinary people do in reporting what they see and hear.[86]

This is not *merely* a social standard, however. We should indeed use language in ways that others do. We should conform not merely through time, but across the community, including the ordinary people. And Mozi's use of the standard (in talking about ghosts, for example) is clearly of this testimonial variety. But that does not, I think, capture all the force of the second standard. It reminds us of a focus that we have noted in all of Mozi's talk of standards. The standards must not merely be shared, but, like utility, and like measurement standards in general, they must be easily accessible. People must be able to apply them reliably simply by the use of their eyes and ears. The *fa*[standards] should be objective and easily projectable and not rely on vague or controversial intuitions. The standards of correct use must be available to people who use their eyes and ears. They should not be the property of an elite class of chanting priests.

The *eyes-and-ears* test, then, is a test of word application. We should not use words or make distinctions that the people do not or cannot make using their eyes and their ears. We understand the test as a test of the social *applicability* and hence the usefulness of terms and distinctions. If people cannot apply the terms on the evidence of their eyes and ears, then the terms are too abstruse for beneficial general use.

The third test further confirms the hypothesis that Mozi's linguistic concerns are pragmatic rather than semantic. We have already touched on what is wrong with making Mozi sound like a modern pragmatist—proposing, that is, a pragmatic test of truth. Ancient Chinese philosophy so far has no project involving a truthlike concept. So there would be no reason to propose a reductive translation of a theory no one had yet advanced. Neither Mozi nor the Confucians address the abstract question of how language corresponds to the world. They do not wonder about the semantic property of sentences. This standard flowers naturally out of Mozi's language utilitarianism. We must use language in ways that yield benefit. We apply the standards so we can *bian*^{discriminate} in utilitarian ways.

If we mistakenly attribute propositional concepts to Mozi here, it will lead us to ask whether Mozi *really* believed in spirits. Perhaps he merely found the belief useful. The text as written cannot easily settle such a question. His moral position is so thoroughly social that the question of an individual perspective on these issues is not even addressed. He bases his proof on language and words rather than on rules, theories, or beliefs. As we argued, he is advocating that we rectify social names to gain general well-being. He proposes, as a means to this, that society adopt the practice of saying *you*^{have} of spirits instead of *wu*^{lack}.

He argues that the proposal is both useful and appropriate. It meets the standards of community agreement and historical precedent. The sage-kings of antiquity spoke that way and acted on that *dao* of appropriate language. Ordinary people speak of the things they see and hear in that way. That way of talking has useful effects. Past writers have filled the literature with morality-inducing stories that speak of spirits. If we do not speak appropriately, we would waste these good, traditional stories. Putting *you*^{have} before *gui*^{ghosts} and *shen*^{spiritual energy} motivates people to appropriate behavior; therefore we should *constant* this linguistic usage.

Mozi does not have a notion of his own belief. He concerns himself with the much more voluntarist and social issue of how we ought to speak of these things. He assumes that the way we speak of them will affect how we act. So we ought to speak of them thus and so.

The Social Character of Language

Dictionaries of Chinese use both *language* and *words* in translating the character *yan*. Like *mu*, which we can translate as either *tree* or *wood*, *yan*^{words:language} has the summing property of mass nouns. The most basic unit of *yan* is the word and any sum of *yan* is *yan*. We can understand most of what Chinese philosophers said about language as being about the word-unit of language. Riveting attention on the character or word underlines the pragmatic character of Chinese theories of language. Words are social in ways that sentences are not.

Notice how we criticize someone's use of words. We can say that words are inappropriate or improper in three ways. First we may say that the person has used a word which the community does not recognize as a word or has used it in an inappropriate situation. For example someone points to a writing tablet and says "Hand me the phill." Or someone stands in a room with the door closed and says "Close the door." Although neither imperative sentence is *false*, they both fail to conform to community standards for the appropriate use of language. Conformity to some normative standards seems necessary even to claim to have a language.[87] From the Chinese perspective, if there is no communal regularity, we would lose the defining function of language (regulating and coordinating behavior). You would have simply have a group of noise makers.

Secondly, we can complain that the use of the word—even though the community shares it—does not conform to past usage. We recognize this criticism from our own traditionally oriented English teachers and media gurus of language who deplore the debased state of modern popular usage. This claim is the key element of a Confucian theory of language. It is the emblem of historicism, the historicist's way of asserting the autonomy and objectivity needed to criticize the *actual language practice* of the community. This privileged critical status is only open to historical *scholars*.[88] We deplore the decline from a golden age of clear and beautiful language. Deviation from past language use is a sign of vulgarity.

The third way that we can criticize the use of a word is the reformer's way. It is pragmatic in the popular sense as well as in the linguistic-theory sense. A word, used in a particular way, marks a particular distinction. Making that distinction can be useful or not. Discriminating in different ways can help us to achieve some goal and hinder us from others. Some tastes and ways of assigning value are more expensive than others. Some distinctions are worthless.

Sentences, on the other hand, are less obviously social. Suppose someone told you that the sentence you had just written was not one used by others in the community (though the words were)? You might feel justifiably proud of your originality rather than feel criticized. You would feel the same if someone tried to criticize your sentences as different from those used by the past masters. Traditionalism in sentence usage is appropriate mainly in religious systems. In sentences, but not words, we more routinely value individualism and autonomy. The possibility of valuing creativity in sentences rests on valuing conformity in word use and meaning. We value saying new and original things *as long as* they are meaningful.

If someone criticizes your sentences using a pragmatic standard, you have an obvious defense. Whether or not your utterances are useful to society, they may be true. Sometimes the truth hurts. Our Greek tradition fostered valuing truth (knowledge) *for its own sake*. Along with individualism and autonomy, a focus on sentences underwrites a semantically defined notion of integrity: truth at all costs.

Notice that the three standards Mozi enunciates make sense as standards for the use of terms. If he is talking about whatever the standards are standards of, then he is talking about appropriateness, not truth. These standards are implausible on their face as applied to sentences, theories, or beliefs. As tests of truth, the three standards fail miserably. As tests of word use, of what distinctions to adopt, they are all interesting and plausible proposals. The historical theory is not the weakest, but arguably the strongest of the tests. A plausible account of our use of terms is that we intend to mark the same distinction marked by those who taught us the term. We assume that this chain of emulation of distinction making and term use goes back to the original coiner, for Mozi, the ancient sage-kings. The Chinese typically credit their culture heroes with the invention of language—both of terms and of the distinctions they mark. A proposal that we continue to mark the same distinctions by those terms is not naive.

Operational Test of Knowledge of Words and Distinctions

That Mozi used a pragmatic conception of term meaning rather than of sentence truth is evident in the following passage. It also illustrates how the concept of know-how applies to language:

Now a blind man says, "What shines with brilliance is white." And "What is dark is black." Even those whose eyes are clear would have no reason to change what he said. Now put black and white together and ask the blind man to pick— he does not know how. So my reason for saying the blind man does not know black-white is not with regard to his naming but with regard to his choosing. (83/ 47/5–6)

This is similar to the claim that while the blind man deploys as others do the names *black-white* he cannot distinguish among the objects. Thus, how can we say he has the distinction? (31/19/5)

The Mozi constantly worries about the ability to make discriminations in the real world. Do people have command of important distinctions such as black-white, sweet-bitter, good-bad? If he had used Western folk theory for talking about mind and language, however, we would expect him to approach this question of word use rather differently. He would state his worry about whether the blind person knew the *meaning of black and white* by asking if he had an *idea* of black-white. He would then presumably incline to say that the (congenitally) blind person did *not* know the meaning of the terms because he had no inner mental picture.

Notoriously, we can not define colors. We suppose it obvious that knowing the meaning requires having some inner, phenomenal *feel* of black and white. Western folk theory gives a less satisfactory account of language use than does Mozi's approach. Blind people can, as he points out, use color words and use them perfectly competently as far as their linguistic mastery is concerned. They may become as fluent as anyone. It is puzzling to say that a blind person does not know the meaning of terms when his use, from a linguistic point of view, is the same as mine. His limitations seem to have nothing to do with his ability to learn language.

From a Chinese point of view, the role of language is to guide behavior. Given Mozi's more behavioral and objective view of mind, he accepts the obvious. A blind man can define and use *black* and *white* exactly as well as one who sees. He has part of the know-how associated with names. The blind man lacks another part of that know how: the ability to distinguish black and white objects in response to instructions using the names. He lacks the ability to guide his conduct, make discriminatory adjustments based on instruction using *black-white*. That is all that Mozi talks about and, arguably, that is all that is important.

The Unity of Mozi and Confucius

Mozi gave more detailed shape to the implicit Confucian theory of language found in *The Analects*. Both schools agree that culture heroes created language. The sages showed their acuity in the guiding distinctions they bequeathed to us for ordering society. We can achieve order through our use of language if we continue to mark the same distinctions. The importance of precedent flows from this focus on using words to guide action. Social agreement and historical continuity are both inherently useful in this project since guidance is both social and accumulated in literature. Rectifying names, agreement with the superior, and the test of antiquity all grow out of the same background theory. We must sustain the system of distinctions that informs our existing guiding discourse. The idea of historical rectification of names underlies the Mohist system as much as it does the Confucian. The key difference is that Mozi regards it as *one* standard of appropriate use among three. It is a consideration in determining appropriate usage, but does not, by itself, justify a pattern of use. It affirms the conservative principle I noticed above. We want to find a way to reform *dao* that does not waste *dao*. Our reform must maximize the benefit to be drawn from traditional *dao* even as we reform it.

An important reason for studying Mozi is to identify these shared presuppositions about mind and language. Since he opposes Confucianism so vehemently and has a clear affinity to classically important Western philosophical positions, those points of agreement take on special importance. They recommend themselves as plausible candidates for basic assumptions of the period and for the most meaningful contrast with Western philosophy.

Indeed we have found a sizeable cluster of such basic contrasts:

1. Humans exist in natural social hierarchies. They incline to adopt and act on some conception of social or moral good: some *dao*.

2. Humans learn essentially by imitating accepted models who are above them in the hierarchy. The salient case of such learning is learning to use a shared system of names: a language.

3. Both the instinct to master names and the instinct to use them in guiding one's action and coordinating social activities are natural. The most powerful way to direct human behavior is by modeling a pattern of language use. Society naturally uses rectifying names or agreement with the superior.

4. Learning names involves acquiring the disposition to differentiate among objects. The test of successful learning is that we differentiate in the same way others in the community do (or the way others in the past have done). This agreement is essential for the adequate functioning of language. That, in turn, is essential for the adequate functioning of society.

5. We can change the distinctions a community marks by names by having the leaders exemplify a different pattern of usage. We determine language usage by authority, custom, and social habit.

6. Negatively, Mozi and the Confucians *agree* in talking of language solely in terms of *words* or *names*. They do not theorize about sentences, propositions, beliefs, thoughts, or ideas. They do not talk of *meaning* apart from the ability to use words and guide action. They do not talk about subjectivist notions so familiar in Western philosophy. There is no hint of a theory of inner representations or images or abstract, intellectual concepts as essential elements in their account of language or of human mental functioning.[89]

The shared assumptions interest us especially since they differ so markedly from the assumptions of both the Indian and European philosophical traditions. Traditional commentaries have not totally ignored these features of Chinese theory of language, but they have downplayed them instead of developing them. A common sinologist's reaction to these features of the classical view of language and behavior is embarrassment. The standard view tends to treat the Chinese view of language and its relation to human behavior as a belief in word magic. They are embarrassed for Chinese philosophy because they accept Western folk theory of language and assume that the theory of ideas and belief-desire explanations of voluntary free moral action are self-evident. So they charitably pass over what they take to be *superstition* in the Chinese theory without exploring how thoroughly it informs the entire philosophical approach of classical China.

Language, on the Indo-European view, is an inert epiphenomenon. Ideas are what are really important. We require ideas to learn language, but not vice versa. If we accept this Western picture, then we will find it charitable to excuse Chinese theories as primitive beliefs in word magic or excessive voluntarism that stress too much the role of language in shaping personality and behavior. From the Western folk-theory perspective, social conventions in general come into the account of human functioning at a much later stage. They constitute relatively mild (and slightly objectionable) intrusions into natural human functioning.

The mind-body distinction that undergirds the subjectivist Western view of human nature and the structure required to make sense of it has been a persistent problem for Western philosophy. We have never successfully explicated the claim that humans can reliably extract the same set of concepts from reality. The view that humans are psychological egoists requires a widely known verbal sleight-of-hand. The eighteenth-century philosophers (especially Butler) analyzed and permanently punctured the doctrine of psychological egoism. The attempt to explain human action by reference to belief and desire inevitably sneaks in dispositions or skills. The Indo-European conceptual scheme, I submit, is the one committed to magic!

II

THE ANTILANGUAGE
PERIOD

5

Mencius: The Establishment Strikes Back

Indeed, when one reads the book of Mencius one has the impression of a man securely embedded in the Confucian tradition who, while he is thoroughly alert to the challenges from without and thoroughly immersed in the intellectual discourse of his time, remains superbly unshaken in his faith.

Benjamin Schwartz[1]

. . . It is difficult to believe that a thinker of Mencius' calibre and reputation could have indulged consistently in what appears to be pointless argument or that his opponents were always effectively silenced by *non-sequiturs*. The fault, we suspect must lie with us. We must have somehow failed to understand these arguments.

D. C. Lau[2]

Background: The Double Challenge to Confucianism

Mencius was an aristocrat from the *Ru* culture center who was born about one hundred years after Confucius died. He shares with Confucius the distinction of having zi^{master} incorporated in the latinization of his name (Confucius' name comes from Kongfu-zi; Mencius' from Meng-zi).[3] He was arguably a greater influence on Confucianism than was Confucius himself. Mencius turned the attention of Confucianism to moral psychology—the theory of human nature. Confucius' disciples had complained they "could not hear" the master's theory of human nature. That shift in focus and Mencius' innatism came to define Confucianism.

We postulated that two warring interpretive strands of Confucianism motivated the composition of *The Analects*. I argued that we most plausibly identify Confucius with the more traditionalist wing of Confucianism. Mencius is the main representative and theorist of the innatist interpretation. His motivation, however, was more complex. In Mencius' hands the doctrine had to deal with more than the problem of interpretation of li^{ritual}. It had to deal with the Mozi's moral-reform challenge to the traditional content of the Confucian *dao* as well. Innatism provides a rhetorically easy defense against any moral reform, Innatism became the orthodoxy for Neo-

153

Confucianism. Confucian interpreters, from the Song and Ming dynasties up to modern American *Third Wave* Confucians, all view Confucius through Mencius' prism.

Accordingly, in the orthodox theory, Mencius' reputation is stellar. He had, however, had a less impressive reputation among his contemporary philosophers.[4] Even other Confucian thinkers pilloried his naive, innatist position. Mencius actually had more success with the rulers—and that was typically little more than a polite hearing. We should, therefore, be suspicious of orthodoxy's reverence for Mencius. It should not be taken as evidence that there is more to Mencius than meets the eye.

What meets the eye is what Waley said in a more candid period in sinology: "As a controversialist [Mencius] is nugatory."[5] The dynamics of Confucian interpretation are clearly in evidence here. They have toiled as assiduously to augment Mencius as they have to diminish Mozi. Mencius can only appear the giant they desire if his main interlocutors are reduced to dwarfs. In both projects the ruling view struggles against the obvious. We were easily able to list a string of philosophically interesting arguments and positions from Mozi. We can equally easily provide a list for Mencius—but it would be a string of defensive, irrelevant, sophistical argumentative dodges. His argumentative style is full of embarrassingly loose analogies, non-sequiturs and apparently deliberate confusions and distortions. He did, however, have an aristocratic writing style!

The stereotype that Chinese philosophy depends on intuition more than on reason stems almost totally from Mencius. We often compare his one doctrine, innatism, with that of Plato. Plato motivated his doctrine with a challenging theory of meaning. The main motivation for Mencius was that it enabled him to opt out of the demand to debate about moral reform. It gave him an apparent basis from which to criticize Mozi without having to meet Mozi's challenge that Confucians justify the traditional status quo.

Paradoxically, Mencius' philosophical ineptitude may be the secret to his eventual cultural dominance. In a scholastic tradition, nothing is more useful and inviting than a vaguely incoherent text. Mencius' elusive mystification is a positive plus. A massive body of Confucian commentary, analysis, and interpretation tries to tease sense out of Mencius' obscure obfuscations. As Lau notes, when we find it inane, our faith that he deserves his reputation convinces us that we must reinterpret it. Scholasticism thrives on such challenges.

Mozi had defined the terms of the philosophical debate with Confucianism. The key term was *bian*[distinction]. The *Ru-Mo*[Confucian-Mohist] dispute is about which *bian* to use in social programming. To engage in philosophical dispute was to argue about what distinctions to adopt. Mencius acknowledges that defending Confucianism forces him to *bian* along with his opponents. Mencius insists that, like the Roman virgins, he did not enjoy it. He complains that he does it only because "the language of Yang Zhu and Mozi fills the empire."[6] If we cannot stop the guiding discourse of Yang and Mo, we cannot spread the discourse of Confucius. If heretical phrases and sayings get into the *xin*[heart-mind] it will be damaging to social affairs and correct administration.

Mozi's influence shapes far more of Mencius' theory than the ruling interpretation ever allows. Mozi pulls Mencius out of his dogmatic ritual trance and theoretical passivity. Mencius abandons the absorbing seclusion of purist role playing, waiting for heaven to direct the concert, and joins the philosophical debate about what *dao* we should follow. Even though this theory justified doctrinal status-quo passivity, he does advance a theory.

But Mencius' training was in ritual absorption, not philosophical theory and argument. He joins the debate because he agrees that *yan*[language] *can* affect behavior—and he thinks that it holds a danger. Inevitably, however, he borrows from the language of his enemies, Yang and Mo. Mencius puts *ren*[benevolence], *yi*[morality], and *shi-fei*[this–not this] in his "four seed" theory alongside *li*[ritual], which slips down to third position and plays a peripheral role in the theory. Mencius' theory of *ren* is universalist and implicitly utilitarian. (Benevolence is the virtue counterpart of utilitarian duty.)

Mozi set the terms, but Mencius' Confucian training in reciting poetry in court did not prepare him to adopt Mozi's argumentative essay style. He settled for a hybrid adaptation of something closer to *The Analects*. The dialogue fragments are conspicuously longer. Mencius makes more sustained speeches than Confucius seemed to. His arguments and theories in those speeches almost make us miss the cryptic aphorisms.

Tradition credits Mencius with compiling his book himself with the help of a disciple.[7] Although Mencius had disciples and students, his book may be the only one that consists mainly of the original teachings of a single person.[8] Since no textual school coalesced around his text, no one annotated and augmented his book.

The terms of the debate were not favorable to Confucianism. Once Mozi had introduced the argument that a social *dao* could not rest on purely traditional standards, early Confucianism was on the defensive. Mencius' rhetorical strategy was to use one of his enemies against the other. The language of Yang Zhu provided Mencius with a way to sidestep the Mohist challenge. However, he had to modify the content that came with the Yangist strategy. He adapted Yang's version of divine-command morality and created an innate, naturalistic defense of Confucianism. This strategy carried Yang's antilanguage implications which account for Mencius' preference for silence and his apologetic attitude for participating in *bian*[distinction-dispute].

We have discussed the language of Mozi extensively. We should now look briefly at how Yang Zhu's distinguished between *shi*[this] and *fei*[not this]. Unfortunately, we do not have direct access to Yang's own language. We know of Yang Zhu's positions primarily from reports in other sources, principally *The Mencius* and the *Lu-shi Chun-qiu*.

The tradition classifies Yang Zhu as an early Daoist.[9] The accepted view, following the interpretation in *The Mencius,* is that Yang Zhu's ethical philosophy is egoistic. In the style of philosophical debate, this amounts to saying he takes *wo*[I:me] as the *constant* term. In Mencius presentation, Yang Zhu *wei*[do:deem] *wo*[I:me]. His actions and deemings are governed by the term *wo*[I:me]. An alternate reading of *wei*[do:deem] is *wei*[for the sake of] (different tone in Mandarin dialect). Yang Zhu, in other words, advocates using the self-other distinction to guide action with self as the dominant, constant term. Mencius cites as Yang's guiding formula ". . . not pluck one single body hair for the benefit of the empire."[10]

Graham, however, has argued that Yang Zhu's philosophy is more altruistic than Mencius' account allows.[11] He reads Yang's statement as "one should not sacrifice one hair *in exchange for* the benefit *of getting* the empire to govern." The *Daode Jing* (ch. 52) traces this Yangist line of argument. Arguably, like Confucius,

Yang Zhu justified rejecting political involvement on moral grounds. The world, he felt, would be better off if everyone refused the empire. We should refuse, that is, to take positions of power and to govern. Graham treats Yang Zhu as an altruistic anarchist, not as a callous egoist.

I will not try to resolve this interpretive issue. Since we have only second-hand reports, our interest in Yang-Zhu really lies mainly in what *Mencius took him to be saying*. Mencius' theory is a response to *his perception of* Yang Zhu's doctrine. He borrows from the view as he understood it.[12]

On either account, Yang Zhu, in rejecting all traditional social values and social-political activity, radically departs from both Confucianism and Mohism. He *fei*s the value of hierarchy, of modeling, of conformity and all the social benefits they provide. What justification could he offer for such a radical way of *bian*ing *shi* and *fei?*

Graham reconstructs Yang's justification largely from the *Lu-shi Chun-qiu* account. It starts from an evaluative basis that Yang shares with Confucian and Mozi—*tian*[nature]. Confucius and Mozi agree that nature's *ming*[command] or *zhi*[will] should guide our *dao* of behavior. They disagree about which *dao* heaven would choose. Yang Zhu's contribution to the debate is to suggest a new way to decipher heaven's choices. He spells out a theory of *ming*[name-mandate] that links it to the length of life. Whatever is *ming* is heaven's will. His theory ties *ming* to *sheng*[life]. The modern compound *sheng-ming*[life] refers to the duration of one's life.

Like other theorists, his *tian*[nature] is less a person than a constancy that is prior to our deliberation about what *dao* we should follow. It sets the conditions, one of which is when we will die.[13] The length of one's life was one of the things commanded or fated by nature. But this was not fate in the sense of events causation. Nature *names* the time of your death at birth by giving you a constitution that has a fixed potential.

Popular Chinese *medical* theory treated life and death as signaled by the presence or absence of *qi*[breath:ether]. *Qi* will later emerge as the *basic-stuff* concept in Chinese metaphysics. But *qi*[breath] is not inert matter. On the contrary, like breath, it is the animating fluid. The traditional test for death in China was to hold a mirror in front of your face. If *qi*[breath] frosted it, you were still alive, you still had *qi*. When you have breath you are alive, when you run out of it you are dead!

So we can represent Yang Zhu's view by analogy. The time of your natural life is fixed by the quantum of *qi*[life force] that nature gives you at birth. The more you have the longer you live. Heaven did not purposely intervene to kill you at the appointed time. *Qi*, once instilled, governed the time of your *natural* death. This gives the moral bite of Yang Zhu's theory. Your actual death is not fated in the sense that it is inevitable. It is named in the sense that you cannot exceed it—but you can fall short.

If some violent physical trauma released your *qi*, you might die before your mandated time, thus disobeying heaven! Absent frequent auto accidents, one met premature, violent death most noticeably in ancient China by getting involved in politics. One wrong word or disastrous piece of advice, getting in with the wrong faction, or just being an innocent victim of someone else's intrigue and power schemes could lead to *zhan*—execution. *Zhan*, often translated as beheading, was cutting the person in two, around the heart and lungs, thus releasing the remaining *qi*. You have thus lost your *qi* and disobeyed heaven in the bargain!

Heaven, Yang Zhu argued, thus implicitly directs us to withdraw from active politics. Our duty to *tian*^{nature-heaven} is to preserve our *qi* and die when nature has intended us to.[14] Egoism is a moral duty.

We do not know much more about Yang Zhu. He was not a Daoist in the important sense that *dao* is not a central theoretical term in his scheme. His egoism seems to counsel opting out of the social task of constructing and instilling *dao*. We can identify Daoist elements in his thought, especially his antisocial and anticonventional attitudes. But two other elements are important to Mencius. One is the fatalistic resignation that counsels acceptance of the limits of the status quo. The other is reading the prescriptive authority of *tian*^{nature} into our inborn endowment. Mencius learns from Yang Zhu the internalist, original constitution strategy of reading *tian*^{nature's} moral guidance. These ideas carry the seeds of the antilanguage perspective in their wake.

Mencius' Philosophical Calling

We noted earlier a familiar analogy that tempts us: Mencius plays the Plato to Confucius' Socrates. The parallel is apt in several ways. In both cases the disciple is so influential that we have a hard time distinguishing between the original figure and the image the follower passed on to us. The parallel is also apt in that both Plato and Mencius synthesized an earlier and rather more sketchy, vague philosophical *attitude*. They developed an incipient tendency into a closed idealist and innatist system. Confucius' doctrines are chaotic and quite lacking in elaborative argument. This invites the natural tendency to interpret him along the lines of his first systematically inclined defender and elaborator.[15]

The parallel breaks down in one important respect, however. Plato lived, walked, ate, and talked with Socrates. Mencius was at least a second-generation disciple of Confucius, living nearly a hundred years after the person he worshipped as a sage. So we can acknowledge the enormous influence of his version of Confucianism and we can hardly avoid it in our own efforts to reconstruct Confucius. But the warrant for any claims that Mencius had special insight into Confucius resembles that of someone today writing the first commentary on Kant.

Facing now a double challenge to engage in philosophical discourse, Mencius tried to formulate and defend Confucianism in the then-current terms of philosophical debate. Mencius' defense eventually did more to shape historical Confucianism than Confucius did. However, I shall argue that in doing so, Mencius fundamentally changed the nature of the Confucian *dao* from literature to genetics.[16] I do agree that Mencius' system is a theoretical development of the *intuitive wing* of Confucianism. Xun-zi represents the parallel development of the traditional wing. Thus, we could, in fairness, regard Mencius as elaborating at least one-half of the doctrine of Confucius.

Time had passed, and political and philosophical developments radically separate Confucius and Mencius. Confucius wanted to save the weakening Zhou dynasty. Mencius accepts its obvious collapse. Mencius deplores what has taken its place but deals with what comes next.

Machiavellianism typified the interim political system. States jockeyed for political and military advantage and, within shifting temporary alliances, they vied with each other for dominance. In large loose alliances, a leader would emerge. This was the *ba-wang*, variously translated as tyrant, overlord, paramount prince. The short-range aspiration of most of the kings with whom Mencius spoke was to enrich their states, have a strong army, and become a paramount prince. They used the stock strategies of deception, alliances of convenience—strike while iron is hot, divide and conquer, and so forth. Mencius deplored the gusto with which they played at their game of diplomacy.

The intellectual milieu had changed as well. Intellectuals in Mencius' time were in both greater supply and greater demand. They did not have to seek regular bureaucratic appointments as Confucius' disciples might have done. Competition for expertise had become so vigorous that the various warring states invited thinkers to come and "think under their gate." This system produced much greater variety in thought and forced Confucianism into a discourse with alternate philosophical systems. Mencius gained from his exposure to different philosophies, although he seems loath to admit it. Still, the authoritarian context of philosophical debate reinforced his argumentative inclination. He relied heavily on persuasive storytelling and the predominantly figurative analogy that might move rulers to action. His writings recall more conversations trying to persuade rulers of the wisdom of his policies than debates with other philosophers. What debates there are, as his disciples recorded them, are notoriously enigmatic and obscure; they require inordinately inventive interpretations.

Emulating Confucius, Mencius wandered from king to king. He allegedly hoped to find one who could carry out his idealist strategy for restoring unity and peace to China. And he taught.[17] His disciples are not as famous as those of Confucius and he seems not to have been as charismatic a personality. (No one in the Classical period was anxious to pronounce Mencius a sage. This had to await his resurrection by Neo-Confucianism.) Mencius himself cultivated modesty in his self-description. He said that Confucius was a sage; that sages come round in cycles; and that it was time for one now. When directly asked if he was a sage, he called it a strange thing to say. Then he pointed out that when anyone asked Confucius directly if he were a sage, Confucius denied it. Denying it is clearly the proper thing for a sage to do.[18]

The political competition produced a variety of opposing political ideologies and strategies. Several powerful minister-statesmen were experimenting with dismantling feudalism and constructing an imperial bureaucracy. They came to be known as *fa-jia*[standards school] and incurred the eternal enmity of Confucianism. In the state of Qin, which eventually unified China,[19] the Lord of Shang (Shang Yang) instituted standard based reforms. He strengthened the king and organized the state into a more centralized power. His policies were a direct attack on feudal institutions. They included economic measures which concentrated power in the government bureaucracy rather than rich families, forced movement of families, conscription, alienation of land, and other measures that weakened the links of powerful families to their base of support.

The heart of the reform became a lightning rod for Confucian criticism. It was the substitution of clear, measurable standards, particularly an explicit, objective published code (devised by current leaders) in the place of traditional books on ritual.

This both undermined a cherished theory of virtue and removed the main pillar justifying the Confucian scholar-priest's claim to power. If knowledge of ritual was no longer important, Confucian training would lose its competitive advantage over utilitarian (military, diplomatic, or agricultural) expertise. Thus Mencius abhorred the Qin reform movement. The growing power of the Qin state threatened other kings, and Mencius' criticisms found some welcome ears.

The political reforms and Mozi's moral reform proposals had a common feature that Mencius opposed: they used explicit, nonintuitive standards to deal with the interpretive issue. The use of deliberate, especially linguistic, standards to direct how we both construct and interpret *dao* becomes the crucial target of Mencius' attack. Practical interpretation must be left to cultivated intuition.

Mencius called his doctrine the kingly *dao*[way], as contrasted with the way of the ambitious, power-seeking *ba-wang*. The doctrine has the same end, unification and control of China, and Mencius links it to the imposing traditional idea of the mandate of heaven. The heavenly *ming*[mandate], as we saw, put moral content foremost. Mencius also referred to his political strategy as *ren-zheng*[benevolent administration].

Ren-zheng emphasized the moral character of the ruler. Mencius inherited the social optimism of Confucius and Mozi. The leaders *could* achieve social harmony by setting models for the people to emulate. Mencius argued that if the ruler was truly virtuous (as opposed to merely putting on the facade of virtue for its strategic value) he could become a *king*. Mencius, thus, began to rectify the term *king*. Only a ruler with the right behavior and character merited the term. If he has the character and behavior, he will, in the natural course of things, get the name *king*. This rectification maps on to the doctrine of the mandate of heaven: only a true king will get the name and the mandate to rule the world.

Mencius' character ethics has its own paradox. He presents it in a way that reminds us of the paradox of happiness: You can achieve your ambition to rule the world only if that ambition is not your basic motivation. In 1A:1, chosen as the first conversation with a ruler in *The Mencius,* he illustrates the point. I cited this argument earlier as containing the charge that utilitarianism is self-effacing. The king's using the Mohist benefit-harm distinction *out loud* to *shi-fei* things will lead to harm. Those below the king will copy his language and interpret it to motivate seeking for *private* benefit. Chaos rather than order will result. Mencius *fei*[wrongs] talk of *li*[utility] by applying the *fa*[standard] of *li*[utility].

Mencius' point is familiar. Critics of utility note that a utilitarian morality *may* fail a publicity test. Consider this case: A president who really is a utilitarian *would never* launch a retaliatory nuclear strike. If the evil empire is evil, then the president cannot let his utilitarian proclivities become known. Going public with his utilitarian sympathies could lead to a disastrous outcome in utilitarian terms. The evil empire would destroy us with impunity! Thus one's moral system declares telling the truth (about one's accepting it) immoral by its own lights.[20]

The social focus is still implicit in the debate between Mencius and Mozi. What is moral for an individual does not concern them. The reflective question at issue is rather this: "What system of public guiding discourse (what *dao*) should we adopt?" Mozi advocates a morality of utility (*li-yi*[utility morality]) and Mencius advocates a morality of benevolence (*ren-yi*[benevolence morality]). Confucius and (later Xun-zi) advocated a morality of ritual (*li-yi*[ritual morality] with a different character *li*).

In Confucius' case, we hesitated even to translate *ren*. For Mencius, translators read *ren* as *benevolent* with some confidence. His idea of *ren-zheng*^{benevolent administration} is of a ruler who shares with the people. Even more than Confucius, Mencius argues that a policy of economic welfare is the backbone of the kingly way. The king should recognize that the people's desires are similar to his and help them achieve them. Mencius speaks of reducing taxes, sharing hunting lands, and sponsoring musical concerts. In one of his more persistent exchanges on this theme, he even includes the king's desire for the enjoyment of women (IB:5). The king should concern himself about famine relief and care of the aged. He should ensure the planting of ample mulberry trees to support enough silkworms to clothe everyone. He should preserve draft animals and ritually discriminate *spring* so that farmers plant and cultivate at the right time (IA:7).

Mencius advocated a return to the *well-field* system, which looked like a land equalization scheme.[21] It divided land up on a tic-tac-toe model (which resembles the character for well). In principle the well should be in the middle plot (where you should play your X on the first turn). Eight families would farm the outer, equal-sized plots. All the families would work the center plot. Its produce would go to support the hierarchy—those above who worked with their *heart-minds* rather than with their muscles.

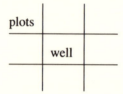

Mencius either lost influence or heart in preaching to the more powerful kings and spent a lengthy period in a small weak kingdom. There he emphasized even more the voluntarist and democratic elements of his political theory: winning the heart-mind of the people. This slogan, for Mencius, as for Mao, meant that public morality determines the competitive outcome more than does objective power.

Mencius continues the tendency to understand *tian*^{nature:heaven} as a kind of natural constancy, a background against which we define our sphere of action. His argument was that the ruler with the correct character would achieve his ambition in the natural course of events. The constant background is human psychology. If the king would adopt Mencius's *dao,* his power would grow because popular support would grow. People would clamor to move to his kingdom, soldiers to fight in his army. They would fight with purpose, moral courage, and commitment. The king's political and military power would inevitably increase.

Finally, his power would be greater if he were benevolent and unselfish than if he directly sought power. Not only would his soldiers fight with real commitment, his virtue would attract the opposing soldiers who would defect and join his forces. Winning battles would be easy even with the smallest force. If he concentrated on the welfare of his people, on lowering taxes, on avoiding aggressive wars he would win. And he would do so faster and easier than if he aggressively fought for power, especially using the techniques of the *fa-jia*^{standardizers}. Thus even the weakest king of the smallest area could become the ruler of all China. He must simply win the *heart-mind* of the people (1A:3,5–6 and 4A:10).

Mencius thus democratized and naturalized the theory of the mandate of heaven. Heaven names you *king* when the word is on the lips of everyone in the world. The evidence *and* the causal efficacy of the mandate flows from the people's acknowledging your status and character. They pour into your kingdom and into your armies. People vote with their feet. Mencius' political arguments, however, implicitly include the intensity of the people's approval, not merely the number of people approving. Victory comes from the dedication of the soldiers as much as from their numbers.

Mencius' political theory was in these respects more progressive than Confucius'. The Mohist movement had affected moral intuitions in China and Mozi's universal-concern morality clearly had influenced Mencius. Mencius' naturalized account of the mandate fills out one unexplained step in Mozi's theory. Mozi simply announced that the most moral person "would be selected" as the *tian-zi*[natural master].

In other ways, still, Mencius' dependence on existing political power led him to compromise with the elite views of the ruling class. He defended traditional privilege against the egalitarian thrust of standardizers' reforms. He opposed all reforms that weakened aristocratic power. He opposed disinheriting the landed aristocracy and rewarding military merit by advancing commoners into bureaucratic power over the hereditary aristocracy (1B:7). His advocacy of the well-field system even had a conservative edge. It was an argument for going back to Zhou land laws in which landowners could not alienate their land. It stayed, in principle, in the hands of the ruling class even as it equalized the plots allowed for farming.

Mencius even watered down the strong Confucian-Mohist commitment to the employment of the worthy. Mencius supported aristocratic retrenchment by requiring an extreme burden of proof before either removing an aristocrat from a position or employing a commoner (IB:7).

Part of his motivation, no doubt, was a desire to compromise enough with royal prerogative to gain a hearing for his doctrine of benevolence. Another is his tendency to overreact to his opponents' views. Among the schools Mencius most stridently opposes is a group called the Agriculturalists. Their equalizing impulse led them to advocate ending all divisions of labor. The rulers, rather than living off the peasants through taxation and slave-household labor, should till the fields themselves and make their own clothes.

Mencius reacted by asserting that a basic division of labor is a natural constant. Some work with their *heart-minds* and others work with their muscles. The former feed and the latter are fed. This justifies the tradition of a scholar elite. The discriminatory output of the scholar's *xin*[heart-mind] determines how the ordinary worker should *shi-fei*. This doctrine earned Mencius sharp criticism from Chinese Marxists—who nonetheless seem committed to the same doctrine.

The core of Mencius' political conservatism lay in his opposition to standard-guided institutional reform. He argued that the key to effective government lay in the character of the rulers and their modeling to the rest of society. The inherited faith in the social power of model emulation made institutional structure seem irrelevant.[22] This became a characteristic theme of Confucian-Standardizer debate. It shaped even Chinese response to modern Western political and military power. Mencius was not a Zhou loyalist, but he saw no reason for changing the basic institutional structure of feudalism. All *his* political utopia needed was rulers with strong moral character!

Mencius' Theory of Moral Psychology

Borrowing Yang Zhu's Naturalism

Mencius' political strategy made certain assumptions which go to the *heart* of his theoretical response to Mozi and Yang Zhu. Mozi had attacked the authority of the classics, the curriculum of Confucianism. These books are not necessarily a source of knowledge of what to do. Yang Zhu had attacked the very idea of engaging in social-political life. While Yang Zhu's attack is more extreme, it is also less threatening. Those who follow Yang Zhu's advice will not show up in court to argue with the likes of Mencius. It is easy to see that Yang's position is politically impractical. Given the terms of the debate—what *dao* should *society* follow—egoism hardly provides a plausible answer.

Mozi, on the other hand, engages Mencius head on and on his weakest point. He challenges the Confucian conception of morality and offers a moral-reform alternative. We can't dance to the old songs indefinitely and passively hope that nature will straighten things out at the top. We have to reform the guidance from the past so we can get some good out of it. Mencius must respond more urgently to Mozi's attack because they are playing in the same theoretical ballpark.[23]

Mencius borrows the structure of Yang Zhu's argument to construct his answer to Mozi. Yang Zhu had taken right to consist in obedience to heaven—as virtually all disputants agree up to this point in the debate. However, Yang did not find the content of this duty (what heaven *materially* desires) by looking at classic texts. Nor did he appeal to heaven's actions in raining benefits equally on everyone. He found the content in our natural inborn capacity, specifically our capacity of life force. Heaven's will is that we realize and fulfill our length-of-life capacity. Yang Zhu had argued that the natural prescriptions are embodied in our inborn physical structure.

All Mencius has to do to borrow this argument structure is to note that nature has instilled in us other capacities and dispositions besides life. This allows him to answer Yang Zhu in a simple way, and gives him a more complex and seemingly invulnerable response to Mozi. The essence of Mencius' addition to Yang Zhu's theory is that nature has endowed us with *moral* capacity. Our physical *xin*[heart-mind] is an organ of moral direction. This he combines with the Yangist assumptions. Guidance comes from nature's *ming* and we can determine nature's *ming* from our inborn dispositional structure. A similar appeal to natural dispositions, as I argued above, was also implicit in Mozi's appeal to nature's will to justify using the benefit-harm distinction as our natural standard.

Now the structure of Mencius' refutation of Mozi will be this: You agree (with the rest of the schools) that *tian*[nature] is the ultimate authority. *Tian* demonstrates its preferences via natural endowments. Then he takes *a bit* of Mozi's position: Heaven has instilled a certain preference structure in us and that is heaven's will. But Mencius expands the point: Heaven has instilled *a detailed inclination to moral judgment and action* in us, not simply a preference for life or benefit.

That detailed natural inclination happens to coincide with the traditional practices and *li*^ritual required by the classics (under the correct interpretation). Mencius argues, surprisingly, that this is because the *moral instincts give rise to the traditions* rather than vice versa. The *li*—rituals and conventions—grew up among people because of our natural inclinations.[24] Conversely, therefore, behavior in accord with the utilitarian criterion is unnatural.[25] We are not natural altruists. We are natural traditionalists; we naturally bury our parents and we naturally favor our own families. That is what heaven wants; those are the inclinations that we should preserve and cultivate.

Mencius has unwittingly borrowed some trouble too, since he has implicitly adopted a potentially troublesome proto-Daoist notion that whatever is natural is correct. Confucianism, tracing out the implications of Mencianism, doomed itself eventually to wrestle with its own adherents, for example, Mad Chanists. Some became *too Daoist* in their *spontaneous, natural* behavior. This comes from the decision to *treat as constant* the distinction between natural and unnatural—to use that distinction to determine *shi-fei*.

It also requires Mencius to mark the natural/unnatural distinction somehow. His anti-Mohist use of a proto-Daoist analysis led him to mark it with the phenomenon of language. Behavior that is engendered by language, by public discourse, is unnatural. Only behavior that emerges naturally from inborn instinct is natural. The natural-unnatural distinction threatens to become a natural-conventional distinction. It thus can be seen as a radical betrayal of the essence of early Confucianism. The attempt to counter Mozi forces Mencius to abandon the aspect of Confucianism that Mozi had attacked. Mencius and the ruling theory never admit this surrender.

The detail of Mencius' theory is rich with insights into human nature. It is easily the strongest, most appealing, and most persuasive part of his idealist theory. It is also the most influential. Eventually, this theory of the heart-mind became so dominant that it became the locus of the debate in medieval Chinese philosophy. They abandoned normative theory entirely and submerged it in debate about moral psychology and metaphysics. Neo-Confucians assume that Mencius dominated the classical period in the same way that he dominated the medieval. They assume that human nature became the only philosophical topic in classical China. I will argue that the classical philosophers quickly saw through Mencius' dodge and that he was marginalized in the truly philosophical period in China.

In fact, part of the reason for Mencius' low status among classical philosophers comes because his contemporaries continued to address the normative question and they saw that Mencius' detour through moral psychology did not answer that question. Let us look at some of the detail of Mencius' psychological theory before returning to the problems of his naive naturalism. We will then consider what Mencius' implicit normative theory must be, whether it is sound, and whether it answers Mozi's ethical challenge.

The Heart-Mind

Mencius assumes that every human has an *organ* that guides action: the *xin*[heart-mind]. Confucius and Mozi would agree on this key point: some natural structure underlies our disposition to discriminate and act in certain ways. They both assume, however, that we *actualize* the heart's disposition by internalizing culture, by language. Social superiors can train us in certain ways of dividing and reacting to things. Confucius and Mozi both conclude that modeling and education, mimicking our parents and older siblings, shape and give content to the natural motivational structure. The novelty in Mencius' version of his view lies in the claim of innateness. The organ comes with *all* the internal dispositions to moral behavior innate in its own structure. It is not that children are moral sages. The innate dispositions grow and flower like a seed. Deliberate socialization can only do two things: it either *reinforces* or *interferes* with what is already there; it should not give independent content to the dispositions.

The Four Fonts

Mencius says the heart consists of four seeds.[26] The seeds are innate, morally discriminatory inclinations or dispositions to action. In certain situations, they incline us to certain actions. The seeds consist of dispositions to select and pursue a range of moral behaviors in concrete situations. Each range of dispositions constitutes a virtue, a group of related dispositions and inclinations. The four seeds, under appropriate cultivation, will grow and blossom into the four classical virtues. These four virtues, in turn, together make up a mature moral character. Mencius has developed an alternative, nonconventional, theory of character cultivation.

The first of the seeds is compassion. All humans naturally feel compassion for other humans. The seed of compassion will naturally grow into the virtue of *ren*[benevolence]. The second seed is the seed of shame and disgust, which will grow into *yi*[morality]. The third is the seed of deference, compliance, and respect for superiors, which will grow into *li*, internalized ritual behavior. The fourth is the seed of *shi-fei*, which will grow into *zhi*[wisdom].

Mencius discusses the seed of compassion at greatest length. This discussion gives us the best account of how the doctrine is supposed to work. It provides the link between his moral psychology and his political theory of *ren-zheng*[benevolent administration]. His stock example of the natural inclination to compassion in people is the story of the child by the well (2A:6). Mencius says that any person seeing that the child might fall in the well has an instinctive natural urge to try to prevent it. Even if the person is a coward—even if he has ignored his sympathies—he will always have the seed, that little bit of a motivational tug to save the child. Mencius expressly rules out that the person motivates himself by the desire for gain, for fame, or for approval of the parents. The only motive is an innate, other-regarding compassion.

His claim parallels David Hume's[27] observation that humans have a natural sympathy for each other. Any normal human dislikes being aware of another human's suffering and enjoys the contemplation of another person's pleasure or happiness. The difference from Hume is the absence of the conceptual apparatus of subjectivity we noticed in Mozi and Confucius. Mencius does not make his point using notions of subjective, inner states of pleasure or pain, desire or intent. He puts the issue in terms of inner behavioral dispositions, impulses, instincts.[28] The heart simply has these reactions to situations in the world. The substance of compassion is the inclination to act, not some inner feeling.

The connection of compassion and *ren* is intuitively clear. The full development of this innate concern for other humans consists in benevolent concern for all humankind. This is the virtue required of a true king. One with this virtue will naturally practice sharing, benevolent government showing concern for the welfare of everyone in the world. *Ren* is the virtue of universal altruism.

The connection between the second seed-virtue pair is less intuitive. If you gave a Western Kantian moralist the following words: (1) shame, (2) respect, (3) morality, and (4) convention, she would normally pair *respect* with *morality* and *shame* with *convention*. Mencius does just the opposite. The virtue of *yi*[morality] arises from shame, ritual from respect. Our contrary intuitions seems connected with our distinction between shame and guilt. A European innatist would say that moral growth results from guidance by our conscience or natural feelings of guilt. Shame, on the other hand, reminds us of peer pressure, not morality. We do not treat morality as public discourse, but as individual commitment. Our transcendent religious ideas and abstract conception of a rational morality lead us to distrust conventions. We inherit a strong sense of the purity of moral conscience as distinct from social approval.

It is easy to exaggerate the difference. I doubt that there are two distinct raw feels: the guilt feel and the shame feel.[29] More plausily, the intuitive difference is a function of our contrasting theories of morality. The Western theory postulates an idealized code: either God's commands or the maxims of pure practical reason. This contrasts with social practices and mores. For a Confucian *or* a Mohist, morality is a social practice consisting of a linguistic *dao* together with institutional arrangements that guide interpretation. When Mencius says that shame leads to *yi,* he most likely follows Mozi in identifying *yi* with an idealized social practice. We have a natural inclination to master and conform to socially acceptable practices and behaviors because we are shame-motivated social animals.

On this assumption, we can see the connection between this germinal disposition and moral virtue. Shame is the natural tendency that motivates us to learn morally acceptable behaviors. The final outcome of letting this feeling have its sway is that we will become moral people *in a conventional sense*. This concept of *yi*[morality] is, thus, still slightly different from the traditional Western one. Mencius views morality as social conformity. Humans incline toward picking up such social behavior patterns and their social nature deters them from doing what public discourse judges to be wrong. No one is an island. No ordinary human can totally ignore the judgments of others.

As I said, the connection between the third seed, respect, and its associated virtue, *li*[ritual], also seems tenuous at first.[30] This is because we have concentrated on the conventional form of *li,* but not on its hierarchical content. If we remember that Confucian *li* dealt mainly with the relation between hierarchical levels, then we will get Mencius' point. Respect for superiors is the basic instinct that motivates us to learn special forms of address, ritual approach, and self-abasing ways of dealing with those in exalted positions. This seed leads to *li*[ritual behavior] because of the essentially hierarchical nature of the *li* in Confucianism. It is not a respect for rational personality or for the moral agent, the individual per se. It is not the kind of respect that marks Kant's egalitarianism.

Note in passing that Mencius' discussion of *li* as a natural virtue is implicitly relativistic. We do notice a natural inclination to learn and practice communal conventions of address and respect. However, this inclination does not require that we treat any particular society's *li* as more natural than another's. In fact, talking of this *seed* almost explicitly reminds us that *li* are relative to society and one society's hierarchical structure and codes of propriety may differ from another's.

This, of course, is Mozi's point. Perhaps Mencius is sensitive to it. It certainly is interesting that Mencius makes a good deal less of *li* than Confucius did. Where Confucius talked more of *li* and *ren,* Mencius talks of *ren* and *yi*—the very concepts that Mozi used approvingly in *attacking* Confucius and his traditionalist assumptions. Yet *li* has to lie near the crux of his answer to Mozi. He needs to claim that *li* behaviors are natural to defend the original Confucian position. Mencius does sometimes stress *li-yi*[ritual morality] in several passages that are strongly reminiscent of *The Analects.*

Mencius slights the last seed even more. He says so little about the theoretically crucial seed of *shi-fei*[this: not this] in developing his theory that one wonders why he included it. Obviously it is crucial for the viability of his innatist answer to Mozi. Mozi's *dao,* remember, resolved the interpretive issue internally by calculating the utility of actual performance in *shi*ing a *dao.* The sum of the utilities of individual acts of *shi-fei*[this: not this] motivated by that public *dao* determines which *dao* to *chang*[constant]. Mencius wants *no* public linguistic *dao.* So there is nothing to interpret. Guidance comes in the form of particular *shi-fei* reactions in actual situations. Mencius' performance-based *dao* consists in following the situational *shi-fei* responses of the heart.

Mencius is claiming that the innate disposition of *shi-fei* grows naturally into *zhi*[knowledge]. This implies that knowledge is innate (albeit, like Leibniz's innate knowledge, it reveals itself, seedlike, as the structure containing it develops and grows). The etelechy or genetic form of the disposition to *shi-fei* must be theoretically complete.[31] As with the other seeds, we must construe the mature virtue (practical wisdom) as whatever emerges after normal cultivation of an innate disposition or instinct.

Shi-fei is a general place-marker for making distinctions—classifying things as this or not this. It also serves as a general term for evaluating—classifying things as approved and disapproved. *Shi-fei* represents the general disposition to distinguish and classify in ways which guide action. We can interpret Mencius as saying that all humans naturally tend to sort and distinguish things. These tendencies result in favorable and unfavorable attitudes toward them which in turn spontaneously guide action.

The mature virtue associated with the *shi-fei* disposition is wisdom, the expert control of important action-guiding distinctions. Wisdom is not discursive or loquacious. All the correct ways to make all the practically required distinctions must be implicit in our heart's disposition in order to assign *shi-fei* to things. The moral seed, like Liebniz's monads, must implicitly contain a potentially complete moral map of my world so that it can generate the right action for me in any actual situation I will encounter.

Reflections on Mencius' Moral Psychology

Most thinkers from the classical period accepted the view that human nature is social. *Their* criticism of Mencius would only be that he exaggerates and idealizes the social goodness of human nature. Typically, Western treatments of Mencius' psychological theory, drawing on traditional Western cynicism about human nature, regard Mencius' views as lacking any empirical support. I disagree; I do not think the problem is that Mencius is morally too optimistic. Western traditional folk psychology, I would argue, is the idealization. We think of *idealized selfishness* as a *realistic* view of human nature.

Our Western bias toward psychological egoism stems in part from the Christian doctrines of original sin and, in turn, from classical Platonic denigration of the physical. We learned to value the intellect as morally transcendent. Reason should control our base, animal feelings and emotions. This tradition influenced Western thinkers to ignore genuine and undeniable social tendencies in humans and to treat moral rationality as an ability to transcend our instinctive nature.

The great works of the Western world give scattered, grudging acknowledgment that humans are social animals, but they reduce most of our social inclinations to a deep kind of egoism. One's *apparent* goals may be altruistic or moral. Our *real* ends, they insist, are self-interested (say, avoiding guilt or gaining approbation). Since we have a desire to be good, we are merely egoistically satisfying one of our desires when we act altruistically.

For two hundred years, Western philosophers have understood the fallacy of these explanations.[32] Naturally it is *my* desire. Otherwise, it would not motivate *me*. This does not make the desire a desire *for my welfare*. The content of the desire is for the well-being of others. That we have such desires is all a psychological moralist needs to show to rebut the psychological egoist. And obviously we do. Despite its continued popularity and *tough-minded* veneer, psychological egoism is empirically naive and typically supported by a conceptual confusion.

Another, more elaborate, argument for psychological egoism instead explains our altruistic desires by social training. The training process, it alleges, inherently relies on selfish desires. At best, this argument shows that our social desires are psychological acquisitions, not that we do not have them. This argument would challenge Mencius' *innatism,* but not the position of Mozi and Confucius. Again, however, this additional premise may confuse the existence of an innate desire with its object. It is not clear that the desire to learn language, to mimic, to idealize our parents, and so forth are selfish in content. They are simple, natural, innate dispositions.

There are other currently fashionable reasons for doubting that the innate structure of human nature is egoistic. Our tough-minded cynics about human nature tend not to notice that sociobiological cynicism contradicts egoistic cynicism. Sociobiology has focused attention on how our genetically implanted dispositions help preserve *a genetic code.* (Writers talk about *selfish genes* to make this theory sound *tough-minded* and *realistic.*) Any parent recognizes that we have an inclination to have, nurture, care for, educate, and then release offspring to the world. This inclination is not in the interest of the individual but the species, the gene pool.

The Chinese view certainly seems to capture something important about our social nature. A dispassionate, unprejudiced view of human nature must, it seems, acknowledge Mencius' portrait of human nature. If his observations are not enough to prove that human nature is good, they are certainly adequate to show that human nature is *social*.

Each of Mencius' seeds describes a plausibly universal feature of a human psyche. All but the most miserable psychopath reacts with feelings for the sufferings and joys of others. Despite the "looking out for number one" pop-psychology view of self-sufficient healthy egos, we are all affected by the praise and blame of our peers. We *do* feel shame and conform our behavior to other's expectations. We conform in manners, dress, political opinions, language—in so many ways that egoistic explanations become empty, uninformative formulas. Better to say that these are part of our natural social nature. There is a natural human instinct to cultivate and internalize social practices and to participate in ritual forms in concert with others. And finally, it is true, despite the self contradictory *advice* of the moral skeptic, we cannot help making value judgments. We would hardly be recognizable as human if we did not.

Problems with Heart-Mind Theory

The problems with Mencius' theory, at this stage, do not lie in its psychological accuracy or realism. His claims, as I have so far explained them, are quite plausible. Any descriptive problems we have with them lie more in our own cultural idealizations than Mencius' empirical inaccuracies. The real problems with his theory stem, rather, from how they *must be interpreted* to make up a normative theory that can even purport to rebut Mozi. The empirical problem is not that his theory is implausibly *optimistic* as much as that it is implausibly *specific* about the *innate judgments of what counts as good*. He must claim that nature writes *specifically the Confucian moral system* into human nature.

The further conceptual problem is this. Mencius confuses his implausibly specific moral psychology with normative theory. Even if he were right that Confucianism is written in everyone's genetic code, Mozi's self-defeating argument would still apply. We can still ask whether we should not try to modify or change this natural programming. So these stronger claims are both blatantly implausible as empirical accounts of human social nature and ethically irrelevant. They beg the very question Mozi raised.

The first seed poses a special problem. Mencius' argument for the pan-human character of the *seed* of commiseration looks like *defense* of Mozi against a standard Confucian attack. Confucians usually take his criticism of Mozi to be this: disinterested altruism is unnatural. The Confucian answer to Mozi *should* be that people have *no* natural inclination to universal love. People naturally show more concern and care for those related by family or other ties. Yet, if Mencius' child-by-the-well example proves anything, it vindicates Mozi's assumption that there is a natural will to *general* human benefit. An innate concern for other humans *regardless of their connection to us is natural*. Mencius' virtue of benevolence, if it is the outgrowth of this seed, seems to correspond to what he despises in Mozi: the standard of universal altruism.

It is, in fact, hard to find an unmistakable statement of the traditional criticism of Mozi in *The Mencius.*[33] Mencius certainly does believe that morality is natural and internal but, evidently, this morality includes an internal inclination to universal altruism. The problem, then, is not so much for Mencius as for his defenders, who treat him as an orthodox defender of Confucian partial-love theory. He certainly does talk about filial piety and the natural inclination to love and respect one's kin. He does not, on the other hand, assert the obverse, that we have no natural inclination to pan-human altruism.

According to Mencius' central theory, *ren* is an outgrowth of a *seed* of *universal* concern for others. According to the traditional notion of Confucian *graded love, ren* should be an outgrowth of partial filial feeling. We take our natural concern for our own kin and "extend it," making it universal. That is the theory of the popular *Classic of Filial Piety.* Mencius, again, does give lip service to filial piety.[34] He shows his awareness that filial piety is a core virtue in the *dao* of the sage-kings. Still, filial piety plays no central theoretical role for Mencius. Specifically, Mencius' seeds analysis contradicts the traditional derivation of *ren*[benevolence] from *xiao*[filial piety]. The seed of *ren* is an *autonomous* virtue rooted in the heart as one of its central natural tendencies, the tendency toward a pan-human moral concern.

Mencius does contradict himself on this issue. Apart from his favored child-by-the-well example, Mencius sometimes identifies *ren* as a primitive element in his system and as distinct from family affection (see, e.g., 7A:45). However, Mencius also appears in places to describe *ren* as *kinning* kin: regarding kin as kin.[35] Other times he describes behavior towards kin as the outcome of *ren*[36] I shall let those defenders of Mencius' logical acumen explain how interpretation can resolve the apparent conflict. This is merely one of many places that Mencius challenges his apologists to heroic logical creativity.

One strategy would be to dismiss the scattered fragments that contradict the central theory.[37] Surprisingly, among admirers of Mencius, the favored strategy seems to be rather to emphasize them to bolster the orthodox criticism of Mozi. They are forced in interpreting to choose between two conflicting accounts. One of them bolsters Mencius most prized claim to philosophical significance, his theory of the heart. The other underwrites the orthodoxy's already bankrupt and irrelevant traditional criticism of Mozi. The dominant line attaches greater importance to these offhand remarks. We must treat them as outweighing his oft-repeated and highly valued seed theory and the child-by-the-well example.

Saving the traditional view is even less appealing than that. Aside from being irrelevant and question begging, as we saw on pages 128–30, that line of argument has strangely embarrassing consequences for Confucianism. Grant that graded love— special-relations love—is a first stage that eventually matures into universal altruism, *ren.* That hardly defends Confucianism against Mohism! Confucians would still have to allow that Mozi *correctly* identifies the content of *mature* morality even if he did not stress how it develops. Confucianism, if it cherishes partial love, stresses what it itself regards as an immature, juvenile *expression* of the innate moral instinct!

Shall we say that while universal benevolence is the ideal, in actual fact, all do love partially? Then we have identified the hated Mohist with the Confucian *ideal* and said that *both* are *unachievable.* This is not much of a refutation of Mozi. We also make Mencius look silly criticizing the Mohist, *Yi-zhi,* for inconsistency in advocating universal love and still showing special concern for his parents. On this interpretation of Mencius, that is precisely what a good Confucian *should* do.

Shall we say that it is the *feeling* which we have for kin that is the specific kind of *love* which we ought to share? It is not clear how to individuate kinds of love to confirm that this is different from Mozi's position (though it clearly contradicts Mencius' child-by-the-well position). Mencius himself is the only plausible target of this criticism. Mencius uses his favorite story to assert that we have a *distinct* disposition to altruistic concern. It is innately situated in the heart as one of its four *seeds,* none of which is filial feeling.

No solution seems satisfactory. That is why the standard defensive Confucian position needs to be bolstered by pretending that the issue is moral psychology or education rather than normative theory. Mencius' normative position is baldly inconsistent with what the orthodox tradition takes to be his core criticism of Mozi. His normative theory of *ren* is hard to distinguish from universal utilitarianism. The performance *dao* of both Mencius and Mozi might turn out to coincide, despite the fact that Mozi *has* and Mencius *eschews* a discourse *dao*.

The difference lies, therefore, primarily in the area of the linguistic *dao,* the one that is used in education. As we noted above, Mencius opposes *using the term li*[utility] *on the grounds that it will result in less utility.* The utilitarian theory is self-effacing. We have to adopt a social practice and an individual attitude of following traditions and intuitions rather than directly applying the utility criterion. Otherwise, we shall gain less utility. We should talk about the *virtue* of *ren* rather than the *value* of *li*[utility]. But, as we saw, the virtue of benevolence corresponds to the utilitarian normative theory of behavior. On this line of analysis, Mencius' difference with Mozi would merely lie in emphasizing a utilitarian moral virtue rather than utilitarian moral language and language-guided action.

A related problem underlies the second seed-virtue pair (shame and morality). Interpreted in a way that makes the pairing intelligible, Mencius seems to accept a Confucian and Mohist view of morality as a social institution. The sense of shame inclines us to conform to social practices and to others' judgments. That conflicts, however, with a traditional understanding of Mencius' argument that *yi* is internal. The appropriateness of a moral behavior should derive from some fact about human nature, specifically the dispositional properties of the *xin*[heart-mind]. That appropriateness should not be dependent on some social-historical convention.

We can avoid this problem if we revise the interpretation of *xiou*[shame]. If we want to credit Mencius with a doctrine of an autonomous morality, we should understand this seed-virtue pair as more akin to *guilt* and *morality* than to *shame* and *mores.* Then we would have Mencius committed to the familiar, but controversial, claim that we all have an internal *moral* guide as opposed to a *social* one, we would have the functional equivalent of a moral conscience that is the only moral source of guidance. Though his claim would also be empirically dubious, Mencius would have at least as sound a position as a traditional Christian moralist with talk of our innate moral conscience. Other deeper difficulties with this second seed-virtue pair come when we consider it alongside the next two seeds.

We are faced initially with a parallel problem in the third seed-virtue pair (deference and ritual). Using the same strategy, where the virtue to be explained is *li*[ritual:propriety], is far less appealing. It is merely empirically *controversial* that we have a pan-human sense of morality and guilt. It seems simply naive to claim that we have a pan-human sense of etiquette and ceremony. Nonetheless, if we are to understand this psychological account as giving the theoretical underpinning of Mencius' answer to Mozi, we should treat these two cases as parallel. We should understand the third seed as we did the second.

If the specific content of morality is accessible from an innate faculty, then so must be the specific content of all the religious ceremonies, eating rituals, naming conventions, and modes of dress. However, the empirical plausibility of this much stronger sense of the innateness of *li* shrinks from low to zero. On the plausible weaker version, we can assume an innate disposition to pick up *whatever* conventions are current in one's community as shame inclines us to pick up community mores. But then Mencius is back in Mozi's ballpark and has to justify the community's mores. On the stronger version, we have to assume an innate disposition in all humans at all times to specifically Confucian behavioral conventions.

Here again, the rest of *The Mencius* does not allow us confidently to settle which reading to follow. Mencius needs the strong sense to answer Mozi. In other sections, however, Mencius slips back to the more plausible weaker version. He treats both *li* and *yi* as things that we teach the common people (1A:4). One standard interpretive solution is to distinguish between an elite and popular theory. Mencius' higher theory describes the ethics of the sage. The weak version describes that of common people who require the sage's guidance.

That elitist strategy, however, comports poorly with the explicit egalitarianism of Mencius statement of the theory of the heart. It turns out that the elite have four fonts and the mass of mankind have the psychology that the Early Confucians and Mohists assumed. And the strong interpretation is no more plausible for the elite, though the authorities will certainly be flattered by it. Mencius, in fact, repeatedly insists on the panhuman character of his analysis. He claims, notoriously, that *all* are like the sages, Yao and Shun.[38]

As a corollary, Mencius implicitly must abandon the claim of semidivine authority for *yi* and *li* (from the sage-kings). He seems to regard his egalitarian claims as entailing that any person could read *yi* or *li* off from her own nature. Only this assumption allows Mencius to link rituals—specifically the Confucian *li* of burial and lengthy mourning for parents that Mozi directly attacked—to innate feelings. Mencius argued, as he had to to answer Mozi, that these rituals evolved from natural instinct. They have a history, but the specific direction of historical development was inevitable. The historically bequeathed burial rituals came to be what they are because our natural feelings *compelled* us to act in those ways. The sages simply behaved as any of us would in giving these feelings ritual form.

> In great antiquity there were some who did not bury their parents. When their parents died, they took them up and threw them into a ditch. Later when they passed by them and saw foxes and wild cats eating them and flies and gnats eating them, their perspiration started out upon their foreheads, they looked askance and could not bear to look straight. Now the perspiration was not for the sake of other people. It was something at the bottom of their hearts that showed in their expressions. They immediately went home and returned with baskets and spades and covered the bodies. If it was indeed right to cover them, then there must be

certain moral principles which made filial sons and men of humanity inter their parents.[39]

But, in a prominent example again, Mencius gives us no reason to conclude that only the *particular* Confucian form of ritual coincides with the *natural human motivational structure*. A cremation ritual—perhaps even a cannibalistic ritual—could have evolved from the vague reaction Mencius describes. Mozi agrees with Mencius that we have a natural human motivation to shared involvement in community practice. We all like singing Christmas carols. It is hard to show that this fact warrants specifically the Confucian *li*. Yet, only this specific outcome can give him an adequate response to Mozi. Mozi, remember, did not advocate abandoning all conventional behavior. He advocated *changing* the Confucian rituals to shared social practices which are more utilitarian. He too envisions a society with accepted, conventional social practices. He did have burial practice: wrap them in a sheet and cover them with three feet of earth. Mencius needs an argument for a *specific* body of ritual.

So we may read Mencius' moral psychology of innate morality in two ways: (1) the weak version, which is empirically plausible, widely shared in China, and compatible with Mohism or traditionalist Confucianism; and (2) the strong version, which is empirically implausible but necessary for Mencius' naturalistic, innatist, internalist response to Mozi.

The weak view is merely a more systematic statement of the assumptions we have found in both Confucius and Mozi. The strong view fundamentally transforms Confucian theory. On that view, Mencius jettisons Confucianism's traditionalist basis. He does this while protesting his adherence to *li*. The *li* ceases to be a transmission of cultural wisdom in linguistic form. It becomes a genetic impulse. Mencius' contemporaries regarded the strong view as untenable. Neo-Confucianism eventually made moral innatism the orthodoxy and developed it into a rival to Buddhist mystical cosmology. Neo-Confucianism read Mencius' ineffable but intuitively accessible and fully detailed moral principles into the moral structure of the cosmos. These orthodox accounts blithely gloss over how remarkably this innatism contradicts early Confucian theory.

The standard view is that Mencius merely fills out Confucius' writings and answers more fully questions that Confucius left implicit.[40] Mozi, it turns out, is theoretically closer to Confucius in his analysis of human nature than (on the strong interpretation) Mencius is. Mencius relies on the weak and widely accepted sense of his claims when he is setting up his psychology. He shifts to the strong sense when he attacks the Mohists.

Now we can see just how crucial the fourth seed *(shi-fei)* is. We can also give it either the strong or the weak reading that we used in discussing his doctrine of both morality and ritual. On the weak reading, Mencius attributes to every human a tendency to classify things as *shi-fei in one way or another* in applying guiding discourse and action. We are programmed to be able to make the distinctions we need to use social linguistic *daos*. We can learn a conventional way to make branching choice responses to relevant stimulus situations.

On the strong reading, the innate bent leads to *only the shi-fei* practical distinctions that Mencius regards as *correct*. On the weak reading, we would relativize the associated virtue, *zhi*[wisdom]. One would know to apply this *dao* or that. One community's wisdom could be another community's foolishness. Wisdom consists in mastery of socially acceptable responses. The strong reading is required to make Mencius a moral realist. Everyone has innate access to *one* ideal pattern of *shi-fei*[this:not this] responses to things. There is exactly one right thing to do in each situation. Each of us has a heart that can *shi* the right action and *fei* the others. The Neo-Confucian philosopher, Wang Yang-ming gives the strong reading its full logical force as a form of absolute idealism. Mencius' heart-mind must tie into a complete moral map of history so each situation will evoke the uniquely correct response.

The strong version lies behind Mencius' more mystical doctrines like that of the floodlike *qi*[material force]. This will become an important doctrine for claiming Mencius as authority for the Neo-Confucian cosmic moral theory.

> May I ask what is called the flood-like *qi*[material force]?
>
> Hard to put into words! Its material force is ultimately extensive and ultimately strong. When cultivated uprightly and not harmed, it fills up heaven and earth. As a material force it coincides with morality and *dao*. Without these it starves. This is born of accumulated morality and not of selections from morality. If your conduct is not comfortable to your heart-mind, it will starve (2A:2).

The passage suggests that the heart's having the four seeds is merely an instance of cosmic stuff's having a moral structure. The heart is an integral part of a total cosmic system and spontaneously *vibrates* with the total state of *qi*[material force] throughout the world. Thus we spontaneously hit on the uniquely harmonizing, homostasis-sustaining thing to do. No set of instructions could be so cosmically sensitive. Following particular, situational intuitions is the only constant *dao*.

Mencius holds that anyone who has fully developed her seeds (a sage) acts with a perfectly situational intuition. Her heart guides her in each unique circumstance to *shi* the right behavior. The Mohist criticism of Confucian tradition cannot undermine this naturalist, innatist conception of moral knowledge. Mencius required neither calculation nor code nor interpretation. A practical, *shi-fei* intuition guides action immediately in any setting.

Mencius' strong version, then, drastically revises Confucian moral theory. Though he dutifully defends the traditional *li* against Mohist attack, Mencius has really abandoned traditionalism. His theory depends on natural intuition as the ultimate standard. (He does not, of course, give up frequent mention of *li*.) We may *use* inherited sage-discourse to describe a *thin and approximate pattern* of *shi-fei* attitudes. Hence the classics are permissible. Our faith that the sage-kings wrote them in response to their intuition ensures us that the classics will not interfere or conflict with this intuition. However, the innate ability to *shi-fei* is strictly independent of external, historical convention. Mere rules could never convey the sensitivity of response available to one who has fully cultivated her innate moral knowledge. Once we have cultivated the heart to completion, we have no need of the picky details of conventional rules.

If we follow the *shi-fei* impulses we have now, they will, in principle, continue to develop until we are all sages. The final criterion of correct behavior, for Mencius, is the discriminatory heart-mind responses of the sage (4A:2). His behavior fixes what is *shi*. Wisdom is the *know-to* the sage has. It is, at best, sketchily expressed in a codebook. Study of the tradition, albeit effective, is a roundabout and vaguely approximate way to moral development.

Cultivating the Heart-Mind: The Plant Analogy

Mencius blurs the weak and strong versions of his theory using his doctrine of moral cultivation and growth. We clearly have not mastered the full skill of feedback discrimination at the moment of birth: an infant cannot respond to the cosmic vibrations of *qi* and produce precisely the correct behavior in the situation.[41] Our inborn morality is a potential. But the ambiguity still lies in *how much detail* is in the potential. Confucius and Mozi accept our obvious and weak potential to *learn morality from our cultural surroundings*. Mencius requires a strong potential to grow into a morality whose entire content comes from the stuff of the seeds.

Thus, Mencius often elaborates his theory of the growth of guiding intuitions and motivation via an analogy to plant growth. We will take the seed-plant analogy seriously. Mencius does not use explanatory concepts like entelechy, essence, final cause, gene, or DNA code. Still, using a plant analogy suggests something important for Mencius. A seed does have a detailed set of directions for growth in it. An acorn does not grow into a pine tree nor a pine nut into a strawberry plant. Our potential is not to acquire some arbitrary *yi* or other, some *li* or other, some *dao* of *shi-fei* or other: it is for specifically the Confucian *dao*. The full knowledge of *shi-fei* is in the seed and comes out as the seed matures into a tree. Note that the analogy of a seed suggests that the final shape of the whole tree is implicit in the seed in *some* sense. That amounts to Mencius' assumption that human nature has a *particular* inner morality.

The content—the detailed structure of the nature of the moral plant—is not a result of the external factors. The external environment may act only to wither, stunt, or distort the growth of the plant. It does not contribute structure; it merely subtracts it. In whatever soil we place it, a pine will not produce an apple tree. Similarly, the seed of our morality will either produce the Confucian morality or some retarded distortion. But if the other factors are present, we do not have to guide the growth of the seed. We don't have to tell it to branch here and here and here. Morality is internal in this sense.

The plant analogy also provides a connection between Mencius' psychological and political theory. The soil—the background condition of any growth—is analogous to a basic level of economic well being. The ordinary people cannot cultivate their moral character if their economic lives are not secure.[42] Hence benevolent government is important as a prerequisite to the specific type of moral growth in the population that leads to perfect order in the state.

Water and nourishment represent introspecting, recognizing, and valuing our moral nature. Noticing it and valuing it (conforming to its seminal responses) are vital germinating stimuli. The feeling of pride and confidence, as it grows in us, reinforces that growth. Similarly, the weeds that grow around it are the other selfish desires. These are the motivations of the other organs of the body that may conflict with those of the *xin*[heart-mind]. If we ignore these they weaken, shrivel, and die while the *xin* grows. If we give in to the bodily desires for food, sex, and leisure, *they* get the nourishment and the sprout of *xin* withers. Every time we follow a moral intuition rather than a bodily desire, we strengthen our *xin* against the weeds and vice versa.

As the character-plant grows, it changes both in its strength and its complexity. When the sprout first appears it is a single point, a simple, intuitive directive like saving a child by a well. As we follow that sprig of intuition and cherish it, it branches—it becomes more complex. Each branching represents a more complex ability to distinguish *shi-fei*. (Picture a branching path through life. We *shi* one branch and *fei* the other as we walk through life.) The first sprout is also delicate and weak. Surrounding weeds easily threaten it. It is easily trampled and killed. As it grows, it gets stronger compared to the other competing plants. Finally, as a full-grown tree, it is both *highly complex* and *secure* against competition from grass and weeds around its base. This represents the moral *xin* of the sage. It makes all the correct, situationally sensitive *shi-fei* distinctions intuitively and never hesitates to follow what is right. The sage is never torn by choice between moral and selfish motives. He still has desires, but none that are incompatible with morality.

Moral sagehood, thus, involves not only heart-mind content, but also heart-mind control. Mencius speaks of his fascination with the *unmoved heart-mind*. He evidently cultivated powers of concentration—perhaps meditation—to achieve that goal. The sage has both precise practical knowledge and infallible self-control. He acts spontaneously without ambivalence or indecision. His intuition is reflexive and inevitably motivates him. A sage never feels torn between morality and self-interest. In the sage, we can allow the selfish desires to exist because they never threaten the tree. Recall Confucius as he follows his heart's desires and never violates the rules. The result of natural, unhindered cultivation is a fully developed moral excellence: sagehood. At that point we have an infallible situational intuition and an undivided inclination to act on it.

Since each of us has essentially the same kind of seed, we all are capable of achieving this sagelike state. All we need to do is start now following our moral dispositions and they will begin to grow in strength and sophistication. Allowing and encouraging that natural growth will result in our becoming sages—always right, always tranquil.

Mencius' account of this moral stage leads us back to the doctrine of a moral mysticism based on qi^{breath}. *Qi* provides the metaphysical underpinning of this idealized moral psychology. Our *shi-fei* response in a moral setting can be perfectly correct and perfectly effective. We can be in harmony with a universal world force. The *floodlike qi* flows between the sage and the world. The *qi* unites the sage's *dao*, the sage's actions, and the *dao* of the whole world. The sage's actions become perfect and natural responses to the total situation. *Qi* is the *life* I bring to my action. It is the force that carries that action into effect, and into practical significance. I control it and am controlled by it. My control depends on my identifying my deepest self with that cosmic moral power. Morality is not only in my mind but in *qi*. The moral sage's *qi*, the scope of the sage's moral concern and effective action, fills the space between heaven and earth.

> This is a *qi* which is extremely vast and unyielding. Nourished with integrity and unhindered it fills the space between Heaven and Earth. *Qi* unites $yi^{morality}$ and dao^{ways} (2A:2).

The sage will know precisely what to do, what small action, right here and now, will prevent nuclear holocaust. (We assume the sage, here and now, would find such a thing wrong.) But, as Wang Yang-ming would say, I distort Mencius' position a little here in separating *finding wrong* from *acting*. We can coherently interpret Mencius only by focusing on the performance *dao*. Do not look at the linguistic formulation of guidance or an assignment of events or objects to linguistic types. The range of *shi-fei* identifications must be individual actions, not named objects. Look at the set of actions, the course through life, that (with names rectified) its guidance would have produced. Mencius' position is that if I were a sage, I would *wei*[do:deem]. My *wei*ing would be *shi;* its effect would depend on the *qi* situation. Along with moral maturity comes harmony with *qi* so those effects will always be optimific. They will promote the natural teleology.

I do not *know* this *dao* as a set of descriptions, names, or distinctions. I know to do *this* when doing *this* is cosmically correct. The set of correct acts (including speech acts) is just the set that an ideally perfect person would do. It follows from no formulae, no language system, no traditional *dao,* no invented *dao.* Still, it is a *dao.* Mencius' *dao* has only an extension, just *that* set of acts. *Dao*'s extension is prescriptive. It consists of *shi*s and *fei*s elicited in a real life context. Humans have a *xing*[nature] for which that prescriptive extension holds. The faculty in which it holds— the faculty capable of grasping and executing that situational *dao*—is my *xin.*

This sensitivity and precision in choosing actions does not come from measurable projections or from a discourse guide. No standard or measurement is sensitive enough: as sensitive as the heart's intuition. The sensitivity must come from the growth of inner moral inclination. The form of awareness is knowing-to: knowing to execute the performance *dao* in the appropriate settings. Knowing it, Wang Yang-ming would say, is doing it. Whatever the internal wiring and programming is, we discover its *dao* output, its *shi-fei* pattern, only in spontaneously responding in specific, concrete situations. We should never impose moral structure from the outside. We must avoid the Mohist error of trying to fashion our moral distinctions by reforming language.

Mencius tells a plant story for this point as well, the story of the foolish man of Song. The fool wanted to accelerate the growth of plants. He went out into the field and gave each one of them a little tug to lift them up higher. Of course the result was to kill the plants. The *deliberate* tug I take to be a figurative analogy to the study of moral philosophy. In doing that one tries to devise, decide on, and then impose an *outside* linguistic standard. One uses language to *train* and direct the moral intuition. You try to shape your intuition to match some *dao* by learning names, acquiring distinctions and practicing discriminating action with them. Then you allow language and theory to dictate and force the direction of the growth of moral intuition. That, Mencius assumes, can only harm moral development.

Language is both unnecessary and, on Mencius' view, positively dangerous. In pulling on the *moral* plant or splitting its stalk (making distinctions that are not innate) you run a danger. The danger that in trying to influence your moral growth, you use some reflective conception of moral behavior. If it is other than that implicit in the plant itself, it will distort the innate moral programming. If it is the same, it can only be a crude and unnecessary guide. Mencius's theory, taking a proto-Daoist as his model, becomes a proto-Daoist theory with an antilanguage bias. Mozi is like the man of Song.

So Mencius' defense of Confucianism *does not* have a language-theoretical level. He says little about it, because his theory of language is antilanguage. This position also forces Mencius to a view of the role of teachers that is controversial within Confucianism. Confucius' disciples thought both *li* and teachers were central to moral cultivation ("If you do not study the *Odes* you will have nothing to say" [Analects 16:13]). They cannot be as central for Mencius if morality is internal. It not only makes the *li* optional; it makes teachers important to Mencius only as stimuli to self-cultivation. What one learns from them, the *content* of their teaching, is superfluous. No structure can be added from the outside. Their modeling either merely encourages the plant growth or inhibits it.

By contrast, we can make perfect sense of *Confucius at seventy* without making the *li* optional or teachers superfluous. As a good Confucian, Mencius does not, of course, *oppose* either of these Confucian symbols. They play a worthwhile role, but only as stimulants to the natural growth of inner morality. In principle, since our nature, our seed, our *xin* is the same as the sage-kings' seed, we should be able to write our own *li*. At least, we should be able to pick out our particular situational performance based on our intuition. In theory, these would conform to the right interpretation of *li*.

Mencius clearly has faith that the properly cultivated execution of the inner content of the *xin* will coincide with the correct interpretations of the traditional *dao*. Mencius does not need an explicit account of rectifying names, however, because the standard is not a traditional codebook. The intuitive ability to select correct behaviors (the ability required to rectify names) allows us to dispose with *li* as a guiding *dao*. *Li*, however, poses no danger and he does not need to condemn it. Unlike doctrines such as those of Mozi and Yang-Zhu, he would argue, the traditional *li* can only coincide with our moral intuitions. Further, as a programming system worked out by moral sages, the *li* could be a stimulus to the inner growth. It is surely better than any substitute we might invent today. In theory, that code is as good as humanly possible. If their code would have interfered with moral growth, the sages would have said nothing. The sages, remember, always executed the act that produced the best result, including speech and writing.

However, intuition has now become the key standard for Mencius. We can find no *formula* that exhaustively generates all of some particular sage's actions. The formulas require intuitive interpretive guidance anyway. The guide, in effect, is inside the sage: his *de*^{virtuosity}. It generates proper actions only in response to particular situations. We cannot translate it into an instruction sheet. His knowledge is not a knowledge of *yan*^{language}, of *ming*^{names}, or of *bian*^{distinctions}. It is *pure practical* know-(how)-to. If we are capable of learning *from* the *li*, then we are capable of learning without it!

Mencius, though he is a situationalist, is not a relativist. Any two sages in precisely the same circumstance will do the same thing.[43] The rightness of the act is not dependent on the *xin*'s response in a subjectivist way. The rightness of their act is real, in the structure of *qi*. Nature programs the *xin* to generate that action. A sage's *zhi*^{knowledge} is of the uniquely and objectively right response to the total situation of *all under heaven*. There is an absolutely correct thing to do in each situation of moral choice. No discourse *dao* can reliably or constantly generate it.

Though Mencius would not approve of this question, we *can* intelligibly ask about the character of that genuine right thing to do. I have hinted that it has, despite his fulminations against Mozi, a utilitarian content. Mencius' universe is a teleology. The end may be order or harmony rather than pleasure. But Mencius' arguments are consistently consequential. No doubt, Mencius' sketch of the good the performance *dao* fosters would differ from Mozi's. I agree, as Tu Wei-ming has argued,[44] that Mencius may implicitly conceptualize the good as a nonnaturalistic and intuitive human perfection. He rejects Mozi's more material conception. However, as his favorite virtue is benevolence, and given the kinds of considerations he offers for his policies, he does not reject utilitarianism itself. That is, his basic position is teleological-consequential and his no-theory theory promotes or maximizes *some* goal.

The appearance of a deontological attitude arises only when Mencius criticizes utilitarian language. His apology for the tradition works *because* he assumes that traditional language will not interfere with the goal of human perfection the way a reflectively generated *dao* would. His criticism of utilitarianism, as we saw, is that in being put in words, it distorts moral motivations. We achieve its goal better by not putting it in language. In fact, Mozi's conceptual structure seems to force Mencius to a deeply consequentialist position. His opposition is not to utilitarian conceptions of what action we ought to undertake but to using its language. The performance *dao* may have a utilitarian direction, but the social *dao* that can effect it is an act deontology, that is, a situational ethics with no stated principles. His arguments actually suggest that we adopt that social stance *for utilitarian reasons*. Act deontology as a public *dao* achieves the good more reliably, his argument implies, than Mozi's explicit utilitarian *dao*.

This antilanguage intuitionism gives Mencius his seemingly defensible position against Mozi's challenge. It condemns anyone's *revising* traditional forms of prescriptive discourse. Deliberate moral reform is *never* justifiable, not because Confucian traditional codes *define* morality, but because our natural inclinations do. There can be no better formulas than those the tradition has naturally generated. Mencius assumes that no reflectively revised language and distinction practices could do any better than the traditional one. In particular, a linguistic practice designed to achieve a utilitarian goal could not do so.

No formula—not the utilitarian calculus, not egoism, not legal systems—no formula can calculate what this action ought to be. The formula, the *dao*, is written as genetic code in our *xin*. We can know it only as it reveals itself in the *xin*'s inclinations in concrete situations of action. If our *xin* realizes its potential—if it becomes a sage's *xin*—then we will know to do such and such in each unique situation. No code (other than the genetic code) generates the actions that constitute Mencius' *dao*.

In summary, the *li* inherently plays a far less central role for Mencius than it did for the early disciples of Confucius. Where *The Analects* speaks most of the time of *li* and *ren*, Mencius drops *li* to a relatively unstressed third place among his four virtues. If Mencius has any implicit standard, it is the spontaneous action of the sage, the person with a fully developed *xin*. No abstract linguistic formula can be a standard. No linguistic formula can be sensitive enough to the situation to take into account the complexity that the sage senses with his responsive *xin*. The *li* are the best approximation but, in the end, only an approximation. If language is inadequate to the task, then Confucius' language can differ from Mozi's language only in degree. What is *fei* for Mozi should be *fei* for Confucius.

The Justification of Intuitionism

Where does Mencius heart-mind theory leave us? We can grant that Mencius' portrait of human nature, construed weakly, is accurate—certainly more accurate than psychological egoism. The four *seeds* form a reasonable picture of the basis of our social lives. We can regard them as psychologically natural. Now we may ask if that theory of human nature can ground Confucian normative ethics. Does it create any special problem for Mozi's moral reform ethical stance? Does it justify either a Confucian traditional normative theory or a Confucian intuitive normative theory?

To the first question, we can now confidently answer no. Taken in their weak and plausible sense, the seeds are as congenial to Mozi's utilitarianism as they are to traditional norms. In fact, in the weak sense there are hardly distinguishable from Mozi's own psychological assumptions except in ways that help him. Taken in the way necessary to underwrite an attack on Mozi, they either beg the question or make wildly implausible claims about empirical psychology.

The seed of shame, in its more plausible elaboration, only explains why we pick up whatever morality is current in our surroundings. It does not provide a refutation of making the morality we teach a utilitarian one. Mozi can simply reply, ''Yes, people should, however, learn to be ashamed of conforming to old practices and not cooperating in efficient ways in jointly beneficial enterprises.'' Although a stronger reading would be familiar given our *conscience* heritage, that we share anything like a detailed universal moral sense is empirically dubious. If we did look for such a panhuman moral outlook, utilitarianism looks to have as good a claim of coinciding with that universal moral inclination as either Chinese Confucianism or Western Judeo-Christian Kantianism.

We do not even have the fig leaf of familiarity for the claim that etiquette and the proper forms for showing respect are panhuman and innate. And Mencius understandably avoids elaboration on the innate pattern of *shi*ing and *fei*ing. Obviously, the strong form of his claim about these seeds flies in the face of actual human disagreement. It amounts to saying that in any dispute, one of the disputants has distorted his natural moral instincts. Mencius calmly assumes that his judgments are all natural, so that anyone who disagrees with him must be engaging in self-deception. (Accusing others of self-deception must surely be the most common strategy of self-deceivers.)

Of course, apologists for Mencius (and Confucius) will accuse us of being unfair. Looking from our modern, relativistic perspective, Mencius' internality of morality doctrine *seems* naive. But that criticism is anachronistic. That relativistic awareness of the multiplicity of ethical systems is a *modern* or *Western* view. Chinese thinkers in classical times, they will argue, had no such insight.

This apology fails. First, since he was replying to Mozi and Yang Zhu, Mencius can't help but be aware that there are conflicting moral views. Even Confucius himself, as we saw, knew that the *li* varied through time and across ethnic boundaries. Mencius certainly knew of a system—the ruler standardized system of Qin—which did not take the traditions, the *li,* as obvious truths. Mozi's attack on Confucian traditionalism discusses the existence of societies with utterly conflicting intuitions about what is right. One can get the logical point without doing the anthropology. Whether or not it was a familiar and widely shared awareness, the theoretical basis of doubt was firmly rooted in the philosophical tradition of the times. In fact, Mencius' system can only make sense *if he thought he was responding to just such doubts.* Mencius is asserting his innatist claims in the face of arguments for changing existing social forms. His position amounts only to *shi*ing his morality as natural and *fei*ing the various reformers.

Even if we grant Mencius the conceit that his moral instincts are the correct ones, we still cannot derive the conclusion he needs. Let us grant the existence of a moral *xin* and grant that it somehow innately contains inclinations to do what Confucian morality requires (with names rectified). We can still ask why we should pay any attention to the *xin* or follow it? Given that Mozi acknowledged that his *dao* deliberately tries to change existing human nature, Mencius cannot simply assume that existing human inclinations are right.

In standard philosophical terminology, Mencius, as much as the reformer, is trying to get an *ought* from an *is.* Why obey the heart? Maybe once we realize we have it, that knowledge should make us free, it should enable us to get a realistic look at it. That detached contemplation may help us free ourselves from its dictation. Zhuangzi will later state the problem as one of justifying the choice of the heart to rule over the other natural organs of the body, the desires which Mencius regards as weeds. Can Mencius give a neutral way to distinguish seeds from weeds? If natural endowment constitutes the moral *dao,* why *shi part* of our natural endowment and *fei* the other part?

From a Daoist point of view, then, Mencius and Mozi have similar weaknesses. Each begs the question against the other. Each purports to speak for heaven and denies that status to his rival. Each takes part of the existing value system, *shis*[that's it] it as natural and *feis*[that's not] the rest. Each appeals to a controversial standard to justify his choice. This is not a productive argument! Both have the problem of justifying the step from nature to guidance. They both treat nature as constant and yet as prescriptive. The natural-nonnatural distinction simply amounts to the keep–throw away distinction for both. The paradox of moral reform plagues defenders of the status quo as much as the reformers.

Mencius seems vaguely aware of the need to answer this challenge. He offers a plethora of different justifications, reasons we should value the heart's inclinations. One of these is the distinguishing feature argument. (Aristotle gave a similar reason for exercising reason: it is virtue in regard to the distinguishing feature of man.) The moral heart distinguishes humans from other animals. Therefore we need to cultivate and focus on it more than we do on organs and appetites we share with animals. You do not want to be like an animal, do you?[45]

Daoists, as we shall see later, do not think the answer to that rhetorical question is obvious. For now, however, we need merely note that many behaviors are unique to the human species. That does not make exercising those behaviors imperative. I suppose humans are the only animals who pick their noses with their thumbs. Need I conclude that we should pick our noses more regularly? Humans laugh. It's a praiseworthy thing, but hardly made obligatory by the mere observation that other animals do not. We are the only animal who can snap fingers—a useful musical skill but not really at the heart of moral rectitude.

But the Daoist reaction is one of puzzlement. Why regard species scope as especially significant for moral purposes. Why isn't our genus of equal relevance? Perhaps we should emphasize primate behavior as against mammal behavior, and mammal behavior as against vertebrate behavior, etc. Or we can raise the same question with smaller scope. Why not emphasize Caucasian behavior, or male behavior, or class behavior, or national behavior? This is another case of Mencius' reading an arbitrary *shi-fei* in (the species distinction) in order to get one out.

Mencius offers a second ground for following the *xin,* an argument from prudence. Mencius suggests that cultivating and correcting our heart is as vital to our health as healing any other part of our body. Any person with a crooked finger would go to great lengths to get it straightened out.[46] Should you not be equally willing to pay and work to correct a malfunctioning moral organ? The answer is "of course." But why should the healthy heart guide the body more than a healthy finger, stomach, eye, or other natural organ? We surely shrink from wanting any organ to be deformed and nonfunctioning!

There is a related argument that is stronger than the one suggested by Mencius' analogy. Having a crooked finger is morally permissible. So is having a weak heart. Still, if Mencius is correct about the heart's epistemological function and capacity, then we have an epistemic *and* moral duty to develop our heart's accuracy. Mencius says that cultivation can make your heart—your practical intuition—a reliable guide *and* motivation to moral behavior. Each of us should undertake the discipline that makes that process accurate and reliable. Still, of course, this leaves open the question as to *which cultivation* is the correct one: a Mohist one, and Yangist one, or a Mencian one, and it still assumes, rather than proves the normative status of the *xin*$^{\text{heart-mind}}$.

Another possible justification is religious. It is implicit in the original argument borrowed from Yang Zhu: we should do what heaven commands; heaven commands whatever our heart dictates; therefore, we should follow our hearts. An appeal to authority, this use of *tian*^{heaven}, gave Yang Zhu's egoism its deontic bite. Mozi also appealed to heaven's authority to motivate his choice of the utilitarian standard for making distinctions. Mencius relies on the same authority so this is at least a justification that Yang and Mo cannot object to. But it, also, cannot settle much.

One of Mencius' most famous statements seems to rectify names in answering Zhuangzi's question. Here Mencius puts the issue most clearly and directly. He acknowledges that various organs of the body tend to discriminate and *shi-fei* among the things they pick out. He gives the discriminations made by his favorite organ, the *xin,* special status by rectifying the terms *xing*^{nature} and *ming*^{fate}.

> It is due to our *xing*^{nature} that our mouths desire sweet taste, that our eyes desire beautiful colors, that our ears desire pleasant sounds, that our noses desire fragrant odors, and that our four limbs desire ease and comfort. But there is also *ming*^{fate}. The superior man does not *say* they are nature. Humanity in the relationship of father and son, righteousness in the relationship between ruler and minister, propriety in the relationship between guest and host, wisdom in the worthy and sage in regard to the way of heaven—these are fate but they are also nature. The superior man does not call them fate.[47]

So there we have the perfect argumentative circle. That one is morally superior consists in his distinguishing among his natural dispositions in this specific way. The justification of this specific way of making the distinction it is that the superior man would do so. So someone who would make just this distinction would make just this distinction. Mo and Yang could hardly deny that!

Zhuangzi argues that Mencius begs the question by presupposing a conventional *shi-fei* implicitly in his appeal to the natural constitution of the heart. Mencius must not only *shi* the heart as the guide, but then *shi* a particular way of cultivating it. This means that his entire *yi*^{morality} cannot be internal to the heart. He must have some standard outside the heart to justify discriminating among hearts (the sage's and the fool's) or heart phases (the uncultivated and cultivated).

Like Mozi, he inevitably has two bases. Mencius, too, must *shi* certain of the discriminations and inclinations of the *xin* and *fei* the others. By treating one set of inclinations as nature, he treats them as something he can and wants to affect. He identifies with a part of the heart. What standards pick the part or phase? By treating the other inclinations as fate, he acknowledges their unmistakable and inevitable presence, but treats them as something external to his deepest being or his nature. He draws a boundary, a *shi-fei* within the self and says this is really me and this is not. Doing this in a specific way is the attitude the superior person—in Mencius eyes. If you want Mencius and other superiors to call you a superior person, you should conform to that *shi-fei* judgment. If not . . .

One interesting way of using the above passage is to remove the question-begging assumption that the superior man makes that particular distinction and choice. We treat it as an argument about motivation and relativistic justification. We are choosing among our lower-level desires. Mencius may be taken as saying that you will find among your first-level desires these moral desires along with the others. You will also find among your second-level desires the desire to cultivate the first-level moral desires. We make that choice from an existing second-level preference. We could question this second-level value and make a third-level choice. But we would still have to do it from an exiting third-level desire, etc.

So we treat the passage as a second-level argument from introspection. Mencius suggests that when we look inside ourselves, we not only see the presence of these four moral feelings. We also, on seeing them, actually have a second-level *shi-fei* attitude toward them. Both the moral seeds and the attitude of valuing them above the other dispositions are there. We do in fact identify with them and want to cultivate them. We want certain of our dispositions to be more reliable both as guides and motivations to behavior. If you introspect honestly, you see not only a motivation to honor, but a motivation to cultivate that *seed*.

So, of course, this argument will have purchase only if you find such a second-level motivation. If you are a counterculture person, you will look inside yourself and see all those conventional values and manners and wish to get rid of them. Mencius then must, as David Hume did, say that he can no longer reason with you. Yet, if you do have that *second-level* desire, then the burden of proof certainly shifts. You need no further justification for cultivating traits of your psyche you find noble. You need a reason not to. Why pretend philosophically that you do not have these second-level desires?

The answer is complex and goes to the meaning of *philosophy*. The philosophical impulse contemplates and compares alternatives. For everyday purposes to say "you want this so get on with getting it" is enough. Having philosophy as a social practice involves making the following linguistic move: "Maybe I should want something else and not this." We can make this philosophical, skeptical move at the level of desires to have desires as easily as at the ground-floor-level of desires. If there were a natural disposition to favor the heart, perhaps we should ignore or modify it. A moral reformer like Mozi has played this game to a point where he is willing to challenge the inclinations to the status quo. Mencius, in the end, bases his status-quo defense on the claim that one should not philosophize.

Mencius' Attitude toward Language and the Heart-Mind

Mencius develops the first antilanguage theory.[48] His answer to Mozi illuminates his theory of language and its relation to mind. His homily about the foolish man of Song who pulled on his plants embodies a view of language and of linguistic *dao*. In other contexts, Mencius puts his view of the relation of *yan*[language] and *xin*[heart-mind] in more theoretical terms. He does this in defining his position against that of his opponent in debate, Gaozi. Scholars normally take their dispute to be about the internality of morality. The hub of their dispute emerges in an aphorism attributed to Gaozi that expresses a plausibly Mohist point of view: "What you cannot get in *yan*[language], do not seek for in *xin*[heart-mind], what you cannot get from *xin*, do not seek for in *qi*" (2A:2).[49]

We can now see a line of interpretation for this aphorism. It suggests a tabula-rasa view of the *xin*[heart-mind]. The inclinations of the mind are all programmed. There is no cosmic, natural guide other than what lies in the heart's inclinations and the heart has no inclinations other than those programmed in via public discourse.

Mencius approves of only the second half of the formula. Recall that he seems committed to the notion of *qi* as a moral force. The innate programming of our *xin* is an integrally related component of the cosmic guide. Our action guiding endowment is lodged exclusively in the *xin*'s inclinations to *shi-fei* that trigger subroutines. There may be more content in the universe, but all that is relevant to human guidance is in this one organ. Conformity to *xin* alone results in vast *qi* linkage.

The second part of this slogan rules out Zhuangzi's view that *qi*[material force] authority might be found in all the natural organs. Mencius and Gaozi agree in seeing *qi* as the motivation *stuff* that vibrates with the *xin*'s controlling intent. *Qi* of the rest of the body is thus naturally subject to *xin*. However, since *xin* can only achieve its effect through *qi*, *xin* must also be in harmony with all the moral force in *qi*. Therefore, no moral aspect of *qi* is relevant to human guidance unless it is in the *xin*[heart-mind]. The full realization of *xin* and of *qi* are thus two sides of the same process. It is the effective realization of the sagelike heart-mind's role in the moral cosmos.

However, Mencius pointedly disagrees with the first half of the formula: that the same relationship holds between *yan*[language] and *xin*[heart-mind]. One should not treat *yan*[language] as a source of what is in the heart. That is to make morality external. The heart-mind contains great detail and accuracy in its discriminatory abilities, its contextual *shi-fei* generation. We could never put it all in language. There must be inclinations in the *xin* that are not in language. Otherwise, practical interpretation of linguistic codes would not be possible.

Mencius' rejects the tabula rasa position. Mencius is, as we argued, right to reject it, whether or not Gaozi held the view. But then Mencius moves to the other extreme. The heart has innate patterning. That patterning will be affected by language. Either language will merely coincide with the innate patterning or change it. If it coincides it is unnecessary. If it detracts, it is wrong. So don't look to language for any guidance that is not in the heart. The danger, therefore, of language is more grave than any reward. We do not require a linguistic *dao* and it may corrupt our *xin*.

Mencius concludes from these reflections that *yi*^morality must be internal.[50] Gaozi disputes this (though he agrees with Mencius that *ren*^benevolence *is* internal). Mencius' position and his long debate with Gaozi is the single sustained argument with a philosopher in *The Mencius* (6A:1–8).[51] Gaozi seems to be a *Ru*[52] who is defending the early Confucian position that moral intuitions are derived from internalizing literature. The two of them run different questions together as Mozi did. One topic concerns what constitutes a *shi-fei* response's being right. Another is how one *knows* which *shi-fei* to generate in a situation. The third is where the motivation to *shi-fei* should come from. We could distinguish thus between the source of morality's legitimacy, the source of its knowability, and the source of our moral motivation. Mencius and Gaozi debate simply and ambiguously about the *source* of morality. Is it internal (from the *xin*^heart-mind) or external (from *yan*^language)?

Mencius, given his focus on moral psychology, can be best understood as concentrating on the third, motivation question. We have had to extrapolate to infer his answers to purely normative or meta-ethical questions. Mencius' position makes most sense on the motivation issue. There, we can understand his view relative to traditionalist Confucianism. Xunzi argues that morality's *content* is a product of artifice and invention. It is a historical accumulation of social practices that people learn and *internalize*. Mozi's position is externalist in this sense as well. He advocates language reform to accomplish moral reform.

Motivation for Mozi is partly internal and partly external. We have a prior motivation to absorb and execute social programs learned from hierarchical society. That prior programming gives some motivation and the content of the teaching—the language—shapes human moral motivation. But Mozi's position is not that the *xin*^heart-mind is a tabula rasa. Any discourse *dao* that can actually take hold and *dao*^guide us requires some prior inclinations. These are the inclinations to accept and operate programming in general and perhaps inclinations to accept some programming and reject others.

Later Mohists, as we noted above, abandon talk of natural will. All existing, functional *de*^virtuosity and all performance *dao*^paths (paths that are actually walked) are equally natural. They are equally consistent with the prior programming of *xin*^heart-mind and equally *tian*^natural. So the Mohists sensed that even a thief could appeal to the natural inclinations in justifying his actions. This insight is the first step to Zhuangzi's pluralism.

The Mohist attitude toward language and morality, our earlier analysis suggests, posed a problem for the Mohists. The problem is a version of a problem we also found in Confucius. If a Confucian can rectify the names in the *li,* they must already be able to recognize a certain *shi-fei* as correct. So the Mohists must assume whatever inner programming makes us able to recognize the utility criterion, and makes that recognition motivate us. If so, we should not have to internalize at least *that*. The Mohists must assume that the *ultimate* moral standards are internal. So Mozi's morality has two sources: a natural will to *shi-fei* using benefit-harm and a whole system of *shi-fei*'s instilled by social conditioning—the discourse *dao*.

Mencius delightedly skewers some Mohists for setting up this problem in a way particularly favorable to his point of view. They advocate internalizing universal love while acknowledging and *demonstrating in their behavior* a *natural* inclination to show favor to their own family and kin (3A:5). This shows they have two conflicting sources of morality: an internal natural *dao* that they divide in two—the acceptable standard and the familial part the standard *fei*[rejects]. They have an external linguistic *dao* that guides the rejection of part of the natural inclinations. Mencius expands the natural internal *dao* to include much more than mere preferences. Mozi, like Mencius, must justify accepting part of our natural preference structure and rejecting the other parts. *Tian*[heaven:nature], Mencius says, creates things from a single source. There is one natural *dao*.

Mencius connects the internal-external disagreement with Gaozi to their respective views about how language should be related to the heart-mind. Then he claims that the strength of his (Mencius') position lies in his "understanding *yan*[language]." Asked to explain this (just after stating the foolish man of Song parable), Mencius proceeds to list the ways in which language can lead one astray: "Obsessions motivate unconventional phrases; licentious phrases lead to traps; heretical phrases lead one astray; escapist phrases lead to exhaustion." Words and phrases are dangers and knowing words consists in knowing their dangers. "Introduced into *xin* they are harmful to its administration. Practiced as administrative edicts, they are harmful to the conduct of affairs." Even if the sages did leave us words (the *li*), if one were to come again he would agree with Mencius' language about language (2A:2).

Mencius seems to have nothing intrinsically good to say about *yan* and *bian* (apart from their instrumental value in countering the bad effects of heretical *yan* and *bian*). However, his theory cannot support a radically antilanguage position. Speaking is a kind of action. The innate disposition to *shi* actions may *shi* turning on the light *or* saying "God bless you!". The source of linguistic acts and behavior alike is the heart-mind. Nothing is more natural, as Zhuangzi notes, than animals making noises. All of nature makes noises. Human noisemaking cannot be contrary to *tian*[nature].

The *xin*[heart-mind] makes practical discriminations and distinctions in concrete situations and produces *shi-fei* responses. Some language, at least, must consist of acceptable outputs of public discourse. For example, uttering the thin prescriptive *shi* must sometimes be an appropriate speech act of the cultivated heart. Only that assumption can rationalize Mencius' own participation in *bian*[distinction:dispute].

What Mencius must *really* object to then is the cultural accumulation of these language responses in a public *dao*. We organize speech acts into *ci*[phrases] that we transmit, accumulate, and teach as a *dao*[doctrine]. Those historically amassed *dao* take on lives of their own *outside* the heart. Then we read them back into the heart to direct the growth of its behavioral inclinations. Internalized back into the *xin* they may in principle conflict with its innate programming.[53] If we use a linguistic *dao* to guide creating a different pattern of distinction making, we run a risk: if we instill approving and disapproving in the heart-mind, we stimulate it to reject itself.

Mencius' *two-roots* riposte to Mozi translates as "How could you recognize the direction or standard to be a good one, unless somehow your heart's *shi-fei* capacity picked it out? If you accept following preexisting inclinations of the heart, why ignore the familial inclinations?" To take some external standard of *shi-fei* and use it to change what is in the heart is the essence of the view that morality is external. That is what it means to have *two roots*. Thus, words and doctrines function as weeds do. They choke the natural and correct maturing of the moral seeds.

Mencius' criticism of Mozi has a flip side. Mozi suggests that his words appeal to the heart-mind to adopt some motivation other than the one it had initially. He both accepts and rejects the heart as a motivational basis of moral standards. But Mencius' *opposition to language* does so as well. If our hearts have innate programming that generates the correct *shi-fei* outputs, then using language to guide us must be one of them. The continuity of the cosmos, the unity of *qi,* suggests that the language too is natural. Its accumulation and its natural implementation in learning, education, and the inculcation of values must be natural. Even the reflective adjustment of tradition—moral reform—must also be the natural effects of the *xin* and *qi.* How can Mencius object to them?[54]

We can translate the question of the motivational source of morality into an epistemological question. We tend to use our own epistemic concepts for this. Mozi did not develop a concept of reason. Mencius does not develop a concept of intuition. The traditional Western *bian*[distinction] was not part of their conceptual framework. We understood Mozi's approach *as similar* to appealing to reason in using objective, measurement standards. He did not, however, formulate a psychological theory of a faculty and use it as an ideal of individual mental functioning. If he had, it would not be a faculty of engaging in proof activity. The closest Mozi comes to a concept like logic and proof is the more general notion of the *necessity of a path given our grasping of a standard.* To accept a basic *shi-fei* is to accept a whole pattern of *shi-fei*s that accord with the standard.

Mencius' epistemological position would be that the source of all knowledge of *shi-fei* was of first-level situational responses of the heart. You could not know what is moral by dividing the heart's *shi-fei* responses into basic, authoritative ones and derivative, changeable ones. The form this mistake takes is that of a linguistic *dao.* Language cannot be either a motivational or an epistemic access to morality.

But Mencius does have a faculty: the innate distinction-making faculty (the seed of *shi-fei*). And we can ask what the faculty apprehends: to what does it give epistemological access? We have been allowing Mencius a realistic answer. Mencius' morality is realistic in a formal sense. There is *one* correct answer to every situational moral problem. Is it also realistic in a metaphysical sense? We have also allowed the *qi*[material force] theory to suggest that it was. The correct answer vibrated somehow with cosmic moral structure. This approximates the Cheng-Zhu *realist* interpretation of Mencius. The rival Wang *idealist* interpretation insists that there can be no such metaphysical separation of *qi* and *xin.* It conflicts with Mencius' insistence that morality was internal! It makes *knowledge* of morality internal, but the *reality* on which the knowledge depends is an external state of *qi.*

But Mencius, again, may not have thought the matter through as deeply as

Wang Yang-ming.[55] His example in discussion with Gaozi is of an elder person. When I *zhang*[elder] (deem and treat as elder) a *zhang*[elder] (one who is elder), what is going on? Gaozi insists that the *zhang*[elder] is outside, Mencius that it comes from inside. Gaozi doesn't raise this difficulty (Mencius may have been supervising the writing) but what would constitute anyone's *zhang*[elder]-ing incorrectly? The motivation and the judgment may come from within, but their correctness or validity seems to depend on what is outside. Mencius can be consistent only at the cost, as I have argued before, of accepting the wild Chanists' conclusion that whatever I *shi-fei* must be correct.

We could understand Mencius as arguing that humans have an entire innate moral grammar. That moral grammar enables them to process any morally neutral external reality structure and produce the morally right line of behavior. But moral rightness has no metaphysical basis other than its situational production by the heart. That would preserve Mencius' claim that morality is *metaphysically* internal rather than external.[56]

We have motivated Mencius' position by noticing a problem in Mozi: the paradox of moral reform. It appears that to propose a moral reform, Mozi must divide the heart in an arbitrary way. Others, with other moral outlooks, will propose dividing it in different ways. The impression that the solution to the paradox of moral reform is status-quo ethics, however, is an illusion. It makes sense only if no debate about *dao* has started, in which case it, of course, it is pointless. Once moral reform has been proposed, one can no longer deny that proposing and debating moral reform is natural. The status-quo answer must itself, therefore, reject a part of natural moral processing. Debating about changing our programming *is* part of our programming. The only *real* status-quo solution *once the problem has been raised* is *"anything goes."*

Of course we *have* innate programming. Our innate programming is to accept social programming. Mozi's concrete position in favor of the *li-hai*[benefit-harm] standard is controversial. But the Mohist position that morality is both external and internal looks quite sound. Mencius cannot show that acquiring intuitions is unnatural. Rejecting Mencius position is not rejecting intuitionism; but only rejecting *innate intuitionism.*

Successful businessmen, doctors, scientists, computer programers, dancers, logicians, and farmers all cultivate reliable intuitions. The intuitions guide them. That entails neither that their intuitions are innate nor that they are entirely socially conditioned. Mozi preferred objective measurement, but his psychological theory followed early Confucian accounts of the growth of intuitions. This produces a way of recognizing how morality—moral motivation and awareness—can be an interaction of both internal and external programming. Mozi's utilitarian moral reform seeks to emphasize objective, external measurement connection. But it cannot rule out both innate and learned patterns of inclination.

Of course, we have no comforting answer to Mencius' worry that a Mohist must alter or erase some his internal programming, his natural concern for special relations. Some settled programming must be changed if we are to effect a reflectively chosen program of universal altruism. We can't comfort Mencius, but we can wonder why he finds the prospect uncomfortable. It can only be his unreflective preference for status-quo Confucian values. We can dismiss the simple condemnation that Mozi is going against nature because Mozi's concern about what programming we *ought to* adopt is a natural concern. Mencius' assumption—that it must be the innate one—simply begs the normative question in favor of a controversial and unreflective conception of the status quo. His position requires that we erase the natural programming to use language and to raise second-level moral reform issues.

Both sides now owe us some reason for normative selection among natural dispositions. Mozi at least gives his self-defeating critique of the Confucian morality he rejects. Mencius relies only on his righteous status-quo bias.

Logic, Language, and Analogy in The Mencius

Mencius has no explicit doctrine of logic or reason of his own. His practice has been the subject of controversy, both intense criticism and dedicated defense. As I have noted, I find myself firmly among the critics. I take the view that D. C. Lau characterizes as "not unusual for a reader of *The Mencius*" that Mencius "indulged consistently in what appears to be pointless argument [and] that his opponents were always effectively silenced by *non sequiturs*."[57] His hostile attitude toward *yan* and *bian* seem to me reflected in his practice as well as his theory. He deploys words almost randomly in facing his philosophical opponents. Mencius' attitude seems to be that, since he knows intuitively what is right, any move that befuddles or embarrases the opponent or gets him to back down is acceptable. He regards argument as wordplay that he has to endure from people of *lesser cultivation*. His only consistent purpose in argument is to fend off challenges, frequently with obfuscation and verbal smoke screens.

To say, as his defenders do,[58] that he depends on a weak form of argument by analogy is already to give him too much credit. I find his analogies atrociously inept and unconvincing. This reaction, however, is also controversial. Graham, for example, says:

> The dialogues with Kao-tzu proceed by a meticulous examination of analogies. Arthur Waley, writing in 1939, declared of Mencius: "As a controversialist he is nugatory. The whole discussion (Book VI) about whether Goodness and Duty are internal or external is a mass of irrelevant analogies, most of which could equally well be used to disprove what they are intended to prove." That few scholars today would share Waley's scorn is a good illustration of our changed understanding of Chinese philosophy over the past half-century. D. C. Lau's paper in 1963 . . . was a landmark as one of the first close analyses of ancient Chinese argumentation.[59]

When all the emperor's wise men agree that his new clothes are of the most exquisite material ever weaved by human hands, one should, I suppose, doubt the appearances. I am not sure, however, that I am in so small a minority in agreeing with Waley's characterization. Even if I were, the reader could guess that I would be more likely to offer Lincoln's analysis than Graham's. Some sinologists can be fooled and intimidated, at least some of the time. I doubt that I will be accused of maintaining that the ruling interpretive view is free from the human tendency to gullibility.

Lau's imperious analysis does seem to have overwhelmed everyone. I am still puzzled about just how his argument goes. In the end, I am most dazzled with his open admission of theoretical motivation. I suspect it explains Graham's alleged majority now convinced of Mencius logical acumen: "[I]t is difficult to believe that a thinker of Mencius' calibre and reputation could have indulged consistently in what appears to be pointless argument or that his opponents were always effectively silenced by *non-sequiturs*. The fault, we suspect must lie with us. We must have somehow failed to understand these arguments."[60]

Lau's study is frequently cited and Graham's praise is *nearly* universal. It is an excellent example of a standard Confucian approach to interpretive theory. He begins with faith that Mencius could not be as bad as he looks: "The fault, we suspect must lie with us." He passes blithely over the implicit admission that *he does indeed appear to be logically incompetent*. Then he attributes background assumptions and hypotheses about meaning that will make sense of Mencius. He reasons that only these assumptions make Mencius look good (and his opponents bad). So the whole cluster "could be assumed to be familiar to the readers of Mencius' day, including assumptions accepted alike by Mencius and his opponents as well as the philosophical views peculiar to each side and also, of course, the method of analogy as used in argument."[61]

This allows us to deny the appearance that Mencius is incompetent at the cost of convicting all his opponents, who apparently make sensible criticisms, of logical and linguistic incompetence. To deny one appearance, we have to deny two. So Lau's study has the form that I have been targeting throughout this book: Start by assuming that the Confucians are deep and profound. Attribute meaning hypotheses and background assumptions that sustain this faith. Claim that your hypotheses are the *real meanings* of the terms and the common assumptions of all Chinese thought. If others seem to have made clear sense—especially if they are Mohists—accuse them of failing to understand the deep meaning of the language or their own assumptions. "At first sight the Mohists seem to have brought order to an otherwise tidy problem. But on closer examination one sees that this is achieved only by ignoring certain factors that Kao Tzu and Mencius took into account."[62]

Graham is right that Lau's paper launched a veritable growth industry in trying to make sense of Mencius' analogies used in his discussions with Gaozi. It is the Mencian counterpart of searching for Confucius' elusive one thread that ties all his aphorisms together. It also has produced an equally diverse range of answers. I do not propose detailed or alternative analyses of Lau's or all these other similarly motivated interpretations. I am again content to let the plethora of warring accounts speak for itself.

I am targeting instead the common assumptions and motivations of that whole pro-Confucian interpretive strategy. It is not my plan to show that any or all attempts at making sense are impossible. I am arguing that the theoretical costs are too great. The cost of countering the *admitted* appearance that Mencius is a logical simpleton is that there must be an enormously complex hidden doctrine which in fact all his opponents know but fail to process as deeply and cleverly as Mencius does. Those who *appear* clear and competent, especially, must be accused of missing the point of the deep background meanings, etymology and assumptions—which they in fact share.

Compare this elaborate dodge with a theory that saves the appearances. Confucians simply do not understand how to do philosophy. Others in the early Chinese culture managed to make more sense of the issues—just as they appear to do. We can make clear sense of *Chinese* philosophy as long as we do not insist that Confucians must be at the forefront. And in the end we even make as much sense of the Confucians. We simply do not persist in the charade that they have to come out right all the time.

So the cost of this heroic Confucian interpretation looks even more foolish when we realize that it still fails. With all the heroic invention of background assumptions, Confucians still do not succeed in making sense of Mencius. Lau's study is widely cited as defending Mencius logical reputation but without explaining *how* Lau's analysis is supposed to have done that. Grant, for the sake of argument, that Lau proposes explanatory hypotheses about the meanings and background beliefs that make sense of Mencius' positions. He alleges that Mencius' dialectical opponents, like the Mohists, didn't understand these points. But how does this bear on Mencius' use of analogy? Lau suggests that the Chinese have a peculiar *use of analogy* in argument. That is another of those shared assumptions that only Mencius, among all Chinese philosophers, understands.

We normally understand analogy as used in an argument or in an exposition. Strict argument from analogy should be like a weak inductive argument. A and B are relevantly alike, so whatever is true of A is probably true of B. The strength of the argument depends on the degree of relevant similarity. Lau's explanation does not turn any of the analogies into argumentative analogies—as he admits.[63] His position is more modest. Elaborately annotating Mencius' theory, he removes the appearance of *total irrelevance* of the analogy. That is not enough to make the analogy carry the weight of an argument. In their role as argument, Waley's complaints remain completely valid.

But could the analogies be expository? Based on his philological reconstruction of Mencius, Lau *explains away the appearance that Mencius' analogies are irrelevant.* He alleges that we can make sense of the analogy *once we accept Lau's way of construing the dispute.* But, one would have expected the direction of explanation to go the other way. The normal purpose of an explanatory analogy is to make the philosophical point clear. If one has to have the philosophical point presented as an abstract theory before he can even grasp what point the analogy makes, then it is not clear *what role the analogy is supposed to play.* It does not argue for the truth of the claim and it does not illuminate it.

All this suggests that maybe Mencius used analogy to challenge twentieth-century interpreters to get his doctrine right. Only by cleverly reconstructing Mencius position can we understand why the analogy had any point! All too frequently, even then the puzzle remains for us. Lau falls back on the fact that, *in Mencius' account of the exchange,* Gaozi doesn't object and allows Mencius to have the last word. Lau appeals to this lack of objection to justify the conclusion that the analogy must have had a point in those days even if we cannot figure it out.[64]

So what can we make of Lau's claim that ancient Chinese thinkers used a unique method of analogy? The Mohists describe (clearly and unmysteriously, as usual) a procedure they call *matching phrases.* Lau asserts that it is a "very good description of the method as it was used by Mencius." But the Mohists' procedure approximates, at best, one argument in the debate with Gaozi. Lau and Graham highlight that argument to imply that Mencius was following a sophisticated logical method. Even if they are correct, it is minimal help. Waley was only minimally wrong—Mencius' arguments were *only largely* and not *entirely* a mass of irrelevant analogies. One argument, it is alleged, was sophisticated.

But is that enough? Was it a valid argument? Was it even logically competent? Let us take a closer look. This exchange with Gaozi is the passage that attracts Lau's analysis.

> Gaozi said, "The inborn is what is meant by *nature.*" "Is that," said Mencius, "the same as 'White is what is meant by *white'?*" "Yes."
>
> "Is the whiteness of white feathers the same as the whiteness of white snow and the whiteness of white snow the same as the whiteness of white jade?"
>
> "Yes."
>
> "In that case, is the nature of the hound the same as the nature of an ox and the nature of an ox the same as the nature of a person?" (6A:3)

At first appearance, Gaozi opens the argument by formulating an obvious and damning objection to Mencius' innatism. *All* the inborn dispositions are equally natural. Why pick out one aspect of nature as the ruling one? Supposedly this is the key to Gaozi's view that human nature is morally neutral. Mencius' response, as Waley observes, seems pointless and irrelevant. Lau's attempt to remove this impression, however, does not depend only on the formal structure of the argument, but the familiar ploy of elaborate and clever interpretive theories about the character *xing*[nature].

Interpretation plays its usual role. It not only excuses Mencius' irrelevance but defangs Gaozi's obvious, sensible, straightforward objection to Mencius' theory. Gaozi's opening move, we come to see, is not the objection to Mencius innatist position that it appears to be. It is instead an irrelevant, pointless, hidden tautology, or pun or some confused expression of the deep, obscure meaning relation between *sheng*[life] and *xing*[nature] (*Xing*[nature] consists of *sheng*[life] with a heart radical.) Traditional suggestions go that *sheng*[birth] and *xing*[nature] might have be written with the same character or have been homonyms. Graham argues that failure to understand the deep meaning of the term *xing*[nature] partly accounts for Waley's mistake.

> Here we may cite another interesting mistake of the truly great Arthur Waley, looking back at him with our superior wisdom half a century later. . . . It has been usual—I did it myself in early publications—to translate Kao-tzu's "It is *sheng* that is meant by *hsing [xing]*" as "It is inborn that is meant by nature." And indeed Hsün-tzu in the next century does identify *hsing* with what we have from birth. But we have seen that in ordinary parlance of the 4th century B.C., the *hsing* of an animate thing, in so far as it was distinguished from *sheng*, meant the course on which life completes its development if sufficiently nourished and not obstructed or injured from outside.[65]

Graham's *plain observation* about our superior wisdom of what the term meant in ordinary parlance of the time does seem the least bit tailor-made for Mencius. And it seems almost to vindicate Waley's accusation that Mencius used terms in idiosyncratic ways if Graham's theory requires that the meaning change takes place just in time to make sense of Mencius' argument and then changes back magically for Xunzi, the Mohists, and the later Daoists. This convenient theory of meaning change is typical when interpreters begin with *the assumption* that Mencius must be truly profound despite the initial appearance of gross confusion.

Somehow, one or the other of these various complicated theories about the deep and constantly shifting meaning of *xing*[nature] mysteriously excuse Mencius' first response. It is not an argument *by analogy*. It is *phrase matching*. Based on this supposed connection, Mencius *properly* says that "What I mean by nature is that which is inborn" is analogous to "What is white is white." In Mencius' telling of the story, Gaozi lets him get away with it. No doubt it shows that Gaozi shared the common but temporarily changed meaning of the character! Forget, for the moment that giving Mencius this inadequate fig leaf has its cost. Gaozi's gambit and response now lose any semblance of intelligibility. No one bothers to explain why *he* would start a conversation with such a pointless tautology or pun.

The fig leaf is inadequate anyway. While it helps explain Mencius' response, it does not remove Waley's objection. If *sheng*[life] and *xing*[nature] were the same character, we could understand Mencius' move, but it would still be invalid. It would now be merely a more understandable error. If they are homophonous then it is a pun—but Mencius move is even more clearly invalid. If it means what Graham says, then I gather that that is supposed to make Gaozi's opening sentence into an analytic truth. Gaozi allows Mencius to rephrase his pronouncement as "What grows is what grows and completes its development if sufficiently nourished and not obstructed or injured from outside." But that is not an analytic truth. If one *reversed it,* it would be. "What grows and . . . and . . . and . . . is what grows" is a little silly, but it is analytically true. But even then it is not analytically true *the way* "White is white" is analytically true. In the end, I simply don't see how all this clever philology saves Mencius from the appearance of logical error.

If we allow that first logical slip, Lau's argument goes, the form of the rest of the argument looks like one later studied by the Neo-Mohists in their analytic theory of language. The Mohists analyzed and criticized an algebraic form of inference. The algebraic form goes as follows: We begin with a simple sentence form: [X is Y]. The inference being tested is, if [X is Y] then is [KX is KY] where K is any constant term. For example, a horse is an animal, the head of a horse is the head of an animal; riding a horse is riding an animal and so on.

The Mohists, as we will see later, show that this apparently cogent inference is *in*valid. Lau needs to show that Mencius was logically competent. He claimed to do that by showing that Mencius knew something about Mohist logic. But the appeal to the similarity with phrase matching leaves us with a dilemma. If Mencius did *not* know anything about logic, then we should accept the plain appearance and say he was incompetent. If he *did* know what the Later Mohist's were up to *but didn't notice* that they had shown the argument form was invalid, then he is still incompetent!

In fact the case for Mencius is even worse than that. Not only does Mencius mimic an argument form that the Mohists knew to be invalid, but he mimics it shockingly badly. He distorts and bungles the form to the point we cannot even imagine how he might have been *tempted* to think it was valid. It looks as if Mencius has no grip of the notion of validity of inference at all. He demonstrates by his incredibly implausible mishandling of the form that he does not even have a clue what the Mohist analysis of the inference procedure was about. If he had heard anything about the Later Mohist's analysis, I'm afraid it just looks worse for Mencius. He is not only incompetent, but unteachable.

Mencius' form is as follows. If you accept [*A* is *B*] (inborn is nature) and that [*A* is *B*] the way [*C* is *C*] (white is white), then if you further accept [*C* of *CR* is *C* of *CS*] (white of white feathers is white of white snow) then you must accept [*B* of *T* is *B* of *U*] (nature of an ox is the nature of a hound). The structure *the Mohists* analyze is tempting but invalid. The structure Mencius uses has so little logical plausibility that I'm at a loss for words! There is a superficial resemblance but it is so far-fetched that it is almost impossible to state it.

Even if we allow the philologists their claim that given some deep insight into meaning, sound, written shape, or etymology, Gaozi's first step really amounts to [*B* is *B*] it does not help Mencius much. The connection between the concession he wrings from Gaozi and the use of [*C*] in step 3 and [*B*] in step 4 still defies any plausible explanation. [*A*] plays no further role in the entire argument.

About a peculiarly Mencian form of reasoning, then, this example tells us little more than that Mencius is incompetent at the logic of his day rather than being merely incompetent period. At best it shows that he has got wind of the logical discussions and hoped to exploit them as a smoke screen. It does show, as I allowed, that Waley is wrong to think that all of Mencius' arguments are by irrelevant analogy. This one may be irrelevant use of phrase matching instead.

Mencius' *pattern* of reasoning is that he will use almost any word trick, equivocation, shifting of his position, personal attack, and haughty dismissive snobbery to get the better of his opponents in exchanges as he reports them in his book. His favorite ploy is shaming with question-begging, leading questions and far-fetched figurative analogies. Consistent with his antilanguage views, he places no faith in words or the idea that there might be morally defensible ways to deploy them. As soon as you get into *bian*[distinction:dispute], all is trickery and delusion. The serious study of inference forms is the business of the school of names, not an antilanguage philosopher like Mencius. Given Mencius' general antilanguage position, we can assume he has no particular use for the school of names or serious interest in their careful logical doctrines.

Mencius' Lasting Influence

Mencius is, in the broad historical picture, the most influential Confucian of the period. Even if he was the laughingstock of the classical philosophers, his eventual influence on Chinese thought was pervasive. The confusion of Chinese thought and Confucian thought typically amounts to confusing Chinese thought with the thought of Mencius. Daoism particularly, I will argue, gets turned into a slightly less specific version of Mencius' intuitive mysticism. Chinese thinkers in the classical period, however, were not much impressed. Laozi's analysis undermined Mencius' assumption that our intuitive judgments must be innate. Zhuangzi's criticism demolished his intuitionism. Even later Confucians were mostly skeptical of his naively optimistic assumptions about human nature. They regarded him as a whipping boy to be brought out for a laugh before they got onto serious subjects.

The weak versions of his claims, on the other hand, were not even controversial. Probably the only novelty in them was the assertion that a panhuman concern was innate. Everyone from Confucius to Hanfei-zi, Mozi to Zhuangzi and probably including even Yang Zhu, shared the view that human nature is social. But Mencius' statement of the detail of the social nature was the most famous and systematic formulation of the claim. The strong version of the doctrine of the goodness of human nature eventually came to dominate medieval Confucianism. So did his conception of the true king and his democratic adjustments to the theory of the mandate of heaven. Even in modern times, both Mao Zedong and his nationalist opponents measured their right to rule by the (frequently manipulated) acclaim and affection of the people.

In theory, the orthodox Confucian establishment usually agreed with Mencius on the political and moral importance of economic well-being, education, and the in-principle moral equality of all people. Those attitudes are still found in modern Chinese revolutionaries and reformers. Mencius' view of the moral cycle associated with the mandate of heaven became almost a self-fulfilling prophecy in Chinese dynastic history. Confucians pretty much took his view of the role of scholars in those cycles. The scholar was to serve his ruler loyally. They usually took *loyalty* in the best sense to mean keeping the ruler as moral as possible. This gave a Confucian basis for criticizing superiors when their policies were not those of *ren-yi*$^{\text{benevolent morality}}$. His political strategy of winning the *xin*$^{\text{heart-minds}}$ of the people has survived to the present day in Mao's successful mass-line strategy, borrowed by Ho Chi Minh. It has even seeped into modern Western culture via the Vietnam war. Finally his doctrine of self-cultivation and its resultant moral mysticism informs the attitudes of intellectuals in China up to the present time.

Mencius does give Confucianism a reflective normative theory, whatever its weaknesses. Confucianism had simply ignored the question that Mozi forced Mencius to face. Thus, Mencius' formative influence on the Confucian establishment is no accident. Act deontology is not a particularly good normative theory. It is an enormously slippery one, easy to flex as circumstances or issues require. It is hard to get a counterexample to it since it rejects consistent commitment to *any* normative doctrine or statement of principles. The heart-mind is the sole source of moral know-how. His theory gave him a reason to refuse to engage in reasoned argument: "In my heart-mind I know it's wrong!" That is all the morally superior man needs. No culture, however, is free from this particular brand of sophistry.

The instinct-based position, not surprisingly, turns out to be a magnificent defender of tradition. It gives Mencius a glib rejoinder to Mozi, whether or not a philosophically adequate answer. Mencius holds that moral knowledge cannot come in a system or be any form of calculation. We respond to a particular situation with a cultivated moral skill. By the time we can understand the theory, we have already absorbed a social morality. So this doctrine still strikes defenders as a good way to block raising the Socratic question and proposing moral reform. Whatever our moral instincts are, we regard them as right. Most of Graham's appreciative herd of Mencius worshipers still think that the problems of moral reform dictate Mencius' status-quo solution.

The distinctive part of Mencius' theory is his denial that one can enhance the heart's reliability by learning and consciously following some discourse *dao*. The *dao*, for Mencius, is the performance *dao*: the contextually generated pattern of *shi-fei* judgments of the properly cultivated heart-mind. Language cannot capture it. Theory cannot guide it.

Notice especially that the formal structure of Mencius' antilanguage perspective is close to that of the Neo-Confucian portrayal of Daoism. His mysticism is moral, to be sure, but Mencius, not Lao Tzu, was the original Chinese, intuitive, antilanguage advocate. He presents as his standard of guidance an absolute, instinctive, morally obligatory *dao* which language cannot capture.

Following that inner *dao* amounts to following one's inner nature and acting spontaneously. One who has cultivated her skills to the highest point requires no conscious thought to act. The actions just spontaneously flow out of her. She unites mystically in her actions with a universal force that fills the entire universe. Language distorts that inner natural *dao*. As we shall see, Laozi does more to undermine that position than to formulate it.

We should not be surprised at these parallels between Mencius and immature Daoism. Mencius, after all, copied the structure of Yang Zhu's argument in order to deal with Mozi. Naturally his use of the argument structure will commit him to a version of Confucianism with proto-Daoist theoretical outcomes. Confucians are fond of claiming that we can harmonize Confucianism with Daoism. There is, they smugly intone, no conflict. Mencius' system in particular promotes harmony with Daoism. Neo-Confucianism came to understand Mencius and patterned its interpretation of Daoism on him. However, the alleged compatibility is an artifact of Mencius' transforming Confucianism along Daoist lines—not because Daoist insights are compatible with initial Confucian theory. And the Daoism Mencius copied was the proto-Daoism of Yang Zhu. Daoism grew through three levels of sophistication beyond Mencius.

My real objection to these claims of compatibility comes in the insipid and primitive Neo-Confucian conception of Daoism. Confucians tend to read all Daoism as staying at the immature level it was when Mencius borrowed it from Yang Zhu.

About that, as we shall shortly see, they are dead wrong!

6

Laozi: Language and Society

Beginning, however with the mystical dimensions of Taoism, we are immediately struck by the use of the word *tao* as the dominant term of this Chinese mysticism. How does a term which seems to refer in Confucianism mainly to social and natural *order* come to refer to a mystic reality?

BENJAMIN SCHWARTZ[1]

From these passages we can see that the entity called the *tao* existed before the universe came into being. This, for the author, is an absolutely indisputable fact. It has an essence which is genuine, and this genuineness is vouched for by the existence of the universe which it has produced and continues to sustain. But beyond this there is nothing we can say about the *tao*.

D. C. LAU[2]

Theoretical Interpretation

An interpretation, like an explanatory scientific theory, explains some aspect of the world. We use interpretive theories when we want to explain some language—whether the language of dolphins, aliens from space, poets, philosophers, mathematicians, or mothers. To understand some principles of interpretation let us suppose we came on the following text carved on the walls of a cave:[3]

! ∧ ! & @
@ & # * !
$ ∧ % & ! ∧ !

Notice that we start with a theory. We are treating the marks as text or inscriptions rather than as water stains or wind carvings. That means that we will adopt a special way of explaining them. We call our explanation an interpretation when we suppose that the marks are a language. For ease in making my point, let me stipulate that we further theorize that the marks are mathematical statements. To interpret or explain them, we would look for an assignment of values to the parts. We make the exercise out to be code breaking.

First notice that one symbol (&) occurs once in each formula. This suggests the hypothesis that & translates to = . We presuppose a lot in this hypothesis—the mathematical language may not have an explicit equal sign (just as classical Chinese has no *is*). Given that hypothesis, however, we might guess that ∧ and * are also mathematical operators and the other symbols are numbers. Again we presuppose a particular arithmetical syntax in this hypothesis. (The authors of the inscription might not write their operators between two numbers.) The hypothesis does make the symbols intelligible. We can understand the scribbles as mathematical formulas. Let's try substituting letters for numbers in a couple of forms.

$$a/a = b \qquad a + a = b$$
$$b = c - a \qquad b = c - a$$
$$d/e = a/a \qquad d + e = a + a$$

Both make the text we found intelligible in our mathematical scheme. Intelligibility is a minimal requirement—a necessary but not sufficient condition on an interpretation. Notice now that we already have two intelligible forms. We need a principle that selects among the intelligible value assignments. Consider the two translations of the last formulas.

$$d/e = a/a \qquad d + e = a + a$$

The left-hand translation into our notation presents a problem. Since $a/a = 1$, d/e must also equal 1. So, if we choose the first assignment, then d and e must be the same number. Now that *is* possible! d might be *twelve* and e *a dozen*.

Still, we prefer the second assignment. Why? We could say that the second assignment of operators fit the symbols more neatly—that is, more elegantly and simply. We assigned a distinct number to each symbol. In science, we prefer the most elegant possible explanation. Of the theories which make sense of the inscriptions, we similarly prefer the one which makes sense most economically. Implicitly, our interpretive theory assumes that a mathematician carved the symbols and took some care in doing so. We further assume that our unknown mathematician values nonredundancy in her mathematical system as we do. She *thinks like us*.

None of these assumptions is sacred. All are defeasible. If we knew a lot more about her, we could use external evidence to confirm the different assumption. However, we only have the text to go on. Someone could rebut our guesses by offering a more elegant set of guesses that explains the inscriptions better. At this point, given our evidence, we would say the second interpretation is the better.

Now substituting numbers for letters, consider the following possibilities:

$$0 + 0 = 1 \qquad 1 + 1 = 2 \qquad 2 + 2 = 4$$
$$1 = 2 - 0 \qquad 2 = 3 - 1 \qquad 4 = 6 - 2$$
$$3 + 4 = 2 + 2 \qquad 4 + (-2) = 1 + 1 \qquad 3 + 1 = 2 + 2$$

Considering just these three, we would not pay much attention to the first one. Why not? Why do the other two seem preferable? Because they make every formula in the text true. You could probably think of many interpretive theories that would make all the formulas true. Remember that we have only the text to go on. So we would prima facie regard one of the latter two as a better explanation of the symbols.

Notice the element of relativity in our interpretative choices. We prefer an interpretation that makes the text something we could imagine ourselves writing. We could change our minds about the assumption about the apparent arithmetic. With other evidence, we might conclude either that she was an atrocious mathematician, that she intended to confuse us, or that she was merely doodling. Perhaps if we had a whole book we could theorize about many of her other beliefs. Then we might have reason to say that the first assignment was the correct explanation of the text. We could imagine that an atrocious mathematician with all those other beliefs might have produced that sort of thing. But given what we have to go on, absent such additional information, the truth-preserving translations are better.

Notice that we still have *two* truth-preserving theories. Which of *them* should we accept? Intuitively, again, we prefer the second. Why? Because the last formula bothers us:

$$4 + (-2) = 1 + 1 \quad 3 + 1 = 2 + 2$$

Our explanation would be more *elegant* if we postulate assignments only to positive integers. We are perhaps making assumptions about the concept of zero and the natural ways of representing negative numbers. We are assuming that the mathematical language, if it had developed enough to have negative numbers, would have evolved a certain economy in representing them. It would have some regularized system for differentiating negative numbers. Otherwise it would use negative symbols that had no relation to their positive counterparts.

These appeals to simplicity, elegance, or economy in an explanation are other elements of relativity in interpretation. What counts as simple depends partly on what we already accept and partly on how we could imagine ourselves operating with this scheme. When we offer interpretation as an explanation of someone's production of a text, our theory may seem to include an implicit psychology. Do we assume that the writer reasons as we do? Do the principles for choosing among possible interpretations reflect these assumptions? If they do, they seem like giant empirical presupposition. Why assume that we all reason alike?

We do not, I think, make *that* assumption. It is, of course, empirically possible that other beings process things differently. Some may process so differently that their communication could be impossible for us to understand. That is, what seems to be their language will have computational rules or conditions of use that we could never master or understand given our human capacities. How would we discover that to be true of hyperintelligent space beings or dolphins? I suggest the only way to test that hypothesis about other creatures is to try to identify their communication patterns and interpret them. Each failure would tend to confirm the special-logic hypothesis. One success, of course, would more decisively disprove it. *Our attempts to interpret would follow the same constraints as before*. We would strive for a simple, elegant, coherent explanation.

It is empirically possible that we could never succeed. Our intelligence is limited and there could be things and beings we could never understand. Their intelligence may be so much greater than ours, or of such a different nature that we could simply never comprehend, even with computers, how their language worked. To them, we may seem like parrots, able merely to make selected noises with no sense of how the noises fit together in a system or into their lives. The same could be true of creatures of lesser intelligence and radically different goals and purposes.

Proving that the target of our interpretation is fundamentally different in its reasoning process is proving that interpretation is impossible. Saying that they are *fundamentally* different in their reasoning process is really saying, "I give up!" If we have made an assumption about common human reasoning, we have made it in choosing to interpret rather than choosing simply to chant the sounds. So the irrationalist claim cannot be a coherent objection from someone who *simultaneously proposes a rival interpretation*. It can only come from someone who has chosen a different line of work. Coming from a rival interpretation, it is simply asking to be excused from any theoretical constraints—especially those that require that his interpretive theory be clear and coherent.

Our reflections have already pointed toward two different versions of the constraints guiding our choice of interpretive theories. The principle of charity says our interpretations should maximize the truth in a language. The principle of humanity says we should maximize the reasonableness. The core of both principles is this: we assume that the rules of syntactical composition and logical entailment *work*. Over time, a language must achieve recognizably human goals in the real world.

However differently our languages work, they must work for a human community in *the real world*. This motivates the principle of charity. We assume we use the language to talk about our world and so we choose the interpretive assignment that best fits the world, the interpretation that maximizes truth. Of course, we can measure fit with the world only through our own scheme. This principle leads us to prefer agreement with our own ideas and beliefs.

The principle of humanity arises from the worry that the principle of charity forces *too much agreement* in the content of our interpretation. A computational language could work in the world as *we* understand it with concepts and assumptions quite different from those we now hold. Truth-based charity is not charitable enough. We ought to allow that our interpretation attribute what seems to us error to our hypothetical authors *as long as* that error is humanly explicable. That is, if we can understand how different assumptions might lead another human culture to that belief. This shifts our focus from the truth of individual statements to how some beliefs lead to others.

We assume that we can come to see how other humans reason from one statement to another. Instead of maximizing truth, we maximize some kind of humanly understandable harmony among the beliefs. This is an informal assumption. We carry it out informally by contemplating various sets of beliefs. We do not appeal to any particular logical theory. If an interpretation of a statement otherwise links the statements in the language in an elegantly understandable way, we need not reject the interpretation because we do not believe the statement. We call this principle of interpretation the principle of humanity.

Notice that we use both principles holistically. We do not use the principle of charity or humanity to make *each* statement true or rationally to connect small fragments. We maximize the truth or reasonableness of the *entire corpus*. We do not change the assignment of numbers to inscriptions *on each line*. Our cave corpus was small. But we contemplated how we might revise our assumptions in the light of more information, a fuller text or some other knowledge of the tradition. The principle of humanity is inherently holistic since it looks for logical connection among attributed beliefs.

In many cases, the two principles coincide. The principle of humanity would normally attribute true beliefs about the world to the author. Both principles could make sense of a claim that a text is contradictory. The principle of charity rules out contradictions (because they are untrue) *except* where no more consistent interpretation is possible. The principle of humanity directly seeks consistency but we can *humanly* understand the tricks, motivations, and deceptive arguments that generate philosophical paradox. Absent independent information about the author's theoretical inclinations and motivations, *humane* interpretation normally selects coherent (consistent) readings over incoherent ones. Its threshold is lower, but the principle of humanity does not allow one to attribute a contradictory theory to a text on purely speculative grounds. We may not appeal simply to an unsupported a priori assumption that the school to which we attribute the text "believes in contradiction."

Now, suppose that someone lived in the cave. He had been studying the text for a long time, had a long beard, hypnotic eyes, and a deep authoritative voice, and a special cap, which he claimed helped his intuition. He told you that the first reading which we had rejected was the traditionally accepted one. However, he did not give any evidence other than to say that his father told him that his father told him . . . what the correct reading was. When you asked why his tradition had preferred the strange interpretation, he replied that the author was an unorthodox mathematician. Her brain patterns were not like Western rational brain patterns. You asked why the tradition had concluded this about her. He replied, simply, "Well, look at the text!"

Do not let the long beard intimidate you! His argument is a non sequitur. The text proves she is unorthodox only if you accept his interpretation of it. Better interpretations do not make her unorthodox at all. The long beard and the tradition do not change the nature of interpretation. His interpretation stands in need of the same justification as ours. Of course, the long beard's interpretation will still be of interest. For example you may want to know more about him and to discuss the other books he has in the cave. Knowing how his tradition read the text will help you understand *his* philosophical system. It may be relevant to understanding *his ancestors* that they accept the contradictory interpretation. Still, you do not lessen the explanatory burden on an interpretive theory by observing simply that the orthodoxy accepts it. Realism in interpretation is like Mozi's realism in morality. The ancestry of a bad interpretation does not make it a good interpretation.

The Text of the *Daode Jing*

You may have guessed the point of my story. We have in the *Daode Jing* a terse text. Confucian gentleman tell us that according to their tradition of interpretation, this text describes something that it simultaneously claims can not be described. Knowing that Confucians take this view is certainly important to understanding *that* school and especially the Neo-Confucian school. Since it defines its position *in contrast to* Daoism, you must know what it took Daoism to be to understand Neo-

Confucianism. That is not the same thing as understanding Daoism. As a logical and semantic matter, Neo-Confucian traditions of interpretation carry no special weight in determining the correct interpretive theory.

Given that it attributes contradiction as a general feature of Daoism, the Neo-Confucian interpretive theory shoulders a heavy burden of proof. It needs to show that the attribution is required to make sense of the rest of classical philosophy. It will not do merely to say that the incoherence of Daoism follows from meaning hypotheses that make Confucius and Mencius free from any possible rational criticism. The holistic nature of meaning requires a unified theory.

Notice that we are relying on our own practice of interpreting. The Neo-Confucian way of dealing with texts may differ enough from ours that we would not even want to call it *interpretation*. But if the question *is* interpretation, then noting that it is the traditional theory does not lighten the burden of justification. The tradition treats Daoism as a rival theory and criticizes it for this inherent contradiction. When you protest that the traditional interpretation is implausibly contradictory, the standard reply is that the author's mind did not work according to your limited Western rationality. The Daoists used a different logic which accepted contradiction. Now that claim surely requires proof. You ask how we can prove that Daoists use a different logic and tradition says, "Look at the text."

Before we do so, notice that in talking of the *Daode Jing,* we should clarify our background assumptions. We share with Neo-Confucianism the assumption that the text is a philosophy text: that it fits into the philosophical milieu we have been talking about. We have seen that Confucius, Mozi, and Mencius have psychological and linguistic doctrines which differ from Western folk theory. Our assumption amounts to saying the theory of the *Daode Jing* should emerge *from some of the same presuppositions* and focus on *the same issues*. The holistic principles of interpretation rule out the image of a philosopher as a *private thinker* reflecting on the world *de novo* from innate Platonic concepts.[4] The Daoist is not going to start, inexplicably, talking of *truth* and *meaning,* definitions, proof structure, reality and belief. He is not proposing how to further the debate between Parmenides and Heraclitus. He would be reflecting on the *Ru-Mo*^Confucian-Mencius dispute about *shi-fei*^this:not this, names, *dao,* guidance in language, and social organization.

My concern in this chapter is interpretive theory, not textual theory. I accept, in broad outline, the dominant current textual theory. It treats the text as an edited accumulation of fragments and bits drawn from a wide variety of sources—conventional wisdom, popular sayings, poems, perhaps even jokes.[5] And the implicit conclusion of this textual theory is that there was no single author, no Laozi. Further, several versions of the text still compete for our interpretive attention. Two recently found buried in a Han-dynasty tomb, the Ma-wang Dui silk scrolls, differ significantly from the various traditional versions of the texts.

We could undertake to interpret each separate text or we could construct an amalgam of one or more of the earlier versions. We normally hope that our textual hypothesis produces a version that is *closer to the original*. Obviously, we cannot make that claim on the basis of direct comparison! I accept the current textual theory but not necessarily because I have great confidence in their evidence. I do it because an interpretation needs a text to work on.

I will be resisting the current temptation to substitute the Mawang Dui texts for the traditional one.[6] This procedure does not commit us to the view that the traditional text was the original. My goal in this book is to challenge traditional interpretations. There is no tradition of interpretation of the heretofore missing text. But since I do intend to explain classical thought by relating the issues of different schools, I do assume that at least as good a case can be made for the traditional text being the correct version as for the Mawang Dui texts.[7]

If someone offered a well-confirmed textual theory that the new texts were closer to the original *Daode Jing,* we would then have a stronger reason to interpret those texts. But it would not be an irresistible reason. We have outstanding interpretive disputes about this traditional text. The new version would be irrelevant to answering which is the best interpretation of *this* traditional text. Each text, since it contained different words in different places, would have a different *best* interpretation—it would say different things. We would interpret *each* against the background assumption that it fits into the philosophical milieu someplace. In principle we could theorize more or less independently, about the best interpretation of each text.

We assume further that the text is a Daoist one. This assumption is particularly troublesome since there was no clear Daoist school in the sense in which there was a Confucian and a Mohist school. Han historians coined the term *Dao Jia* hundreds of years later. The philosophers in question do share some attitudes and doctrines. What justifies the term is that both central texts (*The Daode Jing* and *The Zhuangzi*) focus on second-level metadiscussion of *dao* itself. Daoists were intrigued by the $Ru\text{-}Mo^{\text{Confucian-Mohist}}$ dispute about which *dao* to follow and by the problems of interpreting *dao* in practical action. They began to question the premise of the $Ru\text{-}Mo^{\text{Confucian-Mohist}}$ period. Should we even be trying to construct, propose and effect a positive *dao?* They began to reflect on the very nature of *dao* and on deep puzzles in the proposal to guide guiding discourse.

A unified theory of the *Daode Jing* as a Daoist text would give it a coherent role in the development of Daoism in the context of ongoing philosophical disputes. I follow the outline given in *The Zhuangzi.* The *Laozi* lies between the theory of *dao* attributed to Shendao and the mature Daoism of Zhuangzi. I regard this as more a theoretical placement than a textual one.[8] It *may* also be historical. The view that most tempts me, however, is Graham's speculation that Zhuangzi borrowed the figure of Laozi as a mouthpiece for a critique of the *Ru-Mo,* moralist period.[9] His would be an anti-language version of a Daoist critique—one crucially like that of Mencius. Zhuangzi may especially have enjoyed casting Laozi in this fantasy dialogue because the historical Lao Tan was a much revered Confucian figure. As Confucius' teacher, he could talk down to Confucius. At the same time, he could expose both the radical anti-Confucian nature of Mencius' anti-language innatism and its theoretical weaknesses. Zhuangzi's discussions between Laozi and Confucius may first have associated Lao Tan's name with Daoist content. That opened the door to the tradition of attributing this developing anthology of iconoclastic, antimoralist aphorisms to Zhuangzi's fantasy character.

Still, Laozi's position, either as the genuine author of the *Daode Jing* or as the figure in Zhuangzi's fantasies, remains a way station in Daoist development. It theoretically represents a primativist antilanguage version of Daoism, the one that would logically have to come *before* the analytic period. The analytic philosophers decisively rebut either the Confucian or Daoist versions of the antilanguage innatism. He may have felt a deep sympathy for primitive Daoism, but Zhuangzi obviously knows the Neo-Mohist objection to it and avoids the error himself. Laozi represents the Daoist counterpart of Mencius.

I identify Daoism as a philosophical focus, a trend of thought that includes a number of different theories as it grows. But those traditionally identified as Daoists tend to share an iconoclastic social-political attitude. Daoists lean away from society and convention. That common attitude, however, is not an explicit doctrine. Daoism has also been compared to relativism in science, mysticism in religion, emotivism in ethics and aesthetics, and anarchism in politics. An interpretive theory should be able to *explain the appearance* of these similarities, even if it rejects the fantasy that Laozi viewed the world of particle physics as Einstein did after he formulated his general theory of relativity.

The doctrinal opponent of antilanguage Daoism is positive or constructive *dao* theories, either Confucian or Mohist. Both advocate positing a social, conventional form of discourse to guide behavior. That is the shared feature that Daoists question. Laozi targets directly the traditionalist Confucian theory. He shares many assumptions with Mencius. Both represent a critical response to a common aspect of the first stage of classical Chinese philosophical thought. Yet it undermines Mencius by demonstrating that antilanguage assumptions do not vindicate status-quo conventions.

Laozi was, like Mencius, a mystic in one key sense: he was antilanguage. But Mencius backs into that position, where Laozi seems to be fascinated with paradoxes of trying to state the limits of language in language. His theory of those limits however, reflects the Chinese view of the role of language. Language purports to express *dao*. *Dao*, as we have argued, is guidance. Laozi discusses the limitations of language as a guide, not as a descriptive system. Laozi shows his mysticism, as Mencius did, in rejecting the prescriptive role of language The theory of the limit of language and the mystical tenor is practical, not metaphysical.

Laozi, no doubt, was aware of the real world. That, by itself, does not justify attributing to him an implicit and unmotivated change in the then current *account of* the role of language. He has no motivation both to start treating the role of language as representing reality and then denying that representation is possible. He certainly does *not give any of the familiar Buddhist or Western arguments* for the inability of language to describe reality. Traditional interpreters see the focus on limitations of language and the mystical paradoxes and *supply* the Indo-European justifications as the obvious deep explanations. This requires them to *reinterpret dao* as a metaphysical object.

The text is perfectly compatible with the view that language is a tool for human organization. It provides guidance. *Dao* guides differently when the language is different. Constructivists assume that increasing the amount of language—enlarging *dao*—increases the amount of guidance, hence the accumulation of texts. The Mohists probably agreed, though they worried about which *dao* to select for the task. Laozi develops the interpretive puzzles and invites us to see how traditional slogans or formulas of language can lead us astray. One can never guarantee that people will reliably pick a given path by offering them language guidance.

We see some of the Zhuangzi's playfulness in Laozi's probing into the realm of paradox and in his ideal of absolute spontaneity, creativity, and wonder. Associating Laozi's views with Western and Buddhist descriptive mysticism distorts the role of the mystical here, however. The mystery of Daoism springs quite rationally and coherently from the philosophical concerns of the constructive moralist period. Viewing Daoism a descriptive way plays into Neo-Confucian theoretical purposes. It renders its critique of Confucianism irrelevant and lumps Daoism with Buddhism. Our own religious interest encourages us to extrapolate to Christian or Platonic mysticism. We twist Laozi into a celebration of language's inability to describe some mystical reality.

Given what an interpretation is, we have to view the traditional claim that Daoism is illogical as initially suspect. We can accept it only if we find no coherent, intelligible way to understand the text in its context. The view that Daoism is incomprehensible actually comes from isolating Daoism by proposing a *meaning-change* hypothesis. The word *dao* is supposed to change meaning whenever a Daoist uses it. That hypothesis makes Daoism irrelevant to the debate about *dao* that divided the two schools Daoism criticized. The standard interpretation instead tries to force the text into a set of Western or Indian assumptions—specifically the assumption that language and mind have an essentially descriptive role and structure. The result is the notorious declaration of Daoism's inherent irrationality.

Historical Background of Daoism

We may view the intellectual forerunners of the Daoists as the hermits who challenged Confucius. *The Analects* mentions several encounters with these antisocial types. The upshot of their view seemed to be similar to that of Yang Zhu: one should avoid politics. Withdraw from society and preserve what is valuable rather than getting into the mud of political chicanery where you can not really improve things much anyway.[10]

Tradition sometimes includes hedonists and their opposite, ascetics, in the Daoist movement. The former clearly rebelled against conventional mores, the latter must have disapproved both of the former and of conventions. Conventions do, after all, afford some pleasure. Yang Zhu's egoism also manifests the antisocial, anticonventional spirit. Not all Daoist theories, however, accept self-preservation or survival as a final goal. Yangzhu's is merely one expression of the anticonventional impulse that links early Daoists together.

What all share is the suspicion that social practices are not authoritative. We see no evidence of a shared *doctrine* so far. We mark the *doctrinal* beginning of Daoism when the concept itself becomes the focus of a second-level theory. We have offered an implicit distinction between discourse-level *dao* and performance-level *dao* to help make sense of Mozi and Mencius. The performance sense of *dao* has become very important in the argument. Daoism begins, I argue, when the performance *dao*—the precise course of action being aimed for—becomes a focus of theory. Let us trace the Daoist line of argument.

Shendao and the Beginning of Daoist Theory

Mature Daoism, conceived of as a coherent theoretical development of the Daoist impulse, begins with Shendao. He is another philosopher we know only from indirect reports and fragments. Shendao plays a pivotal role in *The Zhuangzi* summary of Chinese intellectual history (ch. 33). *The Zhuangzi* story places Shendao between the Mohists and Laozi (Lao Tan). Like Mozi, they appealed to the larger perspective of nature to motivate their antilanguage theory. Now, however, they abandon the notion of an authoritative *tian* and substitute great *dao*. Shendao's reflections thus mark the beginning[11] of Daoist theory. I start the theoretical story of Daoism with Shendao because he first reflects directly on the nature of *dao* as a course of action.[12]

Dao as a Philosophical Topic. Let us retrace how the notion of a performance *dao*—a concrete pattern of behavior—grows out of the discourse sense of *dao*. All the philosophers we have discussed so far have used the term *dao*. We teach, master and follow *dao*s. Confucius fixed his *dao* using the classical texts, especially the *Book of Li*. Although those texts stated his *dao,* following that *dao* required interpreting the text's language into action: rectifying names. The intended performance *dao* is a course of action (or a set of possible courses of action) *intended* or *expressed* in literature. Between *discourse* and *course,* as we saw, lies interpretation.

A performance *dao* is a possible course of action. The same discourse may generate different courses of action. The regulative ideal of the constructivist period was that a single body of discourse should guide behavior in a single *constant* course. Mozi proposed a different discourse from that of traditional Confucianism. He proposed to identify the constant discourse by selecting that one that produced proper behavior. Whatever is in his discourse, therefore, his real emphasis is on the standard applied to behavior, to the course of action resulting from making that language constant.

If we focus now on this course of behavior sense of *dao,* we can conceive of Mozi's performance *dao* as a possible world history.[13] It is the course of events that comes about when everyone acts according to the utilitarian criterion. Part of the course of our action, naturally, includes what we say and write. The course of speech and writing should be precisely that which optimizes universal utility. We should make *something* constant, viz. those patterns of assigning words to distinctions which this standard picks out. His discourse is both *subject to* and the *source of* his utility criterion. Remember that this feature led to the possibility that his *dao* might be self-effacing and that Mencius might actually be a performance utilitarian.

Mencius, too, had a *dao*. He gave us lots of discourse, but technically his moral *dao* had no public-discourse form. It was simply the unique world history in which we followed our innate *shi-fei* guidance. No discourse required practical interpretation for Mencius; he needed no rectification of names. His *dao* emerged from situational intuitive guidance. We follow his *dao* when we all actually behave as we would were we sages. Beyond that we can give no discursive account. (At least, we can do no better than the sages did with *li*.) Mencius clearly regards exactly one course of action, one performance *dao,* as correct and constant. All sages would perform alike in similar circumstances.

Notice, then, that we can think of each of these accounts of *dao* as a prescriptive, future social history. A different possible course of human events would eventuate if we *realized* (made real) Mozi's *dao* or Yang Zhu's *dao* or Confucius' *dao* or Mencius'.

Each potential pattern of behavior is a way, a path. So is Christianity, Liberalism, supply-side economics, Fortran, and punk-rock music. Knowledge is knowledge of *daos*—of what to do or how to act. (The modern Chinese compound for *know, remember,* is *zhi-dao*^{know the way to}.) Any system that guides behavior selects a way (a *dao*) of behaving. There are infinitely many possible prescriptive *daos*. There are as many as there are possible world histories generated by varying human normative theories and their possible practical interpretations.

Remember that *dao* is a social concept. It guides everyone, not just an individual. So a performance *dao* is also a social history, not an individual one. The result Mozi's criterion evaluates is an overall utility function. Remember further that *dao* is a mass term. Thus we can sum across the *daos* of different regions and get the *dao* of the state, the nation, and the world. The sum of individual performances is a social performance. Each rival thinker has advocated his *dao* as the one to guide social life in the world. Each therefore prescribes a different world history: one where the *Book of Li* is correctly performed, one where the utility standard is accurately applied and followed, one where each person successfully dies only naturally, one where innate, unreflective *shi-fei* judgments flow forth. Clearly, there are other possibilities—Christian, Buddhist, pragmatic, pluralist, cannibalistic, Marxist, etc.

Given this picture of the many possible paths human history could take if we realized the different *daos* advanced by the contending philosophers, we can now easily see how Shendao proposes to naturalize the concept. His is a Daoist response to the assumption of Mozi and Mencius that takes *nature* as the standard. Shendao first draws the "anything goes" conclusion. Whatever is *actual* is obviously *natural*. Exactly one of that set of possible paths is the *actual* path. If *natural* is the standard, then we all *necessarily* conform to the standard. Shendao says even a clod of earth does not miss the *dao*.[14] We need not guide our behavior by terms in a prescriptive *dao*.

> The great *dao* can embrace but it cannot distinguish. We know that all things have a basis from which they are acceptable, and from which they are not. Hence the saying: "If one selects then one is not thorough. If one teaches, one never reaches one's object. *Dao* is that which leaves nothing out." So Shendao abandoned knowledge, discarded self and flowed with what could not be changed. He regarded coolly letting things carry him along as the pattern of *dao*. He said, *know to not know.* He was one who started to diminish knowledge ended in wiping it out. Ineffectual and irresponsible, he laughed at the world's *exalting worthies;* licentious and lacking (appropriate) conduct, he disagreed with the world's great sages. . . . [H]e gave up *shi* and *fei,* mixed *admissible* and *forbidden* and did not treat deliberate knowing as a pilot. He did not know to use the before/after distinction, he loftily withdrew—went where he was pushed and came where he was pulled—like a feather turning in a strong wind, like a bit of sand in a grinding stone. He was complete and *feid* nothing, acting or still, never erred; never transgressed. . . . Even a clod cannot miss the *dao*. (*Zhuangzi* 94/33/43– 50)

The Meaning-Change Hypothesis. This is the crucial shift that leads to the appearance that Shendao uses *dao* as a metaphysical concept. I have argued that it quite naturally extends the traditional use of *dao* as *guidance*. It arises out of considerations already noticed in earlier philosophers. It plays on the central trend from Mozi through Yang Zhu and Mencius to treat their dispute as being about which guiding scheme is the natural or heavenly *dao*. Traditional accounts suggest that the Daoist use is simply an inexplicable departure from its normal meaning. Here are some examples.

> Whereas in other schools *dao* means a system of moral truth, in this school [Daoists] it is the One, which is natural, eternal, spontaneous, nameless and indescribable.[15]

> Each school of philosophy had its *dao,* its doctrine of the way in which life should be ordered. Finally in a particular school of philosophy whose followers ultimately came to be called Daoists, *dao* meant *the way the universe works;* and ultimately something very like God, in the more abstract and philosophical sense of that term.[16]

> There are instances in which the *dao* refers to a metaphysical reality; there are instances in which the *dao* refers to a kind of natural law; and there are instances in which the *dao* refers to a kind of principle or pattern for human life.[17]

Notice that all these interpretive hypotheses that *dao* changes meaning are explanations offered by translators, not reports of something found in the text. The texts contain exactly the same graph, and nowhere do they say "Let's change the subject." The hypothesis that *dao* mysteriously changes its meaning for Daoists entails that the subject-matter and style of philosophy must have changed *simultaneously.* And the change must have been imperceptible to the participants. Philosophical interest must have shifted from practical, pragmatic concerns to Western-like metaphysics, epistemology, and semantics while everyone slept one night. That a tradition should so radically redefine itself with no clear motivation is, on its face, a wildly implausible interpretive hypothesis.

But the holism of meaning gives it other consequences. For example, the meaning of knowledge must now change. Where it has been know-how or know-to, it must now be descriptive knowledge of some object. Having changed it, the ruling theory cannot explain why Shendao advocates abandoning knowledge or what that slogan has to do with the other attitudes expressed in the passage. A familiarity-based interpretation of Shendao would say he was like our Western Stoics, a fatalist who advocated Stoic acceptance. But the Stoics certainly valued knowledge. Their only rational justification of their accepting attitude lay in the claim that we could know that reason was determining everything, therefore everything that happened was morally right.

But that is not Shendao's position. He abandons judgment of *shi-fei,* and *ke/bu-ke* acceptable-unacceptable. He does not declare whatever happens right; he stops declaring! Despite one reference to "what cannot be changed" it is hard to show he is a fatalist. He doesn't say that nothing can be changed; he simply says that he accepts what cannot be changed. What looks like fatalism is, again as we saw in Mozi, really an assertion that no natural standard requires *shi-fei* assignments.

Contrary to these orthodox views, then, I argue that Shendao's use of *dao* is continuous with the earlier developing theories of *dao*. The Daoists notice that despite appeals to *tian* nature:heaven to justify the philosopher's conflicting *dao*s, the real source of their attitudes is their acceptance of different *dao* prescriptive discourse. They advocated learning, mastering, and knowing the *dao* of their masters. Participants in philosophical disputes appeal to their own discourse *dao*. They start from different guiding perspectives which makes things look obviously different to them. Neither side can understand why their opponent does not see what is obvious. It is so obvious that each side thinks it is natural. Shendao simply reflects that if that is the case, then we can dispense with knowledge. The natural *dao* does not have to be pushed on anyone!

The reverential attitude—the awareness of the compelling power of a discourse *dao*—prompts the popular view that assimilates Daoism with familiar Western forms of mysticism. Daoists supplement their philosophical wonder at the role of language in shaping our lives with the awareness that this is natural. Finding an assertion of incommensurabilty, we assimilate Daoism to Western mysticism. We then attribute to Daoist writers something quite alien to their philosophical scheme, an inner experience. This has seeped into our common consciousness. Daoism, the ruling theory concludes, starts from a mystical inner experience of an incommunicable ultimate, from a blissful mystical experience of incomprehensible oneness. ''The Eastern traditions constantly refer to this ultimate indivisible be reality which manifests itself in all things, and of which all things are parts. It is called Brahman in Hinduism, Dharmakaya in Buddhism, *dao* in Daoism. . . .''[18]

A reality concept does stand behind Shendao's use of *dao*. It is the actual event-world made up of the choices and actions we actually do make. The great *dao* is the actual course of world history conceived of as a guide.

The parts of that reality are not things, but more particular histories. So Shendao could accept that the *great dao* has parts and is a sum. The numerical features of Shendao's *dao* come from (1) seeing it as an actual course among possible courses of events and (2) seeing it as a sum of the entire course of nature or natural history. It is not inherently a mystical concept, but it is natural and totalistic—and paradoxes lurk near by.

We have understood Shendao's doctrine as a development of the implicit Mohist and Mencian appeal to a natural or heavenly *dao* coupled with the truism that whatever is actual is natural. The natural *dao* is the actual way things happen. One doesn't need to follow guiding discourse to conform to the actual *dao*. His ''abandon knowledge'' slogan rejects guiding doctrines. Following the actual *dao* requires no discourse guide. That is Shendao's antilanguage point. He makes no claim about an ineffable reality or an experience of oneness.

The Rejection of Egoism. The meaning-change hypothesis also fails to explain the other side of Shendao's slogan: discard self. An explanation emerges immediately from retaining the guidance sense of *dao*. Shendao wants us to abandon knowledge, to abandon guiding doctrines. Still, as we noted before, *dao* is a broader concept than is mere $yi^{morality}$. It includes all guidance and this encompasses egoism or prudence. Yang Zhu's egoism and Mozi's utilitarianism are essentially alike from Shendao's great *dao* perspective. They are alternative prescriptive systems based on different ways of making guiding distinctions. An egoistic prescriptive system stresses the distinction between *self* and *other* as the utilitarian one does that between *benefit* and *harm*.

Our ability to distinguish *self* from *other* is as linguistically based as any other guiding distinction. Making that distinction as our linguistic community does is a complex social skill which we must learn. It is a skill used in guiding our course of action. Learning those words underwrites learning either a morality of selfishness or of unselfishness. Making that distinction enables one to follow one pattern of desires, approvals, and behavior and to miss others.

Egoism, thus, is not a purely natural or spontaneous response to the world but a prescriptive doctrine which involves focusing on the name wo^1. A *dao* of self-interest, for example, is distinct from following whims, inclinations, or even dominant desires. Different concepts of self-interest (different ways of making the distinction between self and other) produce different egoistic *dao*s Some may focus on economic well-being, some on spiritual, or intellectual well-being, some on one's status in history. As it were, these different egoisms draw different boundaries around the self—make a different self-other distinction.

The doctrine of self-interest guides action as surely as moralistic doctrines do. If we should abandon, as Shendao suggests, all such systems, then we must abandon Yang Zhu's. The two parts of Shendao's slogan are theoretically linked. Because Yang Zhu's egoism is a *dao:* ''abandon knowledge'' *entails* ''discard self.'' Note that already we are seeing that as Daoism matures, it critiques its own earlier forms. Daoism is not a static philosophy.

The Paradox of Primitive Daoism. Because he shares the concept of *zhi*[know] with his tradition, Shendao's slogan generates a prescriptive paradox. Remember that ''abandon knowledge'' does not mean give up scientific beliefs about reality. Shendao seemed to have a fistful of metaphysical claims and observations about what was actual. ''Abandon knowledge'' must instead mean give up or forget prescriptive doctrines—no knowing deliberation, no models, sages, or worthies. Do not abide by prescriptions, but let things take their course.

The problem is that ''Give up prescriptions'' prescribes something. ''Abandon knowledge'' is a prescriptive *dao,* a bit of guiding discourse. If you obeyed it, you would be disobeying it! We have our first Daoist paradox. Shendao's *dao* is a *dao* that cannot *dao*[guide] us.

Shendao's contribution is to naturalize *dao.* Once we understand *dao* as a possible course of history, we can treat the *actual* course of history as a *dao.* As soon as we see that, it is easy to make the case that is the most viable candidate for the title of *natural course of history.* What could be more natural than the actual? But, we can put another paradox in Shendao's way. The actual *dao* includes all the existing doctrinal *dao*s and our tendencies to follow them. What we *do* is use knowledge of *dao*s in acting. It includes all the possible *dao*s as *possibilities.* Nothing in his argument requires us to give anything up.

Daoism's developing theory thus analyzed *dao* in a way that was continuous with prior philosophy. Laozi, in the *Daode Jing,* follows Shendao in the paradoxical prescription that we abandon guiding behavior with knowledge. This means abandoning all discourse *dao* which can guide. His is also an antilanguage point of view. However, he does not base it on the notion of an actual or natural performance *dao* or even a hint of fatalism. In fact, I will argue that Laozi turns his analysis back on the discourse *dao.* The *Daode Jing* analyzes the way in which discourse *dao*s *shape and polish* us and our behavior. However, what Confucius took as their value, Laozi treats as a tragedy. He supports this by a theory of the mechanisms by which lan-

guage guides us. It explains in greater detail the current theory of how names contribute to the guidance inherent in *dao*s and how they influence behavior. This is the
explanation that undermines Mencius' status-quo claim that his existing inclinations
are natural or innate.

In sum, Daoism is a *dao* about *dao:* it discourses about discourse, prescribes
about prescription. It is a series of theories about *dao*s. Laozi, like Shendao, wants
to escape the socializing effects of language. Daoists carried out this study in both
awe for and puzzlement about the process by which language and *dao*s influence us.
The striking new insight of Daoism is that our discourse is the *real* authority, not
nature. Nature was a universal shield behind which philosophers hid what they were
really doing. Nature is neutral in the disputes between moral philosophers.

Laozi: Nonlife and Tradition

Tradition identifies Laozi as the author of the *Daode Jing*. As with Confucius, Mencius, and Mozi, we do not know much about the person Laozi. In these other cases,
however, we did not seriously question that the author existed. We assumed the book
had some inheritance relation to things a person had actually taught. The *Daode Jing*
does not attribute any of its doctrines to a master Lao and it shows evidence of being
mainly a compilation of beautiful poetic fragments. Some scholars resist the consensus,[19] but I accept the dominant view that no actual Laozi ever lived.

The traditional biographical information about Laozi is largely either fanciful
(he lived to be 160 to 200 years old), historically dubious (he taught Confucius), or
contradictory (his hometown, official posts, age). So in the sense that *Laozi* refers to
the single author of the *Daode Jing,* there may never have been one. There were
more likely many.

Still, the text does have consistent *tone* and develops genuinely Daoist themes.
Even if only an edited collection of axioms, proverbs, wise aphorisms, sayings of
elders, and sardonic popular aphorisms, we can try to explain the theoretical message
of the book. The intentionality may be on the part of the editor or the interpreting
reader. Whatever we may think of the authors, editors, exploiters, and readers of the
book, we can try to account for the role the fragments play in the structure of the
text of the *Daode Jing* and in the development of Daoist theory.

I have placed the *Daode Jing* as *The Zhuangzi* did, between Shendao and
Zhuangzi. This is an antilanguage version of Daoism which attacks mainly discourse
dao theories. One tradition has it that an eighth generation grandson of Laozi lived
at the time of Sima-qian, which would place Laozi about one hundred years after
Confucius. Some stylistic considerations place the *Daode Jing* close to *The Mencius*.
I shall argue they are also close in content. They are respectively Confucian and
Daoist versions of the antilanguage reaction to Confucius and Mozi.

The traditional story of Laozi gives an important insight into the *Daode Jing*
even if it is purely fanciful. That story has it that, far from being a gradual compilation of various sources, the *Daode Jing* was written impromptu. Laozi was trying
(perhaps in disgust) to leave China and the keeper of the pass, cognizant of Mozi's
doctrine that we should not waste good teachings, required (or requested—depending
on how much you think he held Laozi in awe) that Laozi write down his *dao*. He

forbade him to pass without leaving his words behind. Fluidly and spontaneously Laozi dashed off this textual treasure. It has delighted, puzzled, frustrated, and intrigued scholars for two millennia. The point is that he had no intrinsic motivation to write. He does so under mild duress but also does it quickly and without deliberation.

Basic Interpretive Hypothesis: Shendao and Language Analysis

The Zhuangzi tradition treats *The Laozi* as developing Shendao's theory. It elaborates the antiprescriptive knowledge position. The text contains echoes of Shendao's anti-knowledge, antisage sentiments but expands the range of things we put in the discard bag. Now it includes *learning, desires, distinctions, names, language,* and *deliberate action along with knowledge* and *sages.* These terms figure in the more elaborate theory of how a discourse *dao* works. In the *Laozi,* the attack comes from familiar antisocial, anticonventional, antiauthoritarian attitudes—not from fatalism or the notion of the actual course of events. Daoist antisocial anarchism motivates this next stage of Daoist theory about language. Since language is an instrument of social control, we should avoid it—and everything that goes with it.

Laozi is, if anything, *less* metaphysical than Shendao. He does occasionally employ the notion of a natural-course-of-history *dao.* But his point is how conventional discourse and names constrain us. He does not treat the natural world history as a solution, the uniquely correct guide. He seems more to relish its paradoxical implications.[20] Or, he uses the natural or great *dao* as an *alternative* perspective from which one can question conventional guidance. Shendao's concept is only one step in Laozi's more complicated argument for the reversal of opposites.

Distinctions and Opposite Names. The text is most interesting on the subject of opposite names. The famous reversal of opposites character of Daoism starts from Laozi's contrast theory of names. He assumed that names come in pairs.[21] Opposite terms are "born together." To have or learn one is to have or learn the other. You cannot have mastered *water* unless you also know what is *not water.* Knowing any term is knowing how to distinguish. Thus we learn each word and its opposite together. And the learning consists in acquiring a spontaneous ability. When we make our familiar linguistic distinctions, we hardly take time to think.

Each pair of terms thus has a single source. *One* distinction gives rise to *two* terms. Where Mozi had a name giving rise to a thin, indexical, *shi-fei* pattern of response, Laozi sees a distinction giving rise to a name pair: the opposites. Knowledge is mastery of a vocabulary, not definitions but spontaneous, conditioned inclinations to discriminate. So his philosophy stresses the bond between the word pairs, and this changes the picture of language slightly. It is not merely an amorphous set of terms; rather, the terms come clustered in pairs of opposites.

What is pragmatically salient about the distinctions between two opposites lies in how they guide us. Here Laozi makes desires central to the account for the first time. The opposites guide our preferences. Distinctions shape attitudes. The focus is still on practical guidance, but he adds an affective mechanism. Socialization produces behavior-influencing desires. They are not innate. I shall argue that *what* the reversal of opposites *reverses* is the socialized desire or preference assignment to each of the pairs. Laozi teaches us to value what convention teaches us to disvalue.

Daoist theory here makes explicit what we have argued was implicit in the theories of language of Confucius, Mozi, and Mencius. The twist, however, underlies a reversal of attitude. Now Laozi rejects the previously valued *shaping and polishing* worked by language and tries to provide a heuristic to undo it.

Distinctions and Desires. Laozi thus makes more explicit something that lay in the background in Mozi. It is not enough to have learned simply to make a distinction in absorbing a system of guidance based on names. We had left it that the word-assignment triggered program control. Laozi identifies the control mechanism as a desire. We learn to desire one discriminant to the other (perhaps only in certain contexts).

To see that the *Daode-Jing*'s view is still distinct from Western psychology, imagine a nonmental account of teaching a distinction. We will pick one of interest to Laozi. Suppose I am an art teacher. My goal is not to teach a theory of art appreciation but to try to shape and polish my students aesthetically. To keep things simple, imagine that my classes consist of bringing in a series of paintings each day and pointing to each and saying either "beautiful" or "ugly." No definitions allowed! By model emulation I gradually train the students to make the distinction between beautiful and ugly paintings. They copy my model of the use of words like *beautiful* and *ugly* until they can apply *beautiful* and *ugly* to paintings they have never seen before essentially as I would. Beautiful/ugly is a social distinction and, as the model, I would set the standard they try to embody.

Suppose at the final examination they all properly classified a series of paintings they had never seen before. In reward, I offer to give them one painting each. If each promptly showed a preference for the ugly paintings, I would certainly regard my work as unfinished. Mastering my aesthetic *dao* is not exhausted in applying the terms correctly. It requires not only correct distinctions, but correct desires associated with the distinctions.

The Daoist twist is this. Learning social distinctions typically involves internalizing society's preferences. Distinguishing between having and lacking, we learn to prefer having. Distinguishing between beautiful and ugly, we learn to prefer beautiful. Learning names shapes our behavioral attitudes, our desires. This is because we learn names by mimicking their use in guiding choices in ordinary contexts. We do not learn them in classes by recitation. Hence we learn to let names guide us to make the same choices that our social models (teachers) do.

Our learning consists in daily increasing our mastery of the system of names. We master the accepted system of names, distinctions, and desires. Every day we add more to the system and become more conditioned and shaped by it. Some people develop the ability to distinguish by mere feel the difference between polyester and cotton. Polyester pants can no longer satisfy them. Their discriminating ability affects their actions. They stop patronizing Zayre's and K-Mart and go only to the *fine* shops that carry natural fibers. These cost more and thus they have to strive for more lucrative jobs. Their motivation is not anything as crude as a slave-master with a whip—it is their cultivated, cultured tastes that drives them. The distinctions they have learned to make and the names they use in structuring what they desire affect their tastes, their lifestyle, and their need to work to satisfy those tastes.

In the ordinary sense, we say these people are following a *dao* of fashion or of taste. They want to appear to have a cultivated, learned taste—to be discriminating.

We would be ashamed to praise a movie we should have known to hate! The sign of class and character is rejecting certain things. Thus language and discriminations carry social class constraints into our very psyches. Acquiring the right desires is crucial to our worth in a social system. Language is a tool in society's project of shaping our behavioral motivations.

Laozi, like Shendao is implicitly antagonistic to those posited *dao*s composed of names. Laozi's image of the nameless *pu*^{simplicity}—the uncarved block that is freedom from desire—captures the essence of his view. Nameless, it is uncarved, undivided. Freedom from names and distinctions is freedom from desire. As soon as it is cut—as soon as there are distinctions—there are names.

Keep in mind that what we would think of as moral theories—conventional *dao*s—are naming systems that guide us. *Dao*s are not so much *theories* that guide us as they are *conceptual perspectives* that guide us. Laozi expands on how, at the level of names, *dao* affects behavior. His account is not at the level of sentences. The mechanism is not like that of rules, evoking a descriptive state of affairs for us to bring about. It affects us more by shaping our taste, our discriminating attitudes. Society trains us in how to draw certain distinctions and act on them. It instills the point of distinction and the associated pattern of desire.

The introduction of *yu*^{desires} into the debate has an implication that the usual translation conceals. Laozi marks the behavioral impulses as products of socialization. If we think of desires in the Indo-European sense as presocial, we may not notice how Laozi's analysis undermines Mencius. Mencius had treated the behavioral impulses, the *xing*^{nature}, as inborn or as products of the natural growth of our behavioral guiding organ—the *xin*^{heart-mind}.

Wei and Wu-wei. Laozi must sense that the ways society shapes us are pervasive. So pervasive that any *thorough anticonventionalism* will generate paradoxes. Laozi's famous *wu-wei*^{nonaction} slogan evokes this paradox: ''*wu*^{lack} *wei*^{do:deem} *er*^{and:yet} *wu*^{lack} *bu*^{neg} *wei*^{do:deem}.'' Let us examine this paradox.

We have discussed both key characters before. The character *wu*^{not exist} we mentioned in Mozi's discussion of spirits. Its opposite is *you*^{exist}. The character *wei*^{do:deem} we discussed in looking at the alternatives to grammatical belief structures. Its role in the term-belief structure is roughly equivalent to *deem to be* or *regard as*. We also noticed it in mencius formulation of Yang Zhu's egoism as *wei-wo*^{for me}. The striking thing about the character *wei* is the apparent complexity of the role it plays in classical Chinese. Chinese writers use *wei* as a verb. We translate these uses as *to act, to make,* or *to do.* When it is used as an adjective, we are drawn to *artificial* or *manmade* as translations and, because writers like Laozi opposed it, even as *false.* Finally, the character plays a role as an auxiliary verb[22] that we typically translate as *for the sake of* or *in order to.*

Laozi did not use English equivalents when he theorized about *wei.* In particular, he did not have one English equivalent in mind for one use and a different English word for another use. He saw a single term and what would have seemed like a unified concept. To *wei* is to assign something to a name-category in guiding action. This is the closest equivalent in Laozi's conceptual scheme to our notion of purposive action. But it still focuses less on the action than the evaluative categorizations that guide actions. *Wei*^{do:deem} is not ''purposeful'' in the sense of free, rational, conscious, or voluntary action. On the contrary, for Laozi *wei* signals socially induced, learned, patterns of response—the opposite of autonomous or spontaneous response. The character links deeming, unnatural artifice, doing or making and purpose. Laozi's prescriptive paradox involves the whole complex role of *wei*. We should avoid any action based on artificially induced or learned purposes or desires—those that result from deeming things to be such and such. Its conceptual role in this slogan is continuous with the theory of a guiding conceptual perspective and Laozi's attitude that being guided in this way is an unnatural artifice.

Our familiar forms of mysticism induce us to adopt a different analysis of the Laozi's nonpurposiveness. Buddhists and Christians interpreting Laozi see him attacking the ego. That is because they see desire, purpose, or meaning as residing in or belonging to the individual. They see desires as natural, individual, and ego based. Laozi sees them as social and linked to names and distinctions. Getting rid of *wei* is freeing us from *society's* purposes, *socially induced* desires, *social* distinctions or meaning structures. We are to free ourselves from social, artificial, unnatural guidance, guidance by a system of distinctions and name pairs. That, notoriously, leaves us able to act naturally. If the Buddhist-Christian inspired understanding were true, we should find celibacy a Daoist value rather than a disvalue.

Thus the conclusion follows from the analysis that learning consists in learning names, distinctions, and desires and then having them guide us. Our natural spontaneity requires us to give up the whole complex. That is Laozi's version of "abandon knowledge." Thus to follow *wu-wei* is to give up names, distinctions, desires, and any deliberate action based on them. *Wu-wei* and "abandon knowledge" are linked slogans.

This leaves Laozi with a more complicated version of Shendao's paradox. His writings still constitute the very thing he opposes, but not simply because it is language. It is because his language has added to our guiding conceptual perspective. He relies on a name pair, *natural* versus *conventional,* and a way of making the distinction (language-based socially induced dispositions are not natural). If we understand his teaching, we are induced to prefer the natural to the conventional and thus to *wei,* to undertake actions guided by that distinction and preference. The purposive part of the book recommends *forgetting* instead of *accumulating.* Taking guidance from the book should teach us not to take guidance from the book. This is another *dao*^{guide} that cannot *dao*^{guide}.

The famous opening line of the first chapter, in effect, admits the paradox, as does the *wu-wei* slogan. No other *dao*^{guide} is any better off. All guidance that *can* come from a *dao*^{guide} will be inconstant.

The First Chapter: The Interpretation

With this background, let us look carefully at the first chapter.[23] Whoever edited the traditional Daoist version of the *Daode Jing* decided to start with certain words. These set the background against which we should read the other fragments. That is, we assume that the editor intended to put key philosophical claims early as a précis to guide our understanding of the sayings to come. The first chapter also contains a classic example of the ambiguities of philosophical Chinese. We may be tempted to the hypothesis that this was not accidental. Still, I will accept its invitation and try to solve the puzzle of which reading to adopt.

The chapter opens with a famous but almost universally misconstrued couplet. The standard translation is: "The *Dao* that can be spoken is not the constant *Dao*." Kaltenmark gives a standard assessment of the opening line "The ineffability of the *[dao]* is affirmed in the very first chapter of the *[Daode Jing]*. This extremely important chapter is unfortunately one of the most awkward of the whole book, for the possibility of punctuating the text in several ways, the character variants, and the uncertain meaning of particular words justify several quite different translations."[24]

The Single, Ineffable Dao

Strangely, practically everyone agrees with Kaltenmark's profile of the first line. They assume, with Kaltenmark, that it asserts the ineffability of the metaphysical, mystical object called *dao*. That is, the first line expresses the contradiction of which I spoke earlier. It speaks of something of which it claims it cannot speak.

That consensus is wrong. The first line does not assert that *anything* is ineffable. It entails neither the existence nor the ineffability of a single metaphysical *or* prescriptive *dao*. Let's look carefully at the first two lines. Notice that *dao* occurs three times in the sentence. We must read it as both a noun (doctrine) and a verb (prescribe, advocate, speak).

$$dao^{\text{way:speak}} \; ke^{\text{can-be}} \; dao^{\text{way:speak}} \; fei^{\text{not}} \; chang^{\text{constant}} \; dao^{\text{way:speak}}$$

$$ming^{\text{name}} \; ke^{\text{can;}}x = {}^{\text{be}} ming^{\text{name}} \; fei^{\text{not}} \; chang^{\text{constant}} \; ming^{\text{name}}$$

The standard translation of the first line is "The *Dao* that can be told is not the constant *Dao*." (Translators usually capitalize *dao*—as they would *God*.) Note first that nothing in the Chinese corresponds to the definite article *the*. Translators conform to their own community practice of always putting *the* before *dao*.[25] We could, in principle, take as interpretive hypotheses that the subject was *a dao* or *any dao*, or simply *Daos*. The translating convention embodies an ancient interpretive hypothesis that all Daoists must worship a mystical godlike *dao*. Thus they presume in translation what they cannot find in the original: assertion of the existence of a single, ineffable *dao*.

It all seems so innocent. How can such a little, *nothing* word matter so much? The answer has been familiar to students of philosophy since Bertrand Russell. The usual effect of a definite article in English is to make a general noun, in this case the term *dao*, into a logically singular noun-phrase: *the* + general noun-phrase = a phrase that entails the existence of a unique object answering the description. Capitalization, on analogy with God (as against gods), has the same implication. It makes a general term a proper noun.

Remember that previous thinkers have used *dao* as a general term of Chinese, not as a proper name. The test of singular versus general in Chinese is whether the term can be modified. This text modifies *dao* exactly as both *The Analects* and *The Mozi* do. The *Daode Jing* refers to heavenly *dao*, great *dao*, and water's *dao*. The very sentence we are discussing modifies *dao*. It is preceded by the adjective *chang* ^{constant}! The concept must in principle encompass both constant and inconstant *dao*. It is merely implausible to assume that Daoists radically change the usual reference of *dao*. It is outlandish to assume that they changed its grammar from that of a general term to a singular name.

So we have no more reason to insert *the* in the translation than *any* or *a* or even simply to use the plural, viz., "Ways that can be told are not constant ways." The second line has exactly the same grammar as the first. Here, however, more translators switch and use the plural *names* in translating that line.

I concentrate on the issue of the definite article to give the reader who is dependent on translations a way to bracket this consistent translator bias. Wherever the translator uses *the Dao* (or *the Way*) substitute *a dao*.[26] However, in this particular structure, even with *the* in the translation, the English sentence does not entail the existence of a single *dao*. Because of the restrictive clause, "that can be told," the logic of this particular English sentence cancels the definite article. The logical force is the same with *the* as with *any, a* or with the plural, *ways*. Consider "The chef who breaks yolks is not the ideal cook." It neither asserts that a unique chef who breaks yolks exists,[27] nor that one who does not break yolks exists, nor that there is an ideal cook. Logically the sentence is equivalent to "Any chef who breaks yolks is not an ideal cook."

The typical English translation asserts that no *dao* which can be spoken is a constant *dao*. Thus, the first line gives no grounds for the assumption that there is some object called *dao* which is ineffable. Read without the assumption that *dao* changes meaning, it makes the rectifying-names point that any prescriptive system put into words gives inconstant guidance. We can understand this line as directed straight at Confucius and Mozi or as expressing the felt paradox of Shendao's or Laozi's discourse *dao*s.

The Inconstancy of Prescription in Language

Even without considering the *the* issue, the usual translation is grammatically wrong. English, but not classical Chinese, has "which" clauses. In Chinese, modifiers precede the terms they modify.[28] One grammatically acceptable parsing *dao ke dao* is as a verb-object structure. (Remember that subject terms are optional in classical Chinese.) Hence: *speak the speakable*. The conclusion may be, first, that doing so *is not constant speaking*. (Remember that *dao* speaking is guiding speech. Guiding speech will change.) Or it may be, second, that doing so would not yield a constant performance *dao*. The passage reminds us of the interpretive problem: *no* linguistic guides give constant guidance.

So the first line, as we predicted, deals with language and action, not metaphysics. We can corroborate this feature by looking at the second part of the couplet. It is uncontroversially about language. The second line explains the first. Speaking the speakable is not constant speaking because naming the nameable is not constant naming. The pattern of word use—the discriminatory *boundaries*—may change over time. The words may change and the distinctions they mark are not constant. So the social practices triggered by names will also change. The inconstancy of guidance by discourse recalls the two established worries in the *Ru-Mo* debates about which discourse *dao* to follow.

The first worry was about projecting or interpreting which triggered the theory of rectifying names. After we have learned to use a name, we have to project it to new settings before we can use the guiding discourse. The projection problem affects both making the distinction that triggers action *and* correctly naming the actions themselves. This familiar interpretive gap between codes and actions arises because we can worry if we have projected our pattern of naming on the world correctly. The action aspect of this interpretive worry recalls Mencius' worry about the austerity of discourse guidance. Situations will always arise in which any prescriptive discourse will misguide us. Names are not sensitive enough to the complexity of the moral situation to provide constant guidance in making distinctions. On either ground, guiding discourse consisting of names can not guarantee a constant course of behavior.

The second worry, the standards issue, is the worry we raised in analyzing the $Ru-Mo^{\text{Confucian-Mohist}}$ debate as debate about moral reform. There appears to be no neutral, constant ground for a standard to which we can appeal to mediate between conflicting *dao*s. The reigning assumption was that the natural or heavenly is constant. Thus a natural *dao* should be a constant *dao*. But, as Shendao's reflections showed, *nature needs no discourse guidance* and *nature seems neutral* between all rival moral systems.

We may be tempted to treat Daoism as making the stronger claim that all *dao*s are self-defeating in Mozi's sense.[29] But this is far from obvious and certainly does not follow from Mozi's way of putting the case. Or we may be tempted to treat Daoism as the forlorn view that any *dao* ends in paradox—as Shendao's does. That would give Shendao a feeble *tu quoque* retort to his critics. But nothing in Chinese philosophy has shown that to be the case and it is neither directly stated nor even hinted at in this first line. Laozi simply notes that *dao*s and names lack *constancy*. He does not distinguish between these two historically traceable ways of failing to be constant. He certainly has not *formulated* any version of this more desperate criticism of language. He does not allege that all *dao*s are self-defeating, paradoxical, or contradictory. He has said only that all *dao*s and names are indeterminate.

In the context of Chinese philosophy, then, this first couplet throws down the gauntlet to the joint *Ru-Mo* ersatz positivist ideal. Both Confucius and Mozi try to select some prescriptive discourse to be made the constant discourse guide for society. Both understand that the guidance must include training in the use of names—rectifying names—to make the discourse *dao* generate the intended performance *dao*. This constancy goal, Laozi announces, is hopeless. We have no way to fix how we may project our use of names in new circumstances. We cannot know whether we have chosen to mark slightly different distinctions or the same. Our social training (learning the code or following models) has no clear implication about how to project in new circumstances. So we cannot guarantee constant guidance from any *dao* that is generated by following a discourse consisting of names.

The second line explains the first because the relation between dao^{way} and $ming^{\text{name}}$ is a part-whole relation. *Dao*s consist of names (not sentences). They guide behavior by means of learned skills in discriminating, desiring, and performing associated with the names. Because names are not constant, language-based guidance cannot be constant. This use of *dao* is continuous with its use in pre–*Daode Jing* literature. No meaning-change hypothesis is necessary to explain Daoism at this point. As we shall see later, the later Mohists, Zhuangzi, Xunzi and Han Feizi also use *dao* in this sense. We will find no evidence of a Daoist linguistic revision of the word *dao*.

The Daoists do focus on and *analyze* the notion of *dao*—they find it both interesting and important. They, like other classical thinkers, treat it as a system of name use, a system that regulates and influences our lives. Since the name use is changeable, the system of guidance consisting of names is changeable.

Worries about both interpretion and standards justify the claim that anything speakable is inconstant. Neither entails that anything in particular is either unspeakable or constant. Laozi may be aware of, but is not relying on, Shendao's theory of the natural *dao* as the actual course of world history. Shendao's way of talking about *dao* is *consistent* with the first line. His *dao,* as we saw, turned out not to guide. Some *daos*—ways of human, rule-guided social behavior—are what they are because of how we speak. Other *daos*—ways things naturally happen—are what they are regardless of how we talk about them. The former, one might argue, can be changed and does not give constant guidance. So far, the *Daode Jing* has not discussed the latter nor said anything to show why nature must be thought of as either changeable or unchangeable.

The very possibility that the actual *dao* might be thought of as constant may be a kind of Daoist comfort. Perhaps, assuming that our skills and practices have their life in a constant nonsocial reality will give us reason to deny that our skills are *utterly* random.[30] Only certain kinds of performance will be successful in the actual world. The constancy of nature is the only assurance we could have of the constancy of our social practices associated with naming. If that is the point behind what Laozi is saying here, it certainly is not directly asserted. His tone is distinctly more skeptical than comforting.

We have discussed the term *chang*[constant] in earlier chapters. There, too, its use was as a linguistic pragmatic concept. Mozi said to *chang* language that promotes good behavior. Chinese philosophy had not made *chang* a metaphysical concept prior to this point. The standard interpretation needs to claim that it too now becomes a metaphysical concept. It appeals to the Greek and Indian metaphysical assumption that only the permanent is real to buttress their metaphysically monist interpretation that the *dao* is the only reality. Guided too quickly by the principle of charity, these interpreters grasp for the familiar before they explore the earlier pragmatic, linguistic reading of the term. We should trace out how *chang*[constant] would be coherent with the Chinese theory of language rather than with the Indo-European one. They treat the *Daode Jing* as merely another metaphysical claim that the apparent world is in flux but the monistic real world is unchanging.

For Laozi, what lacks constancy is not the experienced world of particular physical objects, but the system of name use. No unchangeable systems of discourse exist. This is so not because things change, but because names (and their distinctions) do. We are, so far at least, not dealing with a Chinese Heraclitus reflecting on how rapidly *things* change. I do not mean to assert that Daoists *doubt* that things change; obviously they do. Only Buddhists and Ionians ever seriously thought that they did not.

Bracketing this Indo-European tradition, it is hard to show that Daoists have any reason to treat the obvious facts of natural change as a philosophical problem. What is problematical about so obvious a feature of the world? The problem of permanence and change would be an important philosophical problem only if you begin (as Ionian and Indian philosophy do) with quite peculiar linguistic or epistemic assumptions. The epistemic view (1) that knowledge is of reality and (2) that knowledge must be of things that are true and (3) a nonindexed notion of truth—that is, truth is eternal—leads to the view that reality must not change. The linguistic view would be that words name objects. It treats the projection problem as a question of how it names the same object over time unless something—its objecthood or underlying substance—continues unchanged while its properties or apparent manifestations change. So language attaches to the world in the required way only if *real reality* does not change.[31]

The Daoists make none of these assumptions. Names mark distinctions, not classes of objects. Their knowledge is of ways to do things, including making distinctions and using names. That knowledge *must* change since each situation is unique. Daoists interest *themselves* only in *this* observation. Independently of any actual flux in the world itself, our systems of guidance attach to the world in constantly changing ways depending on conventional, and therefore changeable, practices. That is the philosophical problem about constant guidance that captures the attention of Chinese theorists.

The Paradox of the Terms Being *and* Nonbeing

If the first two lines are the announcement of metaphysical monism, then lines 3 to 6 are an irrelevant aside.[32] These four lines have been the focus of centuries of interpretive controversy. The lack of punctuation and sentence-function marking make two parsing hypotheses possible. Each grammatical parsing suggests a different interpretation of the four lines. Both interpretations are interesting continuations of the opening theme only if we construe the topic as linguistic rather than metaphysical. One interpretation considers the subject of discussion as the relation between having names versus lacking names and having desires versus lacking desires. The other treats the topic as the basic distinction between having and lacking (*being* and *nonbeing*) as an example of an inconstancy in distinction making. Let's look at lines 3 and 4 first:

wu^{lack} $ming^{name}$ $tian^{heaven}$ di^{earth} $zhi's$ $shi^{beginning}$

you^{have} $ming^{name}$ $wan^{10,000}$ $wu^{thing-kinds}$ $zhi's$ mu^{mother}

The parsings identify different grammatical subjects. Should we treat the first two characters of each line as a two-character subject or as subject plus verb? Since Chinese requires no *is*-like connective, this produces the following two readings of the first two lines:

1. *Wu-ming*$^{lacks\ name}$ [is] the beginning of the universe. *You-ming*$^{has\ name}$ [is] the mother of all things.
2. "*Wu*^{lacks}" $ming^{names}$ the beginning of the universe. "*You*^{have}" $ming^{names}$ the mother of all things.

The first analysis hints at a theory of linguistic idealism: names create the world. Having a name for something is the mother of things. Without names, we start creating our universe from scratch. It is a little difficult to elaborate this view plausibly with the creation ex nihilo reading. The most common elaboration of this theme is the chaos interpretation. We characterize the prelinguistic world as undifferentiated kapok. We *organize* it *for all practical purposes* by the use of names. Our system of dividing it up creates thing-kinds. There are no natural *kinds* but there is a natural ur-stuff. This would vindicate the traditional interpretation of *dao* as the undifferentiated kapok (chaos). Call this the names-create-reality theory.[33]

The second parsing does not lead to as much speculative metaphysics, although it deals with the concepts of *being* and *nonbeing*. This parsing requires us to treat *wu* and *you* as mentions, rather than as uses. It focuses specifically on the two opposite terms as an important example of the inconstancy of distinction making. In this case, trying to think of being and nonbeing (arguably the most basic distinctions in a language) as opposites based on a single distinction leads to deep paradox. It is *puzzling* in a way that shows the distinction is *inconstant*. If *you* and *wu* mark a distinction in the kapok, where could that distinction lie? Surely the entire kapok belongs on the *you* side, so there is no distinction. If there were a distinction, it would be part of what there is and should be included within *you*. *Wu* names the beginning—the logical edge—of the universe. The implicit distinction cannot be drawn—it can distinguish nothing.

The various discourse *dao*s of *you-wu* do sort things into both categories. Confucians allegedly *you ming*[fate] and *wu shen*[spirits] and Mohists' discourse reverses this. So they have a conventional application. But we have no way to decide who is correct on this because we cannot give any coherent characterization of the background against which to apply this distinction. We cannot find a *constant* (neutral) place to draw the *you*[have] *wu*[lack] distinction. *You* and *wu* are relative to different discourse *dao*s. Call this the inconstant-distinction theory.

"We can draw no boundary between being and nonbeing!" would be the closest Daoist equivalent of saying that there is no nonbeing. Unlike Parmenides, they conclude, however, that we cannot make sense of being, either.

Constant nature does not give us this distinction. It is a distinction that arises out of inconstant conventional *dao*s. Thus, where we draw it depends on the *dao* we use. It is not constant. Where would the boundary be between what is and what is not? Is it part of what is? Or of what is not? Now we can see that metaphysical interest arises out of the linguistic theory, not as an arbitrary assertion. The interest in the question of being and nonbeing arises *directly* out of the interest in the contrast theory of language.

So far both parsings are possible and lead to interesting and plausible interpretive accounts. But the next two lines, I will suggest, are slightly more coherent with the inconstant-distinction approach (IC) than with the names-create-reality interpretation (NCR). Let us look at lines 5 and 6:

gu[therefore] $chang$[constant] wu[lack] yu[desire] i[use] $guan$[observe] qi[its] $miao$[mysteries]

$chang$[constant] you[have] yu[desire] i[use] $guan$[observe] qi[its] $jiao$[manifestations]

Parallelism argues in favor of using similar parsing theories in 5 and 6 to those we used in 3 and 4. So parsing NCR should take *wu-yu*[lack desires] and *you-yu*[have desires] as units here too: "Therefore constantly lack desires in order to view its mysteries. Constantly have desires in order to view its manifestations."

This creates a problem. The resulting interpretation seems to have Laozi advocating both constantly having desires and constantly lacking them. This doesn't fit well with the attitude toward desire found throughout the book. Further, we need a plausible motivation for this theory of the effects of desire. Nothing in the theory as we have presented it so far justifies these claims about the effects of constantly having and lacking desires. Finally, this parsing does not give *chang*[constant] linguistic theoretical reading that has been central to our interpretation in lines 1 and 2.

The IC interpretation, which uses the *you-wu* distinction as an example, makes a point about the different purposes and desires that is continuous with the theory explained above. We may either treat *you* or *wu* respectively as *constant,* be attracted to that side of the distinction. If we treat *wu*[lack] as constant, we desire to use it to view mysteries. If we treat *you*[have] as constant, we desire to use it to view manifestations. That is a plausible claim to make about the distinction. Treating nonbeing as a constant term will lead to paradox and mystery. Treating *wu*[lack] as naming something is inherently paradoxical. Treating *you*[have being] as constant will manifest itself in desire to study the sequences of events, essentially the study of science.

Why is *wu* associated with mystery? I have argued that the structural approach to the issue is different in China than in the West. But the issue has a common source. Consider this delightful account of the inherent puzzles about non-being from a Western point of view. You can find it under the heading "Nothing" in the *Encyclopedia of Philosophy.*

> NOTHING is an awe inspiring but undigested concept, highly esteemed by writers of a mystical or existentialist tendency, but by most others regarded with anxiety, nausea or panic. Nobody knows how to deal with it (he would of course), and plain persons generally are reported to have little difficulty in saying, seeing, hearing and doing nothing. Philosophers, however, have never felt easy on the matter. Ever since Parmenides laid it down that it is impossible to speak of what is not, broke his own rule in the act of stating it, and deduced himself into a world where all that ever happened was nothing, the impression has persisted that the narrow path between sense and nonsense on this subject is a difficult one to tread and that altogether the less said of it the better. . . .[34]

One could also go to *Alice in Wonderland* for similar lessons. The point is that if you concentrate on *wu,* you will be quickly dazed by philosophical puzzlement.

Notice that this interpretation uses *chang*[constant] in its linguistic sense and derives a coherent *and* consistent consequence about desires. To have this distinction is to have a pattern of desiring, in this case an interest toward different intellectual enterprises. It does not recommend or reject either. It merely notes the effect of constanting one term or its opposite.

At this point, theoretical coherence favors parsing IC. But both may be regarded as live hypotheses. The next line settles the matter.[35] We will look here to the end of the chapter:

ci[this] liang[two] zhe[that:which] tong[same] chu[exit] er[and:yet] yi[different] ming[name]

tong[same] wei[call] zhi[it] xuan[dark].

xuan^{dark} zhi^{it} you^{also} xuan^{dark}

zhong^{crowd} miao^{mysteries} zhi'^s mu^{mother}

It says "These two come forth together and are differently named." On parsing NCR, we have just talked about four items, not two. We have discussed having-names, lacking-names, having-desires, and lacking-desires. On interpretive hypothesis IC, we have discussed only "you^{having}" and "wu^{lacking}." These two contrasting terms are *born together,* as the *Daode Jing* regularly notes. Their being tied in this way as complementaries creates mysteries and ever deeper mysteries. This is one gate into the mystery of language.

Looking at the whole book we confirm that the *you-wu* reading is most consistent with the rest of the book. Pairing or contrasting of *wu*^{lack} and *you*^{have} is a common theme in the *Daode Jing.* By contrast, we allow that the *Daode Jing* does discuss *wu-ming*^{lack names} and *wu-yu*^{lack desire}. But we should find it inconsistent with the antilanguage, anticonventional spirit of the text to treat the opposites—*you-ming*^{having names} and *you-yu*^{having desires}—as Daoist goals. So we accept the second analysis. It furthers the discussion of how *ming*^{names} work in *dao*^{ways}. Focusing on either *you*^{have} or *wu*^{lack} constitutes having different desires or attitudinal points of view. We associate *wu*^{lack} with desire for mystery and paradox (what is nothingness?). We associate *you*^{have} with the desire to understand objects and events—manifestations.

The first chapter, then, announces a skeptical theory about *dao*s, about prescriptive discourse. It supports this skepticism with a claim about names. It follows from the implicit theories we have used in making sense of all the philosophers we have studied so far. And then it considers a basic and puzzling name-pair: being and nonbeing. They seem as opposite as can be and we associate them with different inclinations for *dao*ing, with a mystical and a practical goal.

Yet the very existence of this distinction is a mystery. How can we learn a distinction between something and nothing? What do we divide off from everything? And puzzling about the mystery generates deeper mysteries. Let us see what these are.

Reversal of Opposites in the *Daode Jing*

As I promised, we will understand the rest of the book in the light of the beginning to contrast the traditional Daoist reading of the text from the Huang-Lao cult-of-the-ruler reading. Compelled to write something, Laozi continues by illustrating his view. He draws on attractively stated aphorisms, poems, and the like that express popular *dao*s which reverse the dominant views of how to act. Thus illustrating the point that they sometimes guide well, sometimes badly. In the second chapter, he introduces the concepts *you wu* again. Now his use of them as one among many examples of opposing terms is clear. Thereafter, this collection of sayings is overwhelmingly practical in tone. Interpreters have long puzzled about the practical, political focus of the text. If the central doctrine is mystical metaphysics, what is all this political advice doing?

We avoid this interpretive quandary if we do not treat the central doctrine as mystical metaphysics but as linguistic skepticism. That skepticism arises against a background assumption that language is a social mechanism for regulating people's behavior. The political doctrines thus play a role in the *Daode-Jing's* pragmatic theory of language. Their point is to illustrate the inconstancy of any guiding terms and discourse. He illustrates his point in the common language of Chinese philosophical discussion: political policy. His political and practical advice is almost invariably the reversal of *conventional* political and moral attitudes. He reverses conventional values, preferences, or desires. His advice signals, as well, continuing acceptance of the *Ru-Mo* psychological model. Whatever practical outcome we achieve will flow from social leaders. This part allows the *Daode Jing* to be used by political theorists as advice to the ruler.

This practical advice is the Daoist theory of reversal of opposites. Political advice is only one manifestation. Apparently personal advice, metaphysical speculation, religious pronouncements, anything from here on may be used to illustrate the inconstancy of linguistic guidance. The pragmatic (as opposed to metaphysical or semantic) difference between each pair of opposites lies in our preferences. A single distinction creates both names. We learn some pattern of preference or desire for one and aversion for the other. Laozi's political doctrine illustrates the inconstancy of names and of *daos'* consisting of names. He shows us that we *can* reverse all these conventional *preferences*. They do *not* provide constant guidance. There are cases where opposite guidance (reversing the value assignments) is better. He even treats *you* and *wu* as having reversible pragmatic implications. Learn to notice the value not-having. Nonbeing invites us to create.

The text, then, consists of wise, obvious, or well-known sayings that take the traditional Confucian distinctions and flip-flop the preference ordering. Where conventional wisdom normally invites us to value *you*[have], Laozi invites us to reflect on the value of *wu*[lack]. Where all previous *daos* have agreed in advocating *ren*[benevolence], he notes that heaven is not benevolent. Where all conventional *daos* inevitably stress purposive action and involvement, his sayings illustrate the wisdom of quietude: *wu-wei*[lacks deem:do]. Where conventional value assignments favor the upper, the strong, the wise, the dominant, Laozi's sayings help us appreciate the value of the lower, the weak, the ignorant, the submissive. We normally value being sharp and discriminating. Consider the value of being dull and indiscriminate. Traditionalists value the male; Laozi emphasizes the female. For each conventional distinction, Laozi shows us that in our own proverbs, we have a way of talking that would have us reverse the value preference in each pair of complementary terms. Let us call the *dao* expressed in this deluge of unconventional advice the *negative dao*.

The enormous appeal and influence of the book in Chinese culture and our own testifies to how reasonable that opposite advice is. It is, no doubt, sincerely recorded. Still, if we are reading it in the spirit of the opening lines, its theoretical point must be more subtle than merely reversing conventional guidance and dogmatically pushing the negative discourse *dao*. We should not take the negative *dao* as a constant *dao* either. Its point can only be as a series of examples of how we can reverse whatever guidance we get in language. Each item merely helps us realize that we can never take any fixed discourse as a guide in all circumstances.

The author lays the basis for this theme in the second chapter. For each name pair, there is one distinction. For each distinction, there is a preference ordering.

Some of the examples he chooses are *thin* guiding terms. (See pages 126–27.) They are clearly evaluative: good, bad, beautiful, ugly. The thicker term pairs guide us in more complicated ways. Which we prefer depends on where we are in executing a program and on the setting. These terms include above and below, before and after, having and lacking, and so forth. Laozi's collection of evaluative slogans should suggest that no term-based guidance is constant.

If that preference ordering is not constant, what can we say about each distinction? Is Laozi opposed to distinctions per se? We do assume that his citing of *negative* advice is sincere advice even if not alleged to be a constant *dao*. All learning of distinctions comes with dispositions to prefer one or the other. This insight does give us a perspective from which to raise the question of the point of distinction making. Becoming a discriminating consumer seems to consist in being conditioned and controlled by preferences instilled by society. The preferences are the *practically significant reasons* for the distinction creating the two terms. The terms, however, are not constantly reliable guides to behavior. The implication is that accepting training in discriminating preference is potentially as harmful as it is helpful. This, again, is a pragmatic, not a metaphysical, reason for rejecting distinctions.

The pragmatic argument suggesting skepticism of distinctions starts from a kind of assertion of the identity of opposites. There is only one distinction for any two contrasting terms. That distinction does not reliably guide our preferences. The point is not the descriptive one (that distinctions distort the world); it is the pragmatic one. Trained discriminations are not a constantly reliable guide to behavior. Culturally motivated preferences based on those distinctions are, on the whole, unreliable. And they control us in insidious, unnatural ways.

Thus Laozi moves toward the position of Shendao by a different route, one consistent with the antisocial, anticonventional spirit of the hermits and Yang Zhu. He does not depend on the notion of a single actual *dao* as either a fatalistic or, naturalistic argument for abandoning knowledge. He argues instead merely that knowledge of *daos* cannot be reliable or constant. We could reverse all the guiding $zhi^{\text{know-how-to}}$ we have and perhaps do as well. (Contrarian strategies in the stock market seem to have an impressive pattern of success.) To appear to be stupid in conventional terms might be the smartest thing to do! To *misuse* the distinctions could frequently be a superior strategy. The point of reversal is to see the benefit of forgetting distinctions, not the bald advocacy of some opposite discourse *dao*.

In pursuit of $zhi^{\text{know-to}}$, one adds everyday. In pursuit of *dao* one decreases every day (ch. 48).

Negative Discourse, Negative Know-how

Chapter 3 of the *Daode Jing* goes on to develop the reversal theme. Throughout most of the rest of the book, Laozi exhibits a pattern of discourse leading to the reversal of conventional values. Do not accumulate; do not educate. Learn the value of the negative side of all values. We can even learn to value emptiness and nothing.

This project leads to several recurring ambiguities in the *Daode Jing*. Laozi seems sometimes to value $zhi^{\text{know-how-to}}$, sages, learning, and intelligence and sometimes to disvalue them. We can sort these out by postulating three kinds of know-how, of learning, of sages and of intelligence. Conventional know-how-to consists in mastery of the distinctions and preferences in some shared social guide, Confucian or Mohist. Negative knowledge is *knowing to do the opposite* of conventional wisdom. We implicitly conjecture that Laozi assumes a third level of $zhi^{\text{know-how-to}}$ which he, *ex hypothesi,* cannot put into the book—the guidance *dao* cannot be stated. The book's exercise is reversal. The point of that reversal is not expressed.

When Han Feizi and the Huang-Lao cult read Daoism, they took the negative, anti-Confucian *dao* seriously as *the correct discourse dao* and read all the antibenevolent passages and the appeals to leave people ignorant as endorsing their ruler-oriented, manipulative political ideology. Similarly, when Daoism became a religion merging with Buddhism, people forgot the critical point of reversal. This negative *dao* came to be thought of as the whole of Laozi's theory of *dao,* hence the claim that *dao* is identical to nonbeing—and it exists! Tied to the Buddhist doctrine of *emptiness,* it has become enshrined in traditional interpretations. But it is in direct contradiction to the tone of equality of opposites. The emphasis on *wu,* submissiveness, the Yin, female, dark, waterlike values is not there because these distinctions *are* constant. It is there only as a heuristic corrective to our conventional presuppositions of what has positive value.

Wherever they stand in that third level of knowledge, *wu* and *you* are on a par.

Scheming Political Methods

So the anarchist *Daode Jing* does present a doctrine of government. Laozi gives advice to rulers. The advice is frequently stunning in conventional terms. The ruler keeps people ignorant, empties their minds and fills their stomach, does not try to make them clear and enlightened but stupid and simple. Han Feizi picked up these passages, as we shall see later, as Daoist support for the rulers' arbitrary, manipulative strategy.

Even more surprisingly, the advice is often blatantly dishonest. Appealing to a theory of constant political reversal, the text appears to advocate aiming for the opposite goal of the one you really have. So to become dominant, you should be submissive. You want to become powerful? Then act like the most submissive and unambitious servant of the ruler. The Confucians, looking at this advice, have gleefully accused the Daoists of *scheming methods.*[36] Their analysis furthered the persistent view of Daoism as a metaphysical theory of cyclical flux. According to this Confucian interpretation, the *Daode Jing* supposes that *things* change, specifically that they constantly reverse themselves. So you can get to point A best by heading for not-A.

Daoists, I have allowed, are aware that situations do change. What seemed like a calamity can turn out to be a blessing and vice versa. Success and failure are not always what they seem. Events may surprise us. Contrarian strategies may sometimes work. Or, we may be using too restricted and conventional a notion of success. However, that is not the basic point of the text. At most it contributes to the conclusion that one cannot follow one codified guide in all situations.

We do not need to take this Confucian attack seriously since it assumes the least charitable reading of the text. Laozi could not consistently hold the scheming-methods doctrine as the Confucians present it. First it takes the traditional valuation for granted: domination. Second it supposes a constant and statable *dao:* reversal. Third, it takes only a moments reflection to notice that getting on top in this way is meaningless anyway. By being on top, one will inevitably come back down. Such a strategy is curiously shortsighted.

Laozi includes those sayings among the rest. They do not state the *absolute dao* of government. They illustrate ways of talking that reverse conventional Confucian values. Laozi, I hypothesize, did not intend merely to state a rival *dao,* certainly not one that Confucians can so easily ridicule. He does not want to *join* the *Ru-Mo* debate with a third authoritarian alternative. He wants to *critique* the whole activity. The Confucian interpretation incoherently takes Laozi's stated negative *dao* as his unstatable constant *dao.* That supposed paradox in Daoism is merely a paradox of the Confucian interpretation.

Opposition to Use of the Senses?

> The five colors make man's eyes blind;
> The five notes make his ears deaf;
> The five tastes injure his palate;
> Riding and hunting make his mind go wild with excitement;
> Goods hard to come by serve to hinder his progress.[37]

Another common misinterpretation by modern Western Confucians (and latent Buddhists) has Laozi opposed to sense experience. This imposes a Western fixation on Chinese thinkers for which we so far can give them no plausible motivation. We have found no interest in the question of sense experience anywhere in the tradition so far. We do not even find our concept of *experience, consciousness,* or any theory of cognitive events in a mental medium. Besides, Daoists as nature worshippers could hardly oppose nature. The senses are our access to nature and its natural effects.

Like the concern with metaphysical flux, interpreters impose this philosophical problem on the Daoists in the absence of any credible motivation beyond the familiarity of the problem in the Indo-European philosophical tradition. They assume that *all serious philosophy must share a common set of problems.* If the problem of sense skepticism intrigued Western thinkers, it must have intrigued Chinese thinkers. My argument, on the contrary, is that if we understand how those problems arose in *Western thought,* what the background concepts, metaphysical theories, and so forth were, we will find it quite plausible that no parallel problem plagued Chinese philosophers. This problem of sense skepticism was pursued ad nauseam in seventeenth- and eighteenth-century Western philosophy and in Indian philosophy. But it is not *the paradigm* philosophical question. It's not even a particularly interesting one.

So how can we understand fragments like "The five colors blind the eyes?" (ch. 12). Is that not an appeal to close down the senses? Shouldn't we learn to see with our Buddhist inner eye or our Christian conscience or some other mystical inner insight? I admit I have trouble being objective about the sense-skepticism interpretative line because I simply cannot understand how that view of the sense of the line would even spring to mind, let alone seem plausible.

If we understand the passage as referring to sensible colors, it becomes absurd on its face. The suggestion that the experience of five colors at once makes one blind is so obviously false that even poetic license does little to justify it. I have at least that many colors in my visual field at this moment. Maybe if I keep only four in view at once, I will be safe. But five and your eyeballs burst! Is the Daoist lover of nature really telling us to limit our involvement with nature so we do not see bright colors? Hear different sounds? Taste natural flavors?

That interpretation violates both the principle of humanity *and* the principle of charity. Not only is it blatantly false, but our usual experience is that exposure to more experiences, tastes, and sounds refines rather than destroys our ability to appreciate fine differences.

An initially more obvious reading, consistent with the theme of the whole *Daode Jing,* is easily available. What *blinds* you figuratively is not exposure to color but the *conventional categorizing* of colors into *five.* That conditions us to ignore all the richness of hues and shades in nature. (The alternative saddles Laozi with the strange view that there are exactly five natural colors! And by some miracle of nature, exactly five tastes and tones!) It is society's imposing a gross social distinction that blinds us to the infinite richness of natural hues and shades. We practically ignore all the other possible ways of distinguishing and discriminating color in our conventional instructions. Commitment to the conventional five colors leads you to miss infinite variety of shades and hues presented in nature. It blinds you to the richness of visual experience.

The whole passage is an attack on social embellishment, on socially structured activities like hunting and valuing of rare objects that distort our natural functioning. We should stay with what is essential to our natures and not try to embellish nature with appealing decoration and fashion. Those are based on instilling conventional tastes and attitudes.

Buddhists truly are sense skeptics. They operate with a familiar mind-body dichotomy. But the point of this passage seems to be precisely the opposite of sense skepticism. It prefers the undistorted natural sense to the conventionally conditioned one. Daoists could be more coherently understood to respect and want to preserve unsullied natural experience. Of course, a Han Confucian, sure that the conventional five colors are the key to the five elements that give the ruler power over nature and therefore over us, cannot brook such a heresy. He welcomes the Buddhist interpretation. Nature really does come divided into these neat clusters of fives! Anyone who understood Daoist philosophy would have found that dark ages superstition absurd,

Primitive Daoism; Mysticism and Mencius

I have challenged here the accepted view of what Daoism is. That accepted view treats Daoism as a metaphysical mysticism. The interpreters allow that what they see in the text is incoherent gibberish, but they seek to explain it by calling it deep and profound mysticism. Of course anything they try to say will be incoherent, but somehow the interpreter divines that behind this screen lies a theory of reality and language. The interpreter does not tell us how *he* managed to extract meaning from gibberish. But he confidently tells us that like all mystics, the Daoist absolutely claims the existence of a single *dao* and holds a theory of language such that language can't . . . something or other . . . the *dao.*

What do interpreters divine in the unspoken theory of reality and language that justifies writing this mass of contradictions? I cannot claim to know. I have tried without success to follow a number of accounts. I shall only try to mimic what I take to be what I am hearing so the reader can understand my frustration.

The most common version asserts the unity of mysticism.[38] If we can use the word, there must be something in common among all mystics. So Daoist theory must be like that of the mystics of India and the West. That theory of language starts with the assumptions of Platonic semantics. Every term is meaningful if and only if it points to an unchanging reality. Interpreters place that theory of language alongside a metaphysical assumption that reality consists of objects. But the objects we see are constantly changing. So language can't refer to any of those. Mysticism gets its paradoxical character, then, from claiming, again as Plato does, that there *is* some unchanging object. The mystic, unlike Plato however, incoherently claims this *is* an object of experience—albeit a mystical experience, which since it is unlike ordinary experience must not be an experience—but never mind. Now that we have this monistic and unchanging object, however we got it, one would expect that the conclusion should be relief. Language must be about that unchanging object. But no. They now conclude that language can*not* pick out that object. It can only point to the ordinary objects which the theory had earlier denied that language can properly refer to. Now they turn the tables and insist that language can only distort the only real, unchanging object there is—the *dao,* Buddha Nature, Brahman, Absolute, or God.

I cannot be sure I have stated their position correctly since it seems to contradict both their theory of language and their theory of reality. I shall struggle with it no more. I just insist on this: as long as we are evaluating interpretive theories as explanations of a text, we can always dismiss such theories on their face. The mystical interpretation is a cry of despair. The evidence for it is the alleged unintelligibility of the text as it stands! But a mystical explanation cannot help if we are so frustrated. If the interpretive theory is not coherent, there is no point in seeing if it explains the text. It couldn't explain anything since it has no coherent truth conditions itself. It can't be a consistent explanation of the text because it can't be a consistent explanation of anything at all. Between an incoherent theory and a coherent one, there is no point in asking which best explains the phenomena. At best it explains why we can't explain it, which we need to do only if we really can't.

I say we can. I have proposed an alternative interpretive theory of Daoist claims about language and *dao.* It does not start from the prior acceptance of baldly incoherent assumptions about language and reality. It has paradoxes, but they are the kinds of philosophically interesting paradoxes that flow from considering assumptions that other philosophers or schools take as obvious truths. The paradoxes do not result from arbitrary, capricious, ad hoc, *prima facie* contradictory, and apparently pointless assumptions that have no purpose other than to license the production of verbal gibberish. They do not involve changing the meaning of all the key terms solely to make what one says *un*intelligible.

Both the linguistic and the reality aspects of the view typically attributed to Daoists must be wrong. Daoism is consistent with the direction of Chinese thought at the time. It makes no drastic jump to an Indo-European conceptual scheme. Its assumptions and problems are continuous with the assumptions and problems exercising other philosophers in China. The theory of language is pragmatic. It deals with language as a regulative social mechanism shaping our attitudes, desires, and actions. It does this by training us in making distinctions in a common shared way: a guiding social discourse. It has said very little about an ultimate reality and less about experience, mystical or otherwise.

I understand *dao* in Daoism as I understand it in Confucianism, Mohism, and elsewhere. It is a guiding way. The distinctive Daoist skepticism comes from the fluidity of convention. It does not result in a theory that language cannot capture the *Dao*. The skeptical claim is merely that any prescriptive discourse—any *dao* that language can express cannot be a constantly reliable guide to behavior.

This change in interpretation does not presuppose that a single author—Laozi—wrote the chapter. It does, however, take seriously the challenge to find a coherent interpretation of the text in its cultural context. The present interpretation does make sense of Laozi's legendary reluctance to write his *dao* for the gatekeeper. He opens with a disclaimer that any guidance can be constant. Then he assembles axioms and proverbs, wise sayings of elders with rich life experience. What can be the point? He cannot, consistently, be trying to provide a constant guide to life by this collection of sayings.[39]

What is the point then? What are we to do, Laozi? What advice can you give us? What is the third level of knowledge? Should we abandon distinctions and conventions?

Chapter 80 of the *Daode Jing* describes the utopia of the Daoist primitivist.[40] Daoist primitivists essentially rest with the Shendao interpretation of the *Daode Jing*. Their goal, however, is neither stoicism nor ruler-oriented arbitrary authority. It is *radical* anarchy. As anarchy, it rebels not only against political authority, but *all social authority*. The way to remove the authority of society totally from your life is to remove language. If that were done, it would leave us only our innate instincts. The primitivist optimistically feels these instincts will be peaceful, village oriented, nonimperial, nonagressive. His position is similar to that of Mencius except that the innate, prelinguistic instincts are far fewer. They are capable only of supporting a simple agrarian life in communion with a small clan village.

The primitivist, like Mencius, must assume a natural goodness in our presocial instincts. Without language we would still make distinctions, but they would be *natural* ones instead of *conventional* ones. The difference is this. Mencius' theory entails that all the distinctions necessary for empire building and ruling are implicit in our innate structure. The primitivist says that only those fitting for agrarian village life are natural. For Mencius unified world government is natural, for the primitivist only small villages. The Mencian sage would know innately how to rule all within the four seas. The primitivist sage would know how to plant potatoes and feed pigs and be absorbed in village life.

I argue that Laozi and Mencius come in the same phase of Chinese thought—the antilanguage phase. They, therefore, share an approach to the philosophical issues they addressed. They have a lot in common. Still, Laozi's analysis fundamentally undercuts Mencius' position. Laozi shares the antilanguage attitude, but gives a more plausible explanation of our ordinary moral judgments. Mencius assumed that all our ordinary judgments reflect innate, heavenly ordained moral dispositions. Laozi shows how those reactions in the heart can come from socialization. He shows that the entire process of learning language is a process of absorbing a conventional, social pattern of desires. Our moral attitudes are learned, not innate. After Laozi, classical Chinese philosophers no longer took the strong version of Mencius' position seriously.

Our own romantic tradition clearly favors Laozi's village utopia. But should we treat this as Laozi's goal? Perhaps it is merely another example of a line of discourse designed to see the value in what Confucians *fei*[not this] and the disvalue of what they *shi*[this]. Treating it as a constant utopian idea makes the text incoherent. It presupposes a distinction between distinction making that is *natural* and distinction making that is *conventional*. This distinction leads to attitudes and desires (avoid unnatural distinctions) and to action (retire to the village). If Laozi truly opposes these and also advocates primitivism then he traps himself in only a slightly more complex paradox than that of Shendao.

And what of the borrowed Shendao advice? Can we take "abandon *zhi*[know-to]" seriously? We must treat that, too, as another example found in the tradition for not valuing knowledge and sagehood. We should not treat it as a *constant dao* lest we land in absurdity. We must treat "abandon *zhi*[know-to]" and the antisage passages as showing reasons for reversing conventional evaluative attitudes toward these terms. They cannot be the end of the Daoist story.

So Laozi points mysteriously to some other knowledge. And what of those mystical passages that talk of a metaphysical *dao? Dao* as a creator, as a divine incomprehensible mysterious thing? These passages, like all others in the book, have implications for action, usually implications of reversal. Nourish things without trying to possess them! Nature-worship talk is also discourse. It leads to the reversal of some conventional values. Monism merely motivates another part of the heuristic negative *dao*. It is not the Laozi's constant *dao*.

The *dao,* the discourse, presented in the *Daode Jing* is all changeable. We should throw Laozi's parables and poetry away, like Wittgenstein's ladder of argument, once we have climbed through them. If you understand them, you understand that you do not need them. You understand not to value them as constants.

> The higher scholar hears *dao*—he diligently practices it. The average scholar hears *dao*—it's as if it's both there and not there. The lower scholar hears *dao*—he laughs at it. If he did not laugh, it could not be regarded as *dao* (ch. 41).

Which *dao?* Which scholar has the right response?

We still have no final answer to the question, "What should we do?" Can we coherently see this book as giving the answer? Is this all we can expect when you force a sage to write down his *dao* before he leaves the country? Perhaps he is driving at something else. Something he can point to only by expressing a paradox. "Do nothing arising from deeming and yet nothing can be done without deeming." If there is some advice, some point, Laozi could not state it. And so neither can I.

But Zhuangzi can! Daoism must still mature more.

III

THE ANALYTIC PERIOD

7

The School of Names: Linguistic Analysis in China

The first stage of the answer is simply that the Chinese looked into formal logic and found it less important than other concerns in philosophy. . . .

FREDERICK MOTE[1]

Since means are dependent on ends, it is inevitable that on the Chinese scale of value the wise dicta of Confucius and Lao-tzu are primary, the practical rationality of Mo-tzu and Han Fei is secondary, the games with logical puzzles of Hui Shih and Kung-sun Lung are at best tertiary.

A. C. GRAHAM[2]

Theory of language was a key focus in all the early Chinese schools. Their theory of philosophical dispute focused on names. So, unsurprisingly, adherents of different views began to defend their positions by claiming to have more analytically adequate theories of naming. I will argue that the school of names had Confucian, Daoist, and Mohist versions. The Mohist theories of naming moved the study of language from a pragmatic to a more semantic focus. They embed their semantics in the larger project of Chinese philosophy—getting constant guidance from a *dao*. They tried to describe a realistic base of naming. They sought a reality-based answer to the question, "What is the *right* way to project distinctions in new settings?" The right way, they thought, responded to real similarities and differences in the world.

In the earlier *Ru-Mo*[Confucian-Mohist] period, a social and implicitly relativist outlook dominated the discussion of the right use of terms. However, their arguments drew them toward realism. Confucius began with a purely conventional point of view. He justified his *dao* mainly by its pedigree and the threat of anarchy if we did not maintain the conventional regularities. Implicitly, therefore, his position allowed that we could equally well have another *dao* if everyone agreed and followed that. As we saw, Confucius and his school still had to face a realistic question internal to even his traditional *dao:* What is the *correct performative interpretation* of that conventional ritual scheme? This problem pushed early Confucianism to a realistic doctrine of the correct *application* of the names and of correct performance triggered by the names. Confucius may not have been conventionalist about the *application* of his inherited *dao.* Had he been willing to accept any workable solution that produced a shared agreement, changes in performance interpretation over time should not have bothered him. The realist urge led early Confucians to develop the concept of an intuition that guides interpretive performance: *ren* ^{humanity}.[3]

From the Mohist (and the Socratic) view, Confucius was *still* too much of a conventionalist. He considered the canonical *content* of the received *dao* to be conventional. He gave similar treatment to the roles and ritual competencies denoted by traditional terms. Human guidance came from human history and culture. So Confucians stressed scholarship and mastery of literature. One could raise questions about the interpretation of the transmitted forms, but not its formulaic content. Flexibility came from interpreting the code, not from amending it.

Mozi accepted much of the conventionalist framework, but he directly raised the realist's question. His utilitarian language convention rested on a reality standard. It was not that the distinctions were to mark *the joints of reality,* abstractly and neutrally considered. He introduced reality indirectly through the standard of utility. Certain conventions are more useful than others given the *real* context. Mozi's introducing the pragmatic perspective altered Confucius' focus: We should prefer the *most beneficial* set of conventions. Mozi justified the distinctions marked by names according to their utility in practical guidance, not their descriptive accuracy. Reality only indirectly set the boundary conditions for correct naming.

If we think of something's being conventional only if it is *one of a set of* equally serviceable shared practices, Mozi then accepted the conventionalism of language. He merely argued that Confucius' conventional practices were not as serviceable as alternative conventions might be. This moved him in a realistic direction. He had to appeal implicitly to an extraconventional *authority* and at least one naturally fixed (guiding) distinction. This gave him a realistic causal base for his system of names. It still allows that there might be equally useful conventions and it still depends heavily on the social need for order and agreement.

As we saw, Mozi did pay attention to descriptive distinctions (e.g. black and white) but he used them as action-guiding distinctions. He treated that distinction as an analogue to the distinction between moral and immoral. He also proposed the ideal of measurable *fa* ^{standards} for names and guiding discourse. We are to attach names to things in virtue of features of those things that would be accessible to ordinary people, features that require only use of their eyes and ears. He applied that ideal mainly to prescriptive terms. The measurable standard was *li-hai* ^{benefit-harm}. It makes it easy to project heaven's will, almost like measuring something. What for Bentham was a moral calculus was for Mozi a moral compass.

The urge to realism also motivated the antilanguage theorists. The threat of relativism in Confucius' conventionalism drove Mencius toward innatism. He adopted the *formal* realism of *one right answer* to concrete moral questions. His defense of Confucianism against Mozi required Mencius to offer an equally realistic account. He too based it on our natural dispositions to make distinctions. Like Mozi's distinctions, his natural *shi-fei* amounted to natural practical guidance. He merely dispensed with all derivation. Where Mozi had one distinction guide all *shi-fei* activity, Mencius allowed only the innate, formally unguided *shi-fei*s. Mencius implicitly accepted the conventionalist view of language. It explained his hostility to language and his need to transcend it altogether. Defending Confucianism against Mozi required some extralinguistic guide. Once he had it, language could only be a threat. The intuition directly guided the application of the thin guiding terms, *shi-fei* ^{this-not this}.

Laozi's antilanguage views also seem to stem from a discomfort with the relativity of convention. Most critical is this: conventions could all be otherwise. All distinctions are reversible. His conclusion is not as confidently realist as Mencius' unless we construe him as a primitivist. (In which case, as we saw, the differences with Mencius shrink to a difference in where to draw the boundary between innate and conventional, language-induced guidance.) Speculating about his unspoken third level of knowledge easily tempts us to *mystical* realism. The typical account of Daoist mysticism is realist and absolutist. Reality is the basis of right and wrong. That reality, in fact, makes all language wrong. In a sense, the absolute truth is there is no absolute truth. Shendao's metaphysical *dao* is a natural, unconventional, and therefore constant guide to behavior. The absolute guide to behavior cannot guide.

My theory is that what traditional accounts call the school of names is not *a* school, but the culmination of a trend. Specialists began to pursue more systematic linguistic argument. They defended all three political points of view. Each more directly addressed the abstract relation of names and the world. We can see Laozi as a crucial precursor to this more abstract concern. He showed how guidance required separately discriminating and desiring. One could reverse the desires while holding the discrimination patterns constant. This yielded the chance to look for a neutral account of the discriminations appropriately marked by names. So we also know these writers as specialists in *bian*^{discrimination}. The writers did not share any single political or moral doctrine or attitudes beyond their specialized interest in language and distinction making.

The impetus for this realism differs from that familiar in Western traditions. They do not seek a *causal* explanation of linguistic discrimination—a sense that the world makes our language have the shape it does. They, rather, are still searching for a constant way to project guiding distinctions. The problem with purely conventionalist distinctions is that the very awareness of their conventionality makes them inconstant. That is, once the Mohist has made his point (that traditions could be wrong), any purely conventionalist system will be unstable. Any *dao* can change if our social purposes change.

The other way in which Chinese realism differs is that its underlying theory of language has no clear counterpart to the familiar conceptual structure of Western semantics. We find no concepts of *beliefs, concepts, ideas, thoughts, meanings,* or *truth.*[4] Mohist thinkers create realist semantics out of the project of finding constant guiding discourse. They wonder how to project guiding conceptual schemes. Their analyses use the pragmatic term *ke*^{admissible} as pivotally as Western analyses use *truth.* They still do not focus on sentences but on names or longer strings of names (usually character pairs). The deep concern continues to be guidance, not description.

The Neo-Mohist Text: Importance and Problems

The impetus toward a realistic theory of names manifested itself most obviously in the Mohist school. It was an outgrowth of Mozi's focus on standards of measurement and the idea of a preconventional natural or heavenly standard. Mohists became interested in the intellectual problem of constructing a coherent scheme of conventions.

This led them even to abandon Mozi's emphasis on *tian*^{nature:heaven}. They also avoid any appeal to Mencius-like inner projections of feelings from the *xin*^{heart-mind}.[5]

The Mohist dialecticians were a group of followers of Mozi sometimes also called Neo-Mohists. Clusters of Mohist disciples operated in groups. The individual groups seemed to maintain tight discipline and organization but the various groups differed widely in their concerns. Some dealt mainly with defensive engineering and warfare, others with formal philosophy.

One faction followed Mozi's interest in objective standards of language use and technology. They conveyed their teachings by reciting a summa of terse *jing*^{canons}. Each *jing*^{canon} consists of a short formula dealing with ethics, language, and various sciences (optics, geometry, economics). Copyists incorporated these canons, called the *Mohist Canon,* into the middle of *The Mozi,* where it was preserved but not studied. The tradition effectively lost the key doctrines of this school for two millennia.

The story of how the tradition both preserved and lost this dialectical text is arresting. It should defuse any skepticism that the medieval Neo-Confucian culture could have failed to understand such a crucial part of its own classical philosophy. Further, it illustrates the theoretical nature of textual reconstruction and its implications for interpretation.

A common writing medium in ancient China was bamboo strips. The Chinese laced the strips together and rolled them into a *juan*^{roll}, which we translate as *book* (usually within *volumes*). Chinese was traditionally, therefore, written vertically and one unrolled the *juan*^{roll} right to left. One could then scroll through the book easily. There was probably an inclination to use the strips as natural breaks, like punctuation. The medium imposed a natural approximate standard length and a practical limit on book size. Our traditional *Daode Jing,* remember, emerged as the *Dedao Jing* in a Han school.

These publication practices, coupled with the cost of copying to distribute the book, made writers value terseness. When, however, a scholar copied a text for himself, he probably felt free to annotate, expand, and comment on the text on the strips. These comments sometimes found their way into subsequent copies.

The Later Mohists' texts include six *juan*^{rolls}. They called two simply the first (upper) and second (lower) *Canon.* Two others, they called the first and second *Explanations of the Canon.* The final two were seriously corrupted. Archivists may have gathered them from disbursed fragments and called them (appropriately) the *Greater* and *Lesser Picks.* The *Lesser Pick* was a remarkably coherent essay fragment. The *Greater Pick* was a more random selection of fragments of varying length. Graham postulated that the two picks had come from an earlier and a later Mohist book. He argues that the Mohists had titled the originals the *Canon of Sayings* and *Names and Objects.*

We find the core of the linguistic theory in the two *Canons* and their *Explanations.* Orthodox hostility to Mohism only partly accounts for the traditional neglect of these doctrines. The theory was both singularly sophisticated and tersely expressed. It was inimical to Confucianism but also to the dominant primitivist and absolutist interpretation of Daoism. The immediate cause of the loss of understanding was the way the *Mohist Canon* was written and included in the *Mozi.* The first *Canon* was made up of terse theories of various key terms in the system. The second consisted of only slightly longer conceptual, ethical or, scientific claims, each also explained by a key term. Neither was an essay but a detailed look at a recommended conceptual scheme. As both sets of term-based fragments were shorter than the bamboo strip length, the Later Mohists wrote them across the upper half of the bamboo *book*. Then, to save space, they started again on the bottom half of the strips. The scribe placed a terse instruction at the end of the top half (the middle of the book) to alert readers to this arrangement

At some point in the transmission an unthinking copyist copied straight through each strip. This interlaced the fragments like shuffling a deck of cards. Then successive copies preserved this mistake in the archival paper or silk versions. The absence of punctuation, lack of both understanding and appreciation of its importance reduced the shuffled text to an almost random string of characters. Confucian transmitting theory favored preserving the text, so collectors copied and recopied it. Collectors dutifully preserved it despite no one's understanding or valuing it. Of course it was particularly susceptible to copyist mistakes, skipping, or doubling characters, losing one's place, and duplicating lines. The form delivered to the Qing dynasty scholars, who started the process of reconstruction, was a bona fide jigsaw puzzle.

Fortunately, in the second pair of books, the *Explanations of the Canon,* the Mohists had inserted indices to connect each *Explanation* with its *Canon.* They wrote the first word of the pertinent *Canon* beside the strip containing the explanation. The mechanical copyist inserted these into the text string, usually as the first or second character. This garbled the grammar of the explanations, making them less intelligible. But it also eventually provided a key to unraveling the puzzle. Those characters signaled the beginning of each original fragment and the crucial relation between the two texts. For two thousand years, the archivists treated the *Canon* and *Explanations* as separate texts.

The Neo-Confucian school of the Qing dynasty, the back-to-the–Han movement, developed an empirical, scientific interest in old texts. The process of reconstructing the Neo-Mohist canon began then and continued through the modern period. A. C. Graham published the first English translation of the whole in 1978. Graham's *Later Mohist Logic, Ethics and Science* completed the textual reconstruction. Now, understanding the text that is the key to the last half of classical philosophical period has finally become possible. I argue that it changes the philosophical landscape completely. It is now clear that their advanced theories of language influenced both Zhuangzi and Xunzi. It exposed the blatant incoherence of the antilanguage positions of Mencius and Laozi which Neo-Confucianism took as the apex of Chinese philosophy. It also became possible to trace how this intense interest in terms arose from the theories of the earlier philosophers.

The Neo-Confucian tradition had lost the essence of the classical theory of language. As medieval Neo-Confucianism emerged, following the philosophical dark age and the Buddhist period, its adherents worked from their own implicit theory of language. It consisted of the combination of some vague, intuitive insights of the classical Chinese view combined with the utterly different Indo-European theory that Buddhism had imported. This, coupled with the superstitious, cosmological focus of a sterile, eclectic Confucian orthodoxy effectively obliterated the language insights of the classical thinkers.

The superstition-influenced Han produced a precocious teenager, Wang Bi, who constructed his own theory. It combined the *Daode Jing* and a divination manual (the *I Jing*^{Book of Changes}). This turned the *Daode-Jing* into a cosmogony, Wang Bi's conception of deep thought. He explained that the reason *we cannot name Dao* was that we cannot see it! That the Confucians should take so shallow and silly a theory of language, developed by a superstitious teenager in the philosophical dark age, to be the view of the geniuses of the greatest period of Chinese thought testifies mainly to the power of the Confucian doctrine of respect for antiquity. Still, it had the advantage of fitting in with the Buddhist theory of language and mind. Buddhism introduced attention to epistemology and sense skepticism. But, as we shall see, it had little relation to the sophisticated theory of the philosophical giants of the classical period.

The Centrality of Bian

We sometimes use *Mo Bian* to refer both to the school that produced the text and the texts themselves. The most uncorrupted text in the set of six highlights the importance of *bian*. The authors regard *bian*^{discriminating} as the key to all intellectual activity. *Bian*^{discriminating} makes clear the division between what is *this* (the named category in question) and what is not—*shi-fei*. All investigations involve *bian*, from politics (the distinction of order and disorder) to science (the points of similarity and difference). A theory of *bian* is a theory of the principles of naming, fixing benefit and harm, and resolving difficulties and disagreements.[6]

Names pick out stuff, phrases convey intentions, explanations give the inherent way things are. We then choose and reject according to similarity and difference. What we have in ourselves, we do not condemn in others. What we lack in ourselves, we do not demand in others. Coherence in attitude is the Mohists' basic commitment in developing a guiding *dao*.[7]

The Neo-Mohists give the *standards* of *bian* a new task. We must *bian*^{distinguish} in a way that coherently assigns *ke*^{admissible} to phrases or strings in discourse. Since the discourse includes the discourse about standards of *bian*, this generates a regressive spiral for *bian* and an implicit realistic ideal. If we treat *bian* as *merely* conventional, then we have to regard one set no more correct than another. This threatens our system of discriminations and terms with incoherence or inconstancy because each of the actual systems does accept the realistic goal. They regard the alternatives as disagreeing with them. All our conventional language of discriminations have included the principled goal of finding an ideally best place to mark distinctions. This place the Mohist finds in the *gu*^{inherent way things are}

Western theory expresses this realistic urge in terms of the truth of sentences. Graham and others take *bian* to mean argument and the Mohist enterprise to include logic. This, as I have argued before, is a mistake. At least one of its roots is Graham's failure to appreciate the ambiguity of the English word *argument*. On the one hand an argument is something you have—synonymous with a quarrel—on the other it is something you give—synonymous with proof. Plainly, *quarrels and disputes between schools involve bian*. Classical philosophers, as I have argued, take differences in discrimination to lie at the heart of the disagreements between philosophical schools. However, *bian* has nothing to do with the Euclidian model of proof, as sequences of sentences arranged so the conclusion inherits truth from the premises.

The Mohists do not discuss either logic or sentential semantics in any explicit sense. They do not separate sentence structures from other complex strings or phrases compounded out of words. They do not postulate special sentential semantics—truth—governing the assertability of sentences. Graham disagrees. He has argued that the Mohists discovered the syntactical form of the sentence. He describes this as the "last and most difficult of the Mohist discoveries."[8] His argument is not convincing *unless* one regards a sentence as an obvious natural linguistic kind.[9] In any case, if the sentence is the *last discovery,* then the Mohist could not have discovered argument form since it depends on *a prior notion* of truth-bearing sentences. Arguments consist of sentences with some acting as premises and one as the conclusion.

A similar problem affects the understanding of *yi*[intention]. The text ties it with the *ci*[phrase]. Graham treats *ci* as sentences and then treats *yi*[intention] as *idea* in the Fregean sense, as the thought or proposition. This strips the theory of its pragmatic core and turns it into a British Empiricist conceptualism, complete with its blurring of the word counterpart of an idea and the sentence counterpart. So the Mohist writes that the heart-mind takes what the ear hears and by examination discovers the *yi*[intent]. Graham's English ear hears echoes of Locke. This is so despite the fact that Graham himself shows most convincingly what *intent* amounts to in the Mohist enterprise. The intent in using language involves a commitment to use the term up to a certain point and stop. It is the disposition to project terms onto things (and to stop the projection somewhere).

Phrases develop from the *gu*[inherent] (the way things are in themselves) to embody patterns that guide conduct. The system that guides conduct is a *dao.* The Neo-Mohist, like Laozi, inherits the guiding model of what *dao* does. But he adds theoretical detail. Between names and *dao* lie the dispositions to project terms on the world. Unless we correctly combine the terms and phrases with interpretive intentions, we will miss the performance *dao.* Our guidance will be inconstant. Compound phrases should develop according to the inherent nature of things named. Unless we heed this external basis of our commitments in using terms, we will have difficulty.[10] It is this doctrine that Graham takes to be a theory of sentence form.

The author of *Names and Objects has* seen that a *dao* requires more than mere names. The way we string names together and the way we project distinctions based on them governs the way we perform in following social guidance. The author bases the principles of stringing terms together on making proper distinctions—*bian.* They do not involve the sentence, the thought, idea, or truth. Nonetheless, *bian* has an unmistakable realistic thrust. In the end, however, in trying to state clear, coherent principles for combination, the Mohist admits that they fail. The principles of order are even less regular and discernible than those for names. The Mohists' arguments for realism doom Confucianism and primitive Daoism. The Mohists show them to be incoherent. This, however, leaves a path for a more sophisticated relativism—through which Zhuangzi drives a white horse, snakes, and a praying mantis.

The Realist Move

We should not contrast realism in classical China with either idealism (the view that the world is merely our mental construction) or nominalism (the denial of universal abstract properties). Its contrast in China was linguistic relativism, the view that language, not the world, determines kinds. The Mohist argues that the measurable differences in the world are the basis for making distinctions. Science, for example, does not fix the range of *mammal* merely by linguistic habit and custom. Reality fixes the range of natural kind terms. Hence, whether any culture realizes it or not, dolphins are mammals. A whole linguistic community can be wrong about its linguistic types.

The Neo-Mohists continue original Mohist argumentative themes. They accuse the Confucians of airy apathy toward the actual world. In the Neo-Mohist's view, the Confucians are the ones guilty of excessive focus on conventionality of names. They attend only to mastery of the language in their ancient ritual texts. The Mohists introduced a sciencelike concern with the actual similarities and differences in the world. Confucians assigned names prescriptively, basing them on tradition and intending them to guide proper behavior according to a traditional code. They were theoretically indifferent to the actual similarities and difference in things. They did not advocate assigning names on that basis. They preferred their historical reflections on how the sage-king authorities used names. The Neo-Mohist attitude was that Confucians ignored the real world and based their action on mere cleverness in using traditional names.

The opening formula in the *Canon* introduces the term *gu*^{in itself}. Graham has argued that *gu*^{in itself} played a role in Yang Zhu's egoist nativism. *Gu* is what grows to determine our *ming*^{fated length of life}. It is the heavenly endowed natural constitution.[11] Grammatically, *gu* precedes a conclusion. Translators tend to treat it as *therefore* or *reason*. We could explain its role as well, however, by *inherently*, ''from the constitution of things.'' This explains its vague similarity to object cause. *Gu*^{in itself} shares the term-based conceptual structure of Chinese philosophy. It neither signals a lawlike linking of events nor introduces a sentence that follows from earlier sentences. Its force for Mohists is ''arising from nonconventional natural sources.''[12]

The basic structure the Mohists projected on reality was a *ti-jian*^{part-whole} structure. The parts are divisions within some whole.[13] The *ti*^{parts} are more important to language. When we apply some name we apply it to a part. (We distinguish it from the rest, as Laozi thought). When we pick out a *ti* we do so in virtue of its *gu*. We must, then, *zhi*^{commit} ourselves to *xing*^{proceed} according to *lei*^{similarity}. This means there is a place at which we will *stop* applying the term. In this sense the world controls projection of linguistic expressions from the outside. But that control depends on the impact of the *gu* on us—the *qing*^{feeling:reality}.[14] Naming involves examples—paradigms. Examples are standards of the thing. Anything that *dang*^{hits} the example is the thing in question and whatever does not is not.[15]

One basic way that we name *ti* uses *shape and characteristic*. Two linked senses of this claim emerge from the *Canon*. The names (characters) themselves are quite literally *shapes*. Furthermore, in Chinese, they are shapes that derive from registered differences in shapes of *ti* in the world.[16] The ability to use language thus depends *twice* on the ability to recognize shape. The same ability explains how we can apply terms to *ju*^{pick out} objects and how we can use language symbols: reading and writing. The practical notion of *ju*^{pick out} or *qu*^{choose} gives the Mohist semantics a more pragmatic, purposive tone than would the closely related but more abstract notions of *denotation* or *reference*.

The Neo-Mohists recognized the compositional nature of language. Still, they did not have a syntactical conception based on sentences and parts of speech. We string names together to form larger units, *ci*[phrases], which people used to express *yi*[intentions]. They reintroduce the guiding focus now at the combining level. They reflect on how people use words to guide them in a reality rather than on how pure language fits pure reality.

The Neo-Mohists' doctrine of the *force* of language finally arrives back at the notion of a *dao*[way]. The nature of things together with our nature in registering them, fixes the path we must walk, at least linguistically. This is especially true in the construction of *ci*[phrases] out of names. If we are not clear about *lei*[similarity classes] these constructions will not guide us correctly.[17]

The Mohist's realism gives him an objective perspective on commitment in using names. The Confucian rectification-of-names theory made names too fluid. The standard was social agreement and conformity. The Mohist account is realistic. We call one thing by a name. The external similarities and differences then determine what else we must call by that name. We thus accept a *dao* using names. We must *xing*[walk] along it. (Notice that dao involves the application or interpretation of names.) The text uses the metaphor of turning off the road to discuss verbal *cleverness* (say the unrestricted creativity of rectifying names based on a claimed intuition). The Mohists characterize this in practical terms as *dangerous*.[18]

A Western student of semantics will find interesting how reliably the Mohists embed their realistic theory in a pragmatic framework. From the notion of commitment, to picking out or choosing, guiding intent, and finally arriving at a practical *dao*[way], the social conception of language informs the semantic theory.

The Paradox of Relativism

Pure conventionalism, I argued, is unstable. The problem of practical interpretation, as we saw, pushed early Confucianism toward interpretive realism. Mozi showed that the Confucian *dao* was unstable because it was self-defeating. The Neo-Mohists take on the later antilanguage views that try to escape Mozi's challenge to construct a constant conventional guide. Primitive Daoism and Mencius regard language as inherently inadequate. All language is *bu-ke*[not assertable] in that it distorts guidance— the Dao! The traditional explanation of the Daoist opposition to language assumes that the Dao is inherently one. It therefore has no parts and is nondivisible. Since language inherently marks distinctions, all language distorts the Dao.[19]

The Mohists notice something *perverse* about any antirealist claim. Consider the English sentence, "This sentence is false." It is false only if it is true and vice versa. Now consider the sentence "All sentences are false." It is not a paradox. It is simply false. If it is true, then it is false. If it is false, it is still false. (There are some true sentences, but it is not one of them).

Now the Mohists, for reasons I have explained above (pages 43–44), do not formulate their criticism of the antilanguage position as I just did. Instead of talking of *sentences, truth* and *falsity,* the Neo-Mohists speak of their more familiar *yan*[language]. Instead of false, they use the term *bei*[perverse]. They define *bei* as *bu-ke*[not permissible].[20]

> *Canon B 71:* To regard language as all *bei*[perverse] is *bei*[perverse]—the explanation is in his own language.

Explanation: bei[perverse] is *not-permissible*. If this person's language is permissible then it is not perverse and there is permissible (language). This person's language is not-permissible. He has obviously not examined deeply enough how it *dang*[maps onto things].

They developed a parallel proof rebutting the antidistinction version of the claim.[21] Since every distinction is a *shi-fei*, denying distinctions is denying *fei*. The Mohists rebut the claim that nothing could be *fei*[not this:wrong]. This amounts to *fei*ing *fei* and it must be *fei*. (Consider: "You shouldn't tell anyone what they shouldn't do!" or "It's wrong to say anything is wrong.")

They attack the antilearning positions of Laozi's primitivism and Shenadao's stoicism by the same technique. To teach that learning is useless is *bei*[perverse].

The Pragmatic Focus

So, although we find something close to familiar Western semantic paradoxes, we should treat them as pragmatic paradoxes. The Mohists formulate them in terms of word use and the social criterion of acceptability-perversity. They use *ke*[acceptable] as the main term of analysis and evaluation. They view language as a system with a distinction of acceptable and unacceptable use that is embedded in our social life and reactive nature. The underlying intuition of the discussion is that it cannot possibly be practical policy to allow a language to say certain things.

The Neo-Mohist is not explicitly using the concept of *truth*, but he is using an analogue of the principle of excluded middle. His argument presupposes that an expression is either permissible or not permissible of any stuff. However, the Mohists' discussion here touches mainly on terms, not truth-bearing propositions. They give excluded middle an explicitly conventional role via a stipulative notion of *bi, opposite* or *other*.[22] We form a *bi* by putting the negative *fei* in front of a term. All terms implicitly have such a *bi*. Learning the distinction necessary to use the term means being able to identify what is X and what is not X.

A *bi*[other] is a logical gate. For any given thing and arbitrary name, the thing either gets that name—*shi*[this:right]—or gets its opposite—*fei*[not this:wrong]. This is the *shi* commitment involved in using a name.

Using this notion of *bi* the Mohists argue for a realists' view of *bian*[discrimination:dispute]. A *bian* is a dispute about a *bi*. That is, in a dispute, one party is saying something is X and the other is saying it is not X. Take the Mohists' example. Consider our disagreeing about whether an animal in front of us is a bovine. We construe our positions as "it is" *(shi)* and "it is not" *(fei)*. If, instead, one party says it is a horse and the other says it is a dog, the Neo-Mohists say *that* dispute is not a *bian*. When there is a *bian* in this strict sense, then, one of the parties will always be right. One of them will *dang*[map onto it].[23] This is a proof only of formal realism, the realism of *one right answer*. The Later Mohists seem committed to substantive realism as well. Not only is there a winner in disputes, but the world, not mere social convention, determines the winner. The animal before us really is like other bovines or it is not.

The Mohists may have been aware of Hui Shi's objection that we can find *many* kinds of *likeness*. Someone may project in a way that links horses and oxen as one type. The Mohists do not object to treating horses and oxen as a *whole* of which *horse* and *oxen* are the parts. On the other hand, that whole (draft animals), they suppose, has *nature-given* partitions. The range is compounded just as the term is so the object is a composite object made up of two *ti*[parts]. The existing terms correspond to the proper *ti*[parts] of reality. There is *one* suitable way to break ox-horse into its parts. They label unorthodox ways of *dividing* horses and oxen *kuang-ju*[wild picking out].[24] But this is just a label. The Later Mohists never offer a general theory of which similarities and differences count when we are deciding where nature draws the lines between *ti*[parts]. This is the Achilles heel of their realism.

The realist Mohist commitment to use a word up to a point and then stop is a commitment to apply measurement standards in using words. Otherwise, it falls into the category of a realist version of rectifying names. But the Later Mohists are critical of the Confucian project. The implied part-whole structure of reality requires that names have variable and overlapping scope. The Later Mohists object to the Confucian theory's implied commitment to a formal principle of one name–one thing. Recall the derivation we noted above (pages 65–67). Allowing names to overlap in decision contexts introduces conflict into any complex system of guiding discourse. That formal requirement entailed by the Confucian view of rectifying names, the Mohists argue, is an impractical and unrealistic view of prescriptive clarity in language. It is a wrongheaded way to seek the goal of linguistic reform.

The *Mohist Canon* argues that the realistic interaction between language and the world makes it acceptable that some words overlap. That is, there are going to be cases in which two names refer to the same thing and others in which one name refers to two things (two *ti*[parts]). In the first case, the stock example is of *dog* and *puppy*.[25] Clearly these are two names for essentially the same thing. They discuss the second case by stressing the *indexicality* of *shi-bi*[this-other]. We can call anything *this*. We can call anything *other*. Only we may not do both simultaneously.[26] Such ordinary features of language do no *harm* to its function. Trying to reform them is unnecessary. They do not make guidance incoherent. On the contrary, they foster pragmatic, efficient guidance using language.

The Mohists see that the functioning of names requires that we have both more and less general terms. The more general will *name* the same things the less general ones name. They distinguish among three scopes names can have: a universal scope, a distinguishing scope, and a particular scope.[27] All three types *ju*[pick out] their scope in the same way, by marking it off from its complement. What is striking about this theory is that the Mohist ostensibly views each term as related to its appropriate reality-part in exactly parallel ways. All *picking out* resembles the relation of proper names to particular objects. I have argued that this suggests a mass-stuff picture of reality consisting of noncontiguous, scattered objects.[28]

So the Mohist gives a straightforward, realistic analysis to explain the use of individual terms. We apply them to similar stuff in nonwild ways. We do not know what makes some differences wild and some not. We do know that we are supposed to apply measurement standards. The measurement results come from the real similarity difference structure in the world. The standard may be a model (actual or remembered) or a measurement tool.[29] Similarity and difference must generate a natural structure of both *ti*[parts] and *lei*[similars]. Of these two, the *ti*[parts] are metaphysically basic. *Lei*[similars] can be drawn to link things as long as there is some coherent similarity.[30] We thus pick out parts of or divide the whole using names. What satisfies the name after we make a commitment to the example or a measurement standard is an objective matter. It depends on the world.

Strings and Reference: Extending the System

Satisfied with their theoretical base, the Neo-Mohists move on to the next puzzle. How do we extend the system of natural scopes and ranges from individual terms to strings of terms: compounds, and phrases? They start with the minimally longer compound ci^{phrase}. They look first at extensional compounds. An extensional compound is a phrase that has a scope, just as individual terms do. Its scope is *some kind of* function of the scope of individual terms. What function is it? How do we use compound terms to pick out the precise scope we want? A term (general or particular) picks out or selects a substance or stuff (however scattered and distributed) within a certain range. How is the range of a compound term related to the range of each component term?

The Mohists do not make our familiar sentence-functional distinctions. They do not analyze units of the compound as adjectives and nouns. Adjectives and nouns (general or particular) both pick out a range of stuff. The Later Mohist's question is simply this. How does the range or scope of the individual terms determine the scope of the compound?

Notice that our most popular Western theory accepts a metaphysical analysis of descriptive structure. We assume that the world consists of particulars (objects or substances) and abstract, repeatable properties. The world, that is, reflects our noun-adjective structure. This analysis yields our familiar solution to the problem of adjectival modification. It employs the bent-elbow theory that postulates a meaning for each word. That meaning ties the term to its scope, extension, or denotation. When we compound terms, we associate the compound with a *more complex* idea or meaning. The more complex the idea, the *smaller* the range of things that satisfies it. We have an individual horse, say, and can assign to it the properties *white, old, large, blind, mean, lame, hungry,* and *stupid.* Each one makes the associated idea more complex. What becomes more complex, we call the *intension* (sense, meaning, connotation), the set of properties assigned to the object. And the term has an *extension* (denotation, reference), the physical range to which the modified term applies. As the intention grows, the extension shrinks (that is fewer objects have all the properties included) and vice versa.

The Neo-Mohist, however, worked with only the notion of range or scope. He does not share our assumption of *natural* division of stuffs into individuals, objects or particulars with properties. He also does not talk of sets or collections of individuals. He does not see the conceptual contrast of individuals and universal properties. His analytical structure is a part-whole structure. The natural structure of similarity-difference divides the world into kinds, not into particular objects. Each term, no matter how broad, is associated only with a trained ability to pick out a particular scope (to make a distinction between what is and what is not). Individualization is merely a limiting case of distinction making. Individuals are one variation on the theme of divisions within the whole. This is the key structuring principle announced in the second canon: Ti^{parts} are $fen^{divisions}$ within $jian^{wholes}$.

The relation of part and whole *is* somewhat context sensitive, as we saw. A part can be a whole from another perspective. Our purpose might dictate another division. And we can see a whole as a part of some larger whole. Mass nouns have no privileged principle of individuation. The individual-property metaphysical structure is more rigid. Our folk theory assumes that individuation is given in nature prior to any particular denotational purpose. Our common-sense view of the world reflects our focus on count nouns that have one privileged principle of individuation built in. The Mohists regard individuality as built into the world only in the same sense that the other types of similarity and difference that guide distinction making are in the world.[31] Individuation is just another way of dividing wholes into parts.

The object-property solution also works for English because most normal, extensional compounds are what we can call *intersection compounds*. That is, the range of denotation always shrinks as we add words.[32] There are fewer white horses than there are horses. ''White horse'' names an individual with the properties whiteness and horseness. It divides its reference to each individual that has both properties. The adjective-noun compound embraces, therefore, a smaller class than either term itself would. That is, the class of white objects is always larger than the class of white horses.

Chinese extensional compounds are *not* all intersections. As a result, compounding is particularly challenging for a classical Chinese linguistic theory. There are *two types* of term-term compounds. One resembles typical term modification in English. In Chinese, bai-$ma^{white\ horse}$ picks out a smaller scope than ma^{horse} alone.

In Chinese, however, term modification may have an opposite effect. Where *white horse* narrows the scope of *horse,* other compounds may broaden the scope. For example, the compound $tiandi^{heaven\text{-}earth}$ does not name the *intersection* of heaven and earth. It names their union, hence its translation as *the universe*. Similarly zi-$nü^{son\text{-}daughter}$ does not name the (empty) intersection of sons and daughters. It names their union, hence *children*. These are not rare and insignificant examples. Classical writers fill literary writings with these union compounds. Some familiar examples include *shan-shuei* (mountain-water)^{scenery,} *da-xiao* (great-small)^{size,} *qin-shou* (bird-beast)^{animal}.

English *has* union compounds but employs a distinct syntax for the two different kinds of compounds. We use the plural form together with *and* ''Cats and dogs,'' ''boys and girls,'' and *Field and Stream* are examples.

So the individual-property analysis of compounding would not be as helpful to Chinese theorists as it first appeared. First, they do not take individuation as given. The natural ontological theory of the language is a shifting part-whole analysis, not one based on fixed ontological particulars. Second, the theory accounts only for the intersection compounds, not the union compounds.

Syntactically, the Chinese union compounds are hard to distinguish from intersection compounds. The question for the Later Mohist was what determines whether a compound increases or decreases scope. Their answer appeals to the nature of the paired stuffs. If they *can* overlap and the intersection is not empty, then the compound picks out the intersection. If the intersection is empty, then the compound picks out the union of the parts.

So, the Mohists generate a metaphysical theory[33] to explain how is it that a compound term sometimes picks out the sum of the two scopes and sometimes the product. Let us call these the mass sum and mass product (corresponding to the union and intersection of sets). The mass sum comes from the logical *or*—it names whatever is X *or* Y. The mass product comes from the logical *and*—it names whatever is both X *and* Y. When does a compound have the range of the mass product? When does it have the range of the mass sum?

Their metaphysics reflects their views of reference. The analysis starts with ranges or extents rather than with individuals having properties. They call the physical ranges *wu*^{objects}. I recommend that we think of these *objects* as scattered stuffs. They embrace properties like *white* and *hard* alongside mass objects such as water or wood and natural kinds such as horse and ox. Names refer to these masslike quasi-objects.[34]

Their answer to the question of compound reference starts from noting differences among these ranges. Some ranges or scopes of stuff can interpenetrate. Others do not. *White* and *hard* are examples of terms whose ranges can interpenetrate; the stuff named by those terms fill or *exhaust* each other. *Ox* and *horse* are examples of terms whose ranges do not interpenetrate; they exclude each other.

We will come back to problems with this extensional approach later. For the moment, attend to how the Neo-Mohists tests this theory. They use pragmatic vocabulary: ask what expressions are *ke*^{permissible}. They use *hard-white* and *ox-horse* as names of the two opposite metaphysical types. They check the metaphysical theory by seeing if it can explain the *conventional assertability* of strings of words in various contexts. Can this explain how we would normally speak? Their linguistic analysis has this resonance of ordinary language philosophy. When we apply one expression to an object, does ordinary usage allow another expression to apply?

The Analysis: What Phrases Are Assertable of Others?

In their most thoroughly discussed case, the Neo-Mohists conclude *not-ox* is assertable in cases when *ox-horse* is assertable. How can this be? Well, consider how sum-compounds work. Suppose I asked, "How many brothers and sisters do you have?" Suppose you answered, "Three." Then I ask again, "How many are brothers?" You would not violate the rules of English to answer, "None." The way *brothers and sisters* works in English is like the mass sums in Chinese; it picks out an *either-or* range. Any part of that range counts as *brothers and sisters*—even if you have no brothers. So, in the Mohist phraseology, "*brothers and sisters* no brothers" is admissible. Your *brothers and sisters* happen to include no brothers.

Think of *ox-horse* as a compound term for *draft animal* (like thinking of *brothers and sisters* as an idiomatic replacement for *siblings*.) The Neo-Mohist argues that in these mass-sum compounds whose ranges do not interpenetrate, the parts retain a metaphysical status as *ti*^{parts}. This case does not force a level shift of the part-whole analysis. Even if we call the whole *ox-horse*, each part is either ox or horse—not both. The parts, in Mohist terminology, *exclude* each other. In that case, not X is *ke*^{permissibly predicable} of the stuff named by the compound term XY. The parts keep their distinctness in these compounds. The Mohist calls them *separable* compounds.

The others—the hard-white combinations—in obvious contrast, are the inseparable compounds. In these compounds, the parts interpenetrate so that "wherever you go in the compound, you find two.'' *White* does not keep a constant scope in combinations. *White* picks out different parts of its range in different compounds. It does force a change in the part-whole structure. And it raises problems for their analysis of names. A name, remember, is whatever picks out a range. If a symbol picks out a different range then, despite its symbolic structure, it is a different name.

The Neo-Mohist's theory of compounding is thus inimical to the rectification-of-names ideal of one name–one thing. The relationship between a term and its range changes for the hard-white combinations. *White* in *hard-white* does not have the same range that it does alone. The naming paradigm (a name uniquely picks out a range) now gives us problems. We have to say that *white* ceases to be *the same name* when used in a compound.

The *ox-horse* compounds, by contrast, cause no difficulty for the naming ideal. The divisions they mark keep their scope integrity even in the compounds. *Ox* still picks out ox-stuff exactly the way it does uncompounded. So, even though ''ox non-ox'' is never admissible, ''ox-horse non-ox'' is. In fact, ''ox-horse non-ox non-horse'' is also admissible. (Hint: *non-ox* picks out the horse stuff; *non-horse* picks out the ox-stuff).

Ethics and Realist Language

This realist language analysis still functions in a Mohist ethical structure. The realistic appeal arises pragmatically, not from an abstract commitment to truth. A language adapted to reality in the Mohist way should be more useful in guiding behavior. The problem is that the Mohists do not use the scientific conceptions that could spell out why this would be the case. Why should we assume that a language that cuts things according to natural similarities would serve us better than some alternative? If we were to adopt a causal criterion of similarity, we could start to get an answer to the question. Such a criterion selects the similarities that are important for prediction and explanation. However, the Mohists appeal mainly to the overall coherence this realist ideal gives. It avoids the self-refuting paradoxes of relativism.

That is no small plus. Beyond that coherence, the Mohists (like the Confucians) are appealing mainly to the utility of shared agreement. Basing names on measurement like standards applied to the world results in a clear, more obviously projectable and constant *dao*. The distinctions are still the base of desires and dislikes. By grounding them in the world, we avoid the problem of free-floating conventions of interpretation. Otherwise, the interpretive variability threatens to make any guiding code into molding clay. The realistic appeal gives us a *constant basis* for projecting distinctions on the real world.

Graham concluded that many of the specifically ethical fragments were in the earliest portion of the Neo-Mohist works. It was hardest to reconstruct with confidence. The corruption process we discussed on page 237 must have destroyed much of the original text. What remains is fragmentary and suggestive. Still, the hints are interesting and worth noting. Presumably Zhuangzi and Xunzi did have access to these lines of argument and to their key insights.

The moral system emerges transparently from the scope analysis of terms. The best the Mohists can do is to defend the coherence of the moral naming pattern as they do the coherence of a realistic naming scheme. They slightly revise the original distinction-based utilitarianism. The basic claim is that yi^{morality} is li^{utility}. They no longer treat $ren^{\text{benevolence}}$, however, as a neutral, shared moral concept. Mozi had used ren as if it were simple utilitarian benevolence. The Neo-Mohists now treat it as having acquired Confucian connotations. They describe $ren^{\text{benevolence}}$ as $ti^{\text{part}}\ ai^{\text{love}}$. This suggests an obvious contrast to Mohist $jian^{\text{whole}}$ love.

Most interesting, as Graham first noted,[35] is that the Mohist seems to have abandoned both the authority of $tian^{\text{heaven}}$ and any reference to the $xin^{\text{heart-mind}}$. The natural or realistic warrant for the guiding aspect of language rested not in authority or an interpretive faculty, but in objects and reality. That is the most efficient way to guide word distinctions. Supposedly, seeing Yang-Zhu and Mencius both claim the natural authority has made them aware of how empty the divine-command appeal becomes. Anyone can project shi-fei assignments on heaven and claim that they are natural or spontaneous reactions of the $xin^{\text{heart-mind}}$. This form of reasoning, however, cannot justify rejecting any naturally occurring alternative view of proper guidance. The Mohists think the way to select among the alternatives is to examine the constancy and coherence of the various dao. If they could exhibit a constant, coherent dao, that would be a significant accomplishment. They, in effect, abandon Mozi's appeal to authority.

The coherence of utilitarianism comes from its use of measurement in evaluating outcomes. The Mohist seemed to have worked out a notion of comparative balance of benefit and harm. They use $quan^{\text{weighing}}$ in a positive sense. (Mencius had treated it mainly as an elastic excuse for breaches of propriety.) For Mohists, weighing is an integral part of their calculation or measure-based moral system. To prefer a lesser to a greater harm is a coherent extension of a utility definition of yi^{morality}. Other formulas suggest that they noticed a distinction between intended utility and actual utility. Li^{benefit} is not what you desire, but what pleases you when you get it.[36]

They may have designed some of their system of concepts to deal with Mencian or innatist moral doctrines and criticisms of Mohism. Love should be universal, they still insist. $Lun^{\text{human relations discourse}}$, however, differentiates between people to whom we have *thick* or *thin* responsibilities.[37] The social system has the general goal of universal benefit. We have an abstract commitment to that goal—hence, universal love. The social system makes it *my* role, in pursuit of that universal love, to spread benefit *thicker* on my kin. They even argue that universal love requires self-love. They thus modify the total self-abnegation that frequently brought criticism to Mozi.

They inherit Mozi's view that human nature is socially malleable. Conventional training can instill many different types of moral character. Therefore, no natural $gu^{\text{in itself}}$ settles issues of guidance. Guiding depends on the scope of our concern— that range for which we $wei^{\text{do:deem}}$. $Wei^{\text{do:deem}}$ contrasts with $qing^{\text{feeling:reality}}$. This recalls our result on pages 126–27 that the distinction between convention and nature, constant and inconstant, does much of the work normally done by our description-prescription distinction.

The fragments take a terse position on the Mencian problem of the internality or externality of $ren^{\text{benevolence}}$ and yi^{morality}. The Mohist position is that these moral concepts refer to something both internal and external. Supposedly, this means that the Mohists application depends in part on the external world and the $gu^{\text{in itself}}$ character of the objects of our moral concern. Acknowledging that they are internal seems to require a projection of human reactions—joy or revulsion—on the real world. The scope of our concern must combine with the $gu^{\text{in itself}}$ character of the object of our concern. Both are necessary to have any realistic guiding concepts.

Thus, we have the real, external, in-itself, elderliness of some things. Without the inclination to regard elderliness as deserving of respect, that reality yields no guidance. The similarities and differences *that are relevant to our prior or conventional attitudes* become, therefore, especially significant. Guidance requires more than purely descriptive similarities and differences.

Rectifying Intentional Phrases

The Neo-Mohists can tolerate some wavering on these meta-ethical issues. After all, no rivals have a rock-solid theoretical base for their ethical projections. But the Neo-Mohists will not tolerate incoherence in their guiding projections. They must at least make the universal altruistic utilitarian picture *constant*. Here they run into serious difficulties—difficulties related to the familiar interpretive problem that motivated rectifying names.

The Neo-Mohists cling to the view that the real world fixes the boundaries of the scope of terms. Accordingly, they cannot accept rectification of names as understood in Confucius. That involves having the boundaries fixed by conventions, specifically the conventional guiding discourse (li^{ritual}). We manipulate the conventions by deliberate use of social superiors. For the Mohist realist, objective similarity and difference in the world fixes the scope boundaries of terms. This means the term framework does not guide by itself. The terms must be combined into phrases that guide by expressing a yi^{intent}.

"Killing Thieves Is Not Killing Men." How then, do they deal with the problems which rectification of names tries to solve? They refuse to rectify names to achieve coherence of conventional guidance. Reality alone gives the correct way to project distinctions. Opponents must have challenged their moral consistency and given their abandonment of authority for *constancy;* this is a serious criticism. One obvious challenge goes as follows: You claim to love all people, yet in your own communities you kill thieves. How can this be consistent?

The Mohists' analytical answer draws on their study of compound terms. They had already noted that the relations of compounds to their components was more complex than simple one-name–one-thing analysis suggests. There had to be two quite different models of what compounding did. They now argue at length for the even greater irregularity of moral compounds, ci^{phrases}. Where they had been guided by the ideal of *extensional* constancy, they now emphasize the *opacity* of guiding compounds.[38]

> Her brother is a handsome man. She loves her brother. She does not love a handsome man.

She does not, that is, *handsome man* her brother in the act of loving him. She follows the guidance of *love your brother,* not that of *love handsome men.* Thus, the

Later Mohists rectify the guiding *phrases* rather than the referring terms. In effect, the terms are extensional and realistic. But compounding them with verbs in guiding structures, they argue, does not exhibit regular and uniformly predictable effects. Like the Confucians, they put flexibility into their system of deriving behavior from rules. We rectify not names but phrases that combine names in guiding actions.

The Mohist discussion of this issue makes up the single sequential, intact essay among their works—the *Lesser Pick* (Graham's *Names and Objects*). It starts by emphasizing the role of *bian*[discriminating]. *Bian* now includes the search for *bi*[comparability] in *ci*[phrases]. The comparability illustrated in the essay resembles what we would call an inference. Western logic says that two sentences have an inference relation if the truth of one entails the truth of the other. The Mohist, however, will give a pragmatic analysis of when *ci*[phrases] are *bi*[comparable].

The Mohists find a truly ingenious way to do logical analysis using pragmatic concepts and the notion of ordinary language. We start with an ordinarily assertable phrase of a noun[1] noun[2] *ye* form ("Noun[1] *is* noun[2]"). The Chinese counterpart of our predicate nominative sentence uses no connective. It negates with *fei*[not this:wrong] rather than *bu*[negation]. The Neo-Mohist calls the negated form a *fei* and the nonnegated form a *shi*. Then, we construct an ordinarily assertable form of the same sentence that expands the term to a phrase by adding the same character to both nouns. The added character is typically a verb, but the Mohist, of course, does not make that observation. The effect is to turn a predication into two action descriptions. Term[1] is term[2] but verbing term[1] is not verbing term[2]. I have dubbed this *algebraic inference*.

$$X\ Y\ ye^{\text{X is Y}}$$

$$KX\ KY\ ye^{\text{KX is KY}}$$

In the intended standard case, the relationship exhibits a kind of constancy. The phrases *match* if both the antecedent and resulting phrase lack (or both have) a *fei*[not this:wrong]. In easy cases this neat, constant parallelism holds. "White horse is horse" and "Riding white horse is riding horse." If the appropriately assertable form of the base sentence (the first one) lacks the negative we call it a *shi*[this:right] phrase. Otherwise we call it a *fei*[not this:wrong] phrase. If the resulting sentence (in its appropriately assertable form) lacks *fei*[not this:wrong], we call it *ran*[so] otherwise *bu-ran*[not so]. Ideally a *shi*[this:right] base sentence should generate a *ran*[so] result and a *fei* base a *bu-ran* result.

Now in intensional contexts, this does not happen, at least not reliably. The *Lesser Pick* treatise consists of a plethora of examples where the hoped-for reliable relation fails. One's parents are people, but *serving your parents* is not *serving the people*. Thieves are people, but *loving thieves* is not *loving people*. Now the answer to the assumed criticism is at hand. Essentially the Mohists assert a counterpart of the claim *"execution* is not *murder."* Thieves are people. Killing thieves, however, is not killing people.

A thief is a person because of the way the world is. These terms must be allowed to overlap. But the guidance in the phrase *killing thief* differs from that in *killing people*. So the *dao,* which has "kill thieves" and "do not kill people," is consistent. Mohists purchase that consistency at the price of constant, regular relations between simple names and complex phrases. Their conclusion, thus, has a decidedly paradoxical flavor. The logician finds constant inference relationships among sentence structures. The Neo-Mohists find that the relationships are inexplicably inconsistent. Their conclusion is that we cannot rely on language parallelism to give guidance.

So in constructing the *dao* that will guide our behavior, we must rectify at the guiding (compound) ci^{phrase} level. That makes guidance consistent with a realistic theory of naming. The coherence of the system comes from using the utility standard to guide phrase construction. We cannot rely on formal relations of language to settle matters of guidance. Algebraic inference, the Neo-Mohists conclude, is not reliable.

Once they show that these inferences do not hold universally, the Mohists have their logical defense of their moral *dao* and their realistic theory of meaning. Thieves *are* people, but killing thieves *is not* killing people. It simultaneously allows them to fix name reference realistically and deal with the interpretive problem at a different level. It allows them the excuse flexibility and conflict avoidance benefits of rectification of names. It also shows that they still understand language as guiding behavior through canonical formulas. The referential semantics is a component of a theory of language that still treats guidance as the final function of language.

Defense of Universal Love

The Neo-Mohists thus have a more complicated apparatus to show that their universal love ideal is *constant*. The kinds of challenge they contemplate are not simply doubts about moral psychology. That traditional Confucian attack, as we saw, was just a misunderstanding of the Mohist point. They worry more about the semantic coherence of their ethical position. It raises what they see as a semantic question: can we interpret the phrase "love people" as referring universally? Clearly, what counts as loving people is doing something appropriate with the people with whom *one can have contact,* but that is never all people. So can one's love ever be universal?

The Mohists answer that the term in a complex action description—for example, people—*does not fix* whether it requires universal behavior or particular behavior. But this is not a problem only with their moral *dao*. For example, I count as someone who "rides horse" if I *sometimes* ride *a* horse. Conversely, I count as someone who does *not* ride only if I *universally* do not ride horse—do not ride even one. Similarly, I count as loving people if I love all with whom I come in contact. I count as not loving people if I fail to show love to "even the least of these."

The Neo-Mohists assimilate these two answers to problems of guidance phrases to a pessimistic paradigm. Both seem to them to undermine the ideal of extensional regularity in language. Mohists describe these cases as instances in which the parallelism of phrase construction breaks down. Thus the dialectical analysis ends on a pessimistic Daoist note. We cannot regard language as a constant guide to behavior. No account of language can avoid these vagaries of reference. The Mohists' refuge from this indeterminacy lies in their realism in fixing descriptive terms and their coherent use of the utility standard to structure guiding strings. They admonish us constantly to return to the objective world to check our use of terms. We must follow the similarities in the world.

This admonition reminds us appropriately that we have to use the world to check our *dao*. It solves none of the problems of *how* we do this. It does nothing to show that reality requires their particular ethical system. In fact, the referential principle itself may be seen to presuppose the utilitarian standard. It is a way of constructing language that does have pragmatic advantages. Its consistent, objective, mechanistic standards produce more reliable, accessible guidance. Still, the reliance on the principle of utility in constructing *dao* out of language remains as arbitrary as it was for Mozi.

Neo-Mohist Epistemology

The first *Mohist Canon* gives at least six formulas concerning *zhi*[knowledge]. The first cluster of four follow immediately on the key realist definition of *gu*[in itself] and the part-whole metaphysical apparatus. The world is out there independent of our language. Linguistic activity follows the part-whole structure of reality. With these basic assumptions, the *Mohist Canon* then turns to *zhi*[knowledge]. How do we know in such a world?

Know-(How)-To

The first definition simply says "knowledge is skill." This definition reminds us that the ancient use of *zhi*[knowledge] resembles our *know-how* or *know-to* more than it does our more familiar *know-that*. None of the formulas treat knowledge as propositional or contrast it with belief.

The classical Chinese concept is, in other respects, like our English *know* in its realistic implications. Know-how is not simply *any* disposition to behavior. *Know*, as the ordinary-language philosophers urged, is a *success* verb. *Zhi*[knowledge] is what *correctly* guides behavior. The correctness may be correct interpretation or it may be successful in a real-world context. It must be a reliable guiding mechanism to count as knowledge.

The explanation of this formula uses *zhi*[knowledge] in the sense of a capacity to exercise skill.[39] Other fragments make it clear that the capacity is not merely intellectual but includes an attitudinal ingredient: desires and aversions. For the Mohists, *zhi*[knowledge] replaces *xin*[heart-mind] as the substantive collection of motivation skills. It functions in ways that Western translators convey with terms such as *consciousness* or *awareness*. Again, however, I urge that we resist the translator's impulse to postulate two barely related meanings for the term. We should instead, notice what the pattern of use suggests about the Mohists' view of human intelligence. In the place of these receptive states with a passive abstract content, the Mohist puts a notion of alert, skilled, responsiveness. They define sleep as the *zhi* not *zhi*ing[40] and *ping*[tranquillity] as *zhi* without desire or aversion.[41]

Zhi[know] replaces the notion of will as much as it does consciousness. The Mohists' second formula defines deliberation as seeking. The *Explanation* treats the *zhi* as having a seeking inclination. Deliberating is the *zhi*'s seeking. Although the skilled seeking is reliable, they say, it does not necessarily *get it*.[42]

We can characterize the Neo-Mohist position by adopting an apparatus to talk of this less familiar concept of know-(how)-to. Know-to is prescriptive knowledge as it has been for all the earlier philosophers we have discussed. The assumption has been that *zhi* is knowledge of what to do. The knowledge is expressed in actions (including, of course, speech actions).

We can contrast a theory of this know-to that explains why it has the parallels it does to our concept of knowledge. It does not, however, contrast with propositional belief. We can translate the Platonic conditions of knowledge as practical concepts.

X knows ({how, when, where, why}) to do action A if and only if:

1. X is disposed to do action A ({how, when, where, why}).
2. X's will carry out action A successfully.
3. X's doing A is produced by a reliable (constant) skill or dispositional capacity.

This definition states the *success* principle. (For propositions, it would have been the truth of the belief.) It contains a reliability principle. (Western philosophy has assumed that rational justification is the reliable procedure for producing successful propositional beliefs.) This is why *zhi*^{know} can be primarily a practical ability and still be acceptably translated as *knowledge*.

The next formula treats *zhi* as successful in its search for triggering clues. *Zhi*^{knowledge} is *jie*^{contact}. When our *zhi* encounters a triggering *wu*^{object}, it can *type* it or put descriptive words on it that trigger program execution. It assigns the *shi* and *fei,* the 1 and 0, that must be input for the program to run in a real world.

The third formula also underscores the realist basis of knowing descriptive terms. Knowing is contact with objects and the ability to associate them with our learned model.[43] When our knowing capacity *comes across* objects, we are able to apply standards to them. This is to know the objects.

Finally, the Mohists' fourth formula alters the *zhi* character. They add a *xin*^{heart} radical to *zhi*^{know} and define it as *ming*^{clarity}. We have met this notion of clarity in the earlier Mozi. He sought to be *ming*^{clear} about *bian*^{discrimination} and argued that we must use the distinction between *li-hai*$^{\text{benefit-harm}}$ to get *ming*^{clear} about *shi-fei*. The Later Mohist *Explanation* expands on this. Knowing how to grade or sort things in language[44] is *zhi*^{wisdom}. If we know (how) to do sort them, we know things. Knowing is knowing to sort things in discourse.

After this sequential analysis, the Neo-Mohists use *zhi* in other prominent places throughout the *Mohist Canon*. One especially interesting fragment is this one:

Zhi^{know}: Hearing, explaining, experiencing, names, stuff, union, *wei*$^{\text{do-deem}}$.[45]

This seems to be a list of sources and objects or outcomes of knowledge. The sources of knowledge are hearing, explaining, and experiencing. The objects or outcomes of *zhi*^{know} are names, stuff, uniting the two, and acting. The second and third outcomes clearly signal the Mohists' realistic views. We must combine knowledge of names with knowledge of stuff, things in the world. Only then can language guide deeming action. The most plausible model of know-how for the first two outcomes is Mozi's discussion of the knowledge of the blind man. The blind man knows how to use the names but does not know how to discriminate the stuffs. His knowledge lacks the realistic base that comes from being able to *come across* the stuff and associate it with a learned model.

Knowing names and stuffs should still be thought of on the analogy of skills. The two skillful outputs must be combined for real knowledge. The realist Neo-Mohists, then, stress the importance of knowledge of stuff just as Mozi did in criticizing Confucianism. But they accept the tradition that includes mastery of names as the other important element. Names enshrine the guidance that society has accumulated as discursive practical wisdom. It makes it possible to extend our knowledge to other cases where we hear of things being *like this*. We cannot ignore or abandon the community's skill in the use of names. This is not antilanguage realism.

These two skills must be *he*^{combined} before they can guide action. Skill at naming alone is hard to distinguish from mere *qiao*^{cleverness}. Distinguishing between them requires close examination of the *gu*^{the way things inherently are}. Only when one combines knowledge of things and knowledge of names should one undertake action. We characterize correct action as the final object of knowledge. I have been characterizing it as *knowing-to* (as in *knowing to come in out of the rain.*).[46]

The Mohists' four objects of knowledge correspond closely to the structure we used in explaining Laozi's antilanguage, nonaction position. The difference is this. Laozi's antilanguage analysis treats language as free-floating and changeable convention. The correctness of a distinction is a matter of social convention that may be other than it is. The Mohists insist on a learned skill at discriminating stuffs. This skill has a social element, but its outcome depends on the world. There are objective, prelinguistic differences and similarities that guide our application of social-naming conventions. We should harmonize names to these real similarities and differences before undertaking action. Mohists insist on basing action on something other than mere convention. If we do not, then the Laozi would be correct. We could regard no system of know-how-to as constant.

The other difference is Laozi's focus on the emotional ingredient—desires. The Neo-Mohists seem to regard action as deriving directly from knowledge. Laozi plays the Hume to the Mohists' Kant. Motivation is internal to practical knowledge. But the Mohists' *zhi* is inherently practical, so their knowledge-based position is less striking than Kant's pure religion of reason. They still have a Hume-like commitment to a prior, presocial will to *li*^{benefit}.

Neo-Mohist Logic

The standard account of the school of names assimilates the school's interests to logic. Members of the school are frequently characterized as logicians. While we have certainly found the Mohists' reasoning acceptably logical, they have only flirted around the area of logic in their defense of their ethical *dao*. The theories have been mostly of semantics, or more properly a semantic fragment within the dominant traditional pragmatic theory.

Strictly speaking, little actual development of logical theory emerges from the dialectical chapters of *The Mozi*. The Neo-Mohists do not discern anything more about logical form beyond the algebraic analysis discussed above. Even that they develop mostly in examples and, as we noted, they end up rejecting phrase matching as a reliable (valid) form. They were aware that something resembling inference can extend know-how. Suppose you have hearsay knowledge, say, that the room you have never seen is the same color as this one. Your skill at discriminating the color of this one enables you to know how to *color* the one you have never seen. The Neo-Mohists regard this as a case where name knowledge and thing knowledge can combine by inference. It explains their view of the role of language in the accumulation of knowledge. Names are valuable tools for extending and generalizing action-guiding knowledge.

Otherwise, claims that sound like logic reflect mostly a vague pragmatic view that when you have committed yourself to use a linguistic expression in a certain way, you constrain future commitments. Constancy comes from the standards of measurement for applying terms. The Mohists do not explain anything about how commitment to propositions (sententials) leads to commitment to other sententials which logically *follow*. The matching phrases analysis clearly comes closest. I have argued, however, that it falls *within the general problem of the extensionality of compounds*. Can we add elements to terms in a constant way? We test the proposal, as before, by seeing what phrases we can use of situations in which we use other phrases. What phrases preserve guidance when substituted?

Their main logical terminology (followed by most Chinese reasoning about reasoning) evokes the notion of practical absurdity. Certain combinations of verbal commitments are practically inconstant. They defend the consistency of some of their challenged views by arguing that holding one does not *hai*[harm] holding the other. Otherwise, Neo-Mohists merely express only vague perplexity at how people can "say both these things" or "cling to this and still reject that."

Neo-Mohist Semantics and Chinese Logic

The algebraic argument schema considered by the *Names and Objects* may have been the model for Mencius' famous logical analogy. (See pages 191–93.) From accepting X is Y, accept KX is KY. The algebraic argument form is one that traditional Aristotelian syllogism cannot capture. Do we have any reason to suppose that attention to that form of argument is distinctly Chinese?

First, note that both classical syllogisms and propositional reasoning are frequent in Chinese philosophical writing. The famous Chinese sorites is the most familiar example: "If names are not rectified, then language will not be in accord; if language is not in accord then affairs cannot be accomplished. . . ." They cast even sophistical *invalid* arguments in syllogistic form: "A yellow horse is a horse; a yellow horse is not a white horse therefore a white horse is not a horse."

The algebraic structure, however, is the only one the Neo-Mohists studied as a form and evaluated for validity. That structure focuses on compound terms rather than on truth-functional sentences. We can explain this by their philosophical interests. The infrequent use of logical connectives exacerbates the haziness of sentential structures. Typically, Chinese writers rely on context to make the logical relation between sentences clear. They have a clear conditional connective *ze*[then] but no single character for disjunction. The conjunction *er*[and:yet] is usually limited to contrastive contexts. The focus on names rather than on sentences could have been influenced by features of Chinese language that drew attention to names—graphs, characters— and less to sentential structures (absence of regular subject-predicate form, sentence-functional inflections, punctuation, and syntactical mobility). But a theoretical focus on names as opposed to sentences could exist without such overdetermination. Remember that propositional logic (though noticed by the ancient Stoics) did not dominate ancient Western logical interest either. Aristotle's syllogism showed his own focus on term relations. The influence of mathematical models informed the construction of modern propositional logic mainly in this century. So we can easily explain the absence of propositional logic in classical China.

Explaining why Indo-European philosophical traditions focused on syllogistic forms and Chinese did not is rather more interesting. Indo-European grammars usually require an explicit subject term or case marking that suggests its grammatical presence. This reflects and reinforces the Western focus on assertion as the role of language. We call the descriptive sentence *complete*. We characterize prescription as having deleted the subject. (We could, instead, regard prescriptive form as normal and say that descriptive sentences insert a subject to block the normal prescriptive force of language.) Also the regular use of the verb *to be* reinforces the syntactical requirement that all sentences have a main verb. A writer of classical Chinese could see a term[1] term[2] *ye* sentence and regard it as an instance of compounding. Chinese traditional grammar treats the *ye* is an *empty* character. It alerts us that this *compound* has assertion force while others might not.

The cult of the sentence as a *complete* unit (expressing a *complete* thought) draws attention both to differential syntactical and semantic function and to the phenomenon of compositionality. Together, they infuse Western logic with the traditional, asymmetric, subject-predicate structure.

Chinese quantifiers, by contrast, seem to attach to the predicate: the Mohists *universally love* people.[47] They found matching phrases inconsistent when it added distributives to verbs: "Thieves are people; many thieves are not many people." When they add an explicit scope term, it usually affects the predicate. The grammar is more like that of an equation and the algebraic proposal as an inference schema seems natural.

In theorizing about realistic scope phenomena, the Neo-Mohists *do* discuss inference patterns and use sentential examples. They do not, however, extend their realist semantics to discuss the sentence as a semantic unit or truth as its semantic value. Nor do they shift the focus of language to assertion rather than guidance. Their views reflect off the sea of traditional pragmatic-moral interest. Can skill at manipulating names lead to constantly reliable results in regulating behavior? Can you get moral guidance from name manipulation?

I do not mean that their argument is illogical. The rejection of the algebraic argument form is valid. If it goes wrong in even one instance, then (in its simple form at least) it cannot be a valid argument form. They correctly undermine the inference procedure that makes "killing-thief not killing-person" *appear to be a paradox*. The matching of phrases is not reliable. Their solution involved reading the phrases nonextensionally. They had a logically impeccable argument for rejecting this proposed inference form.

Minimal as it is, the argument in *Names and Objects* is the only discussion of the reliability of structural inference patterns (formal logic) in the known corpus of classical Chinese philosophy. The conclusion of their single effort before the onset of the philosophical dark age was that it does not work. And their motive for under-mining, rather than refining, the inference pattern was ethical. They were trying to support a moral-political doctrine of the Mohist school. Historically, then, minimal logical theory emerged in classical China—and what there was did not succeed. No one knows what might have developed had not the Confucian orthodoxy in concert with the dynastic repression exterminated Mohism (and the crafts) as an intellectual force in China.

Gongsun Long: The Defense of Confucian Language

The school of names, as I noted above, is not a school with a shared prescriptive doctrine, but a collection of theorists who pursue their separate moral and political doctrines by reflections about language and names. Tradition includes other figures in the movement it calls the school of names, the most famous being Gongsun Long and Hui Shi. I shall argue, however, that Gongsun Long and Hui Shi represented different ethical schools and developed their doctrines by more focused theories of language. They diverged, therefore, in their theories of language. One supported Confucian naming principles and the other a more Daoist philosophical position. Neither follows the realistic Neo-Mohist theory.

The *Gongsun Longzi* contains an introductory chapter with stories of Gongsun Long motivating and defending his doctrines in actual discourse with other scholars. Then there are five essays on various subjects surrounding the topics of naming and language. Graham has argued[48] that only two of the five chapters ("White Horse Dialogue" and "Dialogue on Pointing to Thing-Kinds") are plausibly genuine doctrines of Gongsun Long. Some forger plagiarized the others from the *Mohist Canon*. Unfortunately, the plagiarizer did not understand the way in which the *Mohist Canon* had been corrupted. He read two canons together where they had been interlaced and read the index characters as part of the text of the explanations.

The introductory chapter contains interesting hints about the motivation for Gongsun Long's theorizing. He represents himself as defending a Confucian position with his "white horse not horse" thesis. He is not, I think, merely trying to get sympathy by associating with the divine sage. His theoretical position on language *is* a defense of Confucian theory of language, in particular the formal corollary of the rectification of names. He pursued the one-name–one-thing ideal that the Neo-Mohists had criticized.

In that introductory chapter and in other references to Gongsun Long in second-ary literature, he is cited as famous for his "White Horse Dialogue," for *separating the inseparable,* and for *separating hard-white.*[49] We shall understand these formal positions in the context of the Neo-Mohist theory on compound terms. We will con-struct his defense of the Confucian formalism out of these Mohist concepts.

The formal rectifying names slogan is *one name–one thing.* Confucians rectify names to make the rules apply without conflict or exception. They do this by calling things only by the name or description used in the correct rule of *li*. Rectifying fixes which rule applies in the particular setting. We identify the rule by deciding which of the terms applies to the objects in the situation. So we have to decide whether the last king of the Shang dynasty is appropriately named *ruler* or *mere fellow*. Then we can decide whether the action of the Zhou conquest violated the *li* of loyalty to rulers.[50] If the *li* are to guide action unambiguously, then only one of the action-guiding terms can apply to a person or event in each context of judgment.

Of course, the Confucians would rectify names primarily by assigning valuative or grading terms to persons. They based the grade (official rank, ideally) on one's virtue. The *li* spelled out their role description in the hierarchy. Your *moral* duties were the duties of your rank or grade, not of persons in the abstract. The *li* of some other rank just did not concern you. Gongsun Long, however, wrote in a dialectical context in which descriptive terms had become a concern at the heart of semantic theory. He defends a formal, descriptive, general version of this theory. Hence his commitment to *one name—one thing*.

The White Horse Paradox

We have already seen the Neo-Mohist defence of the *ordinary language* position against the *Ideal language* principle of *one name—one thing*. Language does not (and need not) work like that. Combining terms, forming action descriptions, applying terms of size or location—all frustrate the hope that there can be a constant combining principle. Still, language works for our purposes. Changing or reforming the ordering principles is not necessary.

Gongsun Long, like ideal-language theorists in the Western tradition, is proposing a language *reform*. He has an antecedent theory of strict clarity and wants to rectify ordinary language. He requires language to conform to a general principle of strict clarity. The difference between Gongsun Long and Western ideal-language theorists lies in the practical conception of that clarity. Western ideal-language theorists want a language that transparently conforms to scientific descriptions of the world. Gongsun Long wants a language that transparently and invariably guides behavior.

Obviously the reflections of the Neo-Mohists undermine the hope that such guidance can ever be transparent. The particular issue on which the debate between Gongsun Long and the Neo-Mohists focuses is the tricky matter of compound terms. Recall that the Mohists allowed that compounding terms had two effects on the range of things the compound picked out. One compound sums across the two ranges. It picks out the *union* of the stuff picked out by the component terms. The other compound intersects the two ranges. It refers to the range of *interpenetration* of the component terms. The Mohists call the former—*ox-horse*—compounds *separable*. The stuffs did not mix. (You can, as ranchers say, *cut* cattle from sheep). They call the latter—*hard-white*—compounds *inseparable*. They do mix; they interpenetrate. No matter how much you break down a rock, its parts will be both hard and white. You can not *cut* the white from the stone.

Of these two effects, Gongsun Long surprises us by objecting to the one more conformable to our own linguistic practice—intersection compounding. Western philosophy has explained this, remember, as the inverse relation of intension and extension. (See pages 245–46.) As the list of properties increases, the number of individuals who match the list decreases. This had led commentators to the mistaken conclusion that Gongsun Long is theorizing about properties and count nouns. However, his theoretical apparatus is probably like that of both the Daoist and the Mohist.

There are names (mass nouns that function syntactically like proper nouns) and ranges. Gongsun Long cannot accept that a name could change what it picks out while remaining the same name. If it picks out a *different range* (in effect a different object) then it is a *different name*.

So for Gongsun Long the ox-horse (separable) compound conforms to his principle of order and clarity in language. Both terms keep their standard range while combined in a compound. They name the same thing (the same range). The compound's range or scope *expands* as we add terms. Separable compounds conform to the one-name–one-thing regularity ideal. Thus, all compound terms must be separable if we are to follow the Confucian principle of order in language. We must also construe *hard-white* compounds as separate.[51] Either we must regard hard-white as naming the *sum of the two ranges* or deny that it is a *combination of fixed names*. The components do not play a constant role used singly *and* in combination.

Gongsun Long wants to unify the treatment of the two kinds of compounds. He puts his point, therefore, by using one term from each compounding paradigm, *white* and *horse*. Recall what the Neo-Mohists concluded about *ox-horse* compounds. The compound picks out the sum of things that are either ox *or* horse. So the predicate *not ox* could be assertable of the range described as *ox-horse*. Gongsun Long insists on treating *white horse* as a separable compound. He argues by analogy that *not white* is assertable of the range described as *white horse*. The Neo-Mohists had defended their claim by saying that the horse is non-ox; Gongsun Long defends his by saying that the white is non-horse.

The alternative is to *deny* that *white horse* can ever be analyzed. Despite the surface similarity, the terms in combination have no essential relation to the names *white* and *horse* taken separately. Thus the *white* of *white horse* is not the *white* of *white feathers*. Since they pick out different ranges, they cannot be the same name.[52] His argument is a dilemma. The two horns are treating *white horse* as a separable compound or treating it as a syncategorematic term with no systematic relation to its components. On either alternative, the expression "white horse not horse" will be $ke^{\text{assertable}}$.

The Dialogue on Pointing to Things

The other authentic dialogue of Gongsun Long, the *Zhi-Wu Lun* (Dialogue on pointing to thing-kinds) has been the object of much fruitless speculation. The difficulty is that the dialogue is form rich and content poor. That is, while its language is superficially logically tight (filled with *necessarily if . . . then not,* etc.), it lacks content. That is, aside from logical and quasi-logical phraseology, there are only three terms used pivotally: $zhi^{\text{finger:point}}$, $wu^{\text{thing:kind}}$, and $tian$-$xia^{\text{the world}}$. On top of that, the opening sentence contains a straightforward syntactic contradiction. The dialogue has several apparent contradictions.

Scholar after scholar proposes interpretations. Many employ the apparatus of the first-order predicate calculus. They all aim to show how some of its claims follow from others. Their motivation is the charitable one we felt in the cave. They propose interpretations of *zhi* that make the dialogue's claims seem true. Then they use the logical apparatus to show that the dialogue is logical. Later statements of the dialogue follow from earlier statements.

Many of these assign abstract theoretical terms such as *universal* or *property, characteristic* or *class* to the term *zhi*. The interpreters argue that they thus have proof of Chinese theories of abstract objects. Thus Chinese philosophy is as profound as Western philosophy since it has the same theories. This apologetic strategy does not work and, as I argued in the introduction, it leads to disjointed interpretive theory. We cannot allow ourselves the luxury of making up a meaning theory for each separate philosopher to make that philosopher's doctrine come out right. The simple reason is that they were talking to each other. If Gongsun Long comes out right, then everyone who expressed amazed disagreement must have been wrong. The cost of making Gongsun Long into a Platonic abstract theorist is that he fails to communicate with anyone in his linguistic community.

Because of the syntactical contradictions in the dialogue, it is no trick to derive all the sentences from each other. Everything follows from a contradiction (in classical two-valued propositional calculus). In proposing interpretive theories, most translators end up giving *zhi two* interpretations. This removes the explicit contradiction in the opening.[53] Far from proving that any one theory is correct, the very multiplicity of interpretations should warn us of the problem. Any two meanings would eliminate the contradiction. Merely eliminating it, therefore, cannot prove you have the correct meaning. Nothing constrains interpretive theory choice *except* our understanding of Chinese philosophy *outside of this dialogue*. We have noted a striking absence of the concept of meaning in Chinese theories of language. We, therefore, lack justification outside our own familiarity for using that semantic apparatus in explaining this dialogue. Given the Mohist theories, it would not be objectionable to treat *zhi*[point] as reference. The dialogue certainly could not stand by itself, however, *as a proof* that Gongsun Long had a theory of *meaning*- or *sense*-based semantic theory.[54]

We do, however, have good reason to suppose that Chinese writers used *zhi* in explaining the semantics of terms. There is the fairly obvious connection of pointing to things. The Neo-Mohists use *zhi*[point] in suggestive ways. We can imagine that it stands for the notion of symbolic pointing. The meaningful pointing gesture works as the rhyming *shi*[this:right] does. They reserve the term *ju*[pick out] for semantic denotation by a term-type. Other philosophers of language are less careful. Both Zhuangzi and Xunzi use *zhi*[point] in the sense of semantic reference. We take a term to point to a thing. (Remember that a *wu*[thing] is not an *individual* thing but a thing-kind.) So we can identify *zhi* closely with semantic reference. Note that in both the Mohists' and the more general use, *zhi* carries the notion of separating out from a background what is *shi* and what is *fei*.[55]

Graham's latest approach (1978) is, accordingly, the most promising.[56] He does tie the dialogue to a concern we will see emerging in Zhuangzi. The concern could have obvious roots in the Neo-Mohist semantic paradoxes. The pragmatic paradoxes implicitly point to the problem of language's talking about itself. This may have led to a worry about any chance of language's having an *everything* concept. Can we put in language the claim that the part-whole metaphysics ends with some ultimate *whole*? If theorists use the word *zhi* as Graham suggests, then one cannot *zhi*[point] to everything. If every term separates one thing-kind from what is not the kind, then there can be no term that does not exclude something. In particular, the *zhi*[pointing] cannot point to itself. This the line followed by Zhuangzi. He argues that if we say, "All is one," we still have the one and the saying so—and that makes two. Furthermore, the issue of whether there can be an *everything* concept is a plausible development of traceable themes in the analytic school. It grows naturally out of the framework of *ti*[parts] and *jian*[wholes] found in the Neo-Mohist canon.

Now the reason for not being able to name everything is not Laozi's distinction-based worry. It is not that a term like *you*[exists] marks something off from a paradoxical nothing. It is that the *zhi*[pointing] itself is something. It cannot refer to its own referring. Pointing to the whole cannot point to the pointing to the whole. It therefore leaves something out and is not an *everything* concept.[57]

Graham's other insight is that we should not take the phrase "tian xia[the world] wu[lacks] zhi[pointing]" as equivalent to "wu zhi" by itself. This suggests that *world* may be a more crucial term in Gongsun Long's argument than it seemed. The holistic cosmos can contrast only with the things that compose it. We saw a version of this concern in the *Daode Jing*'s characterization of *wu*[non being] as the beginning or edge of *tiandi*[the world].

If a term points to the whole world, then the pointing cannot be part of the world. Linguistic reference must be nonnatural. Hence *the world* does not have that particular pointing. The dialogue may take this to mean that the world does not include *any* pointings period. The world has names and things but not the pointing relationship. This is a suitably skeptical thesis about language with just about the degree of paradox and slippery use of ambiguity characteristic of Gongsun Long's white horse argument. It does not, however, follow. We can point to pointings; we can even have a pointing that points to itself.

The world includes language (names) and things, but it does not contain their relation. The relation we call *reference* (and Gongsun Long calls *pointing*) is not a proper part of the world. If we include pointings within the everything concept, then we cannot express it.

Graham's interpretation, necessarily, is highly speculative. It has the advantage of being a speculation that we can tie to the philosophical issues of the day. It also has a conformable conclusion about the thrust of Gongsun Long's theorizing. His defense of Confucianism against Later Mohist realism defends a kind of linguistic idealism. There is no natural realistic relation between names and things. They depend on conventions. So we can construct the conventions according to whatever ideal principles we want. We can have a language in which *white horse* is not *horse* if this will help achieve a more elegant guiding discourse. Metaphysics is at the mercy of names, not vice versa.

Hui Shi's Paradoxes—The World Is One

Gongsun Long's *defense* was so far from common sense that the Confucians did not welcome it. His attack on the realist conception had mainly curiosity value. The third *wing* of the school of names, arguably, was much more important. This wing has one dominant figure, Hui Shi. Hui Shi was a debating companion and close friend of Zhuangzi. His analyses are much more damaging to the realist enterprise. We will think of him as representing the Daoist wing, although Zhuangzi clearly saw Hui Shi as having a seriously flawed linguistic theory. We know little about him except that he was an expert on the theory of *bian*^{distinction making}. He is credited with ten theses and associated loosely with a cluster of paradoxical statements.[58] The ten theses argue for a nonrealistic position. Hui Shi argues that distinctions are not in the world.[59] The ten theses are:

1. The greatest has nothing outside it; call it the great one. The smallest has nothing within it; call it the small one.
2. That which has no thickness cannot accumulate though it can be as large as a thousand *li*^{miles}.
3. Heaven is as low as earth; mountains and swamps are level.
4. As the sun is once in the center, once on the side, so thing-kinds are once living, once dying.
5. There is a great similarity and it is different from a small similarity; call this *small comparison*. All thing-kinds are ultimately similar and ultimately different; call this *great comparison*.
6. *South* at once has no limit and has a limit.
7. Today I go to Yue and yet yesterday arrived there.
8. Interlocked rings can be untangled.
9. I know the center of the world: north of Yin (a northern state) and south of Yue (a southern state).
10. Exhaustively love all thing-kinds. Heaven and earth are one *ti*^{part}.

These puzzles come without explanation. Traditional literature offers many explanations. Again, we need to make sure that concerns we have already uncovered in Chinese thought constrain our explanations. Hui Shi shows an obvious fascination with problems of comparison (3 and 5) and indexicals—time words, place words—that change their reference with each use (6, 7, and 9). Comparisons are hard to fit into an extensional account of language (is a large flea large?). Indexicals tend to draw our attention to how much the relation between words and reality can shift.

The most important of Hui Shi's theses for understanding Zhuangzi's response to the Later Mohist realism is 5. The use of similarity and difference to justify distinctions in language gives us no unique set of distinctions. We can find some point of similarity in any two things called by *different* names. Conversely, we can find some point of difference in any two things called by the *same* names no matter how much alike. So if we focused on these other similarities and differences, we would draw distinctions elsewhere.

The series starts and ends, however, with a simple mistake. Thesis 1 and 10 both envision some kind of everything concept, an absolute monism. Monism does not follow merely from the relativity of our distinction making activity. The suggestion that it does confuses what we can know with what is real. It suggests that a difference exists only if we can know or prove it does. We can justify no naturally coherent, realistically required, place to draw a distinction. That does not show that there is none any more than it does that there are many. The premises amount to saying we cannot know the independent ultimate structure of reality, and the conclusion then baldly declares what that structure is. Hui Shi's conclusion, ''The world is one body,'' is an example of the verification fallacy.

Hui Shi's conclusion states an interesting problem that reminds us of the problem of an *everything* concept. In thesis 9, he uses the term *tian xia*[the world], the term found in the *''Zhi-wu* Dialogue.'' But in the last thesis, he uses the mass-sum compound found in the *Daode Jing, tian di*[Heaven-earth]. He asserts that heaven-earth is a single *ti*[unit].[60] We can justify no particular pattern of distinctions among things to guide action (loving). Hence he concludes that we should love all thing-kinds without exception.

This conclusion, I believe, is more primitive Daoist than Mohist. The Mohists, remember, did make an implicit distinction between human society and the rest of nature in arguing for utility. We could, in principle, have a utilitarianism that embraced all mammal life, or all vertebrate life, or all animal life, or all life, or all matter. But that was not the Mohist version. What reason do we have for stopping at one of these levels? Hui Shi appears to argue that we have none. He draws the Daoist-like conclusion that we ought to love all of nature rather than giving human society a special significance. But as I will argue, Zhuangzi rebuts this fallacious monism.

Summary: The School of Names

Philosophical discourse takes an analytic turn at this point in history. Chinese thinkers have discovered that the arguments about ethics and politics rest on difficult issues about language and they focused directly on those issues. The natural impulse to realism drew with it a host of implications about reality and mind. These implications developed their established views of words. They described reality and knowledge in ways that flowed from their earlier views of language. They assumed that the heart-mind embraced a kind of skill at applying terms and using them to guide motivations and behavior. So the different language theorists usually saw themselves as defending one of the major guiding theories of the day.

They all treated the world as a part-whole structure. That assumption, however, presented problems. We had the local problem of showing the consistency of part-whole reference when one strung terms together in various ways for practical guidance. Then we saw a hint of a global problem of the great whole and the relativism of the parts and distinctions. It began to be clear that nature was not a sufficient basis of guidance. Nature or heaven will lose its authority once Zhuangzi faces this gap between the world and guidance.

The key problem lies in justifying any *particular* standard for making distinctions above any other. We have this problem *even when* we agree that objective similarities and differences exist *and* agree to base names on them. The problem is that too many ways can be proposed to do this. The Neo-Mohists have not given us any reliable way to classify the *wild* ones.

However, there have been positive results from the analysis. Any competent Chinese philosopher will now see that the antilanguage position is simply incoherent. Some linguistic utterances must be correct, however hard it is to say which they are.

They have begun to notice degrees of more guiding and more descriptive language. They notice that guiding usually comes in more complex structures.

Both the problems and the developments suffuse the writings of the remaining philosophers of the period. Many scholars regard Zhuangzi and Xunzi as the most sophisticated thinkers in this ancient tradition. Graham has shown that both were well versed in the issues and concepts of the analytic turn. The traditional interpretations, however, are theoretically mired (as Neo-Confucianism was) at the antilanguage position of Mencius. They treat Zhuangzi and Xunzi as adopting the same positions that philosophers had adopted before the school of names or as offering inferior theories. They ignore that the analytic period clearly discredited both the antilanguage and the absolute monism theories. Any criticism of what they *take to be* Daoism and intuitive Confucianism they condemn as *Western* or *modern* anachronisms. Neo-Confucian interpretations assume that these later philosophers from the mature period of Classical thought learned nothing important from the analytic school.

Nonetheless they are right that Zhuangzi and Xunzi both thought that the elaborate analysis of names turned out to be an unexpected failure. It did *not* yield the firm foundation for language for which the theorists had hoped. But, I shall argue, the antilanguage position never again tempts these philosophers. Both see the incoherence of pure relativism. We must understand their positions differently now that we understand what they learned from the school of names.

8

Zhuangzi: Discriminating about Discriminating

"Chuang Tzu never knew he was a 'Taoist.'"

ANGUS GRAHAM[1]

Graham has demonstrated that the closer we come to an understanding of the technical vocabulary of those engaged in the dialectic and logical debates of the school of names . . . , the closer we come to an understanding of the issues which lie behind Chuang-tzu's deep engagement with these sophists.

We shall again begin our account of the historic Chuang-tzu with the mystical vision which he shares with Lao-tzu. Chuang-tzu's constant efforts to describe the indescribable in many ways simply amplify and enrich what we have already found in the Lao-tzu.

BENJAMIN SCHWARTZ[2]

An Interpretive Manifesto

Zhuangzi floats over the landscape of Chinese thought like a philosophical phantom shrouded in a self-created mist of elusive style and analytical skepticism. He defies us to interpret his critique of interpretation. There is always room for disagreement and I will claim my share. My account will diverge fundamentally from the ruling interpretive theory.

Zhuangzi had a unique philosophical style. He wrote philosophical fantasy. This style is at once irresistibly attractive and yet maddeningly frustrating. How he presents his positions counts as much as any explicit thesis we find in his fantasies. This style injects insecurity into interpreters. Yet it attracts us like philosophical honey. His combination of brilliance and elusive statement frustrates, delights, and challenges those who want to interpret him.

He puts positions up for consideration as if endorsing them, then reflectively abandons them.[3] He may do this in the form of an internal monologue or as a fanciful conversation carried on among fantastic creatures, rebellious thieves, distorted freaks, or converted Confucians.

In his typical fantasy dialogue, Zhuangzi seemingly dares us to say which voice is really his. Sometimes Confucius, for example, emerges as a target of ridicule, sometimes as the expositor of Zhuangzi's message.

Typically, his philosophical dialogues end without a conclusion. In the place of a conclusion is a double rhetorical question, "Then is there really an X? Or is there no X?" Every interpreter feels sure she knows which answer is correct and attributes it to Zhuangzi. Interpreters, predictably, disagree on what that obvious point is.

Zhuangzi's style signals his status as the premier philosopher of perspective. His staging of fantasy dialogues releases him from trying to make any transperspectival conclusions and yet allows him to philosophize freely. He challenges us to realize that in reading him, we do so from different conceptual perspectives. Working with the text becomes an object lesson in the message of the text. If we think Zhuangzi is saying A, we translate the passages differently than if we are convinced he is saying B.

The Neo-Confucian perspective interprets Zhuangzi's theory as essentially like that of Mencius. One should follow an innate, intuitive, natural guide to action, an absolute, unspeakable *dao*. Thus Neo-Confucians triumphantly assert the ultimate compatibility of Confucianism and Daoism. The ruling theory regards acknowledging this compatibility between the two schools as the sign of mature insight into classical thought. Its Neo-Confucian perspective blocks the Later Mohist awareness that Mencius' or any other antilanguage absolutism is incoherent. It does not *see* Zhuangzi's arguments *as* a refutation of the position.

To see the arguments as one thing rather than another is also a matter of accepting an interpretive perspective. I learned the ruling Confucian perspective as a student. It took years to unlearn portions of it. Now I have a more Daoist perspective. This intrigues me. It makes me sensitive to one of Zhuangzi's frequent observations about perspective. When we have shifted perspective, it is hard to see how we could have been tempted to the earlier one. So it is hard to do the other perspective justice even if one remembers having held it. We cannot assume, simply because we held one perspective earlier, that we now *know better*.

A realistic approach to interpretation assumes that some interpretive perspectives are better than others. The key is *to justify* a shift in perspective. I have argued that the argument must appeal to the overall coherence of the interpretive explanation. An interpretation must first be coherent before it can be a coherent explanation of the text. Schwartz urged that our Western view of what is coherent may be different from the Chinese view. But we have found that other Chinese philosophers themselves clearly raise the objection that antilanguage monism is incoherent. The problem with the dogmatic mystical-monist interpretation of Zhuangzi is that it isolates him from his philosophical culture. It ignores the challenge to integrate Zhuangzi coherently into the philosophical debate.

But perhaps Schwartz's objection can be put differently. The concept of rational coherence itself, not the particular conception of coherence is the issue. Appealing to coherence as the standard is a Western fetish. Chinese interpreters have a different interpretive practice. They may appeal to an interpretation's impact on the community's moral behavior or to its conformity with a tradition of interpretation. It has been alleged[4] that this blatantly Western realistic perspective discredits my interpretations in general. I should learn to make interpretive judgments as Chinese scholars do. I should master and present competently the ruling theory and justify it in the way sinologists normally do.

I do accept that traditional scholarly standards of interpretation in China have a different feel. At least part of that difference lies in the more authoritative status of the community. But I regard that as a particularly conservative *Confucian* phenomenon within Chinese thought, not the Chinese *way of thinking*. It can hardly be alleged to be the method of the antisocial Daoists. Even Neo-Confucian methodology seems more subtle than the argument assumes. The Song-Ming traditions certainly rejected simple conformity to conventional viewpoints. Like Confucius, they allege that *correct* interpretation depends on moral intuition. That position, as I have argued, is also a version of interpretive realism.

This Confucian realism, however, cannot survive Zhuangzi's emphasis on perspective. The assumption that humans share a single moral intuition is a controversial assumption in Chinese thought. A Mohist could be reasonably expected to object. A Daoist who draws conclusions from the irresolvability of the Ru-Mo Confucian-Mohist debate would also be skeptical.

The principle of conformity to scholarly-community perspective is internally incoherent. It is incoherent in modern Western academic communities because *our* community rejects the principle. Conformity to our community standards requires that we do not cite conformity as evidence of correctness. Our community shares a higher-level community commitment to scientific realism. But the community-conformity principle would also be incoherent in any community in which Mozi's point had been made. I have argued that hypertraditionalist version of Confucianism fell under immediate attack in China. It certainly would not have been the perspective of the antisocial Daoists. It is hardly likely to have been Zhuangzi's methodological perspective.

In any case, I note here, for any adherents to communitarian principles, that the unanimity of the scholarly community is hereby broken. I reject the monist, intuitionist interpretation of Zhuangzi.[5]

Do I reject the mystical interpretation? Since by definition it has nothing to say, it seems unnecessary to reject it. But proponents both describe it as incommensurable with language and then proceed to spell out its theoretical content in language. They do it in ways that Zhuangzi would have recognized as incoherent or ways that are alien to the conceptual perspective of classical China. I certainly regard as implausible that Daoist mysticism should have either monist, intuitivist, antilanguage, nihilist, or experiential content.

I reject any conception of Daoist mysticism modeled on Buddhist or Western mysticism. I would also insist that Zhuangzi is not a primitivist or absolutist on the grounds that he directly criticizes both these theories. Their deficiencies were known to the school of names and, by hypothesis, to Zhuangzi. Zhuangzi was both conversant with and competent in the analysis practiced by the school of names. His close association with Hui Shi warrants both the conclusion and our respect for his logical acumen. He should be aware of the problems with an everything concept, an antilanguage position, and with pure nihilism.

I will treat the maximally coherent collection of doctrines expressed by his speakers as Zhuangzi's theory. This appeal to coherence is limited only by the principle of humanity. I am not saying that Zhuangzi could not have made a mistake. But if a mistake has been analyzed in the tradition (in particular by the analytic school), then I will prefer interpretations that do not attribute that mistake to Zhuangzi. No one who respects Zhuangzi as a thinker should object to this assumption.

My account of the content of Zhuangzi's theory draws on the analysis that informs the previous chapters. The same interpretive principle of humanity guides the interpretation here. The ruling view, by contrast, takes a perspective based on a *static conception* of Chinese thought and a fragmented schools approach. The static view treats antilanguage intuitionism as the apex of Chinese philosophy. Hence it views Mencius as the high water mark. It regards crediting Zhuangzi with compatible intuitionist views as a *sign of respect*.

The fragmented schools view also infects the ruling interpretation. Having decided that Daoism is antilanguage monism and that Zhuangzi is a Daoist, it concludes his doctrine must also be mystical monism—whatever he happens to say. This conclusion depends on the fragmenting assumption that *Dao* has a special Daoist meaning, that it is a singular term and has changed its meaning from guiding discourse to the unspeakable name of some metaphysical absolute. It ignores the important influence of the school of names on Zhuangzi.[6]

Zhuangzi's use clearly signals this key mistake in the traditional analysis. In *The Zhuangzi dao*s are many and *dao*s are linguistic. *Dao* remains a general term in the *Zhuangzi,* not a singular one. *The Zhuangzi* contains references to great *dao*, extreme *dao*, mysterious *dao*, heavenly *dao*, the ancient king's *dao*, its, his, or their *dao*, emperor's *dao*, human *dao*, sage's *dao*, the *dao* of governing, moral *dao*,[7] the *dao* of long life, the master's *dao*, the *dao* you cannot (or do not) *dao*,[8] the gentleman's *dao*, this *dao*, authentic *dao*, artificial *dao*, my *dao*, ancient *dao*,[9] The Yellow Emperor's and Yao and Shun's *dao*, Shendao's *dao*,[10] Confucius' *dao*, and Mozi's *dao*.[11] He speaks of learning, hearing,[12] saying,[13] forgetting, having, lacking, losing, gaining, naming and *dao*ing *dao*. Every occurrence of *dao* in the crucial second chapter he either explains within his theory of language or uses to explain something about language: about names, about saying, or about *shi-fei*ing.

I remind the reader of the strategy I recommended earlier for reading translations. You can remove a translator's monistic prejudice in translations by deleting the *the* in *the Dao* and substituting either the plural or an indefinite article *(a, some, any)*. That is, change every *the* Dao or *the* Way in your favorite translations to *a dao, some dao(s),* or *each, every,* or *all ways.* Then think of the paradigm *dao* as some version of guiding discourse. Remember the chronic problem of practical interpretation and how it require some prior guidance, some natural hard wiring. This gives a clear account of any references to an unlearned, unspoken, or natural *dao*. It is the prior, internal, natural guide required in order to absorb any socialized guidance through language.

Zhuangzi, like the rest of the classical tradition, uses *dao* as a concept of guidance rather than a reality concept. His perspectivalism focuses on the awareness that we have many different, incommensurable guiding *dao*s.

Again, despite its deliberately iconoclastic tone, my view of Zhuangzi does have roots in the interpretive tradition. That tradition has always recognized the elements of skepticism and relativism in Zhuangzi. The disagreement between my interpretation and the ruling one lies in what we think is a coherent conclusion to draw from skeptical premises. The ruling theory fallaciously draws a dogmatic monistic conclusion from relativist or skeptical premises. In effect, if we are aware that we all draw distinctions in different ways from different perspectives, we could draw them in many other ways than we do. Then the ruling theory claims that Zhuangzi makes the *perspective-free judgment that absolute reality itself has no distinctions in it.* How could Zhuangzi have understood perspectival skepticism in a way that allowed such a dogmatic conclusion?

The assumption that Daoists are monists mesmerizes traditionalists, who assume that, as Daoists, Zhuangzi and Laozi are monistic mystics. Zhuangzi simply "amplifies and enriches"[14] what Laozi said. Traditionalists model mysticism on Buddhist or Western mysticism. The Confucian tradition cherishes the thought that Daoists agree with Mencius except for ignoring the moral nature of the mystical whole. All this continues as if the school of names had never existed or had influenced anyone. Even Graham, the person most responsible for proving Zhuangzi's mastery of the school-of-names analysis, insists on imposing the antilanguage position on him.

> Although it is not easy to offer a definition of Taoism, thinkers classed as philosophical Taoists do share one basic insight—that while all other things move spontaneously on the course proper to them, man has stunted and maimed his spontaneous aptitude by the habit of distinguishing alternatives, the right and the wrong, benefit and harm, self and others, and reasoning in order to judge between them.[15]

An interpreter who thinks that this inference is valid will not be strict in requiring *an explicit statement* of the position before attributing it to Zhuangzi. All I find Zhuangzi saying explicitly is that for any natural distinction we focus on, we ignore a great many others. That is a statement of pluralism, not monism. Any translator who thinks that monism follows from the relativity of perspective will not notice the crucial difference. He will see all comments about the relativity of distinctions to perspective as allegations that there are no distinctions. Therefore reality is one. We should abandon distinctions. Consider again, for a parallel example, the first line of the *Daode Jing*. It does not, as we saw, assert the existence of a single, constant *dao*. The widespread presumption that it does shows the power of the ruling interpretive perspective. It fixes *Daoism* as being about an incommensurable, monistic, unspeakable object. That is precisely the assumption I challenge again here.[16]

I have been building the argument in the previous chapters. The serious consequences start here. I choose a unified interpretive theory that fully incorporates the analytic school. I reject the fragmented ruling theory. I concentrate on a practical, social conception of language. I avoid projecting the theory of an inner mental life, consciousness, experience, and any mentalist theory of meaning. I credit all Chinese philosophers with the view that language is a social mechanism for shaping human behavior. These arguments invite us to change the interpretation of Zhuangzi and, with it, our understanding of what Daoism is.

Zhuangzi's Place in the Pre-Han Dialogue

The relation of Zhuangzi and Laozi is a puzzle. Graham toys with the idea that Zhuangzi may be partially responsible for *inventing* Laozi. Laozi's role in Zhuangzi's fantasy dialogues is frequently to lecture Confucius. He does that from a perspective that he could share with Mencius except for his view that intuition is socially ac-quired rather than innate. Zhuangzi accepts this part of Laozi but without drawing the incoherent antilanguage conclusion. Zhuangzi also differs form Laozi externally in that his serious dialectical *opponents* are no longer the conventional Confucians. Naive traditionalism is now philosophically obsolete. Zhuangzi simply uses the Confucius-Mozi debate as an illustration of the irresolvability of philosophical dis-putes. His targets are realism and absolutism of many types.

Zhuangzi's first victim is the innatist absolutism of Mencius. He disposes of Mencius easily and disdainfully. Zhuangzi's more challenging opponents are the real-ist dialecticians, especially the Neo-Mohist realists. Developing a coherent way to meet their challenge requires more of Zhuangzi's subtlety and analytical ability. He also uses the results of the analytic philosophy of language to refute absolute Daoism.

His debating companion,[17] Hui Shi, is also the target of both jokes and criti-cism. Zhuangzi rejects Hui Shi's formulation of monism. He shows that Hui Shi's study of names ends in incoherence. Still, much of Zhuangzi's skepticism comes from Hui Shi's reflections on the indexicality of distinction making and similarity and difference (see page 262). Zhuangzi also highlights Hui Shi's comparative eval-uations, those most subject to indexical application. Indexicality, the relativity of reference to speakers' perspective, gives Zhuangzi the key to dealing with Mohist realism. External similarity and difference cannot provide a realist justification for any *particular* way of dividing things into types. That is not because reality justifies *no* distinctions, but because it justifies too many. All the distinctions we can actually draw have *some* basis in reality. Any two things are similar from some point of view and different from some other point of view.

This is where interpreters get lost. The argument can show that Zhuangzi finds no way to show which scheme of distinctions is correct. Its thrust is skeptical. We cannot know which way of dividing the world is correct. We cannot know whether the scheme that makes ten thousand distinctions or one that makes five thousand distinctions is correct. In that case, we also cannot know if the scheme that makes two or one or *none* is correct. The assertion that making no distinctions is the correct way is as dogmatic and unwarranted as any other alternative. Graham makes the standard reasoning most explicit.

> But it is also clear that if he is taking this position Hui Shi has come dangerously close to discrediting his own tool, analytic reason. He wishes to discredit only spatial and temporal divisions, but it will take only one more step to observe that all reasoning depends on making distinctions, and *to reach the conclusion that we should abandon reason for the immediate experience of an undifferentiated world,* transforming "All are one" from a moral into a mystical affirmation. It is in "The sorting that evens things out" that Chuang-tzu takes this step.[18]

But that conclusion simply does not follow. Zhuangzi certainly does not *explic-itly* draw it. The argument is a non sequitur. *We* can reach that conclusion only if we are logically careless. That there are infinitely many possible ways to classify things based on similarity and difference does not entail that none of them is correct. Far less does it entail that a specific one of them is correct, to wit, the one that makes no distinctions.[19]

Interpreters who think that inference valid attribute it to Zhuangzi. They explain the absence of any such formulation as Zhuangzi's mystical refusal to state his conclusion. They thus seem to acknowledge that Zhuangzi realized that the conclusion was incoherent. So the only basis for attributing that conclusion to Zhuangzi is the interpreter's error in reasoning. The agreed textual fact is this: Zhuangzi studiously avoids the mistake of asserting the antilanguage position. When he formulates Hui Shi's monistic conclusion, he criticizes its incoherence. I explain the absence of any such statement straightforwardly. Zhuangzi never drew the invalid inference. We can assume that he is clearly aware of the Neo-Mohist proof that any statement of mystical (ineffable) monism is *perverse*. "All language distorts the *Dao*" distorts the *Dao*.

Zhuangzi's interest in *dao*, like Laozi's takes the essential form of a linguistic theory and theory of mind. Like Laozi's theory, it treats moral intuitions as learned. We learn our intuitions in the process of learning language. His linguistic account shows the further influence of the Neo-Mohists. He sees how language shapes our distinctions, our conception of what thing kinds there are. He saw the practical outcome too: that different languages guide differently. A different guiding consequence accompanies different assignments of names. Each clusters similarities and differences in a distinct way. His theory takes its pluralistic perspectival form because he is trying to deal simultaneously with two results from the school of names. The first is Hui Shi's discovery of the infinitely many ways of clustering similarity and difference. The second is the Neo-Mohist demonstration of the incoherence of the suggestion that we therefore ought to abandon language.

Because he makes fun of Hui Shi and Gongsun Long, most interpreters assume that Zhuangzi recommended against *bian*. But to reject distinctions is to *fei* treating anything as *fei*[not this:wrong] (not of a type). The Neo-Mohists have shown us that that view is incoherent. Our confusion of two English senses of *argument* further betrayed us. The ruling theory *finds* a Zhuangzi opposed to quarrels and *paints* a Zhuangzi opposed to proof or reason. I find no evidence of deliberate irrationalism in *The Zhuangzi*. I do find evidence that he thought any attempt to base naming on real similarity and difference would fail. He thought the Later Mohist's ground-up referential semantics would not work. Even they had concluded that compounding names into phrases did not follow a regular, reliable pattern.

The school of names had simply confirmed Laozi's view. Naming is not constant, especially within any guiding *dao*. But it had also shown that any recommendation to abandon distinctions, to abandon learning, or to abandon language itself was incoherent. The ideal of a correct assignment of names to things was at least coherent. The Mohists' appeal to similarity and difference did not provide a single correct assignment. The sense of lost, humorous, paradox in Zhuangzi's reflections about language comes from this dual awareness. We can neither justify our system of language as uniquely correct, nor can we coherently abandon it. His unresolved fantasy dialogues and double rhetorical question conclusions are a statement of his dilemma.

Graham has shown[20] that Zhuangzi was intimately familiar with the technical terminology of the Neo-Mohist *Canon* and that he used it correctly. Once we have understood what the school is trying to say, we appreciate Zhuangzi's unmistakable skill at dialectics. So we assign low initial probability to the hypothesis that he commits the basic error (all language is perverse) criticized so plainly in the *Mohist Canon*. We see realist faith coupled with a skeptical perspective. There must be a correct conceptual perspective. We could, however, never be sure of having found it. These combined with his playful approach to issues and his respect for our small place in nature yields the apparent mystical tone. We see some disappointment in the failure of direct study of names but Zhuangzi avoids the hand-wringing self-pity of most skeptics. Zhuangzi playfully ridicules the hope of formulating what it is that language cannot state. He describes what it can state—the pluralism—and regards that as his liberation from social convention. Zhuangzi's theoretical advances in this tradition lie in theory of language. The mystical tone has no other theoretical content.

Zhuangzi: Textual and Historical Issues

We know about Zhuangzi personally only what we can infer from his text. That text, scholars have long agreed, is not the product of a single theorist. Scholarly tradition has divided the text into *inner* and *outer* chapters. We presume that the inner chapters contain Zhuangzi's actual writings. The outer chapters consist of writings that some later, more eclectic school considered related to Zhuangzi's themes. Graham classifies the other lines as syncretist, primitivist, and Yangist.[21] The outer texts are historically important. The last chapter, especially, formulates a *Daoist* intellectual history of the period.

The outer chapters do not express a coherent or sophisticated Daoist position They show far less technical mastery of theory of language.[22] Where they express a conflicting or inferior philosophical insight, I will treat the inner chapters as authoritative. The more eclectic outer chapters combine Daoist ideas with the more superstitious and dogmatic positions that proliferated toward the end of the classical period. Where Zhuangzi was a pluralist, they tend toward an frankly superstitious intuitive dogmatism. Dogmatic intuition, even without Confucian content, is not a great improvement over Mencius.

Within the inner chapters, one stands out as the theoretical core of Zhuangzi's writings. The other chapters consist of richly detailed parables whose moral is (perhaps deliberately) ambiguous. I must admit to having being baffled, since my first exposure to the *Zhuangzi,* that anyone could think the stories are unambiguous statements of an absolutist or dogmatic Daoism. When we think of the relativity of comparative distinctions, surely the most obvious is the relativity of large and small. The stories of the first chapter deal with the great and small. Zhuangzi tells of a large bird, and goes on eloquently about its barely comprehensible size, its power and the range of its flight. Then he describes the counterpart world of small flying creatures.

The absolutist interpretation trivializes Zhuangzi's point. They present him as saying that little creatures are limited but big creatures know everything. Zhuangzi puts his own point in careful linguistic terms. We would not construe an animal as talking about things that could never play a role in *its* activities. Words play roles in real lives. Our concepts are tied to the different practical worlds we inhabit and have to deal with.

The traditional interpretation sees these stories as illustrating the authoritarian claim that "bigger is better." The emperor's perspective is better than yours. What can your little, puny mind comprehend of the vastness of universal insight? Zhuangzi's description of the small bird's world, however, is too rich and empathetic for us to explain it by a simple minded *bigger-is-better* absolutism. Zhuangzi's point is the inaccessibility of other points of view from this one. It is just as impossible for the great bird to understand what flying means to the small bird, flitting joyfully from branch to branch.[23] It is just as impossible for the giant sea turtle to know the frog's life in the wonderfully slimy, cool well as vice versa.[24] That certainly suggests the inaccessibility of any universal point of view.

Rhetorically, of course, the point intimidates us more when made in the *greater* direction. Zhuangzi seems not to have been intimidated when rules offered him the chance to take a more universal position, to leave his fishing and go to the capital to share the emperor's concern with the whole empire. Zhuangzi's free and easy fantasy wandering regularly goes the authoritarians one better by appealing to an even greater perspective than they claim. From this even greater perspective, things look different. We should, however, not miss his point; he makes it in terms of blindness and deafness. The things we can put into words depend on the words' being able to play a role for us in our lives. We cannot treat our language as having a free-floating, absolute relation to the world.

Zhuangzi's stories with their dual or ambiguous moral illustrate his philosophical point by their effect on us as much as by their content. What we see in the stories will depend on what perspective we use in reading Zhuangzi. Absolutists see him arguing that we should take the point of view of a cosmic *dao*. They treat the cosmic perspective as an authoritative point of view and one that we can adopt. I see precisely the opposite point in the stories.

If we want to prove which one of these accounts of what Zhuangzi's *dao* was is correct, we shall have to concentrate on the single chapter with detailed philosophical reflection and argument. That is the second chapter in the traditional text. Even its title is subject to interpretation. Depending on what we find it saying, we can read the title as either "Ordering thing-discourse" or "Ordering-thing discourse." It is either a pluralist account of the different ways of dividing the world into things in discourse or it is the single correct discourse that authoritatively orders things. Terminology and reasoning from formal dialectics fills that second chapter.

Despite the strange-creatures-talking-in-riddles-to-each-other motif of the second, chapter, I see an argument being developed in an intelligibly logical way. The chapter announces a pluralistic and naturalistic perspective on language. Then it reflects on the puzzles inherent in three versions of absolutism: innatist absolutism (Mencius), external realism (Later Mohists), and monistic absolutism (primitive or absolute Daoism).

Language and Its Adequacy

Zhuangzi puts the initial statement of his theory of language in the mouth of Nanguo Ziqi. He leans on his armrest and breathes serenely, as if, the text suggests, he had lost his *opposite*. We can understand the loss of *opposite* in the tradition of analysis of names found even in the *Daode Jing.* The Neo-Mohists continue the same analysis. To have lost one's opposite is to have lost the distinction of self and other.[25] This distinction lies between the world to which names, distinctions, and attitudes apply and the point of view that applies them. Because we can apply our language to ourselves, we can shrink to a point of view within ourselves. We can look at what from an ordinary perspective is ourselves, as an *other.*

An onlooker likens his state to that of being dead: "Your appearance is like dried wood and your heart-mind like cold ashes. You cannot be what you were?"

Nanguo Ziqi answers, "Good question. Now I have buried *wo*^{myself}, you know. You know the pipes of men, but not those of earth; know of pipes of earth, but not those of *tian*$^{\text{nature:heaven}}$?"

The onlooker asks, "Could you unpack that just a little?"

Zhuangzi's lyricism flows into his answering description, filled with creative onomatopoeia and allusions. He mentions a *clod,* recalling Shendao's clod that cannot miss the *dao.* The pipes of earth are the physical structures through which the wind blows to produce all manner of natural sounds. He illustrates it richly with invented characters for *whee, oooh,* and the like. This he contrasts with the sound of haunting silence when the wind ceases.

So we are to understand the pipes of earth on analogy to pipes of men. They are blown at the whim of the windmaker and silent when the windmaker stops. These are all natural sounds. Language, like other animal noises, must be treated as a natural sound. But then why separate the pipes of heaven from those of earth? The authoritative heavenly part is the alleged distinctions attached to these noises of curious animals. The pipes of heaven "blow out the ten-thousand *not-alikes*" (the differences, the distinctions) and makes them seem naturally given, or self-chosen.[26] Graham interpreted this passage as meaning that heaven *blows* out the ten thousand different utterances of the philosophers.[27]

We should give a consistent Chinese analysis to Graham's reference to utterances. Heaven (nature) creates *all* the *systems* of discriminating things from each other and of choosing using that discrimination system. The system of natural sounds includes human languages marking these distinctions. Language is on a par with the sound of waves, the twitter of birds, and the slapping of beavers' tails on the water.

Realist semantics relies on a language-world distinction. This story underwrites skepticism about that distinction. It reminds us that the systematic net of our language, our distinctions, and the way it functions to guide choice and behavior is part of nature. It encourage us to focus on how language works as a natural phenomenon instead of on the abstract separation of language and its object. Every *dao* (doctrine) about what distinctions to make and what choices follow is equally natural and equally a part of the natural world. The natural *dao* includes *all* linguistic *dao.*

Shendao's and Laozi's primitive, absolute Daoism were implicitly antilanguage. Zhuangzi's opening goes in precisely the opposite direction. Language is neither unnatural, inherently wrong, nor inimical to the cosmos. On the contrary, all language is *equally* natural. All doctrines are *equally* the pipes of heaven. Heaven blows on all the pipes, not just one, preferring neither the Confucians' nor the Mohists'.

The reversal this approach offers the Daoist is enticing. Without embracing the incoherent condemnation of language, Zhuangzi can puncture the pompous pontificating of philosophical dogmatists. He simultaneously gives them exactly what they want (a heavenly or natural warrant to their way of making guiding distinctions) and strips it of rhetorical value. Heaven *does* dictate their system of making distinctions and acting on them. Each is a heavenly or natural *dao*. Mozi's is. Confucius' is. Yang Zhu's is. However, since all doctrines are pipes of heaven, none has any special status in having this heavenly or natural source. The antilanguage philosophers say that all doctrines are wrong. Zhuangzi grants (in the sense the various philosophers claimed it) that all are equally in accord with heaven:nature.

Knowledge and Language

If language is part of nature, then so are the systems of guiding knowledge based on language mastery. Knowledge consists in mastery of one of these systems of names, one of the *daos*. Of course the only mastery we recognize as knowledge is mastery of systems with which we agree. We distinguish between *great knowledge* and *small knowledge, great words* and *small words*. We learn to make these distinctions about our different schemes of distinctions. We even make Laozi's troublesome distinctions between reality and nonreality. Where do we draw this distinction? For one, we learn to distinguish between sleep, where spirits interact, and waking, where bodies come in contact with a real world.[28] From this distinction we construe a different structure of things than we would if we made no sleeping-waking distinction or a different one.

We philosophers from different schools daily go out and do battle with our guiding heart-minds. These organs of know-how are also our centers of language skill. We battle with evaluations: grandiose, sly, petty. We defend with distinctions: great fears and small fears. These classifications issue from the heart-mind like "bolts from a crossbow." That is the analysis of how the heart determines *shi-fei*.[29]

We make these differing *shi-fei* assignments. Something else, however, happens with each one, something related to habit, logical implication, and character shaping. The *shi-fei* patterns stay with us as if we had made an oath or a treaty.[30] Some kind of precedent, convention, or custom bind us to the *shi-fei* system that wins in our hearts.[31] We cannot use them without implicitly wanting others to agree how obvious and externally directed they appear to be.

Characterizing this tendency of the heart-mind, Zhuangzi employs the term *cheng*[complete] in a theory-laden way.[32] We usually translate the character as *complete* or *success*. Zhuangzi uses it to refer to the *cheng*[completion] of a linguistic habit in the heart. We noted in discussing the Later Mohists that the notion was an externalist one: what things come to be. Zhuangzi uses it of what our heart comes to regard as the boundary of a thing, hence a prejudice. Zhuangzi's use of *cheng*[success] signals the interdependence of what is in-itself and our varying purposes in drawing a distinction. It's what we, in our various ways, make of things. We can understand it by analogy to the pragmatists' *what works*. There are two caveats in this comparison. First, what we are testing are not beliefs or theories, but conceptual schemes (systems of guiding names, that is, *daos*) and discrimination patterns. Second, Zhuangzi never thought there could be a neutral test of success. What works depends on the evaluative standards internal to one's *dao*.

This is one of Zhuangzi's crucial insights. It undermines the Mohist attempt at a pragmatic way of answering which system of distinctions is right. Confucians and

Mohists would think of different social outcomes of a linguistic perspective as success. We have different ways to interpret the pragmatic standard. We never reach rock bottom. The *test* of these is not so objective as successful navigation of a maze to get to the food at the end. A *cheng* is just what wins *given the prior commitments*. It then gets fixed in the heart-mind. The winning distinction is the one parents, peers, or priests successfully implant in you. Many translators have noticed that, for Zhuangzi, *cheng*^{success} carries a connotation of prejudice, bias, or predisposition.

However these patterns get *cheng*^{fixed} in the heart, they persist and accumulate. Discrimination patterns (language) are easy to learn in youth. When we grow old, our commitments to settled patterns begin to weigh us down. We cannot as readily absorb new ones. In learning, therefore, the heart-mind, as it grows complete, advances inevitably to its old age and death. It is daily suffocated by more language.[33] It gradually drowns in its *deemings* and *regardings* and can never recover or turn back. Language makes it old and we can never restore a heart nearing ruin to vigor. The more we amass competencies, the more rigid a structure our heart takes on. The young thus master things—languages, Rubik cubes, computers—faster than *more sophisticated* adults. To be *young at heart* is to have room to absorb new know-how. Children can catch on to Chinese tones easily. Those rigidified in a Western conception of language never get them down.

This may sound to us like a condemnation of making distinctions since making distinctions blocks up our heart and leads to its rigidity, old age, and death. They don't notice that any argument this gives for valuing having no distinctions depends on *valuing distinctions*. The reason the young are better off is simply their openness to learning other distinctions. Having learned distinctions is bad only if learning distinctions is good. Without the value of distinctions there could be no valuing of openness to distinctions. All this argument can justify is openness, not emptiness. Such openness is instrumentally valuable, but when employed, intrinsically less available.

In reacting to the world with progressively more sophisticated schemes of discrimination, the heart-mind always relies on *qing*^{reality feedback}. Zhuangzi also puts this concept in a central position. As we noted above, translators render the character most often as *feelings*. We noted that Graham treats it as *authentic reality*.[34] I have argued that *qing*^{reality feedback} suggests reality as it registers on us. If it were, as Graham suggests, reality itself, its connection to *feelings* would be less clear. My meaning hypothesis, as usual, eschews multiple, unrelated meanings. This cluster of translations can be understood if we think of *qing* as the heart-mind's reaction to reality. Zhuangzi lists joy, anger, grief, delight, worry, and regret as paradigm *qing*. He later calls *shi-fei* the essential human *qing*. Zhuangzi finds no more reason to think of *qing* as arising from within or without. Wherever they come from, he says, they simply crop up before us.[35] That is what we must deal with.

My statement presupposes something Zhuangzi does not assert—a real world context, a thing-in-itself independent of our systems of *shi-fei*. Zhuangzi simply says these are *qing* like music from empty holes, pipes of heaven, mushrooms growing spontaneously. They come like the alternation of day and night. We just do not know where they come from. The world in itself is nothing more than a possibility of doubt, the chance of our being wrong. And it does not matter where the *qing*^{reality feedbacks} come from. We have the reactions. They shape our lives. Without them, we would have no notion of *I* (as distinct from a reality outside us). Without the *I* there would be neither the notion of choice nor of the objects of choice.[36]

This sounds like all we can say from a neutral point of view, but it is dissatisfying. We have based this view of ourselves on an awareness of other points of view. That awareness introduces the realist's realm of doubt. The other points of view may seem as externally based as ours seem to us. Ours may seem to them as strange and counterintuitive as theirs seem. We experience our own as if something outside is directing it, as if there were a deep ruler, a ruler of whom we can in principle have no evidence. We can follow this ruler of the emotions (the real world). We rely on it, but we never see its form. It has felt reality *(qing)* but no form.[37] With the very notion of feedback results to our discriminations that are *ours* comes the notion of an external source of their correctness. But we can never get outside our actual responses to check on it.

The Refutation of Mencius

The heart-mind that has these *qing*[reality responses] is one of many organs of the body. Other organs also make discriminations, have motivational structures, and get feedback response—eyes, skin, taste buds, ears, digestive system among others. Which one of *them* do I regard as akin to *me?* What self-other distinction should we make among them? Are we equally satisfied with them all or must we be partial to one? Do we pick one as *me?* Then we treat the others as part of outside reality?[38] Are their responses internal or external?

Here is another manifestation of our realistic impulse to postulate a *ruler:* one organ must be in charge. It rules the others. We typically pick something like my conscience, my spirit, my reason—these are *really* me. Free agency requires that these control my animal appetites, which I acknowledge as somehow in me, but not as really me. I treat these appetites, in effect, as part of the external natural world. These are things *I* take as objects of my control.

Must we make such a distinction? Can the organs not, Zhuangzi asks, take turns being ruler and ruled?[39] We feel like there must be a true ruler among the organs but, as Zhuangzi noted earlier, we have no evidence of one.[40] Our persistent belief in a true ruler survives even the failure to get any distinct feedback response from it. All our *qing* come as they are and we *give them* their external interpretation.

Mencius, of course, is the classic expression of the attitude favoring one organ. He assumes that the order of nature is a form of guidance. The reality is an inner rule supplied by *tian*[nature:heaven]. And that the content of its rule *is* given in the *shi-fei* reactions of one organ, the heart-mind. Its pro and con distinctions projected on the world *should* rule over all the rest of the body. Mencius remember, calls the heart *nature* and the other organs *fate.*[41] We treat the pros and cons of the other natural organs as a *fate* with which we must deal. He identifies himself with the heart and treats it as an obvious *true ruler.* Furthermore, only that heart enables us to pick out the uniquely correct way to *shi-fei*, the one intended by heaven.

However, the heart comes to us with the rest of the body. It moves and grows, as does the rest of the body, inexorably toward exhaustion in registering reality as we brush against it. It is an organ that wears out just like our other organs. Our acting is like a stampeding horse that cannot be headed. We do not know what the point is or where we are going. (Something must be in control!) Sad! People call it *not dying,* but of what use is that? Our minds govern the body, but this merely enslaves it to a limited, arbitrary purpose.[42]

> As the body changes, the mind does so as well. Is this not the maximum tragedy?
> Is human life this tragic or is only mine?[43]

The absurdity is that the mind purports to govern, but is itself governed by, the inexorable changes of all natural organs. Zhuangzi thus treats the claims of the heart, like the claims of language, as just another manifestation of natural process. It has no special warrant, either among other organs or in the scheme of things. That the heart tells us to do something does not make that thing significant or meaningful. Having the heart-mind enslave us is no more *elevated* in the cosmic scheme than having our taste or appetites enslave us. These are all merely physical parts of us that change, decay, etc., according to the effects of time and nature.

The Mencian theory, remember, both asserts the authority of the *natural* heart and also the authority of the *correctly cultivated* heart. This relies on *two* arbitrary *shi-fei* distinctions: the first between the heart-mind and other organs, the second between the Confucian cultivated heart-mind and the hearts cultivated by other schools or doctrines. The first authority conflicts with Mencius' claim to be in accord with natural endowment. Nature equally endows us with all organs. If Mencius appeals *to the heart* to justify preference *for the heart* among natural organs, he begs the question. This justification of idealist Confucian intuition is circular. Zhuangzi first challenges Mencius' assumption that one organ naturally deserves to rule the others.

Then Zhuangzi notes that, even if we grant for the sake of argument the heart-mind is appropriately the governing organ, that does not vindicate the Confucian view. If we follow the heart-mind that grows with the body as the authority, then no one lacks that authority. By Mencius' hypothesis, we all follow our heart-mind. We define it functionally as that which guides and selects among the attitudes. On what basis do we elevate and *shi* the heart-minds of Confucian historians and scholars? Why does it matter who knows what *age* we are in? Why is *their* heart's guidance special? The fool's heart-mind governs her just as surely.[44] This justification of Confucian cultivation not only begs the question against other schools. It also contradicts Mencius' own moral doctrine that makes the heart the standard of right and wrong. We now clearly require some standard to distinguish among differently cultivated hearts.

If Mencius intends to argue that the heart is the standard for *shi-fei*[right–wrong] judgments, then Zhuangzi's first objection is that Mencius begs the question. The second is that he contradicts himself and appeals implicitly to some noninnate standard in order to distinguish between a properly cultivated and improperly cultivated heart. In both cases, he has presupposed an arbitrary and controversial *shi*[this:right] in his attempt to justify a natural *shi*[this:right].

Finally, Zhuangzi rejects outright the Mencian claim that *shi-fei* pro and con attitudes are innate. His position probably arises from Laozi's analysis. We acquire, he says, our *shi-fei* attitudes in the process of learning language. We start accumulating them from the moment of birth and continue accumulating them until death. For there to be *shi-fei* attitudes which are not grown *(cheng)* into the heart is, Zhuangzi says, like going to Yue yesterday and arriving today. Call this "regarding what is not as what is." Even, Zhuangzi says, the divine Yu cannot make sense of it; how would I be able to.[45]

The upshot of this three-part criticism is an insight parallel to Mozi's. A normative theory can not follow simply from claims of moral psychology. The existence of the heart does not entail that we ought to cultivate and follow it. This is so even if, as Mencius insists, nature intended it as the ruler. That simply asks if we should be guided by nature or by *dao*. We have other organs.

Second, no cultivation that actually occurs can be unnatural. All actual social *daos* that fix the heart-mind are natural. All offer equally natural guidance. Even an uncultivated heart can still offer guidance.

Zhuangzi's conclusion is his version of the Humean dictum, "You cannot get an *ought* from an *is*." But Zhuangzi states it without a concept of *ought*. You cannot get a *shi* response out of the heart without having one *cheng*[completed] in it. Your appeal to the cultivated sage's heart presupposes that we *shi* the heart over other organs. Then we *shi* a particular kind of cultivation of the heart's *shi-fei* reactions.

Now consider the claim that translators typically attribute to Zhuangzi. We should accept guidance from an even more abstract inner source of guidance than the heart: THE *Dao*. The mystery about what *Dao* is does not insulate this position from the same argument. That the heart was subject to decay was *not* the logically crucial part of the argument. The point was that to pick any organ, any standard, any distinction, any *dao* as a guide is to make a prior *shi-fei* judgment. Some arbitrary standard must be assumed before selecting any guide. That is why we can never find the true ruler. Any picking of a standard will have presupposed a prior standard. We can only think that turning back to some mysterious spontaneous nature is the answer if we do not understand Zhuangzi's argument. We can attribute such a view to Zhuangzi only if we assume that he did not understand his own argument.

Nor does it help to say that we should not make such distinctions. That judgment itself makes one! Nor can we conclude that it all starts in some mysterious place. That is merely another way of saying that *we do not know* where it starts and that we cannot possibly get behind it. No absolutist, dogmatic, authoritarian naturalism can provide a better answer to Zhuangzi's argument than Mencius can. The three problems with Mencius' theory of the heart as an inner source of guidance with conclusive moral implications apply mutatis mutandis to any inner Dao.[46] It does not matter how sublime, mystical, obscure, or incommensurable it is. So I have this inner guide; why should it rule my nose? Why preach about it since everyone has it, cannot fail to have and follow it? Besides, Zhuangzi, like Laozi, sees that we learn our *shi-fei* from growing up in the world, not from some prior, antecedent reality. We *do* follow *dao*, but there are many of them. *Dao* does create things—in multiple and constantly changing ways. Zhuangzi would have to be wholly incapable of reflective self-criticism to believe in an inner manifestation of some absolute Dao after refuting Mencius the way he does.

If we have followed this argument aright, we can see that Zhuangzi saw what the traditional interpreters do not. No nativist, antilanguage, intuitive conclusion follows from his analysis of language. Far from condemning all language, he treats it all as natural. It can hardly follow from this that we should stop using language. His image and his argument allow him to regard the use of language, distinctions, conventions as perfectly natural, indeed tragically unavoidable. He sees that we have a powerful impulse to *postulate* some paramount basis of our desires, reactions, and feelings. He also says that we *can never find* that *true ruler*. He knows Hui Shi's argument does not follow. He knows, I shall argue, that its conclusion is incoherent.

The Refutation of the Neo-Mohists

Despite the obscurity of putting doctrines metaphorically, poetically, and in the mouths of various figures, Zhuangzi's essay develops in a logically natural way. His position is that all the different ways of dividing similar and different and acting on those discriminations are equally natural. Two natural objections to this view in his philosophical milieu concern Zhuangzi. The first was Mencius', which argues that the heart-mind has an innate structure of *shi-fei* attitudes. Heaven wants us to follow uniquely these responses in action. Having dispensed with Mencius' innate idealism, Zhuangzi turns to a more serious challenge.

The Neo-Mohists conceptually structure their intended reality. They assume a pattern of similarity and difference that is independent of language and that provides an external standard to which our language should conform. This formal realism gives them a regulative ideal for our system of names. It allows the Mohist escape from relativist incoherence. Our language should reflect the similarities and differences in reality. Thus the *shi-fei* of language ought to conform to the real structure of things.

The Neo-Mohists, holding this realistic semantics, would also object to the pipes-of-heaven metaphor. It does not explain why we take our *bian* seriously. Why do we think that we disagree when we make different noises? We do not disagree when I sing an A-flat and you sing a C. Language must be more than natural noise.

Zhuangzi puts the realists objection in this way: "Language is not merely blowing breath."[47] Language has, Zhuangzi says, *something it languages,* an intended reference. Language is about something. The essential difference between language and noise, then, is its *aboutness.* Language picks out thing-kinds. The structure of reality undergirds and informs where we should draw the line of discrimination among thing-kinds.

Zhuangzi does not directly contest the view that language has a relation to things. He notes, instead, that the relation between language and the world is never fixed. So, if the aboutness relation is constantly changing, is language finally about something or is it not? Does reliance on its aboutness distinguish language from the sound of a baby bird emerging from its egg? Is there a *bian*[distinction] or no distinction?[48]

If one way of relating language and reality were *correct,* then the others would be wrong. If there were such a distinction between *dao*[doctrines] as *authentic*[49] and *artificial,* how could we fail to notice it?[50] If language really had *shi*[this] and a *fei*[not this], what could hide it? Why would we would have trouble telling whose language had the appropriate privileged relation?

Zhuangzi shifts the focus of the argument from the realist regulative ideal, to the problem of knowledge. He does not dispute that one language *might* have a better fit with reality than another. What explains why it is so hard to tell which one it is? What good can this regulative ideal do us if we have *no way of telling which* conceptual scheme has the privileged relation to reality? He questions the usefulness of the regulative ideal of realism.

Given the shared pragmatic focus on language and *dao,* how could nature *intend* only one. How can we walk a way that does not have a relation to what exists? How can a language exist and not be appropriate?[51] All languages must fix on some real patterns of similarity and difference. All languages involve what we called thick concepts that are strongly world guided. Each appears to its adherents to be the obviously correct way to carve things up. They all work in a real context. Of course all *dao*s and language internally determine their own pragmatic standards. For there to be a language *is* for there to be a standard of appropriateness which it meets in application to the world. How will we find a neutral basis to judge between these warring standards of appropriateness in the application of concepts? What use can the regulative ideal serve in settling disputes about how to make distinctions?

Zhuangzi's barrage of questions reminds us that language is not merely a picture of the world but part of a guiding *dao.* He thus reminds us that the fit of names to reality is always in the context of a guiding form of discourse. It always presupposes some value, some purpose. Is the standard of value itself part of the pattern of similarity and difference in things?

Zhuangzi's questions about *dao* and *yan*^{language} are parallel. How can either fail to be what it claims. Any *dao* that we actually practice will exist (hence be natural or *heavenly*). Any language that exists will be *ke*^{permissible}.

What misleads us about prescriptive doctrines or theories is that each comes with its own standard of *cheng*^{accomplishment}.[52] We cannot decide which is more successful because the standard of success is internal to the *dao* in question. From some other view it may be small and unimportant. Any doctrine serves some purposes and practicing it can give a sense of accomplishment (after all the goals of a practice are internal to the practice). Similarly, what misleads us about a language is that we can elaborate on it endlessly. We can spell out any form of language use in ever greater detail. Creative language users can mesmerize their followers to almost any degree. No amount of exercise of a conceptual pragmatic perspective is going to settle which is the really correct one.

Zhuangzi's favorite example of this phenomenon is the contrast of Mohism and Confucianism. Here are two *dao*s of life underwritten by two ways of deploying distinctions of *shi-fei.*[53] They each, with total sincerity and assurance, find the other wrong. Confucian partisans can spell out the Confucian use of language in immense detail. We can turn it in either the Mencius or the Xunzi direction. The Mohists, similarly, can elaborate and develop Mozi's use of language. Zhuangzi is not going to launch a direct attack on these two languages. His point can more easily be made by merely observing their conflict.

Zhuangzi does offer us a *dao* of his own, then. He develops a language in which to discuss the functioning of languages: a *dao* of *dao.* This metaview of the role of language in governing distinctions and attitudes he calls *ming*^{understanding} or *clarity.* If you want to *shi* what others *fei* and *fei* what others *shi,* you always can, once you *ming*^{understand}.[54] Understand what? Mystics think the reference is to some transcendental mystical form of knowledge. I think it is understanding the nature of perspectives: his theory of the indexicality of language.

Language and Indexicality

Indexicals are terms in a language whose reference changes with features of the context. An obvious example is *wo*[I]. It picks out a different individual depending on who uses it. Similarity, *shi*[this] and *bi*[that] are indexicals even when used by the *same* person. They pick out different objects depending on the speaker's position in relation to the objects. By moving the speaker's reference point, we change what is *shi*[this] and *bi*[that]. Time words—*today, tomorrow, now, before*—change their reference to moments of time as each moment passes.

Such indexical terms are the basic context-dependent terms of language. My hypothesis is that Zhuangzi's *ming*[enlightenment] is that all language is indexical. Ordinary terms have their reference fixed by context as well. If I am talking about *the cat* you can only know what cat I mean by studying the context—previous reference to or proximity of some cat. In Chinese, without the clear marking of indexical and universal significance of nouns (the cat versus a cat, all cats, some cats) context dependence is even more striking. Even reference using proper names is highly context dependent. This is especially true where there are a hundred basic surnames and conventions of referring to individuals as *third sister Liu*.

Obviously, introducing indexicality is a way for Zhuangzi to reassert the pluralistic and pragmatic character of language. It vitiates the impact of the claim that language has aboutness. The Neo-Mohists had, themselves, paid some attention to the standard examples of pragmatic reference.[55] Zhuangzi makes context dependence the focal point of his attack on semantic aboutness. It buttresses his claim that nothing fixes the aboutness of language. It helps us see the deep linguistic point behind the story of big bird and little bird! The use of language depends more on our position than on the world.

Zhuangzi grants a semantic aspect of language. Language has aboutness, intentionality. But the particular setting determines its aboutness. Language has only indexical aboutness. What we refer to depends on the social and physical context in which we learn our words. In themselves, all thing-kinds are both *shi* and not *shi*.[56] From different points of view we cannot *see* something's being *shi*, the right thing or the thing referred to in the context. If we were in the context with another conceptual, grading perspective, we might *fei* it.

Thus Zhuangzi's perspective is not merely physical or visual perspective. Remember that *dao*s themselves and language are part of the natural world. Our having adopted or followed *some* pattern of language use (Confucian, Mohist, Christian, scientific, or conservative) puts us in the world with a different perspective. We will *shi* things differently and *bi*[that:other] things differently. *Shi* and *bi* are born together.[57] *Shi* and *bi* have complementary usage. They come into being and pass away together, both are permissible and impermissible of any object in itself.

Zhuangzi's argument moves smoothly from the indexical, demonstrative use of *shi* (where it contrasts with *bi*[other]) to the more evaluative use. The evaluative use contrasts less with *bi*[that] and more with *fei*[disapprove:wrong:not this]. With our different language perspectives we *shi*[assent] and *fei*[dissent] differently. We do not assent to sentences or truths, but to guiding distinctions. We apply and withhold terms with prescriptive significance to contextually selected segments of reality. We thus divide the real world as we walk in it.

When a *sheng*^{divine} of any tradition projects his *shi-fei* onto heaven, he is still basing his judgment on a perspective.[58] Having taken that perspective, it comes to feel like the perspective of heaven. Even if the purported heavenly perspective is one that treats *shi* and *fei* as one, there must be a language that licenses *oneing* them. So, in the end, is there really an aboutness in language, a real *shi-fei,* or is there none?[59]

The antilanguage interpretation assumes that the answer to the rhetorical question is none! All the arguments have shown is that there are many. Zhuangzi, however, merely leaves us with the double rhetorical question and precedes to further puzzles. Let us talk, he says, about talking about something, and about not talking about anything. Zhuangzi invites us to consider an Ur-perspective, a view from nowhere. That is the perspective from which *shi* and *bi* do not contrast and complement each other. He calls it the *hinge of* dao*s (dao-shu).* This is a hypothetical, unbiased, purely nonpurposive perspective that is prior to *any* system of language. Each pattern of prescriptive *shi*ing and *fei*ing starts from the center of a circle of infinite possibility. The view from the axis of *dao*s is not where nothing can be said. It is rather the point from which *anything* can be said with equal warrant. Once we say something, we step off the axis onto a particular *dao*^{path}. From the axis, we can go out at any angle. We can place no a priori limit on the possible pattern of *shi-fei* discriminations.[60]

I have used Zhuangzi's language to describe the relativity of name assignments to language perspective. Zhuangzi refers to the perspective this metalanguage gives us as *ming*^{clarity}. It allows us to see how we can reverse any prescriptive position. Any *fei* can be a *shi* and vice versa. We can abandon the elaborate and tortured sophistries of Gongsun Long. There are possible perspectives from which everything is a horse. From this universal perspective, this hinge of *dao*s, any pattern of *shi-fei* is a possible path. We can understand Gongsun Long's linguistic gymnastics with *zhi*^{finger point} and *ma*^{horse} better simply by contemplating directly the relativity of *shi* and *fei*—by *ming*^{clarity}[61].

In language, we permit the permissible, forbid the impermissible and thus generate a *dao* that action completes.[62] Things become the things they are (get separated from the undifferentiated kapok) because we distinguish and refer to them by terms in a language.

Now, can we make sense of a concept of *things as they inherently are?*[63] Are some things inherently permissible?[64] Are any distinctions right independent of languages in which we use them? Inherently, no thing can fail to be what it is or to be permissible. Zhuangzi's metalanguage speaks of the other languages. From the cosmic perspective all things (and all systems of classification of things) simply *are.* In that sense, nature permits them just as they are. Our talking about talking equalizes all discourse about things.

So from some perspective for *shi*ing we distinguish stalks and pillars, lepers and beauties. Yet, for things however strange and incongruous, some *dao* passes through them and treats them as one. In distinguishing and ranking them, they become *cheng*^{complete} in our mind.[65] By becoming complete or fixed they are damaged.[66] The only way to avoid being complete and therefore damaged is to avoid stepping off the hinge. We would have to go back to where every assignment is equally possible. But, what does that get us?

What is the point of this language of universal perspective, this perspective on perspectives? That we should say nothing? Do nothing? I have argued that Zhuangzi pointedly reverses this quietist mystical conclusion. The point is not to avoid language but to appreciate that many languages, many ways of *shi-fei*ing are possible. The useful advice is that we should be flexible, tolerant, aware of the infinite range of possible ways to respond to life. Getting locked into one makes us unable to see the benefits (and defects) of others. Is this flexibility possible? Can it be *dao*ed from within any *dao* other than a metalevel one, from this perspective on perspectives?

One who understands this metapoint does not use it. (It is of no use by itself except to give us a perspective on multiple perspectives). Finally, Zhuangzi cannot *recommend* his metaperspective as more natural than the others. All recommendation presupposes one among alternative perspectives. This was the point of the refutation of Mencius. Instead he says we can rest on the *usual* ways of talking.[67] These conventional ways are useful because they are shared and underwrite exchange with others. They unite us. We can claim success in the context of a shared agreement, a union with others. That is as much as we can expect.[68] If there is any recommendation by Zhuangzi here it is to do both at once. We see the vast evening out of all perspectives and still use ordinary *shi-fei*.

Beyond this sense of accomplishment relative to some shared *shi* perspective, we do not know the way things are. Zhuangzi's metaperspective does not lead to nonperspectival knowledge of things. It is not a window on the thing in itself, but on the bewildering range of possibilities. It leads us to a conception of the limits of knowing. We cannot know which *shi-fei* knowledge system to *shi*. If we use *dao* in Shendao's sense as the absolute, unknowable, inherent thusness of things, then treating *dao* as one presupposes that we *do* know the unknowable. What mystics treat as one is, by definition, what we cannot know.[69]

Kant seemed to think of his parallel conception of the thing in itself as a manifold. It was a multiple source of *feedback responses* or sensations. Daoists are theorizing in a tradition that does not stress constructing concepts out of sense experience. They deal with using language to make distinctions. A Daoist form of transcendental idealism would naturally tend to characterize the thing in itself counterpart as a *one*. Where Kant imagined knowledge as unifying a manifold, Daoists imagine it as distinguishing a whole into its parts. Zhuangzi, like Kant, allows that we cannot know anything about the absolute object of our conceptual systems. We cannot know, in particular, that it is either one or many. Our metalanguage of a higher or onceremoved perspective shows us only a perspective on the plurality of perspectives. Mysticism and skepticism emerge together. What might be one is what we cannot in principle know, given this concept of knowledge.

The difference between skeptics and mystics is not that we do *shi* and *fei* in one and do not in the other. Skeptics and mystics have exactly the same *shi-fei* content: none. But, practically, we cannot avoid *shi*ing and *fei*ing. The difference between them is merely a difference in attitude toward the *way* we *shi* and *fei*. The skeptic furrows his brow critically and experiences the failure of absolute knowledge as a disappointment. The mystic revels in the very incomprehensibility of it. Put in emotional language, the skeptic *hrmmph* and the mystic *aah* are responses to the same realization of the limits of language, like the monkeys who object to "three in the morning four in the evening, but are perfectly content with four in the morning three in the evening." [70] There is no difference in the substance or amount but a great difference in their emotional reaction.

David Hume appealed to a similar insight in his *Dialogues Concerning Natural Religion*. He made his skeptic, Philo, and his mystic, Demea, join forces. They jointly attack the rational theist, Cleanthes. [71] Both agreed that Cleanthes could not legitimately make any of the claims he was trying to make. Philo argued it was because he could not possibly have knowledge of God; Demea because no human concepts can apply to the incomprehensible deity. Both justify saying the same thing about God—to wit, nothing. The skeptic can say nothing about reality because we cannot prove it. The mystic can say nothing in principle about incommensurable reality. They thus say the same no-thing. One smiles more and has an awestruck look in his eyes. The other furrows his brow a lot.

A parallel comparison helps to capture the similarities between existentialism (especially Nietzsche's) and Daoism (especially Zhuangzi's). Both *discover* the practical pointlessness of universal or absolute *meaning* (purpose). Nietzsche, from his perspective as a disappointed Christian yearning for absolute, transcendent, dependence on God, experiences this awareness with existentialist *angst,* a sensation of looking off a cliff into a bottomless abyss. The angst is caused by the vertigo impulse, the fear we will jump or drop off our perch into that nothingness. Zhuangzi, from his Daoist sense of the constraint of conventional authority, does not think of any cliff as a reference point. If the abyss is bottomless, then there is no such thing as falling. The cliff and Zhuangzi are both floating free. Leaving the cliff and entering the abyss is weightlessness—free flight—not falling. From his relativistic perspective, the cliff is floating away. Zhuangzi's reaction is not "Oh no!" but "Whee!"

The Refutation of Absolute Monism (Primitive Daoism)

The problem comes when the monistic wears out his wits trying to say "All is one." He tries to turn mystical or skeptical silence into an assertion of monism. His position is like that of the skeptic who dogmatically expressed the impossibility of knowledge. Zhuangzi sees both as mistakes. The mistake is essentially that of the primitive Daoist that was diagnosed and criticized by the Neo-Mohists. If all is one, then there are no real distinctions and since language marks distinctions, all language must distort the *Dao*. All language, then, is perverse and all distinctions are *fei*[wrong].

Zhuangzi's wording of his skepticism shows that he recognizes the problem in postulating monism. He formulates monism as an ancient form of knowledge and he ranks it below nihilism.

> The knowledge of the ancients had a zenith. Where was it? There were those who regarded it as having nothing. That was the zenith. It exhausted it. Nothing could be added. Next to them were those who regarded it as having bound-

aries but no *shi-fei*. The emergence of *shi-fei* is the deficiency of *dao* and the *cheng* [completion] of desire.[72]

Shi and *fei* make any *dao* leave something out. They are also the formation of desire. Should we abandon this kind of distinction making? Can we avoid deficiency and *cheng* [completion]? Zhuangzi leaves us again with a double rhetorical question. Characteristically he regards completion and deficiency as a package. No guiding scheme can have one without the other. That does not mean we can regard this combination of completion and deficiency as *bad*, still less that there is a *dao* of avoiding it. (Any such *dao* would also have deficiency with its completion.) We must recognize that all the famous masters of knowledge of whatever skills were both completed *and* deficient. All have accomplished something and neglected something else. To avoid the pair is for them never to practice their skills.

Zhuangzi's reflections expose a paradoxical attitude toward *cheng* [completion]. Any bid to be complete must leave something out, have some deficiency. We have already seen that his attitude of openness and flexibility cannot be intelligible without *favoring* learning to *bian* [distinguish]. He has also refused to condemn the ordinary usefulness of conventional ways. We cannot ask for anything more profound than such interchangeable usefulness in our language. So, far from drawing the passive-withdrawal conclusion, Zhuangzi seems to celebrate pursuing some particular *dao* to mastery. Graham has appreciated this unexpected turn in Zhuangzi's worries about completion and difficulty.[73]

> Skepticism and relativism as extreme as Chuang-tzu's are not in themselves unfamiliar to a modern reader, far from it. What is perhaps strange to him is that there is no vertigo in the doubt, which pervades the most rhapsodic passages of a philosophical poet who seems always to gaze on life and death with unwavering assurance. But there is anguish in ethical skepticism only if one feels bound to choose in spite of having no grounds to choose. For Chuang-tzu, to pose alternatives and ask "Which is beneficial, which harmful?" or "Which is right, which wrong?" is the fundamental error in life. People who really know what they are doing, such as cooks, carpenters, swimmers, boatmen, cicada-catchers, whose instruction is always available to any philosopher or emperor who has the sense to listen to them, do not go in much for analyzing, posing alternatives, and reasoning from first principles. They no longer even bear in mind any rules they were taught as apprentices. They attend to the total situation and respond, trusting to a knack which they cannot explain in words, the hand moving of itself as the eye gazes with unflagging concentration.[74]

Graham's statement, however, attributes an unattested disdain for logic and reasoning to Zhuangzi. Zhuangzi puts the zither player, the music master, and the debater together. Why would he think the logician or the mathematician is less able to "know what he is doing" as than the dancer and the milkmaid? Posing and testing alternatives are what philosophers do as much as setting and driving nails is what carpenters do. Both gain a skill, apply their minds, and reach levels of performance at which they transcend any conscious processing of the first steps of this learning. What is Zhuangzi to say of himself as a philosopher theorizing about the indexicality of language? Can a cicada catcher pursue his craft without making distinctions? He must *shi*[is] cicadas and *fei*[is not] cockroaches. A carpenter must *shi* nails and *fei* screws for some tasks.

Zhuangzi seems to give unequivocal praise of skill mastery in the third chapter. In the tone setting piece for its title, "The Secret of Caring for Life," Zhuangzi draws a favorable portrait of skill-transcending specialization. His expression shows that, like Aristotle (or Confucius) he seems to recognize that human life offers no more fulfilling activity than the exercise of some acquired skill. Well-honed skills seem to invite paradoxical, mystical description. The performance itself pulls us along in a unity of actor and action. It is a way of *losing myself* that one may experience also in contemplation or trance. Our own actions sometimes mystify us. We do not understand how we did it; we certainly cannot explain it to others. Zhuangzi's description in this chapter is a classic:

> Cook Ding was slicing up an ox for Lord Wen-hui. At every push of his hand, every angle of his shoulder, every step with his feet, every bend of his knee— zip! zoop! he slithered the knife along with a zing, and all was in perfect rhythm, as though he were dancing to Mulberry Grove or keeping time as in Jing-shou music.
>
> "Ah, this is marvelous!" said Lord Wen-hui. "Imagine skill reaching such heights!"
>
> Cook Ding laid down his knife and replied, "What I care about is a *dao* which advances my skill. When first I began cutting up oxen, I could see nothing that was not ox. After three years, I never saw a whole ox. And now—now I go at it by spirit and do not look with my eyes. Controlling knowledge has stopped and my spirit wills the performance. I depend on the natural makeup, cut through the creases, guide through fissures. I depend on things as they are. So I never touch the smallest ligament or tendon, much less bone."
>
> "A good cook changes his knife once a year—because he cuts. A mediocre cook changes his knife once a month—because he hacks. I have had this knife of mine for nineteen years and I've cut up thousands of oxen with it. Yet the blade is as good as if it had just come from the grindstone. . . ."
>
> "Despite that, I regularly come to the end of what I am used to. I see its being hard to carry on. I become alert; my gaze comes to rest. I slow down my performance and move the blade with delicacy. Then zhrup! It cuts through and falls to the ground. I stand with the knife erect, look all around, deem it wonderfully fulfilling, strop the knife and put it away."

This story, though a nearly universal favorite, poses a problem for the absolutist.[75] They like the mystical sound, the reference to a *dao,* and they read the claim that *dao jin*[advances] skill as the claim that it *guo*[surpasses] skill. The traditional commitment to a mystical, monistic *dao* conflicts with Zhuangzi's conception of a *dao* that advances skill.

The last paragraph undermines any absolutist reading of the parable. It makes clear that Ding has hold of no absolute way of doing his thing. His way is constantly developing. He continues to progress in pursuing his skill by tracing his *dao* to points beyond his previous training. He comes to a hard part and has to pay attention, make distinctions, try them out, and then move on. The absolutist monistic interpretation cannot brook the suggestion that Ding knows his *dao* and *still improves*. How can you have part of a *dao* that has no parts? The "Star Wars" view of *Dao* makes grasping it an all or nothing matter. When you have it you suspend entirely all thought and sensation. Surrender yourself to the *Dao* and you can be saved! Cook Ding's is not a good story for those with religious-salvation views of Daoism.

The choice of a butcher for this parable seems significant too. Butchering is not a particularly noble profession. Zhuangzi's equalizing tendency shows us that this level of expertise is available within any activity. Further, note that his activity is cutting. Dividing something into parts. When he has mastered his guiding *dao,* it gives him a perception of the world in which the ox appears before him already cut up. He *comes* to see the holes and fissures and spaces as the inherent nature. That seems a perfect metaphor for our coming to see the world as divided into the natural kinds that correspond to our mastery of terms. Mastering any *dao* that works yields this sense of harmony with—control of and control by—the external world.

We may advance skill by learning any *dao*: dancing, skating, playing music, butchering, chopping logic, love-making, skiing, using language, programming computers, throwing pottery, or cooking. At the highest levels of skill, we reach a point where we seem to transcend our own self-consciousness. What once felt like a skill developing inside us begins to feel like control from the natural structure of things. Our normal ability to respond to complex feedback bypasses conscious processing. In our skilled actions, we have internalized a heightened sensitivity to the context.

We all recognize the sense of responsive awareness that seems to suspend self-other consciousness. It is natural to express this ideal of skill mastery in language that suggests mystical awareness. It *does* normally involve suspension of self-consciousness and ratiocination and seems like surrender to an external force. That language should not confuse us, however. Zhuangzi's *ming*[illumination] should help us see that the full experience is compatible with having his perspective on perspectives. Cook Ding can be aware that others may have different ways to dissect an ox. He simply cannot exercise his skill while he is trying to choose among them. We lose nothing in appreciating the multiple possibilities of ways to do things. In real-izing a *dao* of some activity in us, we make it real *in us*. It is neither a mere, inert cognition of some external force nor a surrender to a structure already innate in us.

The butcher does not say that he *began* at that level of skill. He does not report any sudden conversion during which some mystical insight flowed into him. He does not say that he could just *get in tune* with the absolute *Dao* and become a master butcher automatically. And he does not hint that by being a master butcher, he is in command of all the skills of life. He could not use his level of awareness at will to become a master jet pilot or a seamstress. His is not an account of some absolute, single, prior *dao* but of the effect of mastering some particular *dao*.

These reflections lead us to problems with *achieve dao mastery* as a prescription. I shall argue that the problems are both textual and theoretical. The text of the second chapter reflects a more equivocal attitude toward mastery. Any mastery, Zhuangzi notes, must leave something out. Most particularly, to master any skill is to ignore others. Zhuangzi remarks that masters are frequently not good teachers. They fail to transmit their mastery to their sons or disciples.

Zhuangzi directs our attention to this problem with the glorification of total skill dedication and mastery. We trade any accomplishment at one skill for ineptitude at some other thing. The absent-minded professor is our own favorite parody. If the renowned practitioners have reached completion, he says, then so has everyone. If they have not, then no one can. From the hinge-of-ways perspective, we no more value the world's top chess player than the world's finest *jack of all trades*. We should not read Zhuangzi as advocating specialization per se.

The theoretical problems begin when we address the consistency of this advice with the relativist insight behind *ming*^{enlightenment}. Zhuangzi's principle is that you cannot get a *shi* out without already having a *shi* prejudice *(cheng)*. It seems to block straightforward advocacy of sublime mastery. How can he *shi* skillful action and *fei* clumsy action? What counts as *cheng*^{successful} action is internal to the *dao* of the selected activity. There are even conflicting *styles* of the same thing: Ding, we may say, has mastered a butchering style, not butchering itself. Zhuangzi criticizes idealist Confucians for saying the heart cultivated in the sage's way is better than the fool's. How can he, then, turn around and assert a dogmatic standard distinguishing between the cultivated skilled butcher and the clumsy one?

Zhuangzi's metareflections lead us to wonder whether we have made the *right* distinction between knowledge and ignorance. This must, therefore, entitle us to doubt that we can distinguish between skill and clumsiness. (If we remember that *zhi*^{know} has the basic practical sense of know-to, these amount to the same thing.) Chinese martial arts movies sometimes glorify a fighting style known as drunken-style, which excels precisely because it looks so clumsy and out of control. Zhuangzi notes frequently the usefulness of being useless. That makes it hard to accept the claim that he thinks the standards of skillful *cheng*^{accomplishment} are perspective-free *givens*.

Again, how can Zhuangzi *fei* conscious monitoring without presupposing a value (a *shi*)? One can be a highly skillful practitioner of Hitler's *final solution*. Now we find the boast that one does it without any conscious reflection makes it more disgusting rather than more appealing.[76] One's state of mind could be like that of the highly skill rat exterminator. (Lest we forget to see the *beam* in our own eye, I should mention the skillful Indian fighter, Vietnam jet bomber pilot, CIA commando, and the *natural* politician who praises such *heroes* to get elected.)

The problem with Graham's contrasting the ethical philosopher who debates and considers alternatives with the cooks, carpenters, and cicada catchers has a familiar ring. It resembles the problem with Wittgenstein's *ordinary language* criticism of philosophy. We can practice philosophy, including ethical philosophy (searching for first principles), as a language game. We can reach a high level of skill and total absorption in that activity as surely as ballet dancer can. Where could Zhuangzi (or Wittgenstein) get off condemning philosophy as a legitimate activity while practicing it so sublimely themselves?

Consider chess mastery. It illustrates how the mind can be simultaneously applying conscious standards in deliberation while eliminating superfluous lines of play by virtually unconscious parallel processing. Chess is a *dao* in which eminent masters can *lose themselves* as surely as cicada catchers. One could hardly advise a chess master to *give up conscious thought,* yet he requires, as a photographer does, that cultivated intuition, total absorption, and awareness before he can reach a high level of performance.

Now Zhuangzi's *ming*^{illumination} is a *way* of viewing *ways*. It cannot imply Shendao's paradoxical conclusion that we should give up all ways. That all perspectives are partial does not mean that we should not adopt any perspective. Nor does it *shi* any particular subset of ways as naturally *better* (or worse) than others or even that all are equal. The perspective of nature makes no evaluative judgement at all. The Nazi exterminators were indeed horrible from our human moral perspective. If we were cockroaches we might have the same view of scientists who devise hormonal spray which could result in extinction of cockroaches. We are deficient in appreciation of these hearty and adaptive creatures. Must we suppose the cosmos shares our evaluative bias? The nuclear holocaust in Hiroshima and the genocidal holocaust in Europe were both a result of natural social laws in different social systems.

A more objectionable mistake is the converse. Some accuse Zhuangzi of a view which entails that Hitler was just fine. That comes from reading him as if he were Mencius. Mencius, not Zhuangzi, thinks that whatever is natural is good. Zhuangzi intends, I argue, to *undermine* that naive naturalist ethics by observing that whatever is actual is natural. He does *not endorse*, but *questions* the valuation of the natural. All valuation, he would argue, comes from *within* some *dao* perspective. Zhuangzi's relativism does not allow us to say that Hitler's perspective is *just as good* as our own. All it says is "Hitler happened." It was a consequence of natural laws that it happened. One cannot get *any* particular evaluation from the hinge of *dao*s, the cosmic perspective.

Evaluations of equality presuppose perspectives as much as evalutions of higher and lower. Strictly speaking, Zhuangzi's *ming*^{illumination} cannot evaluatively *equalize* different discourse about things.[77] It rather puts them in a nonevaluative perspective, one prior to any *shi-fei*. Any evaluation—*okay, equal, lower than, wonderful*—presupposes a *shi-fei* point of view. The extermination of the human species is plausibly a good thing from the view of other large mammals. I have an oceanographer friend who regards the basic form of pollution to be plant life that creates oxygen! Still, neither of these larger-than-human points of view qualifies as *the* cosmic perspective.

Zhuangzi would, no doubt, condemn Nazi skills from many of the perspectives he regularly adopts. Each would be a limited or partial perspective. The cosmic perspective neither approves nor condemns *nor treats as equal*. So what? It only gives us the healthy reminder that Hitler had a point of view and felt as righteous as Pat Robertson or Ronald Reagan. Zhuangzi does not say, "Say nothing." He does worry that we do not know when our saying is really saying or is not. The alleged sage's schemes dazzle us by slippery and dubious positions. Do not try to be sagelike and project your attitudes on heaven. We rest, as before, in the ordinary, convinced that is as far as we can go. Zhuangzi calls this reduced theoretical expectation *using the ming*^{illumination} perspective.[78]

Is all this metatalking different from other talking? Other talking generates a *shi-fei*. Is the *ming*^{clarity} perspective on perspectives unique in avoiding this? Zhuangzi observes that classing it as like or unlike is itself taking a sorting perspective on language levels. *Ming*^{clarity} must be like other use of language.[79] This perspective must see itself as *merely one perspective* on perspectives. However, Zhuangzi continues, let us experiment with saying something:

> There is a beginning. There is not yet beginning to be beginning. There is not yet beginning to be not yet beginning to be beginning. Suddenly we have not having and we do not know if having not having is having or not having.

Now I have just said something but I do not know if what I have said really counts as saying something or not saying anything.[80]

If we toy this promiscuously with language and our ordinary rules for language, do we still say something? Are these now just noises? Can I deny the law of excluded middle and still have my language be about something? If I violate the law is my language then about nothing? Neo-Mohist realism, recall, relies on the law of excluded middle. Can we talk without it? Zhuangzi merely raises the question and ends, as usual, with the double rhetorical question.[81]

There are other slippery, sagelike things we can pretend to say. There are profound expressions of Monism, like this Hui Shi–sounding pronouncement:

> The world includes nothing larger than the tip of an autumn hair and we can regard Mount Tai as small. No one lives any longer than a stillborn child and yet we can regard Old Peng as dying young. Heaven and earth were born together with me, and yet the ten thousand things and I are one.[82]

Now Zhuangzi reminds us of the problems of an *everything* concept. From already *wei*[deeming] it as one, can there be language as well? Does the claim that all is one mean that language cannot describe it? Having called it one, can it fail to include language? If it does include language, then the saying says something. The one and the saying make two, and two and one make three, and three and one make four and. . . .[83] We cannot, Zhuangzi concludes, coherently say that one thing exists as opposed to nothing. Even if we say there is nothing, we get something. Nothing is one, and something makes two and two and one make three, and off we go again. Better, Zhuangzi says never to start. Do not make any metajudgment about what there is.[84]

Thus monism cannot be the point of Zhuangzi's mysticism. What about the opposite: nihilism?

> Before *dao*s began there were boundaries. Before language began there was constancy.[85] If we accept this then there are guidelines. What are they? They are left and right [obvious indexicals], human relations and morality, divisions and distinctions, contention and strife. We call these the eight virtuosities! The sage picks and chooses his virtues according to his realms and periods.[86]

This suggests that there certainly are prelinguistic structures in things, even guiding structures. The problem for Zhuangzi is not attributing boundaries, but selecting *one* way of marking them from all the other possibilities. Even if there are natural boundaries, then for all the divisions we make, there are some we fail to make. For every distinction we draw, there are distinctions we ignore.[87]

So what do we do? The sage tries to embrace it all. The ordinary man makes distinctions to see some things together. So we say, those who make distinctions fail to see something. We do not try to enunciate an absolute *dao*. We do not try to put the ultimate distinction in language; we do not try to exercise some ultimate benevolence; we do not try to whole the great whole; we do not cultivate ultimate bravery. A *dao* projected on nature gives no guidance. We cannot make a distinction beyond the boundaries of language. Zhuangzi lists the absolutes that cannot make practical sense. Knowing our knowledge is limited and that there are other possibilities is as far as we can go![88]

> Who can know an unspeakable distinction? How can a non-guiding *dao* be a *dao*? Having this kind of knowing ability would be being able to put nature in storage. There would be no filling or draining the storehouse. That's the mystical boundary—the shaded light.[89]

The ordinary, usable conception of *dao*s is pluralistic. A *dao* guides the distinctions and discriminations we make and it measures the *success* of our response. Zhuangzi accepts the real context in which *dao*s operate. But that reality can only be an unknown, mystical *other,* the unknown context of our ways of knowing. We cannot know that it is one, that it is many, or that it is none. A real way things are is just another name for the context in which we exercise skills. The context provides the feedback responses that guide the execution of some internalized program of action.

However, the reality is not part of any *dao*able *dao*. No characterization of it is neutral with respect to the implicit purposes of various *dao*s. Reality is a purpose kapok. A particular *dao* consists of one pattern of discriminations and *shi-fei*ing of outcomes. The kapok then determines what course of events consists in a practitioner's following her *dao*. Even the distinction between a *dao* and the *Ding-an-sich* in which it operates is one made from within a *dao*. Specifically, the *dao* is Zhuangzi's metalanguage, a *dao*-of-*dao*s perspective. Best not even to mention it, he warns.

Dreaming and Skepticism in Zhuangzi

So far Zhuangzi's skepticism has been very different from that familiar to beginning students of Western philosophy. Our traditional paradigm form of skepticism has been skepticism of the senses, not of language. In a typical argument for Western sense skepticism, one finds the argument from dreams playing a central motivational role. The argument usually goes like this: when I am dreaming I seem to be experiencing a real world, but it turns out I am not; now I seem to be experiencing the real world, but it could similarly turn out that I am not.

The sense skeptic uses the argument about dreams to motivate a special meaning to the term *experience*. Western thinkers use *experience* to refer to an inner, private sensation linked to the notion of a subjective, cognitive mind. The received sense items have an evidential content. They are *data*—the building blocks of ideas, beliefs, thoughts, and concepts. Nonphilosophers, by contrast, use *experience* in a nonmental sense as our actual, physical undergoings. An experience in the nonphilosophical sense is some bodily interaction with the world. The dominance of epistemology in Western thought has blended the ordinary and the philosophical uses of the term. *Experience* (philosophical sense) is supposed to be the indubitable evidence available to any individual who may doubt that *experience* (normal sense) has taken place. The argument from dreams together with this special sense of *experience* undermines our confidence that knowledge is ever possible. It makes us unable to prove or guarantee that our experiences are of the external world, since we might have such internal mental states when nothing is actually going on.

Not all dream arguments, however, must presuppose this cluster of mental concepts. Zhuangzi's discussion of dreams, by contrast, comes at the *end,* not at the beginning, of his skeptical reflections. The problem of dreams does not *motivate* his skepticism but is a consequence of a deeper prior skepticism. He does not use the argument to give a special mental meaning to *experience* or to argue for a private, subjective inner mental notion of knowledge or evidential data.[90]

Let us look more carefully at the character of Zhuangzi's skepticism. It faces the same challenge as pyrrhonism. Is the skeptic herself not making a dogmatic claim? She claims to know that we do not know anything. Zhuangzi's version reminds us again of the parallel he draws between skepticism and mysticism. Neither can be coherently stated. His formulation makes clear the difference between his skepticism and Western skepticism. He does not doubt a belief, the belief that we know nothing. He questions instead whether we $zhi^{\text{know-how}}$ to use $zhi^{\text{know-how-to}}$ and its opposite correctly. How do we know that we correctly apply the (know-how-to-use-the) distinction between $zhi^{\text{knowledge}}$ and $bu\text{-}zhi^{\text{ignorance}}$?

> Gaptooth asked Wang Ni, "Do you know what all things agree in *shi*ing?" Answer: "How would I know it?" "Do you know that which you do not know?" Answer: "How would I know it?" "In that case, nothing has knowledge?" Answer: "How would I know that? Still let me try to word it. How could I know that what I call *knowledge* is not *ignorance* and what I call *ignorance* is not *knowledge*?"[91]

Gaptooth's question reminds us that the basis of Zhuangzi's skepticism is the multiplicity of perspectives and the way those different perspectives project term distinctions in novel contexts. If all things agreed on their projections, would that not be certain? Wang Ni's answer goes to the problem of interpretation. How would I know that all things agreed in their *shi*ing? It cannot merely be because they accept the same codebook. Learning a *dao* is learning to interpret it in action. There are multiple *ways* to do this, just as there are multiple ways to do any other action. Thus, even given some particular *dao,* we cannot tell when someone has knowledge of it without presupposing a *dao* of interpreting the first *dao.* Then we can worry about how to interpret the interpretive *dao* and so on.

Does the multiplicity of perspectives enable us to know that we do not know? Obviously not. It does not follow from there being other ways of life that ours is wrong. (Notice that if we were discussing propositional knowledge, it would undermine the knowledge claim. Even if our beliefs were true, the chance that we have not considered some alternative perspective may undermines the justification of the belief).

Is the conclusion, then, absolute skepticism, that nothing knows anything? To know *that* requires knowing that we are using the right concept of knowledge, the uniquely correct way of distinguishing between know and not know. If judgments of knowledge come from within perspectives, then there are many knowledge-ignorance distinctions. Even if everyone *shi*ed alike, we could not know it to be the absolutely correct way to *shi.* We cannot even know that we do not know.

An important feature of the Chinese concept of *zhi* knowledge is that it marks the continuity of human and animal knowledge. Zhuangzi then exploits that to undermine our assumption that even human unanimity in guiding preference provides a basis for absolute value distinctions.[92]

> Humans eat the flesh of hay-fed and grain-fed beasts, deer eat the grass, cen-tipedes relish snakes, owls and crows crave mice; which of the four has a proper sense of taste? Gibbons are sought by baboons as mate, elaphures like the com-pany of deer, loaches play with fish. Mao-ch'iang and Lady Li were beautiful in the eyes of men; but when the fish saw them they plunged deep, when the birds saw them they flew high, when the deer saw them they broke into a run. Which of these four knows what is truly beautiful in the world?[93]

That leaves us, again, with Mozi's basic natural standard. There is still the pragmatic preference for benefit over harm. Might that be what any person *must* take for granted in pursuing guidance? A pragmatist would confront Zhuangzi's skeptical relativism with the observation that certain *dao*s, in the real context, promote survival and others risk extinction. Without claiming that some perspectives are ultimately right, we surely can claim that some are more practical than others. Zhuangzi would allow this objection, but he would point out that the preference for life over death is a preference based on a distinction from a point of view. That preference might in principle be wrong: death might be preferable to life.[94]

> So Wang Ni answers, who knows what the ultimate human may take as beneficial and harmful? He may not be burned by fire, ride in a chariot in the sky, cross the seas and find ways into and out of death so they no longer mean anything to him.[95]

Then Zhuangzi turns to parody the effort to turn this awareness of the infinite possibility of perspective into an antilanguage, quietist, Shendao-like wu-wei no deeming affirmation. If we try reversal and do not worry about benefit and harm, do not have any purpose, do not follow any *dao,* do not call anything anything, we miss the point. The questioner attributes the quietest proposal to Confucius and Zhuangzi rid-icules it as trying to draw an easy conclusion.[96]

The point is that we presuppose something in preferring life to death. That does not mean we should stop! Still, we were just as dead before we were born as we will be after we die. Why would we lament the limit of our lives in one direction and not the other? How do we know that our distinctions mark *real* preferences? It is in the context of this worry that Zhuangzi finally introduces the subject of dreams. The distinction between dreaming and waking, like the distinction between life and death, good and bad food, comfort and pain, attractive and repulsive, is a distinction we may query. What do we leave out when we make that distinction? What purpose does it serve? Do we always draw it at the right place? Do we put it to the best practical use? Dreaming divides part of *what happens* from other parts of what hap-pens.

> When we dream, we do not know to apply the term *dream* to what is going on. Within a dream, we may treat part of our dream as *dream*. When we wake, we

know to *dream* the whole episode. How do we know that we will not come to a perspective from which we will *great dream* all of this? And only the stupid regard it as *awake*?[97]

Notice that Zhuangzi's argument *generates* dream skepticism out of linguistic, distinction-marking skepticism. Zhuangzi does not use it to propose a new meaning of *experience* or any hypothesis about subjectivity, inner minds, privacy, indubitability, or any other of the familiar apparatus of Western sense skepticism. His point is that the distinction of dreaming and waking is one we use in talking about what goes on. We may be using it rightly or wrongly. Maybe we should have a three-way distinction between dreaming and waking and a totem walkabout. Maybe someone will come along who will have a better distinction altogether.

Maybe we misuse the dreaming-waking distinction? Maybe the category of dreams, instead of licensing us to discard the thing we have undergone, should license treating it as an avenue to transhuman archetypes. We should cherish dreams as a window on our chaotic sexual impulses or as a way to correct our psychological problems or as a way to pick a spouse. The skepticism is about distinctions and their use, not about sense data and their representational character—or lack of same.

Zhuangzi's answer to the Neo-Mohists ultimately then must be only the skeptical one. He cannot say that no distinctions are real or that all are equally good or even that all is one. Indeed, his position implicitly allows for a real world that interacts with our *dao*s to yield *cheng*[successes] judged from within the *dao* itself. He offers no reason to reject the Neo-Mohist's abstract demonstration that there is a right way to distinguish. If we disagree, the Mohists showed, at least one of us must be wrong.

His answer, instead, is pragmatic. What good can it possibly do us to know, in the abstract, that one perspective is right and one is wrong? It is impossible to get outside of a perspective in trying to find out which is right and wrong. How can we judge between different systems of making distinctions? Their standards are internal to their *dao*s. Disputes are disputes about how to discriminate. We have no way to find a perspective that yields an absolute judgment about them. If we go to the absolute perspective, we get silence (or white noise, which we cannot tell from silence). We find no way of seeing who is right and who is wrong. We will always find ourselves preferring certain points of view, but we can never know that they are ultimately right.

> Suppose you and I *bian*[dispute:discriminate] and you convince me and I do not convince you. Does that make your position *shi* and mine *fei*? If I convince you and you do not convince, me, is my position *shi* and yours *fei*? Is one of them *shi* and one of them *fei*? Could they both be *shi*? or both *fei*? You and I together cannot know this and others must be even more confused. Who would I get to rectify it? If I got someone different from both of us to rectify it, since he is different from both of us, how can he rectify it? If I got someone like both of us to rectify it, since he is like both of us, how can he rectify it? So you and I together with others cannot know it. Shall we wait for some *bi*[other]?[98]

Graham regards the Neo-Mohist argument about *bian*—the proof that in any *bian* one of the parties will be right—to have answered Zhuangzi. Technically, however, Zhuangzi does not contradict that result. His position is not a metaphysical one rejecting a right way to make distinctions (that would be a dogmatic claim). He shows only that any *shi*ing of a way of making distinctions presupposes some other *shi*. He is making the epistemological claim that we do not and could not occupy a perspective from which we could know that a given perspective is finally right.

Zhuangzi's argument undermines all forms of authority. An authority—your teacher, your school, total human agreement, even nature—is just another perspective. It cannot settle who is right. Even an absolute *dao* (a divine-command morality, for example) would fall to the same argument. How do we know God is right?

The relation of *daos* ^{doctrines} and interpretations is like the relation of penumbra and shadow. You cannot cut a guiding *dao* loose from its interpretation in performance—a relation of dependence on some other dependence on some other, on some other, on . . .[99]

Then returning finally to dreams in a famous closing passage, Zhuangzi for the first time refers to himself.

> Once Zhuang Zhou dream-regarded [himself] as a butterfly—a fluttering butterfly fulfilling its desires and purposes who did not know Zhou. Suddenly he woke and plainly was Zhuang Zhou. We do not know if Zhou dream-regarded himself as a butterfly or a butterfly dream-regarded himself as Zhuang Zhou. Between Zhuang Zhou and the butterfly there must be some division. This is called the transformation of things.[100]

As I argued in connection with Laozi, we more plausibly regard the transformation of things as linguistic flux than as natural flux. *Dao* is constantly changing; that is not a metaphysical claim but a claim about discourse. Constant nature privileges no *dao* uniquely. Each *dao* projects a different nature. Zhuangzi is a clever enough skeptic and philosopher to avoid going beyond his evidence. His evidence, however, is not inner experience, but language. His skepticism is skepticism of how we use language in shaping our heart-minds' assents, dissents, desires, aversions, and behavior. In doing it, we project distinctions on the world, create a framework of things to which we react. There *may* be a right and wrong way to do that, but from where (from what *dao* perspective) would we know which it is?

Science and the Division of Fact and Value

One way to put the point of relativism is to deny that apparent disagreements are real. That is to place the perspective of the judgment within the judgment itself. We normally treat the Mohists and the Confucians as really disagreeing. One treats something as *shi* and the other as *fei*. Now imagine that we read them as judging the thing as *shi*-from-my-point-of-view and as *fei*-from-my-point-of-view rather than simply as *shi* and as *fei*. Then they do not really disagree because both could be right. The judgments do not exclude each other. The appearance of a disagreement arising from *bian* is an illusion. We are, after all, merely *blowing breath*.

This is a version of the antilanguage view. It treats all discriminations as matters of taste. The apparently conflicting views are really fully coherent. They together constitute the natural *Dao*. The *Dao* is the sum of whatever goes on, and these ways of speaking *go on*.

I had once been tempted to the view that such was Zhuangzi's position. *Dao* is a sum concept and the *dao*s of individual schools are part of that *Dao*. But that requires the notion of an all-embracing *Dao*, a notion Zhuangzi suggests cannot be made coherent. The ordinary guiding *dao*s do take themselves to be disagreeing. They seek for an ideal of resolving disputes. They take the disputes to be *real* disputes. The realistic urge is part of the content of at least some *dao*s. Those who use them cannot coherently view themselves as having no real disagreement.

Thus, I now read Zhuangzi as taking a position that does not reject metaphysical realism. He is merely skeptical about the *usefulness* of the realist, regulative ideal of one right answer. Our inability to get outside of our purposive conceptual perspectives to determine which is right makes building a transcendent ideal into our *dao*s useless. But a limited ability to step back from our perspective may help us to achieve purposes that are already part of the perspective. Perhaps there *are* ways to select among *dao*s.

The least appealing way to do this is a kind of Darwinian natural selection of *dao*s. We cannot say the fittest *dao*s survive. Daoism, after all, declined in the face of orthodox Confucianism, a convincing reductio (from the present perspective) of Darwinist Daoism. More appealing proposals would try to discern some more grandiose but still limited purposes in which to embed *dao*s. We could adopt a perspective from which we view ourselves as bit actors in the attempt by the solar system to save the sun from extinguishing its nuclear fuel. Still, from the larger point of view of the galaxy, the *shi-fei* of this solar system is a matter of indifference. It would be so even if it happens to be the only one with life (let alone intelligent life).

The point is that purposiveness is always pluralistic. All purposiveness presupposes a *shi* standard. It picks some range that it approves and some it disapproves. Cosmic absolutism cannot yield purpose. There can be no necessary preference for breadth of purpose. From a God's-eye view, Hitler must have been fulfilling God's plan and purposes. Taking such a point of view is irrational for us, however. It can at most provide a technique for reducing anger or filling idle time with provocative conversation, etc. It yields no argument for revising our existing point of view that Hitler was evil.

Accordingly, we should not view Zhuangzi as an individualist. He does not ground his view in the theory of the value of individual agents. The basic units of his pluralistic theory are indices of perspective. Individuals may share the same perspective, and one individual can successively adopt quite different ones in different times and places. The first question is not "Why avoid egoism?" (a learned, sophisticated form of response). It is rather "Why not follow erratic perspectival whim?" We could just follow this perspective here now rather than cultivate an awareness of perspectives we may have later in life. The Confucian awareness also focuses on a limited base but one broader than the egoists—the family. The Mohist starts from a still broader area of evaluative concern (the people and state). The Buddhists start from a *still* broader perspective (life or sentient beings). However, that does not make one of them really *shi* and the others really *fei*.

We can also adopt a familiar purpose that I think did not present itself to Zhuangzi. We may develop a *dao* guided by the purpose of accumulation of purely explanatory knowledge. We may be looking for constant regularities in the real world. That goal may be independent of any other purpose except that accumulation of descriptive knowledge which may be useful from a variety of purposive perspectives. This would be to adopt the *dao* of science. Those who adopt such a *dao* may be able to ride chariots in the sky, revive people from death, create hearts from plastic, and work many other wonders—except perhaps, preventing their own self-destruction.

Evaluation and Reason

Zhuangzi had neither a concept of science nor of a rational faculty. Thus, I reject portraying Zhuangzi as an *anti*rationalist. One could only project what he would say about rationality or what he would say about science. Rationality, as Kant saw it, is an attempt to transcend particularity. It resulted in universal, constant prescriptions (categorical imperatives). This perspective should give a neutral, universal, autonomous ground for settling disputes.

Zhuangzi would, supposedly, be skeptical that any perspective satisfies that description. In this general sense, Mencius' heart-mind is like the concept of reason, a purportedly universal source of ethical judgment. Western ethics frequently called on a notion of rational intuition. Zhuangzi's analysis of the rise of intuition from training would probably incline him to object to such a concept as he did to Mencius.

But the Western concept of reason is not just of *any* neutral perspective. Its paradigm is a particularly highly structured linguistic process. The paradigm model of reason is the deductive proof structure first developed in geometry. The Western tradition elevated this powerful notion of rational process to a central place in philosophy. It thus focused on the logical process, sentential information, and truth.

Although the conception of reason has had a long history of association with ethics, it has been a troubled history. One source of the problem has been the observation that the outcome of a rational process in ethics should be an action. The deductive proof structure, however, typically produced only a sentence. That seemed adequate for epistemology. It explained how one belief rationalized another belief.[101] The practical syllogism was an adaptation of the proof format to deal with actions as it did with sentential beliefs.

The practical syllogism, therefore, required that the premises include some motivating element that could produce action as a conclusion. This conception led to the traditional Western explanation of action as based on desire and belief. Western theories accordingly treat desire as sentential, as desires for states of affairs. They could not function with beliefs in the structure if this were not true. Zhuangzi has no such sentential conceptions either of desires or belief states. But we could construct a doubt about this conception of practical reason out of some of Zhuangzi's concerns.

The conclusion of a practical syllogism with sentential desire (or statements of value or obligation) and beliefs will be a sentence. It may state an obligation, assert that a state of affairs has value, or express a derived (and rationalized) desire. The gap between this sentence and an action will still require the practical interpretation that grounds most of Zhuangzi's skepticism. How will we know what consists in acting on this desire or value conclusion? To do that, we will need to be able to rectify the terms in the sentence. And that will presuppose an interpretive standard that cannot itself be proved by the same deductive structure.

But this would not amount to opposing or condemning *reason*. It is *no worse off* than any other perspective guiding action. In many ways it is a product of a search for greater constancy or reliability of process.

Zhuangzi's supposed attitude to modern, rationalized *dao*s such as science, rational morality, or the rule of law would be that they all presuppose something. All rational *dao*s are systems of *shi*ing and *fei*ing based on the desirability of calculation and the realist's regulative ideal, the assumption of a single correct answer. But it does not follow that he would reject them. We can take Zhuangzi's fanciful discussions of the people who can survive in fire, be warm in freezing temperatures, fly in the clouds, stride on the moon, and wander beyond the four seas as speculative predictions. There could be ways of assigning *shi* and *fei* which would lead to such accomplishments. Science is an example of such a *dao*.

In making that point in ancient China, however, Zhuangzi was urging exploration of new *dao*s. He did not have a clear conception of the scientific *dao* of hypothetical-deductive reasoning. Meeting science now, he might applaud this marvelously beneficial *dao*. He may also note that we measure its success using its own internal standards of *cheng* ^{completion}. Who knows, after all, what other ways of getting skill over nature might still be possible? Why rest satisfied with science as a *dao*? Something, as much more powerful than science as science is more powerful than peasant divination, may still be discoverable.

Should that possibility justify skepticism of science? Zhuangzi's answer, I suggest, would be no. For us, science is the usual, conventional, shareable system of settling *shi-fei*. There is certainly no reason to abandon it, in fact, one can get as proficient in its evaluative standards as in any other craft or skill. Thus there is no reason to regard Zhuangzi as either antiscientific or antirational.

Practical Advice

Ming ^{clarity} (a metalanguage view of pluralism of linguistic perspectives) cannot *shi any specifiable* way and advocate practicing it to the point of spontaneous response: "So what?" We cannot *help* having a *shi-fei* system. The way to deal with Zhuangzi's ambivalence about accomplishment and defect is that we cannot neutrally *shi* specialization and advocate skill mastery. We also cannot neutrally *shi* nonphilosophical *dao*s, or *shi* jack-of-all-*dao* *dao*s. One could follow one *dao* or many. We cannot, admittedly, follow none. From our meta–point of view, we cannot justify preferring any one to another.

So far, then we have been able to get the following qualified advice out of Zhuangzi's metaperspective. We must carefully state it, point by point. Each, as we saw above, involves potentially paradoxical conflict with the others.

Flexibility. There are many possible *dao*s, ways of distinguishing in action and in grading results—*cheng* ^{accomplishment}. Zhuangzi favors being open to that awareness. That awareness connects Zhuangzi to the traditionally Daoist anticonventional attitudes and the Daoist conception of freedom. When Zhuangzi talks of it, he associates the flexibility that goes with awareness and ability to switch *dao*s with youth. He associates the total commitment to one that prevents us from seeing the value of another with old age and death.

Convention. Zhuangzi clearly sees that his *detached* point of view does not justify condemnation of convention. If he equalizes *lun*^{theories} of things, then he has to regard the usual, conventional ones as equal. There is no reason to avoid them; in fact, because conventions yield agreement, interchange, and usefulness, they do all that any *dao* can do. What more can we ask of a *dao*?

Mastery. We must adopt some *dao*. Even mystical monistic or skeptical ways of talking are *ways of talking*. They affect our attitudes, emotions, and actions. Given that we do adopt some perspective, we spontaneously appreciate the accomplishment of skill mastery in that *dao*. That consists in following a *dao* to the point that we get beyond its words and conscious deliberate guidance to the point of second-nature, spontaneous, aware responsiveness.

We can characterize Zhuangzi's position using the Chinese epistemological concept of know-(how)-to. We know to do things in contexts set by our reality feedback (*qing*^{feelings}). The outcome of knowledge is an action that *cheng*^{completes} the act according to a presupposed system of *shi-fei*. Our *knowledge* consists in making real our chosen *dao* (course of action). Mencius taught that a full knowledge of this sort was in our innate potential. Zhuangzi thought that it comes with instilling, learning a *shi-fei* pattern that guides action.

Zhuangzi says *"Shi-fei is what I call qing."* The feedback responses are reality sensitive directing attitudes. But even *qing*^{reality responses} are conditioned by linguistic perspective. My inner process does not supply me with beliefs about where valued objects are which then combine with desires to direct my course. My intuition functions in the context of an action with *shi-fei* feedback. This indexical feedback directs my motor faculties.[102]

Zhuangzi's conception of action at a high level of skill stresses the spontaneity of the response to a total situation. That response is nearly immediate because the feedback process becomes second nature. In initial training we learned distinctions consciously, deliberately, and with frequent correction. When we have picked it up, we shift the distinction making out of consciousness. It is as if our consciousness were the central processing unit and the distinction is made by an unconscious parallel processor. The parallel processor sends the *shi-fei* result to out consciousness. We come upon things as *such-and-such*. Our response to it is *as if* we had responded unmediated to the world in which the the distinction was a given.

Realized in us, then, the *dao* of whatever we are learning is a skill structure. The structure in us that guides action in response to the situation is *de*^{virtuosity}. We can speak of this guidance as *intuitive,* but not as innate. We learn it as our *dao* advances our skill. Remember again that the intuitive knowledge is knowing-to. It is not intuitive prediction or representation of other's thoughts, unseen events, and so on. Intuition, like knowledge, is practical, not cognitive. So understood, Zhuangzi's departure from Laozi is that he does not propose to abandon the socially acquired, intuitive know-how. He recommends only maintaining a certain openness and flexibility. We can benefit (from our own perspective) from awareness that ours is not the only way to structure things. Beyond that, he pragmatically accepts the ordinary, shared, useful programming and accepts the satisfaction of mastery. We do learn to act on intuition, second nature. We experience this mastery of a skill as a loss of self—total absorption in the activity. We become the expression of the *way* of archery, motorcycle maintenance, and stock prediction. We have seen this ideal in Confucius (who acquired the ability at age seventy to follow his heart and not transgress the moral rules). And it is in Mencius (though he thought it was innate and not learned).

The achievement of skill mastery becomes the mature Daoist notion of spontaneity. Intuitive, immediate, nonself-conscious, intimately aware sensitivity to context in performance marks this mastery. In cybernetic terms, our actions involve constant feedback mechanisms which operate at such speed and accuracy, that they resemble massive parallel processing. It is not that I should turn my mind off. The point is that a parallel processor now handles my walking, which once took my full concentration. It frees the central processing unit for other activities: concentration on reading the map or carrying on the philosophical argument. Central processing consciousness also *kicks in* whenever we are learning or coming to a *hard place*. Sometimes I have to pay attention to my walking and cannot continue the philosophical conversation. In normal skilled action, the mind is processing a vast number of clues at once. It guides our action without routing the information through our conscious central processing unit. Our mind is both shut off (the central processing unit) and yet fully turned on (the parallel-processing feedback guidance of action).

This computer analogy of the Daoist view of intuition or spontaneous action gives us a way to illuminate the contrast in the theory of mind in the two traditions. The Western concept of mind and of the computer is of the *information* processor. The CPU takes in information. The processor exists relative to a cognitive stuff, information. The unit stores information in memory cells, operates on the information, and reports the result, information output. This reflects the Western focus on conscious thought, deliberation, and choice as cognitive.

The Chinese view of heart-mind focuses on guiding behavior. The mind receives reality-feedback inputs (*qing*) and processes them all at once (paralleling processing). The output is not a computational result stored in some memory cell or reported out as information. The output is an action. When we have learned to do anything *like second nature,* we constantly adjust our performance to myriad clues in the environment. We do not mediate the fine adjustment of motor skills by conscious choice. We act, it seems, directly in response to the external environment without CPU involvement.

The Western concept of the cognitive mind is the information processor with its emphasis on content and storage. The Chinese concept of the heart-mind is closer to robotics—the task-oriented computerized system. For both, we can think of the CPU as the language processor. Its typical manifestation is in talking to ourselves. Thus we think of it as *me*. The inner voice is our self-consciousness. The paradox of skill is that we function best when we lose the *I* in this sense. When the skill functions most effectively it bypasses the CPU, it leaves *me* out. That is why the experience is like surrendering to the world or to some external *dao*-force.

The difference between skill and conscious guidance is, to consciousness, like the difference between a basic action and a generated action. A generated action is one we do *by* doing some basic action in a proper context. A basic action is one we do without doing anything else. I switch on the Walkman by moving my finger. In a sense, I move my finger by tensing certain muscles. I could not obey a command to move those muscles, yet I could obey a command to move my finger. We, in effect, know-how-to move the finger. We do not know-how-to move the muscles or send the nerve impulse as such.

Zhuangzi's *ming*[illumination] about this intuition is this. In the process of getting skills, our distinction between basic and generated actions shifts. Our repertoire of basic actions increases and we *forget* what we had learned in acquiring them. A child obviously focuses immense concentration on walking at first. No adult (except in rehabilitation therapy) could walk by putting one foot down, shifting balance, and so on. Walking becomes a basic action. Similarly, typing the word *the* no longer consists in typing the letters t-h-e.

Speaking, eating, tying shoes, driving a car, riding a bicycle—all these become basic. To our conscious processing we do not do them by combining basic actions. We move our conscious processing to a level that treats these as basic actions, as input for further conscious processing. We do other things by doing them. Purposive subsumption (*wei*ing) marks conscious actions. We can redefine the slogan, *wu-wei erh wu pu wei* ("no action and yet nothing is undone") in this light.[103] We operate at the level of skill intensity at which our most skilled behavior is basic action.

Zhuangzi's alternative to primitive, antilanguage withdrawal directs our attention to accomplishment that has the following characteristics which are attractive to the anti-Confucian Daoist tradition:

> 1. Any activity can be an arena for heightened skill. Zhuangzi plausibly chose butchering as an example because it was a low-status occupation. One is not limited to political, official conceptions of virtuosity.
>
> 2. It comes by a potentially infinite process of advancing skill by following a way. In each early stage, I learn that *dao* by discipline and by learning conscious rules. Then we reach a point where "we do not know how to go on." We use this developed guiding intuition to guide the continuation of our skill in each new *difficult place*. Knowledge is unlimited.
>
> 3. One's skill responses appear to us as natural responses, not as choices. It appears to the practitioner that he goes beyond skill and submits or conforms to an external guide, a true ruler. Internally we experience it as a way that takes over conscious movement so we no longer analyze or contemplate actions.
>
> 4. The activity performed in this way is intrinsically satisfying. The skill continues to grow as we move to new hard places and use our developed intuition for further accomplishment. Developing this skill is also satisfying.
>
> 5. Otherwise, self-consciousness, deliberate choice making, is likely to interfere with the performance of the skill at this highest level.

None of this, I argue, justifies the antirationalist interpretation of Zhuangzi. That interpretation gives aid and comfort to the right-brain–left-brain school of interpretation of comparative East-West thought. The parallel-processing part of our mental functioning and the CPU probably never operate in isolation. Certainly in mathematical, philosophical, scientific theorizing, there is parallel processing going on as we are reasoning consciously. And in our skills, even if we do not consciously monitor our basic acts, we monitor higher and higher level aspects of our performance.

Consider again the example I offered earlier, playing chess. This is certainly a higher, intellectually absorbing human activity. Notoriously, linear processing computers with all their computing power cannot beat a human master at chess. The human responds with a finely honed *intuition* about chess positions. She processes (and drops) many lines of play unconsciously while calculating about a few central ones. The so far unmet challenge to programmers is programming that sophisticated human pattern matching into the computer. (The analogy would be even stronger for Go. There computers are even less successful. All teachers stress that an intuition for the beauty of the game is needed for mastery.)

Zhuangzi says that knowledge (know-how) is infinite and life is finite. There is no point at which we cannot further use our conscious processing to increase skill. When we reach a hard place, our mind clicks into solving mode. It draws on all our stored skills but is still conscious, direct, and aware.

It would, admittedly, be easier if we could just vibrate with the *Dao* and solve all problems effortlessly. But evidence is lacking that Zhuangzi thought it was so simple.

IV

THE AUTHORITARIAN
RESPONSE

9

Xunzi: Pragmatic Confucianism

> There was no lack of intellectual power; Hsün Tzu was, without qualifi-
> cation, one of the most brilliant philosophers the world has ever produced.
> But he lacked faith in humanity. This flaw, like the fatal weakness of the
> hero in a Greek tragedy, went far to nullify his best efforts. It not only
> blighted his own fame but did much to impose upon later Confucianism a
> strait jacket of academic orthodoxy.
>
> HURLEE CREEL [1]

> Hsun Ch'ing (c. 298–238 B.C.), the last of the pre-Han thinkers, was in
> many respects the greatest, as he was in all respects the most philosophical,
> of the Confucianists.
>
> E.R. HUGHES [2]

The Interpretive Dilemma

Xunzi figures centrally in the shift from the classical to the imperial culture. He
produced a version of Confucianism that could be a minion of imperial rulers and an
ideology for totalitarianism. He lived near the end of the Warring States period and
studied and taught at the Jixia academy. Supported by the dominant state of Qi, the
academy had become firmly established as a center of political and philosophical
discourse. Xunzi became a teacher in that academy and a spokesman for the non-
Mencian wing of Confucianism.[3] He criticizes and addresses more philosophical positions by name than any earlier philosopher. Much of his thinking focuses on how
different doctrines emerge from people's biases—and why Confucian biases are not
biased.

Xunzi's teachings centered on political philosophy. He probably earned a large
stipend and state honors as a philosophical expounder in Qi. He adopted a comparatively servile attitude toward the rulers and their growing ambition to unify China.
In contrast with Confucius, he savored ruthless, swift, and reliable punishment. He
adopted the Mohist pragmatic attitude toward the need for social authority. He often,
however, slipped into calculating utility only from the point of view of the rulers or
high officials. Mencius' criticism of $li^{utility}$ calculations as tending to narrow biases
applies with far more justification to Xunzi than to Mozi.

Xunzi also adopted Mozi's concern with fixed, public $fa^{standards}$. He bequeathed this concern for standardization, along with his authoritarian bias, to his students. *Fa*^{standards} became a central doctrine of the *fa-jia*^{standardizer school}. His two most famous disciples included the synthesizer of that school's Machiavellian doctrines, Hanfei-zi and Lisi, the person most responsible for the political organization of the first Legalist empire. Lisi's political mold shaped every Chinese dynasty up to 1911—some would argue up to 1989. This link of influence, however, has done more to damage than to enhance Xunzi's reputation. The *fa-jia*^{standardizers} became anathema after the fall of the Qin dynasty. The Confucian orthodoxy treated the *fa-jia* philosophy as the chief cause of the swift decline and shattering destruction of the first empire.

The medieval triumph of innatism as the orthodox interpretation of Confucian moral psychology kept Xunzi from prominence until the modern period. Modern Confucians appreciate the appearance of philosophical and logical sophistication in *The Xunzi*. Xunzi seems to have absorbed some Daoist and Neo-Mohist arguments, which brought about a new, more sophisticated version of Confucianism.

The tradition expresses little doubt about the authenticity of the major segments of *The Xunzi*. There seems, however, to be at least two different thinkers writing there. One is a philosopher, aware of the philosophical issues motivating Zhuangzi's skepticism. The other is a dogmatic, toadying, propagandist for a draconian authoritarian social-political *dao*. He panders to rulers who are looking for ministers and a governing strategy. The central terms occur in both contexts. The philosopher sounds like a pragmatist faced with a form of relativism that he fully understands. The political dogmatist sounds as though he has no grasp of the philosophical problems of realism and relativism.

Robert Eno has concluded that *The Xunzi*, like most other texts we have discussed, was the collective product of another text-based community. This school was built around Xunzi, whose doctrines, no doubt, formed the base of the textual tradition. We could charitably assume that the circumstances of Xunzi's life partly explain his two faces. We could suppose that his political patrons required the dogmatic, assertive tone in support of their authority. I will also argue that his philosophical doctrines may seem to him to justify both the political dogma and the emphatic tone.

That only handles one aspect of the problem, however. Xunzi's treatment of the deeper issues from the school of names is much less responsive than was Zhuangzi's. The basic form of Xunzi's reply is "Let's not talk about such things." Friends of Xunzi assume that he has good reasons for ignoring the issues that generate the paradoxes. These good reasons, however, do not show up clearly in the text. The explicit reasons more often show that Xunzi (or his disciples) simply missed the point.

It would have been gratifying, as a Daoist, to have been able to praise at least one Confucian philosopher. Traditional scholars have often wondered why Mencius and Xunzi had so little political impact in their own time. Xunzi reportedly died in obscurity.[4] I will argue that there would be no reason for surprise if Xunzi had negligible philosophical stature outside of Confucian circles. The evidence is that the judgment of their contemporary philosophers is probably accurate. Confucian training in ritual performance, chanting, and dance, was not intended to produce good philosophers. They did cultivate elevated style, and Xunzi, like Mencius, is often cited as a model of literary style. Even when informed by the best non-Confucian philosophy, Confucians remained best suited as stylistic apologists for authoritarian practices and points of view.

Xunzi's Intellectual Influences

Xunzi develops the conventionalist line of Confucian thought. Zhuangzi had thoroughly undermined Mencius' innatist position. Xunzi thus considered Mencius' view that nature builds innately correct value reactions into the heart as naive. He began to doubt any purely naturalistic basis for values. Values, he argued, were products of cultural tradition, not of nature.

The tradition has acknowledged a robust Daoist influence on Xunzi, though on trivial grounds. It remarks mainly on his use of terms such as *emptiness, stillness,* and *oneness.* We need to look at his arguments and theoretical positions. Awareness of Daoist *arguments* is unhealthy for the worship of Mencius. Philosophical Daoism did influence Xunzi, as did the Neo-Mohists' theory of language. Linguistic analysis and the analytic philosophical style clearly show through in Xunzi's thought.

Xunzi appreciated the force of Zhuangzi's attack on Mencius. He also appreciated that Zhuangzi's skeptical, pluralistic reflections did not entail that we must abandon convention. He, like Zhuangzi, turned the tables on the antilanguage version of his school and celebrated the unavoidable conventionality of any scheme of values. This led him back to the assertion of a *li-i* ritual morality and a more vigorous defense of traditional, conventionalist Confucian theory. His knowledge of Neo-Mohist doctrines, however, forced him to reformulate and develop the required doctrine of rectifying names.

But the other Xunzi—the political absolutist—also comes through even in philosophical sections. This theorist is an uncritical absolutist. He asserts the possibility of direct access to the correct *dao.*[5] This Xunzi doctrine differs from Mencius only in nuance.

The absolutist Xunzi takes the authority of the *junzi* gentleman and the political leader for granted. Their choices are the unquestioned standard of *shi* this:right and *fei* not this:wrong. This Xunzi ignores the philosophical demand that had driven classical thought from Mozi to Zhuangzi. He talks as if he has no need to justify the dogmatic assertion of traditional authority. Even the occasional humanizing provisions we find in Xunzi's authoritarian position, he justifies mainly as in the ruler's self-interest. As Schwartz puts it, the gratification of the strong would be *poisoned by anxiety* if the mass of people were left too badly off.[6] This is a Xunzi preaching to the converted, the ruling elite already convinced of the moral superiority of their perspective.

Xunzi pandered to the tyrannical passion for punishment with hardly a hint that he understood the original Confucian objection to it.[7] Even given the opportunity to soften his draconian association with the most physically debilitating and mutilating punishments (amputations), Xunzi intones the ruling power's familiar refrain that without such obscene measures people will be bad.[8] Perhaps he secretly thinks cutting off a nose is an exercise in moral edification.

From Mozi's first assertion that unanimous agreement of a society's leaders cannot make a doctrine right to Zhuangzi's doubts about any natural authority, philosophers have brought authoritarianism under explicit attack. The later Mohists had even abandoned their founder's second-level reliance on heaven's authority. If, as Schwartz argues, Xunzi simply assumes the justification of authority, then we can explain his failure only in two unpalatable ways. Either he was ignorant of the philosophical developments of the period or he deliberately shaped his doctrine to grovel for the favors of the rulers of the day.

I choose a more charitable interpretation. The conventionalist Xunzi does try to justify authority on pragmatic grounds. It was a good try. In the end, however, neither position successfully salvages Confucianism in the face of the combined philosophical critique of the reforming Mohists and the pluralistic Daoists. I am most tempted to the hypothesis that Xunzi reverts to authoritarianism in the awareness that the analytical conventionalist argument does not get him home. His absolutist conclusion then uses the doctrine of a privileged preconventional vantage point. This brings him very close to Mencius, but since he looks *outward* with this special mindset, he claims to read the correct *dao* in nature. Here he uses the language of *empty, unified,* and *still,* the allegedly Taoist terms. But the doctrine is not pluralism; it is absolutism.

The Xunzi's use of Daoism in the context of its absolutist turn is mainly responsible for the absolutist line of interpretation of Daoism. It generated a view of Daoism linked to the unprovable assertion that some inner technique *is available* to reach Zhuangzi's hinge of *dao*s, the all-round perspective from nowhere. Since then, the tradition has viewed Daoism as including the unstated mystical claim that some can cultivate a state from which they can identify the absolutely correct *dao*. The authoritarian Xunzi-school view of Daoism was developed in the school of his even more ruler-oriented disciple, Han Feizi. From there it flowed into the recently discovered Huang-Lao ruler-oriented Daoist sect. This view of Daoism became the ruling view in the Qin-Han period and resulted in the incoherent traditional interpretive theory that Daoism is simultaneously skeptical-relativistic and dogmatic-mystical.

Outline of Xunzi's Thought

The conventionalist Xunzi is represented in the larger body of the book's doctrines. I would attribute to the conventional, pluralist Xunzi an integrated social-political theory with four related aspects:

Naturalism. He accepts Zhuangzi's nonprescriptive concept of heaven:nature. He also accepts, and stresses more than Zhuangzi does, the natural constraints on conventions that human and environmental conditions impose. He models a vaguely evolutionary theory of conventions.[9]

Economism. The basic environmental constraints inform Xunzi's view of the natural circumstances of justice: economic scarcity in a cooperative society. The conventions preserve cooperative society by solving the scarcity problem. Otherwise scarcity would produce destructive strife.

The Chain of Life. Xunzi offers a theory of human (the species) nature and its place in the cosmic scheme. His analysis provides an implicit species-survival justification of Confucian conventional standards.

Rectifying Names. Xunzi grounds his pragmatic Confucianism on a theory of the relation of language, human morality, and the real-world context. He revises the Confucian *dao* of language in an attempt to answer both Neo-Mohist and Daoist criticism.

Naturalism

Confucius' pragmatic agnosticism started the process of naturalizing *tian*^heaven. Mozi associated *tian*^nature:heaven with normative authority, but separated nature from language-based conventions. The conventions are matters of social choice. Zhuangzi continued the naturalizing trend. He followed the Later Mohists in rejecting the normative authority of *tian*^nature. The opposite of *tian*^nature is not the transcendental *supernatural*, but the conventional, the social. Mozi, Yang Zhu and Mencius had all argued that nature dictated certain *shi-fei* responses. Shendao and Laozi stressed that nature itself gives no specific guidance. The Neo-Mohists tried to resurrect the notion of realistic guidance by basing *shi-fei*s on natural similarity and difference. But they avoided direct appeal to nature as an authority. Both this semantic project and their effort to extend their system to larger guiding phrases failed. Zhuangzi then reminded us that all *shi-fei* systems are equally natural and that we can get no specific guidance from that trivial fact.

Xunzi's theory of heaven also identifies it with what is constant. He used this claim to *deny* that it is *directly* relevant to moral questions. Heaven's *behavior* does not depend on the moral character of things in the realm of men.[10] He contrasts this constancy with the conventional *dao*^way. Xunzi pointedly never characterizes any *dao*^way as constant. The gentleman, however, does incorporate natural constancy as *a given* in shaping his *dao*.[11] No *dao* which can be spoken is constant, but nature (the actual course of nature) is constant. That constancy, therefore, does not convey normative force. Heaven's metaphorical association with constancy derives from its link to the regularity or constancy of heavenly bodies. Xunzi uses the movements of the sun, the moon, and the stars, and the succession of the seasons as standard metaphors of constancy.

The term *tian* also functions as the natural element in Xunzi's triad of *heaven, earth,* and *human society*. Heaven and earth together set the background conditions to which human society (human-stuff) must accommodate. The regularity of that real-world context underwrites the pragmatic argument. Social life has to respond to non-social regularity if we are to live and grow on the earth. Still, the *dao* that guides us is not heaven's or earth's *dao*,[12] but one that consists of the human conventions, the *li*^ritual.

Xunzi's school loyalty committed him to the view that the Confucian convention—the *li*^ritual—is the uniquely efficient mechanism of social order. In principle, we can imagine that many conventional forms *could* underwrite a workable society. It is hard to find an argument in the *Xunzi* for his favoritism other than hints about *li*'s age and semidivine pedigree. A convincing practical argument for this special status never explicitly surfaces in the text. Even the *sophisticated* Xunzi's practical justification of Confucian *li*[ritual] seems to rest on the *shallow* Xunzi's blind faith.

> Rites are the highest expression of hierarchical order, the basis for strengthening the state, the way by which to create authority, the crux of achievement and fame. By proceeding in accordance with ritual, kings gain possession of the world; by ignoring it, they bring destruction to the altars of the grain and soil. Stout armor and sharp weapons are not enough to assure victory; high walls and deep moats are not enough to assure defense; stern commands and manifold penalties are not enough to assure authority. What proceeds by the way of ritual will advance; what proceeds by any other way will end in failure.[13]

How do we know that the Confucian *li* uniquely offers this positive outcome? It is hard, as I said, to find a direct argument, as opposed to these elaborate statements of faith. The direct argument he gives for *li* is his claim that *li* controls and channels desires. He must assume not only that *li* does this, but that it does it in a *uniquely efficient* way, the only way that preserves order and social harmony given human psychology and the background conditions. We could, as Mozi and Zhuangzi argue, achieve this goal using many alternative sets of rituals, some devised deliberately, say, to maximize benefit. Xunzi simply asserts that the *li* is the source of all these good things, that without it one faces anarchy. That indicates that he is preaching to the converted.[14]

Given Xunzi's assumption, his *dao* still derives indirectly from heaven. Heaven sets the natural regularities that make some *dao*s promote stable, harmonious, satisfactory human life more effectively than others. The configuration of the forest dictates a forest path as much as does the intended destination. Given a social goal, the natural structure (the forest) determines the optimal *dao*. But it does so via the creative work of the pathfinder.

The goal, Xunzi thinks, presents no special problem. Xunzi wastes precious little time with Zhuangzi's observation that pragmatic arguments presuppose the value of the survival of the human species. "Fine," he says, "so we presuppose it." There may be some point of view according to which human life ought to die out. Why should that possibility be of any more than abstract philosophical interest to us? Zhuangzi's reflections are interesting but irrelevant to Xunzi's task. We had best get on with life. If we grant that obvious goal then we can begin to make sense of Xunzi's position. He combines awareness that guiding systems are conventional with his article of faith in the Confucian sage-kings. The creative sage-kings have blazed the uniquely efficient path to that goal in the natural context.

Unfortunately, Xunzi nowhere clearly formulates such a direct rebuttal of Zhuangzi. He does frequently allege that the issues central to the school(s) of names are of mainly nuisance value. Aside from the vague sketch of a Zhuangzi as someone who "knew heaven but did not know people," he sidesteps the Daoist pluralistic perspective. His explicit textual goal, in fact, is *only sometimes* general well-being and cooperation. More frequently the shallow Xunzi comes out. He simply assumes the authority and interests of the ruling class. He all-too-frequently starts his arguments from the *obviously* correct and cultivated sensibility of the *junzi*[superior man]. The closest he comes to acknowledging that the form of cultivation begs the question is when he drops it, finally, for the claim that a mystical, unbiased, apprehension of the correct *dao* is possible to Confucians.

A *dao* of correct action therefore depends on coordination with heaven and earth. When the social sphere is *following the* dao, heaven and earth *respond* by advancing human well-being. They do this in virtue of being constant. They do not *intend* that we be moral or seek to reward us for good deeds. The test of *moral* is what is so in harmony with that constancy that it *naturally* yields the most nourishing outcome. Xunzi takes *good* to be whatever, in the context of natural regularity and earthly limitation, best promotes human social well-being.

Thus the king, by following the correct ruling *dao,* brings about the correct pattern of social behavior. That, in turn, brings it about that heaven and earth nourishes his people and their lives go on without injury. This does not involve an explanatory science of the natural regularities. Xunzi defines *knowing heaven* purely pragmatically.[15] Xunzi does not encourage theoretical or metaphysical speculation about the mechanism of nature. All that matters is that we chart the outcomes, not that we understand why they come about. Perhaps his worry here is that any speculation will focus on heaven's desires or willing and draw attention away from the sages' conscious creation of convention.

The various naturalistic formulas of the mandate-of-heaven doctrine work well in Xunzi's naturalism. However, the mandate specifically does not depend on either the satisfaction or the choice of a personal, anthropomorphic heaven. The human portents—starvation, riot, and depopulation—are what signal that the mandate is coming or leaving. Such occurrences mean that society has lost harmony with heaven. From these occurrences, a natural, *social,* causal chain leads to disorder and the loss of effective government power.[16] Good government is government that works, naturally.

Xunzi comes closest to explicit pragmatism when he identifies the thread of *dao* to be whatever is the same for a hundred kings.[17] If they all agree on some institution, then it is crucial to *dao.* He uses this definition to justify his otherwise unConfucian fondness for mutilating punishments.[18] He alleges that we have no other explanation of the origin of such practices. A succession of a hundred kings cannot be wrong about the pragmatically best social policies.

Xunzi focuses mainly on practical economics. This may partly reflect the conditions of the times (the importance of economic strength in political-military survival during the Warring States period). And it partly reflects the influence of Mohism and the *Fajia* on practical political thought. These latter doctrines, both of which emphasized utility, usually calculated in terms of economic benefit. They had become the chief rivals to a Confucian political vision. The basis of economics was foodstuffs. This prerequisite of population growth was, by implication, also a prerequisite of military power. More food meant more people and more people meant more soldiers. We saw a similar focus in *The Mencius.*

Xunzi resembles Mozi more than either the *Fajia* or Mencius in the theoretical importance he placed on education. Xunzi stresses learning more than Mencius does because he views the source of moral doctrine as cultural rather than innate. Like Mozi, he assumes that only education can create a moral population. Morality involves *more* than a natural growth of human nature in a fertile environment.

Good government gives good training and creates good people. But Xunzi adds a new economic element to the justification of li^{ritual}. Xunzi argues that human desires always outstrip the material resources available for their satisfaction. Distributing and allocating these goods in ways that achieve maximum satisfaction requires deliberate, creative social policy. He argues that Confucian training, in particular, not only brings about order, but deals practically with the distribution of scarce economic resources.

Xunzi's justification of li^{ritual} starts from the classical scarcity condition of justice, but his solution is not simply equal distribution. Xunzi does not move to an assumption that individuals have inherently equal value. Instead, in classical Confucian style, his approach is to *give* certain roles differential worth and status. This socially bestowed role status guides his distributive policy. The $li^{rituals}$ simultaneously create the distinctions of noble and base among the people *and* determine and distinguish what objects each rank may appropriately seek.

So Xunzi's goal is ambitious. More than merely rationing goods to equalize satisfaction, he hopes actually to achieve general satisfaction of desires by directly manipulating the dispositions to fulfil those desires. His argument parallels one we found in Laozi's and Zhuangzi's philosophy of language and philosophy of mind. Daoists suggest that words, distinctions, and *dao*s give us our desires. Xunzi insists that desires are part of nature, but that we can control the seeking behavior these desires generate. The desire impulse is an amorphous urge that can be channeled by ritual, language, and convention. We do not create the desire, but we can control what it is a desire *for*. So we can use language to regulate desires. Thus we can achieve social order and harmony in the face of economic scarcity without desire deprivation. We channel desire differentially in the different classes of people so that the desires are for the right things. The right desires are those that match the things available.

> If men are of equal power and station and have the same likes and dislikes, then there will not be enough goods to supply their wants and they will inevitably quarrel. Quarreling must lead to disorder and disorder to exhaustion. The former kings abhorred such disorder and therefore they regulated the principles of ritual in order to set up ranks.[19]

Xunzi celebrates this proposal as fulfilling the classical formula "Equality is based upon inequality." By having inequalities of status, everyone can achieve a roughly equal satisfaction of desires.

Thus the justification of li^{ritual} changes slightly in the *Xunzi*. Li still undergird the hierarchical structure, giving the role expectations for each position in the hierarchy. Now, however, he has the Daoist-inspired awareness that language (organized into $dao^{prescriptive\ discourse}$) shapes desires. He can use the role structure to make rationing effortless. In internalizing the *dao* of their position, the various levels in society will desire the things appropriate to the role they play. Their desire will fit their ranks.

> If matters pertaining to food and drink, dress, domicile, and living habits proceed according to ritual they will be harmonious and well regulated.[20]

Thus society can nourish everyone because not everyone will want lobster. People in some status positions will prefer wild rice with swamp grass. Notice that Xunzi does not take these tastes as evidence of natural superiority. They are neutral, rational adjustments to the expectations of one's social position and role. We have some sociological evidence for his theory. Socioeconomic studies of economic-class stratification support the claim that such a *class* harmonization of tastes does occur.

Again, however, we long for Xunzi's argument that the Confucian *li* is the *uniquely* effective way to achieve this *equality with inequality*. Given any set of goods and a population, there must be many ways to define classes and to instill desires in them. Those whom we train to like lobster, for example, we might also train to like sackcloth. That way, those living on swamp grass can have silk. Laozi's argument that we could forget the cultivated desire for rare goods would make inefficient social policy. Those goods would then go to waste and there would not be enough swamp grass to go around. Xunzi's view of the hierarchy as being narrower at the top probably contributes to the assumption that the top group should be trained to desire the rarer goods.

All his goal—the equal satisfaction of everyone's desires—requires in principle, however, is that we find a way to differentiate the desires. We cannot have all the money chasing the same goods. The combination of the natural social hierarchy and the Confucian *li* of appropriate desires and behaviors solves the economic problem. But Xunzi dogmatically assumes it is the *one dao* that results in adequate levels of satisfaction. We have to look elsewhere for the justification of the specifics of the Confucian *li*^ritual. Xunzi's anti-Confucian disciples, the *Fajia*, delete this unproven assumption from their version of his political program.

The Chain of Life

Xunzi then draws on the Daoist theory of language and the heart-mind in order to base morality on convention. His theory, however, gives humans an un-Daoist special status in the natural scheme. The special status flows from a parallel pragmatic rejection of Zhuangzi's worries about *shi*ing our values as opposed to those of other animals. Xunzi takes for granted that humans *rightly* dominate animals. The domination is a result of both natural regularity and our heavenly given capacities.

Xunzi's doctrine that humans represent an apex of nature has parallels in Western philosophy. But his account of what distinguishes us from animals reveals again a basic difference in our respective theories of human nature. The classical Western definition of human was as a *rational animal*. That definition placed the difference between humans and animals in the faculty of rationality, intelligence, or knowledge. Xunzi finds the capacity of *zhi*^know-how in all animals. The human difference lies in our ability to make distinctions (especially in *wen*^language)! This is the foundation of our aptitude for yi^morality. It makes us able to develop and to subscribe to conventions.

> Fire and water have energy but lack life. Grass and trees have life but no intelligence. Birds and beasts have intelligence but no yi^morality. Man has energy, life, intelligence, and in addition yi^morality. Therefore he is regarded as the most noble under heaven. He is not as muscular as the ox nor as fleet as the horse and yet

he makes the ox and the horse serve him. Why? Because he can group and they can not. Why are humans able to group? Because of divisions. How can divisions influence conduct? Because of yi[morality]. In itself, morality using divisions entails harmony. Harmony entails unity; unity entails great strength. Strength entails power to conquer things. So people can live in houses and halls, can order the four seasons, cut out the ten thousand thing-kinds, and bring universal utility to the world. There is no other inherent basis—it is achieved by a morality of divisions.[21]

Now, Xunzi's notion does not amount to a Darwinian survival-of-the-fittest explanation of the human species. Still, he does hint that humans survive and prosper more because of their social nature than of their intelligence. This manifests the deep difference between Chinese and Western views of knowledge and mind. Obviously, we share the capacity to gain know-how and use it in guiding behavior with animals. The *distinguishing* characteristic of humans is the ability to establish conventional distinctions, the kind that underlie language.[22] That enables them to coordinate their behavior and to store and transmit know-how. We should not think of mind and knowledge, as they function in this argument, as the individual's capacity to process information. The essence of mind is not the capacity to collect cognitive content.

The specific human capacity that allows the move from intelligence to a shared conception of yi[morality] is the capacity to divide and discriminate. Xunzi uses the word *fen*[divisions] along with our more familiar *bian*[discrimination]. The core divisions are those into social ranks. But, as the quotation shows, the divisions include the seasons and the *cutting* of things into kinds. Social distinctions require ritual distinctions of proper objects of desire and appropriate actions. Ritual shapes the proper desires, inclinations, and consequent actions of role players.

Our ability to internalize social standards of dividing things underlies human social character. We humans organize ourselves using conventional ritual codes. To have a ritual code requires that we learn from among the possibilities one shared way of making distinctions. We then learn to act on it in concerted, coordinated, communal fashion. That requires distinctions of rank, distinctions in desired objects, and distinctions among things we deal with in general. Morality, in this broad structural sense, is conventional. And, as a result, Xunzi accepts the corollary that the division of things into types is conventional. It is a purpose-guided, agreed-upon way of clustering things intended to coordinate our actions and our *seekings*.

When we *dang*[hit on] the clustering *dao* then, of the ten thousand thing-kinds, each gets its proper role. The six domesticated types grow from this. The group of growing things all receive their *ming*[name:commands].[23]

This theme embellishes Xunzi's justification of rites. His account of the role of *li* in society develops Confucius' view of *li* as regulative. It also combines that with insights from the pragmatic Mohist and the skeptical Daoist approach to convention. Xunzi's synthesis resembles that of a modern structural-functionalist. Rites *are* important because they reinforce our sense of social togetherness and harmony. They do this even when they do not achieve any more direct pragmatic benefit. Xunzi justifies funerals, for example, in social, functional terms. Funerals give us a stable framework for expressing our natural grief in harmony with each other while reinforcing a sense of social unity. We appropriately express grief in socially shared ways.

The implicit premise is that the Confucian *li*^{ritual} *better expresses* human emotion than does the Mohist's more theoretically unified alternative. Unfortunately, again we look in vain for any argument for this claim. We find only an expression of Xunzi's faith that Confucius' *li* are better. Still, to Xunzi's credit, we do now have at least the explicit formulation of the claim.

Thus our conventions or our rituals bind us together in pragmatically functional groups. Without the social *central nervous system* provided by conventions, the human species could not work in concert.

Language and Morality

The sophisticated Xunzi relies on explictly embracing conventionalism. He rhetorically meets Mozi's challenge head on. There are indeed many possible coordination solutions. We do need a standard of correctness, but he never gives the pragmatic argument. Instead he now uses Zhuangzi against Mozi. We can find no natural standard that does not presuppose some convention. What makes the use of a word correct is the group agreement, not the natural structure of similarities and differences. We cannot get *behind* conventions, cannot find a purely natural standard of judgment. Then he departs from Zhuangzi as well. Any skepticism of conventions is simply an invitation to conceptual anarchy, which Confucians equate with social anarchy. The established conceptual structure, the traditional *dao*^{way}, is the final source of behavioral guidance. If discourse is diverse, social harmony is impossible. We should not, by our words, allow it to get out there are other possible discourses. Since there is no way to settle which to choose from among them, we had best *act like* dogmatists.

Xunzi's argument here has a pragmatic character, but he does not appeal explicitly to Mozi's *li-hai*^{benefit-harm} gnomen as much as to the more Confucian *zhi-luan*^{order-disorder} gnomon. The utilitarian appeal is implicit, but the interpretive *standard of utility* seems mainly to be order. This partly accounts for Xunzi's more authoritarian conclusion. His calculation of the outcome from adopting any *dao*^{way} rests on a ruler's bias. Order is the good to be maximized. This particular calculation of benefit presupposes the standards of evaluation of the existing elite, the *junzi*^{superior man}.

The combination of this pragmatic argument and the elitist assumption accounts for Xunzi's dogmatism. In criticizing Mozi, Xunzi simply asserts that Mozi is blind to the value of cultural embellishment![24] Xunzi's adoration of the *junzi*^{superior man} certainly follows his Confucian background, but it simply begs the question when used against Mozi and Zhuangzi.

His strongest defense of this arbitrary assertion of superior insight comes in the theory of names. It pushes him very close to making an explicit distinction between fact and value. This distinction emerges from his use of the familiar Mohist terms *fa*^{standards} and *lei*^{similarity}. He criticizes Shendao for elevating *fa*^{standards} but having no *fa*.[25] This criticism seems to suggest that in drawing explicit reflective attention to standards of interpretation, Shendao abandoned the assumption that one was correct.

There is merely the one that *shi*^{circumstances} have favored here and now. Xunzi also criticizes Hui Shi for failing to *fa*^{model} himself on the sage-kings in *shi*ing the *li-yi*^{ritual morality} [26]; Hui Shi rejected all distinctions. Those who hear cases, Xunzi argues, must proceed on settled *fa,* where we have *fa* available. Where we have none, they must follow the natural distinctions of *lei*^{similarity}. [27]

The *lei*^{classes} therefore must have some realistic basis. The *fa,* Xunzi insists in contrast, must follow *yi*^{morality}. [28] The *dao*^{way} for the kingly government must not go beyond that of the three traditional dynasties. Very ancient texts fix the wording of the *dao.* The *fa*^{standards} for the interpretive application of terms in that *dao* in action come from ensuing history. The *fa* are the interpretive standards of the later kings. [29]

So one way to explain the movement from the sophisticated to the shallow Xunzi is to credit him with an insight into Mozi's first standard of language: antiquity. The proper use of words depends on prior usage. The standard of usage for moral terms *must* be historical. This justification supplements the unproved claim of unique pragmatic usefulness and Xunzi's biased evaluation of hierarchical order. It comes from the historical nature of conventions and the inextricable involvement of language in convention. It banishes philosophical doubt on pain of conceptual anarchy.

This gives us a deeper insight into Xunzi's assumption that anarchy is the alternative to *li*^{ritual}. We presuppose some standard when we prefer any one alternative to another. Any attempt to create a new standard will also presuppose one. It will be neither more ultimate nor more valid for being new. It will be merely another self-approving choice. So there can be no real basis for preferring an alternative other than the standard we have when we start out to consider it. The standard we have is the settled, historical standard. Thus, unless we stick to the established conventions, we will have a plethora of equally arbitrary systems of valuation. The only characteristic that uniquely picks out one system from the others is its settled, conventional character. We could not possibly justify change. It is best, thus, never to acknowledge doubt.

Xunzi's argument would not persuade anyone from a tradition with a concept of reason. Reason symbolizes the faith that a certain kind of thought can improve on tradition. Neither the Daoists nor the Mohists, I have argued, have offered a clearly identifiable notion of such a transcultural reason. If Zhuangzi is right, all these systems are internally self-*shi*ing and other-*fei*ing. We have no access to an Ur-perspective from which to judge one as superior to another. So, Xunzi concluded, we do now, in historical fact, *have* a basis to approve the existing conventions and to resist change. We have no basis for any alternative.

In the text, Xunzi does not rest calmly on this cool, intellectual reductio of radical change. At best, as I said, explains *part* of his dogmatism. Xunzi has a much more passionate attachment to the Confucian tradition. He values, worships, and loves the traditions in the true Confucian fashion. Extremely intelligent men—the sage-kings—devised them. Wise men have honed and shaped them using conscious activity for generations. Tradition thus contains collected wisdom that the deliberate social tinkering of the liberal utilitarian would not even notice. In trying to reform traditions, the liberal rationalist is likely unwittingly to throw out parts of the ritual whose functions and importance he cannot readily understand. Thus the ritual will break down. Any reform will make it worse and the ultimate outcome of the reform impulse is skepticism and conceptual anarchy. Xunzi's conservatism (like all conservatism) comes from a heightened sense of the systematic working of tradition. It induces a fear that change will affect the system's performance in ways we cannot predict.

Unfortunately, this passion is the undoing of his position. The passionate defense makes the status of the conventions depend on the intelligence and superiority of the sage-kings. The cool defense rested on a historical theory of the proper standard for name use. If intelligent insight justifies the standard then equally intelligent people today could devise alternatives. The passionate defense requires the assumption that people are dumber today than they used to be. Because the circumstances change, an equally intelligent king would almost certainly follow *the tradition* of past intelligent kings precisely by going out and *creating* standards. That is the argument of Xunzi's *fa-jia*^{standardizer} student, Han Feizi.

New Rectifying Names

Xunzi's theory of names mirrors his position on ritual. Xunzi uses *dao* as a general noun. *Dao*s can be fraudulent, illicit, or correct. *Dao*s are rival conceptual moral structures: guiding discourse. His own favorite *dao* is the sage-king's ritual *dao*. It consists of written, transmitted *wen*^{literature}. Xunzi, thus, must deal with the lingering issue of practical interpretation. He can no longer rely on either the discredited one-name–one-thing principle or the elusive ideal of socially constant use. The Daoists and the schools of names have undermined both.

Xunzi's developments and changes in the theory of names do recognize those attacks. He adopts a prescriptive, social doctrine of rectifying names that does not rely on a claim of constancy. He cannot show that proper usage is temporally constant. He does not acknowledge any need to. The standard of correctness is historical tradition. As long as he is within that tradition, he argues, he is right. Nothing but that tradition could be a standard of rightness. Appeals to conform to the sage kings are appropriate, and there is a correct standard of doing so. That is conforming to the existing conventional standards of what conforming is. No other abstract nonarbitrary standard is available. Thus the standard is the current advocate of that tradition—the Confucian *junzi*^{gentleman}. Xunzi solves the problem of rectifying names by becoming a conventionalist about both *dao and* interpretation.

Xunzi does draw heavily from both the content and the style of the Neo-Mohist *Canon* in his theory of names. He begins with explicit theories of his key terms: *nature, emotions, intention, deliberate activity, completion, knowledge, ability,* and *fate.* Further, his discussion touches on many of the issues raised in the dialectical tradition, including Gongsun Long and Zhuangzi. The key terms function crucially and consistently in much of the rest of the book.

Xunzi introduces one important innovation in his account of names. He suggests two categories of names. He uses *gui-jian*^{noble-base} of names that deal directly with social guidance. He uses *tong-i*^{similar-different} of names connected with the natural, real world. He treats these two divisions, which resemble value and fact, in a generally unified way. Both have the social purpose of guiding and coordinating human behavior. Both depend for their application on real-world feedback. Both cluster that feed-back in conventional, customary ways to create intelligible names. The main notice-able difference is that current sage-kings could change the factual names. The social value distinctions must conform to past, inherited standards.

Xunzi initially divides the evaluative terms into the names of the Shang punish-ments, the names of Zhou official status titles, and the li^{ritual} terms that give cultural refinement. He calls the descriptive terms *miscellaneous terms*. We attach them to the ten thousand thing-kinds. The names of things stem from the customs of the mythical, culture-creating Xia dynasty. Interestingly, Xunzi says they provide a basis for communicating with people of distant cultures who have different customs. This culture neutrality and the consequence that current kings can make new names signals an assumption of some natural basis for miscellaneous naming. Xunzi seems to be strongly committed to historical, conventional conservatism only for the names and $fa^{\text{standards}}$ that are value based. For the others, he allows development based on $lei^{\text{similarity}}$.

Xunzi's Definitions

Xunzi's philosophical purposes center on names that deal with human nature—phi-losophy of mind. These terms are central to his account of how the heart-mind uses language for social coordination. He concentrates on the natural-conventional distinc-tion. Xunzi fixes the reference of $xing^{\text{nature}}$ as that which comes about as a result of $sheng^{\text{birth:growth}}$.[30] He intends to use $xing$ sometimes of acquired intuitions—second nature. Call those refined, unified, felt responses that grow in us $xing$ as long as we do not consciously discriminate or calculate benefit. Xunzi calls them $xing$ when they come forth $ziran^{\text{of themselves}}$. This linking of $xing$ and spontaneity thus pointedly avoids distinguishing between *learned* and *innate* skills. What counts as something's being $xing^{\text{nature}}$ is that no deliberate processing accompanies the skilled behavior.

Xunzi also follows Zhuangzi in the way he talks of $qing^{\text{reality responses}}$. He lists Zhuangzi's standard ones: likes, dislikes, happiness, anger, sadness, and satisfac-tion. With these $qing,$ the heart chooses a course of action. The act of choosing is $lü^{\text{deliberation}}$. Both $qing$ and $lü$ follow the Neo-Mohists usage (except the Neo-Mohists used a language radical rather than a heart radical on $qing$).

Notice that $lü^{\text{deliberation}}$ does not evoke any pattern like a Euclidean proof. Delib-eration is not mental arguments-on-paper. Xunzi offers no theory of a practical syl-logism. Xunzi treats deliberation as a simple, basic reaction of the heart after it receives a reality input from our nature mingling with the world. He does not analyze it as a proof structure producing reasons for acting.

When we deliberate and regard the outcome of deliberation as an action, Xunzi calls that wei^{artifice}. The character is formed by a combination of $wei^{\text{do:deem}}$ and a ren^{human} radical. Translators frequently translate wei^{artifice} as *false* or *unauthentic*. Xunzi, however, treats it as a positive concept. Wei^{artifice} is cultural creativity. Wei^{artifice} contrasts specifically with $xing^{\text{nature}}$ and is crucial to Xunzi's account of the conventionality of language.

We would again mislead ourselves if we placed this account in the context of our familiar individualistic psychology. We should not take Xunzi to be advocating that each person develop a unique creative idiolect. *Wei*^{artifice} belongs to *culture* and is mainly an activity for social leaders—the sage kings or *junzi*^{gentlemen}.

Now these definitions will not do what Xunzi wants unless we notice that *xing*^{nature} does not coincide with the more general notion of *tian*^{nature}. We cannot use the English word *natural* in its most general sense. Using language and making choices in shared social ways is natural in that Daoist sense. His definitions cannot rebut Zhuangzi's objection that everything—including all competing doctrine—is natural. We are social animals who operate with shared signaling systems! Xunzi's *xing*^{nature}, however, is not that broad. He does not use the concept, as Mencius did, to get a cheap normative claim: be natural. On the contrary, Xunzi will conclude, *be artificial!*

We can grasp Xunzi's distinction if we think of *xing*^{nature} as human nature only. Its mixing with nature writ large yields *wei*^{artifice}. Artifice *is* natural in this larger sense. Still, it is useful to distinguish the cultural store of products of artifice from the natural and learned spontaneous responses. We can practice and transmit artifice. Artifice leads to Zhuangzi's *cheng*^{completion}. Xunzi pragmatically ignores Zhuangzi's concern that any cultural accomplishment of this type leave some other accomplishment behind. He simply values this cultural product of acts of *wei*^{artifice}.

Calculation[31]—specifically utilitarian calculation—is the mark of *shi*^{affairs}. Xunzi used *shi* in contrast to *ziran*^{self so}, again distinguishing natural actions from artifice. He now contrasts *shi*^{affairs} with *xing*^{conduct}. The latter comes from rectifying with *yi*^{morality} rather than *li*^{utility}.

Xunzi's use gives many of his terms a core and an extended meaning. The key examples are nature and artifice. He again follows the Neo-Mohists here in giving *zhi*^{know-how} a dual use both as a process and an outcome. We distinguish between *zhi*^{intelligence} as a capacity and *zhi*^{know-how} as the outcome. (What humans have within themselves and use to *zhi* he also calls *zhi*.) Xunzi explicitly describes *zhi*^{know-how} as *neng*^{ability}, confirming the know-how analysis of the concept. Any defect or harm to the nature he terms *sickness*. Things which we simply encounter we call *ming*^{name:command} (fate). These are the central terms Xunzi introduces to weld together his theory of language, morality, human nature, and the natural cosmos.

Political Control of the Use of Names

Xunzi, having completed his list of miscellaneous names having to do with humans and their behavior in the world, says that these terms stem (like *fa*^{standards}) from *later* kings. His goal is the same as Confucius' was. The role of social elites' use of language is education. Rulers are like fathers. They influence how we speak and act. When we use names, we discriminate things. Then, prescriptive discourse *(dao)* yields conduct and we communicate intentions successfully.[32] Thus the kings can control the people and make them behave in perfect harmony. They key to government is language modeling.

Obviously, given his conception of the role of the king and the political structure, Xunzi will find *splitting* names to be the most dangerous type of antisocial behavior. It is politically subversive; it undermines the purpose of the state. The rectifying-names role belongs only to the social elite, not to the rabble that happens to get philosophical skills. (No Mohists need apply). Allowing open disputation about how to make distinctions causes hesitation and doubt in action. It lies behind the costly litigations that delay necessary social responses to natural conditions that threaten our shared interests (e.g., floods). Xunzi calls this name splitting and arbitrary creation of new names (Daoist conventional-language anarchism) the *great wickedness*. Name splitting is wrong in the same way that forging a check or cheating on weights is wrong.

Xunzi, although influenced by Daoism, has none of the anarchist in him. He supposes that the result of enforcement of name-conservatism will be that the government uses people harmoniously and easily[33] to accomplish a public good. The assumption clearly depends on the dogmatic Xunzi's confidence that the *junzi*[gentlemen] or social elite *is the standard* of that public good. The only other basis he gives for this authoritarianism is that it provides *a* coordination solution. It makes us *one* in our guiding conceptual perspective *(dao)*. The usage standards *(fa)* make people careful and predictable in obedience to orders.

So the traces of the sage-kings survived and continue to affect us today. Sustaining the continuity of this process is the purpose of government. The present government should preserve and bequeath this success in perpetuating names. Xunzi should, as we noted above, accompany this pragmatic sounding appeal with some argument that acknowledges the claims of the other schools. He should argue that his preferred guiding conceptual scheme and standards of usage are better than its rivals. It is hard to find any argument that fills this gap in *The Xunzi* beyond Xunzi's insisting that convention is the only viable standard. If he is aware of the relativistic perspective that motivated the Mohists and Daoists, he must be deliberately ignoring it because it constitutes *a convention of doubting* conventions and of *asserting multiple conventional answers*. I have suggested that he fears that even suggesting the possibility of choosing a different perspective will undermine his goal of unity. We do have a traditional standard, he argues. Semantic *descent* to considering alternatives leaves us with no foundation for a solution. The result will be conceptual anarchy.

Convention and Pragmatic Utility

Since he puts aside any philosophical objections to picking a pragmatic *dao*, Xunzi sounds like an absolutist. Because of the natural conditions of hardship and social danger, one *dao* clearly stands out: Confucian traditionalism. It does not stand out because it is most successful in testing. To allow the validity of a straightforward pragmatic test is to invite open experimentation and competition. The implicit appeal to an ur-perspective of benefit poses the danger of skepticism, relativism, and epistemic anarchy. Confucian tradition, he assumes, is the one that *is* in place. The pragmatic argument is for continuing it and banning philosophical dispute. The abstract consideration of conceptual alternatives cannot help someone be a *junzi*[gentleman] or prevent his being a *xiaoren*[lesser person]. Sages could hardly explain the confusions that would result and no solution to the problems of rule would emerge. From the ruler's perspective, we have no use for this kind of intellectual activity. The Confucian are wedded to the fervent hope that rulers will somehow naturally be wise elites. (The Daoist fixes on the near certain reality that they will punish!)

Xunzi's fawning appeal to the rulers to enforce his favorite, the Confucian *dao*, promises the gift Confucians can bestow on the king: he will get favorable treatment in the historical records. Who could resist such blandishments! Having a long historical trace of good accomplishments is what government is all about. And the king can get this by meticulously preserving the traditional use of terms.

So Xunzi's pragmatism shows some of the influence of Mohism and some of the implicit assumptions we found in Confucius and Mencius. That assumption is the system-utilitarian assumption that the Confucian *dao,* their guiding conceptual perspective, is best for society. Xunzi's version, however, seems to acknowledge that we can find no neutral conception of *best.* Nor should we seek one. The only viable sense of *best* for such a choice of *dao* is the one we currently have in our settled moral intuitions. That is the traditional Confucian standard. The customary morality, in effect, has conceptual priority over any utility calculations.

Xunzi's position appears to be dogmatic because he invariably defends the traditional values. However, we can now explain that shallow dogmatic aspect of Xunzi as arising from the sophisticated, relativistic Xunzi. The position appears more dogmatic to us in part because we would translate it into a traditionalism about beliefs, rules, or sententials. I have argued that from Mozi on, however, the disputants in China take the issue to be about terms and their application. That strengthens the position of conventionalists enormously, as we saw. The social-standards focus better explains how we use names than how we use sentences or beliefs. Xunzi's focus is on names and standards of discrimination, not on sentences and rules.

Xunzi differs from Mozi primarily in his conservative worry about piecemeal tampering with a system that (1) paragons of past wisdom devised and (2) history has honed to fit social needs and heavenly constancy, and mainly (3) that provides the only intelligible standards available to answer metaquestions about the system.

The Creation of New Names

Xunzi, of course, is not a classical conservative. He is a reactionary! His assumption that we have only the Confucian standards is—in his own time—already false. The ancient Chinese linguistic community, as he was aware, already had rival traditions. A tradition of posing metaquestions and trying to answer them in natural or neutral utilitarian terms was already in place in Xunzi's time, though it may not have been at the time of Confucius. Xunzi can get his reactionary justification for erasing all the philosophy of the period only by imagining himself back to the time before Mozi launched the philosophical enterprise.

Given the existence of a reform and a pluralist or skeptical tradition, Xunzi's position requires more than mere conventionalism. His becomes a radical proposal to arbitrarily value the older, prephilosophical traditions. In our current, conventional, customary use of names, we have deviated from the way the sage-coiners used them. We have missed the intentions of the inventors of language and no longer refer to what they intended to refer to. We have to adjust reference so our practical intentions match up again. Since not many sage-kings have been around recently, *name conservatism* has become lax and we have allowed people (philosophers) to erect strange, new names. They have confused the relation of names and stuffs and made the *shape* of *shi-fei* unclear. So even those who intend strictly to follow the *fa*[standards] and even good Confucians are disorderly.[34]

The mission of a sage-king, should he choose to accept it, would be to reestablish the old names. However, there is a nonreactionary part. He does get to create some new names, fact-based ones.[35] This progressive wrinkle in Xunzi's political naming theory is still authoritarian. He allows *only* the king to do this. The philosophers have proved themselves inept with their wild paradoxes and strange conclusions about "Chickens with three legs." There can be new factual terminology but it must come from the central authority, not from disputing schools of philosophers.

The Theory of Naming

If you have political authority and a concern not to disorder things, then you can change names. To do this, you must keep in mind three principles about names. These are (1) the reason for having names in the first place, (2) the basis of classifying things as similar and different, and (3) and the core necessities in regulating names.

The Reason for Having Names. The reason for having names recalls, in a linguistic version, Mozi's argument for agreement with the superior. Different patterns mix around the heart-mind. Different thing-kinds and various stuffs float around out there. *Noble* and *base* are indistinct; we cannot distinguish *similar* and *different*. As a result we have no way to communicate and achieve shared intentions. Coordination in $shi^{\text{social affairs}}$ (beneficially calculated actions) fails disastrously. The situation is grossly inefficient.[36]

Therefore people with know-how made distinctions and regularized names to point out stuffs.[37] This suggests the sensible idea that coiners of terms should be the *scientists* in their various areas. Xunzi, however, does not make our scientific distinctions. His implicit purposes in naming are still the regulation of behavior. The knowledgeable people are not craftsmen (that would be Mozi's inclination), but the social elite. First you have to get the noble-base distinctions and then you have a social standard for fixing the $tong\text{-}i^{\text{similar-different}}$ distinctions for those below. This gives us a stable conventional system that allows sharing of intentions and coordination of behavior. That is the reason for having names.[38]

The Basis for Distinctions of Similar-Different. Xunzi's major theoretical advances over the Neo-Mohists and Zhuangzi come when he discusses the basis of naming. He formulates this advanced position only for the similar-different distinction since he presupposes authoritarian fixing of the noble-base distinction.

The difference in his treatment of noble-base and similar-different partly explains why he seems both reactionary and progressive. He simultaneously insists on preserving old names and allowing kings to create new names. Supposedly the sage-king, arising today, would base his authority as an elite name user on the noble-base distinction. He could not, therefore, treat that distinction as subject to doubt and change. He would then rely on his traditional authority to create as many new distinction of the similar-different type as may be called for.

Still, these new similarity-difference distinctions are not arbitrary whims of the king. Nor does he base these wholly on the objective similarities and differences in reality. As Zhuangzi and Hui Shi have argued, external similarity and difference do not provide an adequate basis for selecting any particular system of names. Xunzi adds to the account the effect these similarities and differences have on our sensuous nature. He expounds a theory of the natural or heavenly organs. In his theory of heaven, he formulated a species-based conception of a thing's nature. Alongside the list of heavenly *qing*^{reality response} he ranged what he called the heavenly *guan*^{input pipes}: the eyes, ears, nose, mouth, and *shape*. Each has the capacity of different kinds of *contact* knowledge. The *xin*^{heart-mind} controls and directs the input pipes and registers all the inputs. Xunzi calls the *xin*^{heart-mind} the heavenly *jun*^{superior}.[39]

He gives no better answer to Zhuangzi's worry about why the heart should rule. That simply is the heavenly, natural arrangement. The heart *does* direct the input pipes. Xunzi takes another anthropocentric value arrangement as heavenly. We treat as *wealth* whatever is not of our species that we can use to nourish our species.[40] This is heavenly nourishment. (Heaven, obviously, does not approve of cannibalism!)

The linguistic basis of similar and different, he will then argue, is not in external nature, but in its combination with *our* nature as a species. Xunzi says those who are of the same species and have the same *qing*^{reality responses} will have heavenly input pipes that register things in the same way. So we receive a range of inputs with a *similarity space* that our species organs contribute. Humans tend to cluster similarities in human ways. This enables us to *tong*^{communicate}.[41] It gives us the basis for the public agreement on names that underwrites agreement in clustering things.[42]

Xunzi's discussion of sense answers Zhuangzi's attack on human-species bias in considering points of view. Zhuangzi, remember, worried that we suppose our human discriminations and responses to be the correct standards of *shi-fei*. Animals of the same species, Xunzi writes, and with the same reality-feedback mechanisms (feelings) register thing-kinds through their sense organs in similar ways. The beautiful Xishi may seem horrible to the deer, but to all humans the image yields pleasant feedback.

Xunzi kept the analysis on a pragmatic level. He has not claimed that our ways of perceiving feedback directly reflect the world or are exactly as they are in nature. The justification for taking our *qing*^{reality feedback} and sensible distinctions seriously is that it gives all humans the basis for shared, conventional communication. Whatever may obtain in reality in itself, humans react to it and cluster thing-kinds similarly and in a human way.

He does not make the *explicit* concession that, in principle, different beings could cluster things into types in an infinite number of ways. He rests on the natural fact that all members of the same species cluster things in a similar way. Thus our sense organs emphasize certain similarities and differences in a natural clustering. He answers Zhuangzi's skepticism by appealing to the pragmatic necessity that we share enough of a perspective to use names harmoniously. However many ways may exist in principle to group things into classes, human nature favors some species-common pattern of dividing and clustering. That fact is essential to our ability to use language and conventions in pursuit of harmonious coexistence and survival.

Xunzi's conventionalism allows him, again, to disregard this source of skepticism. So we're different! The standard of right and wrong is a human standard used in human communication. The human similarity space is a reasonable basis for correct use of language until we take up communication with animals. The combination of our species-natural input pipes and natural nourishment becomes the pragmatic basis of evaluations and names. Our receptive and judging systems have a shared similarity space and a shared bias about which outcomes to count as *success*. This naturalized Kantian argument does not attempt to get us a neutral universal point of view. Anthropocentrism is our unescapable bias.

Xunzi still must allow that we also do some purely conventional clustering. We still have conventional ways of grouping the humanly registered similarities. Multiple conventions are possible. But not all are equally natural for humans with our heavenly input pipes.

Understanding Xunzi in this pragmatic way reduces the temptation to transport Western eighteenth-century empiricism (modern folk wisdom) into the explanation of Xunzi's doctrine. Traditional Western empiricism has sense data justifying and proving descriptive propositions, sentences, or statements. The empiricist starts with the theory of empirical data. These data have a logical form as a picture of a state of affairs. The logical form of the picture is that objects are related to each other. The form of our imagined mental picture is suspiciously analogous to what we take to be the form of the sentence. Nouns refer to objects and verbs denote the relations. Our folk model of seeing is geometrical projection. Western folk wisdom treats the goal of sensation as scientific truth.

Xunzi's theory differs both in its account of the empirical content and its role in the larger human project. The empirical data do not consist of pictures of individual objects in relation to each other. The empirical *data* consist in an inclination to discriminate. He does not represent the eyes, for example, as conveying a picture of position in space, or of temporal succession, or relative size. The eyes make certain discriminations: shape, color, line, and part-whole distinctions. The ears discriminate clarity and murkiness of toe, pitch, contour, and so on, of sounds. The mouth makes its range of sensory taste discriminations—sweet, sour, bitter—and the nose and body likewise.

Xunzi does not focus on vision and visual representation nearly as much as British empiricism or any picturing theory would. He describes the inputs as akin to *qing* reality responses or feelings. They are not cognitive *contents* but discrimination *thresholds*. He models their output less on pictures of the world and more on cultivated abilities to recognize or notice a distinction. Since all humans pretty much have the same feedback range and classifications—we all taste sweetness and saltiness—we have the necessary capacities for learning and mastery of socially created names. We have the feedback registers that enable us to execute social programming in conventional language.

The names make up the conceptual scheme that guides our shared form of life. We achieve a socially consistent way to mark those humanly distinguishable properties. We do not attach names to pictures of objects in the mind, but to ranges of stuffs that our linguistic community uses in conventional guidance. Given our sensory capacity and clustering tendency, we can pick out one object-type from another. What we essentially share, therefore, is the ability to use our sensory input pipes to coordinate social behavior in some conventional way.

The heart-mind plays the crucial role in this social naming process. Its role does not consist in verifying truths from sense data. Rather, it takes the feedback discriminations made by the sense organs (including, presumably its *qing*—pleasure, anger, sadness, satisfaction) and evaluates them according to conventional standards. The heart assigns responses their proper guiding significance. It assigns *ke* [permissable] to the inputs.[43]

However, the heart-mind relies on the discrimination accuracy of the sense organs in mapping the input similarities. If the senses do not make their distinctions correctly, then the heart-mind has nothing to say about how to act. This is failing to know (to). Thus the sensory discrimination range is the basis of similarity-difference in naming.

The Basic Requirements of Regulating Names

Using our discriminatory feedback, then, we name things.[44] Xunzi does not wallow in Hui Shi's and Zhuangzi's worries about the malleability of similarities and differences. Xunzi's consistent strategy in dealing with all such tergiversation is to appeal directly to pragmatic considerations. He does not treat the paradoxes or puzzles of reference as a reason to improve the theory. So, it is by no means clear that Xunzi understands the theories that led to the paradoxes. His diagnosis focuses exclusively on the social results of engaging in such speculation or raising the puzzle. He scorns any attempt to respond to the philosophical challenge. The generalized conclusion is that the paradoxes upset the conventional ways of using terms to mark distinctions. They alter the traditional ways of stringing terms together in guiding action. They must be stopped!

The basic requirement, then, is conventional agreement. Xunzi begins with the touchy question of compound terms and modifiers: the ox-horse and the hard-white issues. He does not give any principle for deciding between a Mohist and a one-name—one-thing semantic account of compounding. Instead, Xunzi merely says that if a single term sufficiently indicates a paradigm and conveys the settled intent, then use a single term. If not, use a compound term. If neither can properly pick out the intended range then go ahead and use a more vague general term; it will not hurt anything.[45]

The point becomes a purely practical one. Xunzi depends on no more than existing community's conventional expectations. He does not try to make the scheme systematic or constantly realist. In fact there can be no ur-standard for correcting names that is not already in the conventions.

Xunzi thus implicitly accepts the verdict of the school of names. A perfect one-to-one correspondence between names and things is impracticable. His way of rectifying names depends on no such abstract ideal. His basic goal is a pragmatic, conventional rectification of language, not an ideal one. If we know the different names that things have, then we know that we do not represent every difference by a different name. That would generate total confusion. Insisting that we mark every similarity by giving it the same name would be similarly unworkable. There have to be some more and less general names for names to work. We may use pairs of names and single names as much as and wherever practicable. The only restriction is that we abide by whatever conventions for application of compound and simple terms we happen to settle on. That is all.

Sometimes you want to denote a broad range and you use a word like *wu* [thing-kinds]. Other times you may want to distinguish or limit your range and you use some dividing word such as *birds 'n beasts*. Xunzi does not treat individual, class, and general terms as distinct kinds of names as the Neo-Mohists did. He reduces them to differences of degree. Names of individuals are merely the most specific of terms. They do not pick out an *individual* in the metaphysical sense any more than the more general terms do.[46] Every term picks out some part and there is some more general term for picking out the whole of which it is a part.

Names, then, simply mark pragmatically useful (and humanly accessible) distinctions. Nature does not draw the lines between thing-kinds. Species sensory clustering selects certain similarities and differences; then convention and custom take over. Social practices underwrite one way of stringing similarities together and assigning names to stuffs. The only *fa*[standard] for *proper* clustering to guide behavior is the judgment of the traditionally educated elite, the *junzi*[gentlemen]. The similarities and differences are in nature, but the way we cluster and group the similarities in naming and where we cut and divide (say between color ranges) are matters first of human nature and then of human convention.

Xunzi thus takes the easy solution offered by Zhuangzi. Some distinctions happen to be well entrenched in conventions. We can find no independently valid standards for changing them. Any other convention would be equally arbitrary and allowing illicit change would involve the risk of linguistic anarchy. Name giving can only be done by legitimate political authority and under strict, conservative principles.

We can regard some ways of giving names, however, as *cybernetically* better than others. They are easier to remember and have a *natural* intuitive connection to their use. These are good names: they work better socially than would conceivable alternatives. These, again are specially fitting for our species. So they can become useful conventional names and, in turn, the only standard of appropriateness. Names have no intrinsic relation to stuffs. That is a function of the conventional, customary clustering of sensible similarities.[47]

Xunzi addressed other problems that do not have prominent treatment in the Neo-Mohist *Canon*. These are problems of location modification (e.g., Iowa corn). Graham's reconstruction of the more fragmented sections of the Mohist works hints at some focus on this issue.[48] Xunzi combines it with another question about number and names. We can distinguish between things with the same discernible traits but in different places. So, although we can unite them in speaking of thing-kinds, we can also regard different parts of them in different places as different things.[49]

The most interesting thing about this passage is the complicated way Xunzi develops this concept that closely resembles abstract individuality. Western and Buddhist linguistic perspectives take the concept of an individual to be a simple, obvious primitive in their scheme. Other metaphysically important concepts (attributes, properties, classes) are defined on individual particulars. The individuals *have* the properties or *belong* to the classes. I have argued that for the language theorists of ancient China, the thing-kind was the primitive. And the metaphysical structure was a part-whole structure. Here we see Xunzi *constructing* the notion of *an individual object* as a special case of distinguishing parts from wholes. What we call an individual is a possibility of regarding the same thing-kind in different places as *two*.

We find a parallel contrast in the concept of metaphysical change. In the Indo-European traditions, the concept of change presupposed the primitive concept of an individual object. We regard the *identity* of a thing as being bound up with its *individuality*. Being the same thing *is* being the same *individual* of that thing. The individual underlies the Western concept of change. It is the subject that undergoes change. In China before Xunzi, sameness was a matter of falling under the same name. The problem of change we have identified repeatedly in the texts was primarily the problem of *classification* change. This made it as much a linguistic as a metaphysical issue.

Xunzi now formulates a theory of an individual object's change as follows: Where a thing's position does not change[50] and yet its discernible character does, we call this *hua*[change]. We can treat such changed stuff as the same stuff. We say there is change but no difference.[51]

This treatment of change accents the different analytical frameworks of Chinese and Indo-European philosophy. Xunzi does not treat change as a sign that a thing is unreal. He shows no hint of reluctance to use the same word for things that change. He shows no inclination to either Buddhist or an Ionian notion that names presuppose an unchanging individual substance. Names are for thing-kinds. A thing, continuous in space for a period of time may undergo change. Even if the name changes, the spatially continuous thing may be counted as one thing undergoing change.

Traditional Western analysis of change posited an unchanging substance, an underlying reality or a particular. This substance *had* properties, attributes, accidents, etc. These are repeatable nonspatial features that could *inhere in* individual things. They corresponded mainly to adjectives or nonindividuating nouns. Change is defined as when different unchanging properties inhere in the particular substance at different times. The names in the language refer to the particular substance and predicates or adjectives refer to the properties. This scheme of unchanging realities underlying the perceptual world of individual objects shapes virtually the entire history of Western thought. These passages show how unfamiliar and derivative their status is in the classical Chinese scheme.

Thus, we have no good theoretical motivation to assimilate Xunzi's conceptual scheme to a Western or Buddhist one. This passage does not show that Xunzi's theory is like the Western theory of how names attach to particulars or individuals. Western individuals are truly abstract and theorized entities, the grammatical substrata of properties. Xunzi's names, by contrast, all attach to concrete, changing segments of reality. Ordinary individuals are one possible range generated by different applications of the part-whole structure. They are merely comparatively small segments, distinctions. Individuals are neither ontologically nor linguistically basic. They are referenced by space-time bases for counting, regarding things as one or *the same*. But they fit into one end of the part-whole scheme.

A familiarity-induced mistake here may infect our view of Xunzi's epistemology. Western theory of knowledge draws heavily on its metaphysics. It commonly leads to the skeptical conclusion that we can never know individuals. All knowledge is of universals (properties, ideas, meanings). The senses can present to the mind only data on the properties. This account posits mental particulars (ideas) which have parallel mental properties (concepts). Skeptics like Hume worried that *common-sense* individuals might be only the cluster of sensible or mental properties. The *syntax* of the properties—their pattern of clustering—thus becomes the essential presentation to the mind.

Xunzi's talk of sensation tempts some to import this mind-body theme to explain his theory. But that can only work if we also credit him with the particular-universal–

property metaphysical analysis. Otherwise it explains nothing about how knowledge can correspond to reality. I have argued that his analogue of sensations must be embedded in a theory of the heart's activity in directing our conduct. His is not a theory of receiving, entertaining, and storing cognitive or symbolic contents. In conforming to a linguistic *dao,* the heart controls the senses to test for the presence or absence of something (to make a distinction). The heart uses the outcome of the sensible capacity for discrimination for its own further discrimination of *shi-fei,* the right and the wrong things to do. It thus applies names in guiding our conduct. The senses are measuring devices for reality feedback to be used in executing social programs. The primacy of the inner individual, subjective point of view is familiar to Western conventional wisdom but it plays almost no role in Chinese thought.

Xunzi's conclusion is a pragmatic derivation of the core Greek assumption. We can, in our naming practices, treat a thing as one stuff when there is change of feedback distinctions from something that has a continuous location. A thing that metamorphoses can still be classed the same thing. This gives us the feedback conditions for using linguistic number. Thus we socially fix the systems of numbering things in our language.

Easy, pragmatic, conventional uses, then, are the basic necessities in regulating names. No king can afford not to examine these carefully if he wants to succeed at naming. What this emphatically does not require, Xunzi argues, is any direct theorizing about the linguistic paradoxes which so fascinated the school of names.

Pragmatic Treatment of the Paradoxes

Despite his debts to them, Xunzi's attitude toward the theories and conclusions of the school of names is contemptuous. He takes an essentially political position. He discusses them, but not as a philosopher concerned with working out a philosophical problem. He takes the perspective of a ruler concerned with maintaining order while scholars in his territory debate about such things. Such men are dangerous to good order.

More generally, his position is that their speculations are pointless from a pragmatic, hierarchical point of view. One inevitably suspects that Xunzi never really understood the issues generating the paradoxes. He certainly studied them, but he does not show a philosopher's appreciation of the use of paradox for focusing conceptual issues. His complaint that even a sage would have a hard time explaining the paradoxes reflects his impatience and frustration in finding solutions to the puzzles.[52]

When confronting the paradoxes, Xunzi argues more for forbidding the semantic paradoxes than for rebutting them. What rebuttal he does offer is essentially to repeat his it-does-not-matter treatment of the problem of compounds. He rests finally and dogmatically on the conventional usage. He classifies the linguistic paradoxes into three groups. Each group violates one of the three insights about conventional naming that he has explained. These, again, are (1) the reason for names (coordinating behavior) (2) the empirical basis for similarity and difference (species-typical clustering of sensible distinctions), and (3) the general necessities for regularizing names (conforming to shared convention).[53]

Xunzi, in this section, does not even insist that the paradoxes are theoretically wrong. Instead, as a good pragmatist, he argues repeatedly that they should not be uttered. The king should not permit them to be uttered and no serious person should say such things.

Using Theory of Naming to Confuse Naming. The paradoxes, he argues, confuse people and the confusion revolves around the semantic relation of names and stuffs. Some people use names to confuse us about the use of names. The example here we have the best prior analysis for is the Neo-Mohist claim "Killing thieves is not killing people." It uses the addition of one name *kill* to confuse the regular relation of the names *thief* and *person*. It is a result of theory of names that dictates a change in the ordinary ways of speaking, confusing names with names.

The other examples of this impermissible form (using names to confuse names) are paradoxes that we know of mainly from Xunzi's discussion. I will speculate below about how Song Xing (Songzi) might have argued for them. Both are value paradoxes: "Being insulted is no shame" and "The sage does not love himself." The former came from treating conventional shame as merely one of many social perspectives on moral judgment. The latter might be an expression of the paradox of altruism (to love everyone is to love oneself too). These paradoxes, also, seem to use the theory of naming—the theory that language is conventional—to *disorder* the existing conventions of language use. If we consider why we have names—making moral guidance easy and clear—we will avoid saying such things. (And, if we are a ruler, we will forbid anyone's saying them). These are spurious attempts to get beyond conventionalism in language. We should merely conform.

Using Perspectives on Reality to Confuse Names. The second set of paradoxes uses *shi*[stuff] to confuse names. We can think of these paradoxes as arising from observations or arguments about reality that we should group and name things unconventionally. The most recognizable and typical example here is Hui Shi's "Mountains equal marshes." This paradox arises form the relativity (supposedly) of perspectival judgments of space. By considering the real-world context, one motivates using names in nonconventional ways.

The other two examples of this paradox are "In reality there are few desire" and "There is neither increased tastefulness in eating flesh nor increased pleasure from hearing bells."[54] Again we have to guess at a plausible justification for these. I will be speculating below that the former could be a reflection, consistent with Daoism, that the innate desires are simple and few. They contrast with those desires created by language-induced ways of construing and social cultivation. The cultivated desire typically include such things as the acquired taste for expensive and extravagant pleasures (meat and concerts).

Such tastes, someone might have argued, are not natural. So construed, we could see both as example of arguments from a theory of what is real. That view of reality inclines us to treat the usual ways of classifying desire and satisfactions as conventional and optional. Again, a king would see how to preserve conventional similarities and differences in guiding desires and prohibit such talk!

Using Theory of Naming to Confuse Reality. Xunzi analyzes the third group of paradoxes as arising from using names to confuse reality. (No problems arise from using reality to confuse reality!) Xunzi views the sophist as appealing to principles of naming or a theory of the role of names to distort straightforward reality. The example is Kung-sun Lung's "White horse is not horse."[55] A sophist makes an absurd reality claim, Xunzi suggests, because he insists on a peculiar theory of purity in name use. He thus uses name theory to confuse reality.

The other two examples are more obscure. One guess—guided again by Xunzi's classification—is "To deny something is to say it" and "The pillar has an ox." The argument for them is hard to reconstruct from Xunzi's treatment because he avoids theoretical rebuttal. The former may be a confused statement of the puzzle of how we can refer to nonexistent things.[56] In order to deny that something exists, you have to refer to it. This seems related to Laozi's worry about how we make sense of the *you-wu* [being-non being] distinction. If there is a Laozi base of this deny-is-to-say paradox, we can see why Xunzi would regard it as using a theory of names (contrast theory) to distort reality (nothing is something).

I have almost no clue about the last paradox.[57] Xunzi's discussion, again, gives no clue about the content beyond this classification. He simply insists that the king is to avoid and prevent such sophistry. It defeats the essential necessities for regulating names, conventional conformity. You do not have to structure language according to some strict principle or conform to any linguistic theory. You need only convey your purpose clearly using the techniques the conventional language has evolved. We need no rigidly designating ideal language, just the actual shared one. The sophist who makes such claims undermines language conventions. By confronting him with the conflict between what he accepts and what he rejects, you can prevent these sophistries, Xunzi concludes.

He presents a more thorough discussion of one pair of paradoxes outside the "Rectification of Names" chapter. It comes in the section I regard as signaling Xunzi's authoritarian retreat after his analysis fails. The argument here is mainly interesting as exhibiting Xunzi's dogmatic frustration with rival perspectives.

This later dispute concerns a pair of paradoxical slogans attributed to Song Xing (Songzi) that are close to two discussed above. Judging from his tone and detailed attack, Xunzi must have regarded Song Xing as a rival among the scholars gathered at Qi. None of Song Xing's writings survive. We know of his doctrines only from other works that discuss them.

Outside of Xunzi's discussion, our main source of knowledge of Song Xing's doctrines is the Daoist oriented history in *The Zhuangzi,* which presents Song Xing as heading a school of thought following the Mohists. His school shared several foci with Mohism. They emphasized freeing oneself from conventions, customs, or cultural embellishments, taking a public point of view, and pacifism. They also agreed on part of the technique, altering culturally induced dispositions. The account in *The Zhuangzi* treats Song Xing as a bridge between the Mohists and early Daoism. His strategy moved toward Laozi's idea of clearing the heart-mind of socially induced desire.[58]

Song Xing's school adopted what Graham translates as a "separating pens" analysis of our *contact* with the ten thousand thing-kinds.[59] This slogan suggests an early pluralistic analysis of the heart's way of marking distinctions. We occupy *different pens,* different worlds depending on the different biases of the heart. Song Xing hoped this awareness would motivate tolerance in the heart's behavior.[60] The analysis should, therefore, reduce aggressive impulses born of competition. On the one hand, the insight makes our disagreements seem less momentous. On the other, it gives us a new perspective from which to recommend adopting heart-attitudes that reduce competition, disagreement, and aggressive behavior.

The Zhuangzi records that properly ordering *qing*^{language responses}[61] and *yu*^{desires} was the key to the doctrines of Song Xing's school. If, for example, we can come to see insults as merely socially induced judgments and therefore treat them as unimportant, we will be able avoid a lot of human conflict. Spreading such attitudes, having them taught in the place of conventional standards, could lead to stopping aggression and warfare and saving the world.[62]

The two slogans for which Xunzi takes Song Xing to task are these: "To be insulted is not disgraceful" and "The *qing*^{reality response} *yu*^{desires} are few and shallow." *The Zhuangzi* account claims that Song Xing and his followers regarded these as *the inside* and "Forbid aggression and disband troops" as *the outside*.[63] This pluralistic doctrine justified tolerance and pacifism. It is an early version of the Daoist doctrine that desires are mostly socially learned. In particular, one *learns to* be disgraced. Many desires are not *qing*^{reality response} desire, but conventionally generated ones. Similarly, like a primitivist, Song Xing regards the natural emotional reactions as a narrow base. On this base, society creates complex, socialized, and far more numerous desires.[64]

If we accept that Daoist reconstruction, then Xunzi's lengthy treatment is disappointing. He does not acknowledge that the theory is an alternative to his own. Xunzi also intended to eliminate competition by controlling *seeking* behavior. He resists analyzing the desires themselves as socially conditioned. What reason could we have for worrying if the desires or the seeking behavior are conditioned by convention? Xunzi's motivation for his theoretical fetish is hard to fathom. One hypothesis is that he senses the danger to even *his* form of Confucianism from relativism about motivation. Neither his nor Mencius' justifications can work if radically different conventions could lead to radically different human desires. His pragmatic argument for convention would be transparently arbitrary and question begging.

Xunzi's argument with Song Xing starts with a Mohist-sounding analysis that identifies yi^{morality} with an ur-standard of correct *shi-fei*. We need standards of correctness to settle any such issues. Then he asserts, without further argument, that the kingly rule is the appropriate standard.[65] All our present talk about yi^{morality} and *shi-fei* derive from distinctions made by the sage-kings. The distinction between honor and disgrace is one of these. He has started right off begging the question against Song Xing's position. He goes on to assert that according to that established usage, the *junzi*^{superior man} makes a distinction between being socially disgraced and being morally disgraced. Since he uses the correct ancient convention, the *junzi* can never be morally disgraced. The *xiaoren*^{lesser man} can be socially honored but not morally honored. But by hypothesis, Song Xing's argument, like Mozi's, was implicitly a challenge to the traditional, habitual, customary way of making this distinction and justifying the kind of righteous moral indignation that Xunzi is taking for granted.[66]

From there Xunzi's argument degenerates. It is alternately obdurate, deliberately distorting, question begging, and finally simply bullying. He concludes that the political power will crush you if you maintain such dangerous doctrines![67] Xunzi seems to have come to appreciate the argumentative advantage that being a favorite of the ruler afforded him.

Again, we should construe carefully Xunzi's attitude toward these paradoxes.

They do not represent intellectual challenges that could provoke a change in our assumptions about language. He represents them simply as threats to the conventional system of naming which structures society and shapes the people's heart-mind. These are merely unorthodox speech patterns that depart from the rectified *dao*. The ruler does not study these three classifications to understand them or to show how to *solve* them, but to *suppress* them. He does not engage in distinction-dispute with the dialecticians, but merely bans them. The apparatus of language theory is for the king's use in suppressing disorderly language that would interfere with the efficacy of his *dao*.

For the king, using language or speaking is getting one's intention accomplished, and only fools analyze names any deeper. Fools both confuse others in taking name theory too seriously and get confused themselves. They lose sight of the practical point of language. that point is that we use language deliberately to make it easy to know how to follow guiding discourse. We judge success in language use totally on the accomplishment of what one desires and avoidance of what he hates. Pragmatics is in command.

Is Human Nature Evil?

Dao *and Desires*

All Xunzi's reflections on language cohere with his basic assumptions about human nature and society. We use language (names, phrases, explanations, discrimination arguments, theories, *dao*s) to guide behavior. We have traced the general outlines of Xunzi's view of the relation of nature and nurture in his economic justification for the *li*[ritual]. He insists most on rejecting Song Xing's or Daoist versions of how desires are instilled. Trying to erase desire or to limit them is a mistake, Xunzi would argue. Any such an effort comes from not knowing how to *dao*[guide] desires.[68]

The existence of a desire is not tied to any specific object. We can have desires for objects that do not exist. The desires cause a seeking behavior.[69] A conception of *ke*[permissibility]—the received standards embodied in the heart-mind—guide and control that seeking behavior. A natural, presocial desire is hard to distinguish from a socially conditioned one. We can even condition people to accept death in pursuing something they feel is a moral goal.[70]

Human nature is part of the background conditions of language. Its reality feedback system is a factor in nature. Xunzi refuses to follow Song Xing in distinguishing between *qing*[reality response] and *yu*[desires]. He treats desire as the responses of those reality-feedback mechanisms.[71] We cannot avoid what those mechanisms feed back. That is up to heaven or fate—an uncontrollable necessity. However, in deeming a sought-for-thing to be in accord with a *dao*, knowledge emerges.[72] That know-to *is* a social construction. We know to pursue that thing or avoid it. We neither can nor should eliminate desires. Nor can we wholly satisfy them. So we use language properly to shape our conception of the proper forms of pursuit. Xunzi does not make clear why this way of explaining the impact of language on behavior is better than Song Xing's way.

Now, a common conception of what is *ke*[assertable] should govern all humans. All are, in that sense, following a linguistic *dao*. The problem lies (as Xunzi's defense of *li*[ritual] argued) in proposing an egalitarian *dao* that makes all want the same thing[73] or of having a plethora of *daos* that generate seeking-anarchy. Xunzi's Confucian, traditional *dao* does not satisfy all desires. It satisfies enough, however, that people actually abide by it. In the face of the threat that we can satisfy few or no desires, we choose a *dao* that provides general widespread satisfaction.[74] Know-to simply amounts to mastery of the discourse framework that provides such general satisfaction.

All choice making involves a mixed strategy of desire satisfaction. We must balance desires against each other. Humans need a standard for that balancing or they will not be able even to discriminate disaster and blessings.[75] A public *dao* gives the standard. Private or arbitrary ways of selecting things undermine social harmony. They cannot, therefore, underlie claims of know-(how)-to. That is, we cannot claim to have knowledge when we know what Xunzi calls a *private* pattern or standard of guidance. Conceptions of permissibility are essentially public and conventional. The correct way, in being public and in augmenting and coordinating our actions, has the effect of "exchanging one for two."[76] No one could rationally reject it for anarchistic private choice.

Either we follow a consciously developed pattern of moral discourse or we will be slaves to the material environment. If we use a way (discourse about what is *ke*[permissible]) to guide seeking behavior, then we will be lost. The objects in the environment that we stumble on during our desire-induced, seeking behavior will control us, instead of being part of a coordinated social pattern of behavior.[77] Anyone who becomes fixated in this way on things in the environment must live in uncertainty.[78] He has no control over the production of those things that guide and take control of his desire-seeking behaviors. Since we recognize this insecurity of getting satisfaction, even eating something we want will not satisfy us. An awareness of the certain onset of further desires that may not so providently be satisfied inevitably accompanies any temporary satisfaction.[79]

By participating in a shared system of control of desire gratification, we achieve a calm security. We feel a sense of satisfaction and ease when receiving minimal gratifications. We are not a slave of things.[80] We can reliably increase our satisfaction without directly striving for it. Being guided by public prescriptive discourse: this, Xunzi calls *valuing yourself and enslaving things*.[81]

The Textual Problem

The Neo-Confucians have shaped the traditional stereotype of Xunzi (like that of Mozi) by contrasting him with Mencius. Xunzi gives us an elaborate moralistic theory of desires. The human capacity for learning social distinctions makes conventional morality possible. A *dao*[discourse] can then shape them. Yet, most know Xunzi as the philosopher of human evil.

The claim that human nature is evil is violently out of tune with the dominant themes of Xunzi's work. It has become a standard exercise to try to characterize the *real* differences between Xunzi's doctrines and Mencius'. This exercise could hardly be interesting if one Confucian simply thought human nature was good and the other thought it bad! Indeed the main problem is resolving the incoherence between a relatively Mencius-like dogmatic, absolutist Xunzi and a sophisticated, convention-alist Xunzi. Neither comes through as a thorough pessimist about human nature.

Several scholars and translators have suggested, consequently, that the repetitive phrase "Human nature is evil; goodness is the result of artifice" is a later interpola-tion in the text.[82] In the offending chapter, the slogan (or a close variant) is repeated a dozen times, frequently introduced with the Mohist sounding phrase "If so, then human nature is evil. . . ." The repetitive phrase occurs only at the beginning and end of paragraphs. We never find it in the course of the argument.

The repetitive phrase disappears abruptly about two-thirds of the way through the essay. Then the theme turns to the essential similarity of all humans and the sage-kings! The essay proceeds to the end with no further recapitulation of the slo-gan.

These stylistic objections, however, are mild in comparison to objections based on the content. Spliced between occurrences the slogan, even where it does occur, is a theory of the neutrality and malleability of human nature and the importance of social-conventional li^{ritual}. There is an attack on Mencius' theory of innate good-ness.[83] But Mencius is wrong if human nature is *not* instinctively good. Contradicting Mencius does not require asserting the contrary thesis. Xunzi is not perfectly consis-tent, but he seldom *so* obviously overstates his argument is such a way. Nothing between the slogans even comes close to proving that original nature is evil as op-posed to neutral. It is, at all stages, an argument for a distinction between what is natural and what is learned. The emphasis is always on the role of learning, not on original nature. His detailed positions between the repetitive slogans in this chapter are quite consistent with the rest of *The Xunzi*.

Outside the suspect chapter, we find no suggestion that human nature in general, the $qing^{\text{reality responses}}$ in particular, or even the desires are evil. In all the book's other discussions of nature, passion, distinctions, the heart, senses, conventions, etc., the offending claim is never even hinted at. The catchy slogan, we conclude, gives a very inaccurate impression of Xunzi's moral psychology. On the scale of views rang-ing from Christian original sin and Hobbesian psychological egoism to Mencius so-cial optimism, Xunzi is way over on Mencius' side of the scale.

If we look, for example, at *The Xunzi*'s views on the place of humans in nature, we will see that it directly contradicts the view that human nature is evil. Xunzi's position is that the natural distinguishing feature of humans is the ability to make distinctions and to cultivate thereby a conventional morality. The only thing that makes human nature look like evil is his direct criticism of Mencius. He always insists that the morality must be conventional, a product of wei^{artifice}. Far from main-taining that human nature is simply evil, Xunzi argues that human nature includes a natural drive to master language and therefore obtain morality.

The crucial difference with Mencius lies in Xunzi's accepting Laozi's analysis of how we acquire morality. Xunzi allows that, in principle, we could acquire a wide range of possible conceptions of yi^{morality}. What picks the Confucian morality from among those possible is not the presocial inclinations of our heart-mind but the nat-ural and social-historical context. The source of morality involves the interaction of internal and external factors. We encounter external reality in the course of acting out a socially instilled program. Reality generates feedback, the $qing^{\text{feelings}}$ of the heart and the physical senses. These feedback responses are classified as *shi-fei* by the program as part of program control—sensitivity to the environment. The sage-kings have deliberated and constructed prescriptive discourse to mesh most productively with human and external nature.

Xunzi insists that only one conventional *dao*—the Confucian *dao*—can yield the material and organizational benefits necessary to human flourishing and survival in this difficult world. Morality is not innate, but a cultural accumulation. The *tendency and the ability to gain and practice what culture bequeaths,* however, is innate and natural.

The focus on the "human nature is evil" slogan obscures this point. I will, accordingly, regard the exposition of the detailed position as telling us what the slogan means rather than using the slogan to color our reading of the position. We will search for Xunzi's theory of human nature in between the assertions of the slogan.[84] We lack any evidence that Xunzi had a Christian view of a positive evil in human nature. Whatever role the slogan might have played in distinguishing his view from that of Mencius, *we* more accurately characterize him as saying that human nature is neutral. It is neutral in principle as to which morality it will adopt, and it quite naturally does adopt one. The strongest coherent interpretation we can give the slogan is that humans would live in chaos and disorder without a social guiding morality.

We have already laid the conceptual foundations of Xunzi's position on human nature. It revolves about the terms *xing*[nature] and *wei*[artifice] defined at the beginning of the "Rectification of Names" chapter. And it emerges equally clearly in his account of humans' position in the scheme of life forms. The ability and tendency to acquire morality distinguishes us from other animals. Xunzi uses our capacity to make and accumulate discriminations in language to explain this moral ability and tendency.

Morality and language are mutually implicated social practices. Language is the tool by which society can collect, preserve, and pass discriminatory skills on to later generations. The purpose of any distinction or name is behavioral guidance, especially in coordination with others. Convention, far from being an evil, is the very essence of humanity. Thus Xunzi's criticism of Mencius is serious and deep indeed. One cannot dispense with teachers and books of *li;* they are the conduits of *dao.*

All humans have a natural tendency to learn language, rituals, shared pronouncements. We are a species with a natural tendency to conformity in a common doctrine, that is, to morality. We desire good because we have that unfilled potential, a natural void in our constitution. We do not desire it because we are *evil,* but because we are *empty.* That unfilled potential is all that Xunzi can mean by evil, if he is indeed the author of that slogan.

If we do not fulfill our moral potential, then the desires operating by themselves will result in the pattern of conduct that, by those traditional standards, is evil. The potential is the same in all people, from the sage-kings to the paradigms of human evil, the wicked last kings of declining dynasties. *Li*[rites] can condition and transform the nature of all. Xunzi belongs clearly on the nurture side of the nature-nurture debate. Mencius, by contrast, is on the nature side. That captures their difference far better than the evil-good slogans.

Philosophy of Heart-Mind

A puzzle—the Confucian problem of evil—remains. For Mencius (and to some degree for Confucius) the existence of evil was a paradox. The Confucian problem does not follow from the existence of some infinitely good creator. It comes from the Confucian conception of a golden age with sage-kings together with their optimistic doctrine about the effects of good (sagely) rule. Confucius' *one person* model-emulation theory of moral growth and Mencius' plant, needing only minimal basic conditions to grow into full sagehood, make the emergence of evil puzzling. If one generation has sage-kings, how can the next generation lack sages? If ever there were sage-kings, then they must have ordered human society under their rule so that all could (and would) become sages. Confucian assumptions make the historical decline inexplicable.[85]

Xunzi's problem is just the converse of Mencius'. Both agree that we are essentially like the sage-kings. If we need the disciplining effects of past deliberate, conventional artifice to become moral, if we need traditional guidance in principle in order to know what is right, then so did the sage-kings. Where did the sage-kings get the wherewithal to become moral? Do we need an infinite chain of sage-kings each teaching those after them? Where does the chain start?

If the chain starts with the sage-kings and we are like them, then Mencius' position is necessary after all. We could each have invented the *li* ourselves from the inclinations of our heart-minds. The other way out is Zhuangzi's permissive view: not only could we have invented the *li* but myriad other *daos* as well. The content of the *li*[ritual] is accidental. Those who claim to be sages "project their *shi-feis* onto heaven." They claim absolute validity for their situational, indexical guides. In that, too, all humans are like the sage-kings.

Xunzi is not willing to give up the characteristic Confucian claim of only one correct *dao*. Nor is he willing to abandon his position that morality is a convention, a shared coordination system that could, in principle, be different. He is unwilling to embrace the innateness view of Mencius that he considers silly and empirically baseless. His problem, then, is how morality ever originated. If he allows the sage-kings to create it, why not us?

We have seen that Xunzi has implicitly allowed that heaven (nature) indirectly selects the proper discourse. He assumes that only Confucian discourse will enable human survival in the natural world. His pragmatism starts from the existence of historically settled standards. The mechanism that makes one *dao* special is not natural selection. Humans make the pragmatic judgment that this very *dao* is necessary in the circumstances. But the preferred *dao* is built into those very circumstances. It is part of natural history that it has come to be the existing conventional standard. Pragmatic success must be interpreted by established standards.

We could, therefore, reinvent the *li*. We must be able to duplicate the sage-kings' creative linguistic activity. We could devise workable social and other distinctions, terms, and discourse patterns. Thus, it follows, we do not have to learn *dao* from the tradition after all.

Xunzi, accordingly, owes us an account of how to make the sage-kings' productive activity consistent with his principles of conformity to tradition. Are their initial creative efforts as private and arbitrary as ours would be? How could the sage-kings, who were essentially like us, have succeeded in producing the absolutely correct *li* and the *dao?* His account will either fail or it will explain how, in principle, each of us could do the same. He cannot make it too easy, or we would not be able to explain why we do not routinely do it.

This problem further explains why in some sections Xunzi moves even closer to Mencius. The extreme case is in his chapter "Dispelling Obsessions." There he discusses the way the heart-mind operates. He argues that *obsessions* interfere with a natural human capacity to apprehend *dao.* This chapter seems drastically to back off from the analysis of the correct *dao* as a convention.

The thesis of the chapter exploits a Zhuangzi theme in criticizing all alternative *dao*s. Any choice of a *dao* involves a presupposed *shi-fei.* The appearance of a variety of competing *dao*s comes from each scholar's obsession with one particular *shi*[this:right]. That standard generates these other guiding *shi-fei*s. Using a standard is a form of obsession (a prejudice in Zhuangzi's sense). Xunzi, however, assumes that from an *unobsessed* perspective, we would find exactly one correct course. Thus Xunzi, not Zhuangzi, makes the illegitimate slide from relativism to absolutism. The sages' minds are alike in apprehending and following the unobsessed *dao.* Xunzi also appeals to the Neo-Mohists' realistic point. Of the various doctrines, some must be *shi* and some *fei.* Xunzi translates that claim pragmatically as, some will produce order and some disorder.[86] Everyone sincerely tries to rectify errors and thinks his own perspective correct. However, Xunzi agrees with Zhuangzi that their prior *shi-fei*s hinder their efforts to apprehend what is correct.

Xunzi argues that the commitment to any particular *shi-fei* so affects our heart-mind that it distorts our ability to see the *real* distinctions. Borrowing heavily from Mozi, Xunzi claims that such obsessions could make us unable to distinguish black and white right in front of us.[87]

Now this is a curiously disingenuous use of Mohist and Daoist doctrine. What is Xunzi to say of himself and his inflated confidence that he sees black and white without the prejudice of some prior *shi-fei?* Why is his Confucian order-based interpretation not an obsession? He seems to be taking the position that any accepted distinction is a source of obsession—desire, aversion, nearness, distance, beginning, ending. Any of the ten thousand differences interferes with the heart-mind's skill. Indeed, as we shall see, he argues that to see the real distinctions, the heart-mind must be *empty.*

This brings him practically in line with Mencius. The heart-mind works best without language! But Xunzi does not quite fall for the discredited antilanguage conclusion. The problem, in Daoist terms, is not in making the distinctions, but in being *obsessed* by one side of a contrast that should be balanced. It is failing to see the reversibility of opposites that makes one lose balance and perspective.

Xunzi's diagnosis of his philosophical rivals characterizes each using one key term, the one that Zhuangzi would call his presupposed *shi*[this:right]. The Mohists would call it that which he *zhi*[grasps] and Laozi would call it the term *he chang*[constants]. Then, an Zhuangzi noted, the emphasis on one side produces a complementary *deficiency* in something else. Not being aware of the value of the opposite keeps us from *ming*[clarity]. For example, the value of use obsesses Mozi so much that he does not see the value of decorative embellishment (*wen*[literature]). Xunzi even criticizes Zhuangzi using this technique.[88] Zhuangzi so emphasized the perspective of *tian*[nature] that he did not see the perspective of *ren*[humans].[89]

Starting from one distinction as the basic *shi-fei,* each rival scholar then gets a *dao*[way] that has some dominant virtue. Each, however, has only one aspect of the sum *dao.* The sum *dao*'s parts are constant and it responds to all changes in circumstances. So no single aspect can pick it out.[90] This inclines Xunzi to approach an antilanguage solution to the problem of standards. He, more than Zhuangzi, concludes that language distorts the *dao.*

Because this analysis draws so heavily from Zhuangzi's own, we have to wonder how Xunzi arrives at his pro-Confucian conclusion. The answer is shockingly Mencius-like. Confucius' *renzhi*[intuitive knowledge], Xunzi baldly asserts, is free from obsession. So Confucius was able to study any *shu*[art] and reach the level of the original kings. He can align with a school in following the Zhou *dao* and avoid any bias toward *cheng*[completed] cultural accumulation.[91]

That argument for an objective access to *dao* makes sense only if intended for internal Confucian consumption—preaching to the converted! That he has a bias toward settled and fixed tradition is exactly the standard *external* criticism of Confucius. The curious thing is that Xunzi's resolution of the difficulty abandons his own bias for settled convention. He ends up celebrating *ren*[benevolence]—the intuitive interpretive principle! His position now, like Mencius', will impale itself on Zhuangzi's argument against innate intuition.

Thus the unreflective dogmatist comes out, in part, because the sophisticated defense of Confucianism flounders. This chapter has a tone of desperation! How can Xunzi expect *us* to agree that Confucius was balanced and Zhuangzi was not? The criterion of whether we have appropriately balanced the opposing distinctions lies in our *dao,* Xunzi tells us.[92] We Daoists would agree. But the trick is to pick *which dao.* For Xunzi, who uses *dao*[way] with modifiers like *jian*[illicit] and *jia*[bogus], the question "which *dao?*" is surely appropriate. Xunzi finds himself in his own version of Mencius' circular justification. You have to know an appropriate *dao* or you will associate with people who approve of a *fei-dao.* But this is simply the preacher urging the flock not to allow doubt to creep in when they contemplate that the world finds them silly.

Now how do we get this cognitive grasp on the correct *dao* with all the alternatives around? If we allow any training, we bias the choice. If we pick out a particular hierarchical class, we bias the choice. Xunzi seems aware of the need for a universally accessible point of view from which the initial grasping of the appropriate *dao* is possible. This forces him in the direction of Mencius. He, however, tries to avoid the innatism which he himself has criticized so strongly. Instead he tries to go about the task via negativa.

This is often touted as a Daoist influence on Xunzi. I shall argue that it is Xunzi's creating the Confucian caricature of Daoism. The central terms—*empty, unified,* and *still*—are considered central in Daoism more as a result of Xunzi than because they play central roles in Zhuangzi's theory. I will argue in the next chapter that his student, Han Feizi, reads *The Laozi* through Xunzi's filter. They both start with the authoritarian assumption of an absolute correct way. They assert what Zhuangzi denies, the possibility of achieving a frame of mind that gives unbiased access to it.

And they preach this authoritarian doctrine to the ruler's welcome ears. Neither fully acknowledges Zhuangzi's skepticism of any attempt to do this.

> How do humans know *dao?* The heart-mind. How does the heart-mind know it? By being empty, one, and still. The mind never fails to accumulate yet it has what can be called *emptiness.* The mind never fails to be full, yet it has what can be called *one.* The mind is never inactive and yet it has what can be called *still.* People have *zhi*[intelligence] at birth (or in living), having *zhi* they have intentions and the intentions are stored up. What is called *empty* is not allowing what is stored up to interfere with future receptivity. The heart-mind has intelligence at birth (or in living) and the intelligence leads to differences. Differences are things known together and at the same time. So it is two and yet something we can call *one* exists. We call our not letting one interfere with the other *one.* When the heart-mind sleeps, we dream; in fantasy it goes where it wants; when we employ it, it plans. So the heart-mind is never at rest and yet it has what we can call *stillness.* We call not confusing fantasy and knowledge *stillness.*[93]

> The process of seeking *dao* when you have not achieved *dao,* is called empty, one and still. Do it! Then the emptiness of those who need *dao* results in entry. The oneness of those who serve *dao* results in totality. The stillness of those who contemplate *dao* results in [good] judgment. To know *dao* and engage in conduct, one embodies (becomes part of) *dao.* Empty, one and still—call these the great clarity.[94]

Xunzi's three factors remind us again how Chinese heart-mind theory differs from the Western theory of mind. The emphasis on *zhi*[know-to] is not on processing and storage. He links the cognitive function of mind directly to intentions, distinctions, and discriminations. The mind's output (in memories, dreams, and fantasy) is intentions and action plans.

The three qualities of mind that Xunzi recommends resembles the doctrine of some modern moral objectivists. Their position, like Xunzi's is that we should judge from a neutral point of view, without prejudice or passion and in awareness of all the facts. Then we could arrive at an intersubjectively valid moral judgment.[95] Xunzi needs a cognitively objective *dao* to answer Zhuangzi. The objectivity, however, is not in scientific description (for which the three qualities would be less appropriate), but in the absence of bias in prescriptive judgment.

The know-how or know-to does involve a reality check (or it would not work in a real context). Xunzi's characterization surely rivals Mencius' in its exaggerated portrayal of the enlightened sage. Arguably, Confucian assumptions require this exaggeration. Both Xunzi and Mencius are trying to justify adherence to a complex set of rules that they claim is the uniquely correct *way.* They both think the mind of sages created that discourse ages ago, and yet adherence to it is always appropriate. And finally, each is committed to the view (required to justify the Confucian *dao*) that every human *could* come to see what the *dao* is.

> Of the ten thousand things, there is no identifying shape that we do not see, none we see that we do not grade, none we grade that lose their [correct] position. They can sit in their room and see to the four seas, be in the present and grade

things far in the past. Glancing over ten thousand things they can know what the reality-feedback would be, perusing order and disorder, they could penetrate the measure, they structure the universe and govern the ten thousand thing-kinds, institute the great principles and the direction of the universe.[96]

Xunzi goes on in even more hyperbolic terms (though with less content). Obviously, the *dao* is the ideal course of conduct. We would all apprehend it if we had control of the universal (unobsessed with any partial perspective) point of view. Xunzi's moral position is a kind of ideal-observer view. But it still differs from Mencius. It does not put the know-to in innate dispositions, but in the capacity to perceive accurately and without distortion the prescriptive order of things. In a sense, the *real dao* still comes from the outside to the ideally receptive heart-mind. Xunzi's objective is a descendent of Neo-Mohist external realism.

As I have argued, the three key terms here are not especially Daoist. Thinking of Daoism as favoring emptiness or stillness requires taking the negative *dao* as the absolute or constant *dao*. I have argued that this contradicts Laozi's opening assumption that there is no perspectiveless point of view. The only interesting Daoist element in this otherwise familiar, absolutist meta-ethical approach is the claim that languages (*shi-fei*s) are image-shapers. Here again, Xunzi's position has a formal similarity with that of Mencius. Since obsession results from adopting a *shi-fei* (stressing or *constanting* one element of a dichotomy), he describes his universal perspective in almost mystical terms. It seems to require that we provisionally abandon language and guiding distinctions in order to discover the correct way to use language and guide distinctions. Xunzi uses only the immature antilanguage version of Daoism if he draws on Daoism at all for this absolutist account of discovery of the single correct *dao*.

Thus Xunzi's position in this section is also at odds with the sophisticated conventionalist Xunzi. He must consider the heart-mind as having *some independent access* to *dao*. If we are all alike, then we are all capable of such access. The *junzi*^{gentleman} is one who correctly exercises the capacity. *Dao* is not, here, regarded as one convention among many, but as the uniquely best path taking everything into account. It is the path that would be chosen with total impartiality, total comprehension, and total intelligence. Those who reach Xunzi's ideal can replicate the creative work of the sages in evaluative as well as descriptive terms. Finally it is only the informed, educated reaction of the *junzi*^{gentleman} that can be a *fa*^{standard} of content as well as interpretation.

For slightly different reasons, then, both Xunzi and Mencius ultimately make the heart-mind more important than conventions, learning, and accumulation of language and other social practices. This potentially sagelike heart-mind grasps the morally relevant nature of the world and guides the production of the conventions. However inconsistent this doctrine is with the conventionalist Xunzi, it certainly excludes entirely any straightforward reading of the slogan "human nature is evil!"

> The heart-mind is the ruler of the bodily parts and the regulator of spiritual insight. It gives commands but is not subject to them. What it must prohibit it prohibits; what it must move it moves; what it must take it takes; what it must choose it chooses; what it must do it does; what it must stop it stops. We can

make the mouth speak or be silent, the body parts bend or extend. But we cannot make the mind change its intentions. What coincides with its internal standards it accepts; what does not it rejects.[97]

This certainly does not sound like the *evil* mind destined to blind gratification of desires whenever it lacks the *control* of cultural artifice. This doctrine of the heart-mind has the same practical conclusion as Mencius'. He even goes back to the "ruler of the other organs" claim ridiculed by Zhuangzi. By its nature, the heart-mind cannot be anything but the ruler. The other parts of the body, by their nature, are to be ruled and controlled.

The heart-mind is an independent route of access to practical wisdom. Mencius' heart-mind is such a route because it has the sum of all that wisdom built in. Xunzi's heart-mind is such a route because it is so empty and receptive that it can take in the entire external situation. After achieving open receptivity to the total situation, however, the heart must also have the correct internal standards of judgment. We cannot, remember, get a *shi-fei* out unless we put one in. Xunzi has not answered Zhuangzi's criticism of Mencius' heart-mind theory. Confucianism, in the end, cannot fully grasp the argument of Daoism and still justify maintaining its essentially authoritarian character.

Xunzi's theory of the heart-mind does as well as can be done. It makes just the kinds of grandiose claims that a Confucian needs to make to justify the Confucian *dao*. If the heart-mind is as he describes it, if it can adopt a universal perspective, totally lack obsession, and achieve the empty, unified, still ideal and then still have any inclination to choose certain standards and *shi-fei*s, then we could at least allow that it is only a philosophically controversial conception of moral objectivity. It would become one of many possible meta-ethical positions (a Confucian version of the ideal-observer theory). But Zhuangzi's argument was that the desired perspective is not conceptually possible *and*, if it were, the meta-ethical theory is still flawed. We have no reason to regard *that* person's judgment as authoritative. The curious thing is that Xunzi should think any Confucian has achieved an unbiased perspective given his own analysis. Both Mencius and Xunzi seem, in the end, either unable to grasp the basic philosophical difficulty of justifying choice among *dao*s or unwilling to acknowledge it.

10

Han Feizi: The Ruler's Interpretation

[Han Feizi's] personal fate, like that of Lord Shang (ripped to pieces by chariots in 338 B.C.) and Li Ssu (cut in two at the waist in 208 B.C.), helps one to appreciate why Yangists and Taoists recommend the relative security of private life.

A. C. GRAHAM [1]

In this book the Legalist School is seen at the peak of its development, a school of thought which . . . is the nearest counterpart in China to West European post-medieval political theory.

E. R. HUGHES [2]

I again suggest, however, that despite the enormous differences in language and metaphor, we may in fact find in ancient China more anticipations of contemporary Western social sciences than of the natural sciences.

BENJAMIN SCHWARTZ [3]

Han Feizi's Life and the Ruling Image

Han Feizi marks the end of the classical period. He not only is the last zi[master] in the traditional list, he arguably played a pivotal role in drawing the fertile Hundred Schools period to a close. He and Lisi, a more organizationally inclined student of Xunzi, became influential advisers of the notorious Qinshi Huangdi (the first emperor of the Qin dynasty). Their advice triggered an intolerant period of philosophical repression and state-supported orthodoxy. The Qin empire marks the beginning of China's philosophical dark age.

Han Feizi's was the first zi[master] certifiably from the ruling nobility. This helps explain why he appreciates doctrines that favor authority. He was a prince of the small kingdom of Han. He apparently attended the Ji academy while it was under the direction of Xunzi. There, we suppose, he met and impressed Lisi, arguably the most influential philosophy student in history. Lisi, Han Feizi's organizationally inclined fellow student, drew Han Feizi's works to the attention of the future unifier of China. Lisi helped arrange a meeting between the ruler and the strategic thinker. Later, he was to point out that the thinker's loyalty (despite the usefulness of his ideas) was with his home state and recommended his execution. The king, in perfect conformity with Han Feizi's theories, followed this advice.[4]

Han Feizi's writings were erudite, rich in historical detail and examples. He had *learned* philosophy, but added little original philosophy of his own. His writings were almost purely practical. They dealt with techniques of rule intended to strengthen the ruler in the competition for military conquest. His writings eschew ethics in favor of strategy. He took the end as given and obvious. The ruling noble's goal was conquering and unifying *tian-xia*[all under heaven]. He probably intended his tactics for his own kingdom but events put them in the hands of the Qin which gobbled up Han early in its expansion.

So this study ends, as it began, with a nonphilosopher. Beyond his dogmatic assumptions about the end of theorizing and his essentially strategic topic, Han Feizi's writing is more polemical than reasoned. A typical pattern is that he recites some story and then concludes that it is an example to illustrate a phrase, about which one might also cite a poem. His cynicism rests on the familiar sneering tone of superior realistic insight. We recognize it from all self-described realists who reject moral considerations.[5] He shows hardly a glimmer of awareness of the unjustified assumptions and contradictions in his theoretical position.

Yet I do choose to include him for reasons that are the mirror image of those I earlier gave for including Confucius. I thereby partly defer to the traditional account in its list of classical masters. Han Feizi also plays an important role in furthering the authoritarian distortion of Daoism that Neo-Confucianism inherited from China's philosophical dark age. But further, as Confucius showed the assumptions that generated philosophical controversy in China, so Han Feizi shows how the philosophical conclusions influenced the political institutions of imperial China that ended philosophy. Because of the nature of that influence, Han Feizi is the philosophical end of this journey through ideas.

I serve another of this book's purposes by including him. Seeing clearly the philosophical background of Han Feizi means once again challenging the dominant Confucian image. The ruling theory casts the *fa jia*[Standardizers] as a massive evil, an oppressor of people. Confucian historians can then cast themselves as the valiant defenders of the people against this ruthless despotism. Their picture of Han Feizi is much more negative than that of Confucianism's other foil, Daoism. In interesting formal ways, however, the traditional treatment of the two schools are parallel.

The parallel is that both schools are after-the-fact inventions of Han historians. Han intellectual history initiated the traditional labels and first clustered classical thinkers under them. Graham offers an interesting insight into the development of *schools analysis*.[6] The identification of a *rumo*[Confucian-Mohist] *bian*[dispute] was the earliest analysis, and arguably, these were the only self-conscious schools in the classical period. In the outer chapters of the *Zhuangzi* we find a purportedly developmental history of thought that does not include any Confucian thinkers. It starts from Mozi to Song Xing, then Shendao, Laozi, and finally Zhuangzi. In other words, the classical period knew nothing of *daojia*[daoism] or *fajia*[legalism] as schools. The later Han classification that has held analysis in a death grip since then identified different schools by what the Han historians took to be a key term in each cluster of thinkers or texts: *yin-yang, ming*[names], *dao*[way], and *fa*[standards].

In the last two cases especially, the tradition treats writers as sharing a doctrine, not merely a conceptual focus. The attributed doctrine centers on each school's single concept—*dao* and *fa* respectively. Further, the orthodox Confucian interpretation al-

leges that each school's ideology *drastically changed the meaning* of its central concept. This turns history on its head and makes them, rather than Confucianism, the
odd men out. Daoists were alleged to have changed *dao* from a moral concept to a
metaphysical one, legalists to have changed *fa* from meaning *standards* to meaning
laws. We, therefore, have since tended to see the clustered writers as bonded by a
stronger theoretical unity than they may in fact have shared and as more focused and
specialized on this one term than they actually were. Standard histories characterize
all the theories so clustered mainly by discussing the change in meaning of the chosen term. The interpretive hypothesis supplies the traditionally recognized essential
doctrine. Once the meaning hypothesis is firmly in hand, all interpreters have to
do is find the word and attribute the traditionally invented doctrine based on the
meaning-change hypothesis to the writer.

In neither case can one find the writers of the heterodox schools showing any
self-awareness of having changed the meaning of their key term. They seem to think
they are using the words and addressing the issues common to other thinkers of the
period. And I find no convincing argument that they were wrong in so viewing
themselves. *We* learn the hypothesis of meaning-change as an article of faith of sinology
supported by numbing authoritative repetition.

Predictably, this meaning-change hypothesis deforms the heterodox schools' critique of Confucianism. It makes the other schools' theory less accessible and the
relevance of their arguments to Confucianism more obscure. This is equally important in the case of Han Feizi. The soundness of his critique of Xunzi's authoritarian
views from the authority's perspective illuminates one of the pervasive weaknesses
of Confucianism, its reliance on the interpretive authority of its own scholarly clique.

The ruling interpretation, based on the hypothesis of meaning change, translates
fajia as *Legalist* and treats the *fajia* as similar to Western legal positivists. This
interpretive hypothesis, again, falls into the translator's trap. The meaning theory
assumes the chosen Western term is univocal. Thus the hypothesis ignores an important ambiguity in the Western term *law*. One sense of law is purely formal. Syntactically *a law* is a universal sentence. Semantically it involves some modal notion
(scientific necessity, moral, or political obligation). The narrower, more concrete
notion of law is of one quite specific use of syntactical laws in a political institution
more specifically called *human law* or *penal law*. The ambiguity is most familiar in
the political use in the contrast between a law and *the* law.

Legal positivism is one of several theories of the nature of human law. It differs
from its main classical rival, natural law theory, in that it conceptually separates law
in this narrow sense from morality. All the schools use the formal concept of *a law*
of both systems of obligation in debating that issue. Obviously, it is implausible that
we will find any counterpart of the syntactic notion of *a law* in ancient China.

Some, but not all, legal positivists doubt that moral law is real or that moral
obligations are objective. The classical Western legal positivist, John Austin, treated
legal obligation (narrow sense) as conceptually dependent on punishment.[7] Austin
defines positive law (as opposed to moral law) as the general command of a ruler
when backed up by threat of punishment. Positivists have been most visible in public
Western disputes as enemies of the concept of natural human rights.

The ruling interpretive theory views the *fajia* [Standardizers] of ancient China through
the lens of this Western dispute. It blends that familiar Western perspective with the

image of the school fostered by the Confucian interpretation. The outcome is a school of legal positivists who advocate draconian cruelty toward the people. Confucian theory depicts itself as standing against a Legalist-inspired, systematic, and brutal reign of terror.

I shall argue that *fa* does not have either of the equivocal meanings of *law*. For legalists, as for the rest of Chinese philosophy, it continues to mean *standards*. Viewing *fa*[objective standards] correctly will help us understand better the moral and practical argument Han Feizi made against Confucianism. It will make it clear that the enemy, from Han Feizi's perspective, is not the people. The scholarly bureaucracy, the ambitious advisers—in a word, the Confucians—are the target of *fa*.

Fa: *Problems about Meaning*

I challenge the hypothesis that *fa jia*[Legalists] changed the meaning of *fa* from standards to penal law. Versions of this challenge have been raised before. Creel[8] first saw that for the allegedly Legalist writer, Shen Buhai, translating *fa* as *law* would mislead readers about his theory. Most writers accept that the translation is sometimes inaccurate.[9] I shall argue the same point for Han Feizi (and indirectly for Shang Yang, Guanzi, and other so-called Chinese Legalists).

The Historical Theory of Meaning. There are some general theoretical reasons to treat all hypotheses of radical meaning change as suspect. They violate the *unity* ideal that motivates interpretative explanation. More importantly, the historical theory of meaning mitigates against such promiscuous changes in meaning. Some commentators claim this meaning volatility is characteristic of Chinese characters. Historical theory agrees with Mozi on this principle: those who use terms typically intend to conform to their teachers' conventions of use. Departures are possible, but the burden of proof is on the claim that there was either a deliberate or accidental departure from established meaning conventions.

The advocates of the meaning-change hypothesis usually do acknowledge that *fa* once meant *standards*. The appearance of drastic meaning change, however, results partly from the inaccuracy of the one-word translation. Mozi first introduced the term into formal philosophy. Two important detailed features of Mozi's use of *fa* are important and, I shall argue, enduring. First, *fa* are standards used to guide *the application of the terms* found in guiding discourse. Second, *fa* are analogous to *measurements*. The idea is that the standards for projecting the use of terms should be definitive and easily accessible. Mozi likens the use of *fa* to the application of a measuring tool. *Fa* should be available to ordinary people merely by the use of their eyes and ears. His utilitarianism was a *fa* because it was both a guide to making distinctions and it was measurable—accessible to nonscholars.

The analytic Mohist dialecticians make it even more explicit that *fa* are the standards for the application of a term. The *Mohist Canon* says a *fa* is that thing F such that a thing's being like F is its being of the type in question. The examples of *fa* (presumably for a circle) are an image of a circle, another circle, and a compass. So we have models and measurement operations that fix a term's use.

Even allegedly *Legalist* antecedents of the use of *fa* conform to this Mohist model. Guanzi was a rough contemporary of Confucius who is classed among the

Legalists.[10] *The Guanzi* lists the foot rule, marking line, compass and square, beam and weight, peck bushel, and grain leveler as examples of *fa*standards.[11] Guanzi could, therefore, consistently advocate both *li*ritual and *fa*. *Fa* was the non-Confucian solution to rectifying names. This rival theory recommended objective, publicly accessible standards of name use. It opposed the cultivated intuition of the leaders of mutual-admiration societies made up of experts at chanting old texts. *Fa* and *li* were, therefore, viewed as compatible. *Fa* could, in fact, complement any traditional guiding scheme of names. *Fa* guides action governed by any *dao* the way measuring tools guide the application of terms like *round* and *straight* in any set of building instructions. The *fa* make it possible to follow the instructions accurately.

The Confucians had not originally used the notion of *fa* because its structure was authoritarian. The core assumption of the Confucian policy of rectifying names was that the ruler, using either an innate or acquired intuition, was supposed to settle correct language use. Mozi's agreement with the superior recognized Shendao's sociological point that the ruler *will* influence usage, but Mozi maintained that *tian*nature should be taken as the ultimate model. *Tian*nature identified the constant, measurementlike, easily projectable standard of utility as a *fa*standard of language use.

The real departure, then, from the traditional theory of *fa* occurs with Xunzi. Like Guanzi, Xunzi discussed *fa* alongside *li* as if there were no conflict. Xunzi distinguished *fa* from both the regulations and the punishments. The *fa*standards, thus, are not an alternative form of social control. They are ways of determining the application of terms in *any* guiding social discourse.[12] Xunzi's position is that the only standard for the use of terms is *convention* and the only *fa*standard for the *correct interpretation* of convention is the *junzi*superior man. Xunzi fixed historical tradition, as embodied in current scholarly authority, as the main source of correct usage.

For Xunzi, then, the first assumption holds: *fa* are standards for the projection of terms.[13] Since *Fa*standards are necessary for fixing the boundaries of terms used in regulations they are presupposed in any application of punishment. They are the standards for the application of a code to particular cases. Chinese calls the officials who make those individualized decisions *faguan*magistrates, reminiscent of Xunzi's *tianguan*heavenly pipes (the senses). Xunzi was arguing that a *faguan* should always be the schooled specialist with a developed intuition. He thus rejects Mozi's goal of objective, democratically accessible standards.

Han Feizi, I shall argue, rejected his teacher's account of what the *fa* should be and developed the rival theory that they should be objective and accessible. He was less traditionalist, but no less authoritarian. He was equally committed to the authoritarian use of punishment. He distinguishes *fa* from *de*virtuosity specifically in that the latter is accessible only to a few and *fa* is accessible to the mass of people.[14] He follows the philosophical tradition in using *fa* with the sense of *objective, public, accessible standards for interpreting guidance into behavior*.

The Distinction of Meaning and Reference. The second general principle governing our theories about meaning is the distinction of meaning and reference. A claim about the meaning or sense of a term should explain the whole extension or reference of the term. If a writer speaks of coins and uses a penny as an example more often than a quarter, she has not changed the meaning of *coin*. Even if her coin theory emphasizes the importance of pennies among coins as a central illustrative case, it does not change the meaning of *coin*. Han Feizi speaks of public standards as guiding performance. His theory sometimes stresses public proclamations with measurement-like precision in describing links between performance and reward-punishment.

Are these laws? Our Western notion of *law* is of a species of public, objective, clear, accessible standards of behavior. Our notion has the formal feature mentioned above. Scientific, moral, and penal laws are formally universal, sentential propositions. Austin noted the requirement that the commands or expression of desire be *general*. Han Feizi never restricts $fa^{\text{standards}}$ to either sententials or universal sententials. His account is notoriously about $ming^{\text{name}}$ and $xing^{\text{punishment}}$. In Western theory, penal laws are specifically those general commands backed by threat of punishment. Han Feizi applies $fa^{\text{standards}}$ to both reward and punishment. We call principles that govern reward or advancement, even if clearly defined and rigorously enforced, *standards*. There are standards of tenure and laws against fraud. In English, all laws are standards, but not all standards are laws.

If Han Feizi uses *fa sometimes* in reference to what are clearly grammatically rules in universal sentential form, promulgated by public authority with punishments attached and *other times* uses it of standards for appointment, measurement, language, reward, and so forth, then his linguistic behavior is only compatible with the interpretive theory that *fa* still *means objective standards*. He may have different *beliefs* about many aspects of how forms of discourse should guide behavior, and he may concentrate in his theory of a specific type of objective, public standard but he does not change the *meaning* of the terms he uses to express those beliefs.

Tang Juni is surely correct. Han Feizi advocates having *fa* posted for public awareness of what punishments will be meted out. He cites the example of Shang Yang's appointment rule that mathematically calculates the rank one will achieve based on the number of heads cut off in battle. In this, Tang concludes, Han Feizi is "exactly following Mozi." [15] He does not change the meaning of $fa^{\text{objective public standards}}$.

Coherence of Nominal and Verbal Usage. A third general principle of identifying meaning applies with special force to Chinese. We have observed that Chinese words have syntactical mobility; they can be used as nouns and as verbs. *Fa*, like *dao*, is a famous example. Just as our theory of meaning should explain the whole range of referential uses of a word, so it should, as far as possible, coherently explain the linked nominal and verbal uses of a term. As I previously argued, we should mirror the verbal sense of $dao^{\text{guide:speak}}$ with the nominal use of $dao^{\text{guiding discourse}}$. The typical translation of verbal *fa* is *to model on* or *to emulate*. The nominal form, then, is appropriately translated as *standard* or *model*.

Meaning Gaps and Meaning Efficiency. Finally, a hypothesis of meaning change is more plausible when a *meaning gap* needs to be filled. In this case, translation accepts that there are many other terms to refer to commands, regulations, and punishment codes. We regard Confucius as referring to public codes when he criticized $xing^{\text{punishment}}$.[16] Han Feizi seems to conform perfectly to that use.[17] Other terms that could be used to refer to penal codes include $ling^{\text{commands}}$ and $zhi^{\text{regulations}}$. Using *fa*, which is their only term playing the crucial role of objective interpretive standards, to duplicate these already existing concepts is, at best, linguistically inefficient.

A related form of inefficiency in translating Han Feizi flows out of the above two conditions. Han Feizi uses *fa* in combination with a number of terms and the compound use makes more sense if we keep the meaning of *fa* general. So for example he refers to *fa-ling* (interpretive standards with commands), which seem closest to standard laws. But he also uses *fa* in compounds where it can almost never mean straightforward penal law, for example, *fa-du* (interpretive standards with criteria), *fa-i* (interpretive standards with morality), and *fa-shu* (interpretive standards with methods).

Bodde[18] notes that the Qin called their legal code *lü*[laws]. The word, he notes, occurred very rarely in earlier texts. Now if Han Feizi was the theoretician and Lisi implemented the theory in Qin institutions, why coin a new term for this institution? The most plausible answer is that for Lisi and for Han Feizi, as for Xunzi and for the tradition before them, *fa*[standards] did not mean law but objective standards. The statutes were *a particular type* of objective standards.

In summary, I am reluctant to credit Han Feizi with a counterpart of the Western concept of law. He shows no special awareness of the prescriptive universal sentences. His conceptual structure is still that which we described in presenting Mozi's utilitarianism. There are various competing bodies of social guiding discourse: *li, i, dao,* etc. The problem of interpreting that discourse into behavior continues to be the central issue. Dealing with the interpretive problem is the essential role of *fa*[standards]. The prescriptive *sentence* itself still plays no specific explanatory role in the account. Nor do we find the counterpart notions of a legal duty, a legal obligation, or a legal right. Han Feizi admittedly has a concept of public, prescriptive codes of behavior. But a *fa* is not a law; it is any objective standard. *Fa* represent reliable, public, nonintuitive standards for the application of terms in prescriptive discourse in general.

Fa[objective standards] *and Elite Intuition*

The *fa jia*[standardizers] do not contrast penal law and *moral law*. They contrast *fa*[measurement standards] and *li*[ritual]. The latter relies on intellectual authorities for its discovery and interpretation. The contrast of *fa* and *li* is a contrast between two rival theories of positive or conventional, public guidance. Neither is formally lawlike. One is intuitive, scholarly, and the province of a small elite. The other is public, measured, and easily ascertained by most people. The issue between Han Feizi and his teacher Xunzi is not about punishment. Both are enthusiastic supporters of punishment.

The target of Han Feizi's techniques of government is control of the scholar bureaucrats, the status to which politically ambitious Confucians aspired. The central polarity in his analysis is the ruler-minister polarity, not the ruler-people polarity. Han Feizi takes the perspective of the ruler in the competition with ministers as rivals for power. I shall argue that all three of Han Feizi's famous techniques—*shi, shu,* and *fa*—are directed at controlling the bureaucracy more than the populace at large.

The people are mostly irrelevant to Han Feizi's analysis. Where they are brought in, it is mostly as tools or objects of the power struggle between the ruler and cliques of ministers. In that context, when Han Feizi does occasionally raise the issue of the people, he actually argues for protecting the people from the ministers by depriving the ministers of arbitrary power. This, note, is not because he takes the well-being or protection of the people as a goal. His goal is still to enhance the ruler's relative power in the struggle with his bureaucracy. The protection of the people is incidental to depriving the ministers of dangerous quanta of the ruler's power.

The Confucians became essentially a civil service union. They adopted a perspective designed to protect their own avenue to power. They, therefore, represent their ideological and institutional enemy as a draconian ruler, the oppressor of the people. From a Daoist perspective, this is a dispute between two authoritarian parties for the authority to punish the rest of us if we do not conform to their favorite standards. We see no liberal democrats in this particular ideological face-off.

So Han Feizi provides us with our final example of familiarity-induced distortion. It is true that Han Feizi advocates a unitary, imperial, social-political order. His opposition to Confucians is only partly because they represent the scholar-bureaucrat class. Confucianism also defends the basis of the feudal system: family ties and complex, ancestral, ritualized political links. The standards of Confucian social control derive from an elite class of scholar-leaders, the *junzi*^{gentlemen}. They claim the authority to educate and shape the character of the people. Han Feizi opposed both the familial and the scholarly drag on the ruler's effectiveness as well as the inference that the ruler has a duty to educate people. Han Feizi accepts the goal of order, but not the *Ru-Mo*^{Confucian-Mohist} means of education. Rather than a substantive and complex traditional conception of *the* appropriate order, he aims merely at the ruler's effective, total control.

Han Feizi's relation to Daoism is complex and speculative. *The Han Feizi* contains the earliest existing commentary on *The Laozi*. *The Han Feizi* borrowed aspects of Daoist writings that spoke of reversing the traditional value of knowledge. He took Laozi's negative political *dao* seriously. From his ruler's perspective, he typically expressed indifference for the people except as resources. His conception of Daoism was partly filtered through Xunzi's theory of the privileged heart-mind perspective. He advocates that mystically empty, unified, and still heart-mind as a ruling technique. That conception justifies absolutism, not Zhuangzi's pluralism. Dogmatic absolutist assumptions are a political response to elitist's dread of relativist-inspired conceptual anarchy. Indeed the roots of Han Feizi's theory lie in his view that anarchy in interpretative performance is a constant danger without *dao* authoritarianism. Han Feizi is the dogmatic Xunzi with a ruler's perspective rather than a scholar's traditional one.

Confucian Rule of Man and Western Rule of Law

That we should think of Han Feizi as a legal theorist is understandable from another perspective. The Confucian ideals that Han Feizi vilified are a classic case of what Western liberal legal theorists regard as the opposite of law: the *rule of man*, in which a bureaucratic, scholarly, elite class of magistrates resolves issues of public concern based on their moral intuition. This elite credits itself with an esoteric, intuitive insight into a broad range of moral decisions. Its members celebrate the flexibility that the heavy reliance on intuitive application of traditional codes introduces into social guidance. But the moral value of the outcome of the system depends entirely on the quality of the men. If we trust their moral intuitions, we may hope the results will approach those of ideal morality. If they do not, however, we have no way to challenge their moral authority. If our moral intuitions are different, they simply declare us hooligans, counterrevolutionaries, or bad elements. Their intuition *determines* right and wrong. The *junzi*^{gentlemen} are the *fa*^{standards}.

Totally apart from the objective question of the validity of their intuition, the Confucian rule of man is morally objectionable. Its heavy reliance on situational human judgment makes it hard for people to plan their lives. We cannot predict when and where officialdom will intrude coercively in our plans and projects. It undermines the ability to plan and execute rationally conceived ventures.

Han Feizi does base some of his criticism of Confucian prescriptive discourse on similar concerns. It explains the core conflict with his Confucian teacher, Xunzi. His alternative theory, however, is not what we know as the contrasting *rule of law*. He also presupposed a *dao,* a body of prescriptive discourse. One difference is that he intended his *dao* to be a more objective, publicly projectable guide. The other is that he rejected the authority of traditional content in favor of a consequentialist *dao* maximizing wealth and strength of the ruler (which he identified with the state). His account of the difference, however, lay mainly in the publicity, objectivity, and accessibility of his *fa*^{standard}. The values and the interpretation of guidance were measurable. Han Feizi shares, in general ways, the Confucian, Mohist, and Daoist conceptual perspective of *dao* as a guiding body of discourse. His quarrel with the Confucian is with the ancient content and the intuitive standard that gives the interpretive authority to a scholar class.

To understand how Han Feizi's theory differs from Western legalism, let us look more carefully at the conceptual structure of the normative theory underlying the rule of law. The Western controversy about the *definition* of law was the vehicle for conventional Western legal theory. The rival legal theories drew on two conflicting moral perspectives. The consequentialist or utilitarian perspective saw law as an efficient means of social control. The deontological perspective tended to view law as directly justified by desert-based considerations. The split turns on their respective attitudes toward retributive punishment. The deontologist views it as intrinsically just; the utilitarian regards it as of no *intrinsic* moral worth.

To be brief, consequentialist theory fails as a justifying theory for the rule of law. It is not merely that empirical evidence does not support the hypothesis that punishment deters crime. The problem is this. Consequentialist theories, such as Utilitarianism, are inherently comparative. More than showing that law and punishment work, it must show that it works *better* than any alternative. Many alternatives or mixtures of alternatives seem more efficient on their face. Psychological therapy, education-indoctrination, social reform, preventative social precautions, and so forth seem plausible alternatives for a rational utilitarian society.[19] Confucius' argument (see pages 64–65) put the consequentialist case *against* punishment admirably well.

Our retributive moral intuitions surrounding law are very difficult to square with utilitarian morality. The problem is that retributivism essentially looks backward and consequentialist theories look forward. Retributivism demands punishing the guilty even where the overall result is harmful to society. The problem with utilitarianism comes not only in justifying specific instances of punishment, but in prohibiting punishment of innocents. Utilitarian calculations threaten to justify prior punishment of those *merely inclined to* harmful activity or punishing scapegoats to deter others. Our retributive intuitions are that any prospective or end-motivated punishing of people who have not actually done anything is morally forbidden.

The concept of retribution includes a rationalizing element that is essential to our concept of law. It requires proportionality in punishment. Further, it presupposes a notion of moral responsibility: rational moral agency and freedom. Punishment should be proportional to the seriousness of the wrong multiplied by the degree of responsibility for it.

Utilitarianism stumbles because, though it tries, it fails to account for these retributive intuitions. Our retributive moral intuitions are deeply rooted in Western Christian dogma, our ordinary moral beliefs, and our historical ethics. Kant's categorical imperatives most elegantly rationalize those beliefs. The moral agent acts on rational maxims. The agent's rationality entails that it wills its maxims universally, that is, it *wills* that every rational being should deduce his action from the same moral premise. Thus treating the agent with Kantian-inspired respect and dignity requires applying her maxims in our treatment of her. An eye for an eye is an expression of deep respect for the freedom and dignity as individual, rational moral agents. Law-based retributive institutions are our moral right.

Thus our usual justification of retributive institutions positively *requires* the notion of rational agency, the power to control one's behavior and to understand and apply moral (or legal) concepts in guiding our behavior. We must be able to appreciate when reasons or principles yield valid practical conclusions. Kantian doctrines entail that we may not apply retributive sanctions to children, animals, and the mentally ill, since they lack the capacity to appreciate *the reasons* that make their actions wrong. We also do not credit them with the rational self-control necessary for the moral status of an agent. Even those who can appreciate that their action is wrong are not subject to retribution if a mental defect makes them incapable of controlling their behavior.

The retributive intuition that pervades our theory of the rule of law is a powerful one. Its justification, however, has proved to be a major challenge to two millennia of Western philosophy. That accounts for the survival of result-oriented moral theories. They are moral reformers who see the retributivist as merely appealing to our retributive intuitions rather than justifying them. The powerful, inherited Western retributive intuitions continue to drive ethical debate.

The urge to vengeance is arguably universal. It may be among the strongest of natural human instincts. Chinese literature probably exhibits as much natural expression of this urge as our own. Still, Chinese historical traditional *moral attitudes* and *philosophical arguments* are *comparatively* free from the Western retributive fixation. We find remarkably few moral rationalizations employing purely backward-looking theories of desert. Their moral theory does not start from the notion of rational free agency but from the goal of social cooperation. The classical theorists do not share the individualist assumptions behind the distinctively Western moral outlook; we find no theories of free will based on one's rationality. Humans are social and their peculiar genius is not reasoning but learning social *dao*s. Chinese theories of *dao* are predominantly consequentialist. Most apparent examples of expressions of deontological sentiment usually turn out to be deeply *consequentialist* in justification.

So we have deep theoretical as well as formal reasons for doubting that the *fajia* theory has much in common with the Western theory of the rule of law. We find little evidence of retributive theories and none of the formal syntactic notion of *a law*. I have argued that the Chinese focus has mainly been on terms. Confucians originally directed their attention to the names society attaches to status roles. The code guides one in role performance, but early theorists did not segment the code into sentential units. The Chinese way of individuating units of guidance differs, therefore, from that of Western theories. Chinese moral and political philosophy does not use the notion of *a* rule, *a* duty, or *an* obligation. Thus it has nothing on which to hang a clear notion of retributive punishment. On similar grounds we can see that it does not include the concept of a reason for acting, that is, a belief or a desire. We act by executing one of a variety of rival social codes. Each requires practical interpretation. Bridging that interpretive gap has been the activity that drew philosophical attention in elaborating the Chinese theory of the human heart-mind. It will continue to be the focus of Han Feizi's theories.

The Confucian Argument against Punishment

Confucius directs his famous argument in *The Analects* against punishment. Confucius argued against coercive government and its implicit assumptions about the role of government. Punishment ensures social conformity at the cost of giving up on educating and developing the natural human inclinations of spontaneous social conformity: shame. Educational techniques achieve the same end more gradually but also more effectively. Education leads to a stable, long-run solution because it relies on and supports our social instincts. Official coercion using laws and punishment relies on, exercises, and strengthens self-interest.[20] In the long run it undermines order.

The Confucian Argument against Publicly Accessible Daos

The argument based on motivation, recall, ties into another of Confucius' arguments. Confucius makes it less explicitly, but it is a strong undercurrent in many of his aphorisms. Confucius repeatedly disparages the rise of litigiousness, glibness, and cleverness, especially among people governed by promulgated, public codes. For Confucius, public, explicit codes pull a worry in their wake. Any formalized code can be subject to interpretive dispute. The interpretive problem takes this form: "The part of the code governing Y does not apply to me because this is a case of X, not Y. Apply the part governing X to me instead." The inconstancy of names and distinctions makes linguistic *dao*s inconstant too.

The combination of promoting selfishness and glibness means that legal institutions pose a double threat to the natural social mechanisms of control. The Confucians' first objection is to punishment's tendency to induce and exercise selfish heart-mind processing. The Confucians' second objection develops into an attack on *publicizing* the code. General accessibility invites the whole population to quibble about which term in the code applies to them.

I have identified these two concerns about law as the motivational concern and the interpretive concern. The interpretive concern is what requires the rectification of names so both *li* or punishments can give reliable guidance to people. This, according to the famous passage, would be the first measure of a Confucius finally placed in office (13:3).

Notice that both these Confucian concerns employ consequentialist arguments against punishment. Confucianism seldom uses desert-claims to justify punishment. As long as we base our argument on social utility, retributive punishment will lack justification. Less coercive, less destructive means will more efficiently maintain social order.

This second argument, however, yielded an embarrassment for Confucianism. The *li*^ritual is also a fixed code, even though not on tripods. We call it a *positive* morality as we call law *positive* law. The *li* obviously gave rise to disputes among Confucians about correct performance, degree of allowed deviation, exigencies, or rectification of names. The only saving grace is that the Confucian strategy confines the controversy within the ranks of the *Ru*. This tempts Confucians to special pleading and to their natural prejudice that they can handle the interpretive task better than the common person. The Confucian solution to the interpretive problem, by limiting the class of interpreters to the historical scholars, carries with it the preference for *li*^ritual as the positive *dao*. Confucians did not express this openly. They merely note that *ren*^humanity is required for correct performance interpretation and let the assumption that Confucian training generates *ren* stay in the background until Xunzi.

This interpretive concern was the engine that drove Confucianism toward an innatist or intuition driven version, the Mencian orthodoxy. Once we have formulated the concern that people might interpret a code into performance in different ways, we have to rely on something independent of the code to fix which of the interpretive performances is the correct one. An authoritative intuition about performance can settle interpretive disputes about whose performance correctly follows the code. However, if one has an authoritative intuition about performance, the code itself seems unnecessary. It becomes, at best, a temporary learning crutch. Like Wittgenstein's ladder, once we have ascended, we see it as meaningless and toss it away. Like Confucius at seventy, we can eventually follow spontaneous reactions of our heart-mind. Mencius' solution is implicitly more democratic and therefore it carried with it the seeds of Mad-Chanism.[21] The only Confucian technique to limit the interpretive ambiguity is to limit the class of those who can do the interpretation. Xunzi wanted it confined to the Confucian educated *junzi*^gentlemen.

The Liberal Western Argument for Rule of Law

A parallel to this interpretive concern is central to a more modern Western normative justification of the rule of law. Some anti-positivists argue that law is not merely a code with punishment attached. Law, this analysis contends, is essentially an authoritative decision procedure for social decisions of all sorts. One key decision is the interpretation of individual laws. Punishment is common, but not essential to something's being a law. Authoritative interpretation of the guiding code is the mark of a legal system.

Here the contrast of positive law and morality emerges. Morality's decision procedure is idealized rationality. Morality has neither authorities nor fixed formulations. No performative moral authority can make something *moral* by finding or declaring it moral.[22] Morality *proper* contrasts with the accepted morality of a group. Mere general acceptance does not make mores moral. Advocacy by socially acclaimed sages does not make conventions right. This view of morality is central to

Western moral individualism. Each moral agent deserves respect as a coequal rational *source* of the moral law.

This liberal theory of law then appeals to ethical individualism to justify the ideal of the rule of law. Those in power *WILL* punish people who displease them. The human thirst for vengeance is a fact about human nature. That they will tend to punish those who displease them is a fact about people who seek power. The moral justification of law is as *a protection* to individuals because it *rationalizes* punishment. It makes punishment more predictable and rationally avoidable. Rational agents can plan courses of action that insulate them from official coercion and irrational vengeance. The publicity, generality, consistency, and precise projectability of the legal code becomes ethically central. With legal institutions, people will know how to act so as to avoid coercive force. Our actual law systems only approximate that ideal, of course.

Still there is a meaningful contrast with *rule of man* where the law is not specifically, clearly spelled out. Under rule of man, the authority decides on the basis of his moral intuition about what kind of person you are. By contrast, we regard any hint of the intrusion of a judge's private morality as a criticism, as evidence that our rule-of-law ideal has broken down. The neutrality of law has to do with the notion of an objective, universally accessible method of interpretation of a public code of rules. Our ideal demands explicit, nonvague rules and *strict* interpretation. Morality demands, in other words, that law *be* distinct from morality. It is morally important that law clearly state its guidance even when the guidance is morally wrong.

If we construe the ancient debate in China as being between the rule of law and a Confucian ideal of moral leadership, we will miss a deep difference between Confucian and Western theories of persons and morality. The difference between the Legalists and the Confucians was not as deep as the Western legal positivist's contrast between law and morality suggests. We find neither side committed to a clear notion of a rationally given morality, specifically a morality of desert. So the debate in the Chinese context contrasted governing by two rival posited moralities. One was an inherited conventional ritual code. The other was a posited code formulated by rulers. Neither side depended on the syntactic (sentential) notion of a rule, a principle, or a law. Accordingly we will not find a conceptually accurate theory of obligations, duties, or rights in either Chinese conception.

In the contrast they do actually formulate, Han Feizi and the Confucians are divided by two issues. First, they disagree about how to achieve flexibility and adaptability of the guiding system so that it can respond to unique situations. Confucians do it by *flexible interpretation* of the fixed, traditional code. The morally insightful scholar class provides the flexibility. Confucian theory effectively puts the power of flexibility in the hands of the ministers. Han Feizi puts it in the ruler's ability to change the code while leaving the standard of interpretation fixed and inevitable. Second, Confucius (but not Xunzi) would disagree about the sanctions used in gaining conformity. (Between Xunzi and Han Feizi, there is little to choose in their enthusiasm for brutal punishment. But even Xunzi affirms the importance of education.)

Again, the issue between Han Feizi and Xunzi is decidedly not one of the dignity and autonomy of the individual person. For both, some authority gives the standards of social conduct, the sole source of people's conceptions of *dao*. The differences are (1) whether this guiding discourse should come from the ancient sage-kings or the modern ones and (2) whether to use punishment alone or punishment combined with Confucian techniques of education and inculcation.

Historical Survey of Statecraft in China

We could describe Han Feizi's position most simply as Xunzi's without the arbitrary commitment to tradition. Xunzi most directly influences the deep structure of Han Feizi's philosophical thought. But Han Feizi himself turns explicitly anti-Confucian. He traces his concepts of political strategy and regulative techniques to a wide variety of pre-Han sources. The Han theory, therefore, classes several of these as earlier *Legalist* thinkers. They include the practical statesmen who express their theories of statecraft in their politics, though tradition sometimes attributed apocryphal texts to them. Han Feizi also draws clearly from other sources for philosophical argument, concepts and inspiration. These include the Mohists and the negative *dao* of *The Laozi*.

The political statesmen and their institutional reform policies predated even Confucius. Such practical measures account for Confucius' warnings about use of *xing*[punishments]. During the seventh century B.C., the state of Ji emerged as the dominant state among the ducal states professing nominal allegiance to the nearly powerless Zhou king. The chief minister and architect of Ji's rise to power was Guanzhong (Guanzi). Guanzi makes an especially interesting case since Confucius seemed to have a mostly *positive* impression of him. (Mencius was much more critical.) One important factor in his theories, possibly the one that accounts for Confucius' praise, was his reliance on traditional legitimacy, based on *li*[ritual]. Further, he was a fellow Zhou loyalist. But to Mencius, he represented the first move toward the realistic techniques of gathering power through alliances among the traditional fiefs. Mencius called the Duke who could do this a *ba* overlord.[23]

Accounts of Legalism frequently treat the book *The Guanzi*, though a considerably later compilation, as an expression of Guanzhong's ideas. Arguably, however, it is a much later expression of ideas in the direction of Han Feizi. If there is a common element, it lies in the book's direct concern with enhancing the power of the ruler. It lies, further, with the view that the ruler's power is independent of his moral virtue. The explicit concern of such practical statesmen is the range of practical techniques that will enhance the ruler's effective power. Guanzi also sometimes suggests that his policies will enhance the welfare of the people. But he, like Han Feizi, pays scant attention to that goal and almost none to justifying his taking the ruler's interests as his prime concern. He, like Han Feizi, is first and last a practical statesman dealing with a practical political problem whose boundaries he simply takes for granted.

The interesting point is this.[24] *The Guanzi* does advocate *fa*[objective standards]. It clearly does not, however, advocate a Western retributive rule of law. Guanzi advocates *fa*[objective standards] as a necessary adjunct to *li*[ritual]. He addresses, as Confucius did, the problem of interpretation of the *li*[ritual]. If no objective standards guide practical interpretation, then the *li*[ritual] will fail as a guidance system. The text uses the word *fa* in the broad sense of standards to guide the application of any conventional scheme of behavior.[25] *Fa*^{standards} guide the interpretation of four other related categories of public guidance: *lü*^{regulations}, *ling*^{commands}, *xing*^{punishments}, and *cheng*^{administrative measures}. To some of these, punishment is central, to others not. Punishment, thus, has no essential tie to *fa*. *Fa*^{standards} is not an essentially retributive notion in *The Guanzi*.

The most retributive-sounding comments attributed to Guanzi concern having the punishments "appropriate to their names." This is also a central theme in Han Feizi's writings. The idea, however, seems structurally to be more Confucian than Kantian. The names could be either the names of roles or of punishments. The basis for assessment of punishment and reward is the role as expressed in the official title. Responsibility is role responsibility, not rule responsibility.

The name of the punishment should control officials too. Guanzi suggests that if we fix punishments to names in this way "the criminal will have no resentment." This does not seem to be a rule of proportionality as much as a requirement of forewarning.[26] If the promulgated punishment is the amputation of the nose, the executioner should not take an ear, too.

One motivation expressed in *The Guanzi* for making punishments appropriate to names is "the good man should not be fearful." This seems to suggest that rare legalist appeal to the value of *fa*^{objective standards} to the masses. Ordinary people have an interest in the security against arbitrary punishment given by explicit, objective standards controlling penal officials. Further, *The Guanzi* does not suggest that punishment is the only viable motivation for people's obedience. Like *The Mozi*, it argues that if administrative measures are precise and a rulerlike attitude maintained, people will conform. People have a natural urge to conform to standards from above. The point of *fa*^{standard} is that the guide must be precise, objective, and easily projectable.

The essence of *The Guanzi*'s legalism is an appeal to stable, strong, public institutions of social regulation. Punishment, however, is not necessarily what backs the regulation. *The Guanzi* writers saw very little principled distinction between the various kinds of social codes. The important differences seemed to lie in the generality or range of application, the source, and the subject matter.

Han Feizi himself lists Shendao (discussed earlier as an inspiration to Laozi) as a legalist forerunner. The interpretation of Shendao presents a special problem, therefore.[27] How could we understand both his Daoist and Legalist elements? One tempting hypothesis is this. Shendao developed the concept of the natural *dao*, the actual course of events. He intended this concept to undermine the conventional appeal to systems of guidance; hence his slogan, "abandon knowledge." He might have supplemented this antimoral attitude with the iconoclastic claim that what we *accept as moral* is merely whatever the authorities champion. There is no standard apart from the *natural influence of social leadership*. And the content of the *dao* advocated by social leadership has no special warrant. It is there only because it has been favored by circumstance. This, at least, is what Han Feizi takes from Shendao's alleged doctrine of *shi*^{situationalism}. Han Feizi treats Shendao as the chief source of the amoralist concept of *shi*.

Han Feizi lists Shen Buhai as a second source of his ideas. Shen was less concerned with either expedient and deliberately formulated standards of conduct or with punishment. He focused on controlling the bureaucracy. He is identified with the second concept of Han Feizi's triad: *shu*^{statecraft}. The Confucians wanted the ministers to control the ruler. The statesmen concentrated on techniques to preserve the ruler's power against his ministers. The conflict between Han Feizi and the Confucian ruling styles probably stems more from this concern about division of power than from either's concern for common people.

> One who murders the ruler and takes his state does not necessarily [force his way in by] climbing over difficult walls and battering in barred doors and gates. [He may be one of the ruler's own ministers, who gradually] limits what the ruler [is permitted] to hear, getting [control of] his government and taking over his power to command, [so that in the end the minister] possesses the [ruler's] people and seizes his state.[28]

Shen Buhai recommended the ruler adopt *shu*^{techniques} to control ministers and prevent the usual drain and flow of the ruler's power to ministers. These he characterized as *wu-wei*, an idea with both Daoist and Confucian antecedents. Confucians use the term to describe rule in which the ministers carry out all the functions and the ruler merely tends to personnel issues. The way to control personnel was to insist on strict performance criteria, a version of rectification of names. The performance of a man must correspond to the post to which the ruler names him.[29]

The third figure whom Han Feizi acknowledges as a precursor is Shang Yang (died 338 B.C.). Again, our knowledge of Shang Yang's theories is mostly indirect. We have already mentioned Shang Yang as the practical statesman who caused Mencius such disquiet with his institutional reforms in the state of Qin. Han Feizi credits Shang Yang with having made *fa*^{objective standards} central to his theory and practice of statecraft. Shang Yang's ruthless acceptance of punishment contributes to the tendency to see *fa*^{standards} as essentially penal. Still, as Schwartz points out, Guanzi regards the focus on *fa* as a part of a "total program of socio-institutional change."[30] Han Feizi credits Shang Yang with the development of *fa* as a technique of rule. In the alleged fragments, Shang Yang justified the publicity condition in a way strongly reminiscent of a rights-based, liberal conception of the rule of law: "The multitude of people all know what to avoid and what to strive for; they will avoid calamity and strive for happiness, and so govern themselves."[31]

Shang Yang proposed an elaborate system to *spread knowledge* of *fa*. He put the moral argument about as well as it can be put without the doctrine of individual rights. "Government officials and people who are desirous of knowing what the *fa* stipulates shall all address their inquiries to these *fa* officers, and they shall in all such cases clearly tell them about the *fa* and mandates about which they wish to inquire." His emphasis on this point goes right to the heart of the Confucian scholar-official's access to privilege and power. "Since the officials well knew that the people had knowledge of *fa* and orders, . . . they dare not treat the people contrary to the *fa*. . . ."[32]

We should also see Shang Yang's position, therefore, as antibureaucracy, not antipeople. It is a precursor of Han Feizi's attack on the power of the advisers. Shen Buhai's *shu*^{techniques} controls their power relative to the ruler, Shang Yang's *fa* limits their power over the people. If they have to abide by measurementlike standards in punishing and rewarding they cannot arbitrarily reward loyalty and punish political enemies in the way that allows them to get a power base. Han Feizi regards both tools, therefore, as necessary from the perspective of the ruler alone.

Han Feizi starts from the Confucian and Mohist theory of society. Society inculcates behavior in people. It does this by acting as an authority on the language that guides action. It fixes the application of names, especially official role names. The language guides role performance. Those who learn it learn to make the proper discriminations in behavior for each different role.

The society uses several techniques in this indoctrination. These include example, training, encouragement of excellence, and punishment and reward. Han Feizi clearly favors punishment. But the key assumption is that the authority figure does shape what people *shi-fei*. Society is an authoritarian inculcator of action-guiding discriminatory capacities and dispositions. Punishment is technically a secondary matter, one of the arrows in the leader's quiver. The central point is that the decision of some social structure or role-player fixes what is correct, not some objective morality. The chief difference between Han Feizi and Confucianism-Mohism lies in his using this sociological theory exclusively in the interest of the ruler. The assumptions about human nature are those we have seen throughout the period. Mozi advocated *constanting* language that yields benefit. He initiated interest in easily interpretable and universal *fa* standards to be used with the guiding discourse.

The difference is that a Mohist consequential justification takes a universal social point of view. Han Feizi's focuses on outcomes benefitting primarily the ruler and state power. The difficulty in distinguishing what is good for the state and society from what is good for the ruler and the military is a widespread politician's disease.

Sorting out Daoism from Han Feizi's use of it has become difficult. The *Daoist* influence is widely alleged and Han Feizi appeals to both Shendao and Laozi. He or his school also wrote a commentary on the *Daode Jing*. We can mainly conclude that scholars at the time did not see the *two distinct schools* that the Han Confucians saw. The connection of the *Daode Jing* to statecraft reform makes more sense if we assume that Han Feizi treats the *negative dao* as Laozi's *constant dao*. Han Feizi pursues the *scheming methods* political advice enthusiastically. He has some but considerably less interest in the philosophical theory of the limits of language.

Recent discoveries have led to the identification of a school that mixes Laozi's and Han Feizi's attitudes: the Huang-lao school. We regard the Mawang-dui texts as representative of this hybrid school. The Mawang-dui editor of the *Daode Jing* placed the second half (the predominantly political portion) before the theoretical first half. Han Feizi's commentary suggests that he had the same focus and read the books in the same order. The school combined this political doctrine with some doctrines of the mythical yellow emperor.

Some genuine theoretical Daoist ideas in Han Feizi include both anticonventionalism and the ideal of constant impartiality. Han Feizi's attitude suggests that he connects *partiality* with *reliance on intuitive inclination. The Laozi* and Han Feizi agree in their suspicion of the validity of the traditional scholar's cultivated intuition. Intuition is merely sophisticated prejudice. This explains their shared antipathy for education. Han Feizi uses the Daoist idea of simplicity in a more Machiavellian way, however. His point has little connection with Laozi's original motivation. Laozi sought to free people from the controlling impact of society's educational structure and to liberate our natural, spontaneous responses. Han Feizi downplays education in order to make people easier to rule and control. He is quite Confucian in his passion to control people and maintain order.

Han Feizi, then, accepts the Confucian-Mohist goal of social order. He proposes a special set of techniques for achieving that goal. The deep philosophical enemy of both these schools devoted to order is the anarchistic Daoists.

Language and the Danger of Interpretive Anarchy

The continuing problem that Han Feizi uses to motivate his political proposals is interpretive anarchy. He observes that traditional doctrines such as Confucianism and Mohism split into incompatible interpretive wings.[33] He regards with horror the possibility of reversal of opposites.[34] Concepts such as *ren*[benevolent], *yi*[morality], and *li*[utility] have been distorted by Confucians, Mohists, etc., so that *shi*[right] becomes *fei*[wrong]. In a parallel way, people interpret status terms or role names in distorted ways. The effect is that the world ends up praising and denigrating, he says, the wrong kind of ministers.[35]

Of course, Han Feizi's horror reflects his royal perspective: that orderly obedience is simply right. The world, he complains, sees dutiful subjects as sycophants. The way people interpret these concepts does not contribute to making the ruler-state rich and strong. Ergo, they have entirely distorted the terms in question.

Han Feizi treats the problem as a language-based one. In the chapter titled *Nan-yan*[difficult language] he recites a long series of analyses of how language gets distorted. He concludes that the basic problem lies in an essential feature of political discourse. One has to be a worthy or a sage to understand it properly.[36] Further, he traces disorder to the tolerance of rulers in allowing the existence of incompatible *dao*s. There should be only one guiding discourse and one standard of interpretation.[37] The words the ruler *shi*s should be publicized and those he *fei*s should be stopped.[38] One must assume that the ruler will *shi* words that serve the ruler and contribute to the strength and wealth of the state. (As we shall see below, this is not a trivial assumption.)

His special target is *li*[ritual], which he declares "empty sounds."[39] Wherever it emerges there is a hidden profit agenda. Han Feizi's analysis involves a theory of the nature of the *xin*[heart-mind] and how it executes its interpretive function. In effect, he denies that Xunzi's ideal of the empty and still heart is realistic. The heart-mind inevitably *calculates*. Like Mozi, he regards the preference for *li*[utility] as natural and even inevitable. But it is not for a *universal* utility. In its interpretation, the heart inevitably skews the outcome to the perspective it occupies. This comes closer than anything in Xunzi or in earlier philosophers to a theory of natural evil in the heart—although it reminds us of Mencius' argument against using the term *li*[profit].

So ministers inevitably incline to interpretations of guidance that benefit their school or clique. Even parents calculate their interests in raising children. As our perspective changes, as we adopt different roles and positions, we change our interpretation of appropriate conduct.

Western accounts, I think, tend to read Han Feizi's point as excessively psychological. Schwartz, for example, understands Han Feizi as "a simple behaviorist model of man based primarily on the elemental tropisms of pain and pleasure."[40] In the *Han Feizi,* however, the analysis seems more sociological. It is my occupying a social position that affects how my heart calculates. When one occupies the position of a wife, one calculates one way, as a concubine another, etc. Han Feizi puts the point in a deliberately antipsychological way. The ruler should not, he warns, trust *ren*[people].[41] The only thing that is reliable is this: whatever their past personal experiences and relationship with you, their heart will calculate according to their position. The ruler must concentrate instead on making the calculations come out the way he wants.

In particular, it is the nature of position that *chen*[ministers] *must* compete with the ruler. They will interpret moral guidance, orders, the expectations of their office, etc., in ways that benefit those in their position, with their name, their rank, their status. So the ruler needs measurement-like standards for dealing with them. He must reduce to nothing the space for intuitive interpretation. The measurement standards must neutralize the heart's intuitive ability to skew words and language in its calculations and interpretation. *Even the ruler* must have unskewable *fa*[standards] so he cannot be manipulated by appeal to his own calculational bias.

The deep enemy of stable order and the ruler's effective control of the state is the opposite of objective standards—*si-qu*[particular twisting]. It inevitably accompanies the formation of interest-group cliques among the ministers. They form parties based on their evaluative perspectives. These cliques are the main technique for draining power from the ruler. The hallmark of the clique is its praise of others in the clique and criticism of those outside. So if the ruler allows himself to be swayed by any kind of consensus evaluation, he loses. He must always base his appointment-dismissal, punishment-reward decisions on strict measurements, not on the advice of moral ministers.

Shi[Situational authority]

The first element of Han Feizi's famous synthesis is *shi*[situational authority]. Han Feizi credits Shendao with the technique of relying on the charisma of actual rank and power. Again, however, the deep assumption seems to be one we have already traced to Confucius and Mozi. Humans are simply inclined to submit to social superiors, to show them respect, to emulate them. We are inclined to internalize a superior's language in guiding our behavior. We emulate it because it happens to be the one exemplified by the actual ruler placed there by circumstance, not because it is moral. This is a tendency on which the ruler must depend. One cannot rule by force alone when the population of a state is a multitude and the ruler a single person. Without the natural inclination to follow hierarchical authority, the state could not get off the ground.

It would seem that Shendao's contribution was his positivist analysis of this widespread sociological assumption. The pull of authority does not depend on the ruler's personal moral qualities. This ability is a function of the stature alone. That is the natural way things happen. The practical problem is how the ruler can sustain and strengthen this natural tendency in people to obey those who end up in honored positions. The techniques Han Feizi emphasizes include sitting the ruler on a high throne, forbidding the use of his personal name, enforcing lots of bowing, kneeling, and kowtowing, punishing anyone who looks at the ruler's face, and publicizing stories of his strength, accomplishments, and skill.

Han Feizi sometimes speaks paradoxically of this as an application of the doctrine of *wu-wei*. The ideal goes back to Confucius, who thought a moral sage could rule without taking any action. His moral virtue would set in motion a chain of emulations that would accomplish the task of government automatically. Han Feizi's ideal of *wu-wei* differs from Confucius's in that it depends on institutional structures rather than the moral character of the ruler. If we set up the institutions properly, the moral character of the ruler should be irrelevant to good rule. Sage-kings such as Yao and Shun are rare in history and we should order the state so it can run well with mediocre or even incompetent rulers. The efficacy of their employing the institutional structure depends finally on nothing more than this natural tendency: people hold authority in awe! They treat the ruler's appointments and institutionalized standards of behavior as legitimate. If this is lacking, the institutions cannot function by themselves.[42]

When the institutions are functioning, they normally tend to strengthen the natural impulse to identify with and adhere to de facto authority. But the institutions could not get off the ground unless some natural impulse started the social engine.

Shu: *Methods to Control the State Apparatus*

The second central concept—*shu*[method]—consisted essentially in skill in controlling ministers. Han Feizi's emphasis here is on secrecy. The result is that we know little about the details of *shu*[methods]. The emphasis of secrecy is a thread that connects *shu*[method] to the notion of *shi*[situational authority]. The mysterious behavior of the ruler is supposed to be another aspect of the statecraft application of the traditional notion of *wu-wei*[nondeeming]. The ministers, like other people, have natural allegiance to authority. The danger to the ruler comes when the psychological authority distance crosses a minimal threshold. Then he loses that distance which enhances awe of authority *and* gives ministers ammunition for manipulating him. Thus the *wu-wei* techniques included in *shu* sometimes do double duty. They help maintain the aura of mystery *and* distance between the ministers and the ruler necessary to enhance *shi*[situational authority].

Han Feizi gives strategic advice which enjoins the ruler to avoid revealing any of his personal biases and preferences for things, policies or persons, though he does not specifically label this as *shu*[method].[43] Even if he cannot avoid *wei*[deeming], he should keep his deeming secret. This prevents cliques of advisers from gaining personal control over the ruler. A flattering adviser is one of Han Feizi's standard worries.[44] Those who advise and inform the ruler wield power by means of their influence on his decisions. If the ministers do not know the ruler's *shi-feis*, they will give better advice. They will have to make careful judgments of what is *in his interest* rather than flattering and pandering *to his prejudices*. The ruler, therefore, never justifies his punishments because that would tip bureaucrats off about his values. He must remain mysterious so that the advisers are forced to be impartial. His enigmatic persona is the functional substitute for impartiality. It is necessary for the system to work up to the *wu-wei* standard. Things work better if he appears to have no purpose.

Now, we must find this paradoxical even if we take for granted the point of view of the ruler. Han Feizi is clear that the ruler *need not* be saintlike. He may be quite evil and filled with desires. If he does not reveal these, the flattering adviser will have to guess. Why would an adviser automatically guess that the ruler was motivated by abstract justice? He would have at least as much probability of success in gaining favor if he guessed the ruler liked young, beautiful women to fall in love with him or sweet cakes to eat.

The secret doctrine must be much more complex than it appears. One possibility is that Han Feizi thinks of the ruler's interest as a more complex function of his actual desires and preferences. Another is that he thinks of the ruler's interest as a sociological function of his role-perspective more than his actual desires. This makes it clear that *shu*^{method} relies on *shi*^{charisma}, for the ruler must convince the ministers that he is in fact a sage ruler—concerned with his rational or higher interest. Otherwise they will continue to look for his actual preferences with, supposedly, a high degree of success. The ministers cannot be as coolly realistic and perceptive as Han Feizi himself or they would see through this shallow trick instantly. It must be possible to fool them with *shi*^{charisma}. Similarly, *shu*^{method} relies on *fa*^{objective standards} because the ruler must not reward anyone for supplying him with *desired things* but only for public, measurable accomplishments. It also makes clear that the *fa*^{objective standards} must be different from the legal positivist's *signification of desire* on the part of the ruler.

Other techniques discussed[45] include those reminiscent of both Guanzi and Shen Buhai. They aim at total, unswerving loyalty. The techniques include detecting treachery early and stopping coups. Han Feizi hints at the institution of interbureaucratic spying, a technique that survived and surfaced even in Sun Yatsen's constitutional scheme.[46] The institutional feature that Han Feizi places at the center of his practical theory is the control of the *two-handles*. The power of weighing and meting out punishment and reward must be kept in the hands of the ruler. If the ministers are allowed to mete out punishments, the power will drain to them. More important, the ruler must safeguard especially his ability to punish and reward the ministers. He must not let it be assumed that anyone is immune from the ruler's assessment of punishment and reward or that any punishment and reward can be meted out without his approval.[47]

The balance of the theory of *shu*^{method} is a *fa*^{objective standards} adaptation of the Confucian-Mohist theory of advancing the worthy. The ruler appoints and advances people based on merit. The calculation of merit, however, is carefully designed to avoid interpretive skewing that undercuts the ruling purpose. The ruler must never accept mere recommendation or fame. Doing that invites cliques of mutually supporting interests to form. They praise each other and censure rivals and thus get power. Besides, as Han Feizi has argued, the world's praise turns worthless ministers into sages and vice versa. For the same reason, the ruler *may not* rely on his own intuition. He must appoint according to *objective standards of consequentialist worth* in enhancing the power and wealth of the ruler (or the state). Thus a key reason for advancing people in the bureaucracy is military accomplishment. Their merit can be measured with accuracy. Han Feizi cites approvingly a *fa* that specifies a rank and salary adjusted to the number of enemy heads cut off in battle.[48]

Favoring soldiers is good not merely because of the ease of objective measure of their merit. More important, they directly contribute to a ruler's strength.

The state supports scholars and knights-errant in time of peace, but when emergency arises it has to use soldiers. Thus those who have been benefitted by the government cannot be used by it and those used by it have not been benefitted. This is the reason why those who serve take their work lightly and the number of traveling scholars increases every day. This is the reason why the world has become disorderly.[49]

Thus, Han Feizi shows scant respect for scholars and philosophical theories in his appointment advice. Han Feizi's practical reaction to the logicians and Daoists shows the short-cut technique of his teacher, Xunzi: "Suppress them!" He supplements this Confucian *method* with another Confucian theoretical interest, the rectification of names. Han Feizi still portrays the bureaucratic structure as a system of roles—names. The ruler *names* people to positions. Their responsibility is to play the role associated with the name. The ruler metes out punishment and reward as this job description is satisfied or not. This is his Standardizer version of rectifying names. In keeping with his taking the ruler's perspective, he, unlike Confucius, placed the burden of harmonizing names and behavior on the named official, not on the ruler. The ruler appoints according to measurement standards, but the harmony of name and performance is the responsibility of the minister.

Whenever a ruler wants to suppress treachery, he must examine the correspondence between actuality and names *[xingming]*. *[Xingming]* refer to the minister's words and deeds. When a minister presents his words, the ruler assigns him a task in accordance with his *ming*^{name:rank} and demands accomplishments specifically from that work. If the results correspond to the task and the task to the *ming*^{rank}, he should be rewarded. If the accomplishments do not correspond to the task or the task to the *ming* he will be punished.[50]

This requires us to think of the *ming*^{names} as an implicit job description. In a famous case, the job description was *dresser*. The ruler was covered as he slept by a well-meaning official with a different job title. Both the official and the dresser were punished. Han Feizi advocates that the ruler punish those who do too much, including too much good. That person is exceeding his job description, exceeding his authority, and represents a threat to the strictly institutionalized system. Notice, again, that the values are not identified with the personal interests or comfort of the ruler but with his institutional or role interest.

This amounts to a particularly severe institutional imposition of values. Still it is continuous with the Confucian-Mohist social schemes of agreement with the superior or rectification of names. The other application of the doctrine of *xing-ming*^{shape-name} is also linked to that historical Confucian concept of authority and duty. A promise or undertaking—especially one to achieve some governmental aim—is also to be taken as the basis for punishment and reward. And in this case as well, succeeding too well is as bad as failing. Whatever performance you pledge, you must exactly measure up.

The ruler controls his bureaucracy, then, using reward and punishment and the language of roles and promises or pledges. As we will see, all of these must be combined with public, objective standards. So these *shu*^{method} techniques also depend on the third concept of social control, *fa*^objective standards. The standards of performance must be universal, impartial, public, known in advance, and not subject to partisan interpretation. These standards are necessary as well, as we saw above, for the first concept. The king's authority should be independent of his personal qualities. His application of the standards of performance should not depend on the degree of cultivation of his moral intuition or the peculiarities of his scheme of desires. Society must mete out punishment to even the crown prince (at least by proxy). The test is the same; does the prince live up to his role or does he violate some explicit standard of performance? The standards of performance for reward and punishment should be so objective as to remove any need for moral or intellectual virtue in the ruler.

Fa: *Public, Measurable Standards*

I have argued that the meaning of *fa* in *The Han Feizi* does not change. That was a theoretical argument. We can have a more coherent account of Han Feizi's thought by using the hypothesis of meaning constancy than by denying it. I gave arguments for both the general intelligibility of his theory and for its coherence with the tradition out of which he emerged.

Han Feizi frequently justifies *fa* by its influence on *yan*^language, *zhi*^knowledge, and *bian*^distinction:dispute. I have argued that his reaction to the dialecticians reflects the influence of Xunzi. The way to prevent *bian*^distinction:disputes is *fa*^objective standards. The result of *fa* is a general impact on the content of discourse and its relation to action. "Thus, regarding people within the borders of the state, their language and conversation will be guided by *fa*^standards, their behavior will be resolved into practical accomplishment." [51]

We should notice, further, that Han Feizi's focus on *ming*^name is as emphatic as that of any other pre-Han philosopher. He shows no revolutionary insight into the nature of either sententials or rules. Even his theory of punishment is linked to the name, specifically the name of a role. We can understand the role of *fa* in the Han Feizi theory of *xing-ming*^punishment-name best if we think of *fa* as explicit measurements of role performance, the ones on which a ruler ought to base punishment and reward.

Understanding *fa*^standards as objective standards to replace intuitive guidance explains best why it is central to his theory of how to control a bureaucracy. As we saw, Han Feizi said the theory of *shu* could make no sense unless there are objective standards of conduct independent even of the ruler's desires. The *fa* therefore, cannot be thought of as expressions of the ruler's desire.[52] What is important about the *fa* to Han Feizi is their mechanical, inevitable character.

If official appointment depends on reputation and worldly knowledge, then the ruler's power slips into the hands of schools of opinion and mutual-admiration cliques. If he relies on his own biases, these can easily be manipulated. His only protection is to appoint people according to measurementlike standards.

We can also understand why Han Feizi would, unlike Guanzi or Xunzi, come to regard *fa* and *li*^ritual as incompatible. He has accepted his teacher's argument that the *only standard* of interpretation of a conventional, traditional code must be the traditional scholar.[53] Accepting such a code therefore is tantamount to accepting scholarly authority. It inherently weakens the ruler's control and strengthens the class of scholar ministers.

Han Feizi presents the doctrine of *fa* in contrast with *si-qu*^{private distortions} and *si-xing*^{private behavior}. This points directly to his analysis of the main problem of political order: anarchy of interpretation into action. "Therefore, at present [consider] those who are able to exterminate private distortions and follow public *fa*^{objective standards}. [Their] people will be pacified and their state well ordered. If [they] can eliminate private behavior and act on public *fa* then their army will be strong and the enemy weak." [54]

This understanding also makes his theory of the ruler intelligible. As we noticed in discussing *shu*^{method}, the ruler cannot use his own reactions to situations in making his judgments. He too must rely on objective, measurable standards. The standards, apparently, cannot be merely his desires. They must yield some objective good to whoever occupies the role of ruler or some good to the state as a whole. The *fa*, in other words, are not merely the ruler's desires promulgated and backed by punishment. They are objective measurements that allow the ruler himself to avoid the trap of interpretive subjectivity.

Han Feizi goes on to argue that "If one has regulations based on objective standards and criteria and apply these to the mass of ministers, then that ruler cannot be duped by cunning fraudulence." [55] Now clearly, laws, by themselves, cannot keep a ruler from being fooled and deceived. Laws, as the tradition has understood since Confucius first made the argument, are themselves subject to interpretive glibness. What insulates a ruler from duplicity is measurable standards against which to weigh words. Their purpose is to deal with the confusion and doubt engendered by interpretive anarchy. The ruler needs *fa*, he says, to clarify distinctions in the relation of ruler and minister. [56] If they were simply laws, we could not explain this role of *fa* in Han Feizi's argument.

We can more fully understand Han Feizi's theory of *fa* as the focus of his departure from Xunzi. Where Xunzi accepted convention—both for content and interpretation—Han Feizi must reject it. *Shi*^{situation}, not convention, must be the authority. Xunzi's alternative drains power from the ruler to the scholars. This rejection of tradition applies, of course, to all the distinctions in language as it did for Mozi. Thus both the allowed guiding discourse and the standards for making distinctions should be removed from tradition and convention. The source of correct usage and content is not historical, conventional agreement, but the ruler's authority and interest. As Tang Jun-i puts it, Han Feizi doesn't use *fa* to make people be good according to the world's antecedent concept of good. He uses *fa to fix* what *is shi-fei*. He cites Han Feizi's aphorism that the *fa* that prevents treachery first prevents it in the heart, then prevents it in language, and finally prevents it in affairs. [57]

Han Feizi's doctrine of *fa* is theoretically independent of his doctrine of the two handles of punishment and reward. Since he thinks all affairs should be governed by objective standards, this, naturally, includes punishment and reward. But, as we noted above, he introduces the two handles as part of his theory of *shu*^{method}. The central application of the two handles, furthermore, is in connection with the *xing-ming*^{punish name} doctrine. The connected and most detailed application is to promises that ministers make. They are strictly held to performance standards they set for themselves in their predictions and promises. This is hardly a standard case of a positivist legal theory.

Finally, as I have noted, Han Feizi occasionally hints that the *fa* would make people secure. This would be strange if the *fa* were the penal measures themselves. The system of draconian punishment is something that would normally not make people secure. The *fa* can make people secure only in virtue of their objective, public, accessible nature. This advantage counts only against the assumed background of regular intimidation by punishment. The *fa* would make people secure if they are understood as preventing ministers from applying punishment arbitrarily, in accordance with their intuitions. In other words, it is in virtue of their objectivity as controls on ministers that *fa* give people security. This gives people greater security than Xunzi's scheme, which also has draconian punishments but has them meted out by specially gifted *junzi* who have better intuitions than the rest of us.

Obviously the Confucian establishment had a conflict of interest as well as an intellectual disagreement with *fajia*. The Confucians like to represent themselves as providing a shield between the ruthless, all-powerful emperor and the people. They seek to draw power from the emperor allegedly to protect the people from his dictatorial and autocratic rule. It is part of this pose that they represent *fa* as directed primarily at the people. In Han Feizi's theory, however, the *fa* seem mainly directed at controlling the ministers. We do not normally find Han Feizi treating the people as the enemy. He is mostly indifferent to them.

> If the ruler has won the hearts of the people, they will exhort themselves without being pressed.[58]

My point is not that he is enormously sympathetic to the people. He does have his own version of the "human nature is evil" thesis. He argues, "The great ministers find the *fa*[standards] odious and the little people dislike order.[59] This suggests he directs control by *fa* initially at the ministers, not the people. Allowing the officials to inflict punishment based on their intuitions makes the people insecure. So does basing guidance on abstruse and complicated moral doctrines.

> What is called wisdom consists of subtle and unfathomable doctrines. Such subtle and unfathomable doctrines are difficult even for men of highest intelligence to understand. If what men of highest intelligence find to be difficult to understand is used to become *fa*[standard] for the people, the people will find them impossible to understand.[60]

People become more secure when there are reliable tests of their behavior that they themselves can understand and apply. The officials should only punish in accordance with such public, clear, standards. The people, then, can choose a way of acting that will avoid punishment. The clarity of the *fa* makes them more secure as long as *fa* restricts the ministers. Without *fa* any scheme of rewards and punishments will be morally deficient.

Two different arguments lead to this conclusion. One is moral. People ought to have clear warning of the kinds of things that might bring coercive force down on them. That is the rights-based justification of the rule of law characteristic of Western Kantianism. The other argument, an argument from efficiency and control, takes the point of view of the ruler. The latter is the more usual direction of Han Feizi's justification. This occasional sympathetic argument is not the dominant thread and it arises mainly in a context in which Han Feizi notices the coincidence of the ruler's goal of control of the ministers and the people's goal of making official coercion predictable and avoidable.

A publicity condition characterizes *fa* as it does Western law. This is the essential distinction from other regulations. This publicity condition is marked in the first historical reference to *fa*, which were *promulgated* by having them cast on tripods.[61] We have seen that Shang Yang justified the publicity condition in a similar way.

Han Feizi's formulation does not consistently follow Shang Yang's theme of protection of the people against the bureaucrats. He more often reverts, as I have complained, to justifying clear standards from the perspective of the ruler interested in reliable, effective order. "The *fa* works best when clearly revealed." Access to information on the *fa* is important.

> Therefore in the state of the enlightened ruler, there is no literature or books and records but the *fa*[standard] serves as the teaching. There are no sayings of ancient kings but the officials act as teachers.[62]

Another difference between Shang Yang and Han Feizi is that Han Feizi stressed reward and punishment equally while Shang Yang, like a Western legal positivist, treated punishment as more important. Shang Yang argued for this by appealing to a minimal conception of the state's responsibility (minimal, that is, in relation to that of the Confucians and Mohists). It is to prevent wrongdoing, not to encourage virtue. Han Feizi's reliance on both punishment and reward reverts to the more totalitarian Confucian-Mohist conception of the role of state leadership. The purpose of rule is to control the whole range of people's behavior. The authority becomes the standard of *shi-fei*.

Further, in his application of reward and punishment, Han Feizi's reasoning is typically more utilitarian than retributive. He does not directly link a specific punishment as a matter of desert to violation of a specific prohibition. Thus he does not employ the retributive instinct about the severity of punishment. Punishments and rewards are general strategies either for maximizing the ruler's benefit or for achieving some more vague balance of good over evil actions. Han Feizi more often advocates making both punishment and reward extreme than for making punishment proportional to harm and responsibility. His arguments are predominantly consequentialist. Extreme punishment and reward more effectively guarantee the desired outcome. "When rewards are generous then what [the ruler] desires to achieve will be speedily achieved; when penalties are severe, then what he desires to prohibit will be speedily achieved."[63] The goal of punishment, he tells us repeatedly, is to end punishment, not to restore some deserved moral balance.

The Confucians' portrait of themselves as the defenders of the population against harsh legalist measures is, I have argued, a self-serving exaggeration. Confucianism's interest was in preserving its special immunity and maximizing its power. It drew power both from the ruler and from the people at large. Its antipathy toward *fajia* theories stems from Han Feizi's emphasis on ways to diminish the scholar-bureaucrats' power from both directions.

The standard account of the Legalist-Confucian debate focuses in the conflict between *fa* and *li*[rites]. It treats this conflict as equivalent to the Western legal positivists' distinction between law and morality.[64] That is doubly misleading. As noted, *li* is not, strictly speaking, equivalent to *morality* and *fa* is not equivalent to *law*. Han Feizi, to be sure, insisted that what passed for morality in the Confucian system, the *li,* had no essential relationship with *fa*. He was drawing a contrast between two kinds of posits. One derives from kings of long ago. Scholars have preserved it in vague writings accessible only to a skilled school of interpreters (the *Ru*). The other stems from a living ruler. The current ruler can change the guiding discourse. Government makes the guiding code open and publicly accessible. Which posited *dao* society uses determines where the society's power lies.

The confrontation between *li* and *fa* is thus a power confrontation, but not only that. The debate, whatever the ambitious motives of the debaters, turns on interesting differences in the two posits. What are the differences? They are not in the fact of codification itself. (This *is* an essential distinction between law and rational or critical morality.)[65] The major difference in codification would be between a code that can change over time and has only one authorized version at a time and a code that is not supposed to change but yields many competing interpretive versions at a time. The ruler's code could be redone as often as was expedient. Scholars should, in principle, transmit the traditional one without change. The scholar's task lies in selecting among different competing versions, untangling textual corruptions, editing, and commenting. They end up with cliques or schools reading the traditional words differently. Han Feizi wanted to eliminate controversy and have a single expedient guide for everyone's behavior.[66]

Han Feizi's conception of this system is philosophically dogmatic. Consider how it too would dissolve in the face of Zhuangzi's analysis. Like Mozi's standard, the ruler's interest requires both *justification* and *interpretation*. Han Feizi never appears even to address either question. He merely adopts and interprets the ruler's perspective. He wavers between incompatible interpretations of that interest. Sometimes he identifies it with the ruling class or the state, sometimes with the ruler himself and his actual desires, other times with his interest *objectively considered,* sometimes with the general good of the government, and sometimes with whatever arbitrary interest is embodied in the fixed *fa*^{standards}.

The idea to use the ruler to eliminate interpretive dispute reveals either Han Feizi's own unreflective dogmatism or his cynical political response to his inability to solve the problem of skepticism. Han Feizi started with a powerful statement of the problem of interpretive special pleading. He never addressed how that problem would apply to the ruler. The idea that a ruler can clearly and objectively see who are good ministers, policies, etc., is a simple application of Xunzi's dogmatism. I suspect his early view was like Xunzi, that the great man can be free from obsession. His later view was cynical, opportunistic pandering to rulers motivated by the philosophical failure to resolve the problem of interpretive skepticism. It doesn't matter if we find the correct solution as long as society has exactly one!

Authoritarian Daoism

Before I end my account of the classical period with the dismal story of the strangling of the creative philosophical voices in ancient China, I want to trace the above corollary to Han Feizi's call for an officially promoted orthodoxy. It inherits and develops Xunzi's appropriation of Daoist-sounding concepts to the un-Daoist idea that the dominant authorities have a privileged or unbiased perspective on things.

The early imperial dynasties drew two equally important practical conclusions from their analysis of intellectual politics. The flip side of the absence of freedom of philosophical expression is the establishment of a favored ideology. We have discussed earlier the archaeological discoveries that revealed new documents from a previously little known school. It emerged as the favored ideology of the Qin and Han ruling class. It combined a superstitious ruler-based ideology with Laozi's writing and was known as the *Huang-lao*^{Yellow Emperor Laozi}. Its preoccupation with political strategy from the ruler's perspective merged with a superstitious focus on the personal goal of long life. The dominance of this school during the philosophical dark age magnified the dogmatic view of Daoism that flowed into popular intellectual history. This essentially superstitious dogmatic ideology is the ancestor of both religious Daoism and the ruling interpretation's inherited view of philosophical Daoism.

In The *Han Feizi* we can see partly how the authoritarian distortion and appropriation of Daoism began. Most scholarship is skeptical that the Huang-Lao interpretation of Daoism is accurate. But it mostly accepts the key thread of that authoritarian account: the absolute metaphysical *dao* and absolute mystical perspective on it. My view, obviously, is that the Huang-Lao dogmatic interpretation that came to affect the historical image of Daoism and has been read back into the texts. I have argued that the only absolutist version of Daoism was in the Xunzi.

The *Han Feizi* contains a key document in the authoritarian transformation of Daoism consisting of two chapters of commentary titled *Jie-lao*^{explaining Laozi} and *Yu-lao*^{illuminating Laozi}. Han Feizi's authorship is not a settled matter. The author seems tolerant of things (sage wisdom, moral concepts) that Han Feizi usually condemns vehemently. Tang Jun-i offers two hypotheses. If it is Han Feizi's own text, then it is early Han Feizi. Otherwise, he speculates, it reflects an eclectic development toward Huang-Lao Daoism that includes The *Guanzi, Nei-ye*^{inner discipline} chapter.[67]

Graham also identifies that *Guanzi* chapter as a key source of the doctrine of a mystical inner state.[68] The chapter turns a reverential celebration of spiritualists into an assertion that the shamen adept can cultivate a perfect clarity. Guanzi's conception suggests the emptiness and stillness characteristic of Xunzi and Han Feizi. Tang Jun-i stresses the parallelism between Han Feizi's interpretation of the *Laozi* and the *Guanzi* doctrine that we can get access to a magically perspective free "view from nowhere."[69] The *Guanzi* chapter treats this perspective, which avoids the biases of a normal completed heart, as a heart within the heart.[70]

The *Han Feizi*'s commentary on the *Laozi* develops the *Guanzi*'s assertion of an absolutist way which for earlier Daoists had produced paradox. The commentary asserts that perspectiveless knowledge is possible.[71] My understanding of Tang's suggestion rules out that the commentaries on the *Laozi* are mature Han Feizi works. We must now assume that text of the *Laozi* circulating at that time was still in flux. As Han Feizi chose to read it, it would be appropriate reading for a student with Xunzi's political views. Han Feizi saw Laozi's negative *dao* as an authoritarian theory of political leadership based on asserting an absolute point of view. Special people can access this point of view using the techniques of "empty, unified, and still." Han Feizi himself mentions only *empty* and *still*.

The absolute *dao* is the outer, metaphysical counterpart of the inner epistemological point of view that somehow transcends situational bias. A certain mental regimen should both surmount the problem of interpretive skepticism and avoid the perceived danger of standards anarchy. The interpretive heart that prevails over interpretive skepticism gives access to a hinge-of-*dao*s from which we can select an unbiased set of *shi-fei* judgments. Authoritarian readings thus assume a transcendent absolute *dao and* a transcendent mental capacity. These are mystically different from the ordinary perspectives criticized in Daoist skeptical or pluralistic arguments. Xunzi and Han Feizi, quite predictably, each separately suppose that this neutral, objective, transcendent, mystical point of view is their own!

Xunzi, I have argued, can be credited with an almost deliberate pragmatic choice to trumpet dogmatism despite his own deep relativism. He fails to refute Zhuangzi's pluralism. So he condemns it as dangerous and resolves to avoid any disruptive hint of doubt. Anarchy is the unacceptable cost of allowing doctrines of relativism or skepticism any place in discourse. Han Feizi seems, by contrast, simply to have *started* his studies as a dogmatist.

We have already noted that Shendao seemed to have a foot in two directions of philosophical development. Han Feizi acknowledges the influence of Shendao, who has the clearest notion of an absolute *dao*. But his absolute is also paradoxical and contentless. Whatever the situation brings is the *Dao*. Thus the correct *dao* is whatever *dao* the authorities whom circumstances have put in place impose. He no doubt viewed the closely related *Laozi* in the same light. Shendao's metaphysical, single, natural dao gives him a realistic *dao* that is also amoral. Validity is a function of social power. Han Feizi uses the *Laozi* to defend Xunzi's claim of access to an epistemological fulcrum. It helps him pry his own authoritarian perspective into a privileged position. The *natural* way for a pattern of usage to become acceptable is for it to be promoted by de facto authority and to be made a basis for punishment and reward.

The *Laozi* would strike someone like Han Feizi as nothing more than another book critical of Confucians and Mohists. Its content is clearly drawn from many sources, including *realistic* political advice. Han Feizi's use of it is not at all surprising.

Han Feizi, at that early student stage, probably shared enough of Xunzi's perspective not to notice the differences of emphasis. Both agree on the unquestioned need for order and authoritarian discipline, and especially for punishment. Both agree that the basis of this order is control of names (especially of role descriptions) and of guiding discourse. At this stage, Han Feizi's later insistence that the order come purely from authority rather than tradition was not fully formed. Both agreed that the authority emerged in some mystical, unspeakable way from the natural order of things.

So, in this early commentary, Han Feizi is remarkably more tolerant of moral and conventional concepts such as *li*[ritual]. He understands in a surprising mild way Laozi's disparaging grading judgments that treat *ren*[humanity], *yi*[morality], and *li*[ritual] as progressively more serious signs of decline. He is also remarkably congenial to claims of the privileged, intuitive insight of the traditional sage. He gives little sign of his later venomous hostility to conventional ritual, let alone to the other moralistic concepts. Indeed, this early study of Laozi might have marked his position prior to his separation from Xunzi on this issue.

His reading of the *Laozi* shows an early and clear dominance of the perspective of the ruler. It gives the impression that he came to the academy with the clear goal of learning the technique of rule. His version of the *Laozi* must have been close to the recently discovered Huang-Lao version. That version reverses the political and philosophical books in the traditional *Daode-Jing*. His reading of the political portions first helped solidify his tendency to take the negative *dao* as *the* point of the text.

This earnest but essentially pedestrian attempt to dredge the negative *dao* part of the text for bits of ruling advice holds little philosophical interest. But it does show the influence of Xunzi as well as the Huang-Lao fascination with long life,[72] which he gives almost equal weight with the strength and wealth of the ruler.

Everyone, he thinks, accepts the obvious pragmatic goal of ruling a unified imperial state. He shows an already well-developed inclination to confuse the well-being of the ruler with the well-being of the state. But the limits of the text and perhaps Xunzi's more moral outlook make him slightly more inclined to appeal to general well-being than he is in his later work.[73]

His political assertion of a fixed goal and his dogmatic acceptance of the ruler's perspective are propped up by Xunzi's epistemology. The concern is with specifying *a state of mind* that accompanies unobsessed reception of an absolute *dao*. His surprisingly positive talk about sages fits in with this focus. The sage is the paradigm of someone who has the appropriately receptive attitude. His mind is mature and his thinking efficacious.[74] Han Feizi asserts mainly that this quality of mind will enable him to survive, get rich, noble and blessed. He presents this in language close to that of Xunzi. He talks of the natural intelligence.[75] He even describes this clear thinking with the Confucian interpretive concept, *ren*.[76]

Xunzi's position cannot be made purely compatible with the *Laozi*. Han Feizi has to reinterpret Laozi's rejection of conventional distinctions as blinding the natural abilities to discriminate. He understands it as a worry that over exercise wears out the natural receptive ability. Over exercise of a receptive ability is analogous to obsession.[77] But in most other ways, Han Feizi seems to stress an empirical approach. His version of neutral, empty reception has an experimental, pragmatic quality.

He combines Laozi and Xunzi to produce an account of a danger in the state of mind that can produce absolute insight. He employs an assumption that he retains in his later work. The heart works by a kind of calculation. His position, here, however, seems unstable. He assumes that the calculation is for self-interest (li^{profit}), yet he seems also to have an ideal of *a correct calculation* that avoids the distortion of desires and self-interest.[78]

Han Feizi throughout the commentary treats *dao* as a general noun, speaking of the ruler's *dao*, orthodox and heretical *dao*, etc.[79] When he starts to comment on the metaphysical part of *The Laozi*, he takes the Shendao *actual dao* as the topic. The *dao* is all that is the case about the ten thousand things. He imports the non-Daoist concept $li^{\text{guiding tendency}}$, of which we have seen very little in the classical period. It plays a somewhat more substantial role in Xunzi's theory, where the li^{ritual} is treated as a metaphysical pattern.[80] This $li^{\text{guiding tendency}}$ was to become a key concept in Wang Pi's commentary on *The Laozi*. From there it moved into Buddhism and Neo-Confucianism as $li^{\text{principle}}$. Han Feizi makes $li^{\text{guiding tendency}}$ the central focus in his explanation. Each kind of thing has a $li^{\text{guiding tendency}}$ that governs its distinguishable attributes and its course of development and completion. He explains the natural *dao* as the compendium of *li*. So the actual *dao* guides nature via a *li* for each thing kind. Of course, this entails that *dao* is divisible. Each *li*, Han Feizi insists, is distinct. They do not involve each other. (This may reflect Han Feizi's refusal to emphasize *oneness* as Xunzi does.)

Now Han Feizi does see that this conception of *dao* makes *li*^{guiding tendency} a guide in human matters too. It guides the production of conventions (the sage's writing of literature),[81] language,[82] and all prescriptive knowledge. So whatever actually brings it about that there is such a convention is in accord with *dao*. This is the middle point between Xunzi and Shendao. The conventions are in accord with *dao* but that is an amoral, circumstantial result. It is *shi*^{situational authority}.

This picture gives Han Feizi's *dao* an air of amorality. The *dao* is in the evil kings as much as in the good ones. No one opposite describes *dao* unless the other one does as well. Clearly, as Tang Jun-i observes, Han Feizi thinks of his later ruling *dao* as flowing in this way out of his *dao of all things*.[83] He reinforces the view of *dao* as having a part-whole structure by observing that one can have too much or just the right amount of it.[84]

This implantation of Xunzi's notion of *li*^{guiding tendency} seems designed more to justify clear objective *fa* than to explain what *dao* is. Han Feizi derives more of his ruling doctrine's structure from the concept of *li* than from *dao*. The value of *ding*^{fixed} *li*^{guiding tendencies} lies in the possibility of measurementlike guides that can be used in directing punishment.[85] This emphasis on empirical accessibility reflects his view that only a cold, objective, emotionless perspective can be free from obsession.

The Aftermath

The Qin dynasty brought the Chinese classical philosophical period to an end by following Han Feizi's advice. Xunzi and Han Feizi had been impatient with skeptical and puzzling linguistic doctrines. They coupled that with the bald and dogmatic assertion of a privileged route of access to an unbiased perspective. These twin doctrines buttressed their dogmatic authoritarianism. They both defended punishment with the righteous assurance either that they had the absolute view of right and wrong or that it was more important to get agreement than to worry about what was right. This, however, was not the height of classical philosophy, but the dogmatic, unreflective cause of its decline. Both justified control of discourse. No one could say or publish or read language the ruler did not *shi*. So the officials burned books and buried scholars alive.

A great deal has been written about the negative effects of the Qin's suppression of other schools, but the establishment of orthodoxy is equally to blame for the Chinese philosophical dark ages. When the orthodoxy became Confucianism, it took over the priority of satisfying the speculative and superstitious inclinations of the rulers as well as the task of justifying and legitimizing their rule. The cost of orthodoxy is not merely the weeding out of other schools, but stunting and trivializing the doctrine that gets the state's stamp of approval.

Several elements contribute to the authoritarian conclusion of the classical period. We began with the father-teacher concept of role of leadership. Political structures were continuous with all other social ways of inculcating human character. The central example of this social determination of character was language. It also came to be understood as the mechanism of socialization as well. Language shaped behavior and desires and was a proper object of political regulation. The presumed need for order entailed that language had to be controlled.

Philosophical reflection and analysis cast doubt on the possibility of determining a neutral standard for this social-engineering project and especially for the language-control subproject. There are no constant names. That intellectual conclusion terrified thinkers obsessed with order. Without a natural source of values guiding *shi-fei* we seemed doomed to value anarchy. Zhuangzi's *Free and Easy* permission to explore the region around one's own point of view was perverted into Xunzi's dogmatic assertion that his perspective was uniquely free from obsession. He regarded the authoritative status of convention as unquestionable. Analytic philosophy, with its word splitting and other deviations from conventionally accepted language, must be punished severely. Han Feizi merely substitutes authority for Xunzi's convention and accepts the rest of Xunzi's attitude. Now, given the prior assumptions, it becomes obligatory for the ruler to promote one form of language and to proscribe all the others.

I do not regard Daoism as inimical to philosophical objectivity or realism. The theoretical realism of Xunzi's and Han Feizi's view is not what I object to. Realism is compatible with Zhuangzi's healthy appreciation of the practical impossibility of showing what the real answer is. What I object to is promoting the culturally dominant as absolute and final and refusing to state (or allow others to state) obvious skeptical doubts. Such a policy is manipulative because it values keeping others from one's own awareness that other perspectives have powerful claims to be as valuable as our own. This awareness does set us a monumental, perhaps endless task of openness, communication, and deliberation. Some, perhaps many, will shrug their shoulders and sink into philosophical relativism. Resolving these conflicting views of things may actually be insurmountable for the human intellect.

Philosophical relativism is a mistake and perhaps something of a danger. But it is less of a danger than the imposition of current dogma as if it were the absolute truth. That is not only a political danger; it is a choice to abandon the intellectual integrity that realism ought to promote. We have to be prepared to deal with the costs of coming to realize that we may have been wrong all along. Those costs do not justify blind dogmatism.

The belief that there is a single correct answer is compatible with the belief that I do not have it and may never be able to prove it to others. The search for objectivity must be tempered with analysis and Daoist irony. If the impulse to objectivity is not tempered with self-critical skepticism and pragmatic, political toleration for other points of view, it becomes a parody of itself. We must be willing to run the risk of value anarchy before we can justify the pluralism that will allow a Daoist free and easy wandering through points of view.

Similarly, although I object to distorting Daoism into a doctrine advocating absolutism and dogmatic authoritarianism, Daoism need not be opposed to the rule of law. Given the very important Daoist rule "avoid punishment" the rule of law may be the best available technique for controlling the universally demonstrated propensity of powerful types to punish us when they feel like it. Short of genetic engineering to root the urge for vengeance out of human nature, an institution to make its coercive effects more predictable does make them more avoidable. But no Daoist would confuse the law with the objectively right. It is merely the most workable way to control the authorities until we solve the deeper twin problems of vengeful and domineering human nature.

Western objectivism is tightly bound up with the notion of reason. As I have argued, no Daoist should find that idea objectionable. They did not develop such an ideology. I suppose Daoists would welcome rationalism as another point of view. They would be most interested in the current Confucianization of reason in the United States. Some who have inherited the Platonic tradition share Xunzi's dread of relativism. Like Xunzi they advocate that we act as if our traditions were absolutely true. They treat objectivity as a political matter and recommend that we drill our students dogmatically in ancient ways. Avoid the weak, spineless surrender to students' demand to understand other cultures and ways of thinking. Let us, by all means, ban skepticism, irony, and self-doubt.[86] The Daoist would be equally offended by the students' demand to enforce a new orthodoxy and *require* everyone to study their current conception of a diversified curriculum. What tragic flaw makes revolutionaries turn demands for freedom into demands for a new regime of conformity?

The great irony, of course, is that both camps of authoritarians are the real relativists. They don't know how to refute philosophical relativism, so they resolve to act as if it were not there. It is to be politically banned. Mature Daoism would accept analytic thinking as the most appropriate therapy. It simultaneously refutes naive relativism *and* slows us from the too easy and tempting conclusion that since there really is an answer, it must be the one that seems obvious to me now.

The tragedy of Chinese history is that it has recapitulated the classical dialectic. The classical period saw the decline of a tradition and the spread of skepticism and doubt. Traditionalists longed for any stable authority and were willing to ban analysis and irony to get it. They got a brief, draconian, empire, then a Confucian orthodoxy that again spawned skepticism and Daoist relativism. The subsequent period of disorder ended with a relatively stable traditional Confucian order that had an objective urge again, but without techniques of analysis and far too little philosophical irony—though the ironic impulse found other outlets. The relativism introduced by Western contacts provoked an instinctive Confucian need to enforce conformity in word and deed. It was carried out by modern practitioners of enforced order, still struggling to understand what law could be for—beyond punishing nonconformity.

NOTES

Chapter 1

1. Northrup (1946).

2. I owe this engaging metaphor to Thomas Nagel (Nagel, 1986). Zhuangzi's counterpart is the hinge of *dao*^{ways of discourse}. But that will take some time to motivate.

3. This skepticism is formulated as strongly by the first Neo-Confucians as by any modern Western critic. See Munro (1988), p. 6. Of course, like this study, each Neo-Confucian thought that he had got it better than his predecessors.

4. Bruce Brooks has proposed a far more elaborate new chronology of classical thought along similar lines. His analysis was presented at the 1990 meeting of the Northeast Conference on Chinese Thought and may soon be published. While our proposals differ in motivation (his is mainly textual analysis) and numerous details, they share the same motivation. We both insist on explaining the development of Classical thought by reference to dialogue among rival philosophers. The essentially religious view of private thinkers reaching deeply inward to tap some fundamental insight about the universe seems implausible on its face.

5. Blackburn (1984), ch. 2.

6. This is not to suggest that this standard view does not come under criticism in some Indian schools. It does. But it is a view that is standard enough to be criticized. I shall argue that in ancient China, the view itself did not even emerge.

7. I adapt this helpful characterization from Kornblith (1985), p. 117.

8. I am assuming that our concept of belief is not merely dispositional but has narrow semantic content. If we allow either a dispositional or wide-causal notion of belief, then we could attribute beliefs in a straightforward way to a computer.

9. For a particularly clear example, see Graham (1989), pp. 7–8.

10. See Stich (1983) and Churchland (1979).

11. Following Lewis (1972), I believe.

Chapter 2

1. Graham (1989, p. 390) appreciates the philosophical interest in this observation. He and Schwartz, 1985, both allude frequently to Jaspers's axial age hypothesis. For Schwartz, the hypothesis assigns special significance to what for Graham is an interesting sociological coincidence—that several great historical civilizations arose at about the same time—between 800 and 200 B.C. Schwartz seems to suggest that whatever explanation we could give of this fact entails that the basic philosophical *problematiques* must have been alike. It was as if there was a moment of global awareness of *transcendental* questions. This partly explains his adoption of the ruling-theory adoration of Confucius alongside Plato, Moses, and Buddha. Each was the selected recipient of this enlightenment in his area of the world. Sometimes Schwartz speaks as if he appeals to this hypothesis only to insist that we treat Chinese philosophers seriously. I have no objection to this. But the axial age observation gives us no special reason to think that philosophical problems were the same in China as in Greece and India.

2. Graham (1989), p. 12. The Gilgamesh flood epic was cited as a cultural universal when I was a university student. Creation myths and cosmology begin to be important during the Han dark ages, when possibly, cultural contacts with the Middle East along the silk road were expanding. Some scholars depart vigorously from this hypothesis of philosophical independence. Victor Mair, for example, speculates that many terms of Chinese are borrowed from Indo-European languages. He cites phonemic evidence. He notes a plethora of words in Chinese that now or sometime (in some dialect) sounded something like some word of Sanskrit or some other European language. He also claims similarity in doctrine between Buddhism and Daoism. That is more a conclusion than evidence. Others may try to prove the same thing by pointing to similar philosophical theories. Obviously, that kind of argument can only work if they have interpreted the Chinese doctrines correctly. My arguments warn against the assumptions that we share philosophical intuitions. Appealing to similar doctrines to prove cultural contact gets the argument backward.

3. Although, for a great many Shang characters, no plausible line of descent has been traced.

4. Robert Eno (1990), app. B discusses this theory. He is critical of it. My thanks to him for pointing out the questions. I make no attempt to resolve the issue here. Eno himself (pp. 19–21), still, appeals to the Shang practices as precursors of the Confucian focus on ritual.

5. This, again, is controversial. See Eno (1990), app. A.

6. For an excellent discussion of $tian^{\text{heaven:nature}}$ in Confucianism, see Eno (1990). Protestant translators choose the Shang *father in heaven* concept for their translation of *God*. Catholic translators use the Zhou deity $tian^{\text{heaven}}$ for their translation for *God* ($tianzhu^{\text{lord of}}$ ^{heaven}). I leave it to scholars of this schism to explain the significance of the choice of different translations.

7. Thomas Nagel, *What Does It All Mean? A Very Short Introduction to Philosophy* (New York: Oxford University Press, 1987), pp. 38 and 43. Nagel's masterfully elegant introduction to philosophical issues starts from our most familiar and common-sense intuitions. This makes it an especially good guide to pervasive Western attitudes.

8. Graham argues that the Mohists adapted ci^{phrase} as a technical term referring exclusively to the sentence (1978, p. 207–9). I challenged that claim in an appendix to my 1985 article "Chinese Language, Chinese Philosophy, and 'Truth.'" Graham theorized that the Mohists discovered the sentence. It was, he said "the last and most difficult of the Mohist discoveries" (ibid. p. 25). I expressed my doubts about that argument in the same article (p. 510 fn.). There is an interesting anecdote associated with that dispute. I wrote that article using the then current technology—Perfect Writer on a CP/M Kaypro II. Originally the appendix was included as a footnote in the text—the next footnote following the one expressing and explaining my skepticism about the alleged discovery of the sentence. It was a much longer footnote since I was trying to show that the use of ci^{phrase} in *Names and Objects* was perfectly consistent with its normal meaning and in several places could not reasonably have been interpreted as "sentence." Perfect Writer, however, could not handle long footnotes. After several failed attempts to format the article, I finessed the problem by deleting the second long footnote and making it an appendix. Graham has since complained repeatedly to me in person and in print that I wrote a whole appendix rejecting his claim that never mentioned his case for the theory that they discovered the sentence. "Hansen, 'Truth' 517, has an appendix rejecting my claim that *Names and Objects* discovers the sentence, but without criticizing or even mentioning my case for it" (1989, p. 394fn.). Of course, I mentioned, cited, and criticized his claim *that* they discovered the sentence in the first footnote. The second footnote addressed the *subsequent question* of whether they had changed the meaning to ci^{phrase} and begun to use it deliberately to refer only to sententials. If the appendix had remained a footnote, the two footnotes would have been consecutive and Graham's complaint would presum-

ably have focused on the content of the issue rather than the perceived slight. As it was he could not get over that the appendix itself did not contain the argument in the footnote. He has never forgiven me and has passed the robe of transmission to Harbsmeier and Cikoski (Graham 1989, pp. 391–92). Naturally, I have never forgiven Perfect Writer—which is shame since it was otherwise a rather good word-processing editor. This text is being prepared in Word Perfect, which, as the reader will note, allows very long notes.

9. Graham repeatedly cites poetry, parable, and aphorism as evidence of antirationality. See, for example, Graham (1989), p. 7. He does, however, note that parallelism helps disambiguate written Classical Chinese. But his explanation confuses things. If both parallel phrases are structurally ambiguous, then the parallelism cannot by itself help resolve the ambiguity. For parallelism to help, it must be the case that, via either sensible interpretation or further clues, one of the parallel sentences strongly favors *one way* of resolving the ambiguity. A better example would be the perennial question of the parsing of lines 3 to 6 of ch. 1 of the *Daode Jing*.

10. See Burge (1975) for an excellent account of how mass nouns figure in the philosophical problem of change. I draw this example from him.

11. See my account in Hansen (1983), ch. 2. Russell and Lesniewski were among the first to use the term *mereology* of the alternative ontology.

12. Number and shape terms and some temporal terms are the most persuasive examples of regular count nouns (e.g., four corners, one day). I owe thanks to Tim Moore for pointing this out to me. The sortals of Chinese may be used as abbreviated nominal structures.

Chapter 3

1. Eno (1990), p. 9.

2. Schwartz (1985), p. 61.

3. Chan (1963), p. 17.

4. See Eno (1990, ch. 1) for a masterful argument for this view of the *Ru* preoccupation with ritual performance and dance. Eno defends the position that the word *Ru*^{Confucian} was *only* applied to followers of Confucius.

5. I agree with those who find the evidence that Confucius studied the *Book of Changes* unacceptably meager.

6. Schwartz (1986), p. 58.

7. See Eno (1990), ch. 1 and 2.

8. Although Confucius did not like *glibness* or *verbal cleverness*. See *The Analects* 1:3.

9. Buddhism also has a similar tradition of arriving at doctrines by inner meditation. Schwartz (1985, p. 60) appears to accept the private-thinker cliché as a criterion of the emergence of philosophy.

10. I am indebted to Robert Eno for motivation and most of the content of this description of *Ru*^{Confucian} communities and to Bruce Brooks for his presentation of the role of the text in classical thought.

11. For stylistic ease, I will conform to the personalized grammar. Readers can translate every reference to Confucius into ''The Confucius as reported in *The Analects*'' for themselves.

12. See Fingarette (1972, ch. 2) for a parallel argument with a slightly different focus. This is not a general feature of Chinese philosophers. The next figure we discuss introduces philosophical argument and debate as vigorously as any Westerner would. And he picks especially on the nondebating Confucians. Then clever debate characterizes the rest of the classical period. The cleverness would be as marked in style, brevity, and humor as much as in argument.

13. This is not only a Western criticism. The tension and ambiguity of *The Analects* have been a topic of Chinese criticism starting from Wang Chong in the Han Dynasty (b. A.D. 27). Schwartz (1985, p. 61) says ". . . it is not easy to separate the founder's vision from the interpretations of his disciples . . ." He takes issue, however, with Tsuda Sokichi, whom he calls "a radical and iconoclastic critic of the text," who "finds the work so shot through with contradictions and anachronisms that it is unusable as a source of the thought of Confucius . . ." Schwartz is right, I shall argue, to reject that pessimistic conclusion, although I am tempted in the direction of Sokichi. The contradictions do make it hard to decide which group of disciples was right about Confucius' original intent since we only have their inconsistent recollections as evidence of his real positions.

14. See Schwartz (1985), p. 104. Ames (1982 and 1985) is another example.

15. See Chan (1963), p. 22.

16. These two lines explain persistent divisions in Confucianism throughout its history. The two lines are manifest in the Classical period in the dispute between Mencius and Xunzi, and in the Neo-Confucian period in the dispute between Zhuxi and Lu Xiang-Shan. All Confucians face a choice between a relatively textual, traditional and a relatively *natural,* innate approach. Eno (1990) objects to the traditional distinction of these two schools. He argues that *all* Confucian schools continued the practice of cultivating ritual performance. That, of course, may be. But they did adopt different *theories* of what they were doing and of its justification.

17. Schwartz (1985), pp. 130–34.

18. This may be due not only to an emerging dispute in the first and second generation of disciples, but to the general tendency of classic books from this period to take on accretions as later thinkers put their views in the text. See Dawson (1981), p. 4.

19. Classical Chinese philosophical works with *Lun* in the title typically contain a dialogue or debate. Other famous *lun* include the White Horse *lun* and the Iron and Salt *lun*. Zhuangzi equalizes *lun* (discussions) about things. This point was first suggested by Jeff Riegel, although he may not agree with the use I make of it here.

20. Schwartz (1985) notes that Han Fei Tzu identifies eight different schools of Confucian thought. We cannot rule out that Confucius' own theory was internally contradictory. But we also cannot prove that it *was* merely by citing the contradictory nature of *The Analects*.

21. This appears to be Schwartz's view. He indeed suggests that Confucius has a "Taoist strain" (1985, p. 128–29). This resolution was also followed by Wang Cong, who suggested that the problem with *The Analects* was simply that the disciples were stupid and asked the wrong questions. Partisans of either approach will object to my interpretive strategy. Like the original disciples, they want Confucius on their side. Conservative scholarship virtually worships Confucius. Accordingly, it cannot accept the possibility that his doctrine might have been flawed, incomplete, or ambiguous. The typical view is that Confucius stated some *rounded, all-pervading* truth at the outset and various disciples merely missed the point. Where Confucians disagree, someone must have misunderstood the divine master.

However, the point is that any such *deeper* Confucian theory is doubly speculative. The speculation requires that he be clear about things he fails to make clear to his disciples and that the interpreter can figure out how the conflicts were resolved while studying only the aphoristic fragments reported by the warring factions who themselves were confused about the issues. This divine Confucius strategy may serve the quasi-religious purposes of devotees. We Daoists have no use for it. The presupposition that an idealized semideified Confucius *must have* developed a *perfect* doctrine undermines the explanatory project. The later split in the school must then be explained by either incompetence or bad faith on someone's part. The history of Chinese Confucianism does not start with a sublime, rounded truth. It starts with an emerging tension and division between two Confucian lines. Typically the orthodox innatist school maintains Mencius got Confucius right and merely elaborated and filled in details. It treats Xunzi as a heretic. Philosophical progress and tension disappear from these quasi-religious accounts.

22. Remember that the methodological requirement than an interpretation be a coherent explanation of all texts does not require that it treat each text as a single coherent theory. Conversely, that a work is a compilation by several authors over time does not entail that one *cannot* interpret it as a coherent theory. The *Daode Jing,* for example, is clearly an edited collection of fragments, none of which we attribute to the mythical author. What makes *The Analects* different is its tone. We get the sense of quotations—which may be genuine—being used on both sides of a dispute. The coherence of my interpretive theory lies in its natural explanation of the division of Confucianism into the two lines: Mencius and Xunzi. Not only is *The Analects* a later compilation, it is a compilation in the context of an emerging interpretive dispute. The tension that produced two Confucian schools I take to be implicit in the original doctrine. I do not treat the later split as one-sided distortions of a fully rounded Confucian truth.

23. One clever Confucian has suggested that the tension between *ren* and *li* was intended by Confucius to stimulate creative Confucian thought. See Tu (1970).

24. Confucius does signal his acceptance of Zhou traditions, although many scholars speculate that he originated from the region that was the original heart of Shang culture. See, for example, Hsiao (1979), p. 107. He declares "I follow Zhou" (3:14) and gets inspiration from the duke of Zhou. (7:5)

25. I am grateful to Donald Munro for the outlines of the account of Confucius' implicit political theory. See Munro (1969).

26. Hsiao (1979), p. 113.

27. Starting from the baseline, the character *tian*[heaven] functioned more like our *nature* than our *God.* The main feature that *tian* shares with *God* is its role as a source of guidance. It does not correspond to a natural-supernatural ontological dichotomy nor imply a separation of idealized perfection and worldly filth. Conventional interpretations regard Mozi as an exception to this naturalism. I shall argue in the next chapter that this conclusion is dubious.

28. Actually, one of the traditional *five relationships* is an equal relationship—friendship.

29. Of course, any moderately cynical liberal will want to know who grades the examinations and decides who has *merit.* Chinese historians tell numerous stories about the struggle between Confucian scholars and *realistic* politicians. Both wanted control of the examination bureau. This system of merit appointment of officials is the remote ancestor of our own civil service examinations. The stress on merit appointment represents a Confucian power grab that worked. The civil service *did* frustrate the emperor. Whether the political leader should be able to manipulate the bureaucracy depends on who the political authority is and how you feel about her policies. Whether considering the Empress Cixi or Richard Nixon, we admire officials who refuse to carry out immoral policies. However, some may not value such moral independence in the Roosevelt Supreme Court. The tendency of an independent bureaucracy is to preserve the status quo moral values of the bureaucratic class. It is important to recognize that to Confucians moralists, such moral stagnation is precisely the goal of the system. They did not have an image of traditional moral values as something that *ought* to change.

30. See Hsiao (1979), p. 113. I noted with interest the continuation of this tradition in Mao's China. A hallmark of Mao's reign was his image as a theoretician. The top figure is not supposed to be an administrator. He appointed Zhou Enlai to be the administrator. Mao was the source of legitimacy. He evoked dedication and seriousness from his subordinates (the actual administrators) by his own model of discipline and sacrifice.

31. One might suspect that part of later Confucian opposition to laws stems from the fact that legal practices dislodge Confucians from the positions of authority and elevate clever people who are trained not in history and tradition but in mere semantics. This would also

reinforce the enmity between Confucians and the school of names. But we do not find that position stated in *The Analects*.

32. Unlike Plato, Confucius does not want protection in some ahistorical objective reason, but protection in fidelity to the historical tradition. Confucians condemn their sophists not because they are inconsistent relativists but because they do not start from a firm historical base of a transmitted *dao*.

33. Dawson (1981), p. 22.

34. *The Analects* 13.3. Waley (1958) and Creel (1960) have both raised doubts about the authenticity of this passage. The technique is important mainly to the traditional wing. The dominant innate wing has little use for rectifying names. Mencius never mentions the doctrine while Xunzi writes an entire chapter on the subject. Since I am not treating *The Analects* as Confucius' anyway, I shall ignore disputes about authenticity and concentrate on the theoretical roles the doctrine plays in both lines of interpretation.

35. This intriguing passage has generated a typical misunderstanding of rectifying names. Many take the passage to show that rectifying names is not about names at all, but about people's responsibility. They read the theory as requiring that we *live up to* our names. This interpretation arises because Confucius' koanlike answer can be parsed in two ways. In each phrase, we have to treat one of each noun pair as a verb. Since Chinese sentences require no subject, we may choose either noun-verb or verb-object analyses. If we read it as verb-object, "you—the duke" is the likely subject. On this reading the duke's task in *zheng* [administering] is to name people to roles on the basis of their merit: to give the name *ruler* to rulers, *minister* to ministers, and so forth. The duke himself, however, replies as if *zheng* [administering] is everyone else's responsibility. In fact his reply seems so incongruous that one wonders if he is not sarcastically objecting to the enigmatic nature of Confucius' answer. His analysis of that koan-like answer is a self-serving one. The rival interpretation accepts the duke's self-serving analysis as fixing the grammar of Confucius' punning formula. Aside from the duke's reply, we would usually give such two-noun phrases the verb-object analysis.

Confucius' answer *is* ambiguous. Interpretively, we have two choices. Either this passage is about rectifying names or it is not. If we parse Confucius' answer as the duke does, it is not about rectifying names. It is also not about the art of administration. It then has no obvious theoretical connection to the earlier passages discussed. If, instead, we parse it as an injunction to the duke, it is both about administration and rectifying names. In either case, it cannot consistently be used to show that rectifying names is really about rectifying people.

36. This, of course, is a weaker technique. The history book is itself subject to interpretation. The *Spring and Autumn Annals* evoked two competing interpretive commentaries and traditions and they, in turn had competing commentaries.

37. This slogan gives us a way to understand Fingarette's observation that Confucius focused on the performative aspects of language and convention. The Supreme Court has performative authority. A performative is a speech act where the saying is the doing. To say, in the appropriate circumstances, "I promise" *is* to promise. To say "I do" in the proper place in the ceremony *is to do it*. When the performative authority says "I declare you man and wife" those words at that moment appropriately apply to the newlyweds. When a court "finds you guilty" you are, for the first time, guilty in legal terms although in non-legal or moral terms, your guilt starts from the time of the action. "The law is what the Supreme Court says it is" is true not because the members of the Supreme Court are omniscient and infallible about law, but because their authority is performative. Their case-by-case declarations fix the meanings of the legal terms for the judicial institutions.

38. The contrast here illustrates the central contrast of the two traditions. Where the issue is that of truth or fact, authority must be of the expert type. No scientific or moral expert can make something true by saying it. In the law, therefore, we can distinguish between two kinds of authorities. The leading constitutional law professor at the Harvard School of Law is an

authority in the way a Supreme Court justice is not. He may understand the history and theory of law better and may reason more deeply about law. But his saying something about law does not make it true. The Supreme Court justice might be less than wise, but his saying what the law is (in the appropriate ritual circumstances) does make it law.

39. See Dworkin (1977).

40. I am using *Socratic* here in a general way derived from his questioning tradition. His own ethics did not involve rules of behavior as much as the rules for use of terms referring to moral virtue. These might, by extension be thought of as moral rules, but Socrates did not seem to be a deontologist. The Euclidean component in his method, however, was important. It can be found in the use of definitions in a deductive structure.

41. Much of this analysis develops from the valuable and ground-breaking analysis of Herbert Fingarette (1972). The crucial step in his approach lies in generalizing from the particular, seemingly trivial *li* to which Confucius referred to the generalized notion of convention. We follow the analysis as a means of spelling out the presuppositions of the tradition. I am less than confident that Confucius had any articulated theory of convention.

42. Hand shaking is a good modern example of a *li*, except that it does not have the superior-inferior structure so characteristic of Confucian *li*.

43. I am stating the Confucian view here, not arguing for it. But I am inclined to agree with this point. If we were to connect every skillful response to an external situation to a practical syllogism consisting of beliefs and desires, the most ordinary act would require an indefinitely large set of beliefs and desires—too many to store in a normal human brain! I find it more plausible that we use our practical intuitions as *evidence* of implicit beliefs which we cite in explanatory justification. The practical intuition may give me evidence for a corresponding belief which could then function in some deductive or inductive reasoning for some other less intuitive behaviors (such as deciding to let the cows go because a box canyon lies in that direction). Notice that the alternative Confucian explanation of human action requires analogues of program execution and environmental variables, not belief and desire. The motivational condition is that one is *executing* an instruction set, a ritual repertoire, in a real context.

44. This is frequently expressed in their contempt for eunuchs who voluntarily mutilate their bodies. Zhuangzi thus delights in chiding Confucians by telling stories of people of enormous *de* [virtuosity] who are grotesquely misshapen.

45. Eno (1990) argues that it derives from the notion of a dance pattern. He points to the interesting fact that *wu* [martial] and *wu* [dance] are cognate terms. The first sage-kings of the Zhou dynasty took the names *wen* [literature] and *wu* [martial dance]. Even the training of warriors consisted of doing a ritualized dance (something, one supposes, like the forms of the martial arts). *Wen* [literature] may thus stand for any conventional pattern to which one refers in physical behavior or performance.

46. This Wittgensteinian notion is a very tempting translation for *dao* [way].

47. I borrow this term from Steven Stitch (1984). Modern Western folk psychology owes an obvious debt to eighteenth-century philosophical psychology and theory of meaning. Stitch traces it back to the Greek philosophers. Socrates and Plato, however, made skill and performance more central to their accounts than the British empiricists did. Still, the Greeks are the original source of the division of the psyche into rational, intellectual versus emotional, feeling components.

48. I borrow this handy term from David Lewis (1972).

49. Fingarette, however, confuses the issue slightly by appearing to deny that Confucius' has *any* psychological concepts. The point is not that people have no psychological properties, but that their psychological states are dispositional states, not inaccessible, inner cognitive ones. He also distracts from his own insight when he slips into describing *ren* [humanity] as an attitude that must accompany performance of *li*. This is to treat it as an inner state. If Fingarette's account is otherwise correct, *ren* is then explanatorily inert. But if it is a *physically*

realized intuition that guides correct performance, then it can have the important role Confucius seems to assign it.

50. Schwartz, for example, falls into this trap when he tries to rebut Fingarette's claims about the absence of psychology by citing a Confucian complaint that *li* consists of more than silk and gems, then asserting that the complaint is a ringing assertion that the *li* has lost its meaning. But that is to miss Fingarette's point. It cannot be given its meaning by some inner mental state of an actor. Its meaning, what must be added to silks and gems, is an active communal practice—at least that is Fingarette's point. Schwartz's alleged refutation merely begs the question in drawing inferences from the notion of meaning in the Western folk-theory way.

It must be noted that Fingarette is partly responsible for this misinterpretation. Schwartz quotes him as saying "The ceremony may have a surface slickness but yet be dull, mechanical for lack of serious purpose and commitment" (p. 73). Fingarette should not have appealed to intentional notions like *purpose* and *commitment*. The dull, mechanical performance would be explained by a defective physical state of the performer—a machine-language translation of the program that still needs debugging.

51. Though we can tell ourselves this elaborate fantasized, mentalist story about inner objects to account for accumulating language, it does not seem plausible when we notice the social character of language behavior. The theory goes from ridiculous to unrealistic when we extend it to animals and children: "She wanted a bottle and believed she could get it by crying." We end up explaining all patterns of thinking by analogy to adult language speakers vocalizing reasons for their actions. The language we use suggests a picture of children and animals talking to themselves in the *language of thought* but deprived by a capricious nature of the power of external speech.

52. An objection: to talk this way is to explain nothing! An inclination is an empty explanation of a behavior. Belief-desire explanations at least have the virtue of not being mere restatements of the phenomena: we learn to speak language. I agree. We are not offering an alternative theory—at least not an elaborate one of the sort appropriate to psychology as a science. We are merely observing that the popular *folk psychology* is a *bad* explanation. It is not merely probably false; it is an explanation that presupposes what it should explain. No explanation *is an improvement* over that kind of explanation. Confucianism, when it offers the claim that ritual behavior is natural, is not offering an alternative descriptive explanation. But, as an observation about the pattern of human behavior to be explained, it is more realistic than the egoist picture. A complete explanation, on the other hand, would probably involve more neurophysiology than anyone knows at present.

53. Fingarette makes this observation into an explanation of Confucius' opposition to punishment. If punishment is used in the pursuit of this goal, it is morally unacceptable. Confucius assumed that this was the goal of government. He therefore had to condemn punishment as a method of government. I don't find the attribution of individualist morality plausible as an explanation of Confucius' opposition to punishment.

54. See Hansen (1985), "Individualism." Western explanation tends toward microexplanation. We explain a macrophenomena (society or ice forming) by describing the behavior of its parts (individuals or atoms). Chinese explanation tends toward macroexplanation. They explain phenomena (individual behavior or a storm) by describing its place in some whole (social structure or yin-yang ether).

55. I suggest that Fingarette's otherwise inexplicable insistence that *li* must be thought of as magical comes from the fact that modern Western culture tends to explain these things in psychological terms. Since Confucius did not feel the need to explain them in this way, he must think they work by some kind of magic. I doubt that Confucius thought that there was anything operating here but the most natural of processes.

56. It isn't necessary that Confucius not believe in spirits—he may or he may not (11:11).

The point is that spirit plays no role in his account of human intellectual functioning and distinctiveness. Humans are social animals of a particular type: ritual accumulating.

57. Another interpretation is possible here as well. Do we extrapolate from the example correctly? What is it to "do the same thing" in these different circumstances? Despite the appearance of greater information, we can raise a parallel interpretive problem about model emulation and rule following.

58. Its optimistic tone is marred slightly by vagueness. *Sheng* refers to the entire course of life—birth and growth. But, as we shall see, Mencius' own theory is not strictly that full goodness is present at birth but represents a direction of natural growth and development. The other vague element is endemic to Chinese texts. The mood may be imperative: humans should grow toward good or disaster is certain.

59. Fingarette (1972), ch. 2.

60. Rosemont argued this in a presentation of the Society of Asian and Comparative Philosophy meeting. I expect that it will reach publication soon.

61. I will argue for translating *yi* as *morality* in Chapter 3.

62. Consider the anthropological distinction between shame and guilt cultures. (This distinction is less clearly marked in ordinary language.) It distinguishes cultures with two views of the status of morality. A shame culture, Confucian traditionalism, treats it as essentially social. A guilt culture treats ethical issues as either supracultural (say from God) or autonomously individual. In social science usage, a shame culture is one that motivates behavior by the disapproval of the group. The fact that everyone believes it is wrong makes it wrong. On this account, guilt is distinguished from shame precisely in being more autonomous and responsible. I feel guilt when I subject myself to my own moral standards as opposed to those of the group. A shame culture exploits and amplifies our fear of *losing face*. Guilt cultures are, in this sense, more individualistic. Shame cultures are conventional and social. An analysis of the ordinary language use of *shame* and *guilt* can be found in Rawls (1971), pp. 442–46.

63. Schwartz (1985), p. 63.

64. Apologists defend the traditionalist position by treating it as implicitly arguing that there can be no complete escape from traditions in answering moral questions. This implies that Confucius *did* understand the distinction between morals and mores, considered the issue thoroughly, and decided that there could be no extra cultural ground for moral theory. That story would be more plausible if Confucius came at the end, rather than before the beginning of the philosophical movement. At this point in China—the beginning of philosophical dialectic—Confucius' disciples simply fail to recognize the import of real moral questions. Both assume that Confucius' curriculum contains the answer to the question, "What should we do?" They debated only how to get people *to do* it. *The Analects* deals with education and moral sociology, not normative ethical theory.

65. *Analects* 2:23.

66. *Analects* 3:14.

67. Confucius, in one snippet of conversation, claims that some thread unites his teaching. Confucius, in that passage (4:15), does not tell what his one thread is (a disciple offers an interpretation). As Chan (1963, p. 27) observes, Confucian tradition never came up with a coherent account of what it was. Modern day interpreters still try to trace out the senior disciples guess to salvage Confucius' philosophical reputation. A spate of modern interpreters have followed Fingarette in proposing theories of what the one thread is. To me, the whole enterprise smacks of forced apologetics. The interpreters end up trying to tease a moral theory out of speculative etymology, comments about the rhyme and graphic structure of the two words in the disciple's answer. The very desperation with which they cling to this slender thread makes the very point. Confucius did not offer his disciples much of a moral theory.

The passage does have some point. It shows that Confucius was aware that his theory

required some coherence, if not a justification. It points us toward a possible connection between the "Confucian negative golden rule" and the interpretive content of the standard of
ren^{humanity}. Unfortunately, that leads us to an interpretation in which Confucius becomes a
utilitarian—like Mozi. The thread should be Confucius' missing normative ethical theory—the
one that justifies studying and following the *li*. Innatist interpretations insist that Confucius
really did not presuppose the *li*. Confucius was systematically critical of *li*. He based his
theory, as Mencius did, on *ren*. I am arguing that Mencius was radically different from Confucius on this issue. Another approach would appeal to the social consequences of Confucius'
worship of tradition. Rituals defined the structure of the Zhou culture to which he was so
loyal. Order and the preservation of the mandate for the Zhou kings was his primary political
concern. Continuation of the ritual was imperative both to social cohesion and to the definition
of culture. This seems like simply admitting that Confucius was no philosopher of ethics at
all.

    68. Herbert Fingarette's influential book on Confucius offers a *way* of dealing with Con-
fucius' acceptance of *li*^{ritual}. He suggests that Confucius' view of *li* does not stem from an
uncritical, prephilosophical conservative attitude. Confucius knew that one cannot answer Socratic skepticism without presupposing some conventions. The superficially naive traditionalist
doctrine is really a philosophically sophisticated doctrine that convention is inherent in human
life. "We must, at least initially, presume that a thinker and a teacher of great stature has
some more compelling and universal basis for the way he frames and answers his central
questions. We shall understand Confucius better if we try to see what such a basis might be"
(Fingarette, 1972, p. 59).

    This amounts to the recommendation that we attribute a *default* moral theory to Confucius
even if he never stated it as such. Take at face value Confucius attachment to etiquette.
Whether or not Confucius had a sophisticated *argument for* conventionalism, his view hints at
ethical conventionalism. How? We reason as follows: Morality is of supreme importance.
Confucius thought that etiquette was of supreme importance. Had he considered the moral
question, he probably *would have* said that following the *li* (perhaps guided by *ren*) was the
moral thing to do.

    We must wean ourselves of such arguments. The orthodox worship of Confucius cannot
be converted into the premise that he must have been a great philosopher. If we allow ourselves to invent his arguments, we will never notice what is philosophically interesting about
the form of discourse he actually used. Confucius does not, for example, even *say* that people
ought to obey *li*. He does not use the explicit language of *ought* at all. The superior man does
thus and so and the inferior man does thus and so. His tone resembles that of an expert on
etiquette. That tone is appropriate to his understanding of the issue.

    I depart, therefore, from the accepted account of the difference between Chinese and
Western philosophy. Popular stereotypes have Chinese philosophy excelling in ethical theory
and Western philosophy excelling in epistemology and metaphysics. For Confucius, at least,
that is inaccurate. Confucius has virtually no normative ethical theory. If we insist on inventing
one for him and talking about that, we will fail to notice what is most interesting in Confucius:
his novel (to Westerners) theory of education and human social nature. Genuinely ethical
questions seem never to have gripped him. As Fingarette puts it, Confucius has a "way without a crossroads." I hasten to add that Fingarette disagrees with me on this point despite the
apt phrasing. Fingarette says that Confucius' *li* embraces all *authentic* convention. He clearly
intends this to include critical philosophical morality.

    Treating the *li* as a general term which embraces *morality* seems wrong for several rea-
sons. First, Confucius still can be criticized for treating *even conventional morality* as being
no more important than etiquette. Second, we want to distinguish morality proper from the
relative mores of any society or group of societies. Morality is not merely conventional. Finally, the morality interpretation of *li* still does not deal with Confucius' lack of plain prescrip-

tive language, his constant choice of etiquette examples, and his dodging of direct moral issues posed by interlocutors.

69. Bao Zhi-ming has argued that it makes sense for some Chinese nouns, at least, to think of one of the possible principles of individuation as privileged. Some of his examples are persuasive but they may be persuasive mainly because our ways of individuating these names seems obvious. Some kinds of things seem hard to individuate in other ways than as continuous spatiotemporal clumps. And there are passages in the Xunzi which treat something like spatiotemporal contiguity as a general case of being a thing. See Graham (1978), p. 325.

70. See Hansen (1983), pp. 30–55.

71. I owe this insight into Confucius' views to the separate influence of Robert Eno and Roger Ames.

72. *Zhi* is also used in the acquaintance sense. There it creates no parallel danger of misunderstanding for us, however, since it occurs in the same grammatical contexts as in English.

73. Roger Ames and David Hall (1987) have stressed this in their aesthetic interpretation of Confucius.

74. Actually, Rawls's reflective equilibrium relies equally on (8) and (1). His intuition seems to be partly innate and partly acquired intuition. Since it can change by the practice of justice and by theoretical reflection, it seems partly acquired. Since it does not merely reflect the theory one follows (or it could not justify revisions in the theory), it must have some innate pull.

75. Schwartz (1985), p. 164. Schwartz does not recognize any continuity between this Confucian concern with names and the discussions of the school of names. Thus he thinks *The Analects'* concern with names precedes the language crisis proper in ancient China. He essentially attributes naïveté about all the issues just discussed to the early Confucians. They thought that "established language . . . accurately reflects the normative nature of things. Language carries its own imbedded reflection of the true order. The crisis is not a crisis of language but of the human abuse and distortion of language" (92). But that human abuse is precisely what motivates this skepticism. If we accept that naive faith in language, how is such distortion possible? How do we know that *we* have not distorted it? How is it to be corrected? What will count as correct? What is rectifying names supposed to correct? Schwartz attributes confidence to Confucius by attributing to him the Western conceptual scheme: "language is [not] used in ways which conform to its correct embedded meanings" (92). Aside from this projection of Western theory, a Daoist, I suppose, need not object if Confucians want to attribute such naïveté to their founder. The problems are still there. Denying early Confucians' awareness of the problems simply results in the conclusion that they had *no* philosophical insights. I have only claimed that they had no insight into issues of ethical philosophy. I shall argue below that Kung-sun Lung's position, especially, is essentially related to the issue of rectifying names.

76. If there is to be an explanation of the *failure* of China to develop science, this lies near its heart. Science operates under the rational ideal of a universally valid set of deductive formulae for describing the world. It applies the Euclidean, Socratic reasoning model to natural *laws*.

Chapter 4

1. Chan (1963), p. 212.

2. Watson (1963), p. 11.

3. This process continues in Western accounts as well. Most begin with some deprecating disparagement of Mozi's inadequate style or lack of grace of high culture. A typical

example is Watson (1963), who recognizes that *The Mozi* "represents *one of the* earliest *attempts at* philosophical writing in Chinese." He then goes on to say, "Nevertheless, making allowances for its antiquity, one cannot help noting that the *Mozi,* whatever the interest of its ideas, is seldom a delight to read. Its arguments are almost always presented in an orderly and lucid, if not logically convincing, fashion. But the style as a whole is marked by a singular monotony of sentence pattern and a lack of wit or grace that is atypical of Chinese literature in general," pp. 14–15.

4. Imagine saying all this to a professional philosopher and adding, "His disciples launched the analytic study of language, logic, geometry, and economics and wrote a behaviorist nominalist essay on language titled *Word and Object.* Oh, and by the way, almost everyone who writes on the subject agrees that he was philosophically shallow and unimportant."

5. There are, of course, exceptions who give Mozi appropriate credit. Graham (1978) observes that prior to the challenge posed by the Mozi and Yang-zhu, the Confucians "had seemed incapable of posing any question more momentous than 'Did Kuan Chung understand the rights?' " (p. 17). And Hughes, inspired by Hu Shi, says, "Mo Ti's mind was not only superbly logical but also brilliantly dialectical. He may be taken to be the father of several new forms of reasoning, in this respect contributing much more than Confucius did, although at the outset of his career he owed much to Confucius in intellectual and moral stimulus."

6. See Feng Yu-lan's account in Feng Yu-lan (1958), p. 53, and Feng Yu-lan (1947), p. 30, 34–40.

7. Fingarette does this by adding *authentic* to *convention* when he discusses *li.*

8. This, despite the fact, as I argued on pages 82–83, that Confucius seemed to be aware that the *li* change over time and in different regions.

9. A. G. N. Flew, "The Cultural Roots of Analytical Philosophy," *The Journal of Chinese Philosophy,* 6 (1979): 1.

10. Schwartz (1985), p. 137.

11. Graham (1989), p. 34.

12. Watson (1963), p. 127.

13. This surmise is supported by the account in the *Huainanzi* as Schwartz points out in Schwartz (1985), p. 138.

14. See Schwartz (1985), p. 139. Mozi's criticisms presuppose the school is predominantly traditionalist. This gives us another reason for our identification of traditionalism as the earlier wing of the school and therefore more likely to have been Confucius' original doctrine.

15. Graham (1978) makes this case best. Schwartz, inexplicably, discounts Graham's craft hypothesis in Schwartz (1985), p. 137. He elaborates using his classic response to revisionist interpretations: P does not logically entail Q, therefore not Q. He notes that the interest in crafts "does not prove that he is a craftsman." The only possible motivation for this idiosyncratic nonargument is to allow Schwartz to indulge in his characterization of Mozi as a *plebeian.* This preserves the Confucian tradition of pointless deprecation of Mozi.

16. Graham (1989), p. 36.

17. Hughes (1942). Hughes stresses this aspect of Mozi's teachings appropriately.

18. Graham (1989), p. 42.

19. *Mozi* 2/2/9–12.

20. *Mozi* 65/39/61.

21. *Mozi* 2/2/8–9.

22. *Mozi* 2/2/3.

23. *Mozi* 27/16/74.

24. *Mozi* 82/47/18.

25. I borrow this notion from Bernard Williams (1985), pp. 129–30.

26. *Mozi* 58/36/1.

27. *Mozi* 63/39/32–35.

28. *Mozi* 2/2/13–14.

29. *Mozi* 2/2/12.

30. The later Mohists' focus on ci^{phrases} is a development toward rules. A typical ci^{phrase} is an action term plus an object. It states a way of acting toward an object.

31. Our current prescriptive language includes both evaluations and directives. The distinction between *is* and *ought* (between prescription and description) still seems to me to be basic. The distinction between fact and value is more problematic. See, for example, Wiggins (1976).

32. I adapt this handy phrase from Nozick (1981), p. 317.

33. I question whether that tradition had a real source. Mozi, I suspect, simply *invented* it for its rhetorical effect in combating Confucian claims. The fact that he uses it so consciously and chides the Confucians for appealing to a less ancient tradition, makes this suspicion plausible. I know of no evidence outside *The Mozi* that anyone followed the traditions he cites. There could, of course, always be an unrecorded oral tradition among the rising craft classes. However, there would be no reason for that tradition to be so deliberately cast in a historical period earlier than the Confucian sage-kings.

34. We can further ask whether rectifying names is justified *purely* pragmatically (on the grounds that it yields a unified and shared interpretation) or realistically (on the grounds that it yields the uniquely correct interpretation). The second alternative is what requires the doctrine of $ren^{\text{benevolence}}$. Without *ren,* what would become of a code of conduct such as $li^{\text{propriety}}$? See Hansen (1972 and 1983).

35. Mozi's usage validates translating yi^{moral} as *morality* rather than the standard Confucian *righteous.* The Confucian translation downplays early Confucian neglect of morality while it furthers the Confucian strategy of portraying Mozi as a religious fanatic. Mozi discusses yi^{morality} much more than Confucians do. Mozi clearly conceives of morality as distinct from mores. He is directly and centrally concerned with ethical issues. Note that yi^{morality} is a system for *evaluating practices,* not a personal virtue or commitment. It contrasts with li^{ritual}, which is a particular set of practices. Mozi's argument undermines the apologists' attempt to excuse Confucian naïveté by saying that Chinese, for whatever reasons, were unable to distinguish the conventional practice of *li* from real morality. Li^{ritual} is as conceptually distinct from yi^{morality} in Chinese as in English.

36. *Shi-fei,* applied *to daos* rather than *within daos,* represents the functional counterpart of the concept of moral *choice* which Fingarette missed in Confucius.

37. The argument attributing a deontological spirit to Confucianism relies mainly on Confucians' rejecting utility—especially egoist utility. Confucius argues that we should follow the *dao* for our role *even though* the larger society may not do so. It is up to heaven to coordinate the concert. It is up to me to play my part. The reason for this purism is a combination of consequentialism and the lack of reflective ethical thought. Even if fate determines that the concert will not come off, we lack any other basis for guiding action. The alternative is merely disorder or selfishness. The appearance of a deontological attitude is mainly a reflection of Confucius' failure to envision alternative *dao* types. His is, in Fingarette's phrase, a *dao* without a crossroads. We should not confuse this attitude, admittedly purist, with Kantian deontology. It involves none of the key Kantian notions such as *reason, duty,* or *desert.*

38. Philosophers will recognize this as a counterpart of Goodman's problem of "Grue" and "Bleen" or Kripke's "Quess."

39. Parfit (1984), p. 95.

40. Notice that this is not a neutral argument for universal concern. It is only an argument of a relative consistency advantage over familial morality.

41. See, for example, Schwartz (1985), p. 142. His political argument, discussed below, deserves special attention. Superficially it resembles Hobbes'. But closer inspection shows that Mozi does not assume that we are psychological egoists. On the contrary, he assumes that

we are psychological moralists. The *state of nature,* for Mozi, comes from our having different moralities, not from our having exclusively selfish motivation.

42. Partisan Confucian accounts distort the structure of this argument—a dangerous one in their eyes. They treat it as a proof that Mozi's utilitarianism is a deep form of egoism. See, e.g., Feng (1947), p. 43. The same distortion affects their interpretation of the political theory of agreement with the superior discussed below.

43. Parfit (1984), p. 95.

44. Notice that is merely a *could,* not a *does.* Mencius suggests that this pessimistic assumption about the natural tendencies of human interpretive is true. If this is his assumption, it conflicts with his usual optimism about human moral tendencies.

45. I owe the distinction again to Derek Parfit. He calls a morality like Confucian morality *collectively self-defeating* and a utilitarian morality *self-effacing.*

46. *Mozi* 18/12/61.

47. Rawls has come to favor a more political interpretation of this reflective equilibrium. See his "Justice as Fairness: Political not Metaphysical," *Philosophy and Public Affairs* 14 (1985): 223–51.

48. Utilitarianism is used almost exclusively to refer to universal or altruistic utility calculation. Mozi is, in this sense, a straightforward utilitarian in the standard Western sense. Mozi tends to draw the distinction between his standard and a Confucian one as the contrast between a universal and a partial *dao.* I stress the universalist component primarily because Confucian accounts, following Mencius, typically treat utility as a selfish or egoistic moral standard. The other criticisms of Mozi show that he was unmistakably understood as an altruist, conceivably even by Mencius. Mencius might have thought the standard, *li*[benefit], was liable to selfish interpretation, although Mozi himself taught it as an altruistic one. Thus they use *universal love* as the specifically Mohist feature of his theory without noting that he regards that moral attitude as *derived from* the utility standard.

49. At one level, this is only a formal difference. The optimific *dao* may have its words arranged into rules. In that case, Mozi's guidance would overlap that of rule utilitarianism. And it may turn out that rule utilitarianism gives the same guidance as act utilitarianism. See Lyons (1965).

50. See Hansen (1985).

51. *Mozi* 80/46/37.

52. The creativity associated with sententials is, I suspect, a central factor in our conception of ourselves as free, rational agents. We look more like social, mimicking, programmed beings adopting a closed and controlling body of social forms when we consider our mastery of words.

53. *Mozi* 49/31/10.

54. Nivison (1979).

55. The three "agreement with the superior" passages differ on how this naming takes place. Two of them have no subject, the *tian-zi*[natural master] *is selected.* The third identifies *tian-xia*[all under heaven] as the selector.

56. Graham (1989, p. 48) offers the more conventional reading of this argument according to which *tian*[nature:heaven] is treated on the analogy to the Judeo-Christian monotheistic God. I acknowledge the pull of the principle of charity (making the other culture's beliefs like ours) behind this widespread interpretive assumption. But the evidence that supernatural monotheism is either natural or rationally irresistible is less than overwhelming. And in this case, the interpretive assumption both requires a meaning-change hypothesis to explain how *tian*[nature:heaven] came to mean nature (which is the usual *contrast* to God) and contradicts the important insight Graham announces on the same page: that Mozi betrays none of the sense of the holy that pervades Confucianism.

57. *Mozi* 41/26/41–42/26/44.

58. The structure of Mozi's chapter on spirits is fascinating in this regard and can be appreciated even from conventional translations, e.g., Burton Watson (1963). It consists less in arguments against the factual existence of spirits as the recitation of popular moralistic fables in which spirits figure centrally. The repeated argument is that these forms of moral education will be wasted if we say *wu*[lack] of spirits.

59. John McDowell (1981) argues that no fact-value distinction is ultimately warranted. Fact and value distinctions alike rest on social consensus. Simon Blackburn (1981) defends the Humean tradition of viewing ethics as *projective*. I am inclined to think that causal principles for identifying natural kinds signal that causal independence from us is a good way to identify distinctions that are natural rather than social.

60. Fingarette (1972, p. 22) points out that even Confucius evidenced this focus. The *bian*[discrimination] he cites, however, does not have the *yan*[language] radical. But Fingarette does argue convincingly that this kind of focus does predate Mozi. Mozi, of course, makes it a central issue. So the dialecticians follow a distinctly central theme in *The Mozi*.

61. *Ju*[picking out] is the Neo-Mohist approximation of *denotation*.

62. The philosopher Xunzi does make such a distinction later in the classical period. He distinguishes between distinctions of similar and different which can be assessed by the senses, shared between cultures, and determined by contemporary *sage-kings* and distinctions of noble and base which rely essentially on traditional standards and can only be assertable if they follow the usage of the ancient, culture-creating sage-kings. (*Xunzi* 83/22/10–15). In Mozi's conceptual perspective no such distinction plays that kind of role.

63. Chan (1963) is a classic example. A not so partisan account also surprisingly suggests this analysis. See Graham (1989), pp. 41–45.

64. See especially Graham (1989, p. 107), which treats Mencius' introduction of this question as the boundary between prephilosophy and philosophy.

65. *Mozi* 26/16/37.

66. *Mozi* 25/16/22–23.

67. The problems here, as we have stressed, are the problems of moral reform. The Daoists will ask how to find a non-question-begging way to spell out what is better or preferable. That is the issue of normative theory. On that question, the Confucians are no better off than the Mohists. Their appeal to human nature is simply irrelevant.

68. *Mozi*, 27/16/69.

69. This point is obscured by translations that either by emendation or assumption assert that it is heaven who selects "the most worthy and able person in the world." There is no subject for that predicate in two of the three versions and in the third the subject is *tian-xia* (the world). No doubt Mozi did not envision an election, but it is consistent with his argument about universal love, etc., that he would regard it as reflectively wise to acknowledge such a person. He assumes an obvious consensus in this matter of having a ruler. "To anyone who examines the matter. . . ." Mencius, again, seems to follow Mozi in naturalizing the mandate of heaven as a kind of popular acceptance. Following Mencius' naturalized account, Confucian tradition has typically regarded universal popular acclaim as the vehicle of the mandate of heaven.

The argument given appeals to the rationality of the society as a whole adopting the utilitarian system administered by modeling upward. It specifically bypasses divine assent. This should be a further embarrassment to the conventional interpretation that Mozi is an essentially religious thinker.

70. See, for example, Schwartz's treatment (1985), p. 142.

71. *Mozi* 15/11/7.

72. *Mozi*, 16/12/15–17.

73. All these authoritarian conceptions of morality—whether the authority is a sage's intuition, a tradition, heaven, or a cosmic principle—were a primary target of Zhuangzi's

skepticism. Prior to Zhuangzi, nearly all Chinese reasoning about morality is authoritarian in form.

74. Commentators frequently err on this issue. They correctly identify Mozi's philosophy as utilitarian, and then assume, incorrectly, that it must be like the classical British hedonistic utilitarianism. Or, like Graham, they assume that his utilitarianism is faulty if it is not (1989, p. 40).

75. There were ethical egoists in China. Yang Zhu was an egoist who based his individualist benefit-harm calculation mainly on survival. The Later Mohists identified *li*[benefit] as that which, when you get it, you enjoy. That is as close as anyone comes to a subjective base of moral conceptions in the Classical period.

76. Critical accounts sometimes accuse Mozi of a *shallow* conception of utility. This judgment comes from a subjectivist utilitarian tradition, an affluent society, and two thousand years later. It would help to remember that for two-thirds of the world's population, Mozi's position still makes perfect sense!

77. *Mozi* chs. 18–2. Translation modified from Hughes (1942), p. 58–59.

78. The best example is Graham (1989), pp. 36–37.

79. I do not mean to suggest that truth and assertability are opposites. In fact, truth can be thought of as a special case of assertability. It is the standard of assertability for scientific or rational inquiry. Assertability is not independent of the way the world is. The assertability of a question or command is affected by the world. A command is inappropriate where the situation requested already exists. Saying ''Close the door'' and ''The door is open'' are both inappropriate utterances when the door is closed.

80. I borrow this very expressive metaphor from my colleague, Hilary Kornblith.

81. This style of philosophy also affects the translation of a number of other common terms. *Shan*[good], for example, is more accurately captured by *good-at*. Scholars normally understand Confucius as *performing* a ritual rather than *following* it. Education is mainly *moral education* and wisdom *is* action. Confucius connects learning and practice, not learning and storing. The cases are legion.

82. Graham trips over this ambiguity. His argument relies on equivocating between the two senses. The key mistake is made in Graham (1989), pp. 36–37.

83. Burton Watson (1963), p. 118.

84. Excepting, of course, the assumption that all philosophical traditions must share our theoretical preoccupations.

85. A number of commentators deal with this by saying that *yan*[language] also means *doctrine* or *theory*. But, since they do not deny that it means *language/words,* this must amount to saying that they do not linguistically draw the language-theory distinction. Failure to draw that distinction is the hallmark of a pragmatic as opposed to a semantic view of language. Translators tend here, as in the case of *ming*[command], *dao*[guiding discourse], etc., to treat their different English translations in different contexts as if the native speaker would not be likely to see any more inferential connection between two uses of *yan* than ordinary English speakers see between the words *word* and *doctrine* or *theory*. This is a version of what I call the English-is-the-only-real-language fallacy.

86. Graham rejects my earlier argument (1985) for this position. His rebuttal (1989) rests on rhetorical questions. ''But the issue being purely factual . . . with the second of the three tests being a direct appeal to reports of seeing and hearing spirits, what would this difference amount to?'' (395). Graham introduces the rhetorical question with an assertion that begs the question against my interpretation—that the issue *is* purely factual *and* then he begs the question of what the reports are. The rhetorical question suggests that there could be no other way to understand them then the way Graham has understood them.

The answer to his rhetorical question is easy even if we assume, contrary to my hypothesis, that the issue is scientific fact. The difference amounts to this: should we talk about what happens in the morning as *a sunrise* or *a horizon dip?* Accepting Mozi's linguistic policy does not mean that Mozi's hypothetical scientific counterpart must *actually believe* that the earth is the center of the universe. Shallow elitist intellectuals, with their elaborate theories, may think that they have good reason to correct the way ordinary people report this event that they witness every morning. Mozi's scientific counterpart simply insists that we should continue to name this event in the ordinary way that ordinary people report the visual event. To bring the parallel back to ancient China, the sophisticated Confucian explanatory theorist insists on saying "there was a brief concentration of *yang qi*^{dominant ether} in the area where an ordinary person reports seeing *shen*^{spiritual energy}." Taking his position does not mean that Mozi *rejects the explanation of the sighting.* To take another current example in sinology, Graham sides with the modern elitists who insist that ordinary people are wrong in calling Chinese characters *ideographs* instead of *syllabo-morpho-phonographs* or *logographs* or some other favored neologism. Mozi is saying that we can perfectly clearly say, "Chinese ideographs carry phonemic information." We don't have to change the words that people ordinarily use in order to convey information about the world.

Then Graham misstates my position again: "Hansen objects that the two other Mohist tests, the authority of the sages and the social consequences, are not for you and me relevant to truth, so truth is not what the Mohists are after." But I object that the two tests are not tests of truth *simpliciter.* Mozi never says that he is talking about truth; he merely gives us the three standards of language. He is talking about whatever the three tests are tests *of.* If Graham wants to insist, in the absence of any text, that he is really talking about truth, then the three tests ought to be tests of truth. If they are tests of something else, then, unless the text gives some other hint, we should conclude that Mozi is talking about something else. It doesn't help to suggest that there is our "truth" and their "truth." We have to wonder what lies between the second set of quotation marks. An English word? No. A Chinese word? It doesn't seem like it. It is a word in Grahamese, used in his gloss on this passage. All we know about it is that it is not the same as the English word "truth." But that is enough! If it is not the same then it is different. Now the task is to say *what* it is.

So in proposing to interpret them as talking about truth, Graham simultaneously convicts the Mohists of a quite silly error. The problem is that Graham convicts them of the error by reading between the lines of the text a doctrine which is inconsistent with the text. Then he criticizes them for his own interpretive inconsistency!

Graham dismisses this objection: "But even in the modern West only the logically sophisticated fully succeed in detaching questions of truth from appeals to authority and to social benefit." We need to make this kind of apologetic excuse, however, only if they are guilty of the error. And at this point, that is precisely what is at issue. Besides, this response assumes that the question about truth is *inescapably there* to be confused with appeal to authority. That is precisely the claim I have challenged. Graham's answer just begs the question again.

It is common, he says, for people to argue fallaciously from authority. That is, of course true, but irrelevant. Graham, for example, frequently appeals to an alleged consensus of sinologists in arguing for his interpretive views (119–20). But while we can understand how that familiar error would slip into Graham's reasoning, one *would be very surprised* to find it explicitly formulated in Graham's methodological preface, say in a numbered list of principles for determining what is the correct interpretation: "Number 2: If more than 51 percent of the members of AAS as of the date of publication of this book think an interpretation is correct, then it is." There is a difference between an ordinary logical slip and a conscious enunciation of a principle of reasoning that is absurd on its face. This is not a isolated argument of Mozi, but a considered ordered and numbered statement of his theory of acceptable language use.

Then Graham asks another rhetorical question: "Moreover if the existence of spirits raised for Chinese only the question whether it was socially appropriate to affirm it, how was it ever possible to doubt *it* [italics mine] since no one denied the social duty of sacrificing to spirits?"

Graham's rhetorical question baffles me, but seems to beg the question still again. We are disputing about what the *it,* the one that could be doubted, amounts to. I am *arguing that* Mozi is talking of the social duty to say *you* [exists] of spirits. He criticized Confucians for adhering to the wasteful social practice of sacrifice, while ignoring the beneficial and cheap social practice of saying *you-shen* [exists-spirits]. Graham seems to go on to say precisely that, although he reformulates the claim about saying *you* [exists] of spirits *as a factual belief* without even noticing that this, again, simply begs the question. I am challenging that between-the-lines attribution of a theory of belief.

Then Graham cites "the common formula posing alternatives," using his translation into conditionals in an English if-then propositional construction, and claims that asking the question *as his translation renders it* "implies that even outside philosophical circles *the question* [italics mine] was widely regarded to be open. . . ." He does not even notice that the issue between us is *what* "the question" is. He simply assumes it is the factual question to be believed. Now, that is the rival possibility. My interpretive hypothesis may be wrong, but it is an illusion that one can rebut the hypothesis simply by begging the question repeatedly in rhetorical questions.

I challenged advocates of the traditional view to produce *an argument* for attributing truth and belief concerns to Chinese philosophers in the face of absence of those terms and their consistent use of exclusively pragmatic behaviorist language. Using rhetorical questions is simply a refusal to meet the challenge and give an argument. The rhetorical question style has the contextual implication that the answer is obvious. Graham assumes that he only has to show that it is *not impossible* that they would have these concerns. But the interpretive problem as I formulated it arises precisely because I claim *both* interpretations are *possible* and that what seems obvious to someone who has absorbed Western folk psychology may not seem obvious to Mozi. We have to argue for the claim that one possibility is more plausible.

87. Wittgenstein's argument against a private language seems to fail. One could make sense of conforming correctly to one's own tradition (and of failing) even though one could not verify it. It would be meaningless to speak of a private language only if one were a verificationalist. A realist would insist that it is meaningful to suggest that I had violated my own past practice in the use of my private language.

88. You must, however, use pejorative terms, such as *the vulgar,* frequently to distinguish the community of historians you recognize and whose usage you want to enforce from those you reject and whose usage you want to eliminate. This is rectifying names.

89. Where there seems to be a hint of such in translations, it is typically a result of the translators regarding such theories as inevitable common sense and supplying them in the translation.

Chapter 5

1. Schwartz (1985), pp. 255–56.

2. Lau (1970), p. 235.

3. There was a fleeting movement to introduce use of *Micius* for Mozi, whose bones no doubt relaxed when the movement failed.

4. Schwartz (1985), p. 290.

5. Waley (1939) p. 194. Graham cites Waley's comment to illustrate what he calls "the changed understanding of Chinese philosophy over the past half century" (Graham, 1989, p. 119). Graham's comment is itself a symptom of how interpretive theory relying on the principle of charity has led the ruling theory to confuse *understanding* and *agreeing-with.* Nowadays, being sympathetic to Confucians is commonly confused with having mastered and understood Chinese. The sympathetic attitude is, of course, required to get the approval of Confucian

teachers. But we do want to preserve the theoretical possibility that classical Chinese philosophers who bitterly condemned Confucianism just might possibly have understood their native language. We can't let Mencius' elevation to official orthodoxy blind us to the possibility that his dismissive interlocutors might well have been able to spot a fraud when they heard one.

6. *The Mencius* 25/3B/9. Citations again follow the Harvard-Yenching Institute Sinological Index Series convention. *Harvard-Yenching Institute Sinological Index Series,* Supplement no. 17, "A Concordance to Meng Tzu," Chinese Materials and Research Aids Service Center, Inc., Taipei, 1973.

7. Hughes (1942), p. 96.

8. Eno (1990), p. 99.

9. An alternate view is Graham's. He treats Yangism and Daoism as distinct but related. Graham speculates that Zhuangzi may have begun as a Yangist. His analysis of *The Zhuangzi* includes large blocks of what Graham regards as Yangist writings. My own preference is to regard mature Daoism as a theory about *dao.* Yang Zhu shares social attitudes with some of those theorists, but in the reports of his doctrines the notion of *dao* does not play much of a role. Thus I regard him as a proto-Daoist.

10. *The Mencius* 53/7A/26.

11. See Graham (1967), repeated in Graham (1978, pp. 15–18, and 1989, pp. 53–64) for the best account and example of this line of interpretation. Graham takes Yang Zhu to be valuing life, and therefore, to value all life equally. I don't find the textual support for this claim at all convincing in the face of the dominant egoistic tone of most of what Yang Zhu is reported as saying.

12. Graham speculates that what he calls "philosophical egoism" may be inconceivable in ancient China. His interpretation, even if correct, cannot support that conclusion. If Mencius wrongly *accused* Yang Zhu of egoism, he must at least be capable of conceiving of it. Graham's discussion confuses psychological and ethical egoism. It probably is true that all the thinkers of this period accepted the essentially social nature of humanity—that there were no psychological egoists. This difference in our popular psychological theories may be partly a function of Western use of private, individualized, mentalistic psychological concepts.

13. Graham took a cluster of terms to have been developed in Yang Zhu's theory. I follow Graham in the assumption that these terms, especially $xing^{\text{nature}}$, are an important background development for Mencius' theory of human nature. See Graham, "The Background of the Mencian Theory of Human Nature" in *Tsing Hua Journal of Chinese Studies,* 6/1, 2 (1967): 215–74. But I agree with Eno (1990, pp. 257–58n.) that the evidence for attributing all of this to Yang Zhu is weak.

14. A closely related argument is frequently shouted to Confucius by miscellaneous hermits and recluses who supposedly represent an early Daoist attitude and philosophical tendency.

15. A stylistic parallel also tempts us. From an Aristotelian point of view, Plato, though the inheritor and advocate of Socratic method, was also a little cavalier in argument. Western scholars have long been puzzled by Mencius' ineptitude in argument, especially his tortured and gauche analogies. D. C. Lau acknowledges the naturalness of this impression and attempts a defense in his "On Mencius' Use of the Method of Analogy in Argument," *Asia Major,* n.s. 10 (1963), reprinted in his *Mencius* (Penguin Books, Harmondsworth, Middlesex, England) 1970, as appendix 5, pp. 235–63. I do not share his motivation stated in the opening to this chapter. On the contrary, I would argue that we have had no trouble understanding Mencius' opponents. Our problem is only that Mencius' analogies are so inept as arguments. Lau simply has an unrealistic assessment of his calibre as a thinker, and of his stature among his contemporaries (as opposed to the medieval scholastic Confucian orthodoxy). We have a perfectly good explanation of Mencius' much later stature and influence in the Confucian orthodoxy without crediting him with some mysterious and impenetrable logical acumen. Con-

fucianism became the dominant school and accepted Mencius as the orthodox interpreter! During his own period, even among other Confucians like Xunzi, Mencius was a philosophical laughing stock and whipping boy. I object to the pretense that he must be good because he is politically acceptable to the imperial masters. The appropriate inference, from an anarchist, Daoist perspective, goes in precisely the opposite direction!

In amelioration, we can observe that in Mencius' case, as opposed to Plato's, the philosophical impulse and terms and style of argument originated in a rival and antagonistic school. Mencius, though the first philosophical defender of Confucianism, is clearly and by his own admission ill at ease in philosophical dispute. When we encounter Mencius' unprincipled and undisciplined use of any verbal trick that occurs to him, we become acutely aware of his lack of a discipline of logic and argument. He distracts, distorts, or trivializes the issue or his opponents' positions. His whole theory is built on a massive equivocation.

In *The Mozi*, argumentative essay style was just beginning. Mozi's plain expression and natural sense of validity make his arguments easy to follow and reconstruct. Mencius, however, remained in the flowery tradition. Lau's study does suggest that he was dimly aware of an independent movement (probably the Neo-Mohists) cultivating standards and style of argument. His feeble attempts to incorporate their argument forms show how poorly he understood them. His Confucian training stressed picking a good poem to recite for rheorical effect. He brought that attitude to argument, which he treated as nothing more than reciting strings of tangentially related expressions concluded with vague slogans. I will look in detail at Lau's and Graham's attempts to elevate Mencius logical status on pages 188–93 below.

16. Confucian scholars typically gloss over Mencius' radical departure. Neo-Confucianism has a Buddhist-inspired fascination with transmission. This, along with the religious proclivity to view doctrines as springing forth in full and perfect form in the first instance, biases them to hide Mencius' enormous contribution to Confucianism. Mencius could not change absolute truth so he must only have elaborated on it.

17. Eno (1990) argues that the content of Mencius' teaching was still ritual performance, not argument or theory. Philosophy, Eno argues, was something one may stoop to given the need to counter all the heresies in the world, but it was not to be included in the curriculum of a good *ru*! Mencius' philosophy is in fact an explanation of why philosophy should *not* be taught.

18. *The Mencius* 2A:2 (D. C. Lau 1970), pp. 78–79).

19. Our name for *the Central Kingdom* is derived from this dynasty—which in old romanizations was Ch'in. The description of this school as *Legalist* is misleading, as I shall argue on pages 347–50.

20. Notice that this difficulty depends heavily on empirical assumptions about how people will react to the revelation. In particular, it assumes that the other does not react in a utilitarian way. This means the problem does not really show a fundamental kind of incoherence in utilitarianism, just a possible problem given certain empirical assumptions.

Parfit (1984, pp. 23–24) remember, calls a moral system with this result (which prevents its public advocacy) self-effacing which differs importantly from being self-defeating. Utilitarianism is still a coherent practical theory. *Correctly* followed, it leads to the best outcomes by its own lights. Correctly following it may merely require not publicly advocating it. Utilitarianism still tells the president clearly and coherently what to do; he must lie about his moral beliefs.

21. *The Mencius* 3A:2.

22. The roots of this orientation may lie very deep. It seems connected to Mencius' skepticism about language. Institutional forms (constitutions, legal systems, ordinances, principles of organization) rely on language to control behavior. Conversely, given any linguistic *dao*, people of good character will interpret it in morally correct ways. Those with evil dispositions can corrupt even the most divine system. The faith of a Western constitutionalist is

exactly the opposite, more like that of the standardizers. We *can* devise institutional forms that will work even if we assume that people who hold power are infinitely corruptible and that all human nature is evil, selfish, and tyrannical. Mencius would have regarded it as naive to assume that a properly worded constitution guiding an institutional structure can control tyrants.

23. I reverse Graham's emphasis here. Graham's view is that the Yangist pose the serious challenge because Mozi is a moralist and Yang is not. He says Yang Zhu provokes a metaphysical crisis which prods Mencius to rise to the truly philosophical level and talk about psychology! I regard Mozi as the serious challenge and contender and Yang Zhu as the source of Mencius way out. For another dissenting view, see Eno (1990), p. 110.

24. *The Mencius* 21/3A/5.

25. *Ibid.* "Does Yi-Zhi sincerely regard someone's regard for his older brother's child as like his regard for his neighbor's newborn?" Neither Mencius nor his defenders ever seem to notice that this argument (interpreted as a claim about natural behavior) begs the question against a Mohist theory. As I argued above, Mozi perfectly understood that his advocacy of altruistic utility required altering existing attitudes and behaviors. He argued that this was routinely done using conventional education; political leadership and social modeling combined with an underpinning of standards for using language and deploying action guiding distinctions could result in utilitarian outcomes. If Mencius' argument is a moral claim rather than a descriptive one, then it *also* begs the question. But under that interpretation, we would not even think of it as a counterargument as much as Mencius' expression of moral outrage.

26. I choose this from the other possible rendering of *duan* [point:edge] (sources, beginnings, fonts, germs) primarily to tie into Mencius' frequent use of the plant analogy in talking of cultivation of the heart-mind. *Germs* could be used if the reader were inclined to think of wheat germ, however, that is a less frequent association and comes too close to Han Feizi's characterization of the Confucian virtues as the four worms!

27. David Hume, *A Treatise on Human Nature,* bk. 2, London 1739. Meta-ethically, Mencius also seems committed to the Humean view that morality is derived from such natural inclinations. It is pointless to ask whether we ought to be like this or ought to follow such inclinations.

28. He does this even when he appeals to the parallel of taste. See *The Mencius* 43/6A/4–5.

29. The difference lies mostly in what kinds of considerations lead to the feeling. If it comes about upon being discovered by someone while doing some illicit act, but is otherwise absent, I would call the feeling *shame*. If, on the other hand, I had such a feeling alone on the mere contemplation of what I had done (or alternately, perhaps, if I considered it known by God), I would call it *guilt*. The difference in the two seems to lie in their different conceptions of what morality is. The shame conception treats morality as a social matter, the internalization of shared group standards analogous to etiquette (I can be ashamed of my table manners but hardly feel guilty about them. I could be ashamed to have it known that I was urinating, but could hardly feel guilty that I was). Guilt appears to be connected with a conception of morality as standards of behavior that one supposes are accepted by the person himself. Thus to the degree that one accepts group standards, shame and guilt are alike.

30. In other treatments, Mencius uses *yielding* as the seed of *li*.

31. This is the view of Wang Yang-ming, the Ming dynasty idealist Neo-Confucian. I believe Wang got Mencius right. I find this assumption the most coherent way to make sense of Mencius. P. J. Ivanhoe has argued that the two Confucians have quite different views of natural morality. Wang's, he says, is a discovery model and Mencius' is a development model. But Mencius does think there is a correct path for developing the seeds. And his normative position is that correct means "in accord with inborn dispositions." So if there is a correct way to develop, it must be *in* seeds as much as is the end state. Otherwise, Mencius would

be required to think that some part of morality comes from the outside—is external. And this contradicts the position he takes in the debate with Gaozi and Mozi. Mencius would not have any plausible answer to Mozi unless he claims intuitive access to the whole range of particular *shi-fei* responses as inborn.

32. The analysis of the stock arguments for psychological egoism can be found in Bishop Samuel Butler's "Three Sermons upon Human Nature," in *Fifteen Sermons,* London, 1726.

33. The frequently cited discussion with the Mohist, Yizhi (see below, pages 169–70) is ambiguous. We may give it either a normative or a descriptive reading. On the normative reading, it simply begs the question by asserting Mencius' philosophically controversial norms: one ought to love one's kin more than strangers.

34. Still, a mere twenty-seven references is shockingly low. He uses the hated Mohist term *li*[utility] more than that.

35. *The Mencius* 47/6B/3 and 51/7A/15.

36. *The Mencius* 4A/27 and hints of this view in 1A:4 and 1A:7.

37. One could, for example, note that these other formulas are merely examples, not Mencius' central theoretical analysis, or speculate that they are later, earlier, a concession to dominant *Ru* opinion, or point out that those that seem like definitions come in the later, more fragmentary part of *The Mencius* and are not in the context of theoretical discussion. One of these deals with interpretation of poetry. These would be ways to explain away the evidence that Mencius did not understand the implications of his four-seeds theory that the interpreter takes to be basic.

38. *The Mencius* 34/4B/32.

39. *The Mencius* 3A:5; Chan, p. 7.

40. See, for example, Mote (1971), p. 55.

41. As I argue above, I think Wang Yang-ming is right in rejecting this claim. Right, that is, if one is to give a consistent reading to Mencius. The situation includes who and what I am. If the baby does not behave like a sage, that is the right thing for the baby to do. In tending and cultivating the heart, the child is doing the cosmically right thing in every case. There can be no coherent distinction between a cultivation and an mature moral action phase in Mencius theory.

The further step to Wang Chi's "existentialist" interpretation seems inescapable to me as well. It is in the basic logic of Mencius' position as borrowed from Yang Zhu. Naturalism as an action theory does not do a good job of ruling anything out. Zhuangzi also saw these implications of Mencius' position. In the end, Mencius cannot coherently justify a distinction between the alleged sage's heart and the alleged fool's!

42. The *shi*[scholar-knight] can, however. This is not an excuse for individual failure to develop. Anyone with enough leisure and money to buy and read this book should not use this excuse. This is a political premise directed at the ruler. The ruler's political actions can bring about the conditions in which general as contrasted with exceptional moral development takes place. Doing that is the *ren* thing which liberates natural human morality which in turn recognizes you as a true king who has this sagelike effect.

43. The circumstances include things about the sage's body and social status, etc. For example, the way an underweight philosophy professor and a professional heavyweight boxer should deal with a mugger are different. The way a policeman and an ordinary citizen should deal with a mugger are also different. The *xin* gives the correct action for one *in our position* in that circumstance.

44. See especially, Tu Wei-ming (1985).

45. *The Mencius* 25/3B/9, 31/4B/19, and 33/4B/28.

46. *The Mencius* 45/6A/12 and 45/6A/14.

47. *The Mencius* 7B/24.

48. Hu Shih thought Yang Zhu's theory was implicitly antilanguage. But reconstructing it from the existing quotations shows neither a focus on *yan*[language] nor *dao*[discourse way].

49. The key insight in this passage I learned from David Nivison.

50. I owe many of the insights of this section to stimulating discussions and exchanges with Kwong-loi Shun.

51. Note that this does not entail that the debate actually took place. See Eno (1990), p. 260, n. 57.

52. See Eno (1990), p. 114.

53. Given Zhuangzi's analysis and Mencius' initial optimism about human nature, it is not clear how this is possible. This is the linguistic version of the Confucian problem of evil.

54. The Confucian problem of evil becomes endemic in Neo-Confucianism. They do not notice the linguistic version. The general form is simply, given the initial goodness of human nature, how could we get in an evil social situation and fail so obviously to correct it? Thomas Metzger refers to its general form as "the Neo-Confucian predicament." See his book by that name, Metzger (1981).

55. This suggestion, of course, is a heresy!

56. Neo-Confucians seem committed to the view of a moral reality, the position Mencius must have rejected. But they harmonize this with Mencius' view that morality is internal by making the world internal to the heart-mind, pure idealism. They rely on the Buddhist distinction between the universal *xin*[heart-mind] and the individual's *xin*. Thus the moral source is the *dao-xin* not the *ren-xin*[human mind].

57. D. C. Lau (1963), reprinted in Lau (1970), p. 235.

58. Ibid.

59. Graham (1989), p. 119–20. The reference to Lau is to Lau 1963, reprinted in Lau 1970.

60. Lau (1970), p. 235.

61. Ibid.

62. Ibid., p. 259.

63. Ibid., p. 257.

64. Ibid., p. 238.

65. Graham (1989), pp. 123–24.

Chapter 6

1. Schwartz (1985), p. 194.

2. D. C. Lau (1982), xvii.

3. Notice that we begin by theorizing that these are inscriptions. I theorize further that we read them horizontally rather than vertically. I owe this way of making sense of interpretation and the principle of charity to John Haugland who uses it in Haugland (1981), pp. 25–30.

4. See Schwartz (1985), p. 60.

5. The methodology of interpretation offered here does not commit one to a single-author theory for the same reason that it does not make a psychological presupposition. A text may be coherent even if worked on by multiple authors. It may be incoherent if written by a single author. We share our writings with colleagues and hire editors. That does not normally make the interpretation harder or the writing less coherent. Cooperative writing efforts do not essentially change the theory of interpretation. But knowing that a group of writers produced the text lowers the threshold at which we will accept contradictory statements between parts we take to be from different authors. Similarly, knowing that it comes from a single author

over a whole lifetime lowers our threshold for accepting contradiction between sections we take to be written in different periods. That the author is addressing different issues, currying favor with religious or political power, taking hallucinogenic drugs at 4 P.M. each day, etc., may also do that. But interpretation tries to make coherent sense first. If we succeed, these factors do not undermine that successful interpretive theory.

6. But I agree with Schwartz in treating the Mawang Dui text as belonging to a Huang-Lao cult that became popular with the ruling circles at the onset of the Qin-Han dark age. What has emerged as the contents of those documents so far does not incline me to class the text among the philosophically interesting schools of the classical period. Part of my choice of text reflects a view that the philosophical interest of the text is diminished and subverted by the structural changes. The prominent one is to place the political, purposive part of the text first and to bury the philosophical reflections on language that explain it in the middle. This reflects a split in editorial intentions. One stresses the political strategy, the other the philosophical reflections. Similarly the Mawang Dui text adds characters that seem designed to force what I will argue is a less successful interpretation on ambiguous passages.

I choose the traditional text partly because it plausibly reflects Daoist and philosophical emphasis more than the Huang-Lau ruler-directed political emphasis. Given the assumptions that have guided this whole work, I treat it as more likely that philosophically interesting things will stem from the classical thinkers than that they will be added during a period of ruler-dominated superstition orthodoxy and suppression of philosophy.

7. I would argue as follows: The new discoveries confirm the previously held view that the text was still circulating in a state of flux as late as the Han dynasty. And they prove the existence of a Huang-Lao cult and render live the hypothesis that adherents of different schools selected and edited texts in different ways. The discovery of one sample neither disproves nor seriously undermines the prior assumption that earlier varieties of the traditional text were also circulating at that time. We should not refer to the Mawang Dui text as *the* state of the text at that time. To draw that conclusion would be to try to determine the batch from one instance— and in this case an instance drawn from a place that marks it as a biased sample: the tomb of a powerful member of the ruling class! Intellectual hermits were not buried in tombs that would preserve their rotting bones into the twentieth century.

To adopt the hypothesis that the Mawang Dui text is *the* early text requires one further to explain the emergence of the traditional text *from* the Mawang Dui text. If we assume that all the samples are like the one we discovered, then we must postulate a radical textual event that drastically changed that text *and became widespread*. It must submerge the Han text to the point that the Han text is extinct or nearly so by the time Wang Pi collates his text from as many as six different versions available to him. I would assign a higher probability to the hypothesis that verions of at least both traditions were circulating at the time that an elaborate tomb burial gave us one sample.

One familiar attempt to explain the radical-textual-event-and-then-extinction hypothesis is that the Huang-Lao version contains a number of grammatical particles that are lacking in the traditional version, especially in crucial places where they can reduce ambiguity. I have heard it alleged that the obvious explanation of this difference is that the particles were eliminated to bring the number of characters closer to the traditionally accepted five thousand. But on the face of things the converse hypothesis is just as plausible. The tradition of five thousand characters may be *explained by the fact* that some earlier version had only five thousand and the particles were *added* in the Huang-Lao version to try to resolve the interpretive difficulties.

When I consider these two hypotheses and look at the particles in the Mawang Dui version, I am struck by how unnatural many of the alleged particles are how artificially they sometimes break strings. In the first chapter (traditional ordering) for example, the *ye* [assertion particle] occurs first in the opening line, so it ought to read, *"Dao* can be spoken.*"* It is a *ye* that is optional, not required. Translators typically ignore or alter it even as they appeal to the existence of the particle to show it is the original. In the third line where it is supposed to resolve an ambiguity, I will argue it resolves it in the wrong way, a less philosophically interesting and coherent way. And it, again, is a slightly grammatically peculiar use. It looks exactly like an interpretive hypothesis *about* the original text put in the form of editing the text. The very frequency at which these particles in the Huang-Lao text seem mildly out of place would tend to support the hypothesis that they were added to a version that lacked them rather than removed from their natural place in an original.

Finally, I do not regard the matter as settled. I do, however, reject the simplistic but widespread assumption that the Huang-Lao text must be closer to the hypothetical original since it is earlier. That assumption explains the sample on a hypothesis that no one believes: that all existing samples at the time are like the ones we have discovered. Accepting that hypothesis requires that they postulate a radical textual event *after* the discovered sample that effects *all* surviving samples and wipes out all the earlier ones. The sample could be explained far more simply by the same textual event in reverse *before* the discovered sample that needs to affect only *some* samples. The reverse event is also psychologically easier to explain. We all punctuate and add comments to the books we read. Only the Inquisition whites things out. In the absence of a sound argument that the Mawang Dui text is the original, I have many other kinds of reasons as well for preferring the traditional one, not the least of which is that it is more philosophically interesting.

8. I will not offer to buttress it, that is, with a theory about the relative dates of composition or textual stability of the *Zhuangzi* and the *Daode Jing*.

9. See Graham (1981), p. 126–28.

10. Three characteristic stories are recorded in *The Analects* 18:5–7. Note that on Robert Eno's view, Confucius may himself share a good deal of this spirit. Confucius may, despite his having a political theory that spelled out an obligation to participate in the political hierarchy, have used that theory to justify political withdrawal. But he does not share the antisocial or anticonventional assumptions that I would also call Daoist.

11. The traditional account fails to see progress in Daoist theory as it fails to see it in Confucian theory. It never sees Daoism as going beyond Shendao. My account merely starts with Shendao. The traditional account, as far as theory is concerned, ends with it. It attributes Shendao's conception of the natural *dao* as the only concept in both Laozi and Zhuangzi.

12. Interestingly, Han Feizi draws on both Shendao and Laozi in his theory of arbitrary ruler's standards. It is interesting that both the *fa-jia* standards school and *dao-jia* way school are retrospectively imposed by later intellectual historians, suggesting that no such distinction was being maintained by thinkers during the classical period. The Shendao fragments in the two contexts pose a particularly challenging interpretive puzzle. I will only point in the direction of a solution in this note. The passive stoicism in the present passage and the focus on circumstance in the Han Feizi passages are compatible, I believe. His citation by Han Feizi does not mean that he is an authoritarian. His position may have been that, since discourse *dao*s have no moral authority (or equal moral authority), the one that the circumstances make dominant will be dominant. It is not evidence of its moral superiority. The ruler, similarly, happens by circumstance to be in a position of authority. It does not depend on his moral worth. Notice that this is the classical counterpart of fatalism. It is not a doctrine of perfect predictability or causal explanation. It is more like a version of moral skepticism. There is neither need nor possibility to justify authority or which *dao*s are dominant. It happens.

13. Note that I rejected this conception for Mozi himself. See pp. 105–6. That is because *he* is still concentrating on the discourse *dao*, the guide that blazes the path through history.

14. *Zhuangzi* 92/33/50.

15. Chan Wing-tsit (1963), p. 136.

16. Waley (1934), p. 30.

17. Chen Ku-ying (1977), p. 2.

18. Fritjof Capra (1975), p. 117.

19. Chan (1963), p. 138.

20. Laozi seems to express some skepticism of the concept however. He wonders if we can intelligibly think of *dao* as an object. *"Dao*'s being deemed *[wei]* an object! Confused! Wild!"* (ch. 22) See also chapter 25, where the passage discusses the *da-dao*[great dao]. Other relevant passages are chapters 41 and 51. Raymond Smullyan is best on this topic. He is the only commentator I know of who has noticed that it must inherently be paradoxical that *dao* could either exist or not exist. See also his excellent discussion of why it might be contradictory for *dao* to have a name. Smullyan (1977), p. 26.

21. The classic statement comes in chapter 2.

22. The pronunciation of the auxiliary verb in modern dialects involves a tone change.

23. The Huang-Lao rulership versions put the entire purposive section first. Some have proposed, therefore, calling it the *Dedao Jing* instead of the *Daode Jing*. The Daoist versions puts the more linguistic section first. We assume both have a reason for their editorial choice. For the Daoists, we should read the purposive sections in the light of the linguistic skepticism. In the Rulership versions, we should read the linguistic skepticism in the light of its political purposes. I shall be dealing with the Daoist interpretation of the *Daode-Jing* here. I will discuss the development of a ruler oriented interpretation in the chapter on Han Feizi.

24. Kaltenmark (1965), pp. 29–30.

25. This habit persists even when translators accept the Lao-Huang version. It has *dao*[way:speak] *ko*[may] *dao*[way:speak] *ye*[assertion particle]. Translators so cherish their *interpretive* assumption that the book is about the unspeakable, mystical *Dao* they cannot bite the bullet and translate what the sentence says: "Dao can be spoken." (See Hendrick 1989) Alternately, they continue translating with the definite article without noticing that they have contradicted their own interpretive theory. (See Lau 1982).

26. Or *some dao, daos,* or *any dao,* depending on the context.

27. I am assuming a *de dictu* not a *de re* reading, of course. That is, I assume that the sentence is not being used with a particular chef as the intended reference *even if he doesn't break yolks.*

28. Linguists call Chinese a left-branching language since, unlike in English, modifiers must precede what is modified. The translation of the subject, "the *x* which can be *xed . . .*" follows the grammatical analysis of the first line done by a teenage Confucian who lived half a millennium later during the philosophical dark age at the end of the Han dynasty. The debased philosophy of the day was dominated by cosmological concerns. It may calm ruffled feathers here to add that Wang Pi was a brilliant teenager. But the point is that argument from authority on this issue is dreadfully weak—weaker than usual. At the least, translators should say that they are following Wang Pi's revision of the text, not his interpretation. The translation of the subject noun-phrase would be correct for *ke*[can-be] *dao*[spoken] *zhi*'s *dao*[way:guide] (Wang Pi's rephrasing of the first line) but not, straightforwardly, for *dao*[way:guide] *ke*[can-be] *dao*[way:guide].

29. Graham (1989, p. 176) takes Daoism as starting from an even stronger assumption that all language is inherently contradictory. See also his discussion of the Later Mohists' answer (1989, p. 185). Graham gives this analysis of Zhuangzi's Daoism in relation to the Later Mohists. I will explain below why I think that analysis is mistaken of Zhuangzi as well as of Daoism in general. The core is that nothing could count as a theory of *contradiction* that did not include some counterpart of a theory of sentences or propositions, truth values, negation, and some propositional operator.

30. This assumption would make sense of Zhuangzi, especially if we follow Graham in emphasizing the importance of a *knack* for performance that can be correct although it cannot be trained or transmitted.

31. For more analysis of the different conceptual schemes underlying these differences in the view of permanence and change, see the discussion above on pages 46–48.

32. D. C. Lau (1982) perhaps takes this posture. He segments all chapters into fragments which he takes to be integral. This suggests that a correct interpretation must therefore treat each fragment in isolation. But we do not want to know what it meant originally (before inclusion in the *Daode Jing*). The point about taking things out of context is that .doing so changes the meaning. The meaning of these phrases (whatever they might have been in another life) is a function of their being embedded in this chapter at this point.

33. The Huang-Lao version of the text helps the case for this reading. One objection to it in the traditional version is that it should have a *ye* [assertion] particle at the end. But it is less appealing stylistically and in other aspects of content. It does not say *wu-ming* is the source of the universe, but, like *yu-ming*, of *wan-wu* [the myriad things].

34. Paul Edwards, ed., *The Encyclopedia of Philosophy*, vol. 5, p. 524. The contributor is P. L. Heath.

35. The prevailing view among intellectual historians is that the Huang-Lao version of the text settles this interpretive issue. Graham's statement is typical—perhaps the authority for the common belief. Graham says, ''The text of the newly discovered Ma-wang-tui manuscripts by its additional particles *forbids* the alternative punctuation by which lines 5 to 8 [my 3 to 6] may be read as about Nothing and Something . . .'' (1989, p. 219, italics mine). The supposition that one text can *forbid* an interpretive hypothesis embodies several levels of confusion.

The key confusion is between textual and interpretive theory. The new version is relevant to the interpretive issue *only* in virtue of the claim that it is the correct or original version. I have already argued that the usual reasons for this textual conclusion are confused. It is an impulsive reaction to an exciting discovery that does not appreciate the logic of scientific inference. The reaction is, ''This is a remarkable find and it is the earliest physical text we have. It therefore becomes the best evidence of what the original text is.'' But the role of evidence is to confirm or disconfirm theories. We have to compare the relative probability of the two hypotheses. And as we saw, the hypothesis that the traditional version is the original version still explains the data as well—in fact slightly better—than the new rival hypothesis. Both must now explain a radical textual event, but the event required by the hypothesis that the traditional version is genuine is the more plausible on its face. Further, the supplementary hypothesis that the additional particles were *removed* to produce the traditional version is no more plausible on its face than the alternative hypothesis that they were *added* to the original by the partisan Huang-Lao cult. (I would argue that the latter is actually the more plausible.) The instinctive reaction is a familiar human tendency to hasty generalization in statistical sampling. We have an actual physical specimen of one obviously biased sample. The excitement about the discovery should not overwhelm the discipline of statistical method. The fact that we are short on evidence should not justify an invalid inductive procedure.

But, the confusion goes deeper. Even if we did accept the claim that the Mawang-dui version is the original version, it cannot *forbid* any particular way of *reading* the traditional version. The question would then be *whether* we should read it, not *how*. If, for whatever reason of philosophical interest, etc., we do choose to interpret the traditional version, it is likely to be because it says something different from what the Huang-Lao version says. That is what having different words in a distinctive order does—it changes the meaning of what is said. One of the effects might be that one version is ambiguous where the other is not. But that ambiguity is a real grammatical and semantic difference between the two texts. The correct reading of one cannot determine or forbid how we read the other.

But the confusion is even deeper than that. Even granting, for the sake of argument, that we should substitute the Huang-Lao wording, Graham's conclusion is simply overstated. We should not read the substituted text as if it were intended to settle an interpretive dispute among twentieth-century Europeans about the traditional text—as if the particles were put there like commas to punctuate the traditional text for us. We should read the substituted text with its full grammatical force. There are two additional ye [assertion] characters in lines 5 and 6 only. It reads $chang$ [constant] wu [lack] yu [desire] ye [assertion particle] . . . . Graham's conclusion supposes that the additional ye simply breaks the sentence where it occurs. But Graham's own theory of ye [assertion particle] undermines this analysis. An assertion marker should not be here if this is to be read as a verbal imperative sentence. "Therefore constantly lack desires ye." (*?) The normal semantic force of ye is to marks strings as noun-is-noun assertions. Once we have the two interpretive possibilities in mind, we can easily read the Huang-Lao version in a way that give the ye its normal grammatical force. "Therefore constant-ing wu is a desire. Use it to view mysteries." But this reading tends to confirm the (IC) hypothesis more than the (NCR) alternate.

The new particles in the Huang-Lao version of the first chapter taken together illustrate my hypothesis that the Huang-Lao text was the product of *adding* particles to an earlier version. The Huang-Lao cult developed a partisan reading of the existing text. All the additional ye [assertion particle] characters in the first chapter are either otiose, grammatically odd, or simply opt for one of two grammatically possible reading of the original. Where they do opt for a reading, it is the less plausible one as judged from the traditional text prior to the addition of the new characters.

36. Chan Wing-tsit (1963), p. 157.

37. *Daode Jing,* ch. 12. The translation is from Lau 1963.

38. Schwartz seems to fall into this category, although he allows that all mysticisms are also different. See Schwartz 1985, pp. 192–201. He says, "To those to whom mystical language in general conveys no meaning, these selections will be as obscure as Meister Eckhardt or much Indian mystical and Sufi literature" (1985, p. 198). I surely fall in the category of those to whom mystical language has no meaning. But the *Daode Jing* selections in fact make sense to me. So to me the implicit premise that justifies lumping these passages with Indo-European mysticism is their lack of sense. That seems a thin reed indeed.

39. It is characteristic of the standard irrationalist interpretations of Daoism to put Laozi in the position of a European romantic attacking classical Western reason. They paint Laozi as saying *logic* cannot capture the divine ineffable Dao, but it can be done in poetry and imagery. (See for example Graham 1989, pp. 7–8, 218–20, 234.) An interesting claim—I think it misguided and false—but in any case, it belongs to an utterly distinct philosophical tradition and is irrelevant to the *Daode Jing.* Laozi's position is that any *dao* in language cannot be constant. Poetry is language as surely as prose is. After all, Confucius studied poetry as well as li [ritual]. Laozi no doubt had encountered poetry. Parables and fables are language. Laozi had no doubt encountered parables and fables. Logic is also language. There *is good reason* to doubt that Laozi ever encountered logic. So if anything, we should conclude that Laozi taught that poetry and parable cannot provide a constant *dao.* But, since he never addressed logic, it is consistent with his teaching that perhaps logic can provide a constant *dao!* If romantics do not like this line of reasoning, they are free to get emotional about it! If the way the world is cannot be spoken, it cannot be whistled or danced either!

40. I borrow the category of *primitivist* from A. C. Graham (1981), who stresses correctly the stratification within Daoism.

Chapter 7

1. Mote (1971), p. 96.

2. Graham (1989), p. 7–8.

3. This analysis coincides with that of Ames and Hall (1987).

4. Truth is a species of assertability. It differs from other members of that genus in several features. First, it concentrates on sentences, not terms. Term assertability functions within sentence truth. Truth is a species of assertability in which logical notions figure centrally. All truths must be *consistently* assertable. Reasoning practices converge in their judgments of which sentences are truth assertable. Truth assertability must depend on something beyond the social standards. This last feature is the one that makes truth-based theories realistic. It is the only one that emerges clearly in Chinese realism.

5. Graham (1978), p. 268.

6. See Graham (1978), p. 475 (*NO* 6).

7. Ibid., p. 483.

8. Ibid., p. 25.

9. I have published my skepticism about Graham's claim that the Neo-Mohists "discovered the sentence" earlier. See Hansen (1985) "Truth." It is true that the Neo-Mohists are interested in larger expression units and worries about how to deal with them. And frequently the main examples in *Names and Objects* turn out to be sentences. But still, as I shall argue, the Mohists' treatment of these examples parallels their treatment of compound terms and complex noun phrases. It stays on the level of denotation, range, or scope. They certainly do not get any closer to the semantics of sentences than the notion of *tang* satisfiability in the context of the discussion of how there can be winners in distinction-disputes. So despite using sentential examples (compounds with verbal units), the Mohists' *theory* does not evidence that they have, in the relevant sense, discovered the sentence. They certainly show no sign of distinguishing between phrases that can and cannot have truth value when used in assertions.

10. Graham (1978), p. 479 (*NO* 10).

11. Graham translates it as "the thing as it inherently is." See Graham (1978), pp. 189–90.

12. The opening formula of the first *Mohist Canon* gives this definition:

Mohist Canon A 1: *gu:* that which, when obtained, *cheng* completes.

Cheng completion has an interesting role. It normally translates well as *success* or *complete*. But Zhuangzi takes it in a way that underwrites a popular translation as *prejudice*. How are these roles compossible? I suggest the following hypothesis. A thing's *ran* so is its role in our conceptual system. The thing, as it inherently is, should ground our term *projection*. We *complete* that projection some way or other based on how that reality affects us. So the account of what completes a thing has a subjective element. People can be influenced by the same in-itself reality and have different *qing* reality registers. Thus they will differ in how they project their concepts on the world. Later Confucian innatist theories also adopt a concept like *cheng* complete with a language radical. We translate this as sincerity. *Cheng* sincerity represents the morally realistic ideal in projecting guidance.

The *Explanation* of this *Canon* distinguishes between greater and lesser *gu*. The lesser does not guarantee that we can attach a *ran* so to a thing though its absence does rule it out. The smaller *gu* is *ti* part of its inherent nature. The greater *gu* are like the sufficient conditions to the smaller *necessary conditions*. Their presence does guarantee that the thing is *ran* so. Their absence, however, also rules it out. That is how seeing becomes *cheng* complete seeing. See *Mohist Canon* A1 in Graham (1978), pp. 263–64.

13. They used *jian* total from Mozi's *jian-ai* universal love. Graham mistook this structure for our familiar ontology of particular objects and translated *ti* part as "individual." *Ti* part otherwise shows up in dictionaries with a bewildering set of translations: substance, part, body part, body, essence, The first two formulas give a good explanation of these. The *ti* parts are fixed by the criteria for fitting the concept. These depend on the *gu* in itself.

14. The Mohists *qing* feelings:reality uses a *language* radical rather than the more familiar *heart* radical. I treat it as the human reaction capacity that grounds the application of a name.

We apply names according to the way the *gu* of a *ti* impresses us. The impact thus comes to embrace feelings and eventually we come to translate the term as "feeling." Graham points out that the term is more accurately captured in pre-Han usages by "reality" or "essence." But this ignores any nonrealist content of *qing*. It should coincide, then, with *gu*. The association with *feeling* would be impossible to explain except with another radical meaning-change hypothesis. I treat it as the way reality registers on us. It is the impact of reality on humans that triggers their naming and choosing. The advantage of this analysis is that it can *explain* human linguistic conventions. Otherwise the inherent characteristic could determine names only by magic. Graham sometimes treats it as essence in the sense of the characteristics in virtue of which a name applies. But this, again, sunders it from any connection with feeling and also leaves unexplained how reality is supposed to affect our name assignments. *Qing* is a close relative of sense data. It is reality's imprint on us, but is not logically separable, as sense data are, from reality.

15. *Mohist Canon* A70 and B46. See also Graham's (1978) discussion of *qing*[reality], pp. 179–82.

16. The Mohists do not think shape is the only basis for assigning terms to things. A second basis is to use measure and amount. Here the constancy or order of normal names breaks down: parts of a large stone are not large. We have already noticed that flexible-scope analysis. But even the breakdown is not particularly ordered; parts of humans are not humans (e.g. a finger), but the finger of a particular person is that person (as opposed to someone else).

A third way names are attached to kapok is by place—residence and migration. There we cannot know whether the name attaches purely by our skill at distinguishing among things. For example we may have a "Qin horse" and have no way of knowing it as a Qin horse except to see it in the state of Qin. When we are in Qin, we know everything there can have this name applied to it—a Qin vase, stone, building, etc. See *NO* 2.

17. Graham (1978) pp. 478–82 (*NO* 10).

18. Graham (1978) pp. 346–47.

19. See Lau (1963), p. 19–21.

20. Graham translates *bei* as "self-contradictory." He acknowledges (Graham 1978, p. 163) that such translations are not exact. He does not say what is wrong with "contradictory," but I would argue that it implies a concern with sentences and truth. No such concern is in evidence here.

21. *Mohist Canon* B79.

22. Graham amends *bi*[other] to *fan*[opposite]. I prefer to keep *bi* to preserve the relation between the Neo-Mohist thesis and Zhuangzi's relativism. Other than its not being necessary, however, I have no argument against the emendation. The point in its context is so clear that the specific character couldn't matter very much. What the Neo-Mohists are talking about is the complement of a term—*other* is a nice parallel and happens to contrast with *shi*[this] as an alternate indexical to *fei*[not the one in question].

23. The Neo-Mohist use of *dang*[map onto] comes very close, as I have argued, to the semantic notion of *satisfaction*. See Hansen (1985), "Truth."

24. *Mohist Canon* B66.

25. See *Mohist Canon* B40 and Graham 1978, pp. 218–19.

26. *Mohist Canon* B68.

27. *Mohist Canon* A78.

28. See Hansen (1983) and (1985, "Individualism").

29. *Mohist Canon* A70.

30. *Mohist Canon* A86–87. See A6 for the kinds of things that cannot even count as *lei*[similars]. They are cases where the word used in trying to compare them cannot even be used *in the same sense* of both items.

31. *Mohist Canon* A87–87.

32. Extensional analysis fails for some adjectives, for example, *phoney priest* and *potential person*.

33. The alternative to giving this metaphysical account would be possible if classical thinkers already had a syntactic reason to distinguish parts of speech. If we already distinguish between adjective and noun, we are more likely to adopt separate metaphysical categories (object-attribute) corresponding to the syntactical distinction. However, we have noted several reasons why part-of-speech analysis and sentence-based grammar would not capture their attention. Classical grammar relies on word order rather than on syntactical role inflection. Characters have a high degree of syntactic mobility. And proper nouns, common nouns, adjectives, and simple one-place verbs have closely similar syntax. All could be used in term positions. They saw the apparent economy of treating all characters as terms with a scope. So classical thinkers were prompted to neither the theory of parts-of-speech nor the companion concept of the functionally complex sentence.

34. To make sense of this analysis, we really need a notion of stuff which is neutral between corporeal and non corporeal. "Stuff" in English is a bit too corporeal. This is what has motivated me to use "kapok"—a term I first learned from John Perry—to refer to undifferentiated, unqualified, neutral stuff. I exchanged with him the name of the sun around which God's home planet revolves.

35. Graham (1978), p. 23.

36. *Mohist Canon* A26–27.

37. *Greater Pick* 2A (Graham 1978, p. 235–36, *Expounding the Canon* 9).

38. An intensional or opaque structure is one in which truth, meaning, or reference becomes inconstant. In English, belief is a paradigm case of an intensional structure. The truth of S believes that P does not depend (much) on the truth of P. The Mohist finds the term-belief structure intensional.

39. Graham suggests that originally the Mohist used distinct graphs for all three senses distinguished here and that the copyists removed the distinguishing radical from the graph used in the accomplishment sense.

40. *Mohist Canon* A24.

41. *Mohist Canon* A26.

42. The Mohists offer *peering* as the analogy, but this should lead us to wonder how they construed looking. We need not assume their theory of sight was of the passive reception of sense-data pictures. Looking, I suggest, is testing the context for clues to program control and *dao* guidance.

43. The example is seeing—and the above caveats still apply. The Mohists seem barely to develop this concept of modeling, but Graham has proposed emendations and noted versions of the text that allow him to trace several other uses. The major one is A94, which uses the same character with a *yan*[language] radical. It discusses how a verbal description may skillfully turn one's linguistic commitments. In these cases one should seek the *gu*[inherent]—the reality base. The Kripke flavor is very strong here, but without the notion of an essence. The explanation then ties committment to word use, especially in these hard cases of projection, to some *fa*[measurement standard]. When different verbal characterizations allow one to treat it as the same or as different, one relies on *fa* to decide which to apply in choosing and rejecting. The standard, the Mohists seem to acknowledge, involves appropriateness. It must include the utility measurement. Again in A71 Graham postulates a corruption that links *mao*[description] and *fa*[standards] and the account of *bian*[dispute] in the *Names and Objects*. We may link it to the doctrine of *fa*[measurable standards].

44. The same character with a *ren*[human] radical rather than the Mohists' *yan*[language] radical is frequently translated as *ethics*—grading in human intercourse. With the *yan*[language] radical used here, the term occurs in compounds for translating "theory" and "debate."

45. *Mohist Canon* A 80. Although the term *qin* suggests intimacy, closeness, experiencing should not be understood as having some inner private *picture show*. No Chinese philosopher develops a theory of an inner mental subjectivity with a private "thought" record of what one has undergone. The intended contrast here is merely between what one knows from ones own encounters as opposed to hearing about things or having them explained.

46. The "unity of knowledge and action" much later became a slogan of a Neo-Confucian idealist, Wang Yang-ming, but without the Mohists' rational and realistic framework. For Wang, an admirer of Mencius, the unity ironically amounted to dispensing with names and expressing one's innate know-how in action. He developed the theory *to oppose* a school of Neo-Confucian thought that stressed paying close attention to things in the world.

47. This point is argued at great length by Graham (1978), pp. 127–36.

48. See Graham, 1957. I recommend this article to students not merely for its relevance to this particular work, but as a model of an argument for dismissing some text. The literature on classical Chinese philosophy is filled with allegations that such and such passage, chapter, phrase, etc., is "not authentic" or not in the "original" etc. None is as convincingly argued as Graham's claim about the *Gongsun Longzi*.

49. This last claim explains why the hard-white dialogue was forged. Given that he was famous for talking about hard-white, the forger copied the sections on hard-white from the *Mohist Canons* and attributed the result to Gongsun Long. It has fooled us for generations. But, as Graham notes, the secondary sources do not refer to any dialogue on hard-white, only to his position on separating them.

50. This example is a famous one in Mencius, who, despite never mentioning the rectification of names, was a most slippery practitioner of the technique.

51. Although I agree with Graham that the dialogue on hard-white is apocryphal and I reject the abstract or conceptualist interpretive hypothesis used in explaining it, the thrust is in the right direction. Gongsun Long needs to be understood as finding a way theoretically to separate hard and white. However the meaning of "separable" is already fixed by the usage of the Neo-Mohist. We more plausibly regard Gongsun Long as separating in the sense of treating the compound as a sum instead of a product. The standard view that he is talking about sense data is a principle of charity projection from modern Western philosophy.

52. Gongsun Long's dialogue suggests vaguely that *white* might be peculiar in this regard. *White* is always fixed or dependent on some thing's being white. He does not, however, develop this suggestion or follow it up. It sounds, indeed, like a suggestion that would lead in the direction of a property/thing analysis. Spelling it out, however, in a context where the "thing" is a stuff or "thing-kind" rather than an individual object, will not be as easy as those who accept the property-individual conceptual structure suppose it will.

53. Graham gives "a meaning" and "the meaning," Cheng and Swain "act of reference" and "object of reference."

54. I am, of course, insisting on the philosophical distinction between meaning and reference. Those who still think of the meaning of a term as anything that bears the name will be misled by such translations only if they equivocate and also consider meaning to be that which is conveyed in a definition.

55. Again, I owe this insight to Graham. See Graham (1978), p. 460.

56. It is interesting and indicative of the malleability of this dialogue that Graham, in his earlier reading, saw two halves to the dialogue and said that the second resumed and developed points raised in the first half. Now he sees it as two contrasting arguments for entirely different points of view. See Graham (1978), pp. 457–68.

57. Raymond Smullyan speculated about this being a possible reason why the *Dao* cannot be named. See Smullyan 1977, pp. 26–27.

58. There is a famous possibility that Hui Shi may have written much more. A biograph-

ical comment claims that he had five cartloads of writings. They may have been sounder than his ten theses.

59. I owe this to Hu Shi (1923), who first suggested that the ten theses are all paradoxes designed to show the unreality of space and time distinctions.

60. We take ti^{part} seriously here as a continuation of the technical usage in the Neo-Mohist *Canon*.

Chapter 8

1. Graham (1978), p. 128.

2. Schwartz (1985), pp. 216–17.

3. This is the key to understanding Zhuangzi. The effect was first appreciated by Graham (1970). The classic case of this technique is the famous restatement of Hui Shi's point: "Heaven-earth and I were born together; the myriad-things and I are one." Historical commentary on the *Zhuangzi* has regarded this as the central statement of his theory. It is a poetic expression of the *everything* concept. We now have reason to doubt that Zhuangzi would try to state an everything concept. Closer inspection of his "thinking aloud" about the statement shows him subsequently finding it incoherent.

4. Mary Erbaugh urged this objection in an AAS symposium on linguistic determinism and again at a similar symposium at Stanford. I think Lee Yearly has urged a similar objection in numerous conversations.

5. Of course, the community can respond in two ways. They may either reopen the interpretive question or define me out of the community. I will not predict which is more likely.

6. Or, as Schwartz's does above, it acknowledges it and then goes back to the assumption that Zhuangzi is a mystical monist without further examination. It limits the ways the analytic school can have influenced Daoism by the a priori assumption that Daoism is about the unnameable thing named *dao*.

7. *The Zhuangzi* 79/28/64.

8. Ibid., 67/24/68.

9. Ibid., 79/28/75.

10. Ibid., 92/33/51.

11. Ibid., 91/33/22.

12. Ibid., 62/23/21.

13. Ibid., 55/21/16.

14. Schwartz 1985, p. 217.

15. Graham (1981), p. 6. He sticks to his view of Zhuangzi in his 1989 book. But does there try to deal with the incoherence of his interpretive theory with his claim that Zhuangzi was fully conversant with the Later Mohist' analysis. Now he says that those sections of the Later Mohist text where the incoherence of antilanguage monism is proved must have come after Zhuangzi.

16. It might appear that I am questioning whether Zhuangzi is a Daoist? That reverses the matter. This whole study challenges the ruling theory's understanding of Daoism. The classification *Daoist* was introduced by a Han historian to refer to the doctrines of Zhuangzi and Laozi. *Daoism* thus refers to whatever theory Zhuangzi actually held. When we know what that theory is, we shall know what mature Daoism is.

17. Graham hints that Hui Shi might have been Zhuangzi's teacher who later became an equal—or less.

18. Graham (1981), p. 9. Italics mine.

19. Graham has Zhuangzi accepting Hui Shi's last theorem—"The world is one"—but making it mystical. Yet Graham recognizes that Zhuangzi is critical of any formulation of monism. Graham's view seems to be that Zhuangzi affirmed it in the face of his knowing that any formulation was incoherent. He sees Zhuangzi as blaming language for the problem, hence as an antilanguage antirationalist. But if Zhuangzi refuses to formulate what he affirms, how are we to know he affirmed it? This is absurdity chasing its own tail. We say he became a mystic because he drew an illegitimate conclusion which, since he also knew to be incoherent, he refuses to formulate. What reason, then, is there for thinking he drew it?

20. See Graham (1981 and 1978).

21. See Graham (1981).

22. The exception is the "Autumn Floods" chapter.

23. *The Zhuangzi* 1/1/15–17.

24. Ibid., 42/17/5.

25. Giles interprets this as having an out-of-body experience which tears the story out of its historical context and places it in a mind-body tradition. Graham identifies a parallel in the later chapters which he thinks of as a discarded version of the story. That story takes one on a regress of lamenting, and lamenting a lamenting, and. . . . Graham suggests that each of the lamenters is a *self* which treats the object of its lament as an *other*.

26. This description takes two terms from the dialecticians:; the *tong*[alike], which along with its opposite is the basis for a realistic analysis of language and is defined in eight ways in the *Mohist Canon*, and *qu*[choose], used of the way in which names affect behavior toward the thing-kinds they distinguish.

27. Graham (1969 and 1981): "Chuang Tzu's parable of the wind compares the conflicting utterances of philosophers to the different notes blown by the same breath in the long and short tubes of the pan pipes and the noises made by wind in hollows of different shapes. It is natural for differently constituted persons to think differently; don't try to decide between their opinions, listen to Heaven who breathes through them." I agree only up to the semicolon.

28. *The Zhuangzi* 3/2/9–10.

29. Ibid., 3/2/11.

30. Ibid.

31. The *Mohist Canon* discusses language in terms of grasping and limiting. We saw in Mozi the notion of language forcing us to have certain commitments to use the terms of things and then to stop at what is not-this. Notice that we might be tempted to think of this psycholinguistic (sociolinguistic?) claim of Zhuangzi's by analogy to the "force" of logic. But no goundwork has been laid in the philosophical tradition so far for any such notion. This is a kind of linguistic consistency grounded in a habitual skill at making distinctions as our teachers, schools, or communities do.

32. *The Zhuangzi* 4/2/13.

33. Ibid., 4/2/18–20.

34. See Graham's argument in Graham (1970) and (1978), and the argument in Chapter 7, pages 405–6 n.14.

35. *The Zhuangzi* 4/2/13–14.

36. Ibid., 4/2/14.

37. Ibid., 4/2/16.

38. Ibid., 4/2/14.

39. Ibid., 4/2/17.

40. Ibid., 4/2/17–18. For a fuller argument regarding the proper reading of these passages concerning the "true ruler" see Hansen (1983), "Tao of Tao."

41. See pages 181–82.

42. *The Zhuangzi* 4/2/18.

43. Ibid., 4/2/20–21.

44. Ibid., 4/2/21–22.

45. Ibid., 4/2/22–23.

46. Graham focuses attention on the "is-ought" problem in Zhuangzi and one form of his conclusion, I think, comes close to mine here, that is, Zhuangzi is not guilty of the is-ought error. In particular, Zhuangzi should not be read, as the tradition has it, to say "do whatever is natural or spontaneous." In other words, Zhuangzi kicks the props out from under all moral systems of the times with their appeal to the authority of *tian*[nature:heaven] or any other natural appeal. It is hard, however, to see how the position Graham attributes to Zhuangzi avoids the fallacy. "Respond with awareness" seems to have a built-in *shi-fei*. How Zhuangzi can disapprove of distinctions and accept "sorting" without making a distinction between them remains a mystery to me. Is the *shi-fei* distinction between *wei-shi*[objectionable *shi*ing] and *yin-shi*[conforming *shi*ing] an objectionable distinction or a sorting? Whatever is wrong with "follow heaven" is also wrong with "follow the natural *dao*."

47. *The Zhuangzi* 4/2/23.

48. Ibid., 4/2/24.

49. This is a tempting place in pre-Han philosophical writings to render *chen* as "true." I am persuaded, however, by Graham's argument and some of my own (see Graham 1978 and Hansen 1985) to render it as "authentic," contrasted here with artificial. Notice the same contrast using *qing*, another graph we have understood in more of a *reality* sense.

50. *The Zhuangzi* 4/2/25.

51. Ibid.

52. Ibid., 4/2/25–26.

53. Ibid., 4/2/26.

54. Ibid., 4/2/27.

55. See *Mohist Canon* B68. I am not wedded to the historical thesis that Zhuangzi was before or after the Neo-Mohists (cf. Graham's view that the Neo-Mohists refute Zhuangzi on indexicality). I do assume that the doctrines were being worked out in dialogue with each other. I put Zhuangzi after the Neo-Mohists only to stress his familiarity with the themes and techniques of the school and to separate him from Laozi to stress the development and maturity of Daoist theory.

56. *The Zhuangzi* 4/2/27.

57. Ibid., 4/2/28.

58. Ibid., 4/2/29.

59. Ibid., 4/2/30.

60. Ibid., 4/2/31.

61. Ibid., 4/2/31–32.

62. Ibid., 4/2/34.

63. Graham first brought to my attention this distinction between *gu*, things as they inherently are, and *qing*, the accessible feedback from things that *cheng* "completes" our classifications. It figures in the doctrine of Yang Zhu (and therefore Mencius) as well. *Ku* is a natural concept for Zhuangzi to use to confront realist assumptions.

64. *The Zhuangzi* 4/2/34.

65. Ibid., 4/2/35. This is where Zhuangzi's use of *cheng*[complete] reveals his view of it as biased completion. He refers to the heart that grows with the body—the one that gallops forward out of control as the *cheng* heart. Ways are made *cheng* by walking them, and so forth. Now it is clear that things become *cheng* by our dividing. We make things by carving them out of kapok.

66. *The Zhuangzi* 4/2/35.

67. Ibid., 4/2/36.

68. Ibid., 5/2/37.

69. Ibid., 5/2/37–38.

70. Ibid., 5/2/38–39.

71. David Hume, *Dialogues Concerning Natural Religion*, 1779.

72. *The Zhuangzi* 5/2/40–43.

73. See Graham (1983) in Mair (1983).

74. Graham (1983), p. 7.

75. Watson states the problem nicely in a footnote in his 1964 translation, p. 47n.

76. Nazi war criminals reportedly did proclaim that they were just skillful practitioners of a task, almost reflecting pride in their efficiency.

77. This is why I prefer "ordering thing-discourse" to "equalizing thing-discourse" to translate the title of this chapter.

78. *The Zhuangzi* 5/2/47.

79. Ibid., 5/2/48.

80. Ibid., 5/2/49–51.

81. Graham sees a similar point here (I think). But he then attributes to Zhuangzi the further claim that there really is something left out between alternatives. He chooses one of Zhuangzi's rhetorical answers. There really is something between something and nothing, whatever it is. Graham (1981), pp. 55–56.

82. *The Zhuangzi* 5/2/52–54.

83. Ibid., 5/2/53–54.

84. Ibid., 5/2/54–55.

85. Ibid., 5/2/55.

86. Ibid., 5/2/56–57. I cannot avoid the impression that Zhuangzi is being ironic here. In general, I think reference to sages in Zhuangzi are ironic. Graham notes that Zhuangzi never says everything is one but always "speaks subjectively of the sage treating as one." I certainly agree, but find bizarre the suggestion that Zhuangzi endorses rather than ridicules that treatment.

87. Ibid., 5/2/57–58.

88. Ibid., 5/2/58–60.

89. Ibid., 5/2/60–62.

90. Kripke (1963) has argued that Wittgenstein's skepticism about following a rule is a "deeper" form of skepticism than sense skepticism. Sense skepticism is a version of rule-interpretation skepticism. In effect, Zhuangzi's skepticism is more like Wittgenstein's (though without focusing on the sentential imperative rule form, but on the name and the *dao* discourse form). That Zhuangzi should discuss dreams last is logically appropriate. It is the application of a deeper skepticism to a particular issue.

91. *The Zhuangzi* 6/2/64–66.

92. Ibid., 6/2/66–70.

93. Translation from Graham (1981), p. 58.

94. Nietzsche argues that the reversal of the usual preference is what marks both Christianity and Buddhism as decadent religions. They hate life and long for death!

95. *The Zhuangzi* 6/2/70–73.

96. Ibid., 6/2/73–77.

97. Ibid., 6/2/80–84.

98. Ibid., 7/2/84–90.

99. Ibid., 7/2/93–94.

100. Ibid., 7/2/94–96.

101. In fact, it does still leave questions about the psychological status of the belief that parallels the problems about getting motivation out of a rationalizing practical syllogism.

102. Graham has written that Zhuangzi's approach bridges the fact-value distinction. This is because, he argues, Zhuangzi's conception of conduct is stimulus-response. In acting one does not make judgments but simply "responds with awareness" to a total situation. Graham's

account presupposes the authoritarian possibility of some perspective free awareness or knowledge. That seems to me inconsistent with Zhuangzi's skepticism.

103. Note that this slogan never occurs in the crucial second chapter and only once in the inner chapters.

Chapter 9

1. Creel (1953), p. 115.
2. Hughes (1942), p. 226.
3. Hsiao (1979), p. 145–147.
4. Watson (1963), p. 3. From our non-Confucian perspective, this is no puzzle. The philosophical action all takes place in Daoism and Mohism. Xunzi, as I shall argue, never really comes to grip with the philosophical issues. Tang Jun-i (1975, vol. 2 pp. 437–38) argues that Xunzi was more influential than Mencius in the Han. This would explain why his authoritarian view of Daoism might have permeated the Han perspective on Daoist thought.
5. Lee Yearly (1983) first drew my attention to this tension in Xunzi's thought. I have no theory about which is the real Xunzi or which came first. I don't have any argument that the authoritarian elements come only from later additions to the text. That is one possibility. Another may be the conservative conversion familiar in disillusioned political theorists. My instinct is that the conventionalist is earlier and the authoritarian (whether in the school or the individual) later. The authoritarian trend is one we have postulated in the case of Confucius and Mozi earlier.
6. Schwartz has noticed this authoritarian assumption. His defense of Xunzi confuses the historical existence of an authority structure with justification of that authority. He notes that Xunzi does not address "how the sages manage to *establish* their authority." See Schwartz 1985, p. 295 (emphasis mine). That verb equivocates between the urgent philosophical demand to *justify* the ruler's authority and the merely historical *explanation* of how it came about. It may be that Xunzi also has a historian's bias that inclines him to blur these distinct questions. Schwartz goes on to assert that we have "no need to wonder why Xunzi, like Confucius and Mencius before him, simply assumes the need for hierarchy and authority. The good order can be inaugurated and maintained only by a vanguard elite." Schwartz's analysis is inverted. No one needs to explain how authority is *factually* established when the rulers monopolize the knives and whips and the hooligans to wield them. That is reasonably obvious and clear. The *justification* of authority by contrast, is what is at issue in the philosophical reflections of the period, and we do need to wonder why Xunzi ignored the philosophical issue of the day.

Of course, if we agree with the need for a social elite, we may consider it *charitable* to attribute to Xunzi the awareness that we need to impose the elite ideas on everyone. But there is *no warrant* for Schwartz's assertion that such a view was natural and inevitable for Xunzi's "world." Schwartz acknowledges that Xunzi even misses the degree to which Mencius' position undermines the assumed justification of authority. There (p. 299) he further grants that it is superficially inconsistent with Xunzi's acceptance that the sage and the ordinary person are essentially alike. And, as we shall see, it is also inconsistent with the doctrine of "empty, unified, and still." If it is inconsistent with what Confucius said, what Mozi said, what Laozi and Zhuangzi said, and even with what Mencius and Xunzi said, then what does it mean to say it is an inevitable assumption for Xunzi's intellectual world?

I would, of course, concede that it is a natural thing to say for anyone seeking an official status that only the elite can grant.

7. Schwartz (1985, p. 295) treats this penchant for punishment far more positively than I would. Dealing with it in his Xunzi section prompted him to discuss Confucius's original

argument against punishment, which he ignored while discussing Confucius. Schwartz here allows that *The Analects* placed a "clear emphasis" on "minimizing" the role of penal law. He then boldly asserts that punishment *is* necessary and charitably attributes knowledge of this obvious truth to the master. This un-Confucian pessimism he justifies on Confucius' behalf by the un-Confucian assumption that there will always be a segment of society "not accessible to control by moral force" (p. 104). Even if we allowed Schwartz to write his favorite justification of punishment between the lines of Confucius, I would resist excusing Xunzi's position as a continuation of that view. The appeal to moral suasion or coercion by the social elite may have been excusable in Confucius, but by the time of Xunzi is simply obdurate in the face of Mohist and Daoist arguments.

8. *The Xunzi* 66/18/35–40. My lower evaluation of the authoritarian Xunzi than the conventionalist is controversial. Others, including Schwartz, start from the dogmatic views and *explain away* the arguments from relativity. My own plebeian origins may have something to do with my own attitudes toward issues such as elitism and punishment. Even in the Western tradition, where we have a tradition of rational, deontological, retributive defenses of punishment available, I have found it curious that there should seem to be a race among some philosophers to be the first finally to be able to justify punishment. It is as if they regarded that as akin to being the first to discover a cure for cancer. I regard punishment as the cancer. I should like to be the last to justify punishment. Perhaps this stems from a deeply Daoist awareness that I may be a target when "social elite" reach for their mutilating knives. I, quite frankly, don't see the point of heroic intellectual efforts to justify their cruelty. The justifications coming from the same elite smack at least slightly of special pleading. But I will not offer a proof that punishment is wrong. For me, it is enough to note that it hurts.

9. Only *vaguely,* because Xunzi treats the *dao* as an invention of the sage-kings that is *verified* by experience. Yet, since he proposes a conventional interpretative theory, the teachers in each generation transmit ways of making distinctions and determine what the correct way is. This makes it impossible to make the distinction between an evolving and a stable *dao.* Note the similar question about the U.S. Constitution: Was it bequeathed as a stable standard by the founders or did it evolve under flexible interpretation by judges?

10. *The Xunzi* 62/17/1–2.

11. Ibid., 63/17/24.

12. Ibid., 20/8/24. In other places the shallow dogmatic Xunzi insists in apparent contradiction that the hierarchial order is a heavenly ordering (26/9/16).

13. Watson (1963), p. 71.

14. Eno (1990, p. 144) argues for a parallel conclusion, but with a distinctly different tone. He suggests that *The Xunzi* is a book designed to *prevent defections* more than to convince outsiders.

15. *The Xunzi* 62/17/10.

16. Ibid., 63/17/34.

17. Ibid., 64/17/46–47.

18. Ibid., 66/18/42.

19. Translation from Watson (1963), p. 36.

20. Ibid., p. 25.

21. *The Xunzi* 28/7/69–73.

22. Xunzi is not an acute observer of animals or he would not allege that there are no other "grouping" animals. There are social animals. But his point can survive because their socialization does not depend, as human grouping does, on conventional distinctions and a guiding discourse using names linked to the distinctions.

23. *The Xunzi* 29/9/75–6.

24. Ibid., 79/21/21. This reminds one of C. D. Broad's moral intuitionism. Anyone who disagrees about what is moral must be morally blind.

25. Ibid., 15/6/6.

26. Ibid., 15/6/8–9.

27. Ibid., 26/9/13. Dubs and most commentators treat *fa*^{standards} as "laws" and lose the point here. Xunzi does advocate using *li*^{ritual} on the good and *xing*^{punishment} on the rest. But *fa*^{standards} make most sense here understood as standards for making distinctions and properly using terms. That is why he contrasts it with *lei*^{similarity}. My suggestion here is that *fa*^{standards} are for application to terms in codes of behavior. His rivals propose *fa*^{standards} as components of *jia-dao*$^{\text{bogus ways}}$. They underwrite immoral ways of making and enforcing guiding distinctions. It has nothing specifically to do with punishment here.

28. Ibid., 26/9/11–12.

29. Ibid., 28/9/48–49.

30. Commentators stress the "birth" side, but the character clearly has both meanings and the latter is necessary to account for Mencius' use of nature to refer to developed capacities which grow naturally in us.

31. This term is slightly misleading as a translation for *zheng*^{rectify} *li*^{utility}. I choose it to underline the deliberate process component. I doubt that Xunzi thought of this as Bentham would have, as a mathematical process, but more as Mozi did, as an objective measurement generating a distinction.

32. Presumably these are the intentions of the sage-kings who set up the system of names and the *Dao* containing them.

33. We must notice how far this moral conception is from Kantianism. The manipulative nature of the shared Confucian and Mohist early conception of human motivation and society mitigate any Kantian conception of individual dignity. Perhaps the slide to the ruler's perspective that we see in Xunzi is predictable given that initial conception of social psychology.

34. *The Xunzi* 83/22/10–11.

35. Ibid., 83/22/12.

36. Ibid., 83/22/12–14.

37. Ibid., 83/22/14.

38. Ibid., 83/22/14–15.

39. Ibid., 62/17/11–12.

40. Ibid., 62/17/12–13.

41. Ibid., 83/22/16.

42. Ibid., 83/22/16–17.

43. Ibid., 83/22/19–20.

44. Xunzi uses *ming*^{command} rather than *ming*^{name} here. The sense of *command* is not entirely inappropriate since the name giver is supposed to be the political authority and Xunzi does take human authority over other animals to be natural. The name, rather than the sentential imperative, is the bearer of prescriptive force. All idioms corresponding roughly to keeping promises, telling the truth, and carrying out orders, refer to names. That focus shows the degree to which Chinese treats the content of a command as implicit in the name (either because accepted traditions are "built into" that name-role or because any native speaker masters the name's imperatives intuitively). Xunzi attempts no solution to the problem that stopped the Later Mohists: how does stringing names together guide people?

45. *The Xunzi* 83/22/21–22.

46. Ibid., 83/22/21–25.

47. Ibid., 83/22/25–84/22/27.

48. Graham 1978, pp. 471–73.

49. *The Xunzi* 84/22/27–28.

50. Xunzi's formulation could be improved. A thing may change its position as long as the spatial positions it occupies are continuous, that is, form a coherent spatiotemporal history of a single object. Of course, this "improvement" *uses* our conceptual scheme of individuals.

Xunzi's more restrictive formulation shows his unfamiliarity with the concept of the individual particular.

51. *The Xunzi* 84/22/28–29.

52. Ibid., 21/8/34–35.

53. Ibid., 84/22/29–34.

54. The latter must have seemed especially paradoxical because the character for pleasure, as observed above, is the character for music!

55. The text actually presents this paradox as Zhuangzi does, i.e., "Horse is not horse." I follow Watson in identifying it as Kung-sun Lung's paradox, though one could justify including it in Xunzi's third group if one followed Liang Chi-hung and parse it to read as the Neo-Mohists' "ox-horse is not horse" (assuming it must be true for the same reason that "ox-horse not ox"). But this makes only two paradoxes and Xunzi has been following a pattern of clustering three examples.

56. Another temptation is to link it to the Later Mohist claim that we can not deny denials. But that would not fit in Xunzi's classification. It has nothing to do with reality.

57. We are tempted to ad hoc explanations such as that some obscure version of the character was written with an ox radical.

58. *The Zhuangzi* 92/33/33–34.

59. Graham (1989), p. 96.

60. *The Zhuangzi* 92/33/35–36.

61. I follow Graham in treating *qing* with a heart radical and with a language radical as closely related. My theory of their relation, however, is slightly different. I suggest the different radicals mark slight differences in emphases about what registers from reality. On the one hand, it is an impression on the heart-akin to a feeling. On the other it is the linguistic class the heart's parallel processor assigns the input before sending it to the CPU for program control.

62. *The Zhuangzi* 92/33/26–27.

63. Ibid., 92/33/41.

64. *The Xunzi* 69/18/93–70/18/122.

65. Ibid., 69/18/102–3.

66. Graham's treatment of Xunzi's response is far more positive. He seems to regard the appeal to the sage-king's usage as an appropriate starting place for a refutation of this blatantly anticonventionalist position. See Graham (1989), p. 97.

67. *The Xunzi* 70/18/113–14.

68. Ibid., 85/22/55–56.

69. Ibid., 85/22/55–58 and 70/19/1.

70. Ibid., 85/22/59–60.

71. Ibid., 85/22/63.

72. Ibid., 85/22/63–64.

73. Ibid., 31/10/1. See also pp. 315–17. This might be another implicit attack on Mozi—the attempt to have an only one standard *dao*.

74. Ibid., 85/22/64–65.

75. Ibid., 85/22/71–86/22/74.

76. Ibid., 86/22/75.

77. Ibid., 86/22/78–79.

78. Ibid., 86/22/79–80.

79. Ibid., 86/22/80.

80. Ibid., 86/22/83–84.

81. Ibid., 86/22/85–88.

82. See Munro (1969), pp. 77–81. Schwartz (1985, p. 292) dismisses this concern. He argues the slogan is wholly consistent with the rest of Xunzi's thought.

83. Schwartz (1985, p. 292) notes these objections, but clings to the accuracy of the "human nature is evil" slogan in describing Xunzi's theory. Schwartz seems to accept the Mencian argument that if goodness is not internal, then human nature is evil. If all that "human nature is evil" means is that human nature is not perfectly good, then I would agree. But that is not what the English sentence means. If that is what the Chinese sentence says then the standard translation is abysmally wrong!

84. We need not necessarily conclude anything about how it got into the text. I am most persuaded by the theory that it is a partisan interpretative gloss designed to color the reading of the argument. But I do not need any textual theory to justify my interpretive strategy. I dismiss the slogan because it is misleading, especially in this comparative context. We may confuse Xunzi's position with those common in Christian and Buddhist pessimism about original sin and life as suffering. My experience is that the slogan induces English readers to assume that Xunzi thought humans were naturally egoists or naturally cruel and vindictive. Neither is true.

85. A Daoist primitivist has the same problem. If we can exist in perfect harmony and happiness in language-free villages, why would language have started? Isn't there a natural (presocial, nonconventional) inclination to invent language? If so, isn't inventing language as good as other natural behaviors?

86. By hypothesis (one which Zhuangzi presumably would find unappealing) the correct *dao* is one that produces order. This tempts us to respond, in Xunzi's style, that Confucians are obsessed with order and don't appreciate the virtues of spontaneity and upheaval! So their *daos* stress authority and control.

87. *The Xunzi* 78/21/5.

88. Ibid., 79/21/21–24.

89. The criticism is intelligible, but far from sound. Zhuangzi recognized the perspective of humans but drew attention to all the other perspectives. He could be accused of imbalance only on the assumption (which no doubt Xunzi makes) that the human perspective deserves pride of place. Balance, for Xunzi, consists in preferring our species perspective over that of other larger mammals.

90. *The Xunzi* 79/21/24–25.

91. Ibid., 79/21/26–27. *Zhou*[comprehensive] may be a deliberate ambiguity between what Confucius admits (that he follows the *Zhou* in preference to the conventions of the Xia or Shang). Xunzi seems to intend it here to be read as *zhou*[comprehensive].

92. Ibid., 79/21/29–30.

93. Ibid., 80/21/35–39.

94. Ibid., 80/21/39–41.

95. See especially Kurt Baier, *The Moral Point of View*.

96. *The Xunzi* 80/21/41–45.

97. Ibid., 80/21/44–47.

Chapter 10

1. Graham (1989), p. 269.

2. Hughes (1942), p. 254.

3. Schwartz (1985), p. 333.

4. This may be one of the few cases of someone's being executed in conformity with Kant's categorical imperative. Han Feizi's teachings dictate Han Feizi's death. The emperor who conquered China followed the philosopher's own instructions in executing him.

5. Commentators frequently praise the "rationality" and "logic" of self-proclaimed realists who are cynically fond of cruelty. I see no reason to accord any such status unless

they really are rational and consistent. On their face, pessimistic or cruelty-based assumptions are no more realistic than their opposites. Idealized evil is just as idea-based as is idealized good.

6. Graham (1989), p. 376.

7. John Austin, *The Province of Jurisprudence Determined*, lecture 1, 1932.

8. See especially Creel (1970), p. 92.

9. See Schwartz (1985), p. 321, and Graham (1989), pp. 273–75. Graham says that *fa*[standard] "*contracts* toward what in Western terms is law; but even among those classed as legalists it can include, for example, methods of regulating the bureaucracy." This is close to my view, but I would deny that the term contracts. Since it is used for the entire range of guiding standards, its meaning never changes at all for the *fajia*. Laws would be merely one specimen of objective standards.

10. The book of the same name, *The Guanzi* is agreed to be a later compilation. How much of it has some genuine basis in Guanzi's actual theories is controversial. However, given the content, we have no reason to doubt that this case of fixing the reference of *fa* is anachronistic since it is so close to Mozi's use. Further, we understand from independent sources that Guanzi advocated both *fa* and *li*. The citation tends to disconfirm the meaning change hypothesis even if it comes after Han Feizi. It shows then that *before and after* Han Feizi the term was used of measurement standards, not penal laws.

11. Rickets (1985), p. 128.

12. *The Xunzi* 26/9/11–14.

13. Especially telling here is his statement that where *fa* (cultivated traditionalist scholar's intuitions) are not available, one can use *lei*[similarity].

14. *The Han Feizi,* "Revealing Learning," ch. 50, SPPY 19:11B–12A

15. Tang 1975, vol. 1, p. 518.

16. Both Schwartz (1985, p. 322) and Bodde (1981, p. 175) identify *xing* as an early term for penal codes.

17. See, for example, *The Han Feizi,* "Revealing Learning," ch. 50, SBBY 19:12B.

18. Bodde (1981), p. 175.

19. A classic argument for this criticism of utilitarian justification of law is Morris (1968). See also my discussion in Hansen (1985).

20. There is an interesting coincidence that two recent, essentially pro-Confucian authors (Schwartz 1985 and Ames 1987) depart from the Confucian orthodoxy in insisting that Confucius was not really opposed to punishment. Both argue that Confucius thought punishment was at least permissible. Schwartz attributes to Confucius the attitude that punishment is an indispensable, albeit not the only indispensable, technique of social control. Ames (pp. 168–76) argues that Confucius' argument against punishment merely shows a *preference* for education over punishment. But, since Confucius is practical, he must realize that punishment is *necessary* as a last resort. Both base their charitable attribution on their own assumption that punishment is obviously necessary. The practical necessity of punishment is, at best, philosophically controversial. Interpreters should not promiscuously attribute their biases to Confucius. While I find Ames and Schwartz giving *their* arguments for why we must tolerate punishment, I can't find Confucius giving any such arguments. All his arguments are against it. Now, since I agree that punishment is stupid and indefensible, when I credit Confucius with practical wisdom, I will say he has argued *correctly*. I agree fully with the argument in the text and that is the end of the matter. Ames and Schwartz credit him with great practical insight—like theirs. I credit him with practical insight—like mine. But the bottom line is that the only arguments we find that clearly address the matter are directed against punishment. What encourages Ames is that there are mentions of punishment *without any argument*. Ames takes that as proof that Confucius tolerated punishment. But those passages show, at best, that Confucius acknowledged the *existence,* not the permissibility of punishment. Obviously Con-

fucius is aware of the *existence* of a practice of punishment and he has the term in his vocabulary.

21. See Fung (1953 Bodde tr.), pp. 623–29.

22. On this conception of, what is sometimes called *critical morality*, no one, including God, makes something morally right by saying "It is right." Moral laws, like scientific laws, are hypotheses tested by reason, subject to rational revision when they lead to unacceptable consequences.

23. See the excellent brief account in Mote (1971, p. 117) and the more extended account in Hsiao (1979, ch. 6). Mencius tried to avoid calling these usurpers *kings*.

24. *The Guanzi* explanation of *fa* is relevant even if the book is later than Han Feizi. If the inspiration is earlier, it shows the historical meaning of the term is linked to measurement and if later, it shows that even after Han Feizi the term has not changed its meaning even during the Qin and among quasi-legalist sources.

25. See Hsiao (1979), p. 334.

26. Hsiao (1979), p. 339–41.

27. The problem is to show how one can be both stoic and advocate abandonment of knowledge and still be an authoritarian. Thompson (1979) argues that Fung Yu-lan's professed confusion about this is cleared up when we reconstruct the fragments from Shendao. Even if one accepts his impressive reconstruction of the text, it is not obvious that he has produced a theory that clarifies the apparent theoretical conflict. Knowing that both halves of Shendao's theories are both authentic does not solve the problem.

28. Translated and quoted in Creel (1960), p. 97.

29. Hurlee Creel establishes this emphasis in Legalist theory in Creel (1960), p. 104.

30. Schwartz (1985), pp. 331–32.

31. Hsiao (1979), p. 399.

32. Ibid.

33. *The Han Feizi,* "Revealing Learning," ch. 50.

34. This point follows Tang 1975, p. 507. He notes both a Zhuang zi and Xunzi antecedent for this attitude in Han Feizi.

35. This is the general point of the *Liu-fan*^{Six Reversals} chapter.

36. *The Han Feizi,* SBBY 1/3/9A. This statement of frustration echoes Xunzi, of course, and reinforces the perception that Han Feizi does not understand the analytic tradition.

37. *The Han Feizi,* "Revealing Learning," ch. 50. SBBY 19:9B.

38. Ibid., SBBY 19:10B.

39. See Tang (1975), p. 509.

40. Schwartz (1989), p. 332.

41. *The Han Feizi,* book 5, ch. 17 (*Pi-Nei*^{Guarding within}).

42. Schwartz (1985) makes this point very nicely, pp. 339–40. I have a small quibble, however. I doubt that either Shendao or Han Feizi would view this conclusion as anything more than a sociological constant. It is not that authority is inherently right. People do tend to revere authority and the ruler wants to enhance and strengthen that impulse. That authority is *mystically* rooted in *dao* itself is some kind of joke as applied to Shendao. For Shendao, that only amounts to saying that *shi* happens!

43. *The Han Feizi,* "Ruler's Dao," ch. 5.

44. See Schwartz (1985), p. 337.

45. Also in "Ruler's Dao," ch. 5.

46. See, for example, the account in De Bary et. al. (1960), vol. 2, p. 112.

47. Schwartz cites the fact that the two handles of punishment and reward are clearly part of *shu*^{method} in rebuttal of Creel's insistence that Shen Buhai was not a Legalist.

48. See ch. 43, *Dingfa* 17/6b/9–11.

49. Chan (1963), p. 259.

50. Adapted from Chan (1963), p. 257.

51. *The Han Feizi*, "Five Vermin," ch. 45. SBBY 19:6B.

52. *The Han Feizi*, "Having Criteria," ch. 5. SBBY 2:3A.

53. Tang (1975) has most fully appreciated this point; see vol. 1, p. 518.

54. *The Han Feizi*, "Having Criteria," ch. 6. SBBY 2:1B.

55. *The Han Feizi*, "Having Criteria," ch. 6. SBBY 2:1B–2A.

56. *The Han Feizi*, "Having Criteria," ch. 6. SBBY 2:3B.

57. Tang (1975), vol. 1, p. 511.

58. Chan (1963), p. 254.

59. *The Han Feizi*, "Mr. Ho," ch. 13. SBBY 4:11B.

60. Chan (1963), p. 259. Substituting *fa* for "law."

61. Hsiao (1979), p. 398.

62. Chan (1963), p. 260.

63. Hsiao (1979), p. 400.

64. Hsiao (1979), p. 401.

65. Bodde (1981, pp. 179–80) cites this as an explicit distinction between *li* and *fa*. This appears to read backwards from the assumption that the debate parallels the distinction between natural and positive law, between law and morality. But, from the first, Confucius seemed to be teaching from a *Book of Rites* and is supposed to have edited it. It is only on the assumption that the *li* have an explicit formulation that the doctrine of rectification of names has any role to play.

66. *The Han Feizi*, book 9, ch. 50(*Xian-xue*[exposing learning]).

67. Tang's two hypotheses about the source of the commentary on the *Laozi* do not seem mutually exclusive; I shall assume their joint plausibility. Han Feizi's reading of Laozi bridges what could have been Han Feizi's youthful affinity for the dogmatic Xunzi's later posture. My argument focuses solely on content, not on style or word frequency. I think authenticity tests of the latter type could be devised, but the gross measures used at present (counting the frequency of a word or compound) seem unreliable given what we know about editing, tabooing, and so forth in the transmission of texts. The more appropriate tests of style would involve grammatical complexity and types of complex sentences and frequency measures on these.

68. Graham (1989), p. 100.

69. Tang (1975), vol. 1, p. 527.

70. See Schwartz's discussion, (1985), p. 273. Schwartz, like Graham, regards this development as informing Mencius more than Xunzi or Han Feizi. He links it with Song Xing as the "discovery of subjectivity." Song Xing, however, states the *problem*. We all have different perspectives. The discussion in *The Guanzi* purports to have discoverd a magical solution. I can mystically produce a perspectiveless inner state of mind.

I follow Tang in seeing *The Guanzi* development as more important for the Xunzi wing. He needs to motivate a notion of a biasfree *receptor* of an external, real *dao*. Mencius does not want an empty or perspective free heart (except empty of distortion by language). I take the difference between the absolutist Xunzi and Mencius to lie in Xunzi's view that the heart-mind can unerringly perceive the *external* pattern of value. For Mencius it is less a matter of *perceiving* it in things that of *projecting* it from one's intuition *onto* things.

71. See Tang's account, 1975, vol 1, p. 535.

72. *The Han Feizi*, "Jielao." SBBY 6:3A–B.

73. Ibid., 6:6A–B.

74. Ibid., 6:3A.

75. Ibid., 6:4B.

76. Ibid.

77. Ibid., 6:7B.

78. Ibid., 6:7B–8A.

79. Ibid., 6:11A.

80. *The Xunzi* 71/19/30–31.

81. *The Han Feizi,* "Jielao." SBBY 6:8B.

82. Ibid., 6:11A.

83. Tang 1975, pp. 506–7.

84. *The Han Feizi,* "Jielao." SBBY 6:8B.

85. Ibid., 6:11A.

86. I sense this as the motive behind Alan Bloom's *The Closing of the American Mind.* One cannot, of course, be sure of such motivational analyses.

GLOSSARY OF CHINESE CHARACTERS

愛　*ai*　love

霸　*ba*　overlord

白馬　*bai-ma*　white-horse

白　*bai*　white

誖　*bei*　perverse

本　*ben*　originally

比　*bi*　comparability, comparable

比　*bi*　other, that, that:other

筆　*bi*　pen

辯　*bian*　discriminate, discriminating, discrimination dispute, distinction, distinction-disputes distinguish.

辨　*bian*　divide

表　*biao*　gnomen

別　*bie*　distinguish, partial

不　*bu*　neg, negation

不可　*bu-ke*　not assertable, not permissible

不然　*bu-ran*　not so

不知　*bu-zhi*　ignorance

常　*chang*　constant

臣　*chen*　ministers

成　*cheng*　accomplishment, complete, completion, fixed, success, successful

誠　*cheng*　sincerity

出　*chu*　exit

辭　*ci*　phrase

此　*ci*　this

大道　*da-dao*　great *dao*

當　*dang*　hit on, hits, map onto, map onto it, maps onto things

道　*dao*　discourse, way, doctrine, guide, guide-speak, guiding discourse, lead, metaphysical absolute, path, prescriptive discourse, way:speak, ways of discourse, prescriptive possible world histories

道家 *dao jia* Daoists, way school

德 *de* virtuosity, power, virtue

地 *di* earth

定 *ding* fixed

端 *duan* point:edge

多 *duo* much/many

而 *er* and:yet

法家 *fa jia* Legalists, standardizers, standardizer school, standards school

法官 *faguan* magistrates

法 *fa* law, measurable standards, measurement standard, model, objective public standards, objective standards, standard, standard

反 *fan* opposite

非 *fei* disapprove:wrong:not-this, dissent, is not, not this:wrong, not the one in question, not, not-this, rejects, that's not, wrong

分 *fen* divisions

故 *gu* in itself, inherent, inherent way things are, the way things inherently are, therefore

管 *guan* input pipes

觀 *guan* observe

貴賤 *gui-jian* noble-base

鬼 *gui* ghosts

過 *guo* surpasses

害 *hai* harm

合 *he* combined

很 *hen* very

化 *hua* change, changed

黃老 *Huang-lao* Yellow Emperor-Laozi

異 *yi* different

意 *yi* intent, intention

義 *yi* moral, moralities, morality

以 *yi* use, with regard to, with

易經 *I Jing, Book of Changes*

家 *jia* schools-families

假道 *jia-dao* bogus ways

兼愛 *jian-ai* universal love

姦 *jian* illicit

兼   *jian*   total, universal, whole

微   *jiao*   manifestations

教育   *jiaoyu*   teaching-nourishing

解老   *Jie-lao*   explaining-Laozi

幾   *ji*   how many

接   *jie*   contact

進   *jin*   advances

經   *jing*   canons

舉   *ju*   pick out, picking out, picking-out

句   *ju*   sentence

卷   *juan*   roll

君   *jun*   superior

君子   *junzi*   gentleman, superior man

可   *ke*   acceptable, admissible, appropriate, assertability, assertable, can-be, permissibility, permissibly predicable, may

可不可   *ke/bu-ke*   acceptable/unacceptable

狂   *kuang-ju*   wild picking-out

孔子   *Kungzi*   master Confucius

類   *lei*   classes, similarity, similarity classes, similars

利   *li*   benefit, profit, utility

豐   *li*   ceremonial vessel, sacrificial vessel

俐   *li*   clever

禮   *li*   convention, etiquette, propriety, rites, ritual/propriety, ritual, ritual behavior

理   *li*   guiding tendency, principle, pattern

里   *li*   road

利害   *li-hai*   benefit-harm

禮義   *li-i* ritual morality

兩   *liang*   two

令   *ling*   commands

六反   *Liu-fan*   Six Reversals

慮   *lü*   deliberation

律   *lü*   laws, regulations

論語   *Lun-yu*   *Analects,* discussion words

倫   *lun*   human-relations discourse

論 *lun* theories

馬 *ma* horse

貌 *mao* description

妙 *miao* mysteries

明 *ming* bright, clarity, clear, enlightenment, illumination, understand, understanding

命 *ming* command, command:name:fate, commands, fate, fate:mandate, fated length of life, mandate, name-command, to name:command:fate

名 *ming* name, name:rank, name:status, rank, terms, words

墨 *Mo* Mohist

母 *mu* mother

難言 *Nan-yan* difficult-language

內業 *Nei-ye* inner discipline

能 *neng* ability

牛 *niu* ox

匹 *pi* teams

平 *ping* tranquillity

撲 *pu* simplicity

氣 *qi* breath, life-force, material force

其 *qi* its

巧 *qiao* cleverness

情 *qing* feeling-reality, feelings, feelings-reality, reality, response, reality registers, reality, reality feedback

請 *qing* language responses

取 *qu* choose, select

權 *quan* weighing

然 *ran* so

仁義 *ren-i* benevolence-morality

人心 *ren-xin* human-mind

仁政 *ren-zheng* benevolent-administration

仁 *ren* benevolence, benevolent, humane, humanity

人 *ren* human, humans, people

儒墨 *Ru-Mo* Confucian-Mohist

如 *ru* be like

儒 *Ru* Confucian

尚同 *shang-tong* agreement upward, agreement with the superior

善 *shan* good

少 *shao* few/little

神 *shen* spirits, spiritual energy

山 *shen* forest

生 *sheng* birth, birth:growth, life

聖 *sheng* divine

生命 *sheng-ming* life

事 *shi* affairs, social affairs

是 *shi* assent, is, right, that's it, this, this:right, this:right:assent:is

始 *shi* beginning

勢 *shi* charisma, circumstance, situation authority, situation, situational authority, situationalism

實 *shi* reality, stuff

士 *shi* scholar-knight

是比 *shi-bi* this-other

是非 *shi-fei* it-not it, right-wrong, this–not this, this:right–not this:wrong

述 *shu* art, method, statecraft, techniques

說 *shuo* explanation,

恕 *shu* reciprocity

私曲 *si-qu* particular-twisting, private distortions

私行 *si-xing* private behavior

俗 *su* custom

體 *ti* part, parts, unit

體兼 *ti-jian* part-whole

天 *tian* heaven, heaven:nature, natural, nature/heaven, nature, nature's

天地 *tian di* heaven-earth, the world

天道 *tian-dao* natural-way

天宮 *tianguan* heavenly pipes

天命 *tian-ming* fate, heavenly mandate, mandate of heaven, natural naming

天下 *tian xia* the world, all under Heaven

天志 *tian-zhi* natural will, natural intent

天子 *tian-zi* natural master

天主 *tianzhu* lord of heaven

同 *tong* alike, same

通 *tong* communicate

同異	*tong-i* similar-different
萬	*wan* ten thousand
萬物	*wan-wu* the myriad things
僞	*wei* artifice
謂	*wei* call
爲	*wei* deeming, deems, deems:makes, do:deem, do:deem:make:for the sake of, for-the-sake-of
爲我	*wei-wo* for me
文	*wen* language, literature, literature:decoration
我	*wo* I, I:me, myself
無名	*wu-ming* lack names
無爲	*wu-wei* non-action, lacks-deem:do, non-deeming
無欲	*wu-yu* lack desires
舞	*wu* dance
五	*wu* five
無	*wu* lack, lacking, lacks, non-being, not exist
武	*wu* martial dance, martial
物	*wu* object, objects, thing-kind, thing, thing-kinds
顯學	*Xian-xue* exposing learning
孝	*xiao* filial piety, filiality
小人	*xiaoren* lesser person, lesser man
心	*xin* heart, heart-mind
信	*xin* trust
行	*xing* conduct, perform, proceed, walk
性	*xing* nature
刑	*xing* punishment
刑名	*xing-ming* punish-name, punishment-name, shape-name
羞	*xiou* shame
虛	*xu* empty
玄	*xuan* dark
言	*yan* language, language:words, words:language:doctrine
陽氣	*yang qi* dominant ether
也	*ye* assertion particle
因是	*yin-shi* conforming *shi*-ing
又	*you* also

有　*you*　exist, have, have:being, having

有名　*you-ming*　having names

有無　*you-wu*　being-non-being

有欲　*you yu*　having desires

漁　*yu*　fish

於　*yu*　in

欲　*yu*　desires

樂　*yue*　music

喻老　*Yu-lao*　illuminating Laozi

則　*ze*　then

長　*zhang*　elder

者　*zhe*　one who, that-which

政　*zheng*　administering, coercion, governing, regulates, regulating, administrative measures

正　*zheng*　rectifies, rectify

之　*zhi*　's, it/it's, it

執　*zhi*　commit, grasp

知　*zhi*　intelligence, intuitive knowledge, know, know-how, know-how-to, know-to, knowing, knowledge

指　*zhi*　point to, point, pointing, finger-point

制　*zhi*　regulations

志　*zhi*　will

智　*zhi*　wisdom

知道　*zhi-dao*　know the way to, know-way

治亂　*zhi-luan*　order-disorder

中　*zhong*　center

衆　*zhong*　crowd

忠　*zhong*　loyalty

周　*zhou*　comprehensive

字　*zi*　character

子　*zi*　master

子女　*zi-nü*　son-daughter

自然　*ziran*　of-themselves, naturally, self-so

SELECTED BIBLIOGRAPHY

Ames, Roger. *The Art of Rulership: A Study in Ancient Chinese Political Thought*. Honolulu: University of Hawaii Press, 1983.

Ames, Roger, and David Hall. *Thinking through Confucius*. Albany: State University of New York Press, 1987.

Bao, Zhiming. "Language and World View in Ancient China." *Philosophy East and West* 40 (April 1990).

Bennett, Jonathan. *Locke, Berkeley, Hume: Central Themes*. Oxford: Clarendon Press, 1971.

Blackburn, Simon. *Spreading The Word: Groundings in the Philosophy of Language*. Oxford: Clarendon Press, 1984.

Blackburn, Simon. "Reply: Rule Following and Moral Realism." In *Wittgenstein: To Follow a Rule*. Christopher Leich, ed. London: Routledge & Kegan Paul, 1981.

Blakney, R. B., trans. *The Way of Life: Lao Tzu*. New York: Mentor, 1955.

Bodde, Derk. *Essays on Chinese Civilization*. Princeton: Princeton University Press, 1981.

Brandt, R. B. "Toward a Credible Form of Utilitarianism." In *Morality and the Language of Conduct*, Hector-Neri Casteneda and George Nakhnikian, ed. Detroit: Wayne State University Press, 1963.

Bruce, Percy. *Chu Hsi and His Masters*. London: Arthur Probsthain, 1923.

Burge, Tyler. "Mass Terms, Count Nouns, and Change." *Synthese* 31 (1975).

Capra, Fritjof. *The Tao of Physics*. New York: Bantam Books, 1975.

Carus, Paul. *The Canon of Reason and its Virtue*. Chicago: Open Court, 1913.

Ch'ien Mu. *Xianqin Zhuzi Xinian Kao*. Hong Kong: Hong Kong University Press, 1935.

———. *Zhongguo Sixiang Shi*. Hong Kong: New Asia Press, 1962.

Chai Ch'u, with Winberg Chai. *The Humanist Way in Ancient China: Essential Works of Confucianism*. New York: Bantam Books, 1965.

———. *The Story of Chinese Philosophy*. New York: Washington Square Press, 1961.

Chan Wing-tsit. *A Source Book in Chinese Philosophy*. Princeton: Princeton University Press, 1963.

———. *Neo-Confucian Terms Explained*. New York: Columbia University Press, 1986.

——— et al. *The Great Asian Religions: An Anthology*. New York, Macmillan, 1969.

Chang, Leo S., and Wang Hsiao-po. *Han Fei's Political Theory*. Monographs of the Society for Asian and Comparative Philosophy, no. 7. Honolulu: University of Hawaii Press, 1986.

Chang Shun-yi. *Mojing Jiangu Jian*. Taipei: Cheng Chung Bookshop, 1959.

Chao, Y. R., "Notes on Chinese Grammar and Logic." *Philosophy East and West* (1955).

Chaudhuri, Nirad. *Hinduism*. New York: Oxford University Press, 1979.

Chen Daji. *Mingli Luncong*. Taipei: Cheng Chung Bookshop, 1956.

Chen Ku-Ying. *Lao-Tzu: Text, Notes, and Comments*. Translated by Rhett W. Young and Roger T. Ames. San Francisco: Chinese Materials Center, 1977.

Chow Tse-tsung, ed. *Wen-lin: Studies in the Chinese Humanities*. Shatin: Chinese University of Hong Kong, 1989.

Churchland, Paul. *Scientific Realism and the Plasticity of Mind*. New York: Cambridge University Press, 1979.

Confucius. *The Analects*. Harvard Yenching Concordance Series, no. 16. Cambridge, Mass.: Harvard University Press, 1972.

Creel, Hurlee G. *Chinese Thought from Confucius to Mao Tse-tung*. Chicago: University of Chicago Press, 1953.

———. *Confucius, The Man and The Myth*. New York: J. Day, 1949.

———. *Shen Pu-hai*. Chicago: University of Chicago Press, 1974.

———. *The Origins of Statescraft in China*. Chicago: University of Chicago Press, 1970.

———. *What is Taoism?* Chicago: University of Chicago Press, 1970.

Dawson, Raymond. *Confucius*. New York: Hill and Wang, 1981.

De Bary, William Theodore. *The Message of Mind in Neo-Confucianism*. New York: Columbia University Press, 1989.

———, ed. *The Buddhist Tradition in India, China and Japan*. New York: Vintage Books, 1972.

———, et al. *Sources of Chinese Tradition*. New York: Columbia University Press, 1960.

DeFrancis, John. *The Chinese Language: Fact and Fantasy*. Honolulu: University of Hawaii Press, 1984.

———. *Visible Speech: The Diverse Oneness of Writing Systems*. Honolulu: University of Hawaii Press, 1989.

Dennett, Daniel C. *Brainstorms: Philosophical Essays on Mind and Psychology*. Cambridge, Mass.: MIT Press, 1981.

———. *Elbow Room: The Varieties of Free Will Worth Wanting*. Cambridge, Mass.: MIT Press, 1984.

Do-Dinh, Pierre. *Confucius and Chinese Humanism*. Translated by Charles Lam Markmann. New York: Funk and Wagnalls, 1969.

Donagan, Alan. *The Theory of Morality*. Chicago: University of Chicago Press, 1977.

Dubs, H. H. *Hsun-tzu: The Moulder of Ancient Confucianism*. London: Arthur Probsthain, 1927.

———. *The Works of Hsun-tzu*. London: Arthur Probsthain, 1928.

Dummett, Michael. *Truth and Other Enigmas*. Cambridge, Mass.: Harvard University Press, 1978.

Duyvendak, J. J. L. *Tao Te Ching*. London: John Murray, 1954.

Dworkin, Ronald. *Taking Rights Seriously*. Cambridge, Mass.: Harvard University Press, 1977.

Eno, Robert. *The Confucian Creation of Heaven*. Buffalo: SUNY Series in Chinese Philosophy and Culture, 1990.

———. *Masters of the Dance: The Role of T'ien in the Teachings of the Early Juism (Confucianism)*. Ann Arbor, Mich.: University Microfilms, 1984.

Fung Yu-lan. *History of Chinese Philosophy*. Translated by Derk Bodde. Princeton: Princeton University Press, 1952.

———. *A Short History of Chinese Philosophy*. Translated by Derk Bodde. New York: Macmillan, 1958.

———. *The Spirit of Chinese Philosophy*. Translated by E. R. Hughes. London: Routledge & Kegan Paul, 1947.

Fingarette, Herbert. *Confucius—The Secular as Sacred*. New York: Harper and Row, 1972.

———. "Following the 'One Thread' of the Analects." *Studies in Classical Chinese Thought* 47 (1979).

Forke, Alfred. *Lun Heng, Essays of Wang Ch'ung*. New York: Paragon Book Gallery, 1962.

Forrest, R. A. D. *The Chinese Language*. London: Faber and Faber, 1948.

Giles, Herbert A. *Chuang Tzu, Mystic, Moralist and Social Reformer*. London: Allen & Unwin, 1981.

Goldman, Alvin. *A Theory of Human Action*. Princeton: Princeton University Press, 1970.

Goldstein, Laurence. "Logic and Reasoning." *Erkenntnis* 28 (1988).

Graham, Angus. "The Background of the Mencian Theory of Human Nature." *Tsing Hua Journal of Chinese Studies* (1967).

———. *Chuang-tzu: The Inner Chapters*. London: Allen & Unwin, 1981.

———. "Chuang-tzu's Essay on Seeing Things as Equal. *History of Religions* 9 (1969–70).

———. "The Composition of the Gongsuen Long tzyy." *Asia Major* 5 (1957).

———. *Disputers of the Tao: Philosophical Argument in Ancient China*. La Salle, Ill.: Open Court, 1989.

———. *Later Mohist Logic, Ethics and Science*. Hong Kong and London: Chinese University Press, 1978.

———. "The Place of Reason in the Chinese Philosophical Tradition." In Raymond Dawson, ed. *The Legacy of China*. London: Oxford University Press, 1964.

———. *Reason and Spontaneity*. London: Curzon Press, 1985.

———. "Review of *Language and Logic in Ancient China.*" *Harvard Journal of Asian Studies* 45 (1985).

Han Feizi. (SBBY edition). Taibei: Zhonghua Shuju, 1968.

Hansen, Chad. "Ancient Chinese Theories of Language." *Journal of Chinese Philosophy* 2 (1975).

———. "Chinese Language, Chinese Philosophy, and 'Truth' " *Journal of Asian Studies* 44 (1985).

———. "Freedom and Moral Responsibility in Confucian Ethics." *Philosophy East and West* 22 (1972).

———. "Individualism in Chinese Thought." In Donald J. Munro, ed. *Individualism and Holism: Studies in Confucian and Taoist Values*. Ann Arbor: University of Michigan Press, 1985.

———. *Language and Logic in Ancient China*. Ann Arbor: University of Michigan Press, 1983.

———. "Punishment and Dignity in China." In Donald J. Munro, ed. *Individualism and Holism: Studies in Confucian and Taoist Values*. Ann Arbor: University of Michigan Press, 1985.

———. "A Tao of Tao in Chuang Tzu." In Victor Mair,, ed. *Experimental Essays on Chuang Tzu*. Honolulu: University of Hawaii Press, 1983.

Harman, Gilbert. *Change in View*. Cambridge, Mass.: MIT Press, 1986.

———. *The Nature of Morality*. New York: Oxford University Press, 1977.

Haugland, John. "Semantic Engines: An Introduction to Mind Design." *Mind Design*. Cambridge, Mass.: MIT Press, 1981.

Hayakawa, S. I. *Language in Thought and Action*. New York: Harcourt, Brace and World, 1939.

Henricks, Robert G. *Lao-tzu: Te-Tao Ching: A New Translation Based on the Recently Discovered Ma-wang-tui Texts*. New York: Ballantine Books, 1989.

Hobbes, Thomas. *Leviathan*. New York: Dutton, 1950.

Hou Wai-lu. *Zhongguo Sixiang Tongshi*. Beijing: Renmin Chuban She, 1957.

Hsiao Kung-chuan. (Mote, F. W. tr.), *A History of Chinese Political Thought*, Volume 1: *From the Beginnings to the Sixth Century A.D.* Translated by F. W. Mote. Princeton: Princeton University Press, 1979.

Hu Shih. *The Development of Logical Method in Ancient China*. New York: Paragon Press, 1969.

———. *Mingxue Jigu*. Shanghai: Commercial Press, 1923.

———. *Zhongguo Gudai Zhexue Shi*. Taipei: Commercial Press, 1968.

Hughes, E. R. *Chinese Philosophy in Classical Times*. London: J. M. Dent, 1942.

Hume, David. *A Treatise on Human Nature*. Edited by Philip Niddich. Oxford: Clarendon Press, 1983.

Ivanhoe, P. J. "Reweaving the 'One Thread' of *The Analects*." *Philosophy East and West* 40 (1990).

Kaltenmark, Max. *Lao Tzu and Taoism*. Stanford: Stanford University Press, 1965.

Kao Heng. *Laozi Zhenggu*. Reprint. Taipei: Commercial Press, 1968.

Karlgren, Bernhard. *Grammata Serica*. Taipei: Chengwen, 1966.

Kasoff, Ira E. *The Thought of Chang Tsai*. Cambridge: Cambridge University Press, 1984.

Katz, Steven T., ed. *Mysticism and Philosophical Analysis*. New York, Oxford University Press, 1978.

Kitagawa, Joseph M. *The Religious Traditions of Asia*. New York, Macmillan, 1987.

Kongzi (Confucius). *The Analects (Lun-yu)*. Taipei: Chinese Materials and Research Aids Service Center, 1972.

Kornblith, Hilary. "Beyond Foundationalism and the Coherence Theory." In *Naturalizing Epistemology*. Cambridge, Mass.: MIT Press, 1985.

Korsgaard, Christine. "Skepticism about Practical Reason." *Journal of Philosophy* 73 (1986).

Kripke, Saul. *Wittgenstein on Rules and Private Language*. Cambridge, Mass.: Harvard University Press, 1963.

Lau, D. C. *Chinese Classics: Tao Te Ching*. Hong Kong: Chinese University Press, 1982.

———, trans. *Confucius: The Analects*. New York: Penguin Books, 1979.

———, trans. "On Mencius' Use of the Method of Analogy in Argument." In *Mencius*. Baltimore: Penguin Books, 1970.

———. "Some Logical Problems in Ancient China." *Proceedings of the Aristotelian Society* n.s. 53 (1952–1953).

Leslie, Donald. *Argument by Contradiction in Pre-Buddhist Chinese Reasoning*. Canberra: Australian National University, 1964.

Lewis, David. "General Semantics." In Donald Davidson and Giblert Harmon, eds. *Semantics of Natural Language*. Dordrecht, Holland: D. Reidel, 1972.

Liang Qichao. *History of Chinese Political Thought*. London: Kegan Paul Trench Trubner, 1930.

Lyons, David. *Forms and Limits of Utilitarianism*. Oxford, Clarendon Press, 1965.

Mair, Victor, ed. *Experimental Essays on Chuang-tzu*. Honolulu: University of Hawaii Press, 1983.

———, trans. *Tao Te Ching: The Classic Book of Integrity and the Way*. New York: Bantam Books, 1990.

McDowell, John. "Non-Cognitivism and Rule-Following." In Cristopher Leich, ed. *Wittgenstein: To Follow a Rule*. London: Routledge & Kegan Paul, 1981.

Mei Y. P. *The Ethical and Political Works of Mo-tse*. London: Arthur Probsthain, 1929.

———. *Mo-tse, the Neglected Rival of Confucius*. London: Arthur Probsthain, 1934.

Mengzi (Mencius). *Harvard-Yenching Institute Sinological Index Series*. Taipei: Chinese Materials and Research Aids Service Center, 1973.

Morris, Herbert. "Persons and Punishment." *The Monist* 52 (1968).

Mote, Frederick W. *Intellectual Foundations of China*. New York: Alfred A. Knopf, 1971.

Mozi. *Harvard-Yenching Institute Sinological Index Series*. Taipei: Chinese Materials and Service Center, 1973.

Munro, Donald J. *The Concept of Man in Early China*. Stanford: Stanford University Press, 1969.

———. *Images of Human Nature: A Sung Portrait*. Princeton: Princeton University Press, 1988.

———. *Individualism and Holism: Studies in Confucian and Taoist Values*. Ann Arbor, University of Michigan Center for Chinese Studies, 1985.

Murti, T. R. V. *The Central Philosophy of Buddhism*. London: George Allen and Unwin, 1960.

Nagel, Thomas. *The View from Nowhere*. New York: Oxford University Press, 1986.

――――. *What Does It All Mean? A Very Short Introduction to Philosophy*. New York: Oxford University Press, 1987.

Needham, Joseph. *Science and Civilization in China*. Cambridge: Cambridge University Press, 1954– .

Nietzsche, Friedrich. *Twilight of the Idols and The Anti-Christ*. Translated by R. J. Hollingdale. Baltimore: Penguin Books, 1968.

Nivison, David. "Mencius and Motivation." *Studies in Classical Chinese Thought* 47 (1979).

Northrup, Filmer S. C. *The Meeting of East and West*. New York: Macmillan, 1946.

Nozick, Robert. *Philosophical Explanations*. Cambridge, Mass.: Harvard University Press, 1981.

Parfit, Derek. *Reasons and Persons*. New York: Oxford University Press, 1984.

Pears, David. *Wittgenstein*. London: Fontana Press, 1971.

Quine, W. V. O. *Ontological Relativity and Other Essays*. New York: Columbia University Press, 1969.

――――. *Word and Object*. Cambridge, Mass.: MIT Press, 1960.

Rawls, John. *A Theory of Justice*. Cambridge, Mass.: Harvard University Press, 1971.

Ricketts, Allyn W. *Guanzi: Political, Economic, and Philosophical Essays from Early China*. Princeton: Princeton University Press, 1985.

Rorty, Richard. *Philosophy and the Mirror of Nature*. Princeton: Princeton University Press, 1979.

Rosemont, Henry. "On Representing Abstractions in Chinese Thought." *Philosophy East and West* 24 (1970).

――――. "State and Society in the *Hsun Tzu*." *Monumenta Serica* 29 (1971).

Rosemont, Henry, and Benjamin Schwartz. *Studies in Classical Chinese Thought* 47 (1979).

Schwartz, Benjamin. "On the Absence of Reductionism in Chinese Thought." *Journal of Chinese Philosophy* 1 (1973).

――――. *The World of Thought in Ancient China*. Cambridge, Mass.: Harvard University Press, 1985.

Schwartz, Stephen P. *Naming, Necessity, and Natural Kinds*. Ithaca, N.Y.: Cornell University Press, 1977.

Simmons, Keith. "Ethical Realism and Anti-Realism. Unpublished manuscript. UCLA Department of Philosophy, 1987.

Smart, J. J. C., and B. Williams. *Utilitarianism: For and Against*. Cambridge: Cambridge University Press, 1973.

Smullyan, Raymond. *The Tao Is Silent*. New York: Harper and Row, 1977.

Stitch, Stephen. *The Fragmentation of Reason*. Cambridge, Mass.: MIT Press, 1990.

――――. *From Folk Psychology to Cognitive Science: The Case against Belief*. Cambridge, Mass.: MIT Press, 1983.

Tang, Jun-i. *Zhongguo Zhexue Yuanlun: Yuan Dao Pian*, vols. 1–3. Taipei: Taiwan Student Bookshop, 1975.

Thompson, P. M. *The Shen-tzu Fragments*. Oxford: Oxford University Press, 1979.

Tsuda, Sokichi. *Rongo to Koshi no shiso* (*The Analects* and Confucius' thought). Tokyo: Iwanami shoten, 1946.

Tu Wei-ming. *Confucian Thought: Selfhood as Creative Transformation*. Albany: State University of New York Press, 1985.

――――. *Humanity and Self-Cultivation: Essays in Confucian Thought*. Berkeley: Asian Humanities Press, 1979.

Tu Wei-ming and James T. C. Liu. *Traditional China*. Englewood Cliffs, N.J.: Prentice Hall, 1970.

Waley, Arthur, trans. *The Analects of Confucius*. New York: Random House, 1938.

———, trans. *Three Ways of Thought in Ancient China*. London: Allen and Unwin, 1939.

———, trans. *The Way and Its Power: A Study of the the Tao Te Ching and Its Place in Chinese Thought*. London: Allen and Unwin, 1934.

Wang Xian-qian. *Zhuangzi Jijie*. Taipei: Sanmin Bookshop, 1963.

Watson, Burton. *Chuang-tzu: Basic Writings*. New York: Columbia University Press, 1964.

———. *Han Fei-tzu: Basic Writings*. New York: Columbia University Press, 1964.

———. *Mo-tzu: Basic Writings*. New York: Columbia University Press, 1963.

Wiggins, David. "Truth, Invention, and the Meaning of Life." *Proceedings of the British Academy* 62 (1976).

Williams, Bernard. *Ethics and the End of Philosophy*. Cambridge, Mass.: Harvard University Press, 1985.

Wittgentstein, Ludwig. *The Blue and Brown Books*. Translated by Elizabeth Anscombe. New York: Harper Torchbooks, 1960.

———. *Philosophical Investigations*. Translated by Elizabeth Anscombe. Oxford: Basil Blackwell, 1953.

———. *Tractatus Logico-Philosophicus*. Translated by Elizabeth Anscombe. London: Routledge and Kegan Paul, 1961.

Wu Kang. *Lao-Zhuang Zhexue*. Taipei: Commercial Press, 1955.

Wu Yi. *Chinese Philosophical Terms*. Lanham, Md.: University Press of America, 1986.

Xunzi. *Harvard-Yenching Institute Sinological Index Series*, no. 22. Taipei: Chinese Materials and Research Aids Service Center, 1966.

Yan Lingfeng. *Daojia Sizi Xinpian*. Taipei: Commerical Press, 1968.

———. *Lao Zhaung yanjiu*. Taipei: Chung Hua Bookshop, 1966.

Yearley, Lee. "The Perfected Person in the Radical Chuang-tzu." In Victor Mair, ed., *Experimental Essays on Chuang-tzu*. Honolulu: Unviersity of Hawaii Press, 1983.

Yu Yu. *Zhongguo Mingxue*. Taipei: World Book Co., 1967.

Zhuangzi. *Harvard-Yenching Institute Sinological Index Series*, no. 20. Cambridge, Mass.: Harvard University Press, 1956.

Zimmer Heinrich. *The Philosophies of India*. Edited by Joseph Campbell. Princeton: Princeton University Press, 1951.

INDEX

Absolutism, 235, 266–68, 270, 273, 297, 310, 339, 351, 375. *See also* Daoism: absolutist interpretation; Han Feizi; Later Mohists, semantic realism; Metaphysics, realism; Xunzi; Zhuangzi

Abstraction, 17, 24, 27, 38, 46, 48, 149, 240, 244, 252, 258, 260, 327–29, 408n.51

Aesthetics, 45, 61, 74, 75, 86, 87, 92, 111, 212, 355, 387n.73. *See also* Dao$^{way:guiding\ discourse:}$ ^{performance} *dao;* Skill

Agriculturalists, 161

Alphabet, 34, 40, 44

Altruism, 97, 114, 130–31, 155, 156, 167–70, 187, 249, 331. *See also* Mozi: partial v. universal; Universality; Utilitarianism

Ames, Roger, ii, 387nn.71,73, 404n.3, 418n.20

Analects, The (of Confucius), 33, 57–60, 71, 78, 80, 82, 84–87, 92, 96, 108, 148, 153, 155, 166, 178, 204, 215, 354, 379n11, 380nn.13,20,21, 381n.22, 382n.34, 387n.75, 414n.7

Ancestor worship, 32, 371

Argument (proof), 16–19, 21–23, 33, 51–53, 70–72, 118, 126, 136–44, 186, 201, 238–40, 242, 255–59, 273, 295–98, 314–22, 379n.12. *See also* Interpretation

analogy in Mencius, 154, 188–95, 255, 395n.15

authority, argument from, 3, 9, 10, 100, 101, 107, 121–25, 132, 133, 138, 171, 181, 278, 296, 307–9, 310–12, 348–52, 355, 363, 365–67, 371, 372, 382nn.37,38, 391n.73, 393n.86, 402n.28, 411n.46, 413n.102

Mohist analysis of, 192–93, 250, 254–58, 396n.15

Aristotle, 16, 141, 180, 255–56, 287, 395n.15

Assertability (acceptability), 64–66, 69, 78, 111, 114, 116–18, 139, 143–49, 173, 185, 199, 206, 216, 239, 241–46, 250–52, 259, 281, 327, 335, 372, 391n.64, 392n.79, 393n.86, 405n.4, 407n.43

Authoritarianism

in Confucianism, 5, 278, 310, 322, 351, 355, 417n.86

Justification of, 65, 69, 89, 90, 123, 125, 171, 181, 240, 278, 310–12, 322, 351, 355, 358, 363, 371, 372, 374, 413n.6, 414n.8

Shendao's conception of, 205, 372, 419n.42

Bai-ma$^{white\ horse}$ issues, 243–47, 255, 257–59, 261, 332, 380n.19, 416n.55

Bao Zhi-ming, 387n.69

Behavior

codes of, 62–70, 80, 86–93, 102, 134, 158, 165–68, 177, 178, 184, 240, 251 316, 335, 348, 349, 354–56, 370, 386n.22, 397n.25, 415n.27

language and behavior, 19, 41, 51, 103, 114, 116–21, 146, 205, 228, 281, 410n.26

theory of, 63, 71, 78–79, 85–87, 105, 119, 149, 150, 164, 166, 185, 204–6, 249–254, 300–303, 316, 360, 383nn.43,45, 384nn.51,52,54, 398n.42, 408n.46

Bei^{perverse}, 241–42, 271, 272, 285

Being and non being, 118, 120, 146, 213, 219–26, 261, 387n.69, 402n.20

Belief

belief-desire explanation, 19, 76, 119, 142, 150, 298, 383n.43, 384nn.51,52

contrasting concepts of, 19, 41–46, 73, 75–77, 118–20, 141–47, 149, 252–53, 293, 298, 377n.8, 394n.86, 412n.101

term-belief structure, 142, 155, 176, 213, 214, 253, 407n.38

Bentham, Jeremy, 234, 415n.31

Bian$^{distinction:dispute}$, 104–8, 116–28, 143, 146, 154–56, 185, 188, 235–39, 242, 250–53, 262, 271, 280, 286, 295–96, 316, 345, 391n.60, 407n.44

Bie$^{partial:distinguish}$, 102

Blackburn, Simon, 17, 391n.59

Bloomfield, Leonard, 34–35

Brooks, Bruce, 377n.3, 379n.10

Buddhism, 14–17, 23–29, 204, 208, 225, 237–38, 373, 378n.2, 379n.9, 399n.56, 412n.94

Cause, 32, 46, 122, 174, 234–36, 240, 391n.59, 401n.12

Chan, Wing-tsit, 11, 57, 95–97, 385n.67, 391n.63

Chang^{constant}, ii, 104, 110, 114, 120, 127, 155, 166, 214–16, 218–21, 230, 235, 339, 404n.35

Cheng$^{complete:prejudice}$, 275–79, 283, 289, 300, 340, 405n.12, 411nn.63, 65

Cheng^{sincerity}, 405n.12

Chinese language. *See* Language

Chomsky, N., 91

Ci^{phrase}, 45, 185, 239, 241, 244, 249–51, 378n.8, 389n.30

Coercion, 64, 354–56, 368–69, 376, 414n.7. *See also* Confucius: punishment and law, *Fa*^{standards}; *Zheng*$^{government:regulation}$

Coherence
  in Chinese thought, 27, 143, 170, 218, 221–22,
    227, 243, 247–51, 256, 259, 266, 270–71,
    274, 385n.67, 396n.20, 409n.3
  in interpretive theory, 7, 8, 26–28, 70, 88,
    197–200, 204, 221, 227–28, 257, 266–67,
    336, 349, 366, 381n.22, 399n.5. *See also*
    Interpretation: humanity, principle of
Computer analogy of mind, 18–25, 91, 105, 301,
    303, 377n.8, 416n.61
  programming and language, 19–21, 24, 51, 53,
    64, 75, 91, 101–8, 115–26, 177, 183–88,
    212, 224, 253, 292, 330, 336–37
Conceptualism, absence of, 11, 16–29, 33, 38–
    46, 75–76, 85, 111, 142, 148–50, 235, 239,
    244, 329, 383n.49
Confucian school (*Ru*Confucianism), 3–7, 9–16, 23–
    32, 57–68, 73–75, 92–96, 107–15, 128–38,
    153–59, 163, 172, 178–80, 187, 195, 200–
    205, 233, 241, 264–67, 281, 307–15, 345–
    61, 368–70, 378nn.4,8, 379nn.4,10, 12,
    380nn.16,20, 21, 381nn.22,23,31, 394n.5,
    396nn.15,16, 399n.53,54. *See also*
    Confucius; Mencius; Neo-Confucianism;
    Xunzi
Confucius (Kongzi), 11–13, 32, 57–64, 153–61,
    202, 204, 210, 233, 266, 311, 340, 345. *See
    also Analects, The*
  dao prescriptive discourse, 20, 82–87, 102, 104, 106,
    130, 138, 205, 217, 321, 323
  educational theory, 2, 20, 57–78, 91–92, 101–
    4, 133, 175, 209, 351–54, 383nn.43,44,
    384n.55, 385n.64, 386n.68, 392n.81,82,
    419n.20
  human nature, 20, 57–87, 130, 132, 136, 164,
    167, 172, 174, 362, 383n.49, 384nn.50,52,
    391n.67
  interpretive and textual problems, 57–60, 82,
    87, 201, 379nn.5,11, 380nn.13,20,21,
    381nn.22,23, 382nn.34,35, 385n.67, 394n.5
  intuition, 59, 68–71, 73, 74, 80, 81, 87, 88,
    89–93, 234, 383n.49
  language, 74–75, 82–92, 102, 103, 115, 128,
    140, 212, 216, 294, 321, 379n.8, 382n.37,
    387n.75, 391n.60, 393n.86, 404n.39
  model emulation, 63, 64, 67–74, 80, 102, 138,
    161, 212, 338, 363
  morality (hypertraditionalism), 52–62, 75–78,
    81–85, 95–97, 107–9, 115, 129, 133, 149,
    165, 189, 234, 323, 353–56, 382n.32,
    385nn.62,63,64, 385nn.67,68, 388n.14,
    389nn.35,36,37, 390nn.45,48
  music and poetry, 20, 36, 45, 52–53, 58, 66–
    68, 85–87, 105, 136–38, 155, 177,
    387nn.71,73, 404n.39
  political theory, 58–71, 122, 133–35, 338,
    356, 359, 363, 381n.25, 386n.68, 391n.69,
    399nn.53,54, 401n.10, 413nn.6,7
  punishment and law, 63–74, 132, 307, 349,
    352, 354–58, 367, 384n.53, 413n.7,
    417n.86, 418n.20
  rectifying names, 64–70, 122, 134–35, 149,

    184, 241–47, 249, 257–58, 382n.35,
    387nn.71,75, 408n.46, 414n.22, 415nn.32,44
  *ren*humanity and *li*ritual, 59, 62, 68–73, 78–81,
    83, 86–90, 87–94, 126, 166, 177, 184, 316–
    17, 340, 355, 381n.23, 383nn.41,42,
    383nn.49,50, 384n.55, 385n.68, 388n.8,
    392n.81, 420n.65
Constancy. *See also* Reliabilism
  of dao or names, 4–5, 42, 52, 93, 96, 100–
    104, 109–12, 114–17, 119–23, 127–29,
    135, 138, 143–46, 155, 156, 163, 166, 173,
    205, 210, 215–59, 269, 271, 296–99, 311,
    319, 339, 342, 348, 360, 375, 404nn.35,39,
    406n.16
  and *truth*, 93, 100, 110, 114, 139, 235, 250,
    407n.37
Contradiction. *See also* Coherence; Truth
  in Chinese thought, 59, 113, 200, 201, 215,
    225, 259, 260, 380nn.13,20, 399n.5,
    414n.12
  classical Chinese concept of, 255, 402n.29,
    406n.20
Convention
  and language, 3–5, 18, 23–26, 28, 34, 38–39,
    40–42, 51–53, 61, 65, 68, 72, 74–5, 79, 85,
    89, 94, 101, 105, 127, 130–32, 136, 143–
    47, 157, 163, 170, 203, 204, 211–29, 233–
    35, 238–48, 254, 261–63, 272–78, 280–86,
    300, 307–42, 348–50, 366–67, 373–75,
    382n.37, 406n.14, 414nn.9,20. *See also
    individual philosophers*
  morality (Confucianism), 4, 82, 97, 100, 109,
    113, 140, 163–66, 170, 174, 222, 223, 233–
    35, 310–16, 322, 336–37, 348, 356, 367,
    383n.41, 385n.62, 386n.68, 389n.35,
    416n.66, 417n.91. *See also individual
    philosophers*
  and truth, 18, 75, 86, 139, 140–47, 180, 198–
    99, 235
Count nouns, 46–49, 72, 245, 259, 329, 379n.12
Cultivation, theory of. *See also* Culture and
    enculturation
  Daoism, 195, 212, 278–79, 289
  early Confucians, 57, 59, 65, 68, 71, 80
  Han Feizi, 348, 360, 366
  Mencius, 158–60, 163–68, 173–77, 180–82,
    185–88, 194–95, 278–79, 289, 397n.26,
    398n.41
  Mozi, 96, 100–106, 110, 113–18, 122, 129,
    136–40
  Xunzi, 308–12, 315, 326
Culture and enculturation, 35, 73, 76, 78, 91,
    100, 102, 108, 119, 120, 138, 164, 211,
    213, 229, 375, 385n.61. *See also* Computer
    analogy of mind; Language

*Dang*hits on, 240, 316
*Dao*way:guiding discourse
  Confucian (conventionalist), 59, 60, 62, 63,
    68–71, 78, 80–89, 91–93, 308–43, 345–61,
    382n.32, 389n.37, 414n.9
  Confucian (innate or intuitive), 153–55, 156,

157, 159, 160, 162, 165, 166, 169–78, 180,
183–86, 187, 195, 381n.29, 385n.64,
386n.67, 387nn.69,75, 391n.67, 415n.33
Daoist, 201–30, 266–71, 273–75, 279, 281–
92, 293–303, 395n.9, 404n.39, 408n.57,
409n.6
discourse *dao*, 84, 205, 209–10, 222, 268,
335, 401n.13, 412n.90
Laozi's negative dao, 127, 222–30, 240, 342,
351, 360, 371–73
meaning and translation, 13, 19, 27, 84, 103–
6, 111–15, 139, 203–11, 215, 218, 222–23,
230, 235, 268, 292, 296, 328, 330, 346,
371–73, 383n.46, 392n.85, 401n.12,
402nn.25,26,28, 415n.27
metaphysical, 27, 38, 114, 139, 172–73, 203–
11, 215, 218–30, 235, 262–72, 282, 285,
287–92, 296, 310, 346, 371–73, 400n.7,
401n.11, 402n.20
Mohist (utilitarian), 4, 89, 96, 100–119, 120–
23, 137–42, 146, 149, 166, 178, 205, 208–
9, 248, 252, 323, 390n.48, 401n.13,
407n.42, 416n.73
moral, 82–83, 106–9, 112–13, 159, 162, 173,
178, 268, 389n.36, 390n.49, 396n.22,
411n.47, 417n.86
and names, 3–4, 20, 68, 104–6, 116–18, 128,
176, 209, 215–18, 239–41, 247, 251, 268,
271, 322–23, 330, 348, 402n.20, 408n.57,
409n.6, 412n.90, 415n.32
other, 69, 88, 102, 109, 127, 155–57, 208–9,
225, 227, 297, 351, 370, 374, 399n.48,
419n.42, 420n.70
performance *dao*, 4, 73, 84–86, 104–5, 111,
117, 140, 176–77, 184, 205–9, 239, 268,
326, 330, 354–55, 379n.4, 308n.16,
383n.45,49,50, 396n.14, 402n.30
Daode-Jing, 212, 223, 238, 373, 379n.9,
381nn.22, 401n.8, 402n.23, 403n.32,
404nn.38,39
Daoism, 2–7, 10–15, 20–28, 32, 50, 53, 90–96,
110, 120–25, 137–38, 155–57, 180–81,
192–95, 239–41, 251, 257–64, 308–21,
331–34, 339–52, 358–61, 365, 371–76,
378n.2, 391nn.67,73, 402n.29. *See also*
Laozi; Zhuangzi
absolutist interpretation, 236, 272, 279, 285,
287, 291, 297
and authoritarianism, 195, 266–68, 272–74,
279, 287, 297, 310, 322, 340–45, 351, 370–
76, 402n.23, 413n.4
mature v. proto-Daoism, 163, 176–77, 195,
204, 230, 266, 342, 395nn.9,14,
401nn.10,11, 409n.6
primitivist version, 229–30, 235–36, 242, 272,
333, 404nn.39,40, 418n.85
De[virtuosity], 19–20, 61–64, 71, 78, 91–92, 103–8,
122, 140, 177, 184, 300, 348, 383n.44,
413n.103
Death, 32, 127, 156, 276, 279, 294, 300, 334
DeFrancis, John, 34–38
Desire, 19, 124, 167, 181–82, 211–23, 235,

314–316, 335–337, 364–66, 404n.35. *See
also* Belief, belief-desire explanation
Determinism
causal or logical (Fatalism), 98, 122, 207, 209,
211
linguistic, 25, 39, 42, 45–46, 65, 69, 85, 102,
117, 122, 128, 142, 149, 166, 240–42, 281,
314, 375
Discourse, 31, 120, 133–34, 163, 222, 243, 249,
253, 261, 347–50, 361, 366–67, 412n.77,
414nn.9,22. *See also Dao*[way:guiding discourse]
Distinction, 20–21, 24–25, 27, 48–53, 90, 92,
103–5, 115–37, 141–43, 147–50, 153–55,
158–66, 170–87, 204–6, 211–49, 253–55,
260–81, 283–96, 312–60, 366–67, 369–71,
372–73, 405n.9, 406n.16, 409n.59,
410nn.26,31, 411n.47, 414nn.9,22,
415nn.27,31. *See also Bian*[distinction:dispute]
Duke of Zhou, 58, 61, 381n.23
Duty. *See* Ought, absence of concept of; Rights,
absence of concept of

Economic thought, 99, 158, 160, 174, 194, 310,
313–15, 334, 388n.4. *See also individual
philosophers*
Education. *See also* Culture and enculturation
Confucius' theory of. *See* Confucius:
educational theory
Daoist views of, 212, 224
general Chinese concept of, 57–59, 78, 91–92,
138, 164, 184, 392n.81
Mencius' theory of, 170, 186
Mencius v. Xunzi on, 313, 321
Mohist and later Mohists on, 100–108, 115–19,
122, 126, 129, 133–34, 138, 391n.58,
397n.25
other theories, 351–52, 357, 360–61
Egoism
ethical, 8, 97, 155–57, 162, 181, 208–9, 240,
297
psychological, 64, 76, 79, 132–33, 150, 167–
68, 178–81, 208–9, 336, 384n.52, 389n.41,
395n.12, 398n.32, 417n.84
Emotion, 18–28, 40–45, 52, 87–89, 101, 114,
119, 129, 135–37, 164–74, 182, 236, 254,
276, 280, 285, 317–19, 325–26, 333–36,
341, 383n.47, 404n.39. *See also* Desire;
Yu[desire]
Empiricism
in Chinese thought, 145, 326, 330, 373–74
Western influence on interpretive theory, 7–11,
14, 37–40, 239, 326–40, 383n.47
Eno, Robert, 57–58, 99, 308, 378nn.5,6,
379nn.4,10, 380n.16, 383n.45, 387n.71,
396n.17, 397n.23, 399n.51, 401n.10,
414n.14
Epistemology
Chinese, 4, 51–52, 73–78, 81, 85–87, 91–95,
110–11, 119, 142–44, 181, 186, 207, 223–
29, 252–54, 265–74, 284–301, 316–19,
325–41, 370–76

Epistemology (*continued*)
Western, 8–9, 15–28, 43, 85, 104–5, 139, 142–46, 236–38, 298
Ethics. *See* Egoism; Etiquette; Individualism, ethical; Law
Etiquette, 71, 83, 85, 100, 171, 179, 386n.69. *See also Li*ritual
Euclidean model of reasoning, 13, 19, 53, 70, 139–42, 238, 320
Evaluation. *See* Mozi, fact and value; Ought, absence of concept of; Zhuangzi: fact and value
Experience, lack of subjective concept of, 16–28, 33–38, 52–53, 75–77, 85, 94, 208, 226–30, 252, 269–70, 284, 287–88, 292–96, 300–302, 330, 410n.25
*Fa*standards, 13, 158, 160, 307–8, 317–19, 322, 345–52, 358–59, 364–74, 386n.67, 390n.48, 391n.62, 392nn.79, 86, 392n.86, 396n.15, 401n.12, 407nn.43,44, 415n.27, 418nn.9,10,13,19, 419n.24
*Fajia*standardizers, 13, 161, 313, 345–47, 353, 397n.22, 418n.9. *See also* Han Feizi, Legalist, Shang Yang, Shen Buhai, Shendao
Falsity, concept of, 16, 146, 213, 241, 320. *See also* Truth
Feelings. *See* Desire; Emotion; *Qing*reality response; *Yu*desire
*Fei*not this:wrong, 67–68, 72, 103–6, 108, 128, 133–35, 215, 242, 250, 271, 279–300, 360–61, 401n.22. *See also Shi*this:right and *Shi-fei*right:wrong
*Fen*divisions, 316
Fingarette, Herbert, 71, 76–77, 81–83, 379n.12, 382n.37, 383nn.41,49,50, 384n.55, 385nn.67,68, 388n.7, 389n.37, 391n.60
Flux, theory of, 11–12, 16, 27, 46–51, 110–11, 216–19, 225–26, 229, 247, 278–82, 296, 328–31, 361, 366–71, 379n.10, 403n.31, 415n.50. *See also Chang*constant; Constancy
Fung Yu-lan, 388n.6, 390n.42, 419n.27

Gaozi (Kao Tzu) 183–85, 187, 189–93, 398n.31
Golden rule, Confucius' negative, 88, 100, 386n.67
Gongsun Long, 49, 233, 257–61, 271, 283, 319, 332, 408nn.49,50,51,52
Graham, Angus, 1–3, 8, 11, 23, 28, 36, 45, 48, 88, 98–100, 125, 145, 155, 156 188–94, 202, 233, 236–39, 247, 248, 257, 260, 261, 264, 265, 269, 270–72, 274, 276, 286, 289, 295, 328, 332, 344, 345, 371, 377n.1, 378nn.2,8, 379n.9, 388nn.5,15, 390n.56, 391n.64, 392nn.74,83,86, 394nn.5,9,11,12,13, 396n.15, 397n.23, 402nn.29,30, 403n.35, 404nn.39,40, 405nn.9,10,11,12,13,14, 406n.15,20,22, 407nn.39,42, 408nn.47,48,49,51,53,55, 409nn.3,15,17, 410nn.19,25,27,34, 411n.46,49,55,63, 412nn.81,86,102, 416nn.61,66, 418n.9, 420n.70
Grammar

case, 42–43, 215–17, 256
complex noun phrases, 4, 45, 239, 244–59, 271, 327, 405n.51
influence on theory of language, 16–51, 76, 83–84, 105, 142, 213–19, 245, 256, 329, 407n.33
nouns, mass, and count, 46–50, 84, 146, 206, 215, 243–46, 259, 329, 379nn.10,11,12, 387n.69
subject-predicate structure, 16, 21, 27, 42–52, 142, 219, 256, 294–95, 329–30, 382n.35, 390n.55, 391n.69
tense, 42
use of nouns as verbs, 8–9, 43, 45–46, 49, 84–85, 105, 116, 122, 142, 213, 215, 256, 349, 382n.35
Greek thought, 5, 13–30, 47–50, 59, 63, 70, 85, 87, 93, 119, 139, 141, 147, 157, 167, 180, 204, 218–21, 228, 253, 256, 329–30
*Gu*inherent, 238–40, 254, 405nn.12,13,14, 407n.43
Guanzi, 347–48, 357–59, 364, 366, 371, 418n.10, 419n.24, 420n.70
Guilt, v. shame, 164–71, 331, 352–54, 385n.62, 397n.29

*Hai*harm, 97, 108–9, 113–31, 187, 234, 253–55, 317, 331, 352–54
Hall, David, 387n.73, 404n.3
Han Feizi, 194, 380n.20, 401n.12, 417n.4, 418n.10, 419n.42, 420n.67. *See also Fa*standards
  daoism, interpretation of, 360, 370–76
  influences on, 344, 347–48, 357–59, 364, 369, 371–72
  intuition, 348, 350–56, 360–68, 372
  language and interpretation, 349–56, 370
  political theory, 350–51, 354, 357–71
  tradition and *li*ritual, 351, 355
Hard-white, 49, 246–47, 257–59, 327, 408n.49
Heart-mind, 16–20, 22–28, 52–54, 75–78, 80, 101–6, 138–43, 160–68, 170–88, 194–95, 213, 226–28, 239, 263, 274–80, 298, 301, 315, 320, 324–27, 332–43, 351–55, 361, 373. *See also* Mencius; *Xin*heart-mind; Xunzi
  authoritarian theory of, 171, 179–81, 226, 248, 278–79, 324, 332–43, 352–55, 420n.70
  computer analogy of, 18–25, 28, 34, 37, 51, 91, 105–6, 142, 187, 198, 276, 288, 300–303, 377n.8, 416n.61
Heaven or nature, 21, 32, 63, 71, 84, 100–101, 109, 120–38, 153–88, 191–96, 205, 207, 239–48, 261–63, 274–85, 310–23, 348, 378n.6, 381n.27, 390n.55,56, 391nn.69,73, 410n.27, 411nn.46,47, 414n.12. *See also Tian*nature:heaven
Heraclitus, 47, 50, 201, 218
Hierarchy, social assumption, 53, 61–72, 102–3, 124, 130–49, 165, 166, 315, 318, 340, 362, 401n.10, 413n.6, 414n.12
Hsiao, K. C., 61, 381n.24, 419n.23
Huang-Lao School, 222, 225, 310, 360, 371, 373, 400nn.6,7, 402nn.23,25, 403nn.33,34,35,36
Hui Shi, 242, 257, 261–63, 267, 270–71, 280,

291, 318, 324, 327, 331, 408n.58,
   409nn.3,17, 410n.19
Hume, David, 109, 119–21, 164, 182, 254, 285,
   329, 391n.59, 397n.27
Hu Shih, 110, 388n.5, 399n.48, 409n.59

Idea theory of meaning, 14–19, 22–26, 75–76,
   85, 111, 119, 142, 244, 292, 298
   absence of in China, 25–26, 38–44, 53, 76,
      85, 120, 142–50, 235–39, 244, 293, 329,
      417n.5
Indian philosophy, 14–33, 41–47, 53, 63, 85,
   139, 141, 149–50, 172, 203–4, 213–19,
   225–28, 237–38, 256, 267, 328–29, 377n.6,
   404n.38
Individualism
   ethical, 62, 70, 108, 135, 147, 297, 353, 356,
      384nn.53,54, 385n.62, 389n.37, 392n.75,
      395n.12, 415n.33
   metaphysical or methodological, 17–18, 38–40,
      47, 50–53, 75–78, 85, 94, 108, 132, 135,
      206, 243–45, 320, 326–30, 415n.50
Innatism, in Confucianism, 4, 11–15, 21, 51, 59,
   63–64, 69–71, 79–83, 87–92, 101, 108,
   118–21, 153–57, 164–94, 201–6, 210, 229–
   35, 266, 270, 278, 280, 288, 300–301, 308–
   9, 313, 320, 331, 336–42, 348, 355,
   380n.16, 382n.34, 386n.67, 387n.74,
   408n.45. *See also* Mencius
Interpretation
   charity, principle of, 10, 132, 150, 199–200,
      223, 227, 310, 390n.55, 392n.86, 394n.5,
      399n.3
   classical Chinese theories of, 4–5, 24, 38, 52–
      53, 59, 64–93, 101, 105–25, 133–34, 138,
      141, 159, 163–68, 173, 177, 184, 203–6,
      216–18, 233–34, 239, 241, 247–52, 265–
      66, 276–77, 293–98, 317–19, 338–42, 348–
      58, 361–67, 370–73, 382n.36, 385n.67,
      389n.34, 390nn.44,47,48, 391n.86, 396n.22,
      398n.41, 412n.90, 414n.9
   humanity, principle of, 10, 11, 88, 199, 200,
      227, 267, 268
   methodology of, 2–29, 37–38, 43–49, 60, 176,
      183, 196–204, 210–22, 228–29, 236, 260,
      265–71, 302, 310, 337, 348–50, 379n.10,
      380n.21, 381n.22, 382n.35, 385n.57,
      391n.86, 399nn.3,5, 401n.12, 403nn.32,35,
      417n.84
   ruling theory of, 1–2, 5–19, 22, 27–29, 50,
      96–97, 143–44, 153–58, 169–72, 186–91,
      195, 200–203, 207, 215, 220, 225–29, 259–
      60, 264–72, 283, 287–88, 302, 307–10,
      337, 345–47, 350, 361–62, 371, 380n.21,
      381n.27, 382n.35, 385n.67, 386n.68,
      390nn.42,56, 391nn.69,86, 394n.5,
      395n.11,12, 397n.25, 402nn.25,28,
      403nn.32,35, 404n.39, 408n.51, 409n.15
Intuition, Chinese (practical) v. Western
   (cognitive), 1–4, 12, 19–23, 40, 43, 51, 97,
   100, 106–12, 126–27, 135, 145, 200, 241,
   264–72, 277–79, 289, 298, 300–303,

378n.7, 383n.43, 387n.74, 414n.24. *See also*
   Confucius; Han Feizi; Mencius; Xunzi
Ionian Philosophy, 16, 218–19, 329

Japan, 30
Japanese, 38
Jian[whole:universal], 102, 245, 248, 405n.13
Junzi[gentleman:superior man], 312, 317, 319, 322, 333,
   342, 368
Justice, 70, 114, 310, 314, 387n.74

Kantian theory, comparisons, 27, 89, 109, 120,
   123, 141, 165–66, 254, 284, 298, 326, 353,
   358, 389n.37, 415n.33
Kapok, 220, 283, 292, 407n.34, 411n.65
Ke[admissible], 96, 110, 207, 215–16, 235–38, 246,
   259, 281, 327, 334–35
Knowledge
   Chinese definitions of, 43, 85–90, 123–28,
      172–78, 204–11, 217–25, 252–55, 275–
      303, 313, 334, 340–43. *See also Zhi*[know-to]
   practical v. propositional, 43–45, 73, 117–20,
      139–50, 252–56, 293, 298, 406n.16,
      408n.45,46, 419n.27
   skepticism and the Chinese concept of, 16, 26–
      27, 66–68, 223–29, 284–87, 292–98, 324–
      27, 341
Kornblith, Hilary, 19, 377n.7
Kripke, Saul A., 5, 389n.38, 407n.42, 412n.90

Language
   Cantonese, 41–42
   Chinese characters, 9, 13, 24, 31–46, 75–78,
      378n.3, 393n.86, 407nn.33,42,43,44
   Chinese dialects, 33, 41–44, 153, 402n.22
   Chinese theories of, 7, 25, 33–57. *See also
      individual philosophers*
   community nature of, 4, 12, 21, 34–42, 50–59,
      62–78, 82, 85, 100–110, 114, 116, 121–28,
      139, 144–49, 171–73, 199, 206–18, 224,
      227, 234, 240, 249, 251, 254, 260, 266,
      267, 280, 308, 322–35, 379, 384n.51,
      390n.52, 391n.59, 393n.86, 394nn.87,88,
      397n.25, 405n.4, 414n.22, 417n.85
   contrast theory of, 211–26, 274, 339, 391n.60.
      See also Bian[distinction:dispute]; Distinction;
      Shi[this:right] and *Shi-fei*[right:wrong]
   declarative function of, 3–4, 16, 23–25, 31,
      37–39, 51–52, 85–86, 103–4, 116, 126,
      139–42, 203, 251, 256–58, 298–300, 326,
      340–42, 384n.51, 386n.68, 387n.76,
      389n.31
   definitions, 13, 20, 67–70, 83, 139–48,
      383n.40, 408n.54
   English, 7–9, 33–51, 82–84, 143, 213–16,
      237–39, 241–46, 252, 271, 349, 387n.72,
      389n.35, 392n.85, 402n.28, 407nn.34,37
   function of, 3–4, 40–42, 51–57, 74–78, 103,
      116, 146–49, 202–3, 234, 280–81, 314–19,
      326–28, 334–35, 382n.37, 396n.22,
      406n.14, 416n.61

Language (*continued*)
  indexicals, 211, 243, 262, 270, 282–86, 291,
    300, 338, 406n.22, 411n.55
  Indo-European v. Chinese, 14–19, 25–30, 33–
    54, 74–75, 85, 93, 139–41, 149–50, 203,
    218, 228, 237, 256, 258, 298, 329, 378n.2
  inflection, 21, 42–46, 256, 407n.33
  phonemics or phonetics, 24, 34–37, 41–45,
    378n.2
  picture theory of, 3–4, 16, 19–21, 24, 37–38,
    53, 105–6, 118, 148, 281, 326. *See also*
    Language, declarative function
  prescriptive function of, 21, 51–52, 103, 115–
    16, 141, 206–10, 215–16, 248, 256, 283,
    350–52, 387n.69, 389n.31, 415n.44. *See
    also* Language, function of
  sentences and sententials, absence of, 2–4, 16–
    21, 40–53, 75–76, 93, 103–6, 115–17, 122,
    126, 139–49, 235, 239–41, 251–56, 298,
    323, 326, 349–50, 378n.8, 389n.30,
    390n.52, 402n.29, 405nn.4,9, 406n.20,
    407n.33, 415n.44
  skepticism of, 4, 16, 40, 51, 92–3, 218–27,
    235, 272, 284–85, 292–96, 329, 372,
    387n.75, 396n.22, 399n.48, 402n.23,
    404nn.38,39
  theory of. *See individual authors;* Interpretation;
    classical Chinese theories of; Semantics
  tonality, 33, 40–41, 384n.51, 402n.22
  transmission of, 41, 57–80, 104–8, 172, 185,
    233, 288, 316, 319–21, 355–56, 370,
    382n.32, 414n.9, 420n.67
Laozi
  being and non-being, 219–24, 261, 332
  constancy and inconstancy, 216–30, 254
  on desire, 212–14, 217, 220–22, 235, 271,
    315, 331–34
  influences, 233, 254, 269, 331–34, 360, 371,
    401n.12, 411n.55
  interpretation problems, 10, 26–27, 195–204,
    208–10, 225, 228, 269, 360, 371–73,
    404n.39, 409n.16
  on knowledge, negative and mystical, 127,
    206–11, 219, 223–26, 230, 254, 342, 351,
    357, 360, 370–74
  life and historicity, 210–11
  meaning of *dao*^way in, 12–15, 96, 103–10, 195,
    204–8, 401n.11, 402n.20
  political theory, 203–4, 223–26, 322, 360,
    371, 400n.6, 402n.23, 413n.6
  primitive Daoism in, 195, 202–3, 209, 227–30,
    235–42, 263–67, 272–74, 285, 321, 333
  reversal of opposites, 18, 211, 222–26, 230,
    235, 242, 283, 294, 339, 361
  on sensation, 226
  text author, 200–204. *See also* Daode-Jing
  theory of language, 211–22, 254, 271, 274,
    404n.39
  wu-wei^non-action slogan, 213–14, 223, 230, 294,
    302, 359, 363
Later Mohists. *See also* Mohism
  bian^distinction, 235–39, 242, 250–53, 262

compound terms, 49, 239, 244–59, 263, 327,
    330, 378n.8, 405n.9
  epistemology, 252–54, 321, 405n.14,
    407nn.39,42, 408nn.46,51
  ethics, 247–49, 392n.75
  logic, 190–93, 238, 249–51, 254–57, 389n.30,
    396n.15
  pragmatic focus, 233, 238–42, 410n.26,
    415n.44
  rectifying names, 241, 243, 247, 249–51, 256–
    57
  semantic realism, 233–35, 239–43, 247–49,
    251–56, 391n.61, 402n.29, 406nn.16,22,23,
    407n.38, 409n.15
  textual problems, 235–38
  Ti^part and *jian*^whole, 50, 240–48, 262–63, 328,
    409n.60
  white horse paradox, 243–47, 250, 258–59,
    327, 408n.51
  Xunzi, relation to, 308, 313, 317, 323, 332,
    342, 415n.44, 416n.56
  Zhuangzi relation to, 271, 264, 267, 270, 281
Law. *See also Fa*^standards
  advocacy in, 53, 59
  Confucian opposition to, 59, 61, 64–65, 74,
    134, 354–56, 381n.31, 414n.7
  interpretive problem, 64–65, 355, 396n.22
  morality and, 65, 346, 350, 355–56, 382n.38,
    384n.53, 401n.12, 414n.7, 420n.65
  and punishment, 61, 64–65, 132–34, 346,
    349–60, 367–69, 376
  scientific or natural, 61, 122, 132–33, 247,
    346, 349–50, 387n.76, 419n.22
  syntactic notion, absence of, 356, 349–50, 354,
    356, 418nn.9,10
  Western theory of, 65, 69, 133–34, 346, 349–
    58, 364, 367, 369–70, 382nn.37,38,
    418n.19, 420n.65
Lei^similarity, 240–43, 317–20, 406n.30, 415n.27,
    418n.13
Legalist, 3–7, 11, 13, 28, 308, 313, 344–48,
    356–58, 365, 368–69, 376, 396n.19,
    418n.9, 419nn.24,27,29,47. *See also
    Fajia*^standardizers; Guanzi; Han Feizi; Shang
    Yang; Shen Buhai
Leibniz, Gottfried Wilhelm, 166
Lewis, David, 377n.11, 383n.40
Li^benefit, 13, 36, 97, 108, 113–22, 131–35, 159,
    170, 248, 254, 307, 321, 361, 371, 373. *See
    also Hai*^harm
Li^guiding tendency, 373–74
Li^ritual, 36. *See also* Convention
  Confucius on, 58–59, 62–93, 378n.4,
    383nn.43,45, 384n.52, 386nn.58,67, 392n.81
  Daoism on, 205–6, 294
  Han Feizi on, 344, 348, 350, 354, 355, 357,
    361, 366, 370, 372–73
  Mencius on, 153, 155, 163–66, 171–74, 177–
    80, 184, 185, 187, 396n.17
  Mozi on, 97, 101, 129, 131, 136, 258, 389n.35
  Xunzi on, 309, 311–18, 337–39, 415n.27
Lisi, 308, 344, 350

Literature. *See Wen*literature
Locke, John, 132, 239
Logic
  Chinese logic, 7–9, 96, 118–20, 138, 186,
    233, 238, 242, 246, 250–60, 275
  Daoism and logic, 119, 202, 220, 265, 267,
    270, 273, 275–76, 279, 280, 286, 404n.39,
    410n.31
  excluded middle, law of, 242, 291
  in language analysis and interpretation, 8–10,
    17–19, 34, 37–39, 42–44, 49, 57, 69, 75,
    88, 143, 198–201, 216, 260, 270, 276
  Mencius' use of analogy, 158, 169, 174–76,
    181, 188–93, 255, 308, 395nn.15,16
  Western models of, 16–19, 141–43, 250, 298,
    326, 387n.76, 405n.4
Lu Xiangshan, 380n.16

Mair, Victor, 378n.2
Mandarin, 41, 42, 155
Mandate of heaven, 32, 58, 61–63, 122, 131,
    159, 161–62, 194, 311–13, 386n.67,
    391n.69
Mass nouns, 46–49, 146, 245–46, 259, 379n.10,
    415n.50
Mathematics, 34, 37, 120, 196–98, 302. *See also*
    Euclidean model of reasoning; Logic
Meaning
  intensional concept of, absence in China, 35–
    40, 75–78, 85, 114–17, 143–48, 235–38,
    244–47, 258–59, 324–30, 384n.50. *See also*
    Conceptualism, absence of; Idea, theory of
    meaning
  meaning-change hypotheses, 8–10, 13–15, 28,
    45–46, 76, 96, 189–90, 201–8, 215–17,
    252, 260, 276, 346–50, 378n.8, 390n.55,
    392n.85, 406n.14
  problems of. *See* Interpretation
  Western theory contrasts, 8, 16–19, 39–40, 45,
    76, 85, 139, 244, 329, 348, 383n.47,
    394n.87
Measurement, 47–48, 99–103, 109, 120–24,
    135–38, 145, 158, 176, 186–87, 234–35,
    243–44, 247–48, 255, 292, 299, 330, 342,
    347–49, 359, 362, 364–67, 374, 407n.43,
    415n.30, 418n.10, 419n.24. *See also*
    *Fa*standards
Mencius (Mengzi)
  heart-mind, theory of, 79, 153–95, 203, 208,
    229, 248, 278, 339, 342–43, 398n.37,
    420n.70
  historical influence, 71, 97, 153–63, 169, 172,
    189–90, 193–94, 308–9, 390n.48,
    395nn.11,16, 397nn.23,25, 397n.31,
    398n.41, 398nn.33,41, 399n.56, 408n.46,
    413n.4
  innatism and intuitionism, 154–59, 170–88,
    193, 195, 205, 380nn.16,21,22, 385n.58,
    398n.31, 415n.30, 420n.70
  language, view of, 154–55, 157, 161, 163,
    173, 183–88, 190, 195, 382n.34, 390n.44,
    396n.22, 408n.50

life, 153–57
logic. *See* Logic, Mencius' use of analogy
mission, 157–62
moral psychology, 162–88, 194, 391n.64,
    397n.27, 399n.53, 417n.83
normative theory, lack of, 129, 153–54, 162–
    63, 168–74, 176–88, 194, 386n.67,
    396n.22, 397nn.27,31, 398nn.33,41,
    399n.56
plant analogy, the, 174–79, 397n.26
political theory, 157–60, 174, 194, 391n.69,
    398n.42, 413n.6
Merit, employment/rule by, 63, 68, 101, 131,
    134, 161, 209, 223, 322, 364, 381n.29,
    382n.35
Metaphysics, 5, 13, 15–18, 27, 38, 46, 51, 53,
    61, 81, 83, 85, 86, 104, 105, 111, 139, 156,
    175, 186, 187, 203, 206, 207, 209, 211,
    215, 216, 218–20, 222–28, 230, 235, 239,
    242–46, 246, 252, 260, 261, 268, 295–97,
    313, 328, 329, 330, 346, 371–73, 386n.69,
    397n.23
abstract objects. *See* Abstraction
mind-body distinction, absence of, 16–19, 52,
    384nn.50,51, 396n.11. *See also* Belief;
    Computer analogy of mind; Desire; Heart-
    mind; Idea theory of meaning
monism, 13, 27, 218–19, 228, 230, 262–73,
    285, 287, 291, 300, 409nn.6,15, 410n.19
part-whole metaphysics, 43–51, 84, 220, 243–
    48, 260–62, 328–29, 384n.54, 390n.48,
    405n.13, 406n.16
realism, 391n.51, 394n.87, 405nn.4,12,
    411n.63. *See also* Absolutism; Daoism,
    absolute interpretation; Later Mohists,
    semantic realism
relativism, 4, 46–51, 54, 80–82, 87–92, 109,
    124, 133, 166, 177–82, 220, 233–35, 239–
    42, 247, 262–64, 268–69, 283–86, 289–90,
    294, 296, 308, 322, 323, 333, 339, 351,
    372–76, 382n.32. *See also* Zhuangzi; realism
    and relativism in
substance-attribute (particular-property)
    metaphysical structure, 16–17, 43, 46–51,
    219, 228, 244–45, 328, 329–30, 407n.33,
    408nn.51,52, 415n.50
*Ming*clear:bright, 36, 253, 283, 290, 299
*Ming*command:fate:mandate, 32, 63, 105, 116, 122, 156,
    159, 162, 181, 220, 392n.85, 415n.44
*Ming*name, 3–4, 21, 49, 66, 104, 116–18, 122,
    126, 215–22, 316, 331, 345, 349, 365–66,
    415n.44
Model emulation, 61–75, 80, 84–85, 87, 101–7,
    114–15, 130–38, 147, 149, 156, 159–64,
    177, 209, 212, 217, 321, 338, 347–49, 362–
    63, 385n.57, 391n.69, 397n.25
Mohism, 391n.67, 413n.4, 414n.7, 415n.33. *See
    also* Later Mohists; Mozi
  centrality to Chinese thought, 1–4, 313, 323,
    331–36
  Mencius interaction with, 154–56, 169–73,
    181–93, 397n.24, 398n.33

Mohism (*continued*)
  orthodox treatment, 11–13
Ru-Mo^{Confucian-Mohist} model (Daoist treatment),
    154–56, 201–5, 216–17, 267, 271, 280–81,
    351–52, 360–69
Moore, G. E., 125
Morris, Herbert, 418n.19
Mozi
  bian^{distinctions}, 96, 104, 116–20, 128, 147–48,
    154–56, 166, 185–86, 212, 220, 324,
    391n.60, 407n.43
  constancy, 100, 110–15, 127, 166, 216–18,
    311
  fact and value, 21, 106, 113–16, 119, 125–28,
    135, 139, 141, 147, 391n.62
  human malleability—instilling *daos*^{ways}, 100–
    106, 113, 116, 118–19, 126–27, 150, 164,
    166, 186, 234, 397n.25, 398n.31, 401n.12,
    416n.73
  interpretive issues, 95–98, 114–16, 120, 132,
    139–43, 389n.35
  language, theory of, 96–97, 101–3, 117–18,
    122–23, 126–27, 139, 143–48, 150,
    393n.86, 410n.31
  measurement standards, 99–103, 109, 120–24,
    135–38, 145, 187, 234, 347–49, 358,
    388n.15, 407n.43, 415n.31, 418n.10
  motivating morality, 113, 119, 120–25, 133,
    138
  names and guidance, 103–11, 115–18, 122–27,
    393n.86, 406nn.14,15,16
  normative theory, 100, 106–17, 121, 125, 128–
    30, 134, 140–43, 389nn.35,36,37,38,
    39,40,41, 390nn.42,43,48, 391n.58,
    398n.31
  paradox of moral reform, 108–13, 118–21,
    159, 180, 184, 187, 391n.67
  partial v. universal, 100, 112–15, 121–25,
    127–30, 169, 248, 389n.40, 390n.48,
    391n.69, 399n.56
  political theory, 101–2, 130–37, 149,
    389nn.41,42, 391n.69, 397n.25, 413n.5,6
  pragmatics in, 110–18, 128, 139–48, 218
  reason and reasoning, 119–23, 138–42, 201
  relation to Confucianism, 95–102, 112–15,
    128–38, 144–49, 388n.14, 389nn.33,35
  role of *tian*^{nature} in, 100–101, 107–9, 121–25,
    127, 131–35, 156, 162, 381n.27, 390n.56,
    391n.69
  social nature of humans, 100–105, 117, 128–
    35, 390n.40. *See also* Mozi; human
    malleability
  spirits and fate in, 118–22, 125, 144–46,
    391n.58
  style, 97–99, 154–55, 387nn.3,4, 396n.15
  traditionalism, attack on, 96, 106–15, 149,
    163, 166, 173, 180, 397n.23
  universal love, 128–30, 169–70, 185, 248–51
  utilitarianism, 97, 103, 108–17, 121–25, 128–
    38, 143, 146, 166, 170–72, 178–79, 185–
    87, 205–8, 234, 237, 307, 317, 323, 347–
    50, 390nn.42,48,49, 392nn.74,76

Western comparisons, 132–33, 138–48
Munro, Donald, 377n.3, 381n.25, 416n.82
Mysticism, 2, 7, 26–27, 87, 172–75, 193–96,
    203–4, 208, 214–15, 221–23, 226–30, 235,
    265–72, 284–93, 300, 310, 313, 342, 371–
    72, 402n.25, 404n.38, 409n.16, 410n.19,
    419n.42, 420n.70

Names, *See also Ming*^{names}; Language; *individual
    philosophers*
  rectifying, 20, 159, 177, 181, 205, 216–17,
    348, 354–55, 359, 365, 382n.35, 387n.75,
    389n.34, 394n.88, 408n.50, 420n.65. *See
    also* Confucius; Language; Later Mohists;
    Ming^{name}; Mozi; Xunzi
Neo-Confucianism, 5, 7, 11, 14–15, 28–29, 96,
    173, 195, 200–204, 236–37, 264–67,
    377n.3, 380n.16, 396n.16, 397n.31,
    399nn.54,55,56, 408n.46. *See also*
    Interpretation, ruling theory of; Wang Yang-
    ming; Zhuxi
Neo-Mohism. *See* Later Mohism
Nivison, David, 118, 119, 184, 390n.54, 399n.49

Objectivity, 3, 43, 52. *See also* Constancy;
    Measurement; Metaphysics: realism;
    Reliabilism; Subjectivism
  Confucian, 341, 343, 374
  Daoism on, 375
  Han Feizi on, 348–50, 352, 360, 366–67, 374
  Mohists on, 99–103, 108, 124, 126, 187
  Western contrast, 43, 126, 343, 349, 376
Obligation. *See* Ought, absence of concept of
Ordinary language, 243, 246, 250–58, 284–92,
    297–301, 331, 385n.62, 393n.86
Ought, absence of concept of, 21, 113–16, 119,
    122, 126–28, 140, 298, 346, 349–50, 354,
    365, 381n.29, 386n.68, 389nn.31,37,
    397n.27, 411n.46. *See also De*^{virtuosity};
    Dao^{way:guiding discourse}; Ethics; Mozi: fact and
    value; Rights; Zhuangzi: fact and value

Paradox
  anti-language, 209, 213–17, 222, 230, 241–42,
    264, 266–67, 409n.59, 410n.19,
    416nn.54,55
  being and non-being, 219–22
  Daoist love of, 203, 213–14, 264, 402n.20
  miscellaneous other paradoxes, 159, 184, 226,
    228, 256, 260. *See also Bai-ma*^{white horse}
    issues; Gongsun Long; Later Mohists: white
    horse paradox; Xunzi
  of moral reform. *See* Mozi; paradox of moral
    reform
  of relativism, 247, 264
Parallelism, 45–46, 98, 220, 250–51, 371,
    379n.9
Parfit, Derek, 112, 113, 390n.45, 396n.20
Parmenides, 27, 201, 220, 221
Partial v. impartial, 169, 276–77, 283, 290, 325–
    26, 339–43, 362–70. *See also* Mozi: partial
    v. universal

Particulars. *See* Metaphysics: substances-attribute
Performance. *See Dao*^way:guiding discourse
Perspectivalism, 137, 266–76, 281–85, 288–300, 322, 330–33, 372–75, 413n.102, 415n.33, 417n.89, 420n.70
Plato, 13, 18, 27, 38, 59, 70, 92–93, 104, 108, 118–19, 167, 201, 204, 228, 253, 260, 376, 377n.1, 382n.32, 383n.47, 395n.15
Poetry, 20, 36, 44–46, 52–53, 58, 75, 85–86, 95, 98, 105, 155, 230, 345, 379n.9, 398n.38, 404n.39
Political theory, 58, 61, 65–67, 73, 80, 95, 122, 132, 160, 161, 164, 174, 310, 344. *See also individual authors*
anarchism, 4–5, 28, 135, 203, 211, 229, 233, 312, 317–19, 322, 328, 335, 351, 361, 367, 372, 375
Pragmatics, 41–43, 51, 222–24, 389n.34, 391n.62, 392nn.79,85, 394n.86, 396n.22, 405n.4. *See also* Later Mohists; Mozi; Xunzi
Prescriptive language. *See* Language, prescriptive function of
Private language, 16–19, 23–26, 38–40, 52–53, 75–77, 85, 94, 111, 142, 149–50, 292–93, 329, 394n.87, 395n.12, 408n.45. *See also* Subjectivism
Psychological theory, contrasts. *See* Behavior; Belief; Computer analogy of mind; Desire; Education; Egoism; Emotion; Euclidean model of reasoning; Experience; Idea theory of meaning; Intuition; Knowledge; Reason; *Xin*^heart-mind; *individual thinkers*

Qi^material force, 156–57, 174–77, 183, 186
Qing^reality response (feelings) 36, 240, 248, 276–77, 300–301, 320, 325–26, 333–34, 336, 405n.12, 406nn.14,15, 411nn.49,63, 416n.61

Radicals, 36, 44, 64, 191, 253, 320, 391n.60, 405nn.12,14, 407nn.39,43,44, 416nn.57,61
Ran^so:thus, 250, 321
Reason, 16–19, 22–23, 53, 70, 72, 86, 93, 167, 198–201, 254–55, 271, 273, 286, 298–300, 353, 382n.32, 383n.43, 384n.51, 387n.76, 389n.37, 393n.86, 404n.39, 405n.4, 419n.22. *See also* Argument; Euclidean model of reasoning; Later Mohists; Mozi; Zhuangzi
Reliabilism, 4–5, 53. *See also* Constancy
Confucian conceptions of, 72–73, 178, 181–82, 307, 334–35
Daoist conceptions of, 93, 187, 203, 224, 229
legalist conceptions of, 350, 354, 368–69
Mohist conceptions of, 100, 105, 109–10, 120, 145, 250–57, 263, 271
Western analogues, 150, 299
Ren^human, 48, 77, 87, 320, 340, 362, 407n.44
Ren^humanity:benevolence, 59, 68–71, 78–81, 83, 86–91, 96–97, 100–101, 107, 129, 137, 155, 159–70, 184, 194, 223–24, 248, 340, 355, 372, 381n.23, 383n.49, 386n.67, 389n.34, 398n.42, 399n.56

Ren-zheng^benevolent government, 159–70
Rights, absence of concept of, 52, 61, 74, 132–33, 346, 356–58, 359, 368. *See also* Ought, absence of concept of
Ritual, 57–59, 62–68, 71–83, 107, 131, 136–38, 163–72, 233, 312–19, 337. *See also* Convention; *Li*^ritual; Traditionalism
Rosemont, Henry, 34, 81–83, 100, 385n.60
Ruler
as target or perspective of theory, 32, 58, 99, 114, 136, 154, 158–60, 225, 273, 307–10, 322–23, 344, 357–74
theory of ruler's role, 61–70, 80, 102, 114, 121–22, 130–31, 158–62, 194, 258, 277, 312–24, 331–37, 350–51, 357–74. *See also individual thinkers;* Political theory; Sage kings
Ru-Mao debate, 4, 12, 137, 154, 201–4, 216–17, 223, 226, 233, 267, 345, 351. *See also* Confucian school; Mohism; *Ru-Mo*^Confucian-Mohist model
Russell, Bertrand, 215, 379n.11

Sage kings, 20, 62, 67–70, 89–92, 110, 138, 144–48, 171–77, 185, 205–11, 312–13, 318–24, 333–42, 363–64, 383n.45, 389n.33, 391n.62, 398nn.41,42,43, 412n.86, 413n.6, 414n.9, 415n.32, 416n.66
Yao and Shun, 63, 122, 171, 268, 363
Sages, Sagehood as moral ideal or authority, 5, 69, 135, 138, 157, 164, 171–83, 205–6, 211, 224, 229–30, 279, 289–91, 338, 341–42, 355, 361–64, 371–73
Sanskrit, 16, 378n.2
School of names. *See* Gongsun Long; Hui Shi; Later Mohists
Schwartz, Benjamin, 6, 11, 12, 57–59, 92, 98, 153, 196, 265–66, 309–10, 344, 359, 362, 377n.1, 379n.9, 380nn.13,20,21, 384n.50, 387n.75, 388nn.13,14,15, 400n.6, 404n.38, 413nn.6,7,8, 416n.82, 417n.83, 418n.20, 419nn.42,47, 420n.70
Science
absence of in classical thought, 31, 53, 69, 78, 86, 93–99, 106, 120, 127, 140–45, 209, 221, 236–38, 240, 247, 258, 282, 296–302, 313, 324, 326, 341, 346, 349, 382n.38, 384n.52, 387n.76, 392n.79, 393n.86, 403n.35, 419n.22. *See also* Argument; Language: sentences and sententials, absence of; Logic; Reason
scientific model of interpretation, 34, 196–97, 237, 267. *See also* Interpretation; Meaning
Semantics
of Chinese language. *See* Interpretation; Meaning
content of Chinese theories of, 49–56, 110, 116, 139–40, 145–48, 223, 233–35, 238–44, 250–58, 280–82, 311, 327–32, 377n.8, 381n.31, 392n.85, 403n.35, 405n.9, 406n.23. *See also* Interpretation; Later Mohists; Meaning

Semantics (*continued*)
  contrasts with Western theories of, 4, 16–19,
    21, 24, 33, 36–49, 75–76, 85–86, 116,
    139–50, 228, 238–41, 329
Shame, 64, 164–71, 179, 331, 354, 385n.62,
  397n.29
Shang Yang, 150, 344, 347, 349, 359, 369
Shen Buhai, 347, 358–59, 364, 420n.47
Shendao, 202–18, 224, 229–30, 235, 242, 268,
  274, 284, 290, 294, 311, 317, 345, 348,
  358, 360, 362, 371–74, 401nn.11,12,
  419nn.27,42
Sheng$^{birth:life:growth}$, 156, 191–92, 320, 385n.58
Shi$^{this:right}$ and *Shi-fei*$^{right-wrong}$, 9, 72, 126, 101–41,
  155–87, 205–7, 211, 230, 234, 242, 250,
  275–300, 311–33, 339–43, 350, 360–75,
  406n.22, 411n.46, 419n.42
Shu$^{statecraft:art}$, 107, 283, 350, 363, 366
Shun, Kwong-Loi, 399n.50
Similarity role in classification, 12, 39, 75, 100,
  104, 120, 126, 128, 138, 148, 160, 190,
  205, 233, 238–54, 259, 262–63, 270–71,
  280–81, 311, 317, 324–31, 391n.62,
  406n.30, 415n.27, 418n.13. *See also*
  Lei^{similarity}
Skepticism
  Chinese, 4, 12, 51, 66, 74, 87, 91–93, 110–
    11, 183, 193, 218, 222–24, 229, 292–93,
    308, 310, 316–17, 322–29, 370–72, 374–
    76, 402n.20. *See also* Knowledge, skepticism
    and the Chinese concept of; Language,
    skepticism; Zhuangzi, skepticism
  moral, 52, 87, 96, 168, 386n.68, 392n.73,
    401n.12, 413n.102
  of orthodox interpretive hypotheses, 2, 7, 19,
    26–28, 236, 371, 377n.3, 405n.9
  sense, 5, 16–17, 226–27, 238, 292–93, 295,
    412n.90
Skill, 72–85, 86–91, 99–106, 138–42, 150, 174,
  194–95, 209, 218, 286–92, 299–303, 320,
  339, 363, 370, 383n.43, 405n.14, 406n.16,
  410nn.31,47, 412n.76. *See also De*^{virtuosity};
  Knowledge; *Zhi*$^{know-to}$
linguistic, 27, 42, 50, 66, 101–6, 126, 217, 252–
  56, 263, 275, 357, 370. *See also* Language
Smullyan, Raymond M., 402n.20, 408n.57
Socialization. *See* Culture and enculturation
Social roles, 32, 68, 77–81, 86, 111, 116, 234,
  314–16, 354–66
Socrates, 23, 70, 83, 92–93, 97, 100, 107–10,
  113, 139, 157, 194, 234, 383nn.40,47,
  386n.68, 387n.76, 395n.15
Song Xing (Songzi), 331–34, 345, 420n.70
Spirits, 94, 275, 277, 287, 384n.56, 391n.58,
  392n.86. *See also* Mozi, spirits and fate in
Spontaneity, 1, 74, 80, 106, 114, 163, 178, 203,
  209, 211, 214, 269, 279, 299–301, 320,
  321, 361, 411n.46
Standards, problem of, 4, 9, 24, 28, 50–52, 68,
  70, 80, 87–93, 96–103, 108–49, 155, 158–
  89, 205–7, 212, 217–18, 234–44, 247, 251–
  55, 266–67, 275–82, 289, 294–99, 308–11,

316–28, 333–40, 343–75. *See also Fa*^{standards}
Stitch, Stephen, 18, 377n.10, 383n.47
Subjectivism, 17–19, 27, 94, 108, 117, 126, 135,
  142, 149–50, 164–65, 177, 292–93, 330,
  392n.75, 405n.12, 408n.45, 420n.70. *See*
  also Experience, lack of subjective concept
  of; Idea theory of meaning; Perspectivalism;
  Private language
Supreme Court, 69–70, 381n.29, 382nn.37,38
Syllogism
  deductive, 16–17, 141, 255–56
  practical, 17, 53, 86, 120, 139, 141–42, 165,
    298, 320, 353, 383n.43, 412n.101
Syntax. *See* Grammar; Language

Ti^{part}, 240, 248, 262–63, 405nn.12,13,14,
  409n.60
Tian$^{nature:heaven}$, 21, 32, 63, 84, 100–101, 107–9,
  121–27, 131–35, 156–57, 160–62, 181,
  185, 205, 236, 248, 277, 311, 321, 348,
  378n.6, 381n.27, 390nn.55,56, 411n.46
Traditonalism, 57–70, 79–82, 87–103, 106–18,
  122–30, 134–38, 143, 146–49, 153–57,
  161–66, 169–86, 194, 200–203, 205, 223–
  25, 233–35, 240, 254, 270, 283, 309–10,
  317–19, 322–24, 327, 333–40, 348, 350–
  53, 357–61, 367, 370, 372, 376, 380n.16,
  381nn.24,29,31, 382nn.32,34, 383n.40,
  385nn.62,63,64, 386nn.67,68, 388n.14,
  389n.33, 391nn.62,73, 394n.87, 415n.44,
  418n.13
Translation paradigm, 7–11, 24, 33, 75, 96–98,
  103, 122, 126, 142, 143–45, 207, 213, 215–
  16, 252, 260, 268–69, 300, 346–47, 349,
  392n.85, 394nn.86,89, 400n.7, 402nn.25,28,
  406n.20, 408n.54. *See also* Meaning:
  meaning-change hypotheses
Truth, 4–5, 8, 16–17, 21, 43, 45, 69, 85, 93,
  110, 116–19, 125, 137–47, 159, 190, 201,
  219, 238–42, 247–56, 283, 293, 298, 326,
  382n.38, 392n.79, 393n.86, 402n.29,
  405nn.4,9, 406n.20, 407n.38, 415n.44
Tu Wei-ming, 178, 381n.23, 398n.44

Universality. *See* Partial v. impartial; Mozi: Partial
  v. universal; Mozi: universal love
Utilitarianism, 4, 88–89, 93, 155, 159, 163, 170,
  178–79, 205, 248–52, 263, 307, 313–23,
  352–55, 361, 369, 389n.37, 390nn.45,48,49,
  392n.74, 396n.20, 418n.19. *See also* Mozi:
  utilitarianism

Virtue
  in Chinese moral theory, 20, 140, 155, 164–72,
    168, 291, 300, 340, 369. *See also*
    Dao$^{way:guiding\ discourse}$; *De*^{virtuosity}; Ought,
    absence of concept
  as requirement for political office, 32, 103,
    134, 159–60, 165, 250, 357, 363, 366. *See*
    also Merit, employment/rule by

Waley, Arthur, 154, 188, 190–93, 382n.34, 394n.5
Wang Bi, 237–38, 373, 400n.7, 402n.28
Wang Chong, 59, 380nn.13,21
Wang Yang-ming, 173, 176, 186–87, 397n.31, 398n.41, 408n.46
Watson, Burton, 95, 97, 98, 388n.3, 391n.58, 412n.75, 413n.4, 416n.55
Way, 3–4, 12, 16, 19, 43, 45, 47–52, 62, 66, 79–90, 105–7, 123, 293, 299, 331, 392n.79, 404n.39, 414n.9. *See also* Dao^{way:guiding discourse}
Wei^{deemido}, 9, 43, 142, 155, 176, 213–14, 248, 253, 291, 302, 320, 363, 402n.20, 411n.46. *See also* Wu-wei^{non-deeming action}
Wen^{literature}, 45, 62, 71, 74–75, 315, 319, 383n.45
Williams, Bernard, 120, 127, 388n.25
Wittgenstein, Ludwig, ii, 5, 24, 43, 71, 72, 88, 91, 93, 230, 289, 355, 383n.46, 394n.87, 412n.90
Wu^{non-being:lack}, 118, 120, 213, 214, 219, 220, 221, 222, 223, 225, 259, 261, 263, 294, 302, 359, 363, 391n.58, 403n.33, 404n.35
Wu-Wei^{non-deeming action}, 213, 294, 302, 359, 363

Xiao^{filiality}, 89, 169
Xin^{heart-mind}, 20, 96, 101, 104, 154, 161–64, 170, 174–86, 194, 213, 236, 248, 252–53, 320, 325, 361, 398n.43, 399n.56. *See also* Heart-mind; Mencius: heart-mind, theory of; Xunzi: Heart-mind; Zhuangzi: and Mencius
Xing^{human nature}, 36, 76, 181, 191–92, 213, 320–21, 337, 395n.13. *See also* Confucius: human nature; Mencius: heart-mind, theory of; Mencius: innatism and intuitionism; Mencius: moral psychology; Xunzi: human nature; Zhuangzi: and Mencius
Xing^{punishment codes}, 348–50, 357–58, 415n.27, 418n.16. *See also* Confucius, punishment and law; Law, and punishment
Xing-ming^{shape-name}, 365–67
Xunzi (Hsun Tzu)
    absolutism, 5, 310, 317–18, 322, 338–42, 351, 370–74, 413nn.5,6, 414nn.8,12, 415n.33, 417nn.86,89, 420nn.67,70
    chain of life, 315–17, 414n.22
    conventionalism, 309–19, 322–33, 336–42, 380n.16, 391n.62, 413n.5, 414nn.8,9, 416nn.66,73
    Daoist aspects, 308–12, 314–22, 324–25, 327–28, 331–34, 336, 338–43, 351, 370–73, 375–76, 413n.4, 420n.70
    desires, 312–16, 325–26, 331–37, 339, 343
    heart-mind, 309–10, 314–16, 320, 324–27, 330, 332–34, 336–43, 351, 361, 373, 420n.70
    historical influences, 307–15, 317–25, 327–28, 331–33, 335–43, 381n.21, 413n.4, 414n.7, 415n.31, 416n.66
    human nature, 311–12, 320–21, 325, 328, 334–38, 342–43, 416n.82, 417nn.83,84
    interpretive issues, 11, 264, 307–10, 329, 335–

38, 381n.22, 413n.5, 414nn.8,14, 416n.82, 417nn.83,84
    intuitionism, 320, 323, 328, 340, 348, 415n.44, 418n.13
    language, theory of, 309, 311, 314–34, 336–37, 339–40, 342, 382n.34, 387n.69, 391n.62, 415n.50, 419nn.34,36
    morality, 309, 311, 313, 315–19, 323, 331, 334–38, 341–43, 352, 372–73
    naturalism, 309–15, 317–22, 325–26, 328, 333–34, 336–39, 342
    paradoxes, 308, 324, 327, 330–34, 338, 416nn.54,55,56,57
    political theory, 307–10, 313, 317, 321–31, 413nn.5,6, 414n.7, 415nn.27,44
    pragmatism, 307, 310–13, 315–23, 325–28, 330, 333, 334, 337–39

Yan^{language:words}, 9, 21, 101, 103, 117, 145–46, 155, 177, 185, 188, 241, 281, 366, 391n.60, 392n.85, 407n.44
Yang Zhu (Yangism), 11, 88, 154–57, 162, 177–81, 194–95, 204–9, 213, 224, 240, 248, 272, 275, 311, 392n.75, 395nn.9,11,12,13, 397n.23, 398n.41, 399n.48, 411n.63
Ye^{assertion particle}, 250, 256, 400n.7, 402n.25, 403n.33, 404n.35
Yi^{intent}, 239, 241, 249
Yi^{morality}, 13, 82–83, 96–97, 101, 107–8, 123, 128, 131–33, 137, 155, 164–66, 170–71, 174–75, 182, 208, 240, 315–21, 333, 336, 350, 361, 372, 385n.61, 389n.35
Yin and Yang, 225, 345, 384n.54, 393n.86
You^{being:have}, 49, 118, 146, 213, 219–25, 261, 394n.86, 403n.33, 404n.35
Yu^{desire}, 213, 220, 333–34, 404n.35. *See also* Desire
Yue^{music:joy}, 86, 136. *See also* Confucius: music and poetry

Zheng^{government:regulation}, 63–64, 68, 159, 382n.35
Zheng^{rectify}, 63, 66, 415n.31
Zhi^{know-to}, 8, 43, 82, 85–86, 96, 104, 142, 164, 166, 172, 177, 206, 209, 224–25, 230, 252–54, 289, 293, 315, 321, 341, 366, 387n.72
Zhi^{object:particle}, 219, 222, 402n.28
Zhi^{point:finger}, 259–61, 283
Zhong^{loyalty}, 36
Zhuangzi (Chuang Tzu)
    anti-language Monism, 202–3, 210–11, 263–64, 266–76, 271, 279, 283, 285–92, 294, 296, 300, 409n.15, 410n.19
    and Confucianism, 202, 266–67, 269–70, 277–81, 301, 383n.44, 412n.86
    dreams in, 52, 292–96, 412n.90
    fact and value, 279–81, 289–90, 294, 296–99, 411n.46, 412n.102
    and Han Feizi, 345, 351, 370, 372, 375, 419n.34
    and Hui Shi, 262–63, 267, 270–71, 280, 291
    interpretive issues, 265–69, 272, 274, 276, 283, 285–87, 292–93, 380n.19, 401n.11,

Zhuangzi (Chuang Tzu) (*continued*)
 402n.29, 409nn.3,6,16, 410n.19
 knowledge, 272–73, 275–76, 277–81, 284–98,
  300, 411n.65, 412n.81
 language, 265, 267–77, 279–86, 289–92, 296–
  98, 300, 405n.12, 409n.15, 410n.19,
  411nn.46,65, 412n.81
 and Laozi, 202–3, 210–11, 217, 269–71, 274–
  75, 278–79, 296, 300
 and Later Mohists, 266, 270–71, 273, 275,
  280–83, 285, 291, 295–96, 411n.55
 life, influences and texts, 272–73, 395n.9,
  401n.8, 406n.25, 409n.17, 410n.19,
  411nn.55,63
 and Mencius, 180–85, 193–94, 198, 277–81,
  284, 290, 300, 391n.73, 398n.41, 399n.53,
  411n.65
 practical advice, 284, 289, 290–94, 299–305,
  402n.30
 realism and relativism in, 264, 266–68, 270,
  273, 277, 280, 285–86, 289–91, 294, 296–
  97, 377n.2, 410n.19, 411n.65
 reason and rationality, 269–71, 273, 277, 286,
  298–300, 303, 410nn.19,31, 412n.81
 skepticism, 265, 268–70, 272, 274, 284–86,
  292–300, 391n.73, 411n.46,
  412nn.86,90,102
 and Xunzi, 308–12, 314–15, 317–21, 324–25,
  327–28, 332–33, 338–41, 343, 413n.6,
  416n.55, 417n.89
Zhuxi, 186, 380n.16
Zi[character], 33, 38, 42, 44–45